THE STATE IN ANCIENT INDIA

THE STATE IN ANCIENT INDIA

BENI PRASAD

GYAN

Published by

GYAN

Gyan Publishing House
5, Ansari Road
Daryaganj, New Delhi-110002
Phone: 011-47034999, 9811692060
E-mail: books@gyanbooks.com

Distribution Network
gyanbooks.com
India, USA, Canada, UK, Australia

ISBN: 978-93-7225-203-3 (HB)

First Published, 1928

2nd Impression 2025

Printed at: Gyan Press, Delhi.

THE STATE IN ANCIENT INDIA
Author: BENI PRASAD

THE STATE IN ANCIENT INDIA

THE
STATE IN ANCIENT INDIA

A Study in the Structure and Practical Working of Political Institutions in North India in Ancient Times

Thesis approved for the degree of Doctor of Science (Economics) in the University of London

BY

BENI PRASAD, M.A., Ph.D., D.Sc. Econ. (London)
Reader in Civics and Politics,
Formerly, Lecturer in Indian History,
University of Allahabad

1928

PREFACE

THE scope of this thesis is confined to the treatment of the structure and practical working of political institutions in Northern India in ancient times, *i.e.*, up to the Muslim conquest. The discussion of the *origines* of institutions is excluded from the work, except in so far as it is essential to an explanation of the structure of institutions in historical times. Social institutions in general, social or political theory, ordinary political history, and the institutions of the Deccan and the south of India are touched upon only as auxiliaries to the main theme. The work is based on a first-hand study of the original sources. In handling Vedic evidence, the Vedic Index of Professors Macdonell and Keith has been useful as suggesting references to original authorities. Dr. Richard Fick's Social Organisation in North-Eastern India in Buddha's time has likewise been extremely helpful for the Jâtakas. A good many of the references in Chapter V (on Jâtakas) are identical with those in Dr. Fick's excellent treatise but the sixth book of the Jâtakas has also been utilised; some new facts are adduced throughout and fresh conclusions enunciated. In connection with Epic data some suggestions were derived from the well-known essay of Dr. Hopkins on the Social and Military Position of the Ruling Caste (J. A. O. S., XIII, 1888). In Chapters X and XII and in a few paragraphs of other chapters, dealing with theoretical books, the material used is much the same as in my Theory of Government in Ancient India (post-Vedic) but the point of view is different and some of the passages utilised are also different.

The radical divergence of my hypotheses from the conclusions of my predecessors renders it all the more obligatory on my part to express my gratitude to them. But for their invaluable pioneer work in the domain of ancient Indian politics, it would have been impossible to write a connected account of the development of Hindu administration or to offer fresh interpretations of its various aspects. My particular obligations are due to my tutor Prof. H. J. Laski and other teachers at the London School of Economics and Political Science who guided my studies in Sociology, Political Science and Public Administration. Prof. A. Berriedale Keith and Dr. L. D. Barnett kindly offered valuable suggestions on the dates of some Sanskrit texts. Prof. C. N. Nallamuthu Ammal, M.A., B.Sc. (London), of Lady Willingdon's College, Madras, brought some Tâmil data to my notice and assisted in their evaluation. Dr. Pran Nath, D.Sc. (London), during his tenure at the India Office Library, extended to me all facilities ot research there and directed me to a number of little known texts which, otherwise, might have escaped my notice. The advice of my colleague Mr. Kṣetreśa Chandra Chaṭṭopâdhyâya, M.A., never grudged on the busiest of days, was always helpful in handling Vedic and classical Sanskrit texts. Another colleague, Mr. Bisheshar Prasad Srivastava, M.A., offered valuable criticism and saw part of the book through the press. Mr. Ram Shankar Prasad, M.A., read the proofs of the rest of the work and also compiled the Index.

The Royal Asiatic Society's scheme of transliteration has been adopted with slight modifications which will explain themselves. The accepted spelling of place-names has been employed but diacritical signs have often been put to facilitate correct pronunciation. The proper names of persons are accented exactly in the manner adopted by their bearers.

BENI PRASAD.

CONTENTS

ABBREVIATIONS

Ep. Ind. . . . . Epigraphia Indica.
Ind. Ant. . . . . . . Indian Antiquary.
J. A. S. B. . . . . Journal of the Asiatic Society of Bengal.
J. A. O. S. . . . . Journal of the American Oriental Society.
J. B. B. R. A. S. . . . Journal of the Bombay Branch of the Royal Asiatic Society.
J. B. O. R. S. . . . . Journal of the Bihar and Orissa Research Society.
J. R. A. S. . . . . Journal of the Royal Asiatic Society.

THE STATE IN ANCIENT INDIA

CHAPTER I.

Introduction.

The Basis of the Study.

The political institutions of the Hindus[1] are, in their origin, as old as those of the Greeks but it is impossible to trace their development or visualise their working with the same clarity and fulness. In spite of the rapid strides of Oriental research during the last hundred years, there is no political history of India, in the strict sense of the term, prior to the sixth century B.C., while the gaps in the subsequent annals are numerous and sometimes cover centuries. The dates of many kings are doubtful, while nothing can exceed the difficulty of fixing the chronological limits of most of the Hindu poets, philosophers, grammarians and legal and political writers. Nor is the raw material available for the study of political institutions so abundant in itself as the size of the country and the duration of its history would lead one to expect. Historical compositions are few. Works on law or polity are certainly numerous but, for the most part, they are theoretical and do not readily yield any information on the practical working of institutions. General literature, religious or secular, gives something only after the most searching examination. The foreign accounts of India by classical, Chinese and Arab writers

[1] Throughout this book the word Hindu is used in a comprehensive sense so as to include followers of the Brahmanic, Buddhist, Jaina and other indigenous Indian persuasions.

are more valuable but they are few and far between and some of them have not come down to us at first hand. The inscriptions and coins which have been discovered and deciphered by a host of scholars in ever-increasing numbers of late constitute the real basis of the study of the structure and working of Hindu political institutions but the interpretation of administrative and fiscal terms therein bristles with difficulties. A discussion, based on scanty and dispersed materials, partly of uncertain dates, is bound to be perfunctory at best. Besides, there is the risk of reading modern or preconceived notions into the terms and documents of ancient times of which the atmosphere is so difficult to re-capture. One may be tempted to dismiss the polity of ancient India as mere "Oriental Despotism" which requires no further analysis and evaluation. Or one may import into antiquity the spirit and ideals of modern times. Again, such is the nature of our documents that isolated statements readily adapt themselves to attractive hypotheses and generalisations. The warning uttered by Professor Keith in regard to the Ṛigveda applies to much else in the range of Hindu literature, epigraphy and numismatics. "It is easy," he writes, "to frame and support by plausible evidence various hypotheses, to which the only effective objection is that other hypotheses are equally legitimate and that the facts are too imperfect to allow of conclusions being drawn."[1] Caution, indeed, must be the governing principle of all endeavours to elucidate the political ideas and institutions of the ancient Hindus For instance, it is desirable to work on the assumption of later dates of books for which higher chronological limits are possible but not at all certain. To antedate any phenomena would be to weaken the very foundations of what ever hypotheses one may build. Another caution, equally

The Method of Study.

[1] Cambridge History of India, vol. I, pp. 78-79,

essential, is to resist the ever-present temptation of "combining information." A picture, constructed from texts separated by hundreds or thousands of years, may be fascinating in its fulness but may not be true of any given epoch. Similarly, documents from regions far apart cannot be used for a single area. In the uncertainty of dates and the obscurity of the whole subject, every document should, as a general rule, be handled by itself and then joined to others only on the surest possible ground. The application of the most rigid critical standards alone can serve to illuminate the subject and, it may be, to add a new chapter to the science of Comparative Politics.

The nature and working of Hindu political institutions were largely affected by geography, racial characteristics, social organisation and economic conditions. Geographical factors have, more than anything else, determined the trend of Indian political history. While the Himâlayas have, for the most part, formed an impenetrable wall on the North, the openings on the North-west have let in successive hordes of immigrants and invaders who brought with them new types of civilisation, new ideas and institutions. Again, the north-western passes facilitated commercial and general intercourse between India and the Middle East. Recent excavations and discoveries, carried out chiefly by Sir Aurel Stein, have proved that the extensive desert which bars inter-communication at present was not so arid two thousand years ago, and that in Baluchistân and Seistân there existed flourishing sites of civilisation which were abandoned, with the gradual drying up of the land, only after the second century B. C. The chances for an exchange of cultural and political influences with Persia, might, *prima facie*, have had something to do with the development of Hindu practices. Within the frontiers of India there are hills and valleys in the North, North-west,

The Influence of Geography.

North-east, in Central India and on the western coast, which afforded shelter to hard-pressed tribes and clans and enabled them to preserve their peculiar institutions. In the North, the vast Indo-Gangetic plains, flat and monotonous, have largely determined the form of political organisation. Here the contrast with Greece is complete. In Greece, as Zimmern puts it, "each little plain, rigidly sealed within its mountain barriers, and with its population concentrated upon its small portion of good soil, seems formed to be a complete world of its own. Make your way up the pasture land, over the pass and down on to the fields and orchards on the other side, and you will find new traditions and customs, new laws and new gods, and most probably a new dialect. You will be in a new nation."[1] In North India, the absence of any hills, lakes or unfordable rivers militated against the permanence of political boundaries. *Prima facie*, every state would tend, as it were naturally, to encroach upon its neighbours. It was not long before public opinion and political philosophy held up to admiration the ideal of the "big kingdom," "the kingdom extending up to the sea," "the universal dominion." Constant efforts were made to realise the ideal in some practical form or other, in reality or in name. The result was almost incessant warfare or readiness for war which was bound to influence the structure and working of governmental institutions. It would promote the monarchy as against other forms of government. It might mean heavy military expenditure and correspondingly heavy taxation. Whenever an extensive dominion came into being, the difficulty of communications,—the standing difficulty of all pre-modern governments—might prove well-nigh insurmountable. The authority at the centre could not easily make itself felt at the circumference. Rigid centralisation would be impracticable. Regional autonomy would

[1] A. E. Zimmern, Greek Commonwealth, pp. 62-63.

tend to be the rule. Nor would an "empire" under such circumstances hold together long even nominally. The outlying regions would constantly be tempted to cut themselves adrift from the main body, to start on an absolutely independent career and, in their turn, to make a bid for supremacy. Once again, at the first signs of weakness or pressure at the new centre, the old process might re-start round another point. Indian political history would thus resolve itself into a ceaseless play of the centripetal and centrifugal forces in which the latter would, on the whole, prove stronger than the former.

The Deccan.

India is split into two halves by the Vindhyas and Satpuras. Nothing like the Himâlayas, these chains of hills and mountains allow free intercourse between the North on the one hand and the Deccan, as the table-land is called, and the country south of the Krişnâ on the other hand. But they have served to make the two regions different in race, language and partly in culture. Within the peninsula again, the Deccan plateau is in geographical configuration different from the extreme south and differs from it essentially in race, language and character. Politically, India is divided into three great entities, each with a system of its own. More energetic and persistent than the quest for the suzerainty of the whole country, has been the quest for supremacy over the North, over the Deccan and over the South as a whole. In particular, the region known as Tâmilakam, extending from the south of Madras to Cape Comorin, has a strong individuality of its own. In spite of centuries of Âryan contact and influence, its civilisation has run an independent career. The admixture of Âryan blood is small; the languages contain few Sanskrit words; the political institutions show many important peculiarities. In the extreme south-west of India the Malâbâr, sheltered by the Western range and the sea from outside influences, is still a museum of sociological curiosities. There is, however, no evidence to prove that its institutions represent a survival of those which once prevailed over the whole of the south or beyond. Further up, the sea and the Western Ghâṭs, running for hundreds of miles along the coast, enclose a narrow strip of land, called the Koṅkan,[1] which reared a hardy, sturdy race and enabled it to preserve and develop its peculiar institutions. Beyond the bounds of India proper lies the island of Siṁhala or Ceylon which, for centuries, shared in the history of Southern India and, to a far lesser extent, in that of India as a whole. Politically, however, it is an entity by itself. It is desirable that in any administrative survey the North, the Deccan, the South and Ceylon should be primarily treated by themselves. Since, however, they frequently influenced one another and since proximity and similarity of certain conditions made their institutions alike in some respects, the administrative history of any of the four areas can be enriched by comparison with that of the others and by illustration from them.

The predominance of Agriculture.

The most striking resemblance between the North of India and the rest of the country lies in the domain of economic life. Agriculture has been the predominant occupation of the whole country. The methods of agriculture have been practically the same everywhere and for the whole of recorded history. The conservatism which the pursuit of agriculture tends to produce has therefore been a common feature. Owing to the absence of any serious economic change, the framework of social and political life has not altered much. Besides giving the institutions a remarkable fixity, the dominance of agriculture has partly determined their form and character. The vast majority

[1] For a graphic description of the Ghâṭs, see Elphinstone, History of India, ed. Cowell, pp. 600-601.

of the population have lived in scattered villages. The proportion of the rural to the urban element was, in all probability, even higher in ancient India than at present. The population itself was much smaller and therefore even more dispersed than at present. The Hâthîgumphâ inscription of Khâravela of Kaliṅga (C. 165 B.C.) puts the population of Kaliṅga, roughly modern Orissâ, at three millions and a half. A comparison of this figure with the figures available for the Kaliṅga army and the casualties in a former war and then a comparison with the numbers of the armies given for other regions, and, finally, a comparison with the present population of Orissâ, indicate, very roughly, a hundred millions as the population of the country. The mention of pastures and forests in Hindu literature and the general tenour of the foreign accounts also leave the impression that the country was not so thickly populated in ancient times as at present. No certainty is possible in a matter like this. But the rough indications are that in ancient times the population of India was about one-third of its present strength. It was thus even more diffused among villages than at present. Such a condition was not favourable to the development of that intensity of life which characterized parts of ancient Greece and which issued in democratic organisation. Not only was this vital condition of democracy wanting, but the usual size of a state and the difficulty of communications put direct or representative democracy as a form of central government out of the question. Besides, the essential moral basis of democracy was destroyed by the operation of caste which cut the population into at least four and generally many more racial, occupational or social groups, held in varying degrees of esteem. Caste, however, also struck against aristocracy as a

Population.

Form of Government.

Caste.

form of government. It distributed the intellectual, martial and economic strength of the community among various sections and prevented that concentration of power in a single group which might enable it to dominate the rest. The elimination of democracy and aristocracy left the monarchy as the dominant type of government. Nothing else could meet the situation created by the conjuncture of geographical, economic and social factors. The monarchy alone could symbolise the union of any considerable area of territory.

The village.

On the other hand, the dominant sway of agriculture made the village the unit of society and, therefore, of political organisation. A village would, of course, share in the general culture of the land. But in the ordinary routine of life, it would tend to be a world by itself. Everything would tend to intensify its group-consciousness. For fiscal and administrative purposes it would be the starting-point of all arrangements. Higher divisions of local government might be formed by grouping successively larger numbers of villages together.

Industry and Commerce.

The guild.

While agriculture was the principal occupation, industry and commerce would be pursued by numbers of persons in every locality. Industry has always shown a tendency to organise itself in guilds. The guild, as a modern writer remarks, "is indeed a structure which, at one period or another, has existed over practically the whole of the civilised world. In medieval Europe, industry was carried on under a system of enterprise at once public and private, associative and individual. The unit of production was the workshop of the individual master craftsman; but the craftsman held his position as a master only by virtue of full membership in his Craft-Guild. He was not free to adopt any methods of production, or any scale of production he might choose; he was subjected to an elaborate regulation of both the quality and the quantity of his products, of the price he should charge to the consumer, and of his relations to his journeymen and his apprentices. He worked within a clearly defined code of rules which had the object at once of safeguarding the independence, equality, and prosperity of the craftsmen, of keeping broad the highway of promotion from apprentice to journeyman, and from journeyman to master; and also of prescribing the integrity and well-being of the craft by guarding the consumer against exploitation and shoddy goods."[1] Conditions in ancient India were, of course, different in many important respects from those in medieval Europe. But the basic principle is the same. Throughout the greater part of ancient Indian history, guilds in some form or other are met with and have an important bearing on the state.

Racial Characteristics.

The influence of race as a determinant of the course of social and political evolution cannot be traced so readily as that of geography or economic conditions. "National Character" has been the subject of some strange theories. As an English political writer puts it, national character is a wonder-worker at the beck and call of every embarrassed historian. Nevertheless, it must be admitted that a mass of men in a given region often differ in important psychological traits from another group. The ultimate origin of these differences may be traceable to geography,—to soil, climate and resulting habits of life and thought—but the presence of a set of deep-seated psychological traits constitutes a series of influences by itself in historical times. The "innate characteristics," as they may be called, have not been the same everywhere in India. For instance, the Tâmil character which has so profoundly impressed the

[1] G. D. H. Cole, Introduction to Terry's Translation of Renard's Guilds in the Middle Ages, pp. xiii-xiv.

whole of South India is an entity by itself. The temperament of the Marâthâs who, of all Indian communities, come nearest to the Teutons in their intellectual and moral makeup, differs much from that of the people of Bengal or the Puñjâb. Yet behind all the diversities it is possible to discern some common characteristics, which, in their aggregate, sharply differentiate the people of India from those of any other country. The Indian temperament displays an emotional flow and vibration which, on the whole, militates against rigidity of discipline and organisation and bars uniformity in associated life. The religiosity of the Hindus is proverbial but there never arose any ecclesiastical organisation like the Roman Catholic Church or the Anglican Church. The Buddhist Saṁgha which represented the maximum of organisation in Hindu religious life, was pervaded by a spirit of intense localism. The Jaina orders were more loose, while the Brâhmaṇas seem to have been positively averse to ecclesiastical systematisation Prayer and worship which have been congregational in Europe have, for the most part, been individual among Hindus. Here culture has been embodied in institutions to a far lesser extent than in the West. It is true that in certain matters, for instance, in ritual and caste, a degree of discipline was prescribed and an amount of organisation attempted, which is unknown in Western Europe. But even here endless multiplicity of forms and diversity of details are apparent. Again, a caste or a subcaste rarely had a definite machinery of government, legislative, executive or judicial. It left a great deal to the operation of custom and the informal working of group-opinion. This lack of organisation goes a long way to discount the Brahmanic claims to supremacy which fill Brahmanic literature. Whatever the theorists might say, the fact remained that the Brâhmaṇas had no organisation, no independent financial resources, no effective means of resisting a king. Ultimately, they depended on the king, the landed magnates or the community at large for grants, fees, and presents. In economic life, too, the organisation was never so strict in ancient India as in Europe. The guilds, essentially local in character, were never well-knit together. In the political conditions which obtained in ancient India, this habit of loose organisation would tend to produce a sort of federalism or feudalism—feudalism which represents want of system rather than a system. This trait in the Hindu character was intensified by the imaginativeness which was another striking feature in the temperament of the ancient Hindus. To soar above the earth was often to lose touch with realities and to drift away from system. On the other hand, the Hindu mind was remarkable for its love of logic. It delighted in classification, division and endless sub-division. In practical life it sometimes pursued logic with extraordinary tenacity and tended to run an idea to its extreme consequences. Here is one of the causes of the growth of caste. Europe stopped at class; Hindu India rushed into caste.

Caste.

Caste, which formed the basis of the social order, was, along with geography, race and economic postulates, a great factor in the political life of the Hindus. Apart from the fact that it ruled out democracy or aristocracy as a form of government for a state as a whole, it deeply influenced the nature, character and working of the monarchical state. Caste resolves function into a purpose, an ethical principle, a religious conception. In the exaltation of the group, it largely sacrifices the individual values. It strikes at the root of individuality and amounts almost to a denial of personality. It refuses to admit that every individual is, in his nature, universal and that he has the right to seek his own self-expression, to determine his own ambitions and pursue his own interests. The principle of caste is the negation of the dignity of man as man. It rules out all idea of individual liberty or rights independently of those which arise from the necessity and desirability of performing prescribed social functions. Hence, there was no effort in the history of Hindu politics to define the spheres of individuality on the one hand, and the group or state on the other hand. "Laissez-faire" had no basis in ancient India. When it liked, society could direct everything pertaining to human life.

The composition of the government.

Caste would naturally influence the composition of the governing body. It would entrust government to the Kṣatriyas and, though the rule was sometimes violated, its prescription was generally effective. At the same time the Brâhmaṇas were, socially and religiously too important and, intellectually, too powerful, to be left out of political counsels. Brâhmaṇa priests or ministers were often by the side of the king. Legal difficulties were often submitted to Brâhmaṇa pariṣads or committees for solution. Attempts were made to enlist the moral support of the Brâhmaṇas for the government. Law, which is an expression of the social spirit, reflected caste at numerous points in ancient India.

Groups.

Caste fosters group-psychology as opposed to an independent individual mentality or national consciousness. It helps the tendency towards functional organisation. Among the ancient Hindus, organisation, though loose in degree, tended to be both horizontal and vertical. There might arise multitudes of local and functional jurisdictions and intermediate associations standing in various, more or less ill-defined, relations with the state. Every group which has developed a consciousness, tends to be independent or quasi-independent in its own sphere. It rests with the state to coordinate the working of these groups, to keep each within its proper limits and, generally, to secure those conditions under which they can flourish to the best advantage of the common good. The extent to which the state can fulfil this function of co-ordination and security is likely to depend on its intrinsic strength and animating spirit and the whole set of circumstances at a given moment. In this whole series of relationships, custom is likely to be the guiding principle, if written positive law is wanting. In such a case, sovereignty would cease to be monistic. In the rigid Austinian sense of the term, it would disappear altogether. It would be essentially pluralistic, diffused among myriads of groups, particulate jurisdictions and influences. Such was the situation which a conjuncture of basic circumstances brought about in ancient India.

Religion.

Religion must be reckoned among the great factors in the history of the Hindus. Brahmanism sanctified caste and entrenched it firmly in the estimation of the people. It made law part of itself and thus tended to impart to it strength, conservatism and permanence. Religion sought to direct the life of the rulers as of the rest of the community. It inculcated charity, gentleness and promotion of popular happiness on the part of the king. It held a spiritual ideal before the state. It could serve as a moral check on the despotism. Occasionally, it might become the animating principle of the policy of the state. Under a king like Aśoka, the state might become actively missionary. Religious change was likely to tell on politics. The rise of Buddhism and Jainism shook the political position of Brāhmaṇas for a while. Incidentally, religion emphasised renunciation of the world and led many rulers to abdicate in favour of their sons or relations.

The starting point of study.

Such were the principal determining factors in the development and working of political institutions in ancient India. They were common to the North, the Deccan and the South and to all, except, perhaps, the most ancient, periods of the early history of India, though their actual force would necessarily vary from time to time and place to place. The history of India as a whole has generally been viewed from the North. But several years ago, a noted Southern scholar, the late Sundaram Pillai, laid down that "the attempt to find the basic element of Hindu civilisation by a study of Sanskrit and the history of Sanskrit in Upper India is to begin the problem at its worst and most complicated point. India, south of the Vindhyas—the Peninsular India—still continues to be India proper. Here the bulk of the people continue distinctly to retain their pre-Âryan features, their pre-Âryan languages, their pre-Âryan social institutions. Even here, the process of Âryanisation has gone indeed too far to leave it easy to the historian to distinguish the native warp from the foreign woof. But, if there is anywhere any chance of such successful disentanglement, it is in the south: and the farther south we go, the larger does the chance grow.

The South?

"The scientific historian of India, then, ought to begin his study with the basin of the Krisņâ, the Cauvery of the Vaigai, rather than with the Gangetic plain, as it has been now long, too long, the fashion."[1]

But if one prepares to depart from the old fashion, one meets with an insurmountable obstacle at the very threshold. It is possible that the Tâmils began their institutional career earlier than any people of the north but their early forms and working are lost to us. The oldest available southern records are considerably later in date than the earliest extant northern documents. A few Tâmil scholars have tried to prove that Tâmil literature embodies tradition as old as 12000 B. C. or even earlier. But their arguments have been contested by other Tâmil scholars. They proceed on the basis of the very tradition of which the

[1] Tamilian Antiquary, 1908, p. 4.

soundness has to be proved. If critical standards be rigidly applied, one can rarely go beyond the Christian era on the basis of Tâmil data. Social institutions and practices which leave their mark on customs and ceremonies may be traced to earlier beginnings, though, even here, the process is beset with difficulties at every step. But in relation to political institutions, the southern material does not carry us, in point of time, beyond the period which is fairly illuminated by northern evidence. If it did, it would be necessary to preface any political survey of the North with a chapter on the South. As it is, even the score of inscriptions discovered in the South a few months ago do not touch the other side of the Christian era. A discussion of Hindu political institutions must still start from the North.

The Raw Material.

The date, authenticity and value of each piece or class of evidence will be discussed as it is used in the following chapters. But a word may be said on the relative value of the data available. The inscriptions must form *the* basis of any study of Hindu political institutions. Here some very remarkable personages proclaim their aspirations, motives, and achievements. Here the actions of numerous kings, officers, private individuals or groups are recorded by contemporaries, with reference to the social, economic and political circumstances of the times. The epigraphic records are supplemented by coins of which the legends, though brief, sometimes settle doubtful dates, introduce new names and titles and occasionally illuminate an obscure political situation. The few seals which have so far been discovered are equally useful. The remains of old buildings, towns, caves or tanks sometimes serve as valuable illustrations. Next in value stand the accounts of foreign observers, Greek, Chinese and Arab, which, in the case of the last two classes of writers, have been transmitted at first hand. The Greek notices, preserved only in later extracts, cannot be accepted at their face value but they are, none the less, very useful. The next place must be assigned to the few Hindu chronicles or biographies, such as the Harṣacarita of Bâṇabhaṭṭa, the Râjataraṅgiṇî of Kalhaṇa and the Vikramâṅkadevacarita of Bilhaṇa, which throw a flood of light on the structure and working of political institutions. Finally, there is the vast range of Hindu literatures, Sanskrit, mixed Sanskrit, Pâlî, Brahmanic, Buddhist and Jaina, religious, legal, political, secular; from which administrative gleanings have to be made. Owing to the uncertainties of the dates of Hindu literary productions which sometimes range over centuries and occasionally transcend a whole millenium, and from the theoretical character of a good many of them, the value of this kind of evidence is largely supplementary, comparative and illustrative. However, it does sometimes reflect the actual state of things or paint an ideal not far removed from reality. It is unfortunate that the epigraphic records and foreign accounts do not begin until the fourth century B.C. For the preceding centuries one has to rely entirely on literature.

CHAPTER II.

The Age of the Ṛigveda.

(BOOKS I—IX.)

The Ṛigveda.

The Ṛigveda is the oldest document and the first of the four Vedas of the Hindus. It has well been said that it "is not a book, but a library and a literature."[1] The date and order of its ten Maṇḍalas or books and of the 1,028 hymns which they comprise, cannot be determined with any approach to certitude. Attempts have been made, notably by Arnold,[2] to fix their order of composition but the conclusions have been challenged by other scholars.[3] The general consensus of opinion is represented by Keith when he remarks that the nucleus of the Ṛigveda is formed by Books II—VII, each of which is attributed to a different priestly family.[4] To this were prefixed the groups of hymns by other families which constitute the second part (51—191) of Book I. Later, the first part (1—50) of Book I and Book VIII which is attributed to the family of Kaṇva were added. When Soma hymns were taken out and put together there came into being Book IX.[5] The tenth Maṇḍala is considerably later. Its metre, language and ideas are conclusive on the point. It is

[1] Arnold, Vedic Metre, p. ix.

[2] Vedic Metre, p. 49, gives a scheme summarising the results arrived at.

[3] See J.R.A.S., 1906, pp. 484—90, 716—22 ; Ibid., 1912, pp. 726—29.

[4] The families are those of Gṛitsamada, Viśvâmitra, Vâmadeva, Atri, Bharadvâja and Vaśiṣṭha.

[5] Keith, Cambridge History of India, I, p. 77.

impossible to dogmatise on the chronological limits of the various sections. Max Müller placed the earlier and more primitive Vedic hymns between 1200 and 1000 B.C. and the later ones between 1000 and 800 B.C.[1] Attempts have been made to fix higher dates on the basis of astronomical calculations and other grounds.[2] The recent discovery of the Mitannian Inscriptions of about 1400 B.C. at Boghazkiöi was seized upon as solid evidence for assigning a higher antiquity to the Ṛigveda, but the discussion which followed left the problem practically where it stood.[3] For the present 1200—1000 B.C. is the safest date for the first nine Maṇḍalas of the Ṛigveda.[4] The scene of the hymns has been held to lie in the valley of the Indus and its tributaries. Some, indeed, might have been composed before the Âryans came to India from whatever their original home might have been. A few others, again, might have come into being after the Âryans had moved a little further east. But the vast majority of them undoubtedly belong to the Puñjâb.[5] The language of the hymns is a highly artificial one and, as many scholars think, could not have been the ordinary tongue of the mass of the people. It is probably the idiom, primarily, of the priests and, secondarily, of the rest of the upper class. The whole of Vedic literature, in fact, is primarily and essentially priestly literature. Its concepts and sentiments are to be judged as primarily those of priests and it has to be remembered that practices are reflected through a priestly medium.

[1] Max Müller, Ṛigveda Saṁhitâ, Vol. IV, pp. vii et seq.

[2] For instance, Jacobi, Ind. Ant., XXIII, pp. 154 et seq. See also Thibaut, Ind. Ant., XXIV, p. 85, also p. 361.

[3] J.R.A.S., 1909, Jacobi, pp. 721 et seq.; Oldenberg, pp. 1095 et seq.; Keith, pp. 1110 et seq.; Ibid., 1910, Jacobi, pp. 456 et. seq.; Keith, pp. 464 et seq.; Oldenberg, pp. 864 et seq.

[4] Max Müller, Prefaces to the Ṛigveda Saṁhitâ; Macdonell, History of Sanskrit Literature, pp. 40—48.

[5] On the Geography of the Ṛigveda, see Macdonell, op. cit., pp. 139—145.

A long course of development lies behind the social institutions reflected in the hymns of the Ṛigveda. On the whole, Vedic society is patriarchal, but kinship, real or fancied, is no longer the only bond which holds men together. The nomadic stage is over and the bond of territory or neighbourhood is plainly in evidence. A third line of organisation is emerging into view. Scholars have long been divided in their opinion on the presence of caste in the first nine Maṇḍalas of the Ṛigveda,[1] but the weight of cumulative evidence lies on the side of those who hold that the institution is taking shape in the early hymns. In a hymn of the fourth Maṇḍala, the god Agni is referred to as possessing the Kṣatriya quality of strength.[2] A hymn of the seventh Maṇḍala invokes the gods Mitra and Varuṇa as Kṣatriyas.[3] Another hymn in the fourth Maṇḍala[4] and another in the fifth[5] refer to the Kṣatriya order. In the hymns which belong to the slightly later groups, the references are clearer. A hymn in the second-half of the first Maṇḍala has the following in the course of a glorification of the Dawn:—

Ṛigvedic Organisation.

"One to high sway, one to exalted glory, one to pursue his gain, and one his labour:

"All to regard their different avocations, all moving creatures hath the Dawn awakened."[6] In the first-half of the same Maṇḍala reference is made to Varuṇa's Kṣatra rule or dominion.[7] In the eighth Maṇḍala divine blessings

[1] For instance, Zimmer, Altindisches Leben, pp. 185 - 203 (summarised in Vedic Index, II, pp. 248-49), holds that the Vedic Indians on the Indus were unbrahmanized. He connects "the change from the casteless system of the Ṛigveda to the elaborate system of the Yajurveda with the advance of the Vedic Indians to the east."

[2] Ṛigveda, IV, 12, 3.

[3] Ibid., VII, 64, 2.

[4] Ibid., IV, 42, 1.

[5] Ibid., V, 69, 1.

[6] Ibid., I, 113, 6; Vedic Index, II, 250.

[7] Ṛigveda, I, 25, 10.

are invoked successively on the men of prayers, the warriors and the people.[1] In several hymns one detects priests receiving Dakṣiṇâ or priestly fee.[2] All through the Ṛigveda the distinction between Âryans and non-Âryans, Dâsas or Dasyus, is clear and fundamental. Thus, even in Books I—VII, and yet more clearly in Books I—VIII as a whole, the elements of caste are present. Caste has not yet acquired the rigidity which characterised it in later times. In the ninth Maṇḍala, for instance, a Ṛiṣi remarks that he is a composer of hymns, his father a physician, and his mother a grinder of corn; they are all engaged in different occupations.[3] But whatever its laxity or fluidity, the institution of caste is there, probably in its initial stages.

Explanation of Caste.

It is not easy to account for the rise and growth of caste. Senart argued with great force that the Âryan practices of endogamy and exogamy were primarily responsible for the development.[4] This, however, can be only part of the explanation. The term Varṇa or colour which denotes caste has rightly been held to supply a further clue. The history of the relations between the whites and the blacks in South Africa and the southern states of the American Union offers an illustration.

Colour.

In ancient India the natural difference of complexion might not have been so great, colour-feeling might not have been so strong and the gulf between the fair and dark races might not have been so wide. But distinctions of colour, emphasised by divergences of civilisation and, for a while by a life-and-death struggle for the possession of land and cattle, would be enough to create an almost permanent line

[1] Ibid., VIII, 35, 16—18.

[2] Ibid., VI, 27, 8; I, 168, 7; VIII, 24, 29; VIII, 39, 5.

[3] Ibid., IX, 112, 3. See also I, 113, 6.

[4] Senart, Les Castes dans l'Inde.

of division. Ever and anon we meet with references to Kṛiṣṇatvac or black skin.[1] Elsewhere, Indra destroys the godless army of Kṛiṣṇa or black.[2] Expressions of contempt, hatred and hostility towards the Dasyus or aborigines and prayers for their destruction are interspersed throughout the Ṛigveda. For instance, Indra is invoked to be cognisant of the hymns of Ṛiṣis, to cast his weapon against the Dasyu and increase the vigour and fame of the Ârya.[3] In the fourth Maṇḍala, the wily and impious Dasyu is to be destroyed and his wealth bestowed on Kutsa.[4] Indra does destroy large numbers of them.[5] Indra has made the Dasyus devoid of all virtues and an object of hatred to all men.[6] "O Âśvins! destroy those who are yelling hideously like dogs and coming to destroy us! Slay those who wish to fight with us."[7]

These aborigines, however, do not seem to have been savages. Not to speak of their capacity to offer tough, stout resistance to the Âryan advance, there are references to their wealth,[8] and their forts.[9] When they had been subjugated and brought under Âryan sway, it was inevitable that, in spite of all the strength of colour-feeling, there should ensue some mixture of blood. The phenomenon would before long arouse anxious thoughts and an attempt would be made to stop the process. Stringent prohibitions against the intermarriage and interdining with the aborigines would be laid down. So the foundation of caste would be laid. Racial mixture, however, would be likely to go on in a legitimate or illegitimate manner and

---

[1] Ṛigveda, I, 130, 8; IX, 41, 1.
[2] Ibid., VIII, 96, 13–15.
[3] Ibid., I, 103, 3.
[4] Ibid., IV, 16, 9–10.
[5] Ibid., IV, 30, 15.
[6] Ibid., IV, 28, 4. See also V, 70, 3; VI, 18, 3; V, 25, 2.
[7] Ibid., I, 182, 4.
[8] E.g., Ibid., IV, 16, 9-10; I, 176, 4; IV, 30, 13; VIII, 40, 6.
[9] Ibid., III, 12, 6. "Indra and Agni have cast down the ninety forts which Dâsas held, together with one mighty deed."

mixed castes would be produced. Meanwhile, the natural process of social specialisation and division of labour would cut the Âryan body itself into sections. It cannot be emphasised too strongly that the whole atmosphere of the Ṛigveda is charged with militarism. The principal gods of the Ṛigveda are great warriors. Indra, the greatest of gods, is the greatest of warriors, slaying and destroying hundreds at a blow. Even references to natural phenomena are clothed in militaristic phraseology. From beginning to end one meets with wars between Âryans and non-Âryans and among Âryans themselves. The dâśarâjya-yuddha, the battle of Sudâs against the ten kings, which fills so many hymns, is perhaps a fair illustration of the prevalent state of things. Society had to organise itself for war. We see the people as such engaged in warfare,[1] but as among the early Germans, there would grow up an order of warriors, a body of men who were constantly ready for the field and who would be the nucleus for the rest of the combatants. The hereditary tendency, so marked in all early society, would convert the order into a class. The Hindu tendency of running an idea to the extreme would convert the class into a caste. The requirements of religion would similarly lead to the development of a priestly caste. While all Âryans should pray and worship the gods, not many could make it the business of their life. Only a few could compose hymns of adoration and devotion and master the technique of sacrifices and ceremonies which were gaining in complexity with the lapse of time. A perusal of the Rigveda leaves no doubt that the Âryans of that age had a keener zest of life than their descendants manifested ever afterwards.

Social specialisation.

Warfare.

Priestcraft.

[1] Ibid., I, 69, 3; IV, 24, 4; VI, 26, 1; VII, 79, 2; VIII, 96, 15; I, 126, 5; VI, 26, 1.

But they have already begun to get anxious about the Unknown Beyond and, on the whole, the religious vein among them is stronger than among the ancient Greeks and Romans. Their spiritual life lent itself readily to priestcraft which gave rise to a sacerdotal order. Once again, under the operation of the hereditary tendency and the logical tendency, the order would crystallise into a caste. The formation of the Brâhmaṇa and Kṣatriya castes —the priests and warriors—would leave viś or people at large as one huge caste. With the Śûdras representing a good deal of the aboriginal or mixed element already marked out, the fourfold division would be complete. It may be added that slavery was known to vedic society both in the period represented by Books II—VII and the slightly later one represented by Book VIII.[1] Beyond the pale of caste, there might still remain large aboriginal tribes or groups.

Divisions and Restrictions.

As society grew more complex and economic development led to further sub-division of labour, the four castes, particularly the last two, would split into numerous sub-castes. The effect of permanent settlement in different regions which could not easily communicate with one another would be further to sub-divide castes on the basis of locality. But this process does not seem to have gone to any considerable length in the age of the Rigveda. Nor is inter-marriage among the three higher castes barred or hedged round with such restrictions as appear in the Dharma Sûtras, not to speak of the Dharma Śâstras, of later ages.[2]

Tribes.

The political organisation reflected in Books II—VII is the same as in Books I, VIII and IX. All the nine Maṇḍalas can, therefore, be utilised

---

[1] Ibid., VII, 86, 7; VIII, 56, 3.

[2] On the whole subject of the development of caste, see Vedic Index, II, 247—71, and the authorities cited there.

together. The Âryans of the Ṛigveda are divided into a number of tribes. The 'Five Tribes,' frequently spoken of, seem to be the Purus, Turvaśas, Yadus, Anus, and Druhyus.[1] Besides them there are others such as the Bharatas, Gandhâris, Uśînaras. Some scholars have worked out a gradation of Vedic society. The Grâma or village, perhaps originally the horde, consisted principally of the branches of a family living together. A number of Grâmas formed a viś or canton; lastly, a number of cantons made up a Jana or people. But as Keith has pointed out, these terms are used with distressing vagueness in the Ṛigveda, that, for instance, the Bharatas can be called at one time a Jana and at another time a Grâma, and that the evidence for the subordination of the Grâma to the Viś is totally wanting.[2] The term viś often means merely a settlement.[3] In the plural it seems to denote subjects.[4] Nowhere has Viśpati the technical sense of "lord of a canton," viś could not be a normal unit of government.[5] So we are left with the Jana and Grâma as possible political organisations. Grâma means a collection, a horde, and it is possible that the term originally referred to the wandering tribe or clan. The derivative grâmaṇî, leader of a grâma, might at first have referred to the leader of the moving group. When the horde settled down, grâma would naturally mean the settled horde. It might be applied to a whole tribe. But in course of time the term seems to have been restricted to the smaller settlement, the unit of society, *viz.*, the village. This seems to be the most likely explanation of the ambiguity of the grâma. In any case, references to the grâma as a unit of habitation are numerous. For instance, in a hymn of the second section of the first Maṇḍala

[1] On their geographical distribution, Macdonell, op. cit., pp. 154—56.
[2] Keith, Cambridge History of India, I, p. 91.
[3] Rigveda, IV, 37, 1; V, 3, 5; VI, 48, 8; VII, 61, 3; VII, 70, 3.
[4] Ibid., VI, 8, 4.
[5] Keith, op. cit., p. 91.

Rudra is propitiated in order that all in the grâma may be well-nourished and exempt from disease.[1] In a hymn of the first section of the same Maṇḍala, Agni is invoked as the protector of the people of grâmas.[2] Even if the significance of grâma be doubtful in the Ṛigveda, it is more than probable that an agricultural people would be divided into villages.

The Jana once settled on a more or less definite piece of territory, probably including a number of villages, formed a small kingdom. It was headed by a Râjan, a king or a chief, normally hereditary.[3] It is just the arrangement which the prevalence of warfare and the totality of social circumstances would, *a priori*, lead one to expect. In a later work of Vedic literature, the Aitareya Brâhmaṇa, one of the true causes of the rise of the kingship seems to have been grasped. "The Devas and the Asuras were fighting............The Asuras defeated the Devas. ....The Devas said, 'It is on account of our having no chief (arâjatayâ) that the Asuras defeat us. Let us create a Râjan (râjânam karavâmahe).' All agreed."[4] Similarly, the Taittiriya Brâhmaṇa records that "the Devas and Asuras joined in battle. Then Prajâpati concealed his eldest son Indra, lest he should be killed by the mighty Asuras. Prahlâda, the son of Kayadhu, likewise concealed his son Virocana, lest he should be killed by the Devas. The Devas went to Prajâpati and said, 'there can possibly be no battle for a state having no king.' Then they courted Indra to be their king with sacrifices."[5] It is hardly necessary to remark that what the gods or demons are supposed to do is only a reflection of what men actually do or are believed to have done. It is possible that the Aitareya passage

The Kingship.

---

1. Rigveda, I, 114, 1.
2. Ibid., I, 44, 10.
3. Keith, Cambridge History of India, I, p. 94.
4. Aitareya Brâhmaṇa. I, 14.
5. Taittiriya Brâhmaṇa, I, 5, 9.

or rather its original, whatever it might have been, enshrines a tradition that the Âryans had at first no regular military chiefs, that their enemies had such leaders, and that the example of the latter was followed by the former as a matter of expediency and necessity. Such a tradition might have been based partly on facts but there is no means of being perfectly sure of it.[1] All that can be reasonably inferred is that warfare which demands leadership and some concentration of authority, tended somehow to originate or strengthen the chiefship.

The Character of the Kingship.

The Râjan is well-established in the Ṛigveda and his character can be inferred from a number of hymns. He is the 'guardian of the people,' their 'ruler.'[2] The gods Mitra and Varuṇa are invoked to keep the splendour of dominion, guarding the dominion that lasts for ever.[3] Again, they are kings, guards of mighty, everlasting order.[4] The authority of the king is binding. A hymn in the first Maṇḍala refers to Agni as claiming obedience like a king.[5] "I am the royal ruler," says Varuṇa, "mine is empire, as mine who sway all life are all the immortals. Varuṇa's will the gods obey and follow. I am the king over folk of sphere sublimest."[6] There, again, Trasadasyu, chief of the Purus, claims divinity for himself. "......The Gods associate me with the acts of Varuṇa:.. ...I am the king Varuṇa; on me (the gods) bestow those principal energies (that are) destructive of the Asuras;......I am Indra, I am Varuṇa, I am those two in greatness......."[7] Obedience seems some-

[1] On the basis of a passage in the Ṛigveda, Zimmer held that in some states there was no king in times of peace but his interpretation has been questioned (Vedic Index, II, p. 216).

[2] Ṛigveda, III, 43.

[3] Ibid., V, 69, 1.

[4] Ibid., VII, 64, 2; VIII, 56, 1.

[5] Ibid., I, 67, 1.

[6] Ibid., IV, 42, 1.

[7] Ibid., IV, 42.

times to be forced.[1] On the other hand, a hymn in the fourth Maṇḍala refers to a Râjan who dwells in peace and comfort in his own house, to whom holy food flows richly and to whom the people freely pay homage.[2] The rule of a king is expected to be beneficent to the people. A king is seen bestowing favours on those worthy of them.[3] When the resplendent Agni is invoked as the protector of the people in grâmas, one detects an analogy with the function laid upon a king.[4] Elsewhere, however, the king is spoken of as the master of the riches of his own subjects and of hostile people. The king was expected to lead in war. A hymn addressed to Soma Pavamâna refers to him as sitting like a king above the hosts.[5] The king is sometimes described as purâm bhettâ, the sacker of forts or such earth-works as were thrown up at the time.[6] The god Indra, doubtless after the earthly ideal, goes intrepidly from fight to fight, destroying castle after castle, with his strength.[7] Agni is to win all the forts and treasures.[8]

The king's pomp and majesty.

Even in the earliest hymns of the Ṛigveda, the king is surrounded by pomp and majesty. A hymn in the second Maṇḍala refers to Mitra and Varuṇa as kings and pictures them seated in their supremest home, the thousand-pillared, firmly based.[9] Again, in the seventh Maṇḍala, "O Varuṇa, thou glorious lord, I entered thy lofty home, thine house with thousand portals."[10] It appears that the king lived in a mansion as splendid as the arts of the times could rear. In the slightly later collections of hymns, Râjans are spoken

[1] Ibid., VII, 6, 5; IX, 7, 5.
[2] Ibid., IV, 50, 8.
[3] Ibid., I, 67, 1.
[4] Ibid., I, 44, 10.
[5] Ibid., IX, 7, 4.
[6] Vedic Index, II, p. 212.
[7] Ṛigveda, I, 53, 7. See also VII, 18.
[8] Ibid., III, 15, 4. See also IV, 27, 1.
[9] Ibid., II, 41, 5.
[10] Ibid., VII, 88, 5.

of as like gold to look upon.[1] They are too terrible to behold.[2] Presumably, they wore shining apparel.

The administration.

The administration was expected to conform to law or custom. "Varuṇa true to holy law, sits down among his people; he, most wise, sits there to govern all."[3] Elsewhere in the course of a hymn to Mitra and Varuṇa, the laws of kings are spoken of as standing firm.[4] The idea of order as dwelling among men has emerged.[5] "Strong is the thought of Ṛita (law or truth), the behest of Ṛita."[6] In the task of administration, the king seems to have been assisted by a number of men. The gods Mitra and Varuṇa are spoken of as having set their warders "who visit every spot and watch unceasing." They keep guard over fields and plants; they find out those bent on evil.[7] Spies are often mentioned in the hymns. They seem to have been more than detectives; they partook of the character of agents general. Varuṇa's spies are pictured as seated round about.[8] Elsewhere they are "ever true and never bewildered."[9] Sent on their errand, they "survey the two world-halves well-formed and fashioned Wise are they, holy, skilled in sacrifices, the furtherers of the praise-songs of the prudent."[10] Agni is implored to send forward his spies.[11] It is possible to distinguish only two officers specifically in the entourage of the king. The Senânî, 'leader of an army," seems to have been a military commander appointed by the king.[12]

---

[1] Ibid., VIII, 6, 38.
[2] Ibid., I, 85, 8.
[3] Ibid., I, 25, 10.
[4] Ibid., VIII, 24, 8.
[5] Ibid., IV, 40; V, 8.
[6] Ibid., I, 68. Cf. I, 152, 1; V, 44, 2; VII, 60, 13.
[7] Ibid., VII, 61, 3.
[8] Ibid., I, 25, 3.
[9] Ibid., VI, 67, 5. [10] Ibid., VII, 67, 3. [11] Ibid., IV, 4, 3.
[12] Ibid., VII, 20, 5; IX, 96, 1. Macdonell and Keith hold that the senânî "was appointed by the king, not by the people, to command in war when the king became too important to lead every little fray in person." Vedic Index, II, p. 472.

The grâmaṇi, leader of a grâma, seems to have been a village officer, presumably exercising both civil and military functions.[1] In the scheme of government, the Purohita or the priest occupied a position second to none in weight and dignity. "The Vedic Purohita," as Keith puts it, "was the forerunner of the Brâhmaṇa statesmen.....there is no reason to doubt that a Viśvâmitra or a Vaśiṣṭha was a most important element of the government of the early Vedic realm."[2] In the first line of the first hymn of the Ṛigveda, Agni appears as the high priest.[3] In a later hymn he is the great priest in sacrifices, as he is "our help in battle-strife."[4] Brahmanspati is also called great high priest.[5] Priestly sacrifices are reckoned helpful to victory.[6] Besides, throughout the Ṛigveda the priests are the rain-makers and therefore command reverence and devotion. Brâhmaṇas as a class must be well-favoured. "The Gods uphold that king with their protection who helps the Brâhmaṇa when he seeks his protection."[7] It was partly as an informal representative of this mighty order that the purohita took his place beside the king. It seems that a king had only one purohita at a time. Purohitas sometimes accompanied kings to battlefields and even took a share in the fighting.[8] On the whole, a purohita may be regarded as an influential advisor who sometimes became the companion of the king.

The Purohita.

[1] Vedic Index, I, p. 247. The Grâmaṇî seems to be identical with the Vrajapati mentioned elsewhere.

[2] Cambridge History of India, Vol. I, p. 95.

[3] Ṛigveda, I, 1, 1.

[4] Ibid., I, 44, 10. See also III, 2, 8.

[5] Ibid., II, 24, 9.

[6] Ibid., VII, 18, 13.

[7] Ibid., IV, 50, 8-9.

[8] Vedic Index, II, 5—8, 263. For Viśvâmitra, Ṛigveda, III, 33, 53; for Vaśiṣṭha, VII, 18, 83. For other references, V, II, 2; VI, 70, 4.

The expenses of the administration seem to have been met by some sort of contribution from the people, particularly the rich folk. In the second section of the first Maṇḍala, Agni is once referred to as eating the woods like a king eating the rich.[1] One finds no trace of revenue officers in the Ṛigveda, perhaps from the nature of the document. It is probable that the king held a considerable area of land as crown-land but nothing can be definitely proved.

Revenue.

The subject of justice is equally obscure. Nowhere does the king appear as definitely exercising civil or criminal jurisdiction. The expression Śatadâya[2] seems to mean one whose wergild was a hundred cows. It is probable that the system of wergild which is imbedded in the later Dharma Sûtras prevailed in Vedic society. For the rest justice might have been an affair of the family, the clan, and, lastly, the tribal assembly.

Justice.

That there was an assembly, Sabhâ or Samiti, is beyond doubt. But nothing can be gleaned about its composition. It might have been supposed to consist of all the free Âryas or of the higher classes alone. Nor are its functions any clearer. The king certainly attended it. But Zimmer's view that he was elected by the assembly is untenable; at any rate, it finds no proof in the Ṛigveda. It is likely that, as Geldner argued, the king was merely accepted by the assembled tribesmen. For the rest, it is "reasonable to assume that the business of the assembly was general deliberation on policy of all kinds, legislation so far as the Vedic Indian cared to legislate and judicial work."[3] Vidatha

The Assembly.

[1] Ṛigveda, I, 65, 4.
[2] Ibid., II, 32, 4.
[3] On the Sabhâ and Samiti, Vedic Index, II, 426-27, 430-31. Ludwig holds that the Samiti included all the people, while the Sabhâ was the special assembly of Maghavans and Brâhmaṇas. Zimmer

is another perplexing term which occurs several times in the Ṛigveda. It has been variously interpreted as an 'order,' a secular or religious assembly, a gathering for war, or even abstract ideas like knowledge, wisdom, priestly lore, sacrifice or spiritual authority. Bloomfield holds that it means primarily the 'house' and, secondarily, the sacrifice connected with the house. From the context in which the term occurs, it is not possible to glean anything about institutions.[1]

A feudal tendency.

Leaving the doubtful Vidatha out of account, the fact remains that there was a popular element in the polity of the Ṛigveda. There are, however, also some indications of a tendency which can only be called feudal. There are passages in which the term Râjan which usually denotes a king is employed in the sense of a noble. Thus we read, "He amplifies his lordly might, with Râjans he slays, even mid alarms he dwells secure. In greater or less fight none checks him, none subdues,—the wielder of the thunderbolt"[2] In the Rigveda the term Râjanya denotes both the royal and noble families. It will appear that a king was often surrounded by a number of nobles perhaps drawn from the same class, perhaps only claiming a similar social status. At the same time there occurs the expression Samrâj several times in the Ṛigveda.[3] It means great or supreme king and implies some difference from the ordinary

believes that the Sabhâ was the village assembly. The authors of the Vedic Index agree with Hillebrandt in thinking that "Samiti and Sabhâ are much the same, the one being the assembly, the other primarily the place of assembly." The Atharvaveda, VII, 12, 1, calls the Sabhâ and Samiti "the two daughters of Prajâpati," and thus distinguishes between them. But apart from the fact that the passage is later than the bulk of the Ṛigveda, it carries us no further.

[1] Vedic Index, II, 296-97. See the authorities and references cited there.

[2] Ṛigveda, I, 40, 8. See also I, 108, 7.

[3] For the references, Vedic Index, II, 433.

king. It may signify either an increase in power or a status of suzerainty. The latter hypothesis is not barred by the absence of large kingdoms. As the sequel will show, the Hindu political system permitted the establishment of the relationships of suzerainty and vassalage even within a comparatively small area. Beyond this it is impossible to go for the age of the Ṛigveda. Sometimes the tribes contracted alliances among themselves. For instance, several of them fought against Sudās but such alliances were not federations.

CHAPTER III.

Gleanings from Later Vedic Literature.

The tenth and last Maṇḍala, distinctly later than the rest, of the Ṛigveda was composed probably after 1000 B.C.

After the Ṛigveda proper.

About the same time three other Vedas took shape. The Sâmaveda is only a collection of chants from the Ṛigveda for Sâman singers and is, therefore, valueless for historical purposes. The Yajurveda contains, besides a number of Ṛigvedic hymns, prose passages of its own. It is a collection of the formulæ and prayers of the Adhvaryu priests who actually performed the sacrifices. It has come down in two main recensions, the Kṛiṣṇa or black and the Śukla or white. Of the former there are three complete texts—the Taittirîya, Kâṭhaka and Maitrâyaṇî Saṁhitâs—and an incomplete text called the Kapiṣṭhala Saṁhitâ. For the White Yajurveda there is the Vâjasaneyi Saṁhitâ.[1] About the same time arose

The Atharvaveda.

the Atharvaveda which was, only long afterwards, recognised as a regular fourth Veda. Its spells and incantations, sometimes grotesque in character, were once held by modern scholars to be primarily non-Âryan in origin and the whole Veda was looked upon as an uncouth mixture of Âryan and "Drâvidian" practices and superstitions. Recently, however, the opinion has been gaining ground that the Âryans had magic and witchcraft of their own and that the Atharvaveda is, like the other Vedas, Âryan in origin and spirit. Only it represents a phase of belief and practice different from what is mirrored elsewhere. About the time that

---

[1] On the composition of the three later Vedas, see in particular Macdonell, History of Sanskrit Literature, pp. 171—92.

the last three Vedas were put into shape or only slightly later, Vedic ceremonial was elaborated and Vedic ideas explained or obscured in the earlier Brâhmaṇas. Of these the Pañcaviṁśa Brâhmaṇa, pertaining to the Sâmaveda, is the oldest. Next comes the Aitareya Brâhmaṇa of which the first five books are probably earlier than the rest. Then comes the Kauṣîtakî or Śâṅkhâyana Brâhmaṇa. Both belong to the Ṛigveda.[1] The ideas and institutions reflected in the tenth Maṇḍala of the Ṛigveda, the three other Vedas and the earlier Brâhmaṇas belong to the same order and, with specification of their sources, can be reviewed in the same strain.

The earlier Brâhmaṇas.

This extensive literature which falls roughly between 1000 B.C. and 700 B.C. belongs not merely to the valley of the Indus but also to that of the Ganges which the Âryans had penetrated in the meanwhile. The chief peoples of this period are the Kurus, Pañcâlas, Śibis, Matsyas, Vaitahavyas, Kośalas, Videhas, Kâśîs, Kekâṭas, Vidarbhas and Aṅgas. The Śriñjayas were closely related to the Kurus. Near the Uttara Kurus were the Uttara Madras.[2]

The peoples.

Caste has developed further and is now firmly established. It is now regarded as divine in origin and eternal in duration. In the well-known pantheistic Puruṣasûkta of the tenth Maṇḍala of the Ṛigveda occurs the standard explanation of caste. At the commencement of creation appeared Puruṣa, endowed with a thousand heads, a thousand eyes and a thousand legs. "Puruṣa is all this world, what has been and shall be." Three-fourths of him is the immortals in heaven and "one-

Caste.

---

[1] Keith, Cambridge History of India, Vol. I, pp. 114—16. Bloomfield, Introduction to the Hymns of the Atharvaveda. Whitney, Introduction to the English translation of the Atharvaveda. Macdonell, op. cit., 202—17. Keith, Aitareya Âraṇyaka, pp. 172-73.

[2] Keith, Cambridge History of India, Vol. I, 118—121.

fourth of his is all creatures." From his mouth sprang the Brâhmaṇas, from his arms the Kṣatriyas, from his thighs the Vaiśyas and from his feet the Śûdras.[1] Hence, the primacy of the Brâhmaṇa, the strength of the Kṣatriya, the utility of the Vaiśya and the low position and dependence of the Śûdra. Henceforward the principle of caste meets us everywhere. It is true that change of caste is occasionally recognised as possible. Viśvâmitra, for instance, who appears as a priest in the Ṛigveda is called a king in the Pañcaviṁśa Brâhmaṇa.[2] There, too, some kings are spoken of as performers of sattras.[3] Cases of intermarriage between different castes are met with.[4] Once at least in the Aitareya Brâhmaṇa the position of the Brâhmaṇa is subordinated to that of the Kṣatriya.[5] But the general trend of the later Vedic literature points to the consolidation of caste. The Brahmanic supremacy is to be buttressed in all sorts of ways. "Him who reviles a Brâhmaṇa, he (the king) shall fine with a hundred; him who strikes a Brâhmaṇa, he shall fine with a thousand; he who draws blood from him shall not behold the world of the Pitṛis."[6] In litigation, the king is required to support Brâhmaṇas against non-Brâhmaṇas.[7] In the Atharvaveda, as elsewhere, the Purohita is exalted. "The rain of Mitra-Varuṇa falls not on him who wrongs the priest. To him no command brings success; he wins no friend to do his will."[8] On the other hand, the Vaiśya is

[1] Ṛigveda, X, 90, 12 Also Atharvaveda, I, 9, 3; X, 6, 31. Cf. Aitareya Brâhmaṇa, VI, 1, 1. Taittirîya Brâhmaṇa, I, 2, 6, 7, III, 2, 3, 9.

[2] Pañcaviṁśa Brâhmaṇa, XXI, 12, 2. On seers of royal origin, Vedic Index, II, 261.

[3] Pañcaviṁśa Brâhmaṇa, XXV, 16, 3.

[4] Ṛigveda, X, 109. Atharvaveda, V, 17. Pañcaviṁśa Brâhmaṇa, IV, 24, 25. Vedic Index, II, 259-60.

[5] Aitareya Brâhmaṇa, VII, 20.

[6] Taittirîya Saṁhitâ, II, 6, 11.

[7] Ibid., II, 5, 12.

[8] Atharvaveda, V, 19, 15. On the priests see also Ṛigveda, X, 66, 13; 70, 7.

described as tributary to another, to be lived on by another, to be oppressed at will.[1] The followers of various crafts sink in estimation and form castes of their own. "The Śûdra is the servant of another, to be expelled at will, and to be slain at pleasure."[2] It is probable, however, that the fall in the status of the Vaiśyas brought them nearer the Śûdras and thus indirectly improved the position of the latter. In any case, however, caste barriers are now definitely set up and constitute a factor of first-rate importance in the political and economic life of the community.[3]

Political Conditions.

It is possible that the ordinary size of a state increased during this period beyond the point reached in the first nine books of the Ṛigveda, but direct evidence on the subject is wanting. The new ideal which has definitely emerged is either that of the big kingdom or of suzerainty. In the Atharvaveda one of the most cherished ambitions of a king is to 'conquer' others. Victory in war is the burden of numerous hymns. For instance, a long prayer to Arbudi and Nyarbudi for assistance in battle breathes a jingoistic feeling of the utmost fervour.[4] The question is whether victory in war ordinarily led to annexation or merely to some sort of vassalage. There are indications which point to the latter probability. The term Samrâj, superior king, occurs in the Vâjasaneyi Saṁhitâ.[5] Adhirâja, which has a similar significance, is met with in the last Maṇḍala of the Rigveda,[6] the Atharvaveda,[7] the Taittirîya Saṁhitâ,[8] the Maitrâyaṇî

[1] Aitareya Brâhmaṇa, VII, 29, 3. Vedic Index, II, 255.
[2] Vedic Index, II, 255-56, summarising the passage in the Aitareya Brâhmaṇa, VII, 29, 4.
[3] On the whole subject, Vedic Index, II, 247—71, and the authorities cited there.
[4] Atharvaveda, IV, 22; VI, 38, 39, 97; VIII, 8.
[5] Vâjasaneyi Saṁhitâ, V, 32; XIII, 35; XX, 5, etc.
[6] Ṛigveda, X, 128, 9.
[7] Atharvaveda, VI, 98, 1; IX, 10, 24.
[8] Taittirîya Saṁhitâ, II, 4, 14, 2.

Saṁhitâ,[1] the Kâṭhaka Saṁhitâ,[2] and the Taittirîya Brâhmaṇa.[3] The Pañcaviṁśa Brâhmaṇa speaks of the Âdhipatya or supreme power.[4] The White Yajurveda also contains prayers to various gods for supremacy to kings.[5] The Kâṭhaka Saṁhitâ and the Maitrâyaṇî Saṁhitâ have the term svârâjya which, though not indicative of supremacy, seems to emphasise the element of independence.[6] The term Ekarâja, literally, 'sole ruler' which is used metaphorically in the Rigveda[7] seems to be used in a distinctly political sense in the Atharvaveda.[8] There are only two possible explanations: either a big powerful ruler assumed a higher title or a king got some other rulers to acknowledge his suzerainty in some rough and ready manner and therefore arrogated the lofty designations. The latter supposition would imply a feudal tendency. It is supported by the references to fights for single villages, to prayers and oblations prescribed for one who desires possession of a village.[9] If there were such small autonomous areas, they could hardly have stood by themselves and those who held possession of them are likely to have leaned on others for support. It may be added that during this period the terms Râjan or Râjya continued as usual to denote a king or a kingdom.[10] It is probable that overlordship was still the exception but that it had emerged as a form of political relationship. It is not possible to carry the discussion further on the basis of the evidence available for this period

[1] Maitrâyaṇî Saṁhitâ, IV, 12, 3.
[2] Kâṭhaka Saṁhitâ, VIII, 17.
[3] Taittirîya Brâhmaṇa, III, 1, 2, 9.
[4] Pañcaviṁśa Brâhmaṇa, XV, 3, 35.
[5] Śukla Yajurveda, IX, 39.
[6] Kâṭhaka Saṁhitâ, XIV, 5. Maitrâyaṇî Saṁhitâ, I, 11, 5.
[7] Ṛigveda, VIII, 17, 3.
[8] Atharvaveda, III, 1, 4, 1.
[9] Kṛiṣṇa Yajurveda, II, 3, 10; III, 4, 8.
[10] Atharvaveda, III, 4, 2; IV, 8, 1; XI, 6, 15, etc. Taittirîya Saṁhitâ, II, 1, 3, 4; VII, 5, 8, 3, etc. Aitareya Brâhmaṇa, VII, 23, etc. A reference to the good government of a Kṣatriya occurs in the Ṛigveda, X, 109, 3.

but as the sequel will show, the whole trend of later development harmonises only with the view here indicated.

The monarchy was the normal type of government. There are, indeed, a few passages which at first sight point to the existence of oligarchy. A hymn in the tenth Maṇḍala of the Ṛigveda remarks, "As the Râjans assemble together in the Samiti, the plants gather together in him who is called physician . . . ."[1] We read in the Atharvaveda, "They that ruled, a thousand, and were ten hundreds, those Vaitâhavyas, having devoured the cow of a Brâhmaṇa, perished."[2] The most probable explanation of these passages is that nobles are meant. In some other passages in the tenth Maṇḍala of the Ṛigveda,[3] the Atharvaveda[4] the Vâjasaneyi Saṁhitâ,[5] and the Taittiriya Saṁhitâ,[6] the term Râjan seems to be used only in the sense of a noble. It shows that round the king there stood a nobility which claimed the same social status as the royal family.

The Nobility.

The evidence at our disposal does not bear out the contention of some modern scholars that the monarchy was elective. No actual instance of election is anywhere recorded. A passage in the Atharvaveda—"To the tenth (decade of life) abide here, formidable, well-willing . . . "[7]—has been interpreted by one scholar as referring to life-long election as opposed to election for one or more generations, but, read with the context, it is only a usual prayer for long life and prosperity. What seems actually to have happened was that the people formally accepted a new king. It is

Popular acceptance of the king.

Ṛigveda, X, 9, 16.
Atharvaveda, V, 18, 10.
Ṛigveda, X, 42, 10; X, 97, 6.
Atharvaveda, XIX, 62, 1; II, 6, 4.
Vâjasaneyi Saṁhitâ, XVIII, 48; XXVI, 2.
Taittirîya Saṁhitâ, V, 7, 6; I, 3, 6.
Atharvaveda, III, 4, 7.

possible that the people might refuse to accept a physical or moral wreck for their leader but there is nothing anywhere in the nature of qualifications for candidates for royalty or indications of habitual choice on the score of merit. When choice seems to be referred to in benedictions and prayers, it only signifies acceptance. A hymn in the Atharvaveda indicates that the people at large, including metal-workers, builders of chariots, etc., signified their acceptance of a new sovereign.[1] Another hymn records the blessings and benedictions showered on him on the occasion. "Unto thee hath come the kingdom; with splendour rise forward; as lord of the people, sole king, bear thou rule; let all the directions call thee, O king; become thou here one for waiting on, for homage.

"Thee let the people choose unto kingship, thee these five directions; rest at the summit of royalty, at the pinnacle; from thence, formidable, share out good things to us."[2]

Consecration.

The acceptance was symbolised by a formal consecration. In the Vâjasaneyî Saṁhitâ the king-designate before his accession steps upon a gold plate perforated with nine or a hundred holes, and the priest sprinkles the waters over his head, chanting the following sacred text :—

"With Soma's glory, I sprinkle thee! with Agni's glow! with Sûrya's splendour! with Indra's energy! be thou the sovereign protector of the ruling powers!"

"Make him, O gods, to be unrivalled for great rulership, for great superiority, for rule of the people," etc.[3]

In the Atharvaveda the waters are supposed to be collected from many quarters. "The waters of heaven that revel with milk, in the atmosphere or also on the earth—with the splendours of all those waters do I sprinkle

---

[1] Atharvaveda, III, 5, 6, 7.

[2] Ibid., III, 4, 1-2.

[3] Vâjasaneyî Saṁhitâ, IX, 40; XXV, 17, 18.

thee."[1] It appears that prior to the sprinkling, the king-designate, attired in bright clothing strode upon the tiger's skin unto the great quarters.[2] In several compositions of this period is mentioned the Râjasûya, a yet more complex ceremony for the inauguration of a king, which consisted of a series of sacrifices lasting for a year or so.[3] In the Taittirîya Samhitâ[4] during the Râjasûya rite of adoration the king is addressed as Mitra, Varuṇa, etc.[4] The rite of consecration raised the king almost above humanity. It is, however, in the later Brâhmaṇas that varieties and details of the consecration ceremonial are fully developed.[5]

Turbulence.

In spite of the consecration, however, a king sometimes came to grief. In the Taittirîya Saṁhitâ, the king emphatically claims the obedience of the people.[6] But the same text elsewhere elaborates a sacrifice to avert the impending expulsion of a king.[7] The Atharvaveda contains prayers for the restoration of an exiled king.[8] Elsewhere the fervent desire is expressed that all rivals must be inferior to the king.[9] All this points to some trouble which might be due to refractory nobles or other subjects or to tactless kings.

The Assembly.

In such turbulence the Assembly appears to have been a factor to be reckoned with. In the course of a hymn in the tenth Maṇḍala of the Ṛigveda which may refer to the assembly in one's own state or in a conquered enemy's territory,

---

[1] Atharvaveda, IV, 8, 5-6.
[2] Ibid., IV, 8, 3-4.
[3] Taittirîya Saṁhitâ, Atharvaveda, IV, 8, 1; XI, 7, 7. Aitareya Brâhmaṇa, V, 1, 1, 12.
[4] Taittirîya Saṁhitâ, I, 8, 16.
[5] Taittirîya Brâhmaṇa, II, 7, 15—17. Śatapatha Brâhmaṇa, *infra*.
[6] Taittirîya Saṁhitâ, II, 7, 18, 2.
[7] Ibid., II, 3, 1.
[8] Atharvaveda, III, 3-6, 4.
[9] Ibid., I, 9.

a proud leader says, "Superior am I and have come here with a force capable of doing all things. I shall make myself master of your aims, your resolutions and your assembly."[1] "Of these that sit together," so runs a prayer in the Atharvaveda, "I take to myself the splendour, the discernment (vijñâna); of the whole gathering (saṁsad) make me, O Indra, possessor of the fortune (bhâgin)."[2] The concord of the monarchy and the assembly was devoutly to be wished and prayed for. We read in the course of a benediction in the Atharvaveda, "Fixed, unmoved do thou slaughter the foes, make them that play the foe fall below (thee); (be) all the quarters (diś) like-minded, concordant; let the gathering (samiti) here suit thee (who art) fixed."[3] Again, "let both Sabhâ and Samiti, the two daughters of Prajâpati, accordant, favour me."[4] The Atharvaveda contains prayers for power of argumentation and eloquence in order to acquire influence over the assembly.[5] Sometimes witchcraft was used to achieve the same end. "What (witchcraft) they have made for thee in the Sabhâ—I take that back again."[6] The assembly itself seems to have been sometimes unsteady in temper. There is a tell-tale passage in the Atharvaveda. "We know thy name, O Assembly; verily, sport (nariṣṭâ) by name art thou."[7] In the last hymn of the last Maṇḍala of the Ṛigveda, there is a fervent exhortation for concord in the Assembly. "Assemble, speak together; let your minds be all of one accord.

The Assembly and the King.

Concord in the Assembly.

---

[1] Ṛigveda, X, 166, 4.
[2] Atharvaveda, VII, 12, 2-3.
[3] Ibid., VI, 88.
[4] Ibid., VII, 12, 1.
[5] Ibid., II, 27; VI, 69.
[6] Ibid., IV, 31.
[7] Ibid., VII, 12, 2.

"As ancient gods unanimously sit down to their appointed share.

"The place is common, common the assembly, common the mind, so be their thoughts united.

"A common purpose do I lay before you, and worship with your general oblation.

"One and the same be your resolve, and be your minds of one accord.

"United be the thoughts of all that may happily agree."[1]

There is no means of gauging the actual power wielded by the Assembly. Nor is the scope of its activities at all clear. From a hymn in the last Maṇḍala of the Ṛigveda it appears that the assembly sometimes acted as a court of justice.[2] Sabhâsad or Sabhâcara seems to mean a member of the Sabhâ, one of those who sat to decide causes.[3] It is possible that the judicial work of the Sabhâ was entrusted to a small committee of its members. The matters of which the Sabhâ probably took cognisance as a court of justice, seem to have been disputes about land,[4] cheating at play,[5] recovery of debts,[6] inheritance,[7] theft, assault and murder.[8] Besides justice, the most important function of the assembly seems to be that of general deliberation. It is impossible to dogmatise on the subject, but from certain references in the Atharvaveda it appears

The work of the Assembly.

[1] Ṛigveda, X, 193, 2—4.

[2] Ṛigveda, X, 71, 10. "All friends are joyful in the friend who cometh in triumph, having conquered in assembly."

[3] Vedic Index, II, 427-28.

[4] Kṛiṣṇa Yajurveda, II, 2, 1.

[5] Atharvaveda, VI, 118-19.

[6] Ibid., VI, 117.

[7] Kṛiṣṇa Yajurveda, II, 6, 1.

[8] Vâjasaneyi Saṁhitâ, XXX, 5.

that the Assembly discussed war,[1] peace,[2] finance[3] and general well-being.[4]

Nevertheless the literature of this period leaves the impression that the centre of gravity had already shifted to the monarchy. It was the king who constituted the real government. In more than one hymn of the Ṛigveda it is recognised that Rita—truth, right or law—is the base on which the earth rests.[5] Beyond the Ṛita, another hymn in the same Maṇḍala of the Ṛigveda, which is reproduced in the Atharvaveda, inculcates firmness on the part of the king. "Here be you firm like the mountain and may you not come down. Be you firm here like Indra; remain you here and hold the realm.

The King.

"Firm is the heaven, firm is the earth, firm is the universe, firm are the mountains, let the king of the people be firm.

"Let the realm be held by you, be made firm by the Râjâ Varuṇa, the God Bṛihaspati, Indra and also Agni."[6]

Round the king there seems to have been a circle of relations, friends, and chief officers, some of whom were called king-makers. "They that are kings, king-makers, that are charioteers and troop-leaders (headmen ?) subjects to me do thou, O Parṇa, make all people round about."[7] The Pañcaviṁśa Brâhmaṇa mentions eight Vîras or heroes, round the king, *viz.*, his brother, son, Purohita, Mahiṣî, Sûta, Grâmaṇî, Kṣatra and Saṁgrahîtri.[8] The Taittirîya Saṁhitâ and the Taittirîya Brâhmaṇa give a fuller list of the Ratnins

The King's friends or officers.

Atharvaveda, VI, 75, 103.
Ibid., VII, 52.
Ibid., III, 29.
Ibid., VI, 107.
Ṛigveda, X, 85, 1; X, 190, 1.
Ibid., X, 173. Atharvaveda, VI, 87-88.
Atharvaveda, III, 5, 7.
Pañcaviṁśa Brâhmaṇa, XIX, 1, 4.

or jewels: Brâhmaṇa, Râjanya (noble), Mahiṣî (first wife of the king), vâvâta (favourite wife of the king), Parivṛikti (discarded wife), the Senânî, commander of the army, the Sûta, charioteer, the Grâmaṇî, village headman, the Kṣatra, chamberlain, the Saṁgrahîtṛi, treasurer, the Bhâgadugha, collector of taxes, and the Akṣâvâpa, superintendent of dicing or thrower of dice.[1] The Maitrâyaṇî Saṁhitâ varies the order of enumeration and adds the Takṣa, carpenter, the Rathakâra, chariot-maker and Govikarta, slayer of cows or huntsman.[2] It is difficult to conjecture the exact status and functions of these notables but it may be surmised that after the age of the Ṛigveda there had ensued a good deal of administrative development, that there had come into being a number of household officers and administrative functionaries, that no clear distinction had been drawn between the two and that probably the same persons acted in a double capacity.

Spies.

There seems to have been a large staff of spies. "From the sky," says the Atharvaveda, "his (Varuṇa's) spies go forth hither; thousand-eyed they look over the earth."[3] From a curious allusion in the Ṛigveda, one is inclined to infer that spies detected or caught criminals. Afraid of spies, Yama rejects the love of his sister.[4] It is interesting that the Taittirîya Saṁhitâ mentions Dûtas as well as Prahitas.[5] Many centuries later Sâyaṇâcârya, the great Vedic commentator, explained that the Dûta was a regular representative of the king while Prahita was a mere spy.

---

[1] Taittirîya Saṁhitâ, I, 8, 9, 1 et seq. Taittirîya Brâhmaṇa, I, 7, 3, 1.

[2] Maitrâyaṇî Saṁhitâ, II, 6, 5; IV, 3, 8.

[3] Atharvaveda, IV, 16, 4.

[4] Ṛigveda, X, 10, 1–6.

[5] Taittirîya Saṁhitâ, IV, 7, 1.

Justice.

The judicial administration still seems to be in a state of flux. Besides the Sabhâ or its committee which seems to have acted as a court of justice in some causes, the king probably performed some judicial functions. A hymn in the Atharvaveda refers to him as a stern corrector.[1] In the Kâṭhaka Saṁhitâ, a Râjanya is mentioned as an overseer (adhyakṣa) of the punishment of a Śûdra.[2] This may be a case of the delegation of judicial authority. To the expression Madhyamaśî, which occurs in the tenth Maṇḍala of the Ṛigveda[3] and reproduced in the Vâjasaneyi Saṁhitâ[4] and the Atharvaveda,[5] divergent meanings have been assigned. Probably it means an arbiter or mediator and thus points to the practice of arbitration during this period. On judicial punishments the evidence is very scanty. The Pañcaviṁśa Brâhmaṇa says that a Purohita might be punished with death for treachery to his master.[6] It appears that treason was already regarded as one of the highest crimes and that it brought the severest punishment on the greatest in the land. A hymn in the tenth Maṇḍala of the Ṛigveda shows that a gambler who lost heavily and got deep into debt found himself bereft of home and reduced to slavery.[7] It is not impossible that heavy indebtedness led to slavery in ancient India as in ancient Greece and Rome. From the Taittirîya Saṁhitâ it is clear that various fines were inflicted for various offences.[8]

---

[1] Atharvaveda, IV, 8, 2.

[2] Kâṭhaka Saṁhitâ, XXVII, 4.

[3] Ṛigveda, X, 97, 12.

[4] Vâjasaneyi Saṁhitâ, XII, 86.

[5] Atharvaveda, IV, 9, 4.

[6] Vedic Index, II, 84.

[7] Ṛigveda, X, 34.

[8] Taittirîya Saṁhitâ, II, 6, 11.

The fiscal arrangements of this period are even more obscure than the judicial. In the tenth Maṇḍala of the Rigveda, the king is called the sole taker of taxes from the people.[1] In the Atharvaveda he can eat the Viś, that is, levy heavy exactions on his subjects at will.[2] It appears from the Taittirīya Saṁhitâ that there was no communal ownership of land, that fields were held by individuals or families and that possession was sometimes disputed.[3] It seems that the land was the principal source of revenue and that regular officers had been appointed for the collection.

Revenue.

It is not possible to form any further idea of the activities of the state during this period. Roads are referred to[4] but there is no evidence to prove that they were constructed or maintained by the king. For the rest, the Vedic composers expected the king to secure plenty and prosperity and applauded those whom they believed to have fulfilled the ideal.

Functions of the State.

Some of the features of Hindu polity revealed in the second stage of Vedic compositions are observed in a more highly developed form in the last stage which is represented by the later books of the Aitareya Brâhmaṇa, the Śatapatha and some other Brâhmaṇas and the earlier Upaniṣads such as the Chândogya and Bṛihadâraṇyaka. This class of compositions took shape, roughly speaking between 700 and 500 B.C. The other Upaniṣads, too, form part of Vedic literature, but they are so late in composition that they cannot be dealt with alongside the Brâhmaṇas.

The latest Vedic Literature.

---

[1] Ṛigveda, X, 173, 6.

[2] Atharvaveda, IV, 22. For other references to Bali or tribute, see Vedic Index, II, 62.

[3] For instance in the Atharvaveda, III, 4, 7.

[4] Atharvaveda, XX, 127.

Caste is gaining in rigour and is dominating the whole of life. The Śatapatha Brâhmaṇa dedicates the representatives of the four castes to different deities at the Puruṣamedha sacrifice.[1] It prescribes different modes of address for the different castes,[2] and different sizes of funeral mounds for them.[3] In the Soma sacrifice the Śûdra is certainly given a place,[4] but elsewhere it declares that he is not at all fit to be addressed by a Dîkṣita or consecrated person.[5] Once, indeed, it seems to regard the Brâhmaṇas, Kṣatriyas, and Vaiśyas as constituting the whole world and leaves Śûdras altogether out of account.[6] Here and there it is true one meets with exceptions. Janaka, for instance, is said to have become a Brâhmaṇa.[7] In the Bṛihadâraṇyaka Upaniṣad Ajâtaśatru is a teacher of the Brâhmaṇa Gârgya Bâlâki.[8] But the general trend of the period is towards the consolidation of caste.

Caste.

In the general political conditions, too, a change seems to have taken place by this time. The ideal of the big kingdom is now more pronounced than ever and the average size of the state also seems to have increased. The eighth book of the Aitareya Brâhmaṇa has a series of terms which denote variety or gradation of sovereignty—Râjya, Sâmrâjya, Bhaujya, Svârâjya, Vairâjya Pâramasthya, Mâhârâjya, Âdhipatya,

Change in political conditions.

[1] Śatapatha Brâhmaṇa, III, 1, 1, 10.

[2] Vedic Index, II, 253.

[3] Śatapatha Brâhmaṇa, XIII, 8, 3, 11.

[4] Ibid., V, 5, 4, 9.

[5] Ibid., III, 1, 1, 10.

[6] Ibid., II, 1, 4, 12; IV, 2, 2, 14.

[7] Ibid., IX, 6, 2, 10. In the Aitareya Brâhmaṇa (VII, 29) the progeny of Kṣatriya who eats in the company of men of other castes rises or falls accordingly.

[8] Bṛihadâraṇyaka Upaniṣad, II, 1, 1. See also the Kauṣîtakî Upaniṣad, IV, 1.

Svâvaśya.[1] Further, the title for the kings of the Southerners, the Satvatas, is Bhoja; that for the kings of the Westerners, the Nîcyas and Apâcyas, is Svarâṭ; that for the kings of the Northerners, the Uttarakurus and the Uttaramadras, is Virâṭ; that for the kings of the people of the middle country, called Kuru Pañcâlas and Uśînaras, is simply Râjan. It is impossible to establish the exact significance of these terms, but when the title of Samrâṭ is applied to the kings of the Prâcyas or Easterners, it seems like an inkling into the first beginnings of the Magadhan imperialism which was destined to affect the whole of India after the 5th century B. C.[2] Janaka, king of the Videhas, is also called Samrâṭ in the Śatapatha Brâhmaṇa[3] and in the Bṛihad-âraṇyaka Upaniṣad.[4] Elsewhere the eighth book of the Aitareya Brâhmaṇa declares that monarchy at its highest should have a dominion extending right up to the natural boundaries, up to the very ends, in fact, up to the sea.[5] It mentions twelve such monarchs.[6] Divested of its obvious exaggerations, the statement means that from time to time some kings had actually developed their power far beyond the average and almost brought a new type of state into existence. It could only be either an empire in the strict sense of the term or a suzerainty. The latter alternative finds support in the thirty-ninth chapter of the same Brâhmaṇa, where the Aindra Mahâbhiṣeka is spoken of. That rite is said to have been performed by great rulers like Janamejaya, Sâryâta, Śatrujit,

---

[1] Aitareya Brâhmaṇa, VII, 3, 14; VIII, 12, 4, 5. The term Ādhipatya also occurs in the Chândogya Upaniṣad, V, 2, 6. K. P. Jayaswal and R. C. Majumdar interpret Vairâjya as absence of royalty, that is, republicanism. Macdonell and Keith take it to denote some form of royal authority (Vedic Index, II, 221). The context supports the latter interpretation.

[2] Aitareya Brâhmaṇa, VIII, 14, 2, 3.

[3] Śatapatha Brâhmaṇa, XI, 3, 2, 1, 6; 2, 2, 3.

[4] Bṛihadâraṇyaka Upaniṣad, IV, 1, 1; 3, 1.

[5] Aitareya Brâhmaṇa, VIII, 4, 1.

[6] Ibid., VIII, 14, 4; 19, 2.

Viśvakarman, Sudâs and Marut, each of whom had succeeded in conquering the whole world. "A Kṣatriya who is consecrated with his Aindra Mahâbhiṣeka, conquers all conquerors, knows all the worlds, becomes *superior to all kings*, gains renown and majesty, becomes self-created and self-ruled, after conquering 'empires,' countries ruled by the Bhojas,..... ....after death ascends heaven and overcomes death." Superiority to all kings supplies the clue. The "conquest of the world" did not mean the extinction of existing kings but merely the acknowledgment of suzerainty. The same conclusion emerges from certain passages in the Śatapatha Brâhmaṇa. It speaks of four royal sacrifices—the Râjasûya, Vâjapeya, Aśvamedha and Aindra Mahâbhiṣeka. The Aśvamedha was to be performed by kings who had been successful in Digvijaya or conquest of all quarters. A horse should be let loose with the words, "Go thou along the way of the Âdityas." Guarded by armed warriors, it should be allowed to roam about for a year, during which period oblations were to be offered by the sacrificer. When the horse returned unmolested at the end of the year, a grand assembly should be held of all the kings and chiefs of the country and, in their presence, the animal should be sacrificed.[1] Here, again, the presence of chiefs and kings at the assembly and sacrifice points to the relationship of suzerainty and vassalage. According to the Śatapatha Brâhmaṇa, this rite had been performed by thirteen kings.[2] The bid for suzerainty might sometimes be rudely checked. The Śatapatha Brâhmaṇa speaks of the Satvatas who prepared a horse for the Aśvamedha but who were defeated by Bharata and lost the horse to him.[3]

Royal sacrifices.

[1] Śatapatha Brâhmaṇa, IX, 3, 4, 8.
[2] Ibid., XIII, 5, 4.
[3] Ibid., XIII, 5, 4,21.

The Vâjapeya and Râjasûya.

Next to the Aśvamedha and the Aindra Mahâbhiṣeka in dignity stood the Vâjapeya and after it the Râjasûya. The Śatapatha Brâhmaṇa says that the Râjasûya sacrifice is that of a Râjan and the Vâjapeya that of a Samrâṭ, and emphasises that the latter is higher than the former.[1] Later, the same text mentions Âsandî, sitting on a throne, as one of the characteristics of the Samrâṭ.[2] In the course of the Vâjapeya, the sacrificer is called 'All-ruler.'[3] Of the net result of the Râjasûya we are simply told that "by offering the Râjasûya he becomes king."[4] Here, too, the performance of the Vâjapeya perhaps implied some sort of suzerainty. In the later Brâhmaṇas both the sacrifices have been elaborated beyond all precedent. Even the Râjasûya is not a single independent ceremony but a series of consecutive rites occupying a year or so and requiring the services of numerous priests. A few of the significant details may be mentioned. Explaining one of the Râjasûya rites, the Śatapatha Brâhmaṇa remarks that the sacrificer is Indra,—he is Indra for a two-fold reason, namely, because he is a Kṣatriya and because he is a sacrificer."[5] Elsewhere it identifies the sacrificer with the god Prajâpati.[6] In the course of the Râjasûya, the sacrificer shoots from a distance. "And as to why a Râjanya shoots, he, the Râjanya, is the visible representative of Prajâpati: hence, while being one, he rules over many."[7] The Vâjapeya equates the sacrificer with Bṛihaspati. "All ruler is he, N. N." says the priest. "All-ruler is he, N. N. Him, thus

---

1 Śatapatha Brâhmaṇa, V, 1, 1, 3, 13-14.
2 Ibid., XII, 8, 3, 4.
3 Ibid., V, 2, 2, 14-5.
4 Ibid., V, 1, 1, 12.
5 Ibid., V, 4, 3, 4. See also V, 1, 4, 2; 2, 5, 3.
6 Ibid., V, 2, 24 ; 3, 4, 23.
7 Ibid., V, 1, 5, 14.

indicated, he thereby indicates to the gods. Of mighty power is he who has been consecrated, he has become one of yours; protect him."[1] Again, in the course of the Vâjapeya, the Adhvaryu spreads out the goat-skin with the words, 'This is thy kingship.' Thus he endows the king "with royal power. He (the Adhvaryu) then makes him sit down, with the words, 'Thou art the ruler, the ruling lord' whereby he makes him the ruler, ruling over those subjects of his;———'Thou art firm and steadfast!', whereby he makes him firm and steadfast in this world;———'Thee for the tilling!———Thee for peaceful dwelling!———Thee for wealth!———Thee for thrift!' whereby he means to say, (here I seat) thee for the welfare (of the people)."[2] As in the Atharvaveda various kinds of waters are taken for the sprinkling.[3] Some symbolic rites are mentioned. A tiger-skin is spread in front of the Maitravaruṇa's hearth.[4] The sacrificer makes a short chariot race,[5] touches a cow as arranged, and stops amid the cows of his relations.[6] He puts on shoes of boar's skin, because the boar had been produced by the gods putting a pot of ghee on the fire.[7] Looking down upon the earth he mutters, "O mother Earth! injure me not, nor I thee." This is done, lest the earth should shake him off.[8] In the course of a sort of dialogue with the priests around in succession, the king is addressed by them as Brâhmaṇa, and also as Savitṛi 'of true impulsion,' Varuṇa 'of true power,' Indra 'mighty through the people,' Rudra 'the most kindly.'[9] The Adhvaryu hands over the wooden sacrificial sword to him with these words, "Indra's thunderbolt

[1] Śatapatha Brâhmaṇa V, 2, 2, 14-15.
[2] Ibid., V, 2, 1, 24.
[3] Ibid., V, 3, 4, 3—28.
[4] Ibid., V, 3, 5, 3, 4, 1, 11.
[5] Ibid., V, 4, 3, 5—9.
[6] Ibid., V, 4, 3, 15—18.
[7] Ibid., V, 4, 3, 19.
[8] Ibid., V, 4, 3, 20.
[9] Ibid., V, 4, 4, 9-13.

thou art: therewith serve me." With the same words, the sword is passed on by the king to his brother, thence to the Sûta, finally to the Grâmaṇî. "And as to why they mutually hand it on in this way, they do so lest there should be a confusion of classes and in order that society may be in the proper order."[1] The Ratnins, as these personages are called, are asked to a symbolic game of dice, the bet being a cow brought by an ordinary man.[2]

Other sacrifices.

There are other sacrifices of which the significance is not perfectly clear but which seem to imply some sort of suzerainty. In the Aitareya Brâhmaṇa the Punarabhiṣeka or the second consecration entitles a king to all sorts of royal dignities.[3] There Janamejaya aspires to universal dominion.[4] The Sarvamedha, mentioned in the Śatapatha Brâhmaṇa, was another grand sacrifice.[5] All consecration, however, was of great moment. Performed in other connections, it made Vaiśyas equal to Brâhmaṇas for the time being. All who underwent it were at least temporarily equal to gods.[6]

The office of the king.

In the Aitareya Brâhmaṇa, at the time of the consecration, the king takes an oath as follows :—

"Between the night I am born and the night I die, whatever good I might have done, my heaven, my life, and my progeny, may I be deprived of, if I oppress you."[7]

At the same time, however, the idea of proprietorship in the kingdom is gaining ground. In the Bṛihadâraṇyaka Upaniṣad, a king offers himself and his kingdom to Yâjñavalkya.[8] Another passage in the Aitareya Brâhmaṇa

[1] Śatapatha Brâhmana, V, 4, 4, 15—19.
[2] Ibid., V, 4, 4, 20—25.
[3] Aitareya Brâhmaṇa, VIII, 5—10.
[4] Ibid., VIII, 11.
[5] Śatapatha Brâhmaṇa, XIII, 7, 1.
[6] Ibid., III, 1, 1, 8 ; 2, 1, 17 ; 2, 1, 39-40.
[7] Aitareya Brâhmaṇa, VIII, 15.
[8] Bṛihadâraṇyaka Upaniṣad, IV, 4, 23.

shows that the hereditary succession was firmly established.[1]

That kings were generally Kṣatriyas is abundantly clear. A passage in the Śatapatha Brâhmaṇa even bars the kingly office to Brâhmaṇas. The Kṣatra takes no delight in the priestly office and the Brahma takes no delight in the rank of rulership.[2] There is no evidence in Vedic literature for the contests between Brâhmaṇas and Kṣatriyas for supremacy which a few modern scholars believed to have occurred on the basis of some later legends and passages.[3] There is, however, one passage in the Śatapatha Brâhmaṇa which seems to suggest that non-Kṣatriya kingship was not altogether unknown. King Marutta Âvikṣita is called Âyogava,[4] which, according to the later testimony of Manu, is a mixed caste resulting from the union of Śûdras with Vaiśya wives.[5]

The caste of kings.

In accordance with the general trend of development, the Purohita has now become more important than ever. He and the members of his order must be kept constantly in good humour. Even a powerful king like Janamejaya was humbled by Brâhmaṇas.[6] The Śatapatha Brâhmaṇa would exempt Brâhmaṇas from taxes.[7] The dictum is reiterated with such complete unanimity through the succeeding ages. The same Brâhmaṇa expounds the dogma of the joint rule of Brâhmaṇas and Kṣatriyas over the people,[8] though elsewhere it restricts them to their several functions.[9] In one passage it derives the kingly power from

The Priest.

[1] Aitareya Brâhmaṇa, VIII, 12.
[2] Śatapatha Brâhmaṇa, XIII, 1, 5, 2, 3, 5.
[3] Muir, Sanskrit Texts, Part I, Ch. III.
[4] Śatapatha Brâhmaṇa, XIII, 5, 4, 6.
[5] Manu, X, 12.
[6] Śatapatha Brâhmaṇa, III, 4, 1, 7.
[7] Ibid., XIII, 6, 2, 18; 7, 1, 13.
[8] Ibid., XI, 2, 7, 6.
[9] Ibid., XIII, 1, 5, 2-3.

that of the priest.[1] It is the royal priest who secures the fall of rain for the crops, says the Ṛigveda in its tenth Maṇḍala.[2] The Aitareya Brâhmaṇa declares that the Purohita is half the Kṣatriya; he is indispensable to the success of royal enterprise. He is the Râṣṭragopa, protector of the kingdom. Along with his wife and son, he is the three-fold sacred fire for the king. If propitiated, he blesses the king with dignity, valour and dominion and ultimately secures him heavenly grace. If he is displeased, he hurls ruin and destruction on the realm.[3] To quote the Śatapatha Brâhmaṇa, again, the Śrotriya or the learned Brâhmaṇa and the king are joint "upholders of the sacred law among men."[4]

Royal attendants.

Besides the Purohita, the king had a number of attendants, sûtas (heralds), grâmaṇîs (headmen),—non-royal kingmakers as they are sometimes called, who formed his entourage.[5]

Justice.

Justice in which the assembly had so far taken a prominent share, now becomes ever more a royal prerogative. At the same time the king is declared immune from punishment. "For Varuṇa Dharmapati (lord of the law)," says the Śatapatha Brâhmaṇa, "he then prepares a Varuṇa pap of barley, thereby Varuṇa, the lord of the law, makes him lord of the law; and that truly is the supreme state, when one is lord of the law; for whoever attains to the supreme state, to him they come in (matters of law): therefore to

[1] Ibid., XII, 7, 3, 12.

[2] Ṛigveda, X, 98.

[3] Aitareya Brâhmaṇa, VII, 26; VIII, 24—27. Vedic Index, II, 5 84, 223.

[4] Śatapatha Brâhmaṇa, V, 4, 4, 5.

[5] Ibid., XII, 9, 3; XIII, 2, 2, 18.

Varuṇa Dharmapati."[1] The Chândogya Upaniṣad speaks of fire-ordeals and other tests for establishing the innocence of the accused who might plead not guilty, but one cannot be sure of the date of the particular passage. It regards murder, theft, adultery and drunkenness as the most heinous of crimes.[2]

Revenue.

Taxation seems to increase during this age. Probably the expenses of government had increased. In the Śatapatha Brâhmaṇa the king is several times regarded as devouring the people.[3] References to Bali or tribute are of frequent occurrence.[4]

The Assembly.

During this period the assembly is occasionally referred to. In the Śatapatha Brâhmaṇa it seems to take cognisance of currency, of coins such as Kriṣṇâla and Niṣka.[5] The Chândogya Upaniṣad mentions the Samiti of the Pañcâlas as presided over by king Pravâhaṇa Jaivali.[6] But the assembly is now less and less in evidence. It is no longer a regular organ of deliberation or justice. Such a change, in fact, was inevitable with the increase in the size of states and the further progress of the feudal tendency. While the king would gain more and more in power, the people would find it more and more difficult to come together.

[1] Śatapatha Brâhmaṇa, V, 3, 3, 9. The White Yajurveda (X, 27) contains exhortations to equal justice and beneficent protection.

[2] Chândogya Upaniṣad, VI, 16.

[3] Śatapatha Brâhmaṇa, I, 8, 2, 17; IV, 2, 1, 3, 17; V, 3, 3, 12; 4, 2, 3; X, 6, 2, 1; XIII, 2, 9, 6, 8, etc.

[4] Ibid., I, 3, 2, 15; 5, 3, 18; 6, 3, 7, etc. Aitareya Brâhmaṇa, VII, 29. Vedic Index, II, 62,

[5] Śatapatha Brâhmaṇa, XII, 7, 2, 13; XIII, 1, 1, 47. Originally niṣka seems to have been a gold or silver ornament. Later, it denoted a gold coin.

[6] Chândogya Upaniṣad, V, 3, 1.

The idea (of) Dharma.

At the same time the idea of Dharma as a moral check on despotism emerges more clearly. The Śatapatha Brâhmaṇa wants the king to uphold the sacred law, "for he is not capable of all and every speech, nor of all and every deed, but that he should speak only what is right, and do what is right......."[1] The Brihadâraṇyaka Upaniṣad says that "Dharma is the Kṣatra of the Kṣatra; therefore, there is nothing higher than Dharma. Thenceforth even a weak man rules a stronger with the help of Dharma as with the help of a king. Thus Dharma is what is called the true."[2] The term Dharma or Dharman defies translation. It covers the whole range and complex of settled principles and forms of conduct. Law, ideal rather than positive, is one of the senses in which it is used. Ancient Hindus never clearly distinguished between religious and moral duty, usage or customary observance.

[1] Śatapatha Brâhmaṇa, V, 4, 4, 5.

[2] Bṛihadâraṇyaka Upaniṣad, I, 4, 11—15. See also Chândogya Upaniṣad, II, 23, 1-2. Cf. the later philosopher Kaṇâda who defines Dharma as the source of welfare and salvation (Vaiśeṣika Sûtras, I, 1-2).

CHAPTER IV.

Gleanings from the Sûtras.

(500—100 B.C.)

Sûtra Literature.

After the Brâhmaṇas and the earlier Upaniṣads, the Sûtras stand out as the next important class of literature. In ancient India learning was generally cultivated in schools and the results arrived at were given the stamp of schools which were often attached to various Vedic sects. Such schools seem to have arisen all over the country by the sixth or fifth century B.C. By this time the Âryans had overspread the whole of northern India and penetrated far into the south. The wider their geographical distribution, the greater were the differences of doctrine, law, custom and ceremonial among them. The Sûtras, though agreeing in certain fundamentals, display innumerable differences of detail. The 'threads,' as the term means, are extremely thin. They represent the very acme of concision which too often renders them obscure and dreary. Nevertheless, they do in a large measure simplify and systematise the complicated theology and ritual of the Brâhmaṇas. Broadly speaking, they fall into three classes, or rather aspects, the Śrauta, Gṛihya and Dharma—the sacrificial, domestic and legal. A complete collection, a Kalpa Sûtra, should comprise all the three but many of them have perished and, generally, each body of Sûtra stands independent of others. Their fundamental object is the same—the regulation of human life. Their full and detailed instructions show the great place which authority occupied in the direction of the Hindu mind. In general, they fall between the sixth and second centuries before Christ but the exact date of each can not be determined. Bühler placed the Dharma Sûtras, which from our point of view are the most important, between the sixth and third centuries B.C. and formulated a chronological order—Gautama, Baudhâyana, Vaśiṣṭha and Âpastamba. Jolly assigns Gautama and Baudhâyana to the sixth or fifth century B.C., and Vaśiṣṭha and Âpastamba to the fifth or fourth century B.C. Jayaswal would attribute the first forms of the Sûtras to about 500 B.C., but in their present shape he would place Gautama at 350 B.C., Baudhâyana at 240 B.C. and Vaśiṣṭha at 100 B.C. Hopkins thinks that "probably the Grihyas represent the earlier Sûtras; the Dharmas as a whole come later, perhaps 300 B.C. would represent the earliest." Âpastamba, he concludes, "probably is not older than the second century B.C.," while Vaśiṣṭha is even later. It is again probable that many of the Sûtras were recast subsequently, and that their text has been frequently tampered with to bring them into harmony with the later Dharma Śâstras. Gautama, in fact, is known as a Dharma Śâstra. Only roughly can the Sûtras be held to reflect the life of the period from 500 to 100 B.C. during which they arose. It will be a mistake to compare the Dharma Sûtras or the later Dharma Śâstras, as Sir William Jones compared Manu, to the Institutes of Justinian. The Hindu texts do not embody any system of positive law and represent no real system of jurisprudence. They are manuals of conduct, of ideal morality or law. Besides, they are pre-eminently the product of priestly brains and tend to look at life from a narrow standpoint.

The Dates of Sûtras.

From this body of literature, extensive as it is, it is possible to obtain only a few glimpses of the actual structure and working of contemporary political institutions. Among

Gleanings from Śrauta Sûtras.

the best known of the Śrauta Sûtras are the two belonging to the Rigveda—the Śâṅkhâyana and the Âśvalâyana. The followers of the former Caraṇa or school were later settled in northern Gujarât and those of the latter in the south between the Godâvarî and the Kṛiṣṇâ.[1] But the beginnings of the Sûtras themselves lie probably in the north. Both describe the complicated ceremonies of the various royal consecrations, the Śâṅkhâyana at greater length than the other. Its account of the Râjasûya is a turgid elaboration of the description in the Śatapatha Brâhmaṇa. In the course of it occurs the interesting statement that "it is Varuṇa whom they consecrate."[2] It enumerates seven kings—four of them being Pârikṣitas—who performed the Aśvamedha sacrifice.[3] The Lâṭyâyana Śrauta Sûtra, the accepted manual of the Kauthuma school attached to the Pañcaviṁśa Brâhmaṇa, remarks that "whomsoever the Brâhmaṇas and Râjânaḥ (kings or nobles) may place at their head, let him perform the Vâjapeya."[4] From this it may be inferred that any ruler could perform the Vâjapeya and that the ceremonies had lost their characteristic value at least in some places. The Kâtyâyana Śrauta Sûtra which belongs to the white Yajurveda and, on the whole, strictly follows the order of the Śatapatha Brâhmaṇa, clearly distinguishes between Râjya and Sâmrâjya, and lays down that the Râjasûya is to be performed by a king who has not yet performed the Vâjapeya.[5] On the other hand, the Âśvalâyana Śrauta Sûtra rules that "after performing it (the Vâjapeya), let a king perform the Râjasûya......"[6] The Âpastamba Śrauta

1 Macdonell, History of Sanskrit Literature, pp. 244-45.
2 Śâṅkhâyana Śrauta Sûtra, XV, 13, 4. See also XV, 1, 11.
3 Ibid., XVI, 9.
4 Lâṭyâyana Śrauta Sûtra, VIII, 11, 1. Also IX 1—3, for the Râjasûya.
5 Kâtyâyana Śrauta Sûtra, XV, 1, 1-2.
6 Âśvalâyana Śrauta Sûtra, IX, 3, 3 to IX, 4, 23. Also IX, 9, 11 for the Vâjapeya.

Sûtra, which belongs to the Black Yajurveda, would restrict the Aśvamedha to the Sârvabhauma **Râjâ** or universal monarch. It records an interesting rite in the course of which the Adhvaryu was temporarily reckoned as sovereign. "He (the king) hands over the kingdom to the Adhvaryu, and says, 'O Brâhmaṇas and princes, this Adhvaryu is your king; whatever loyal respect is due to me, the same from you may be shown to him, whatever he does by you (or to you), the same shall be considered as authoritatively done to you.' As long as the sacrifice lasts, the Adhvaryu becomes the king."[1] The Baudhâyana Śrauta Sûtra which also belongs to the Black Yajurveda and which is older than the Âpastamba gives a slightly different version. "Here (in the Aśvamedha) those who anoint a Kṣatra as the king anoint the Adhvaryu (in his stead). He (the Kṣatriya king) says—'O Brâhmaṇas and princes, the Adhvaryu will be the king these two years; obey him; whoever does not obey him, the whole property of him they will confiscate.' Accordingly, the Adhvaryu is the king these two years."[2] Whether the Brâhmaṇa sacrificial agent ever actually exercised political authority in the interregnum is more than doubtful, but these details furnish a graphic idea of the political importance and prestige of the priesthood. The Baudhâyana Śrauta Sûtra also reveals the tremendous significance attached to the Aśvamedha. None was to meddle with its progress. For instance, if any one, in disregard of the royal proclamation, let out mares to meet the wandering sacrificial horse, he was to be punished with confiscation of property.[3] Incidentally, we learn that confiscation of property was now the recognised penalty for disobedience to the royal command.

1 Âpastamba Śrauta Sûtra, XX, 2, 12, 3, 1-2. See also XVIII, 1, 1; 8, 22.
2 Baudhâyana Śrauta Sûtra, XV, 4.
3 Ibid., XV, 8.

Next to the Śrauta Sûtras stand the Gṛihya Sûtras. Nothing can exceed the minuteness with which they dilate on domestic ritual but they rarely extend their scope beyond it. Incidentally, the Pâraskara Gṛihya Sûtra would grant autonomy to villages in private matters and family concerns.[1] No outside interference is needed. Here, probably, the Sûtra is more or less true to facts. The Parâśara Gṛihya Sûtra has an arresting statement. It declares that royalty does not depend on hereditary right, but on acquisition by the sword.[2] It points to an age of chronic warfare and political disturbance.[3] Caste is firmly entrenched in the Sûtras. For instance, in the Gṛihya Sûtra of Gobhila, there are caste distinctions in fetching fire.[3]

The Gṛihya Sûtras.

It is the Dharma Sûtras which are of real interest to the student of society and politics. Caste is fully developed in all of them. So, too, the Âsramadharma which divides the life of a twice-born man—a member of any of the three higher castes—into four stages, studentship, household, retirement and renunciation. All the Dharma Sûtras and, following them, the Dharma Śâstras, want the scheme of the duties of the four castes and four stages to be enforced by the government. It is, however, remarkable that all of them recognise two sorts of punishments for many sins, one to be inflicted by the government, and the other, a penance rather than a regular punishment, to be undergone by the sinner voluntarily or to be forced on him by those who wish him well in this, and particularly, in the next life. So, the sanctions, to use a modern term, are both civil and spiritual. It is sometimes difficult to say to which class a writer attaches greater importance. Gautama and Baudhâyana

The Dharma Sûtras.

---

[1] Pâraskara Gṛihya Sûtra, I, 8, 13.

[2] Parâśara Gṛihya Sûtra, I, 68.

Gobhila Gṛihya Sûtra, I, 1, 15-16.

lend colour to the hypothesis that a system of penances, voluntary and enforced, was the earliest Hindu way of promoting virtue and punishing sin and that justice in the modern sense of the term was introduced only later. Sir Henry Maine supposed that rules of conduct were first worked out by priestly lawyers who later addressed themsevles to the kingly power to have them enforced.[1] The facts, as known, do not support Maine's theory. From the prominence of penances in the Dhamaśâstras and Purâṇas, it appears that civil and spiritural jurisdictions in moral life ran concurrently.

Gautama.

The school of the Gautamas represented by the earliest of the extant Dharma Sûtra compendiums, is a Caraṇa of the Sâmaveda.[2] It arose somewhere in the north. While basing his ethics on caste, Gautama makes some concessions to meet the exigencies of practical life. In distress, that is to say, in emergencies, a Brâhmaṇa may study under a non-Brâhmaṇa, and may follow the occupation of a Kṣatriya and, failing that, of a Vaiśya. In the last contingency he is to refrain from dealing in certain articles, though in the last extremity even these restrictions may be disregarded. Gautama would not like a Brâhmana to follow Śûdra occupations under any circumstances, but he admits that some had permitted even this when life was in danger.[3] In self-defence, a Brâhmaṇa may always use arms.[4] Kṣatriyas and Vaiśyas, too, may, in emergencies, follow lower occupations.[5] In a later chapter he permits

Caste.

[1] Maine, Ancient Law and Custom, pp. 43-44.

[2] Kumârila Bhaṭṭa, Tantravârtika, (Benâres edition), p. 179. Max Müller, History of Ancient Sanskrit Literature, p. 374. Bühler, Introduction to Gautama, p. L.

[3] Gautama, VII, 1—24.

[4] Ibid., VII, 25.

[5] Ibid., VII, 26.

a Brâhmaṇa to practise usury, agriculture or trade, " provided he does not do the work himself."[1] It may be assumed that orthodox writers would make these concessions only when compelled by the force of facts. It is clear that rules of caste, while recognised in theory by all, were not uniformly observed. In Gautama, the status of Śûdras tends to approximate to serfdom or slavery. A Śûdra should obtain his livelihood only from the higher castes,[2] eat the remnants of their food[3] and use their cast-off shoes, umbrellas, garments and mats.[4] He must support his master, in case of distress, with any savings of his own.[5] On the other hand, he must be supported by his master even when no longer able to work.[6] A regular family life is permitted to him,[7] but all intellectual cultivation and participation in the higher spiritual life is denied to him. Only by permission can he use the exclamation, namaḥ (adoration), as his mantra.[8] " If he (a Śûdra) listens, intentionally, to (a recitation) of the Veda, his ears shall be filled with (molten) tin or lac.[9] If he recites (Vedic texts), his tongue shall be cut out.[10] If he remembers them, his body shall be split in twain."[11] There is no evidence to show how far such maxims were actually carried out. It may be that the Brâmaṇas are painting themselves worse than they actually were. But it is clear that the position of the Śûdras was very hard. It seems that the Śûdras did not always accept their prescribed lot. Gautama invokes the might of the government to enforce

[1] Ibid., X, 5-6.
[2] Ibid., X, 57.
[3] Ibid., X, 59.
[4] Ibid., X, 58.
[5] Ibid., X, 62.
[6] Ibid., X, 61.
[7] Ibid., X, 54, 55.
[8] Ibid., X, 64.
[9] Ibid., XII, 4.
[10] Ibid., XII, 5.
[11] Ibid., XII, 6.

the social order. He is deeply concerned to maintain the supremacy of Dvijas, the twice-born, and to keep Śûdras to the lowest place. "If he (a Śûdra) assumes a position equal to that of twice-born men in sitting, in lying down, in conversation or on the road, he shall undergo corporal punishment."[1]

Government.

In his eleventh chapter Gautama enunciates his maxims on government.[2] His theory lends itself to a few inferences about the contemporary state of things. His precepts would fit only a small state. The state in which he lived was either very small or a small feudatory of a big one. In any case, it was a whole by itself. Gautama wants the king to learn the use of the bow and the management of chariots and to stand firm in battle.[3] He pictures the king seated on a high pedestal surrounded by his subjects who occupy lower seats.[4] In Gautama[5] and other Brahmanical writers, the Purohita is an institution by himself. Later epigraphic testimony helps the conclusion that a king usually had a high priest. There were also other priests at the court for the performance of Vedic sacrifices.[6] When we are told that the king is the master of all except Brâhmaṇas,[7] and that he shall be worshipped by all except Brâhmaṇas,[8] it is legitimate to infer that the Brâhmaṇas occupied a privileged position, though the extent of the privilege was, doubtless, exaggerated by priestly law-givers. Gautama wants that Brâhmaṇas who are versed in sacred lore and live up to its precepts, should be exempted by the king from corporal punishment, imprisonment, fines,

Ibid., XII, 7.

Ibid., Chapter XI, in particular 1, 5—8, 11—14.

Ibid., X, 7—12.

Ibid., XI, 7.

Ibid., XI, 12.

6 Ibid., XI, 18.

7 Ibid., XI, 1.

8 Ibid., XI, 7.

exile, censure and disgrace.[1] Here is an extensive claim to the 'benefit of clergy' but we do not know how far it was admitted in practice. Brâhmaṇas acted as counsellors of the sovereign. "For it is declared (in the Veda): 'Kṣatriyas, who are assisted by Brâhmaṇas, prosper and do not fall into distress."[2] From their ranks, too, were drawn the astrologers and interpreters of omens who seem to have been attached to Hindu courts all through history. Gautama states the opinion of those who declared that 'the acquisition of wealth and security depends upon taking heed of those readers of supernatural influences.[3]

Justice.

In Gautama, as in other Hindu writers, the king is expected personally to administer justice, and to enforce the sacred law. But they all admit the validity of local or group custom. In spite of his ultra-orthodox leanings, Gautama recognised that "the laws of countries, castes and families which are not opposed to the (sacred) records, (have) also authority."[4] Again, "cultivators, traders, herdsmen, money-lenders, and artisans (have authority to lay down rules) for their respective classes.[5] Having learnt the (state of) affairs from those who (in each class) have authority (to speak), the king shall give the legal decision.[6] Gautama thus grants legislative powers to groups or associations of men. It is more than probable that the followers of various occupations regulated part of their life and transactions by the customs which had spontaneously arisen among them and by the rules which were enunciated to meet any contingencies. It is again probable, as the text of Gautama suggests, that in the enforcement of these

Ibid., VIII, 7—13.
Ibid., XI, 14.
Ibid., XI, 15-16.
Ibid., XI, 20.
Ibid., XI, 21.
Ibid., XI, 22.

rules and customs, the royal judicial machinery had a share. A priestly law-giver would necessarily add that these regulations were to be enforced only when not opposed to the Scriptures, but in practice the force of local custom might have proved irresistible. It is significant that cultivators are mentioned among self-regulating groups. In practice it would mean that a village should enjoy a good deal of autonomy. A few provisions concerning agriculture are interesting. Unenclosed pasture-lands were to be used for grazing cattle and for firewood.[1] If cattle damaged fields or crops, the responsibility fell on the herdsman if he happened to be with them, otherwise on their owner.[2] But if the field damaged was unenclosed, its owner was held partly responsible.[3]

Witnesses.

Gautama makes it abundantly clear that during his time witnesses were usually summoned in a case[4] and that some rules had been framed to determine the admissibility of their evidence in particular cases.[5] But his elaborate prescriptions on the character, qualifications and disqualifications of witnesses are so purely theoretical as to warrant no inference about actual practice. Gautama's Twelfth Chapter, on Civil and Criminal Law, is full of details, but is not a statement of positive law. He seems to supply the model which he would like a code of law to follow. But it is permissible to infer from him that caste privilege had invaded public justice at innumerable points and that for the same offences different punishments were inflicted on members of different castes. The lot of a Śûdra might have been really hard.

Caste and Justice.

[1] Ibid., XII, 28.

[2] Ibid., XII, 19-20.

[3] Ibid., XII, 21.

[4] Ibid., XIII, 1.

[5] Ibid., Ch. XIII.

To take a single instance, "a Śûdra who intentionally reviles twice-born men by criminal abuse, or criminally assaults them with blows, shall be deprived of the limb with which he offends."[1]

Gautama, like Vaśiṣṭha, prescribes five mâṣas for twenty kârṣâpaṇas as the rate of interest which, according to the commentator Haradatta, works out to 15 p.c. per annum.[2] For some articles, however, such as gold and flavouring substances, Gautama admits higher rates of interest.[3] He recognises no less than six forms of interest, *viz.*, compound interest, periodical interest, stipulated interest, corporal interest, daily interest and the use of the pledged article.[4] He remarks that when the principal has been doubled, interest ceases and that when the article pledged is used by the creditor, the loan bears no interest at all.[5]

Interest.

Gautama's precepts on taxation probably bear some relation to facts. The land-tax should be one-sixth, one-eighth or one-tenth of the gross produce.[6] One-sixth was the standard fixed by Hindu theory in ancient India. It will appear that the land-tax was always supplemented by others. "Some declare that (there is a tax) also on cattle and gold, *viz.*, one-fiftieth of the stock."[7] On merchandise, $\frac{1}{20}$th was to be paid as duty; on roots, fruits, flowers, medicinal herbs, honey, meat, grass and firewood, $\frac{1}{60}$th.[8] Besides, a merchant should give the king every month one article of merchandise for less than the market value.[9] Even

Revenue.

[1] Ibid., XII, 1-2.
[2] Gautama, XII, 29. Vaśiṣṭha, II, 51. Cf. Manu, VII, 140.
[3] Gautama, XII, 36, 44—47.
[4] Ibid., XII, 34-35.
[5] Ibid., XII, 31-32.
[6] Ibid., X, 24.
[7] Ibid., X, 25.
[8] Ibid., X, 26-27.
[9] Ibid., X, 35.

those who had nothing to give should make some contribution. Gautama wants every artisan to contribute a day's labour to the service of the king.[1] In addition to all this, treasure-trove should belong to the king.[2] The sources of revenue and the rates fixed are likely to have obtained in practice. Gautama, like all other Hindu writers, holds that the justification of taxation was the protection which the king afforded to all and sundry.[3] This is probably a correct representation of the public feeling of those days but there was no constitutional means of enforcing the duty of protection.

Miscellaneous duties of the State.

Besides the protection and promotion of righteous life with which government is charged, Gautama prescribes specific relief measures which a king is likely to have undertaken in an informal manner. He must support needy students, Brâhmaṇas, Śrotriyas, all who are unable to work.[4] A Hindu court might well have been a centre of charity.

Baudhâyana.

Many of the social and political ideas of Gautama are to be found in other Sûtra composers but the latter also present something peculiar to each. Baudhâyana's school belonged probably to the south, where much later, Sâyaṇa, the great Vedic commentator, was a member of it. A reference to sea-borne commerce points in the same direction.[5] The fourth section of the Baudhâyana Dharma Sûtra is probably a late addition, while the date of the third is doubtful. The first two sections alone can be utilised for the Sûtra period. He preserves a record of the old theory of wergild which is likely to have been

Law and Justice.

[1] Ibid., X, 31. [2] Ibid., X, 43. [3] Ibid., X, 28.
[4] Ibid., X, 7—12.
[5] Baudhâyana, I, 10, 18, 14.

grounded partly in the facts of some remote epoch. For slaying a Kṣatriya one should give a thousand cows besides a bull; for slaying a Śûdra, ten cows and a bull. Then in priestly contempt of Śûdras, Baudhâyana adds that the fine for killing a flamingo, a pea-cock, a crow, an owl, a frog, a musk-rat, a dog, etc., etc., is the same as for killing a Śûdra.[1] Baudhâyana, however, knows of state courts and judges. He specifies three sources of law—the Vedas, Smṛitis or sacred tradition and the example of Śiṣṭas—personages who combine moral excellence with mastery of Vedic and subsidiary studies and powers of ratiocination. Failing them, doubtful points of law should be submitted to an assembly of ten, comprising four scholars, each a master of one of the four Vedas, a Mîmâṁsaka, a scholar acquainted with the Aṅgas, a reciter of the sacred law, and three Brâhmaṇas, belonging to three different orders. Failing such an assembly, points of law might be referred to five, three or a single blameless man but never to a thousand fools. A little later, however, he adds that narrow and difficult is the path of the sacred law, that many gates lead to it and that a doubt can never be resolved by a single person, "howsoever learned he may be."[2] Details apart, it is probable that a pariṣad or committee of this type was constituted to give what may be called a jurisconsultum. It might be dominated by priestly lawyers but its constitution would depend on the king, who could 'pack' it at will. It could form a machinery for what must be pronounced a species of legislative business. The sphere of any such body, however, would be strictly limited. Like others, Baudhâyana declares that local customs and opinions, varying in different regions, should be respected.[3] As might be expected, caste privilege enters

[1] Ibid., I, 10, 19, 1—6.
[2] Ibid., I, 1, 1, 1—10, 12.
[3] Ibid., 1, 1, 1, 2, 1—9.

Baudhâyana's judicial system at many points. He would exempt Brâhmaṇas from corporal punishment but he adds that Brâhmaṇas who tend cattle, practise agriculture or who live as artizans, actors, usherers or servants should be treated as Śûdras. It will appear that the caste-law of occupations was often violated and that its violation sometimes implied a forfeiture of the privileges which it conferred.[1] Like Gautama, Baudhâyana summons witnesses and prescribes their qualifications, etc.[2] Baudhâyana's fiscial system deserves a word of notice. He prescribes one-sixth of the gross produce of the land as

Revenue.

the due of the state. On goods imported by sea, a ten per cent. duty should be charged, "after deducting a choice article." Here the theorist might be reproducing facts. He declares that the duties on marketable goods should be fixed according to their intrinsic value and that the traders should never be oppressed.[3] It is probable that the state-demand varied from

The law of war.

article to article. Turning to the law of war, Baudhâyana holds that no king should ever use barbed or poisoned weapons. Nor should he strike women, infants, old men, Brâhmaṇas, those who are insane, intoxicated, terrified or who have lost their armour. From this humanitarian rule, only assassins are excepted.[4] The statement is interesting as the first clear Hindu view of the ethics of war but we cannot be sure that it represents practical politics.

[1] On the whole subject of caste and caste-privilege in Baudhâyana, see I, 10, 18, 2—6; I, 10, 18, 18—20; I, 10, 19, 1—5; I, 5, 10, 23—25; II, 6, 11, 12—16. In prescribing relaxations of these rules (II, 2, 4, 16—20), Baudhâyana contradicts himself.

[2] Ibid., I, 10, 19, 7—16 *et seq.*

[3] Baudhâyana, I, 10, 18, 1, 14-15.

[4] Ibid., I, 1, 10, 18, 10—13.

Apastamba.

The Dharma Sûtra of the Âpastambas, which forms the twenty-eighth and twenty-ninth sections of the Âpastamba Kalpa Sûtra, seems to have arisen in the south,[1] probably in the Ândhra country. Âpastamba admits no absolute finality in law or morality. He confesses that ancient sages had transgressed the present code of morality and law but adds that they had incurred no sin "on account of the greatness of their lustre" and that none could follow them now with impunity.[2] It is clear that there was no permanent, immutable, universal law. It varied from time to time and, doubtless, from place to place. A few details of Âpastamba on kingly duties are interesting. The king should build a town with its gates looking towards the south. In the heart of the town should stand the royal palace with its gates facing the south. In front of it should be a hall, called the hall of invitation, a sort of guest-house. At a short distance towards the south should be erected an assembly-house, with doors on the north and south, to serve, *inter alia*, as a 'gaming-house' for the 'pure and truthful' members of the three higher castes. In the palace, in the hall and in the assembly house, fires should be kept burning and daily oblations offered.[3] Here the law-giver is probably following some existing model. It is noteworthy that gambling was no sin in those days and was even provided for. The state looked more to the needs and amusements of Dvijas than to those of Śûdras.

Local Government.

Âpastamba makes it perfectly clear that a regular system of local government had grown up by his time. He mentions village and town-officers. The jurisdiction of a town-officer covers a radius of a yojana (nearly eight miles) and that of a village officer a radius of a kos, nearly two miles. Within

[1] Âpastamba, II, 17, 17, where he speaks of a practice of the Northerners in a way which only a Southerner would do.
[2] Âpastamba, II, 6, 13, 8—10. [3] Ibid., II, 10, 25, 2—13,

the area of his jurisdiction, an officer should be responsible for order and security and should himself recompense unaccounted thefts. The officers, according to Âpastamba, should be drawn from the first three castes.[1] The injunction does not square with the strict theory of caste and is not likely to have found a place in a Dharma Sûtra if something like it had not been followed in actual practice.

Revenue.

Âpastamba's exemptions from taxation are interesting. Brâhmaṇas, women, minors, students, ascetics, the blind, the deaf, the diseased, and Śûdras who live by washing the feet of others need pay nothing to the state.[2] The maxim may be based partly on facts. On the other hand, on failure of heirs, all property escheats to the king.[3]

Law.

Âpastamba's disquisition on civil and criminal law is as minute as that of the other legal writers, but there is no evidence to show which of his provisions are based on facts. It is safe to conclude that caste had vitiated jurisprudence and that the Śûdras fared worst of all.[4] For the rest only a few maxims need be noted. Âpastamba would exact full damages from a man who does not cultivate his lease of land. If he is rich enough, he must be forced to pay to the state the value of the crop which should have reared on his fields.[5] A servant in tillage who abandons his work shall be flogged.[6] The same punishment should be awarded to a herdsman who forsakes his work.[7] The flock entrusted to him shall be taken away.[8] The owner of cattle may impound trespassing cattle.[9] In warfare, Âpastamba prohibits the slaughter of fugitives, of

---

[1] Ibid., II, 10, 26, 6—8.
[2] Ibid., II, 10, 26, 10—17.
[3] Ibid., II, 6, 14, 5. For inheritance in general, II, 6, 14, 1—13.
[4] Ibid., II, 10, 27.
[5] Ibid., II, 11, 28, 1.
[6] Ibid., II, 11, 28, 2.
[7] Ibid., II, 11, 28, 3.
[8] Ibid., II, 11, 28, 4.
[9] Ibid., II, 11, 28, 5.

those who ave surrendered, and of those who beg for mercy with flying hair or joined palms.[1] It may be mentioned in passing that the law-giver wants the king to support and protect women who had been cruelly wronged by wicked men.[2]

Vaśiṣṭha.

The Dharma Sûtra of Vaśiṣṭha arose in the north. Long afterwards, Kumârila Bhaṭṭa stated that Vaśiṣṭha was studied only by followers of the Ṛigveda but that it was generally recognised as authoritative. On caste, as on many other topics, he is in line with other Dharma Sûtras.[3] He wants the king to enforce the provisions of caste, but he also lays down, like Gautama, that respect should be paid to all the laws of countries, castes and families.[4] So not even in theory is social life to be regulated and controlled entirely by the state. For the king, Vaśiṣṭha has the usual precepts. A Purohita is, of course, essential to the king's welfare.[5] It is for fiscal arrangements that Vaśiṣṭha is peculiarly valuable. The land-tax and mercantile tolls are to be supplemented by a monthly levy from artisans.[6] " No taxes shall be paid on the usufruct of rivers, dry grass, forests (places of combustion) and mountains,[7] or those who draw their sustenance from them may pay something."[8] The law-giver speaks with a divided voice but he gives a clear indication of certain fresh sources of revenue which a government is very likely to have tapped. The king is to provide maintenance to eunuchs and lunatics[9] and inherit their property.[10] In general, on failure of heirs,

---

[1] Ibid., II, 5, 10, 11.

[2] Ibid., II, 10, 26, 22—24. For a few other political ideas, I, 6, 19, 10—12; I, 7, 21, 4; I, 10, 29, 6.

[3] Vaśiṣṭha, III, 24-25; I, 17; IV, 2; II, 40.

[4] Ibid., XIX, 7-8.

[5] Ibid., XIX, 3—5.

[6] Ibid., XIX, 28.

[7] Ibid., XIX, 26.

[8] Ibid., XIX, 27.

[9] Ibid., XIX, 35.

[10] Ibid., XIX 36.

property goes to spiritual teachers or pupils ; failing them, to the king.[1] Elsewhere he remarks that property entirely given up by the owner goes to the king.[2] The theorist would not allow the escheat of a Brâhmaṇa's property in any case but his very imprecations point to the breach of his precept in practice.[3] He himself strongly objects to Brâhmaṇas subsisting by begging. "The king shall punish that village where Brâhmaṇas, unobservant of their sacred duties and ignorant of the Veda, subsist by begging, for it feeds robbers."[4] To the list of exemptions from taxation given by Âpastamba, Vaśiṣṭha would add royal servants, wives of servants, young students, old men, unmarried girls, widows who have returned to parental homes and persons in general who have no protectors.[5] On justice, warfare, diplomacy and other matters, Vaśiṣṭha follows the traditional line. He would admit three kinds of proof in cases of property, *viz.*, documents, witnesses and possession.[6] In a dispute about a house or a field, the depositions of neighbours should be relied on.[7] If they differ among themselves, documents should be resorted to.[8] If the documents conflict with one another, the statements of the aged inhabitants of the place or of corporations should be decisive.[9] A few miscellaneous provisions may be noticed. From fields through which there is a right of way, a space sufficient for a path and another sufficient for turning a cart should be set apart.[10] In the vicinity of new buildings there should be a passage about three feet in breadth.[11] The property of widows, minors, etc., should be administered by the king.[12]

Miscellaneous.

[1] Ibid., XVII, 81—83.
[2] Ibid, XVI, 19.
[3] Ibid., XVII, 84—87.
[4] Ibid., III, 4.
[5] Ibid., XI X, 23-24.
[6] Ibid., XVI, 10.
[7] Ibid., XVI, 13.
[8] Ibid., XVI, 14.
[9] Ibid., XVI, 15.
[10] Ibid., XVI, 17.
[11] Ibid., XVI, 12.
[12] Ibid., XVI, 8-9.

It is needless to notice the other Dharma Sûtras here. Viṣṇu, though in Sûtra form, is so heavily interpolated as to be a product of practically about the third century A.D. The Vaikhânasa Dharma Sûtra, which represents one of the younger offshoots of the Taittirîya school, cannot be earlier than the third century A.D. Besides, it is in its four praśnas, only a treatise on domestic law. The Dharma Sûtra of Hiraṇyakeśin closely follows the Âpastambas from which that school probably derived its origin. It yields nothing fresh to the student of institutions. The Mânava Dharma Sûtra is lost to us, though its ideas may be imbedded in the later Smṛiti of Manu. The Dharma Sûtra of Śaṅkha-Likhita is referred to by Kumârila,[1] and is said to have been specially studied by the Vâjasaneyins but it has not yet been discovered.

Other Dharma Sûtras.

[1] Kumârila Bhaṭṭa, Tantravârtika, p. 179.

CHAPTER V.

The Epics.

I.—The Bṛihaddevatâ.

About the fifth century B.C. was composed a work which, though not included in Śruti or revelation, bears a strong affinity to Vedic literature in spirit, though not in style. The Bṛihaddevatâ, attributed to Śaunaka, is a summary of the deities and myths of the Ṛigveda.[1] It assumes the form of an epic but, as Macdonell shows, it does not borrow from the Mahâbhârata. It has one political reference of some interest. On the demise of a sovereign Ṛiṣṭiṣeṇa, the subjects offer the sovereignty to his son Devâpi, who, however being afflicted with a skin disease, declines it, saying, "I am not worthy of the sovereignty; let Saṁtânu, the younger prince, be your ruler."[2] It will appear that the kingship was avowedly hereditary, that the succession ordinarily went by the rule of primogeniture, that the subjects formally accepted a new king, that they even made a formal offer of the throne, that physical disability was a sufficient reason for departing from the ordinary rule of succession and that, next to the eldest prince,

The Bṛihad-devatâ.

[1] The Bṛihaddevatâ has been edited and translated by A. A. Macdonell and published at Cambridge, Massachusetts, 1904. Macdonell pronounces it later than 500 B.C., but earlier than Kâtyâyana and in no case later than 400 B.C. (Introduction, pp. xxii-xxiii). See also Keith, J. R. A. S., 1906, pp. 1—3.

[2] Bṛihaddevatâ, VII, 156-57; VIII, 1.

the younger had a presumptive title to the sceptre. Beyond this the Brihaddevatâ throws no light on institutions.[1]

II.—THE MAHÂBHÂRATA.

The Mahâbhârata.

The epic style which the Bṛihaddevatâ follows seems to have acquired vogue during the period which saw the composition of the Sûtras which are so entirely different in spirit and form. The Âśvalâyana Grihya Sûtra itself refers to Gâthâs, heroic tales and ancient legends, and mentions a Mahâbhârata, as well as a Bhârata.[2] The Śâmbavya Sûtra mentions the Mahâbhârata itself. The historical germ of the great Epic can be traced to the 10th century B.C.[3] The sources of the literary epic lie in the traditional recitations of bards who probably were neither priests nor scholars.[4] They were however recast and extensively added to for centuries. The chronological scheme proposed by Hopkins is the most acceptable of all that have been propounded. "We may tentatively assume as approximate dates of the whole work in its different stages. Bhârata (Kuru) lays, perhaps combined into one, but with no evidence of an epic before 400 B.C. A Mahâbhârata tale with Pâṇḍu heroes, lays and legends combined by the Puranic diaskeuasts, Kṛiṣṇa as a demi-god (no evidence of didactic form or of Kriṣṇa's divine supremacy), 400—200 B.C. Remaking of the epic with Kṛiṣṇa as all-god, intrusion of masses of didactic matter, addition of Puranic material old and new; multiplication of exploits, 200 B.C. to 100—200 A.D. The later books added with the

---

[1] In a note to VIII, 2, Macdonell notes that some Mss. read Râṣṭra for Râjya in the ordinary sense. It is clear that Râṣṭra did not yet possess the fiscal significance which it has in some later writers. Nor did it mean a province, as distinct from the whole kingdom.

[2] III, 3, 1.

[3] Macdonell, History of Sanskrit Literature, p. 285. On the whole subject, pp. 277—86. See also Hopkins, J.A.O.S., XIII, pp. 58—69.

[4] Hopkins, Cambridge History of India, Vol. I, p. 220.

introduction to the first book, the swollen Anuśâsana separated from Śânti and recognised as a separate book, 200 to 400 A.D.; and finally 400 A. D. +: occasional amplifications."[1] The didactic chapters, though added very late, are not necessarily so late in origin. Probably they were composed by the second century B.C. That there was more than one version of the Epic tale is evident from one of the Buddhist Jâtakas where the names of the Pâṇḍu brothers are given in a different order and the few incidents related are different from those in the great Sanskrit work.[2] But the theory of Holtzmann and von Schroeder that the poem was originally composed in honour of the Kurus and that it was later re-written to favour the Pâṇḍus is exploded. Nor does the hypothesis of Lassen, largely adopted by Weber, that the Epic originally related a war between Kurus and Pañcâlas find support at present.

The character of the Epic.

Though primarily a court epic to be recited before priests and aristocrats at great royal sacrifices, the Mahâbhârata is also meant to be 'sung' to the people at large. According to tradition, it is connected with the White Yajurveda. It calls itself the fifth Veda and a Dharma Śâstra.[3] But it is really an encyclopædia in which divergent and even contradictory ideas on religion, morals and politics are put in close juxtaposition. J. Dahlmann tried to prove that the Mahâbhârata was originally composed as a law-book by a single author in the sixth or fifth century B.C., but his arguments are rather weak. In point of area, the Epic pertains to the western districts of the Madhyadeśa or middle country, where the principal theatre of events is situated. It is true that the later framework of epic brings in the kings

[1] Hopkins, Great Epic of India, pp. 397-98. Also pp. 398—402.

[2] Kuṇâla Jâtaka, V, 412—56. Cf. Darmesterer, Points de contact entre le Mahâbhârata et le Śâh-nâmeh, Journal Asiatique, 1887.

[3] Âdi Parvan, LXII.

of the whole of India, but it is unsafe to draw any conclusions about the rest of the country from material of such doubtful dates.[1]

Theory and Practice in the Mahâbhârata.

Unlike the Brâhmaṇas and Sûtras, the Epic pulsates with life and throughout displays freedom and independence. But from the circumstances of its composition, it cannot be held to represent the customs and opinions of any single generation. Since it is impossible to fix the chronological limits of its various sections, it can only be regarded as indicating that certain practices prevailed on the banks of the Jumnâ and the upper Ganges sometime before the Christian era. The Râjadharmânuśâsana chapters of the epic are invaluable as presenting a synthetic view of Hindu political thought but they seem to stray far from practice. Their precepts are honoured more in the breach than in the observance in the story of the Epic.

Caste.

Throughout the Mahâbhârata the social order is based on caste and a complete theory of it occurs in the Śânti Parvan[2] There is, however, an arresting statement in the Vana Parvan where Yudhiṣṭhira remarks that the intermixture of races had been very great indeed, that castes had been hopelessly mixed up and that, therefore, conduct was the chief thing

[1] On an analysis Pargiter (J.R.A.S., 1908, pp. 334 et seq.) concludes that "the division of the contending parties may be broadly said to be south Madhyadeśa and Pañcâla against the rest of India." See also C. V. Vaidya, Epic India. For some calculations of the date of the Mahâbhârata events, rather wide of the mark, see V. Gopal Aiyar, Chronology of Ancient India; J. F. Hewitt, History and Chronology of the Myth-making Age; C. V. Vaidya, Epic India, the Mahâbhârata, a Criticism. See also D. Von Hinloopen Labberton, J.R.A.S., 1913, pp. 1 et seq.

[2] See particularly Śânti Parvan, LVI, 28-29; LX, 7—16, 20—36; LXII, 4; LXIII, 1-5; LXV, 8—10; LXXII, 4-8; CLXXXVIII, 1—14 CCXCVII, 3-4.

that mattered.[1] Mésalliances were not uncommon in aristocratic circles and were not looked down. Vidura, born of a slave-girl, plays a part more honourable than that of his half-brothers, Dhṛitarâṣṭra and Pâṇḍu. He is married, through the instrumentality of Bhîṣma, to a daughter of King Devaka by a Śûdra wife.[2] Non-Kṣatriya kingship was not altogether unknown. The Sabhâ Parvan speaks of Śûdra kings on the western coast.[3] Beyond the pale of caste lay some border peoples and foreigners like the Yavanas, Kirâtas, Cînas and Barbaras, who, according to the theory of the Śânti Parvan, were entitled to perform certain Vedic rites and make presents to Brâhmaṇas.[4] The claims to Brahmanic supremacy are set forth in the Sânti Parvan in the most uncompromising fashion. In so many words the Brâhmaṇas are declared independent of the state.[5] But in the epic as a whole it is the Kṣatriyas who are most prominent, whose will prevails and who are undoubtedly supreme. In the Śânti Parvan Kṣatriyas are exhorted by heaven and hell to work in constant co-operation and harmony with Brâhmaṇas.[6] We are assured that on the Purohita depends the growth and preservation of the king himself.[7] That every king had a Purohita is perfectly clear from the epic. There are also instances of Riṣis like Nârada being worshipped by powerful rulers like the Pâṇḍus.[8] But in the tale as a whole, the priests hardly exercise any influence on the course of events.

Vana Parvan, CLXXX.
Âdi Parvan, CXIV.
Sabhâ Parvan, LI.
Śânti Parvan, LXV, 17-18.
Ibid., LXXII, 10–17; LXXIII, 29–32. Cf. Vana Parvan, CXXXIII. Also Śânti Parvan, XXXIII, 2–9; XXXIV, 1–4, 6–8; 22–27; XXXV, 1; LXXV, 10–12; LXXVI, 3–13; LXXVII, 2–7; LXXXIX, 3–6.
Śânti Parvan, LVI, 24-25; LXXIII, 8–13; LXXIV, 13–15, 17 LXXVII, 10–17; LXXXIII, 29.
Ibid., LXXIV, 1-2. Also Âdi Parvan, CLXXII.
Sabhâ Parvan, V.

They are simply ignored when momentous decisions are taken.[1] In the Mahâbhârata, the position of Śûdras is better than the Brahmanical legal texts would lead one to expect. The Śânti Parvan awards three of the chief offices of government to Śûdras.[2] In the Sabhâ Parvan there are respectable Śûdras who are invited to the royal consecration.[3]

Feudal elements in the State.

The political horizon of the Mahâbhârata is far wider than that of any works noticed so far. It is in the epics that we first meet with a term—Bhârata or Bhâratavarṣa—which denoted the whole of India. The ideal of universal dominion is there. But in the composition of the state, feudal elements are present in a far greater measure and far more clearly than in the preceding epochs. There were many states, very small in size. It is significant that on a notable occasion Yudhiṣṭhira is ready to make peace if he be given just five villages to form a realm for himself. But every kingdom of any considerable size seems to have included a number of feudatories. The latter were called Râjan and, in contradistinction to them, the suzerain sometimes called himself Samrâṭ. A significant passage in the Sabhâ Parvan has it that there were Râjans in every house but they had not attained to the rank of Samrâṭ, which title was difficult to obtain.[4] It appears that Râjans themselves sometimes came forward for some reason or other to select an overlord. The Sabhâ Parvan has it that Râjans selected Jarâsaṁdha to be their head because he was the

[1] See, for instance, Ādi Parvan, CII ; Udyoga Parvan, I.

[2] Śânti Parvan, LXXV, 6—10.

[3] Sabhâ Parvan, XXIII, 41-42. See the Ādi Parvan, LXIV, for the legend that when Paraśu Râma thrice bereft the earth of Kṣatriya men, the Kṣatriya race was continued by the union of Kṣatriya women with Brâhmaṇas. See the Ādi Parvan, CXXXIV, for Brâhmaṇas teaching the profession of arms to Kṣatriyas.

[4] Sabhâ Parvan, XV, 2.

most powerful of all. Several feudatories became his officers.[1] There was another manner in which the relationship of suzerain and vassal could arise. A monarch could instal a favourite as "king" of some region, have him duly consecrated and thus formally admit him into the charmed circle. It was understood that such a new "king" must be a person of the blood royal, a hero or a high military commander. To overcome Arjuna's reluctance to meet Karṇa in a tournament, Duryodhana creates the latter "king" of Aṅga. "At that very moment," we are told, "seated on a golden seat, with fried paddy and flowers and water-pots............. the mighty Karṇa was installed king by Brâhmaṇas versed in mantras. And the royal umbrella was held over his head, while camaras waved around that hero of graceful mien."[2] But when the untoward accident of his father's entrance revealed the 'fact' of Karṇa's descent from a Sûta, Bhîma exclaimed, "O thou, son of a charioteer! Thou dost not deserve death in fight at the hands of Pârtha (Arjuna) . . And, O worst of mortals, thou art not worthy to sway the kingdom of Aṅga, even as a dog does not deserve the butter placed before the sacrificial fire." Duryodhana, however reproved Bhîma and said, ". . . Might is the cardinal Virtue of a Kṣatriya, and even a Kṣatriya of inferior birth deserves to be fought with. The lineage of heroes, like the sources of lordly rivers, is ever unknown . . . This prince among men deserves the sovereignty of the world, not of Aṅga only, in consequence of the might of his arm and my disposition to obey him in everything." There arose a confused murmur approving of Duryodhana's speech.[3]

A third factor which promotes the feudal tendency in the Mahâbhârata is the usual bid for supremacy symbolised

[1] Ibid., XIV.

[2] Âdi Parvan, CXXXVIII.

[3] Ibid., CXXXIX.

by the Digvijaya. The Digvijayas or "conquests of the quarters," carried out by Duryodhana and Yudhiṣṭhira do not result in any annexations. It was enough that their suzerainty was acknowledged by those whose dominions they or their lieutenants chose to enter. Again, on Pâṇḍu's Digvijaya, "the kings of the earth with joined hands waited on him with presents of various kinds of gems and wealth, precious stones and pearls and corals, and much gold and silver and first-class kine and handsome horses," etc., etc. Pâṇḍu accepted all the presents and retraced his steps towards his capital.[1] Thanks to these factors, a sort of feudalism seems to have become the order of the day. The Sabhâ Parvan brings on the stage a whole crowd of feudatories in whose presence Kṛiṣṇa slays his perverse relative, Siśupâla.[2] In the same Parvan, again many Râjans are seen bringing excellent jars for water for the bath of Yudhiṣṭhira after the great sacrifice.[3] In a private conflict Karṇa and Duryodhana attack and slay many Râjans.[4] In the many Svayamvaras in the Epic, the number of "kings" is legion.[5] In the Aśvamedha Parvan, a prince salutes all his seniors of the Kuru race and the other 'kings' present.[6]

Relations of the suzerain with the feudatories.

As a rule, the feudatories enjoyed autonomy in their internal affairs. But certain passages in the Mahâbhârata indicate that sometimes they chafed under the yoke, real or nominal. Not unoften were their relations with the suzerain characterised by distrust and jealousy.[7] In the

---

[1] Âdi Parvan, CXII.

[2] Sabhâ Parvan, XLV.

[3] Ibid., LIII.

[4] Śânti Parvan, IV.

[5] For instance, the svayamvara of Draupadî, Âdi Parvan, CLXXXVII; the svayaṁvara of Damayantî, Vana Parvan LV—LVII; again, Ibid., LXX-LXXI.

[6] Aśvamedha Parvan, LXXXVII, 27.

[7] Śânti Parvan, LXX, 30-31.

Sabhâ Parvan Nârada suggests to Yudhiṣṭhira that conquest should be followed by earnest attempts at conciliation.[1] In the Aśvamedha Parvan a king depletes his treasury and then the feudatory princes swarm round him and cause him serious trouble.[2] On the other hand, it was sometimes felt that the suzerain power could not be all-sufficing and must allow feudatories to subsist. In the Âśramavâsi Parvan, Dhritarâṣṭra says that a powerful king should never seek to exterminate weak kings, for these do good to the world by cherishing the good and punishing the wicked.[3]

Aristocracy.

Round every suzerain and every feudatory chief there is an aristocracy of warriors. Strife is the law of their being throughout the Mahâbhârata. They evince the highest loyalty to their chief and are always ready to lay down their lives for him. "Sweet it is to die in battle, the path to heaven lies in fighting."[4] The Vana Parvan has it that glory is preferable to life and that a hero's real life is the life of his fame.[5] That was the Kṣatriya way to be observed by royal and other aristocratic families. At the tragic conclusion of the domestic war, the blind old Dhritarâṣṭra says that he does not grieve for his hundred slaughtered sons. "They have all died in the observance of Kṣatriya duties."[6] To Yudhiṣṭhira who, with his brothers, was responsible for the extermination of the old man's progeny, he had already remarked once, "Rise up . . . Do thou now attend to thy duties . . . Thou hast conquered this earth according to the usage of the Kṣatriyas."[7] Instances of such expressions and deeds can be multiplied almost without number.

---

1 Sabhâ Parvan, V.
2 Aśvamedha Parvan, V, 12.
3 Aśramavâsi Parvan, VI, 16,
4 Karṇa Parvan, CIV.
5 Vana Parvan, CCCIII, 20, 31.
6 (Aśramavâsi) Parvan, III, 2 8.
7 Aśvamedha Parvan, I, 7.

It was under such circumstances that government was carried on during the period of which the traditions are reflected in the Mahâbhârata. The administration was presided over by the king who was expected personally to propel the machine. According to the theory of the epic, he was to be the embodiment of all virtues, all beneficence and heroism.[1] But the main story as well as the secondary episodes of the Epic show the average king falling far short of the ideal. The monarchs are addicted too much to gambling and hunting; often they are ferocious, at times licentious. In the Sabhâ Parvan there is a debate on gambling which at last is approved.[2] The Kuru princes use fraud; Yudhiṣṭhira loses his all, including his wife who is wantonly insulted by the winners; Bhîma vows to drink the blood of Duryodhana—a vow which, later, he fulfils to his satisfaction.[3] In the Droṇa-Parvan Duryodhana wants Yudhiṣṭhira to be captured alive so as to entice him to dice and then exile and ruin him once again.[4] Under the fascination of dice, Nala completely neglects the affairs of state. The people of the city and the officers came to the palace "unable to bear the calamity that had befallen their king conversant with

The King.

[1] For the ideal attributes and qualifications of the king, Śanti Parvan, LVII, 21-22, 30-36; LXIX, 3-4, LXXX, 2—113, CXX, 40—43. Sabhâ Parvan, V. For theories of the origin of kingship Vana Parvan, CLXXXIII, Śanti Parvan, CLXCII, 7—23; LIX, 87—89; LXVII, 17—32. On the supreme imperative necessity of government, Śanti Parvan LXVIII, 8—35; LXVII, 2—4, 12—16, LVII, 40; LXIV, 2, 21—30; LXXII, 29; LXXV, 13; LIX, 133-34. On the inherent divine prestige and vigour. of the king, Sânti Parvan, LXXII, 25; LXVIII, 39—47, LXV, 29; LXVII, 4, 8—11; LXVIII, 30—41, 48—50, 32—35; XXXVIII, 110.

For remarks on anxieties inseparable from royalty, Ibid., CLXXVI, 10—12.

[2] Sabhâ Parvan, LVIII.

[3] Ibid., LXV et seq.

[4] Droṇa Parvan, XII.

virtue and welfare." But not even at his queen Damayantî's request would the king see them. "Those councillors of state as also the citizens, afflicted with grief and shame, returned to their homes, saying, 'He liveth not.'"[1] A little later, Damayantî herself called a council in the name of Nala. "When the subjects in a body had come a second time, the daughter of Bhîma informed Nala of it. But the king regarded her not."[2] In the Epic the Pâṇḍus are sometimes spoken of masters of the Vedas and the rest of the sacred lore, but as one traces their career step by step, one meets with no regular intellectual training on their part. On the other hand, they receive a regular military training. Arjuna's son Abhimanyu is a full-fledged warrior and is married at the age of sixteen.

The Succession.

The succession to the throne was hereditary and normally went by the rule of primogeniture. But a grave physical defect was generally tantamount to a disqualification. We are once told in the Udyoga Parvan that the gods do not approve of a defective king.[3] In the Epic a new king has generally to be accepted by the people. The Mahâbhârata embellishes the Brihaddevatâ legend in which Devâpi declines the throne on the score of his skin disease. Pratîpa had three sons, Devâpi, Bâlhîka and Śaṁtanu. The eldest, a leper, loved by the whole family, is about to be installed, when "the priests, seniors, inhabitants of the city and the country forbid his consecration." The king yields.[4] The blind Dhritarâṣṭra is passed over in favour of his younger brother Pâṇḍu. On the other hand, some exceptional reason might induce people to discount any physical defect. Once in the Vana Parvan they insist on having

[1] Vana Parvan, LIX.
[2] Ibid., LX.
[3] Udyoga Parvan, CXLIX.
[4] Ibid.

a blind man as their king.[1] On the death of Pâṇḍu, the sceptre temporarily goes to Dhṛitarâṣṭra, but the question of regular succession comes to the fore when Yudhiṣṭhira, the eldest son of Pâṇḍu, reaches majority. The story of the epic favours the view that the crown belonged *de jure* to the family of Pâṇḍu. The first move to instal Duryodhana, the eldest son of Dhṛitarâṣṭra on the throne raised a wild popular uproar. Much earlier when Dhritarâṣṭra had first inquired if his newly-born son Duryodhana would be king, 'Jackals and other animals began to howl ominously.'[2] The minor episodes of the epic also point to hereditary succession and popular acceptance of the king. In the Aśvamedha Parvan the people dethrone a king but immediately proceed to invest his son Suvarcâ with the rights of sovereignty.[3] In the myth of the early kings when the tyrant Veṇa is bereft of life by the Riṣis, the sceptre is entrusted to his son Pṛithu.[4] In extraordinary contingencies the people practically elect a King. Thus, in the Âdi Parvan all the people chose Kuru, son of Saṁvaraṇa to be their king, for, they said, "he is a virtuous man."[5] Again, Janamejaya, though a mere boy, is elected king by the united voice of the people of the city. He ruled with the help of his priests and ministers.[6] The practice of installing a prince as heir-apparent and even king during the lifetime of his father is in evidence. Thus, in the Âdi Parvan, Nahuṣa instals his son when he has secured the consent of the people of the city and the country.[7] It is

Vana Parvan, CCXCIX.
Âdi Parvan, CXV.
Aśvamedha Parvan, V, 9.
Śânti Parvan, LIX, 87—89.
Âdi Parvan, XCIV, 49.
Ibid., XLIV, 6.
[7] Ibid., LXXXV.

clear that in spite of the recognition of hereditary succession and primogeniture, a king has to be formally accepted by the people. Protest and tumult follow if there is anything radically wrong with the king-designate. In the epic, indeed, people appear on the stage on all extraordinary occasions. When Dhritarâṣṭra proposes to pass over his nephew Yudhiṣṭhira, the rightful heir, in favour of his own son, the people raise a fearful outcry. They meet in assemblies, streets and courtyards and demand that Dhritarâṣṭra should be deposed, that Yudhiṣṭhira should not only be declared heir-apparent but forthwith installed as King. Dhritarâṣṭra, they declared, had long ago forfeited the right to the kingdom on account of his blindness. How could he now have a right to transmit it to his son[1] Towards the close of the story, when old Dhritarâṣṭra leaves for forest-life, he addresses the whole multitude and commends the people to the care of Yudhiṣṭhira who speaks in his turn.[2] When resolved on renunciation, Yudhiṣṭhira arranged that his grand-nephew Parîkṣit should be king in Hastinâpur. He called his subjects together and informed them of his plans. They were disconcerted at the news and unanimously disapproved of the king's intention to abdicate. "This should never be done." But Yudhiṣṭhira succeeded in persuading them to accept his proposals.[3] (The king was expected to be accessible to all, even to agriculturists.[4]) On the other hand, the Epic, in some of its episodes, assumes that the king could do what he liked with his kingdom. At the game of dice which constitutes one of the central events in the plot of the Epic, Yadhiṣṭhira pawns and loses

People in Politics.

---

[1] Ibid., CXLI.

[2] Âśramavâsi Parvan, IX. For moving scenes on this incident see section X.

[3] Mahâprasthânika Parvan, I.

[4] Sabhâ Paran, V.

his city, his country, his lands, "the wealth of all dwelling therein except of Brâhmaṇas and all those persons themselves except Brâhmaṇas, still remaining to me."[1] Nala similarly loses his kingdom and his wealth to his brother Puṣkara who drives him away and proclaims throughout the city that any one showing any attention to Nala would be put to death. As a result none showed any regard to their erstwhile sovereign.[2]

Consecration.

The consecration of kings in the Mahâbhârata is conducted, on the whole, according to the procedure laid down in the Brâhmaṇas and Sûtras but a few additional touches are given. The king-designate 'worships' his ministers.[3] Elsewhere he promises that by thought, word and deed he would protect the earth and religion and that he would observe the precepts of Ethics, Law and Politics in his conduct.[4] To the consecration of Yudhiṣṭhira, Brâhmaṇas, Kṣatriyas, Vaiśyas and respectable Śûdras are invited.[5]

The subjects, headed by the priests, came to see him bringing with them diverse kinds of auspicious articles. They brought earth and gold, many kinds of gems, jars of gold, silver, copper and earth, full of water, flowers, fried paddy, kuśa grass, cow's milk, śami, pippala and palâśa, sacrificial fuel, honey, clarified butter, etc. Seated on a throne of gold, surrounded by Kṛiṣṇa, Dhṛitarâṣṭra, his brothers and others, Yudhiṣṭhira touched the beautiful white flowers, svastikas, vessels full of diverse articles, earth, gold, silver and gems. He and his wife Draupadî sat on the Sarvatobhadra seat, "covered with tiger-skin and blazing with effulgence." They poured on him oblations of

[1] Sabhâ Parvan, LXV.
[2] Vana Parvan, LXI.
[3] Sabhâ Parvan, XIII, 4, 26, 29.
[4] Śânti Parvan, LIX, 106-107.
[5] Sabhâ Parvan, XXII, 41-42.

clarified butter with proper mantras. Kṛiṣṇa and others then poured on him water from sanctified conches. Yudhiṣṭhira who had accepted the presents offered to him now gave many more in return. The priests blessed him with all their heart.[1] Similar but less elaborate accounts of consecrations appear elsewhere in the Mahâbhârata.[2] A consecration was often followed by a Digvijaya. Yudhiṣṭhira sends out armies to make sure of his suzerainty over the surrounding regions. The Aśvamedha Parvan seems to indicate that a successful Digvijaya was followed by a fresh consecration, a grand royal sacrifice, attended by many 'kings' and marked by an exchange of costly presents and by lavish gifts to priests and others.[3] At the time of his own consecration, a king would sometimes consecrate his son or brother as Yuvarâja. Yudhiṣṭhira appointed his brother Bhîma, next to him in age, to that office.[4] Besides the Yauvarâjyâbhiṣeka which is met with throughout Sanskrit literature, the Mahâbhârata furnishes instances of the consecration of military commanders like Bhîṣma,[5] Droṇa,[6] Karṇa[7] and others. Great, indeed, was the merit of sacrifices. At the conclusion of the war Kṛiṣṇa said to Yudhiṣṭhira, "Do thou now celebrate many a sacrifice with suitable presents to the priests."[8] A little later, four sacrifices, the Râjasûya, Aśvamedha, Sarvamedha and Naramedha are recommended to Yudhiṣṭhira partly for purification from the sins of the war.[9] Besides elaborate ritual and charity, there seems to have been an intellectual element about some sacrifices during the epic period. In

[1] Śânti Parvan, XLI, 1—23.
[2] Âdi Parvan, XLIV, LXXXV, CI. Sabhâ Parvan, XLV.
[3] Aśvamedha Parvan, V, LXXII et seq.
[4] Śânti Parvan, XLII, 7.
[5] Udyoga Parvan, CLV.
[6] Droṇa Parvan, V.
[7] Karṇa Parvan, I.
[8] Aśvamedha Parvan, II.
[9] Ibid., III, 1—8.

the Vana Parvan, for instance, Aṣṭâvakra proposes to his uncle Śvetaketu that they should repair to Janaka's sacrifice to listen to the discussions of Brâhmaṇas as well as to partake of excellent food.[1]

Ushered with pomp and ceremony into his office, the king lived in a grand style. His palace was expected to be a knot of paradise. In the Sabhâ Parvan, at the request of Kriṣṇa, Maya undertakes to build for the Pâṇḍus a palace like that of the celestials.[2] When finished, the mansion was all splendour and grandeur.[3] Close to the royal residence was a court of justice, gambling hall, a music hall, an arena for wrestling and brute fights. A spacious area was set aside for markets at the capital. Parks were laid out for the people. Definite quarters were assigned to the common people. The "king's city" should be laid out in six squares, the streets should be well-watered and well-lighted with lamps. Pains should be taken to make it as sanitary and beautiful as possible. A capital city in the Mahâbhârata is defended by battlemented towers and seven moats.[4] Besides the capital there are other towns, multitudes of villages and yet smaller settlements called ghoṣas or pallis in the Mahâbhârata.

The Palace and Capital.

Habitations.

At the capital, the king was assisted in the task of administration by a number of officers of whom seven were the most important, *viz.*, the commander of forces, the second in command, the governor of the citadel, the chief priest, the judge, the physician and

The Administration.

Chief officers.

[1] Vana Parvan, CXXXII. [2] Sabhâ Parvan, I.

[3] Ibid., III-IV. Several descriptions of great Sabhâs, which are here tantamount to palaces and courts, occur in this Parvan: the Celestial Sabhâ (VII); the Sabhâ of Yama (VIII); the Sabhâ of Varuṇa (IX); the Sabhâ of Vaiśravaṇa (X); the Sabhâ of Brahman (XI).

[4] Vana Parvan, CLXXXIV. Virâṭa Parvan, XXII.

astrologer.[1] Subsequently there is mention of eighteen principal officers, including the heir-apparent, chamberlain, overseers of the harem, inspectors of prisons, justice, forests and frontiers.[2] The theory of the Śânti Parvan speaks of more than thirty chief offices.[3] In another section of the same Parvan, a king is advised to appoint officers for mines, salt, Śulka (customs), river-crossings, elephants, infantry, etc.[4] One of the most important of all offices was that of the ambassador. It might be entrusted to any of the chief personages at the court. Drupada entrusts it once to his Purohita.[5] Krișṇa himself acted as the envoy of the Pâṇḍus. Dhritarâșṭra once entrusted a diplomatic mission to his younger brother,[6] and on another occasion to his charioteer.[7] The charioteer was another great personage. Krișṇa himself acted as the charioteer of Arjuna in the great war. Over all the officers and ministers stood a chief minister. "A king without a minister cannot govern his kingdom even for three days."[8] Some of the chief officers were relations of the king. After his consecration Yudhișṭhira bestows many offices on his relations.[9] Elsewhere, too, the Śânti Parvan counsels that relations of the king or persons particularly trustworthy should be appointed to chief offices.[10] In another section of the same Parvan, again, birth is prescribed as one of the considerations in making appointments.[11] There it is declared that to the chief offices as a

Recruitment of officers.

[1] Sabhâ Parvan, V, 38.
[2] Ibid., V.
[3] Śânti Parvan, LXXV, 16–10.
[4] Ibid., LXIX.
[5] Udyoga Parvan, VI.
[6] Sabhâ Parvan, LVIII.
[7] Udyoga Parvan, XXII.
[8] Śânti Parvan, CVI, 11. Sabhâ Parvan, V.
[9] Śânti Parvan, XLII, 8—19.
[10] Ibid., LXIX.
[11] Ibid., CVI, 12.

whole should be appointed four Brâhmaṇas, three Kṣatriyas, twenty-one Vaiśyas, three Śûdras and one Sûta.[1] In the practice of the Mahâbhârata, however, the principal officers are drawn from the aristocracy. It is possible that some of the offices were hereditary.[2]

Position of ministers.

In the Sabhâ Parvan Nârada hints the advice that a king should constantly consult his ministers.[3] In practice, however, the rule was not always observed. Nor was the advice of ministers, when tendered, always followed. In the Bhîṣma Parvan, Dhritarâṣṭra is blamed for refusing to listen to Vidura, Bhîṣma, Droṇa and Sañjaya. Sañjaya himself blames Dhritarâṣṭra for the evil policy he had pursued.[4] When leaving the capital the king might entrust his affairs to the Purohita or some other dignitary. In the Âśramavâsi Parvan, when Yudhiṣṭhira goes out with his brothers, the city is left in the charge of the Purohita and Yuyutsu, a general.[5] When for some extraordinary reason the king was unable or unwilling to perform his duties, the charge of the state might devolve on the queen and ministers. In the episode of Nala, the king forgets all in the fascination of dice. His queen Damayantî meets a deputation of citizens and herself summons a council, though she fails to rouse her husband from his stupor to attend it. Apprehensive of the worst, she asks Vârṣṇeya, the royal charioteer, to take her children to her parents in Kuṇḍina. Before obeying her command, Vârṣṇeya seeks and obtains the approval of the chief officers.[6] In the Mahâbhârata there is no fixed rule about regency during a minority. In one such contingency Bhîṣma alone guards the realm.[7]

---

[1] Śânti Parvan, CVI, 11.
[2] For the ideal qualifications of ministers, Ibid., LXXXIII, 2—50; CXIX, 3—9; CXX, 48.
[3] Sabhâ Parvan, V.
[4] Bhîṣma Parvan, LXV.
[5] Âśramavâsi Parvan, XV, XXIII.
[6] Vana Parvan, LX. [7] Âdi Parvan, CII.

In the Epics, the old popular assembly has altogether disappeared. If the people occasionally make themselves felt, it is not through any constitutional channels. In place of the assembly there has grown up a court consisting of the king's relations, nobles, feudatories, priests, officers and chief men of the capital. In the Mahâbhârata the court is often the scene of festivity and rejoicing. Dancing girls form part of the retinue.

The Court.

In the sphere of local government, the village is the unit. Every village seems to have had an officer, called Grâmâdhipati, who looked after affairs in general and was particularly concerned with the king's share of the produce. In Vedic literature, the office of Grâmaṇî is the goal of a Vaiśya's ambition.[1] The Mahâbhârata furnishes no indication of the caste of the Grâmâdhipati. In the Sabhâ Parvan Nârada counsels the appointment of five officers in each village,[2] but that may be a counsel of perfection. We cannot be certain that even the Grâmâdhipati was regularly appointed by the government. He might sometimes have been hereditary or marked out by village opinion for the office. According to the theory of the Śânti Parvan, groups of ten, hundred and a thousand villages should form the successive administrative divisions. Here theory may be reflecting facts in a rather idealised manner. Each head of a village or an administrative division should keep his immediate superior informed of all happenings and submit regular reports. The officers seem to have been paid in kind. For instance, the superintendent of a hundred villages should receive a large village for his sustenance while the officer of a thousand villages should enjoy the revenues of a small town as his

Local Government.

[1] Taittirîya Saṁhitâ, II, 5, 4, 4. Maitrâyaṇî Saṁhitâ, I, 6, 5.
[2] Sabhâ Parvan, V.

remuneration. Such a practice would inevitably promote the feudal tendencies. From this scheme of local government towns seem to have been excluded. Each town is to have an officer to itself, a Sarvârthacintaka, one who thought or cared for everything.[1] For purposes of defence garrisons were to be stationed along the borders and in towns.[2]

To watch over government servants, feudatories, nobles and the people at large, a host of spies swarmed the land. Bhîṣma declares that the employment and direction of spies is one of the prime duties of the king. They are to be set in cities, provinces and the territories of feudatories. None is to escape their glance, not even the king's sons, relations, friends or counsellors. No place is to be free from their ubiquitous presence. They must frequent parks and pleasure-grounds, courts, houses, shops, meetings of scholars and crowds of common people.[3] One of the functions which fell to the lot of spies in ancient India was that which falls to the lot of journalists at present. They had to submit to the sovereign regular reports on public feeling on the doings of the government in the cities and provinces.

Spies.

Besides those directly concerned with administrative business, there were large numbers of other persons in the employment of the state. There seem to have been state factories in which multitudes of artisans worked. In the Sabhâ Parvan, Nârada advises Yudhiṣṭhira to keep them regularly supplied with materials, to pay them regularly, to examine their work and to reward their merit.[4]

Artisans.

---

[1] Śânti Parvan, CXXXVII, 8–11.
[2] Ibid., LXIX, 6 et seq.
[3] Ibid., LXIX, 8–12, 52; LXXXIX, 14–16; LXXXVI, 20-21; XCI, 50.
[4] Sabhâ Parvan, V.

The sources of revenue in the Mahâbhârata are wider than in the Sûtras. Theory again fixes the land-tax at one-sixth of the produce. This was supplemented by customs again on the theory that merchants should pay for the protection which they received from the state. There was no fixed rate for mercantile dues; they were to be settled after consideration of the purchases, sales, profits and standard of living. Artisans should be taxed on an evaluation of their manufactures, their expenses, receipts and their general prosperity. Justice formed another plentiful source and brought in a good deal by way of fines and forfeitures. In a curious passage, Arjuna remarks that Brâhmaṇas should be punished with word of mouth, Kṣatriyas with restriction to bare sustenance and Vaiśyas with fines and forfeiture of property.

Revenue.

According to orthodox theory Brâhmaṇas are exempt from all taxes. They were expected to live a life of poverty and could not therefore have much to pay. But the Śânti Parvan makes it clear that if they forsook their true vocation and followed any other occupations, they were to be taxed like others. If any group of persons combined to resist taxation, they should be struck down by diplomacy or force. The brunt of taxation fell on the Vaiśyas who are called karapradâḥ or payers of taxes in the Sabhâ Parvan. [2] In the same Parvan we read of 'love-offerings.' Brâhmaṇaṣ, Kṣatriyas, Vaiśyas, Sûdras, outcasts, high and low alike

[1] Śânti Parvan, LXIX, 25; LXI, 10-11, 13-16, 20-23; LXXXVII, 14-15, 18-21, 23, 35-40; LXXXVIII, 2-12; LXXXIX, 24; XV, 4; CXIX, 17; CXX, 43-44; CXXX, 9, 35; CXXXIII, 3; CXXXIV, 3-4; CXXXVI, 1-2; LXXXVI, 3-11.

[2] Sabhâ Parvan, XLVI. Cf. Âdi Parvan, CXCII.

bring tribute to the king, for the sake of love (prītyartham).[1] Euphemisms apart, such offerings constituted a regular source of income. Elsewhere in the same Parvan many semi-civilised tribes, like the Vairamas, Pâradas, Tuṅgâs, Kitavas, living in woodlands or on the sea-shore, present numerous animals of various species to the king.[2] The forests which abounded yielded their products and were a distinct source of income. Forced labour was sometimes exacted. We are told in the Śânti Parvan that all Brâhmaṇas who did not come up to the ideal should be made to pay taxes and render the usual corvée.[3]

The Mahâbhârata makes it clear that in emergencies like war, the king made unusual demands on his subjects.

Emergency Finance.

Abnormal times were regarded as governed by a morality of their own. A king should explain the situation to his people and levy extra taxes. He might force any unwilling subjects to disgorge their wealth. If war exhausted the treasury, he might seize the wealth of all except Brâhmaṇas.[4] It is recognised that to defray the expenses of a sacrifice, a king may seize the wealth of an irreligious rich man.[5] At the conclusion of the war, Yudhiṣṭhira declares that he could not levy dues for celebrating a sacrifice at the moment.[6] He plainly implies that that was the usual practice. A Dasyu's wealth could also be confiscated in case of need.[7]

[1] Sabhâ Parvan, LII.

[2] Ibid., LI.

[3] Śânti Parvan, LXXVI.

[4] Śânti Parvan, LXXI, 23; CXXX, 37-38, 47-48; CXXXII, 5, 9; CXXXIII, 3.

[5] Aśvamedha Parvan, XII.

[6] Ibid., III, 14.

[7] Śânti Parvan, CXXXVI.

It is difficult to obtain any clear idea of the sphere of state-activity during the Epic period. The theory of the Śânti Parvan makes it conterminous with life itself. The state should ceaselessly foster righteousness, guide, correct and control the moral life of the people, make the earth habitable and comfortable for men.[1] It is possible that the theorist had some basis of practice for his counsel when he wanted the government to reclaim land for cultivation, to excavate tanks and lakes and thus make agriculture independent of the caprices of the rains, to make loans of seed-grain to cultivators in time of need.[2] The king should cause wide roads to be laid out and watering-stations to be erected at proper distances.[3] Robbers should be exterminated everywhere.[4] The king is himself counselled to practise boundless charity on occasions like the Râjasûya but he must discourage and punish indiscriminate begging.[5]

Sphere of state-activity.

In the Mahâbhârata the aspiration to create an empire is hallowed into an imperative, sacred duty. Yudhiṣṭhira, the epic embodiment of kingly righteousness, burns to emulate the glory of the kings of old.[6] He must establish a glorious empire and, therefore, make short work of the mighty Jarâsandha of Magadha.[7] Where unprovoked aggression was erected into a moral ideal, it was inevitable that diplomacy should throw all scruples overboard. Reason of state became the one guiding, overmastering principle and justified the extreme of fraud and treachery.

Foreign policy.

[1] Śânti Parvan, LXXXVIII, 14; LXXV, 19; LIX, 114-15.
[2] Ibid., V, 17, 21; LXV, 2. Sabhâ Parvan, V.
[3] Śânti Parvan, LXIX, 53.
[4] Ibid., LXXV, 5.
[5] Ibid., LXXV, 10; XIII, 40-41; LXXXVIII, 16-17; 23-24. For royal gifts see *inter alia* the description of Hariścandra's great sacrifice, Sabhâ Parvan, XII.
[6] Sabhâ Parvan, XIII.
[7] Ibid., XIV. For Jarâsandha and his ancestor Vṛihadratha, Ibid., XVII.

In the course of one of the most remarkable episodes in the epic Jarâsandha declares that it was a Kṣatirya's duty to bring others under his sway by the display of his prowess and that he was justified in treating them as slaves.[1] He longs to make a hecatomb of a hundred 'kings' and had already collected eighty-six for the purpose when he was overpowered by Kriṣṇa and the Pâṇḍus.[2] In the Vana Parvan it is stated that whatever sin a king commits in acquiring dominion, is expiated afterwards by means of sacrifices and gifts.[3] While on this subject in the Śânti Parvan, Bhîṣma, the great exponent of righteousness, takes his stand on pure reason. He quotes Uśanas who, in days of yore, had told the Daityas that scriptures were no scriptures if they could not stand the test of reason. Under the pressure of abnormal circumstances, extraordinary maxims must be applied to the conduct of affairs—maxims which had brought 'blazing prosperity' to king Śatruñjaya to whom they were preached by an ancient sage. One should readily surrender before might and then seize the first opportunity to smash the powerful antagonist or suzerain. A king should remember that vanquished foes are always on the alert and can never be trusted. Secret diplomacy, hypocrisy of all sorts, "divide and rule," corruption of the enemy's forces or subjects, lavish use of gold and poison, ruthless severity, devastation of hostile territory, wholesale destruction of its population—such are the weapons recommended for dealing with enemies.[4] The whole series of chapters on Âpaddharma in the Śânti Parvan[5] remind one of Machiavelli. There are sentences, written with the "point

[1] Sabhâ Parvan XXXII.
[2] Ibid., XV.
[3] Vana Parvan, XXV. See also XXII. XXXIII.
[4] Śânti Parvan CIII, 16, 19-42; CV, 6-9, 21-25; CXXXI, 4-7, 10-12; CXXXVIII, 12-18; CXL, 7-70. CXLI, 70-71, CXLIII, 1-24. For Arjuna's remarks to the same purpose, XV, 16-23, 25, 37-38; also X, 6-8; Sabhâ Parvan XXXII. Cf. Vana Parvan XXIX-XXXIV; For Kaṇikas discourse in the same strain, Âdi Parvan, CXLII.
[5] Âpaddharma begins with section CXXXI of the Śânti Parvan.

of a stiletto" which may pass for quotations from "the Prince." The section, as a whole, may be styled, as Diderot proposed to style certain chapters of Machiavelli, as "the circumstances under which it is right for a prince to be a scoundrel." Like the Italian realist, the Epic poet "strips away the flowing garments of convention and commonplace; closes his will against sympathy and feeling; ignores pity as an irrelevance, just as the operating surgeon does." In both, the purpose is the same, "the secular state supreme, self-interest and self-regard, avowed as the single principle of state action; material force, the master-key to civil policy. Clear intelligence backed by unsparing will, unflinching energy, remorseless vigour, the brain to plan and the hand to strike—here is the salvation of states."[1] The political circumstances which primarily suggested these lines of thought were, in essentials, the same in medieval Italy as in Ancient India. In the Âśramavâsi Parvan, towards the close of the Mahâbhârata, Dhṛitarâṣṭra enunciates to Yudhiṣṭhira the doctrine of Maṇḍala as the guiding principle of policy,[2] but these passages are very late.

Ethics of the battlefield.

In contrast to its precepts on diplomacy, the Mahâbhârata inculcates a high standard of the Ethics of the Battle-field. A Kṣatriya may oppose deceit by deceit but should always be fair in response to fairness. He should not proceed on horseback against a car-warrior and should not wear armour when pitted against one unclad in mail. He should not strike one who has been disabled, who has fallen into distress, whose bowstring has been cut or who has lost his vehicle. A wounded enemy should be sent home or properly treated by skilful surgeons. If a wounded righteous warrior is taken captive, he should be

[1] Morley, Romanes Lecture on Machiavelli, pp. 20-21, 26-27, 33.

[2] Âśramavâsi Parvan, VI, VII.

cured and then set at liberty. "This is the eternal duty." A warrior whose armour has fallen off, who begs for quarter, saying, 'I am thine,' who joins his hands in supplication or who has laid his weapon aside, may be taken captive but should not be killed. Nor should one slay those who are asleep, thirsty, fatigued, or at meals, nor those who are seeking spiritual emancipation, who are mad or who stay trustfully. The lives of camp-followers, menial servants and other people of the sort are sacrosanct. An ambassador is not to be injured under any circumstances. A maiden, captured in war, should be detained for a year and asked to marry the victor. If she does not consent, she ought to be sent back. So, too, with slaves. In the story, this ideal is approached by many in varying degrees. But not seldom do warriors cry fie on it. In the fierce conflicts of Droṇa Parvan for instance, heroes openly throw all ideals overboard.

Military service.

Besides promising heavenly joys to valour, the Mahâbhârata counsels a king to reward meritorious military service by double pay, excellent food and drink, promotion in the ranks and a seat equal to that of the king. The Epic lays down physical, mental and moral qualifications for soldiers, dilates on the time, season and order of manoeuvres and discusses the characteristics, dispositions and chances of success of armies.[1] But the subject lies beyond the scope of the present work.

[1] Śânti Parvan, LXIX, 34—40, 55; LXXXV, 26—28; LXXXVI, 5 - 15; XCIV, 1-2; XCV, 2—5, 7—14; XCVI, 1—7, 11, 16-17, 22-23; XCVII, 8, 11-12; XCVIII, 15—25, 35—48, XCIX, 1—17; C, 6—24, 30; CI, 324-5; CII, Bhîṣma Parvan, I, 24—27 et seq. For the fighting, also Droṇa Parvan, Karṇa Parvan. Hopkins, J. A. O. S., XIII, pp. 191—325, treats the subject of war in the Mahâbhârata exhaustively.

The kingship, tinged with feudalism, is the predominant type of government in the Mahâbhârata. But there are a few passages which point to the existence of Gaṇas or olgarchies. Yudhiṣṭhira inquires of Bhîṣma how gaṇas prosper, how they can manage to keep secrets with so many in the seat of government. In reply Bhîṣma emphasises that Gaṇas must, above all, maintain internal cohesion. If disunited, they will fall an easy prey to enemies. If united, they will attain to prosperity and outsiders will seek their alliance. It behoves their wise elders to nip in the bud any disputes that may arise within the Gaṇas. If the seniors treat rising dissensions with indifference, the members will soon fall into violent mutual wrangling. It is essential to guard against dangers from within. They can uproot a Gaṇa in a single day. Gaṇas are destroyed not by the courage, diplomacy or gold of the enemy nor by the lure of female charms, but by internal dissensions. Harmony is the very law of their being. In every Gaṇa people should be taught to practise their duties, to bow before learned persons. The Executive, consisting of the 'chief persons,' must be trusted and suffered to keep secrets. The Gaṇas should keep their treasuries full, should regulate their policy well, employ numbers of spies and display courage, perseverance and steady prowess on the battlefield.[1] It appears that the oligarchies, non-monarchical, flourished for a while but they were torn by internal dissensions. They had an executive which sometimes found it difficult to make its authority felt. About the Andhakavṛiṣṇi oligarchy Kṛiṣṇa

Oligarchies.

[1] Śânti Parvan, CVII, 10–32. F. W. Thomas (J. R. A. S., 1914, pp. 10–12) shows that Gaṇa implied absence of royalty, though Fleet (J. R. A. S., 1915, pp. 13—19) interprets Gaṇa as a tribe. With a monarchical background, however, the passages in question make little sense.

remarks that though he was entitled to one-half of the executive power, he only received bitter words from his relations.[1]

Besides the state, feudal dominion and regular local government, there appears in the Mahâbhârata another principle of organisation. Guilds of warriors, industrial workers and traders flit across the stage. They are reckoned among the principal supports of the monarchy. A king is enjoined to avail himself of Śreṇîvala which is described as equal to that of hired soldiers. It refers most probably to force which guilds of warriors could supply, obviously for a consideration. Economic guilds depend for their vitality on internal cohesion. Nothing can expiate the sin of forsaking one's duty towards one's guild.[2]

Guilds.

To the Mahâbhârata was appended another work called the Harivaṁśa which describes the exploits of Kṛiṣṇa and his ancestors in 16,000 ślokas grouped in three sections. It is rather late. Nor does it throw any fresh light on political institutions. Cantos 146-7 describe a magnificent royal picnic in which the heroes, Baladeva, Kṛiṣṇa, and others spend the day in feasting, drinking, singing and dancing. Thousands of courtesans enlivened the scene.

The Harivaṁśa.

III.—THE RÂMÂYAṆA.

Along with the Mahâbhârata, the Râmâyaṇa of Vâlmîki ranks as one of the two great Epics of India. It has a unity and individuality which the longer compendium lacks. But its date is almost equally uncertain. In its present form it is certainly later than the kernel of the

The date of the Râmâyaṇa.

[1] Śanti Parvan, LXXXI.

[2] Vana Parvan, CCXLVIII, 16. Śânti Parvan, LIV, 20.

Mahâbhârata. Jacobi shows that the Râmâyaṇa originally consisted of five books, II—VI, though here, too, some cantos are interpolated. The Seventh Book is certainly so late that it cannot be utilised along with the rest. The first beginnings of the real epic may go back to 500 B.C. but extensive additions were made till the second century B.C., and even later. However, the second century B.C. saw most of the work complete. The Râmâyaṇa arose in Kośala, with its centre at Ayodhyâ in Avadha (Oudh). Its narrative leads much further towards the south, though Laṅkâ, the abode of Râvaṇa, the king of Râkṣasas, is hardly likely to be Ceylon.[1] Whatever the locale of Kiṣkindhâ or of Laṅkâ, the Râmâyaṇa, for the most part, illustrates the political conditions only of the eastern districts of Madhyadeśa just as the Mahâbhârata pertains to its western parts. Unlike the Mahâbhârata, the Râmâyaṇa is a Kâvya; it is called the Âdi-Kâvya, the first 'artificial' poem. Its style is certainly polished and graceful, but it has all the naturalness and spontaneity of true poetry.[2] It was meant to be recited before gatherings. The fourth section of the First Book, the Bâlakâṇḍa, says that after composing the Râmâyaṇa the master reflected as to how he should publish it before assemblies. The Buddhist Jâtakas make it clear that there were several versions of the Râmâyaṇa current. In the Daśaratha Jâtaka, Sitâ is the sister of Râma paṇḍita and Lakkhaṇa

---

[1] Jacobi located Laṅkâ in Assam Sardar Kibe has recently located it in the Central Provinces.

[2] Jacobi, Das Râmâyaṇa. Macdonell, History of Sanskrit Literature, 302—11. Griffith, Appendix to his Abridged Translation of the Râmâyaṇa. Keith, J. R. A. S., 1915, pp. 318—28. The statements of Dischrysontonius (50—117 A.D.), and Philostratus (170 or 180 A.D.), that Homer's poetry was sung in India (Eggeling, Encyclopaedia Britannica, Vol. 21, 9th edition, p. 281) can refer only to the Râmâyaṇa and not to the Mahâbhârata as was once supposed. The Râmâyaṇa consists of 24,000 Ślokas and has come down in three distinct recensions, (1) the Bengal, (2) the Bombay and (3) the West Indian.

paṇḍita as the two princes are called and the other details of the story are also different.[1]

In spite of the difference in locale, the chronological approximation makes the social and political atmosphere of the Mahâbhârata and the Râmâyaṇa much the same. Caste is present in either, but it must be added that priestly influence is stronger in the Râmâyaṇa. For instance, at the conclusion of the horse-sacrifice for the birth of a son, king Daśaratha conferred the earth upon Brâhmaṇas. The latter, however, knew their resources and interests better and said, "Thou alone art worthy to protect the earth; nor can we rule it being constantly engaged in Vedic studies. Do thou, therefore, confer on us something instead, as the price thereof. Do thou confer upon us gems or gold, or kine, or anything else, for . . . we do not want earth." Daśaratha then bestowed on them ten lacs of kine, ten koṭis of gold and twenty of silver.[2] Later, the king calls Viśvâmitra his guide and his god, when the latter comes to request him to depute two of his sons, Râma and Lakṣmaṇa, to fight the demons who molested his sacrifices The king is unwilling to part with his tender children for the sake of a hazardous enterprise. Viśvâmitra gets angry with the king and the earth trembles. Vaśiṣṭha, the Purohita of Daśaratha, advises compliance with Viśvâmitra's demand. The king yields.[3] In the course of a dialogue later on, the power of the Brâhmaṇas is affirmed to be greater than that of Kṣatriyas.[4] Describing the ideal kingdom of Ayodhyâ, the poet specially notes that the Brâhmaṇas were obeyed by Kṣatriyas, who, in their

Brahmanic influence.

[1] Daśaratha Jâtaka, IV, 124—31.

[2] Bâlakâṇḍa, Section XV. The later Uttarakâṇḍa, Ch. 74, has a peculiar theory of the development of caste.

[3] Bâlakâṇḍa, XX.

[4] Ibid., LIV. See also VII.

turn, were followed by Vaiśyas, while the Śûdras occupied with their proper vocations, ministered unto the three higher orders.[1]

Feudatories.

The Râmâyaṇa reflects the same type of feudalism as the Mahâbhârata. Daśaratha who is often designated King of Ayodhyâ is quite as often called a universal ruler.[2] It appears that while he actually governed only the region of Kośala with its capital at Ayodhyâ[3] he exercised a sort of suzerainty over a wider area which was parcelled out among a number of feudatories. Daśaratha's court is described as ordinarily crowded with neighbouring kings who come to pay tribute.[4] For Daśaratha's horse-sacrifice, they pour into the city of Ayodhyâ daily and nightly in a long stream and bring with them various kinds of gems for presentation to the king.[5] Elsewhere there is mention of "princes throned as well as those without thrones," that is, ruling feudatories as well as other members of their families, "from east and west, north and south," bringing countless gems for presentation to Bharata.[6] In a remarkable episode, there is an assertion of the suzerain's right to call feudatories to order and to take them to task for misconduct. When the Vânara king Vâlin reproves Râma for hitting him secretly instead of fighting him openly as behoved a Kṣatriya, Râma replies that Kiṣkindhâ was part of Ikṣvâku dominions, that

[1] Bâlakaṇḍâ., VI.

The Uttarakâṇḍa, which is later than the rest of the Râmâyaṇa, records an episode which found an echo in subsequent Sanskrit literature. Śûdras were forbidden to practise religious austerities, lest the Brâhmaṇas and Kṣatriyas should be enfeebled. A Śûdra who dared to transgress the prohibition was killed by Râma with his own hand. (Uttarakâṇḍa, LXXXVII—XCI.)

[2] Bâlakâṇḍa, VII, for instance

[3] Ibid., VI.

[4] Ibid., V.

[5] Ibid., XIII.

[6] Ayodhyâkâṇḍa, LXXXII.

the Ikṣvâkus had the power of awarding favour or punishment on men, beasts and birds alike, and that, as commanded by Bharata who then ruled the capital Ayodhyâ, he was entitled to determine how he would punish those who went astray. Śâstras had sanctioned the destruction of miscreants.[1] In the Râmâyaṇa however, Kośala, the real kingdom of the Ikṣvâkus, is rather small. On his banishment, Râma had quickly passed its bounds.[2] Marriage alliances are of frequent occurrence among suzerains and feudatories alike.

The succession.

The Râmâyaṇa knows only of the monarchical form of government and recognises the succession not only as hereditary but as governed by the law of primogeniture. The heir-apparent was installed Yuvarâja and associated in the task of administration during the lifetime of his father. The yuvarâja as well as the king is formally accepted by the people who protest if any violation of the recognised custom is attempted. At the approach of age, Daśaratha desires to retire into the forest and entrust the kingdom to Râma.[3] He summons a huge assembly of people from the capital and the provinces, lays his proposal before them and requests them to speak out their minds. They heartily approve of the project of Râma's installation and paint his transcendent virtues on which their judgment was based. *Inter alia* Râma had mastered the use of all the weapons known among men, gods and Asuras. Returning from the field on horse-back or on an elephant, he had always enquired after the welfare of the people, after their sons and wives, their disciples and servants, their fire and home and all else. So he must be king.[4] Not long after when people

[1] Kiṣkindhâ-kâṇḍa, XVIII.
[2] Ayodhyâkaṇḍa, XLIX. Yet in the next Canto L, it is called the extensive and romantic Kośala.
[3] Ayodhyâkâṇḍa, I.
[4] Ibid., II.

notice Râma on his way to his father's palace, they exhort him to protect them after the manner of Daśaratha.[1] When Daśaratha, bound by his previous promises to one of his wives, Kaikeyi, is led to exile Râma for fourteen years and to command Bharata's installation in his place, there is general consternation at the departure from the established law. Lakṣmaṇa advises Râma to take instantaneous possession of the government, threatens dire civil war and talks of depopulating Ayodhyâ with sharp arrows and of despatching his father in case of opposition. Râma's mother Kauśalyâ, though devoted to her husband, seriously requests her son to consider Lakṣmaṇa's proposals.[2] When Râma meekly accepts exile, Lakṣmaṇa is beside with rage. "People will mark this thy forsaking of the kingdom for redeeming the vows of thy father with opprobrium." "Do thou perform the rites of installation with things necessary for benediction – do thou engage in these affairs—myself alone shall be able by force to thwart the opposition of the kings."[3] Râma, however, explains that Daśaratha was the lord and master of all people and might do what he liked.[4] This, however, was not the view of the minister Sumantra when he reproved Kaikeyi saying, ". . . . the princes will obtain the kingdom one after another according to age ,---this custom it is your study to render nugatory even while the lord of the Ikṣvâku race is still alive. . . . . . . No Brâhmaṇa will dwell in your dominion."[5] When Râma has departed for the forest and the ministers, assembled, request Bharata to "become our king," the latter replies, ". . . In our line it is ever fit for the first-born alone to perform the task of government . . ." He must bring Râma back.[6] Later when a huge assembly

---

[1] Ayodhyâkâṇḍa, XVII.
[2] Ibid., XXI.
[3] Ibid., XXIII.
[4] Ibid., XXIV.
[5] Ibid., XXXV.
[6] Ibid., LXXIX.

again presses the crown on him he reiterates that "Firstborn, foremost in merit, righteous-souled . . . . Râma deserved the kingdom as Daśaratha did." If he, a younger prince, accepted the offer, he would bring disgrace on the race of Ikṣvâku.[1] On meeting Râma at long last in the forest, Bharata says, "Thou art the first-born; and meet it is that thou shouldst get thyself installed. Râma answers that "the monarch is competent to make me stay in the woods clad in black deer skin, as to establish me in the monarchy."[2] To this view of the case Bharata's reply is significant. "Deprived of the kingdom in consequence of my posteriority in point of birth, what doth regard for morality avail me ? . . . . even this morality has been established with reference to us, *viz.*, that the eldest son of the king existing, a younger one cannot be the king.'[3] Elsewhere, too, in the Râmâyaṇa the same rule is established. In the Bâlakâṇḍa, on the death of Sagara the people make his son Amśuman king. It will be observed that in such transactions popular opinion and feeling counted for something. Nevertheless it could sometimes be disregarded. In the episode of Râma's proposed installation it is to be noted that the people's will, which Daśaratha had so sedulously endeavoured to ascertain and which still favoured Râma's installation, eventually goes unheeded. Sometimes, of course, a popular agitation could redress some grievous wrong. A legend in the Ayodhyâkâṇḍa recalls how a king had been compelled, by the pressure of the people, to banish his son who amused himself by throwing people into the river Sarayû.[4]

---

[1] Ayodhyâkâṇḍa, LXXXII.

[2] Ibid., CI.

[3] Ibid., CII.

[4] Ibid., XXXVI.

In the ordinary course of things, it will appear, the consecration of a new king was attended by festivity on a gigantic scale. The whole city was decorated. Courtezans played and danced all around. Priests, generals, merchants, citizens, provincials—all thronged the palace and made a holiday.[1] The white umbrella was one of the signs of kingship. Sîtâ, before she knew of the abandonment of the proposed installation of her husband, innocently inquires, ... "Why has not thy charming face been placed under the shade of an umbrella, having hundred ribs and white as a watery foam?"[2] Later, the Kiṣkindhâkâṇḍa and Yuddhakâṇḍa describe actual consecrations more or less in the Mahâbhârata style. The Uttarakâṇḍa which is later than the rest of the Râmâyaṇa, has two descriptions in the same strain. In every one of them, auspicious waters are collected from the seas and rivers in golden jars. They are sprinkled over the prince seated on a throne. The crown is placed on his head. Generally he receives presents from his nobles and subjects and offers gifts to Brâhmaṇas. Generally, too, a sacrifice is performed.[3]

Coronation.

Thus installed on the throne, the king was expected to be the embodiment of all virtues.[4] As in the Mahâbhârata, he should run the governmental machine himself. He is the chief executive officer, the chief judge, the chief military commander. None the less he lives a life of luxury and pomp. For instance, every morning eulogists, bards, singers and genealogists present

The King and the Circle round him.

[1] Ayodhyâkâṇḍa, III, XIV, XV.

[2] Ibid., XXVI.

[3] Kiṣkindhâkâṇḍa, XXVI. Yuddhakâṇḍa, CXII, CXXVIII. Uttarakâṇḍa, LXIII, CVII.

[4] For the ideal of kingship Nârada's description of Râma to Vâlmîki, Bâlakâṇḍa I. Also the delineation of Daśaratha, Ibid., VI.

themselves at his palace.[1] His eldest son was generally associated with him in the task of administration. The knightly age for a prince was sixteen when he could be expected to take the field.[2] After his marriage he lived apart from his parents.[3] A king sometimes also gave his brothers high positions. For instance, king Janaka placed his brother Kuśadhvaja in charge of an important sacrifice. At the king's command he occupied a seat worthy of a king.[4] The story of the Râmâyaṇa shows that polygamy, rampant among aristocrats, could occasionally lead to serious political complications. When informed of Daśaratha's command for Râma's banishment, Kauśalyâ bursts out that she had been disregarded by her husband and reduced below the level of her rival Kaikeyi's maid-servants.[5] A queen seems to have had an 'anger-chamber' where she could retire in moments of high dudgeon, like Kaikeyi, to the discomfiture of her husband.[6] The daily 'politics' of the harem must have been disturbing while their occasional repercussions on the affairs of the kingdom might have proved calamitous. Not the least attractive feature in Râma's character is his monogamy.

The Priest. Ministers.

Throughout the Râmâyaṇa the Purohita appears as the right-hand man of the king, his constant advisor. The king had eight ministers, who had served the dynasty from father to son. Here is a strong confirmation of the view that high office was often hereditary. They were expected to be upright counsellors, capable administrators, ever intent on the good of the monarch, skilful in divining the motives of others, adepts in dealing tactfully with the people, ever

---

[1] Bâlakâṇḍa, VI; Ayodhyâkâṇḍa, LXV.
[2] Bâlakâṇḍa, XX. For the ideal of a prince, see the delineation of Râma, Ayodhyâkâṇḍa, 1.
[3] Ayodhyâkâṇḍa, XVI.
[4] Bâlakâṇḍa, LXX.
[5] Ayodhyâkâṇḍa, XX.
[6] Ibid., X.

busy in replenishing the treasury and in enrolling troops for the defence of the realm. They should bear no ill-will towards Brâhmaṇas or Kṣatriyas or the people at large.[1] The priest and ministers could play a higher role in emergencies. When Daśaratha dies of bereavement, they take the situation in hand, send for Bharata from his maternal grandfather's country, press the sovereignty on him, and failing in their endeavour, accompany him to Râma's forest abode and participate in consultations of high moment.[2] Sumantra can reprove the queen herself. From a passage in the Yuddhakâṇḍa it appears that ministers fell into two classes, Sacivas and Mantrins and that the term amâtya was a general one including both.[3] Another passage in the Ayodhyâkâṇḍa divides ministers into three classes—Mukhya or chief, Madhyama or middle and Jaghanya or low. In the same section, the Ayodhyâkâṇḍa speaks of eighteen Tîrthas or heads of departments of superior and inferior categories.[4] As in the Mahâbhârata, one of the most important offices is that of the ambassador. The lives of envoys are sacrosanct.[5] Kings had magnificent courts. The Ayodhyâkâṇḍa mentions one which consisted of a thousand members.[6]

The capital.

The capital was well laid out according to plan. Ayodhyâ is described as two yojanas (about eight miles in length), though in another passage its dimensions are given as twelve yojanas in length and ten in breadth. It was intersected with roads, wide, straight and beautiful. They were regularly sprinkled with water and on the sides were flower—plants which charmed all eyes with their full-blown

[1] Bâlakâṇḍa, VII.
[2] Ayodhyâkâṇḍa, LXXIX, LXXXII, CIV et seq.
[3] Yuddhakâṇḍa, CXXX.
[4] Ayodhyâkâṇḍa, C.
[5] Ibid., CIX;
Sundarakâṇḍa, LII—LIII.
[6] Ayodhyâkâṇḍa, C.

blossoms. The mansions rose high in the sky and glittered with gems. The city was laid out in four squares. The whole was defended by battlemented towers and moats.[1] Generally, there were four gates though Laṇkâ is said to have had eight.[2]

Guilds.

Guilds appear in the Râmâyaṇa as in the Mahâbhârata.[3] There is a reference to Sayodhaśreṇī which most probably implies a corporation of soldiers, or a guild which combined economic and warlike functions.[4]

The necessity of Government.

The imperative necessity of Government is vividly realised in the Epic. In a passage of wonderful eloquence, the poet paints the horrors of anarchy. A realm without a king is like a river without water, a forest without grass and a herd of cattle without the herdsman. The gods themselves frown over kingless regions. In anarchy, there is no rain and no agriculture. Trade disappears. None can feel secure about his property or even his life. The very idea of law goes to the winds. Men prey on each other, like fishes, from hour to hour. Family life and morality fall to the lowest depths. Father and son fight each other, wives get out of hand. Religious practices suffer a woeful decay. Brâhmaṇas do not keep their vows. None cares to perform sacrifices with texts and prayers. Sages can be sure of nothing. In short, a country without a king is perfectly wretched. It can witness no happiness, no festivity, no joviality. From such unspeakable misery, the monarch alone rescues the people. He is the universal benefactor, he is father, mother and friend, he is the hope and mainstay of all, he is the right, he is the truth.[5]

[1] Ayodhyâkâṇḍa, V, VI.
[2] Yuddhakâṇḍa, XCIII.
[3] Ibid., III, CXI.
[4] Ayodhyâkâṇḍa, CXXIII.
[5] Ayodhyâkâṇḍa, LXVII.

CHAPTER VI.

The Jâtakas.

The literary productions of the Brâhmaṇas—the Dharma Sûtras, the Epics and later, the Dharma Śâstras—studiously ignore the heretical movements which had arisen or were flourishing contemporaneously. Each school follows its own tradition in a cloister or grove. None can be taken as an exact reflection of the totality of political circumstances in any given epoch. The Brahmanic data are usefully supplemented by Buddhist tradition. The faith of Gautama Buddha whose career lay between the sixth and fifth centuries before Christ first took root in Magadha. There as in some neighbouring districts Brahmanic influence was less strong than anywhere else in North India. In the orthodox computation, Kâśi and Magadha are excluded from Brahmarṣideśa. Manu includes Magadhas and Videhas in his list of mixed castes.[1] In the course of a few centuries the Buddhists had produced a literature which challenges comparison with that of the Brâhmaṇas. The word of the Buddha, according to the orthodox tradition, is contained in the Tripiṭaka or the Three Baskets : (1) Sutta, comprising the five Nikâyas or collections, (2) Vinaya, giving rules of monastic life for monks and nuns in five works, the Pâtimokkha, Mahâvagga, Cullavagga, Sutta-

Buddhist literature.

[1] Manu, X, 5 et seq. Pargiter suggests that in Magadha, the Âryans met and mixed with a body of invaders from the east by sea (J.R.A.S., 1908, pp. 851—53.) But there is no convincing evidence on the point. According to the Jâtakas, Aṅga and Magadha are conterminous. (II, 211.) On the boundaries of Madhyadeśa see Vinaya Piṭaka, I, 197 ; Manu, II, 21.

vibhaṅga and Parivara and (3) Abhidhamma, comparatively inferior, which discusses metaphysics in seven compendiums. This extensive canon exists in two versions: (1) in Pâli, the hieratic language of the Buddhists of Ceylon, Siam and Burma, and (2) in Sanskrit or 'mixed' Sanskrit, the sacred idiom of Buddhism in Nepâl, Tibet, and, in a way, also China and Japan. The dates of these works, however, are as doubtful as those of the Brahmanical Sûtras or Epics. Rhys Davids, who relied chiefly on the Pâli canon and tradition, worked on the hypothesis that the four Nikâyas—the Dīgha or Long, the Majjhima or Middle, Saṁyutta or Miscellaneous and Aṅguttara or Numerical—representing the sayings of the Buddha, were put together, "out of older material at a period about half-way between the death of the Buddha, and the accession of Aśoka," that is, in the fourth century B.C. Other sayings, ascribed mostly to the Buddha's disciples, were put into a supplementary fifth Nikâya, the Khuddaka or minor collection, to which additions were made as late as the reign of Aśoka. On the whole, both Rhys Davids and Oldenberg referred the Vinaya and Sutta Piṭakas to about the fourth century B.C. But the scheme is no longer accepted. The dates of the Buddhist councils themselves, including that of the third one believed to have been held under the auspices of Aśoka about 247 B.C., have been called in question.[1] The chronology of the Ceylonese tradition is now almost entirely set aside. It is argued that the whole Buddhist canon is posterior to Aśoka and could not have taken shape prior to the second or first century before Christ. Sylvain Lévi and others have shown that the Pâli idiom itself, in which the southern canon is composed, did not arise till sometime after Aśoka. The great Mauryan emperor does not

[1] On the Buddhist Councils see in particular de la Vallée Poussin, Ind. Ant., XXXVII, pp. 1 et seq.; 81 et seq.

use it in his Edicts. The Buddha as well as his contemporary Mahâvîra, the founder or renovator of Jainism, must have preached in some Prâkṛit language, Mâgadhî or Ardha-Mâgadhî. It is impossible to assign any more specific dates to Buddhist scriptures. It is certain that they do not represent the work of a single mind or generation. It is also certain that the Pâli version is earlier than the Sanskrit.[1] The political data which this literature can be pressed to yield have therefore to be used with the utmost caution. Generally, they fall into two classes, either furnishing the names of old states, kings or ministers and recording their deeds, or incidentally reflecting the working of institutions. Facts of the former character are best reserved for treatment in connection with regular political history. The inferential data must be dealt with like those of the Mahâbhârata and the Râmâyaṇa. They are particularly abundant in that portion of the Khuddaka Nikâya which gives the Jâtakas, the 547 stories of the Buddha's previous births and which is one of the noblest monuments of Buddhist literature. Tradition will have it that these stories were taken by the royal missionary Mahinda to Ceylon during the reign of Aśoka in the third century B.C. They were translated from the Pâli into Siṁhalese and back into Pâli by Buddhaghośa in the fifth century A.D. It is in this translation of a translation that the Jâtakas have come down to us. In accordance with the tradition they were long believed to

Jâtakas.

[1] On the whole subject, Rhys Davids, Preface to the Dialogues of the Buddha (Sacred Books of the Buddhists), particularly pp. IX—XXII. For his vews as well as those of Oldenberg, also S. B. E., Vol. XI, p. X, Vol. XIII, p. XXIII. Rhys Davids, Questions of King Milinda, I, XXXVII et seq. Cambridge History of India, Vol. I, pp. 192—97. G. K. Nariman, Literary History of Sanskrit Buddhism (from Winternitz, Sylvain Lévi, Hüber). Sylvain Lévi holds that the Vinaya of the Sanskrit canon was first codified in the third or fourth century after Christ. Kern holds that Pâli was never a spoken language but was an altogether artificial idiom. See also Oldenberg, Introduction to Vinaya Piṭakam, Vol. I, pp. LIV-LV.

mirror the thought and conditions which prevailed before the time of the Buddha. Richard Fick assigned them, as a whole, to the age of Buddha, remarking that "many of the Jâtakas are undoubtedly very old and belong, so far as their origin is concerned, to the pre-Buddhistic period."[1] Rhys Davids inclines definitely to the pre-Buddhistic period.[2] In the last generation of scholars, Max Müller alone perceived that for the text of the Jâtakas we must, strictly speaking, be satisfied with the time of Vattagâmani, 88—76 B.C.[3] In the light of the latest researches, the position may be summed up in the words of Keith : "The Jâtaka book is a strange conglomeration of old and new verses with new prose ; some of its tales, as we know from Buddhist sculpture and a stray citation or two, go back to the Aśokan epoch or shortly after ; as folklore its contents are often of undeniable age, but as Buddhist fables their antiquity is uncertain."[4] So, the Jâtaka material is to be treated as partly pre-Mauryan and partly post-Mauryan. It pertains primarily to Magadha, and the districts round Benares, though, incidentally, it throws light on

[1] Fick, Social Organisation in North-Eastern India in Buddha's time, tr. Maitra, pp. IX—X.

[2] Rhys Davids, Buddhist India, p 207.

[3] Max Müller, Sacred Books of the Buddhists, Vol. I, Preface, p. V.

[4] Keith, Buddhist Philosophy, p. 22.

The Jâtakas have been arranged into twenty-two nipâtas, not according to their contents, but according to the number of gâthâs or verses occurring therein. The first nipâta has 150 stories, the second 100, the third and fourth 50 each, while the others have much fewer. King Brahmadatta of Benares figures in numerous stories, which may have first arisen in or near the sacred town.

For Jâtaka illustrations in the Bas-reliefs on the Bharahut Stûpa, Oldenberg, J. H. D. S., 1897. See also M. Chas. Duroiselle, Pictorial Representations of Jâtakas in Burma, Ann. Rep., Arch. Sur., Ind., 1912-13, pp. 87—119. Hultzsch, Jâtaka at Bharahut, J.R.A.S., 1912, pp. 399—411.

regions as far as Takkasilâ on the north-western frontier of India.

Little need be said here of Buddhist social or political theory. On the whole, it is more liberal than the Brahmanical. It could not ignore the deep-rooted institution of caste but it refuses to set very much store by it. It does not believe in the age-long Brahmanic supremacy. It confers no privileges on Brâhmaṇas. It does not constantly advise the king to enforce the principles of the established social order. Buddhist literature habitually places Kṣatriyas before Brâhmaṇas.[1] For political philosophy the Jâtakas are not particularly valuable. Their utility consists in the light which they throw on contemporary social, economic and political circumstances. The Jâtaka material has been worked out from the economic standpoint by Mrs. Rhys Davids[2] and from a broad social standpoint by Richard Fick.[3] But at least from the political point of view there is room for further research and fresh conclusions.

Buddhist Social Theory.

That caste with its appendage of outcaste prevailed in the country is clear from the Jâtakas. In the Setaketu

[1] For the Buddhist fanciful golden age, its degeneration and the consequent rise of the family, private property and state, see Agaṇṇa Suttanta, Dîgha Nikâya, Vol. III, Section 27; Mahâvastu ed. Senart, I, 347-48; Rockhill, 'Life of the Buddha . . . derived from Tibetan works in the Bkah Hgyur and Bstan Hgyur,' pp. 1—7. Cf. the Burmese Damathat, tr. Richardson, p. 7. Also Spence Hardy, Manual of Buddhism, p. 68. For Buddhist attitude towards caste, Dîgha Nikâya, III, 1, 15; III, 1, 24; Majjhima Nikâya, 90, Kaṇṇakathala Sutta 84; Madhura Sutta; Cullavagga, IX, 1, 4. Dhammapada, Ch. XXVI, tr. Max Müller, 90 - 96. Udânavarga, tr. Rockhill, Ch. XXXIII. Nidânakathâ, I, 49. Rhys Davids, Dialogues of the Buddha, 114—17, 119—22, 144—59. For general political theory, also Lalitavistara, particularly, 14-15, 103, 131, 136. Āryadeva, Catuḥśataka Śâstra (P L. Vaidya, Etudes sur Āryadeva et son Catuḥśataka, H. P. Sâstrî, Memoirs of the Asiatic Society of Bengal, Vol. III, No. 8, pp. 449—514).

[2] J. R. A. S., 1901.

[3] Social Organisation in North-east India in Buddha's time.

Jâtaka (III, 233) a Brâhmaṇa runs away from a Caṇḍâla and seeks atmospheric purification. In the Mâtaṅga Jâtaka (IV, 388) a Brâhmaṇa ascetic finds a tooth-pick, thrown by a Caṇḍâla up the river, caught in a tuft of his hair. "Damn you," he cries, "wretched Caṇḍâla, you bird of evil omen, you shall not live here any longer, move your dwelling down the river."

Caste.

In the next, Citta Sambhûta Jâtaka (IV, 391-2), two Caṇḍâla brothers are beaten almost to death because at their sight two high-class maidens abandon a visit which, incidentally, would have brought food and drink gratis to the people.[1] The unfortunate men disguise themselves as Brâhmaṇas and go to Takkasilâ for study, but when their birth is discovered they are again thrashed. (See also IV, 388.) In IV, 144, a Kṣatriya can't eat with his daughter by a slave, and a discussion is raised whether the children of a Kṣatriya by a low-caste woman are to be treated as Kṣatriyas. At one moment it is recognised that the family of the mother does not matter, that of the father alone is important. In I, 134, a woman who gathered wood is installed as Aggamahesi, chief queen, and the vicegerency is conferred on her son. Considerations of caste rule marriage (IV, 376, III, 422, III, 162, IV, 22, III, 93, I, 199, II, 121, II, 225). In IV, 231, a princess descends from a tree to meet an ascetic prince only when she is assured that he is a Kṣatriya and can recite the Kṣatriya formula. On the other hand, a king offers his daughter in marriage to a Brâhmaṇa ascetic (III, 517). In III, 27, a Caṇḍâla wins the favour of a king by pointing out the impropriety of the latter's occupying a seat higher than that of the priest who was explaining the Veda to him. The Caṇḍâla is made king of the night, that is, town sentinel, nagaraguttika.

[1] For another similar incident, IV, 378.

In III, 194 sq., the Purohita of a Benares king, after a self-imposed test, comes to the conclusion that virtue is better than learning, that birth and caste cause conceit . . . Khattiya (Kṣatriya), Brâhmana, Vessa (Vaiśya), Sudda (Śûdra), Caṇḍâla and Pukkusa will all be equal in the world of the gods, if they have acted virtuously here. Ambâ Jâtaka (IV, 205) also says that among members of all the six divisions he is the best from whom one can learn what is right. In Tittira Jâtaka (I, 217), the Buddha, after an untoward incident asks the assembly of monks, "Who deserves to have the best quarters, the best water, the best food ?" Some replied, "He who was a Kṣatriya before he became initiated." Others replied, "He who was a Brâhmaṇa or a Gahapati." The Buddha, however, would not recognise the claims of birth at all. The caste rules of professions are often violated. There are, of course, numerous 'world-renowned' Brâhmaṇa teachers, surrounded by crowds of, say, 500 pupils each (I, 166, 239, 299, 317, 402, 436 ; II, 137, 260, 421, III, 215), but Brâhmaṇas also work as land-owners (III, 293 ; IV, 276), agriculturists (II, 165 ; III, 163 ; V, 68), merchants (IV, 7, 15 , V, 22, 471), archers (V, 127), hunters and tappers (II, 200 ; VI, 170), wheel-wrights (IV, 207). Many Brâhmaṇas accumulate vast amounts of wealth (II, 272 ; III, 39 ; VI, 15, 22, 28, 237, 325 ; V, 227).[1] Brâhmaṇas sometimes eat with Kṣatriyas (II, 319-20). Aristocrats themselves sometimes act as traders or servants (II, 87 ; IV, 84, 169).

Brahmanic supremacy questioned.

In the Dasabrâhmaṇa Jâtaka a debate between two young men on birth or action as the basis of caste is referred to Gautama who declares that the followers of pastoral, agricultural, industrial, commercial or martial pursuits could not be called Brâhmaṇas. The obvious

[1] Cf. Vâseṭṭha Sutta, No. 35 of the Sutta Nipâta.

allusion is to those who claimed Brahmanic privileges on the score of caste though they had renounced scholastic or priestly callings. In many stories, for instance, in the Sambhava Jâtaka, V, 27, Juṇha Jâtaka, IV, 96, Brâhmaṇas play a rather ignominious role. (Also in I, 425, IV, 484.) On the other hand, the Buddhists themselves occasionally laid emphasis on birth. In the Nidânakathâ (I, 2) the first Bodhisatta is Brâhmaṇa of good family, on both sides, up to the seventh generation. The Jambukhâdaka Jâtaka (II, 438) speaks of descent as implying nobility.

Âśramas.

The rule of Âśramas or the four stages of life stands on a footing with that of caste. It is held to be binding (II, 85, 394; III, 147, 352), but it is not observed in all its strictness. Apart from the probability that numberless persons might have undergone no 'studentship,' nor ever resorted to renunciation, the order of the Âśramas is often violated. There are instances of Brâhmaṇas who take to asceticism on reaching adolescence (I, 333, 343, 361, 373, 450; II, 131, 232, 257, 262; III, 110; IV, 325). In many cases the completion of studies is immediately followed up by renunciation (II, 53, 56, 72, 85; III, 64, 79, 110, 119, 228, 249, 308; V, 152, 193). There are instances of parents offering the alternatives of family life and renunciation to their sons. A Brâhmaṇa boy in his 16th year is thus addressed by his parents, "Son, on the day of your birth we lit a birth-fire for you. Now therefore choose. If you wish to lead a family life, learn the three Vedas; but if you wish to attain to the Brahma realm, take your fire with you into the forest and there tend it, so as to win Mahâ-Brahma's favour and hereafter to enter into the Brahma realm." The latter alternative was preferred by the boy (I, 494). In II, 43, there occurs an almost identical incident. The third stage is often passed over (II, 41, 145, 269; 437; III, 45). The birth of a son, is sometimes the signal of renunciation to

Brâhmaṇas and others (III, 300-301; IV, 220). Untoward happenings sometimes led to the same result. A son of a hunter chief and a daughter of another hunter chief were married against their will. Both turned ascetics (IV, 72). On his parents' death, a Brâhmaṇa forsakes the world (II, 314; also 411). Another does the same on the death of his wife (III, 147). The vogue of renunciation sometimes disturbed political arrangements. A prince turns an ascetic as he is to be consecrated king after the usual processions (IV, 492 et seq.). Elsewhere two princes, bent on renunciation, are earnestly exhorted by their parents to stick to the world but in vain (IV, 121-22). There are other cases of princes spurning all earthly dominion and glory and taking to renunciation (III, 31).

The Ruling Class.

In the Jâtakas there is a ruling class, consisting primarily of Kṣatriyas, which stands above all and which typifies the state. Its members are not to be addressed by name or in the second person by people of low castes. In his pride a king calls a Purohita's son Hînajacca, 'of low birth' (V, 257). For the primacy of the ruling class, I, 177; III, 19; IV, 42, 205, 303, V, 123). Purohitas or their sons, however, are admitted to intimacy with kings, princes and aristocrats (I, 437, 289; II, 47, 282, 376, 437; III, 31, 317, 392, 417, 455; IV, 200, 270; V, 127; VI, 330). Others are also sometimes admitted into the high circle. Thus Prince Brahmadatta and Mahâdhana, son of a rich merchant, are comrades and playmates and are brought up with the same teachers. On succeeding to the throne, Brahmadatta receives Mahâdhana thrice a day. When the latter, losing faith in his courtezan, renounces the world, the king summons "the wicked, vile woman" and commands her to "go quickly to where my friend is and fetch him; if you fail, your life is forfeit" (III, 476).

Kṣatriyas generally wielded the sceptre but non-Kṣatriya kingship was not altogether unknown. Thus in Jâtaka, I, 326, the expulsion of a tyrannical king is followed by the elevation of a Brâhmaṇa to the throne. Similarly, in the Padakusalamâṇava Jâtaka (III, 513) a Brâhmaṇa who instigates a revolt against a thievish king and thus brings about his death is installed king (see also II, 264 et seq.).

Non-Kṣatriya Kingship.

The sons of aristocratic families were educated, along with Brâhmaṇa youths, at Takkasilâ on the north-western frontier. It seems to have been one of the most notable seats of learning in ancient India. On the basis of contemporary Greek accounts, Pliny states that the town itself was situated on a level where the hills sink down into the plain. Strabo praises the soil as extremely fertile from the number of its springs and water-courses. In Ptolemy's geography it is called Taxiala, probably from the Sanskrit Takṣaśilâ, hewn stone or Takṣakaśilâ, *i.e.*, rock of Takṣaka, the Nâga king, though others take it to be derived from the Takkas, a powerful tribe which probably occupied the regions between the Indus and the Chenâb. It seems to have been an extremely rich town. There is a myth in a Jâtaka that a Benares king attacked Takkasilâ, but amazed at the rich glory of its gate tower which he fancied to be the king's residence, he abandoned the expedition (II, 217-8). Jaina literature, which contains numerous references to Takkasilâ, shows that it was at one time adorned with vast numbers of Jaina edifices.

Takkasilâ.

Here were established a large number of teachers who taught for fees and sometimes gratis. On his arrival at Takkasilâ, a Benares prince encounters his future teacher, as the latter is walking to and fro after finishing his teaching. The young man at once takes off his shoes, removes his umbrella, and stands saluting him with respect. The teacher welcomes him and, after he is refreshed, inquires, "Where do you come from?" "From Benares." "Whose son are you?" "The son of the king of Benares." "For what purpose have you come?" "For the purpose of learning the science." "Have you brought your âcariyabhâga (teacher's honorarium) or do you wish to become a dhammantevâsika?" "I have brought honorarium for the teacher." Forthwith the prince placed a purse of a 1,000 gold pieces at his feet. That seems to have been the usual fee (Tilamuṭṭhi Jâtaka, II, 278). Those who paid the fee were treated like the eldest sons in houses. Besides the fees from pupils, the teachers of Takkasilâ received invitations and presents from the neighbouring folk (III, 171).[1]

Hither flocked the sons of kings, aristocrats, priests and plutocrats for education.[2] Sometimes, indeed, princes were educated at home. In the Gâmaṇicaṇḍa Jâtaka (II, 297), a king himself instructs the prince in the three Vedas and in all worldly duties. The Tilamuṭṭhi Jâtaka (II, 277), however, says that "the kings sent their sons, although in their own city there lived a world-renowned teacher, to a great distance over the borders of the kingdom for learning the sciences, and they thought, in this way their pride and haughtiness will be broken, they will learn

Young Aristocrat and Priests at Takkasila.

[1] For Takkasilâ, Takṣaśilâ or Taxila, see McCrindle. Invasion of India by Alexander the Great, p. 342; India as described in Classical Literature, Strabo, pp. 33-34. Also J R. A. S., XX, p. 343. Ann. Rep. Arch. Surv. Ind., 1914-15, Marshall, pp. 1—35; Sukthankar, pp. 36—41; Marshall, Ibid., 1912-13, pp. 1—52; Ibid., 1915-16, pp. 1—38. K. de B. Codrington, Ancient India, etc., 47—49; also pp. 49—56 for the contemporary Gandhâran art and sculpture. Marshall, a Guide to Taxila, second edition, Calcutta, 1921. For a seventh century notice, Yuan Chwang, Watters, I, 240.

[2] For instances of princes going to Takkasilâ, I, 273; II, 319, 323, 400; III, 158, 168, 415, 463; IV, 315; V, 161. For wealthy Brâhmaṇas, sometimes worth 80 crores each, sending their sons to Takkasilâ, I, 463, 505, 510; II, 53, 56, 85; III, 39, 64, 158, 219, 428, 194, 228, 341, 352, 400, 403, 497; IV, 22, 74, 200, 224; V, 247, 263. For sons of plutocrats, III, 375; IV, 475.

to bear heat and cold, and learn also the ways of the world." Here a king gives his son only a pair of sandals with simple soles, a sunshade made of leaves and 1,000 kahâpaṇas and sends him to rough it out at Takkasilâ (Cf. V, 457). The journey to Takkasilâ itself lay through forests (I, 395). Some adventurous youths were not satisfied with the usual experiences. A prince and a Purohita's son, after finishing their education at Takkasilâ, wander about to observe various local usages (V, 247). It was generally at the age of sixteen that princes joined Takkasilâ (I, 259, 262, 273; II, 2, 87, 277; III, 122, etc.). Probably they had already received some literary and military instruction at home. There are, however, cases of princes completing their education at sixteen and not resorting to Takkasilâ at all (e.g., I, 261). The education of a prince was a comprehensive one. In I, 259, and III, 115, the three Vedas and eighteen branches of learning are mentioned as subjects of study. In II, 87, a Benares prince learns the three Vedas, archery and eighteen accomplishments at Takkasilâ. Elsewhere, too, (III, 122, 158), we can see the princes and Brâhmaṇas studying together. In II, 100, the son of a wealthy Brâhmaṇa learns charms at Takkasilâ and then teaches them to Brâhmaṇa and Kṣatriya youths. At Takkasilâ every student studied under a teacher and had to attend on him. If he offended, he could be punished, even corporally. A Benares prince, so treated, vows vengeance and, on ascending the throne, contrives almost to kill his teacher, though, later, he makes ample amends for it (II, 278 et seq.).

The King.

In the Jâtakas the king is a despot. Different stories imply different theories of the foundation of his power. Once a Yakkhinî (Yakṣiṇî) who becomes the favourite consort of a king solicits from him the boon of unrestricted power over his dominion. "My love," replies the king, "in no way do all the subjects of my kingdom belong to me, nor am I their lord; only over those who rise against the king and do wrong am I lord. Therefore I cannot give you unrestricted power over the whole kingdom" (I, 398). Here the king is the guardian and censor rather than the master of his subjects and is not supposed to be capable of dealing with the kingdom as he likes. But elsewhere a king is prepared of his own accord to make over his kingdom to an ascetic (III, 80, also 353). In another curious story, when the queen-mother falls in love with the Purohita, the king makes the latter king, his own mother queen and himself acts as viceroy (III, 392). Once a king actually divides his kingdom with a poor man and the two rule in harmony and friendship until the new half-king embraces asceticism (III, 448-49). In these stories the kingdom is looked upon almost as private property which can be partitioned or surrendered at will. Both the different conceptions may be true of the different places or times.

The character of monarchical rule.

The character of the despotism varied according to the personal equation. The Dasarâjadhamme or ten duties of the king (III, 274, 320) comprise charity, moral rectitude, sacrifice, truthfulness, mildness, self-denial, forgiveness, not to cause any pain to anybody, patience, a yielding disposition. In the Jâtakas, kings are often just, righteous, merciful and charitable. But a king could sometimes be a whimsical tyrant who, as a Jâtaka (II, 240) puts it, "oppresses and puts down his subjects by punishments, taxes, torture and robbery, as one pounds sugar in a sugar mill, who is as odious to them as a particle of dust in the eye, as a particle of sand in the rice or as a thorn that has pierced the hand." An oppressive king sucks the country dry of all wealth (IV, 224). Another capricious tyrant took a dislike to all old things and made cruel sport of old men and women (II, 142). Another seized the wife of a hermit though he restored her later (IV, 23). Numerous other cases of tyranny can be cited (II, 122, 169, 391; III, 178, 454; V, 98). Sometimes the merits of spiritual or temporal ministers could make up for the defects of a king (III, 317) but in the absence of any constitutional check the ultimate remedy for oppression lay in revolt and assassination. In the Saccaṁkira Jâtaka (I, 326) a king is driven out of the town by the enraged

Revolt.

Kṣatriyas, Brâhmaṇas and others who instal a Brâhmaṇa on the throne. In the Padakusalamâṇava Jâtaka (III, 513) a Brâhmaṇa discovers that a king and his priest have stolen and concealed a precious treasure. He contrives to get the people together and proclaims aloud:—

"Let town and countryfolk assembled all give ear,

"Lo, water is ablaze. From safety cometh fear. The plundered realm may well of king and priest complain. Henceforth protect yourselves. Your refuge proves your bane." The people thought, "the king, though he ought to have protected others, threw the blame on another. .... That he may not in future go on playing the part of a thief, we will kill this wicked king." "So they rose up with sticks and clubs in their hands, and then and there beat the king and the priest till they died." The Brâhmaṇa, responsible for all this, was proclaimed king. Another king is persuaded by a hypocritical Purohita to sacrifice his queens, sons, best horses and bulls so that he might go to heaven. The plot is frustrated and only Sakka, the god of gods, prevents the multitude from killing the king. The people agree to spare his life, "but," they decide, "we will not give him rule or dwelling in this city—we will make him an outcast and appoint his dwelling outside this city." So they stripped him of his royal garments, made him wear a yellow dress, put a yellow cloth on his head, and having made him an outcast sent him away to an outcast settlement. But the prince continued to attend to his wants there (VI, 146 et seq.). Elsewhere a significant tradition is recorded that a king who violated righteousness was swallowed up by flames from the earth and his sons had to leave the city (III, 458 et seq.).

The succession.

In the Jâtakas the hereditary succession and primogeniture are firmly established (I, 127, 395; II, 87, 116, 212; IV, 124, 176). In Thusa Jâtaka (III, 121) a prince imprisoned for treason is set at liberty on the death of his father and duly placed on the throne. So not even treason, one of the darkest of crimes in ancient India, was deemed serious enough for a departure from the rule. In Succaja Jâtaka (III, 67) a king says to the prince, "My dear son, so long as I am living, you shall not live in the town; remove your residence elsewhere and accept the reins of government after my death." A few similar incidents occur elsewhere in the Jâtakas (II, 203, 229; VI, 158) It appears, however, that in certain localities or periods reflected in the Jâtakas, a slightly different practice prevailed. The hereditary principle was qualified by that of capacity. In II, 297, the ministers tell a rather young prince that he will be consecrated only on satisfying certain tests which pertain to the administration of justice. In the Pâdañjali Jâtaka (II, 264) King Brahmadatta of Benares—the usual Jâtaka hero—leaves a stupid son behind. The ministers propose to instal him on the throne, but the Bodhisatta, who happened to be the late king's spiritual and temporal adviser, said "the prince is a fool and a good-for-nothing fellow; we will first examine him and then instal him as king." The nature of the test proposed shows that the king must, above all, be qualified to administer faultless justice. The ministers held two courts and gave once the correct and once an incorrect judgment, but the prince, incapable of distinguishing between the two, only bit his lips both times. "This man," said the Bodhisatta, "does not know right from wrong, or good from bad; beyond the biting of his lips be knows nothing." So the ministers consecrated the Bodhisatta himself, a Brâhmaṇa, to the kingship. In such cases the ministers are the judges of the capacity to rule and can deal comparatively freely with the crown. In any case acute physical incapacity was regarded a disqualification for the kingship. In spite of protests a king gives his eyes to a Brâhmaṇa and then thinks, "What has a blind man to do with ruling? I will hand over my kingdom to the courtiers, and go into my park and become an ascetic and live as a holy man" (IV, 407 et seq.) Another king struck with leprosy similarly departs into the forest (V, 88). The people in the Jâtakas are extremely anxious to make sure of the regular succession When after their earnest prayers to the deities the queen-consort of a childless king gets a son, they exclaim, "We were before helpless, now we have a help, we have obtained a lord" (VI, 1). In another tale when a monogamous king had no son, the townsfolk gathered together in the palace courtyard and raised a howl. "What is it?" asked the king "Fault we have none to find," said they, "but this that you have no son to keep up your line. You have but one queen, yet a royal prince should have 16,000 at the least. Choose a company of women, my lord, some worthy wife will bring you a son." The king, however, refused to flinch from his previous promise of monogamy. Then the queen herself presented to him 1,000 Kṣatriya maidens, 1,000 Mahâmatta maidens, 1,000 gahapati maidens, and 1,000 dancing girls. Later, she presented another host of 12,000 women to the king (IV, 316 et seq.) In another story, all decency, morality and prestige are thrown to the winds in order to obtain a son to succeed to the throne (V, 279 et seq.)

Royal idiosyncrasies could sometimes disturb the rule of primogeniture. A Benares king gives a province to each of his hundred sons as his education at the hands of a courtier is finished. The youngest, Saṁvara, however, chooses to live at court. The ministers ask the king on his death-bed, "When you are dead . . . to whom shall we give the White Umbrella?" "Friends," replies the king, "all my sons have a right to the White Umbrella. But you may give it to him that pleases your mind." On the seventh day after the king's death, the courtiers uplift the White Umbrella with its festoons of gold over the youngest prince. On hearing of his accession, his ninety-nine brothers say, "He is the youngest of all; the Umbrella does not belong to him. Let us lift the Umbrella over the eldest of us all." They besiege the capital but Saṁvara offers to divide his wealth among them. Peace is concluded and Saṁvara is recognised (IV, 131 et seq.). In another story, the elder prince at first declines the kingdom but later demands it and gets it from his younger brother who had been reigning in the meanwhile (IV, 168 et seq.). In IV, 84, a kingdom is divided among ten brothers. One of them gives his share to their sister, only stipulating that he should receive the taxes due to him. These stories may relate to a period or a locality in which the practice of primogeniture was arising but was not yet fully established. Elsewhere in the Jâtakas a king resists the importunity of his queen to give the kingdom to their son, because the latter is 'ill-luck.' Not even temporarily for some years or some months or some weeks but only for a single week would he place him on the throne. The prince's seven days' sovereignty is proclaimed throughout the city by beat of drum. He is led round the city triumphantly on an elephant under an umbrella, but on the sixth day his father has him beheaded (VI, 10 et seq.).

On failure of sons, the crown seems to have gone to the eldest of the younger brothers of a king (I, 133; II, 367). In certain contingencies in the absence of direct heirs, the crown seems to go to the son-in-law of a king (II, 323). In no circumstances is the crown formally placed on the head of a woman. There is an incidental statement that "infamous . . . is the land which owns a woman's sway and rule; and infamous are the men who yield themselves to women's dominion" (I, 155). Women, however, did sometimes wield the actual sovereignty. In IV, 105, on Udaya's death no king was set up, the commands of his widow Udayabhaddâ were promulgated and the Mahâmattas administered the kingdom. In IV, 84, a brother gives his own share—one-tenth of a kingdom—to his sister but we are not told that the latter was duly crowned. In a few stories the crown is offered to whomsoever the people think fit (e.g., I, 399). Once on the tragic death of a king of Takkasilâ, the Bodhisatta who happened to be the youngest of the hundred sons of Brahmadatta of Benares, is elected king by the courtiers and citizens who admire his self-control. In another story a childless king and his Purohita vow that if either gets a son, he should succeed to the kingdom and to the wealth of both. Thanks to a deity, the Purohita got four sons. But in spite of all possible precautions, the four young men renounce their claims to the sceptre and turn ascetic one after another (IV, 473). It is, however, significant that this story recognises the validity of a king willing the crown out of the royal family.

Choice by the festal car.

If the succession was altogether unsettled, recourse was had, perhaps only in some out-of-the way regions, to a strange procedure. Seven days after the death of an heirless king, the Purohita let a festal car, the phussaratha, be driven with the five insignia of royalty placed on it. "It will come to the man who will become the king." The man whom the car singled out by stopping near him was made king (III, 238; IV, 39; V, 248). Once fortune favoured a poor woman's son born in the street (IV, 38). This method might sometimes be combined with another. A king on his death-bed leaves the succession to the will of his daughter who is approached by the various officers but she rejects them all and proposes three tests. Meanwhile, the Purohita and the ministers let out the festal car. It selects the Bodhisatta who also satisfies the three tests of the princess and becomes king (VI, 31 et seq.).

Relations between kings and princes.

The whole problem of the succession was complicated by premature ambitions, jealousies and the vogue of renunciation. A prince, acting as viceroy, conspires against the king, his elder brother. When discovered he flies to a frontier district and demands the umbrella or a battle. In the ensuing war the king is slain (VI, 31). Another prince appointed viceroy grows impatient of the crown, conspires and murders the king (V, 263 et seq.). A sixteen-year-old prince tries various expedients to kill his father. When detected, he is imprisoned (III, 122 et seq., also 216). A prince-governor comes to the capital, Benares, to pay his respects to his father. The latter thinks, "This fellow may do me wrong, if he gets an opportunity." So he tells him, "As long as I live, you cannot dwell in this city. Live somewhere else, and at my death bear rule in the kingdom." The prince obeys and leaves Benares with his chief wife (III, 67). In another story too horrible to relate, a Benares king, afraid that his wife might grow too proud of their little son, has the seven-month-old baby torn to pieces, bit by bit, in the presence of his weeping mother (III, 179). A suspicious king exiles all his sons (II, 116). On the death of a king, the eldest prince succeeds to the throne in the regular order and the younger becomes Uparâjan but he grows arrogant as the astrologers have foretold universal dominion for his son. A command is issued for his arrest but he flies to the forest (IV, 230 et seq.). In another story the elder prince at first declines the kingdom but later demands it and gets it from his younger brother who had been reigning in the meanwhile (IV, 168 et seq.). Moral delinquency sometimes went against a prince. Thus a prince who refused to give up strong drink was banished (V, 467). On the other hand, the sway of the gospel of renunciation sometimes led kings to instal their sons on the throne and themselves to retire into the forest (V, 161-62). In VI, 95 et seq., a barber points out the appearance of grey hair on the head of a king. The latter forthwith instals his son on the throne, rewards the barber with a village and retires into the forest. Sometimes a prince, caring 'nothing for glory,' would voluntarily decline the crown in favour of a younger brother, though he may still awaken jealousies (II, 87). In an interesting story a king invites his brother suddenly found out, to come and reign as king (V, 22 et seq.). There are numerous instances, of kings abdicating in favour of their sons and of young princes prematurely following the path of renunciation and refusing consecration (I, 138; III, 364, 393, 515; IV, 7; V, 177). There are other cases of young princes being persuaded only with the greatest difficulty to assume the sceptre (IV, 105).

Popular acceptance of the king.

In some localities or periods, the new king had to be accepted by the people. A wicked prince who is advised in vain by counsellors, Brâhmaṇas and citizens to mend his ways is at last thus threatened by the Bodhisatta, "the people of the kingdom, dreading what a prince so fierce and passionate may become when king, will not place you on the throne but uproot you . . . and drive you forth to exile" (I, 507).

Consecration was an important ceremony in the age of the Jâtakas. As in Brahmanical literature, the Purohita sprinkled the king-designate with water and so raised him high above ordinary mortals (III, 239; IV, 40). In III, 408, the ministers, Brâhmaṇas, gahapatis, citizens and dancing girls, stand round the throne at a distance from each other. In the Pañcaguru Jâtaka (I, 470), the Bodhisatta accepting the kingdom at the people's hands, enters the town, decorated in heavenly style. and passes "into the spacious hall of the palace and there seated himself . . . on his jewelled throne beneath the white umbrella of his kingship. Round him in glittering splendour stood his ministers and Brâhmaṇas and nobles, whilst sixteen thousand nautch girls, fair as the nymphs of heaven, sang and danced and made music, till the palace was loud with sounds like the ocean when the storm bursts in thunder on the waves."

Consecration.

The consecration and its pomp are well-described in the Ayoghava Jâtaka (IV, 492 et seq.) "What is my son's age?" asks a king. "He is sixteen years old," reply the courtiers. The king determines to make over the realm to the prince who is brought out. The whole city is decorated from end to end. "They decked out the state elephant in magnificent caparison, and dressed the boy in his best, and placed him upon the elephant's back," saying, "My lord, make a circuit rightwise about the rejoicing city, your inheritance, and salute your father the king of Kâsi; for this day you shall receive the White Umbrella." After the procession the prince stood before the king. "What do you wish us to do?" asked the courtiers. "Take my son," replied the king, "and put him on a pile of jewels, sprinkle him from the three conches, uplift the White Umbrella with its festoons of gold" (IV, 492 et seq.)

There are other pictures of festivities, dramatic performances, etc., on the occasion of a prince's marriage or accession. The rejoicings were often signalised by a release of prisoners (V, 282 et seq.)

The king lived in great splendour. Once we see him "seated in majesty and splendour beneath a white canopy of sovereignty upon a throne of gold with legs as of a gazelle . . ." (I, 267). On return from expeditions, he generally goes in solemn procession round the city and then enters the palace (I, 305). Seated on an elephant, the king often went round the city in stately procession (II, 122). Kings vie with one another in splendour. For instance, a Benares king thinks, "All over India the kings live in a palace supported by many a column . . . What if I make a palace with one column only to support it ? Then I shall be the chiefest king of all kings" (IV, 153).

Royal splendour.

Sometimes there were glorious wrestling matches. Once we read, "the wrestling ring was prepared in front of the king's gate ; there was an enclosure for the games, the ring was decked out gaily, the flags of victory were ready tied. The whole city was in a whirl ; line over line rose above the seats, tier above tier" (IV, 81). A musical scene is thus described : "At the palace door a pavilion was set up, and a throne was set apart for the king. He came down from the palace, and took his seat upon the divan in the gay pavilion. All around him were thousands of slaves, women beauteously apparelled, courtiers, Brâhmaṇas, citizens. All the people of the town had come together. In the courtyard they were fixing the seats circle on circle, tier above tier . . . " (II, 253). Kings are seen going to the park surrounded by dancers (III, 40). As usual they are fond of hunting (III, 325). The fortnightly fast seems to have been the occasion of great festivity. The place of meeting is decorated ; king, viceroys and others listen to discourses (III, 342). The king sometimes holds wine orgies (V, 13 et seq) There were gorgeous elephant festivals (V, 282 et seq.)

Part of the royal splendour was the harem. When a king and queen of Benares determine to marry their daughter only to a monogamous prince, the ambassadors of a suitor, the king of Mithilâ remark, "Ours is a great kingdom, the city of Mithilâ covers seven leagues and the measure of the whole kingdom is 300 leagues. Such a king should have 16,000 wives at the least . . ." (IV, 316 et seq.) A king of Videha is said to have possessed a harem of 16,000 wives (VI, 220). So, too, Daśaratha, king of Kośala (IV, 124 et seq.) The high traditional number may be taken to imply that almost every king had a large seraglio. The harem had its own 'politics.' A king takes a flower-selling girl into the harem, raises her to the position of chief queen, then disgraces her and finally rehabilitates her (III, 21). Another king raised the helpmate of his troubles to be the chief queen but otherwise neglected her. The Bodhisatta had to exert himself to bring about a thorough reconciliation (III, 68, also 107-108). The rivalries and jealousies of co-wives were proverbial (V, 21). The affairs of the harem sometimes had serious repercussions on affairs of state. In the extremely interesting Jâtaka version of Râma's tale, the queen-consort of Daśaratha is succeeded on her death by another who, in response to the offer of a boon, requests the supersession of the two elder princes by her own son. Informed by soothsayers that he has still twelve years to live, the old king tells Râma and Lakkhaṇa, "My sons, if you live here, some mischief may befall you. Go to some neighbouring kingdom, or to the woodland, and when my body is burnt, then return and inherit the kingdom which belongs to your family . . ." They and their sister Sîtâ go to the Himâlayas. On the king's demise in 9 years, the queen-consort desires that the umbrella should be raised over her son Bharata. But the courtiers did not allow it, saying, 'the lords of the umbrella are dwelling in the

The harem.

forest.' Accompanied by a complete host of the four arms, Bharata himself proceeded to the forest with the fine insignia of royalty for Râma. When Râma refused to return until the completion of the full twelve years, the rest came back but for the next three years the slippers of Râma were supposed to rule the kingdom. The ministers placed them on the royal throne when they judged a cause (IV, 124 et seq.). More unsavoury situations were sometimes created. A prince-viceroy, falsely incriminated by a jilted step-mother, is sentenced by the enraged king to be taken to the thieves' cliff and beheaded. The nobles, the ministers, and many harem ladies protest. But the king is adamant (IV, 191). The harem was strongly guarded (IV, 105). But nothing could prevent occasional criminal liaison. Guilty of misconduct in the harem, a minister is told by the king, "O blinded by folly! you have sinned, and are not worthy to dwell in my kingdom; take your substance and your wife and family and go hence." The minister migrates to Kośala and becomes the confidential adviser of the Kośala king. He instigates border raids and a regular invasion against his old master (I, 262 et seq.). Several such incidents are recorded in the Jâtakas (II, 125-26, 401; III, 13, 168 et seq., 337 et seq). In another story, a royal servant becomes a paramour of the queen, murders the king and buries him. The prince, however, does the same to the murderer and amply revenges the wrong (III, 419 et seq.). There is one instance of an Uparâjan intriguing in the harem of the king, his own brother (IV, 79).

Royal Charity.

A pleasanter side of court life was the charity practised on a lavish scale. It must have gone a long way to win the loyalty of the people and enhance the prestige of the king. A king of Benares "built six halls of bounty, one at each of the four gates, one in the midst of the city, and one before the palace;

and every day he distributed in gifts six hundred thousand pieces of money." The monarch himself went among the needy and the miserable and showered bounties. The whole country was astir with his generosity (II, 118). Identical statements are made of many other kings (IV, 176, 355, 361 et seq., 402; V, 162; VI, 42 et seq.) Beggars and mendicants are often at the king's window (II, 273). In spite of the pomp and glory which surrounded him, a king could unbend on occasions. We see a king moving freely among his subjects (IV, 201). Another greets a mendicant, sets him on his own couch, and offers him all the delicious dishes prepared for himself (II, 273). Another king led an ascetic "to a dais and set him upon the throne under a white umbrella; his own food the king gave him to eat and himself ate of it. Then he took him to the garden, and caused a covered walk and dwelling to be made for him, and furnished him with all the necessaries of an ascetic" (II, 316). Similar incidents are recorded elsewhere (III, 79 et seq.). The king's example of charity was imitated by his wealthy subjects. A Benâres merchant worth eighty crores established six almshouses at the usual spots and in the usual style. We are told that 600,000 beggars partook of his generosity each day (III, 129; also IV, 355 et seq.). A royal treasurer practises charity on the same scale and in the same manner (V, 383 et seq.).

Duties of the King.

The king was the motive force of the whole government. One of his principal duties was the administration of justice. He is often an original tribunal and sometimes open to suggestion or protest from his Purohita or minister of justice (I, 433; III, 232). The king is often prompted to summary justice. A man is brought before him. "What is this, my friend?" enquires the king. They reply, "here's a thief who has been robbing your majesty's treasury." "Away with him to execution." The accused, however, has the courage to expostulate and is released (I, 371). Elsewhere, too, a criminal is hauled up in the very first instance before the king (I, 384; see also II, 298 et seq.) In the Rathalaṭṭhi Jâtaka (III, 104) a Purohita of the king falsely accuses some cart-drivers of striking him. The king promptly commands the drivers to give up their horses by way of punishment. The minister who happened to be the Bodhisatta, expostulates, persuades the king to hear the other side and so leads him to give the correct judgment. There were, of course, many cases which were decided by the officers of the king without reference to him (II, 182; V, 299).

The king must promote morality and sometimes adopts rough and ready homely ways of doing so. Succeeding Brahmadatta as king of Benâres, the Bodhisatta summons his ministers, Brâhmaṇas, gentry and others and, with their consent, proclaims, by beat of drum, that in fulfilment of his princely vow, he would make a sacrifice of a thousand sinners (I, 260). The people believe that everything depended on the king. Figs are sweet when the king exercises his rule with justice and equity. But "in the time of unjust kings, oil, honey, molasses and the like, as well as wild roots and fruits, lose their sweetness and flavour; and not these only but the whole realm becomes bad and flavourless" (III, 111). The king did sometimes play the rôle of a moral teacher. Twice a month, for instance, a king would gather his subjects together and say, "Give alms, practise virtue, righteously follow your business and calling, educate yourselves in the days of your youth, gain wealth, do not behave like a village cheat or dog, be not harsh or cruel, do your duty in caring for mother and for father, in family life honour your elders" (IV, 176-7, also, 361 et seq.). Some kings were particularly anxious to provide for the comforts of hermits and travellers. For instance, one of them provides a park to shelter them, in particular during the rains (IV, 444).

Next to the king stood the Uparâjan, brother or son or other kinsman of the king. In IV, 79, on the death of a king, the elder prince becomes king while the younger is appointed Uparâjan almost automatically. He is the "sub-king," a vicegerent, in constant touch with the king. In the Kurudhamma Jâtaka, the Uparâjan waits every evening on the king and receives the greetings of the people on entering or leaving the palace. On ceremonial occasions he sits behind the king on the back of the elephant, a seat sometimes occupied by the Purohita (II, 374). An Uparâjan, however, did not necessarily act for the king during the latter's absence. Starting on a long hunting trip a king once entrusts the kingdom to the care of his mother (VI, 75). Another whimsical king who sets out on a long journey to discover his faults entrusts the realm to the ministers as a whole (IV, 370).

The Uparâjan.

Every king had a Purohita, who was his adviser in spiritual, and sometimes also, in temporal affairs. The very first king Mahâsammata had appointed a Brâhmaṇa's son as family-priest (III, 454). Often, though not always, the office was hereditary and continued in the same family for generations (I, 437 ; II. 47 ; III, 392, 455, IV, 200). Once some Brâhmaṇas objected to the installation of a young son of the late Purohita. "For seven generations," protested the mother of the boy, "the performance of elephant consecration (hatthimaṅgala) has been hereditary in our family; the old custom will pass out of our hands and our wealth will disappear" (II, 47; III, 400). Sometimes, of course, new men would be introduced (III, 194, 337). A king of Videha has four sages to instruct him in Dhamma (VI, 330).

The Purohita.

The Purohita is the Âcârya, teacher or preceptor (II, 376; IV, 270; V, 127). He is actually seen teaching sacred texts to a king of Benâres (III, 28). We see him admonishing a king who was set on evil ways (III, 317). In the Tilamuṭṭhi Jâtaka, the king makes his Takkasilâ teacher his Purohita, looks upon him as a father and follows his advice (II, 282). Sometimes the king and the Purohita are friends and companions (I, 289). A prince and a Purohita's son born on the same day are brought up together and go to Takkasilâ together (III, 31). Fleeing at night from an invaded town, a king takes with him only his queen, a servant and the Purohita (III, 417). For his maintenance, the Purohita seems to have enjoyed, besides any presents, a Bhogagâma, the revenues of a village (III, 105 ; IV, 475). The consecration of state elephants brings a Purohita ten millions (II, 46). To the Purohita, as to priests in general, land may be given as sacrificial fee (III, 516).

Functions of the Purohita.

The Purohita's functions were extremely varied. He is an astrologer and must ward off any misfortunes threatened by bad dreams or inexplicable natural phenomena (I, 334; II, 46; III, 43. Cf. IV, 364). In the Maṅgala Jâtaka, (I, 371), however, the premonition of signs is condemned.[1] In Dhonasâkha Jâtaka (III, 159) an ambitious Purohita helps the king through a sacrificial ceremony, to acquire a city which is difficult to conquer. He proposes to his lord to pluck out the eyes of the thousand captured kings, to rip up their bellies, take out the entrails and give a bali-offering—to a god. Besides advising the king on all sorts of affairs, the Purohita often performed judicial work. Rectifying a wrong decision of the Senâpati who is supposed to be corrupt, a Purohita receives popular acclamations and is then appointed by the king regularly to try law-suits (II, 186-87). He guards the king's treasure (I, 439). His ambitions sometimes rise higher.

[1] The Tevijja Sutta (II, 8) contains an energetic denunciation of the arts and lying practices of astrology.

Once a Purohita tries to take the entire control of the state in his hands (V, 57). Sometimes he identifies his ambitions with the glory and greatness of his master. "I will make this king conquer all other kings in the whole of India; in this way he will become the sole king and I the sole house-priest" (III, 159). If, however, a Purohita deeply displeased the king, he could be consigned to dire punishment. We see him once dragged to the place of execution by the king's people (I, 439). There is mention of corrupt back-biting priests (V, 2 et seq.). The judgments of another hopelessly corrupt priest were rectified by the prince who is then appointed judge of all suits and earns the bitter hostility of the priest (VI, 131). It goes without saying that, besides the house-priest, other Brâhmaṇas were consulted by the king. We hear of Brahmadatta of Benâres and his queen calling 800 Brâhmaṇas to forecast their child's destiny (I, 272).

Minister.

Besides the Purohita, the king had a number of ministers, amaccas. They seem to form a class by themselves and to regard themselves as distinct from Kṣatriyas and Brâhmaṇas and all others. "I come of amaccakula (a family of ministers)," says one (II, 98, 125). Failing to interpret a dream of the king once, the ministers say, 'The Brâhmaṇas know it, O great king" (IV, 335; see also I, 260; III, 376; IV, 408; IV, 462 et seq.), thus implying that they themselves did not belong to the sacerdotal caste. Occasionally, however, Brâhmaṇa ministers are met with (III, 342). Ministers should be versed in all sciences (II, 30, 74). As a rule they are respected by the king but there are occasional cases of arbitrary treatment (III, 239). The offices are sometimes hereditary (I, 248). On the death of a king the realm sometimes falls to their charge. During the occasional absence or incapacity of a king too the ministers sometimes took charge of the state (IV, 370, 407, 438).

The Senâpati seems to stand at the head of ministers. Having determined on renunciation, a king calls his ministers with the Senâpati at their head (V, 178). "The king cares nothing for the city," once the people say, "we will inform the Senâpati" (V, 459). Once the ministers offer the crown to the Senâpati but he declines it and departing for the forest, bequeaths a testament of laws to be followed in the administration of justice (V, 125). The Senâpati not only wielded the military command as his title implies, but also performed other functions. He decided cases. A corrupt Senâpati is seen accepting a bribe (II, 186). Sometimes a relation of the king, for instance, a step-brother, or a son, was appointed Senâpati (I, 133; IV, 168; VI, 30).

Senâpati.

The regular minister of justice was the Vinicchâmacca who not merely decided cases but also offered counsel on matters of law and morality (II, 380).

Vinicchâ-macca

The Bhaṇḍâgârika or treasurer was an officer of the highest importance (IV, 43; V, 123; I, 248, 252). In the Nigrodha Jâtaka, some one predicts to his friends that on the next day one of them would be king, another Senâpati and he himself Bhaṇḍâgârika. The Bhaṇḍâgârika seems usually to have been a very rich man and is sometimes spoken of as possessed of 80 crores (I, 349, 466, etc.). The Rajjuka or rajjugâhaka amacca, 'the rope-holding minister,' seems to have been the surveyor of land (IV, 169). Next to him stood another survey-officer called doṇamâpaka or doṇa, one who measured with a dry rod (II, 367, 378). The herañño̤ika was the keeper of the king's purse (III, 193). The Sârathi was the charioteer (II, 377). The cashier, sword-bearer, keeper of the umbrella were some of the other officers (VI, 38 et seq.). The

Bhaṇḍâgârika.

The Rajjuka, etc.

Dovârika is the chamberlain and belongs to the lowest rung of the ladder (II, 241 ; V, 250). In the Mâtaṅga Jâtaka, a dovârika's duty is to thrash Caṇḍâlas and other vagabonds who wanted to peep at the palace, with sticks or bamboo-posts, catch them by the throat, and fling them on the ground (Fick, tr. Maitra, p. 156). In the Mahâ-piṅgala Jâtaka, a dovârika speaks of the king giving him eight blows on the head whenever he entered the palace (Fick, tr. Maitra, p. 156). The same title seems to have been borne by an officer whose duty was different. There is a dovârika who has to close the city-gate at night (II, 379).

Police officers.

Some police officers are in evidence. The nagara-guttika is charged with the arrest and execution of robbers and is once jokingly called 'king of the night' (III, 59). The coraghâtaka, 'slayer of thieves,' is another similar officer (III, 41, 179). The city, at any rate, has a large police force. Informed of the doings of a daring robber, the king of Benâres orders the city-watch to post bands here and there (III, 437). The police. however, was not altogether above corruption (III, 437 et seq.). Nor was it adequate for all contingencies. In crises the townsfolk would themselves come out and assist in the maintenance of order (V, 502).

Miscellaneous.

Among the miscellaneous officers and employees at court may be mentioned the valuer of articles—of elephants, horses, precious stones, gold, etc., who valued commodities to be purchased at court (I, 124), archers (II, 87 ; V, 128), elephant-tamers (II, 221), musicians (I, 384; II, 250); dancers and singers (II, 227; IV, 324); potters, basket-makers, gardeners, barbers, cooks, etc. (I, 121, 137, 138; II, 5, 319; V, 290—92; Fick, tr. Maitra, 287—89). At least sometimes Government posts descended from father to son. A few Jâtakas (I, 349; III, 385; V, 383) imply that the post of treasurer was hereditary in a family for seven or more generations. There is mention of an hereditary senâpati (V, 210). In any case many of the higher officers were drawn from the ranks of Mahâmattas or nobles (II, 98, 125, 203, 378).

The court.

The court of a king comprised the higher officers, the Râjaññas as well as other personages. Rich merchants called Setthis, whether heads of guilds or important on their own account, are frequently in attendance on the king (I, 289, 349; III, 119, 128, 299, 300, 444, 475; IV, 63; V, 382). There were courtiers who received grants of land from the king and were termed Râjabhoggas.

The province.

The Jâtaka stories already alluded to make it clear that a kingdom was divided into provinces or districts. Princes were often appointed to govern them. Below this administrative division stood the village, then, as now, the unit of society.

The village.

Village habitations were surrounded by fields and jungles (I, 215; V, 46). Some villages seem to have been fairly large. Physicians go to villages in search of medical practice (III, 202, 204). There is mention of a village which paid a revenue of 1,00,000 (III, 229), another which contained 1,000 smiths families (III, 281). In another village a Brâhmaṇa family worth eighty crores thought it worth their while to take up their abode. The kingdom of Videha is said to consist of 16,000 villages (III, 365). But our ignorance of the exact size and population of the territory makes it impossible to calculate the average extent of a village. The majority of villages are likely to have contained an heterogeneous population, but there were others inhabited exclusively or mainly by members of a single caste or followers of a single occupation. There is mention of Brâhmaṇa villages and Brâhmaṇa farmers (II, 368; III,

293; IV, 276); carpenters' villages (II, 18, 405; IV, 159, 208; Fick, tr. Maitra, p. 274); smiths' villages (III, 281, 86); potters' villages (III, 376, 508); hunters' villages (VI, 71); robbers' villages (II, 388; IV, 430).

In the Jâtakas there is no trace of any village Pañcâyata or any other organ of self-government. The only regular administrative officer was the Gâmabhojaka. The chief of the homogeneous Brâhmaṇa and other villages (III, 281; VI, 71; IV, 430; II, 388) corresponded to the Gâmabhojaka. The office was perhaps often hereditary, though village favour, opinion would naturally count for a great deal. The king's too, might partly determine the ultimate choice. Once the king's chaplain is seen acting as the village headman (III, 105). That the headman might sometimes be a person of high standing is also proved by the designation amacca which he sometimes bears (I, 354). In any case the functions of the Gâmabhojaka were wide and important. He exercised judicial powers, arbitrated between villages and made the guilty pay fines. For instance, he fined a fisherman's wife for stirring up a quarrel. She was tied and beaten to make her pay the fine (I, 483). He imposed and collected fines for excessive drinking, etc., and granted licenses for the sale of intoxicants (I, 198). Or he might issue prohibitions against the slaughter of animals or sale of intoxicating drinks (IV, 115). Elsewhere he is seen distributing food to famine-stricken villagers on promise of receiving a share of their next crop (II, 135).

Village government.

That he could be controlled by the king is clear. In the Kulâvaka Jâtaka (I, 198), the gâmabhojaka speaks ill of the villagers to the king, but on their innocence being proved, the slanderer's possessions are given to them, he is made their slave and, finally, expelled from the village. In the Kharassara Jâtaka (I, 354) a gâmabhojaka is degraded and

The king's control.

replaced by another. In the Pânîya Jâtaka (IV, 14) two gâmabhojakas in the kingdom of Kâśî respectively prohibit the sale of strong drink and slaughter of animals. But the people make a representation that these were time-honoured practices. The proclamations are annulled. Custom must be adhered to. The need for royal supervision could not be gainsaid. In I, 355, a gâmabhojaka, newly appointed, betrays his trust by combining with robbers to plunder his charge (I, 355). If a headman was outrageous in his conduct, the villagers would sometimes take the law in their own hands. For instance, a headman who intrigued with a villager's wife was seized by the lock of hair on the top of his head, dragged into the courtyard and mocked as he cried 'I am the headman.' He was thrashed till he fainted. He was not deprived of his office but he remembered the lesson (II, 135-36).

Corporate activity in the village.

There were many affairs in which the villagers themselves took the initiative. In the Losaka Jâtaka (I, 237 et seq.), Buddhist brethren are supported by village personages, and villagers pay a man to teach them the true doctrine. We are told that under the influence of a popular leader, villagers led ideal lives. " They used to get up early and sally forth, with razors and axes and clubs in their hands. With their clubs they used to roll out of the way all stones that lay on the four highways and other roads of the village; the trees that would strike against the axles of chariots, they cut down; rough places they made smooth; causeways they built, dug water tanks, and built a hall; they showed charity and kept the Commandments" (I, 199). Women sometimes took part in these activities (I, 201).

Cities.

The number of cities in a kingdom was sometimes very large. "Eighty-four thousand cities," says a queen to console her melancholy husband, "chief of which is the royal city of Kuśâvatî, own your sovereignty, sire, set your heart on them" (I, 392). In spite of the patent, gross exaggeration, the number indicates that there were many cities. As usual, men of the city looked down on the rural folk. "These misguided provincials," says the son of a slave, "have no idea of dressing. And as for taste in scents and garlands, they have got none" (I, 452). Cities were surrounded by walls and fortified by watch-towers, etc., and sought to be made impregnable (III, 117). Towns seem to be administered by royal officers. There is no trace of any institutions of urban self-government.

Revenue.

The land-revenue was the chief source of the king's income. Royal servants (Râja kammikâ) seem to have measured the fields and fixed the assessment (IV, 169). There the owners of some fields pray for a remission of taxes. Exemption was occasionally obtained, as, for instance, once by a Seṭṭhi through the king's brother (IV, 169). Raññobhâga is the term applied to the king's share of the produce (II, 378). If taxes were not paid voluntarily they were to be collected forcibly (II, 240; IV, 224; III. 9; V, 98). The taxes seem to have been collected by the gâmabhojakas with the assistance of some royal officers. The latter are called balipatiggâhakas, niggâhakas, bali sâdhakas (II, 17). The collectors are sometimes very oppressive and once reduce a village to desolation. "The men could not, for fear of the king's people, live in their houses; they surrounded their houses with hedges and went after sunrise to the forest. In the day the king's people (Râjapurusâ) plundered. at night the the thieves" (V, 98). The property of those who died without heirs escheated to the king. Once (III, 299) we read that "seven days and seven nights the army of the king took to bring the goods of people dying without heirs to the palace." Sometimes whole families renounced the world and the king took possession of their property. In the Haṭṭhipâla Jâtaka (IV, 485) a Purohita and his wife follow their sons into the forest. On hearing of it, the king exclaims, "Unclaimed wealth comes to us." The rule about treasure-trove is not clear. On the one hand, a farmer appropriates the whole treasure he discovers in a field (I, 277). Elsewhere (I, 398) a king exclaims 'Treasuse-trove is a royal perquisite' and so hastens to appropriate a woman—really an ogress. Petitioners make presents to the king (II, 166). Some other imposts are levied. The king is entitled to "milk money" on the birth of an heir (IV, 323).

Justice.

It is patent that in the Jâtaka administrative system as a whole, the executive and fiscal functions were combined with the judicial. But besides the king, the Purohita and the Senâpati there were also other judicial officers. Sometimes the bench consisted of several judges. We see a court of five counsellors (V, 228.) Incidentally, they are all corrupt (V, 229). In III, 505, a regular hall of justice is mentioned. Ecclesiastical cases seem to have come before state-courts. Thus, the case of a pregnant nun in which the commands of the Buddha and his rival Devadatta were concerned, comes before a king and his ministers (I, 146 et seq.). The investigation of crimes was, at least sometimes, thorough. When a king gives out that he has lost a jewelled crest, the city-gates are shut, all carts are searched and similar other measures taken (II, 122-23; V, 461). The punishments for serious offences were very severe. A robber, guilty of high treason, has his hands and feet, nose and ears cut off, is laid in a canoe and is left to drift down the Ganges (II, 117). Another daring robber is sentenced by the king to be put to death. "They bound his hands behind his back, and led him to the place of execution, scourging him in every square with whips" (III, 436; see also V, 461). An ascetic suspected of robbery at night is, after being reviled and beaten by the owners of the house, carried into the presence of the king. The latter makes no inquiry but merely says, "Off with him, impale him upon a stake." They took him to the cemetery and lifted him up on a stake of acacia wood. There he hung a whole day with gouts of blood falling upon his body (IV, 29). An ascetic, at first appointed judge, is falsely accused of treason and is sentenced to be slain. However, he is ultimately allowed to depart. Later, the queen is accused of correspondence with him and is put to death. When the four princes become enemies of the king on this account and the innocence of the ascetic is established, the king sentences his five accusers—the former judges—to be put to death. The sentence, however, is not executed in deference to the wishes of the Bodhisatta. So, the five men are stripped of their property, disgraced in various ways by their hair being fastened into five locks, by being put into fetters and chains, by cowdung being sprinkled over them and are finally driven out of the kingdom (V, 229 et seq). In another story, two sellers of bad drink are sentenced to be beheaded (V, 13). Accidental homicide however, seems to have been lightly dealt with. A park-keeper who happens to kill a paccekabuddha flies in dread but is pardoned and restored to his office (III, 441). For certain offences imprisonment was the ordinary punishment. Prison life was hard indeed. On release a man looked forlorn and helpless (VI, 8). Imprisonment, in fact, seems to have been regarded as equal to some horrible punishments in its severity. Thus, of four robbers brought before a king, one is sentenced "to receive a thousand strokes from whips barbed with thorns, another to be imprisoned in chains, a third to be smitten with a spear and the fourth to be impaled" (VI, 4). For some heinous crimes the punishment was to be trampled down by elephants. The culprits were made to lie down in a courtyard and the trained beasts broke their bones (I, 200).

The Jâtakas throw little light on the military side of the administration. The army seems to have been recruited for the most part from the natives of a state. A king who slights his own soldiers and favours new-comers finds his troops torn by jealousies at a crisis and suffers defeat. He learns the lesson and once again shows favour to his own men (III, 400 et seq.).

The Army.

The political conditions reflected in the Jâtakas display the same feudal tendencies and the same tenure of foreign relationships as the Epics. The size of a state was, as usual, small but the ever-present tendency towards expansion led to complications. A king would sometimes attack another without any provocation (II, 95). They raid each other's frontier (I, 263 et seq.). Another king finds his city surrounded by numerous potentates because astrologers have predicted universal dominion for his daughter's son. He has to fly to the forest (IV, 230). We are told of a single sovereign capturing a thousand "kings" and seeking to make a sacrifice of them (III, 159 et seq.). Elsewhere we hear of ten brothers slaying on the wheel thousands and thousands of conquered 'kings' (IV, 84). The passion for war is well caricatured in the Cullakalinga Jâtaka. A king of Dantapur in Kalinga, gifted with enormous personal strength and commanding a fine army, could find none willing to fight him. 'I am longing to fight,' said he to his ministers, "but can find no one to war with me." On the suggestion of the ministers he sends his four daughters, bedecked with jewels, round about so as to be able to declare war on potentates who might be tempted to take any one of the damsels into their harem (III, 3 et seq.). Victory in war did sometimes lead to annexation. Thus, the king of Kâśî conquers, annexes and plunders Kośala (III, 116, 153; V, 425). We read of another king

Foreign affairs.

whose territory is annexed and who himself is captured and suspended head downwards on the lintel of the door (III, 13). But sometimes the defeated rulers were suffered to retain their dominions on acknowledgment of suzerainty.

Feudal tendencies.

So arose a network of relationships of overlordship and vassalage. Thus, many "kings" send their daughters to be married to the prince of Kuśavatī, and their sons to serve as his pages (V, 282 et seq.). Another element of feudalism was furnished by the presence of big landholders (III, 155; IV, 220). A Brâhmaṇa magnate was worth 80 crores (IV, 237). Another frontier landowner was estimated equally highly (IV, 370).

These feudal tendencies and this tenure of foreign relations rendered the frontier a scene of chronic disorder and

Border troubles.

confusion. It harboured rebels and conspirators (VI, 31). It was often in a state of revolt or disturbance which called the king from his capital (I, 304, 437; II, 74, 315; III, 400, 497; IV, 189). The departure of the king to set the frontier in order was sometimes the signal for internal trouble.

Besides feudalism there was the tendency towards functional organisation. Traders in various articles, skilled

Guilds.

workers of various categories, such as mariners (IV, 137); garland-makers (III, 405); caravan traders (I, 368; II, 295), mass-troopers (I, 296-97; II, 388; IV, 430); masons, blacksmiths, carpenters, painters, etc. (III, 387; VI, 427), had organised themselves into guilds. Eighteen was the traditional number of the varieties of guilds. Their representatives were invited to ceremonial functions (IV, 411; VI, 22). Definite quarters were sometimes assigned to guilds in a city (I, 320). The state maintained touch with the guilds. Their leaders are seen attending on the king (II, 12, 52; III, 281). The Bhaṇḍâgârika seems to have acted as a judge for guilds in some cases (IV, 43). Within a guild itself, the position of the Seṭṭhi or alderman seems often to be hereditary (I, 231, 248; III, 475).

CHAPTER VII.

Pre-Mauryan Administrations.

Vedic literature, the Sûtras, the Epics and the Jâtakas give an inkling into the administrative practices of different regions and ages but they afford little help towards the reconstruction of regular political history. It is not until the last quarter of the 4th century B.C. that any connected account of political events can be commenced and administrative data examined in the light of well-authenticated institutions. Nevertheless, a few facts can be gleaned about the political transactions of the two centuries which preceded the foundation of the Mauryan empire. The most important sources of information are the Buddhist and Jaina[1] literatures which, though primarily ethical and philosophical, incidentally give some political facts because the founders of Buddhism and Jainism sprang from aristocratic families and came into contact with crowned heads in their career. In several Buddhist works occurs the following list of the sixteen great states :—

Beginnings of Indian Political History.

(1) Aṅgâ, (2) Magadhâ, (3) Kâśî, (4) Kośalâ, (5) Vajjî, (6) Mallâ, (7) Cetî, (8) Vaṁsâ, (9) Kurû, (10) Pañcâlâ, (11) Macchâ, (12) Sûrasenâ, (13) Assakâ, (14) Avantî, (15) Gandhârâ and (16) Kambojâ.[2]

[1] See Jacobi, S. B. E, Vol. XLV, p. 122, for Pârśvanâtha who might have been the founder of Jainism. For the life and teachings of Mahâvîra, the traditional twenty-fourth or last Tîrthakara of the Jainas, see the Jaina Kalpa Sûtra and Âcârâṅga Sûtra.

[2] Rhys Davids, Buddhist India, p. 23; Cambridge History of India, I, 172-73 ; relying mainly on Aṅguttara Nikâya, I, 213 ; IV, 252, 256, 260. Mahâvastu, II, 2. Vinaya Texts, II, 146. The names are given in their Pâli forms.

It is likely that about the sixth century B.C. the whole of North India from Gandhâra in modern Afghânistân to the borders of Bengal was parcelled out roughly among sixteen principal states.

Big States.

Another list in the Dîgha Nikâya divides the central region of the North into seven states.[1] But neither the seven nor the sixteen seem to have constituted a permanent political system. They frequently warred with their neighbours; their boundaries would change and some would be annexed to others. By the beginning of the fifth century B.C. Kośala had conquered Kâśî, Magadha had conquered Aṅga and the Assakas were probably dependent on Avantî.[2] Besides the principal states there were others, dependent or independent, which filled the northern plains. Some of these were clan-oligarchies in their form of government.[3] A list of ten such clans was compiled by Rhys Davids from Pâli records :—

Clan-oligarchies.

1. The Sâkiyas, capital Kapilavatthu
2. The Bulis, capital Allakappa
3. The Bhaggas, capital on Suṁsumâra Hill
4. The Koliyas, capital Râmagâma
5. The Kâlâmas, capital Kesaputta
6. The Mallas, capital Pâvâ
7. The Mallas, capital Kusinârâ
8. The Moriyas, capital Pipphalivana
9. The Videhas, capital Mithilâ
10. The Licchavis, capital Vesâlî.[4]

[1] Dîgha Nikâya, II, 235; Rhys Davids, Dialogues of the Buddha, II, 270. Cambridge History of India, I, p. 173.

[2] Rhys Davids, Cambridge History of India, I, 173.

[3] The Avadâna Śataka (No. 88) preserves an old tradition that some merchants from Madhyadeśa in reply to queries in the south, stated that some regions were under Gaṇas and some under Râjas. Kâtyâyana, IV, 168, also distinguishes between saṁgha and Ekarâja. See D. R. Bhandarkar, Lectures on the Ancient History of India, p. 147.

[4] Rhys Davids, Buddhist India, pp. 8, 9, 22. Cambridge History of India, I, p. 175. Also, Jaina Kalpa Sûtra, ed. Jacobi, p. 65.

All these clans were not necessarily independent. For instance, the Śâkiyas owned the suzerainty of Kośala and, before the death of the Buddha, suffered a complete destruction of their autonomy.[1] Thus, the fundamental political conditions in this epoch are the same as those reflected in somewhat later literature which has already been noticed. It is, however, interesting that autonomy, so long as it lasted, carried with it autonomy of political organization. A monarch might be the suzerain of an oligarchy.

Form of Government.

The Jaina Âcârâṅga Sûtra preserves the old tradition that some regions were ruled by Gaṇas, some by two kings and so on while others had no rulers at all.[2] It is difficult to be sure of the meaning of this passage.[3] Neither Buddhist nor Jaina literature furnishes any instance of dual kingship. If the rule of Gaṇas pertains to these states, it probably means the rule of clans. All the oligarchies are named after clans and founded on the idea of clan. Their assemblies are referred to as those of the Śâkiyas, Mallas, etc.[4] All the inhabitants of any one of these states could hardly have belonged to a single clan and could not have come together for deliberation. Of representation, there is no trace or hint anywhere. Hence this type of polity is to be designated as oligarchy rather than republic. The Jâtakas mention seven thousand seven hundred and seven Licchavi kings. The number is too symmetrical to be authentic but it does indicate that the aristocratic families

[1] Rhys Davids, Buddhist India, p. 8.

[2] Âcârâṅga Sûtra, II, 3, 1, 10.

[3] For a doubtful interpretation, Jayaswal, Hindu Polity, I, 96–100.

[4] Rhys Davids, Dialogues of the Buddha, I, 113. Dîgha Nikâya II, 147.

numbered several thousands. Beyond their pale lay the other inhabitants.[1]

In these oligarchies the assembly seems to have been a living institution. Probably it was a continuation of the Vedic Sabhâ or Samiti. The Saṁthâgâra, as the mote-hall was called, seems to have been a mere roof supported by pillars without walls. Like the Vedic Sabhâ it was the scene of gossip and social life. A Brâhmaṇa thus describes his experiences of Śâkiya Saṁthâgâra to the Buddha, "Once, Gautama, I had to go to Kapilavatthu on some business or other of Pokkharasadis and went into the Sâkiyans' Congress Hall. Now at that time there were a number of Sâkiyans, old and young, seated in the hall on grand seats, making merry and joking together, nudging one another with their fingers; and on a truth, methinks, it was I myself who was the subject of their jokes; and not one of them offered me a seat. That, Gautama, is neither fitting nor is it seemly that the Sâkiyans, menials as they are, mere menials, neither venerate, nor value, nor esteem, nor give gifts, nor pay honour to Brâhmaṇas."[2] The news of the Buddha's death is broken to the Mallas while they are in the assembly hall.[3] Elsewhere too there is a reference to the mote-hall of the Mallas.[4]

The Assembly hall.

It is almost impossible to form an idea of the powers or procedure of the assembly. It is recorded that when the king of Kośala besieged the capital of the Śâkiyas and demanded surrender, they resolved to assemble and deliberate whether they should open the gates. When they

[1] Jâtaka, I, 504; IV, 148.
[2] Rhys Davids, Dialogues of the Buddha, I, 113.
[3] Mahâparinibbâna Suttanta, 6, 23.
[4] Dîgha Nikâya, II, 147.

assembled they discovered that opinion was divided. But the view of the majority prevailed.[1] We are not told whether it was an *ad hoc* gathering or a regular meeting of the assembly. The Aṭṭhakathâ has it that the tocsin was sounded when the Vaisâlians entered the house of law, which may mean the assembly.[2] If the Mahâ-Govinda Suttanta faithfully reproduces earthly conditions in its description of the palaver in Sakka's heaven, it may be inferred that at a clan meeting all sat in a specified order, that the chief laid the business before the assembly and that the recorders noted down the unanimous decisions arrived at.[3] It is not, however, possible to assert anything with certainty about procedure at clan meetings. Jayaswal and, following him, some other scholars hold that the detailed procedure of business prescribed by the Buddha for his Saṁgha or monastic order was borrowed by him from political assemblies where it actually prevailed and where, in fact, it was taken for granted. But apart from the fact that the dates of Buddhist works are very uncertain, it has to be noted that nowhere in Buddhist or Jaina literature is there any evidence of any organic connection between the procedure of the monastic order and the political assembly. In the Cullavagga the Buddha is represented as laying down the law himself for monks and nuns. There is little warrant for assuming that the theroy of the monastic order represents the practice of political life.[4]

[1] Rockhill, Life of the Buddha, pp. 118-19.

[2] Turnour, J. A. S. B., VII, 1838, pp. 994-95.

[3] Rhys Davids, Dialogues of the Buddha, II, 259—64 ; Cambridge History of India, I, p. 176.

[4] The Vinaya Piṭaka is the primary authority for the Buddhist Saṁgha. For the procedure of monastic meetings Mahâparinibbâna Suttanta, IV, 7; Mahâvagga, II ; III, 6, 6, 26; IX, 2—8; Cullavagga, IV, 10, 14, 26 ; XII, 2, 7-8 ; V, 14, 24 ; IV, 11, 12 ; XI, 1, 4, 7; IV, 9, 5; XII, 1, 10. For Jayaswal's views, Modern Review, 1913; Hindu Polity, I, pp. 45 et seq. Also, D. R. Bhandarkar, Carmichael Lectures, 1918, Lecture IV.

The Executive.

In these oligarchies the executive was presided over by a chief called Râjan. There is nothing to show how he was elected or that he was elected at all in the strict sense of the term. The designation Râjan applied to him has monarchical associations. The accounts of the life of the Buddha seem to assume that he might have succeeded his father Śuddhodana in the headship of the Śâkiya clan. A passage, though late, in Kâtyâyana's Kâśikâ is illuminating on this point. It speaks of "Râjanyas being leaders of families consecrated to leadership."[1] The chief point of difference between the oligarchic and monarchical executive seems to be that the former was based partly on the idea of clan and had to take account of the assembly. For the rest, the line between the two is very faint, almost non-existent. Besides the Râja there was an Uparâja, a sort of vicegerent and a senâpati or military commander.[2] Other officers, too, might have been appointed. The Mahâvastu speaks of the Licchavis appointing a Mahattaka to be the envoy of the whole people.[3] Mention is made of peons or police among the Koliyans and Mallas.[4] If a passage in a later work, the Lalitavistara, can be relied on, the clan-executive sometimes found it difficult to carry out its will. "Amongst them (the Vaisâlians) the rule of having respect for the high, the middle ones, the oldest, the elders, is not observed; everyone considers himself to be the Râja; 'I am the Râja, I am the Râja.' No one becomes a follower of another."[5]

[1] Kâśikâ, 546-47.

[2] Aṭṭhakathâ, Turnour, J. A. S. B., VII, 1838, pp. 993 et seq.

[3] Mahâvastu, I, 254.

[4] Rhys Davids, Buddhist India, p. 21.

[5] Lalitavistara, III. Jayaswal, Hindu Polity, I, 52, takes the passage to imply equal right of voting and a universal aspiration for the presidentship.

Besides the organs of government at the centre, there were moots in towns and perhaps also in villages,[1] but of their jurisdiction or working we can gather nothing. Kulas or families also had some regulating powers.[2] Here the state is based partly on the territorial basis and partly on the basis of kinship. From incidental touches it appears that the whole government was rather homely in character. Thus, the Mallas of Kusinârâ imposed a fine of 500 pieces on any one who "went not forth to meet the Blessed One (the Buddha," when, on his tour, he drew near their town.[3]

Local Government.

According to the Aṭṭhakathâ, the judiciary consisted of a graded series of courts, each of which must find the accused guilty before he could be punished. The Viniccaya Mahâmattas formed the first court. Then came the Vohârikas or lawyer-judges; Sûtradharas or masters of law; Aṣṭakula or council of the eight; Senâpati, Uparâja and Râja.[4] The passage is intensely interesting but it is not corroborated anywhere else in Buddhist literature. The arrangements it indicates are rather complicated and there is no means of knowing how they worked in practice. The Aṭṭhakathâ adds that the decisions of the Râja were recorded in a Paveni-patthakân.

The Judiciary.

The clans sometimes formed alliances and even loose temporary confederations. The Licchavis once federated with the Mallas and, together, both set up an executive of eighteen members, drawn in equal numbers from either group.[5] Elsewhere we read that when Ajâtaśatru attacked his grand-

Confederations.

---

[1] Rhys Davids, Cambridge History of India, I, p. 177.

[2] Later, the Basâḍh seals (Ann. Rep. Arch. Surv. Ind., 1903-4, pp. 107 ff; Ibid., 1911-12, p. 56; Ibid., 1913-14, p. 138) speak of prathama kulikas or chiefs of kulas.

[3] Vinaya, I, 247; Mahâvagga, VI, 36.

[4] Aṭṭhakathâ, Turnour, J. A. S. B., VII, 1838, pp. 993-94.

[5] Jaina Kalpa Sûtra, 128.

father's dominion of Vesâli, he was encountered by nine Licchavi and nine Malla confederate chiefs, though in vain.[1] At another time the Licchavis federated with the Videhas and other clans. The confederates as a whole were called Saṁvajjians. It was to the federated Vajjian clans that Gautama Buddha addressed a few precepts. He seems to give a dose of conservatism to those who might be inclined to rush headlong into innovations. He insists that time-honoured customs and usages must be maintained. Nothing that was not already established should be enacted. Nothing that had been enacted should be abrogated. The elders must be honoured, esteemed, revered and supported. It should be a point of duty to hearken to their words. Justice and fairness should always be followed. Women or girls should never be detained by force or abducted. The spiritual interests should not be neglected. The Arhantas should be defended, protected and supported. The Caityas, sacred temples, must be revered and maintained. Turning to constitutional affairs, the Buddha wanted the clansmen to hold full and frequent assemblies. They should "meet together in concord and rise in concord and carry out Vajjian business in concord." So long as these wholesome rules were observed, "so long may the Vajjians be expected not to decline but to prosper."[2]

The Kingdoms.

The clan-oligarchies covered a very small part of the northern fringe. The plains for the most part were ruled by monarchs. One of the most powerful kingdoms in the time of the Buddha was that of Kośala which stretched from Nepâl to Prayâga on the confluence of the Ganges and the Jumnâ. It does not

Kośala.

[1] S. B. E., XXII, Int., p. XIV.

[2] Dîgha Nikâya, Mahâparinibbâna Suttanta, tr. Rhys Davids, Dialogues of the Buddha, II, 79–85. The Buddha repeats the same precepts in Aṅguttara Nikâya, VII, 19.

seem to have been a unitary state. The Śâkyas are mentioned as a feudatory community acknowledging the overlordship of king Pasenadi.[1] The relations of the Śâkyas with the Kośala king are well indicated in a passage in the Dialogues of the Buddha, where the great teacher remarks that "the respect which Pasenadi receives from the Śâkyas is shown by him towards me."[2] None the less, the Śâkyas retained their pride of birth and disdained to give a daughter of their house to the suzerain's family.[3] Elsewhere Pasenadi is said to be the head of a group of five Râjas.[4] Here is an unmistakable indication of feudalism. Pasenadi is said to have been educated at Takkasilâ. He appreciated the teachings of the Buddha and built a Saddhamma Mahâśâlâ, a great hall of the Dhamma, for him. None the less he practised perfect religious toleration.[5] There is an interesting Jâtaka tradition (IV, 152) that once during his absence from the capital to visit the Buddha, Pasenadi left the administration in charge of a minister who proclaimed his deposition and installed his son, Viḍuḍâbha, on the throne.

Kośala was sometimes at war and sometimes at peace with neighbouring realm of Magadha, one of the sixteen Janapadas of Jambûdvîpa.[6] Its king Bimbisâra or Śreṇika who was a contemporary of the Buddha is said to have been the fifth of the

Magadha.

[1] Rhys Davids, Cambridge History of India, I, 181.

[2] Dîgha Nikâya, III, 83-84. Rhys Davids, Dialogues of the Buddha, III, 80.

[3] Rockhill, Life of the Buddha, 75—77.

[4] Saṁyutta Nikâya, Book of the Kindred Sayings, tr. Mrs. Rhys Davids, p. 106.

[5] Kośala Saṁyutta, Saṁyutta Nikâya, I, 68—102. Dîgha Nikâya, 87; Udânavarga, 2, 6.

[6] For Janapada or Mahâjanapada, Aṅguttara Nikâya, I, 213; IV 252, 256, 260. The name Magadha first appears in the Atharvaveda, V, 22, 14.

Śaiśunâga dynasty founded by Śiśunâga or Śiśunâka about the middle of the 7th century B.C.[1] His kingdom is said to have included 80,000 villages, each under a chief or headman.[2] The Cullavagga records an incident pertaining to Bimbisâra's administration, and showing that the king had a number of Mahâmattas or ministers who were expected to give him sound advice. Bimbisâra dismissed some Mahâmattas who had advised him badly, degraded some others with whose counsel he was not satisfied and promoted those whose advice he approved of.[3] An incident relating to the reign of Ajâtaśatru, son of Bimbisâra, shows that the state reserved forests even in those early days. A Bhikṣu's action in taking wood from a reserved forest is noticed by Vassakâra, a minister of Ajâtaśatru, and brought to the knowledge of the Buddha.[4] The Vinaya Piṭaka shows that towns had gates which were closed at night when all entry was forbidden.[5] Both Bimbisâra or Śreṇika and Ajâtaśatru or Kûṇika are claimed by Jainas and Buddhists as adherents of their religions. Probably they patronised both the creeds and displayed that wide tolerance and appreciation of divergent persuasions which characterised so many rulers in ancient India. It is possible to form some idea of the tenure of inter-state relationships in the Buddha's days. Bimbisâra is said to have contracted marriage alliances with the kings of several states. These, we may be sure, were quite common in ancient India. It is said that on Kośala Devî, one of the wives of Bimbisâra, the revenues of an estate in Kâśî had been settled by her father

[1] V. A. Smith, Early History of India, 4th edition, p. 32.

[2] Mahâvagga, V, I, 1. For Bimbisâra tradition, see also the Jaina Harivaṁśa Purâṇa, I, 148-49.

[3] Cullavagga, VII, 3, 5. For ministers see also Mahâvagga, I, 40, 3.

[4] Vinaya Piṭaka, III, 41—45.

[5] Vinaya Piṭaka, IV, 116-17.

Mahâkośala. When the lady died of grief at the tragic end, of her husband, the payment was no longer made to Magadha. Thereupon, Ajâtaśatru commenced a war which, with varying fortune, was closed with a marriage alliance.[1] The diplomatic relations of states already extended over nearly the whole of India. Ajâtaśatru is said to have fortified his capital Râjagṛiha against an apprehended attack from Ujjayinî.[2] Ajâtaśatru actually came into conflict with the Vajjian confederacy. He is represented as saying, "I will root out these Vajjians, mighty and powerful though they be, I will destroy these Vajjians, I will bring these Vajjians to utter ruin." He built a fort at Pâṭaliputra (Pâṭaliputta) on the Ganges on the frontier, treacherously sowed dissensions among the Vajjians, at last overran their territory, destroyed Vesâlî and butchered its people.[3]

Other Kingdoms.

Of the other contemporary kingdoms, those of Avantî with its capital at Ujjayinî and of the Vaṁsas with its capital at Kosambî are

[1] Dîgha Nikâya, I, 86 III, 127; Jacobi, Jaina Sûtras, I, XII—XV; Dîpavaṁśa, III, 56—60; Mahâvaṁśa, II, 29, 30; Rhys Davids, Cambridge History of India, I, pp. 182—85; Charpentier, Ibid., 160-61; V. A. Smith, op. cit., 32—38.

[2] Rhys Davids, Buddhist India, p. 13. Archæological remains prove that Râjagṛiha was a great town in antiquity. The remains of its vihâras and stûpas have in modern times been utilised for temples, mosques and tombs.

[3] Rhys Davids, Dialogues of the Buddha, II, 78; Cambridge History of India, I, 184-85; Rockhill, Life of the Buddha, 127; V. A Smith, op. cit., 37-38.

Jayaswal (J. B. O. R. S., V, 550-51) identifies the Parkham statue of Mathurâ as that of Ajâtaśatru and the two Śaiśunâka statues in the Indian Museum at Calcutta as those of Udaya and Nandivardhana of this line (J. B. O. R. S., V, 402—406). See also his paper on the Śaiśunâka and Maurya chronology and the date of the Buddha's Nirvâṇa, J. B. O. R. S., I, p. 67. For criticism, Ramaprasad Chanda, Ind. Ant., XLVIII, p. 25; R. C. Majumdar, Ibid., p. 29.

noteworthy but we know nothing of administrative importance about them. If Buddhist tradition preserved in later works can be trusted, justice was highly prized at Kâśî.[1]

The Persian Dominion.

It was probably during the lifetime of the Buddha that the Persians under Darius conquered certain districts in the north-west of India and grouped them into the twentieth satrapy of their empire.[2] It stretched along the banks of the Indus and probably included the whole of Sindh and part of the Puñjâb to the east of the river. It paid 360 Euboic talents of gold dust, equal to 185 hundredweights as tribute.[3] But a passage in Xenophon's Life of Cyrus shows that partly at least the Persian dominion fell into line with the fundamental political conditions of India. There is a reference to an Indian 'king' who sent a sum of money through some agents to the Persian king.[4] The passage points not to downright annexation but to the relationship of suzerainty and vassalage. The Persian empire always respected local autonomy and it is more than probable that its Indian tracts

[1] Dhammapada Commentary, I, 251 et seq. For the kingdoms, Majjhima Nikâya, III, 7; II, 83; Vinaya, II, 32, 139; Lalitavistara, ed. Rajendra Lal Mitra, p. 24; Rhys Davids, Buddhist India, 141–46; Cambridge History of India, I, 185—88. The site of Kosambî long discussed (e g., Watters, On Yuan Chwang, I, 366—69; V. A. Smith, J. R. A. S., 1898, p. 503) was identified last year with the village of Kosam, at a distance of about eighteen miles from Sirathu Railway Station in the district of Allahabad.

[2] India is not mentioned in the Behistun Inscriptions of 516 B.C. at Persepolis but is mentioned in the Inscription on the tomb of Darius at Naksh-i-Rustam, 486 B.C. The Indian satrapy must have come into existence during this interval.

[3] Herodotus (Rawlinson), II, p. 403; IV, 177, 207; V. A. Smith, op cit., 38—43; William Jackson, Cambridge History of India, I, pp. 319—341; who may be consulted for further references to other writers.

[4] Xenophon, Cyropaedia, VI, 2, 1—11.

were either left in the hands of old dynasties or at any rate governed on the old lines. About Indian royal houses themselves it is interesting to recall that Aristotle quotes from a book by Scylax of Caryanda (employed by Darius to navigate the Indus) that among Indians kings were held to be of a race superior to their subjects.[1] Here a ruling caste is indicated. The Persian connection probably provided fresh openings for an exchange of cultural influences between India and Persia. The general similarity between the political institutions of ancient India and ancient Persia makes it difficult to estimate the extent of the influence of the latter on the former but that there was some influence cannot be doubted.[2]

The Greek accounts.

During the interval between the death of the Buddha and the invasion of Alexander the Great in 327 B.C., Indian political annals, even after the painstaking research of the last two generations, can show only a few names.[3] Practically nothing can be gleaned about administrative practices. It is only in the later years of the 4th century B.C. that the curtain rises with advent of the Greeks. There were at least nineteen writers who visited the country with Alexander or shortly after his death or who were at any rate his contemporaries. Patrokles states that Alexander caused the whole country to be described by men well-acquainted with it and that the description was put into his hands afterwards by his treasurer Xenokles.[4] But all the

[1] Politics, VII, 14.

[2] Spooner, J. R. A. S., 1915, pp. 63–89, 405–55, exaggerates the general influence of Persia on India. For criticism, V. A. Smith, J. R. A. S., 1915, pp. 800–802; Keith, Ibid., 1916, pp. 138–43; Thomas, Ibid., pp. 362–66; Nimrod, Modern Review, 1916. See also J. J. Modi, Asiatic Papers, II. For a comparison of Indian and Persian political institutions, infra, Ch. XVII, Conclusion.

[3] V. A. Smith, op. cit., 38–43. Rhys Davids, Cambridge History of India, I, 188–90. Jayaswal, J. B. O. R. S., V, 88–106. R. D. Banerji, Ibid., 210–15.

[4] Strabo, IV. McCrindle, India as described in Classical Literature, p. 95.

original works have perished. The extracts probably embellished by successive generations of writers and preserved in a few authors mostly of the first century B.C., or the first century A.D., sometimes indulge in fairy tales and sometimes contradict one another. Strabo stigmatised the Greek writers on India as a set of liars of whom only a few managed now and then to stammer out some words of truth. The charge is sweeping and rather uncritical but it must be admitted that it is difficult to penetrate to the truth in writers who had a love for the marvellous and who borrow or summarise accounts of regions and times far removed from their own. They cannot be accepted at their face value and have always to be used with great caution.[1]

[1] Of the writers, Arrian (Arrianus), philosopher, statesman, historian and tactician, was born towards the close of the first century A.D. at Nikomedia in Bithynia in Asia Minor and died in the reign of Marcus Aurelius. Strabo flourished in the reigns of the Emperors Augustus and Tiberius (27 B.C.–A.D. 37) in Pontos, and wrote a sort of universal geography. Diodorus Siculus, born at Agyrium in Sicily, flourished in the days of Julius Cæsar and Augustus (49 B.C.—A.D. 14) and composed the Bibliotheca Historia, a Universal History. Quintus Curtius Rufus lived probably in the reign of the Emperor Vespasian (A.D. 70–79). He wrote a life of Alexander Plutarch, the famous author of the Parallel Lives of Greek and Roman heroes, was born at Chairo-naia in Boiotia about the middle of the first century A.D. Pliny (A.D. 23–79) wrote the Encyclopædic Historia Naturalis. Claudius Ptolemaeus (Ptolemy) wrote his Outline of Geography (Geographike Hyphegesis) in the nature of a universal survey, at Alexandria. For English rendering, McCrindle, Ancient India as described by Megasthenes and Arrian, Calcutta, 1877 Ancient India as described in Classical Literature, Westminster, 1901; Invasion of India by Alexander the Great as described by Arrian, Q. Curtis Rufus, Diodorus, Plutarch and Justin. Westminster, 1896. For Modern accounts of Alexander's Invasion of India, see V. A. Smith, Early History of India, 4th edition, pp. 52—120; E. R. Bevan, Cambridge History of India, I, 345—386.

Political Conditions.

On the whole, the Greek accounts show the country between the Indus and the Jumnâ divided into a large number of independent and half-independent principalities, frequently at war with their neighbours and all swayed by militarism. The eastern parts of the country seem to have developed the large-state organisation, which, however, was equally militaristic. Of the states in the Puñjâb and Sindh some were monarchical and others tribal oligarchies. Âmbhi of Taxilâ who allied himself with Alexander, Puru or Porus who offered such tenacious resistance and the neighbouring king of Abhisâra, are monarchs of the usual type already considered.[1] It appears that there were many chiefs under a king. At a sort of durbar held by Alexander at Takṣaśilâ, before he met Porus, a number of chiefs came to him with presents from the small territory already subdued. The oligarchies[2] display variety of organisation but it is impossible not to suspect that their institutions have been brought by the Greek imagination nearer to those of Hellas For instance, we are told of the Sophytes (Saubhûtis)[3] and the Kathians (Kaṭhas) that "they do not acknowledge and rear children according to the will of parents but as the officers entrusted with the medical inspection of infants may direct, for if they have remarked anything deformed or defective in the limbs of

[1] Puru seems to have been a family name. At the time of Alexander's invasion, a nephew of the king who is given the same name, was in revolt against him and offered to surrender his uncle into the hands of Alexander. Later, when he found the king an ally of the Greeks, he warred against both (Arrian, Book V, Ch. XXI; McCrindle, Invasion of India, 113-14).

[2] Pâṇini who cannot be later than 300 B.C. mentions Saṁghas in his Sûtras (e.g., III, 3, 42) but we cannot be sure that he is referring to oligarchies or republics. For an interpretation in the political sense see Jayaswal, Hindu Polity, I, 41—44.

[3] For the identification of Sophytes with Saubhûtis, Sylvain Lévi, Journal Asiatique, VIII, pp. 237 et seq.

the child they order it to be killed."[1] This order, adds Strabo, was pronounced by a magistrate according to the law.[2] Diodorus embellishes the details and adds that beauty was highly prized by those people in politics as in marriage[3] Political infanticide is opposed to all we know of Hindu life, character and institutions in any part of the country from indigenous or foreign sources. Nowhere in Hindu literature or inscriptions is there the remotest hint at it whether by way of approval or disapproval. If such a practice really prevailed at this time, Aśoka who came shortly after and who was a humanitarian above all else would be sure to condemn it in his edicts. The fact is that the Greeks, struck by the heroism and endurance of the Kaṭhas naturally compared them to Spartans and then imagined that similar institutions were required to produce similar characteristics. Another stretch of fancy can be detected in the description of Patala by Diodorus. It was a city of great note "with a political constitution drawn on the same lines as the Spartan; for in this community the command in war is vested in two hereditary kings of two different houses while a council of elders rules the whole state with paramount authority."[4] Here, again, the Greek imagination seems to have transplanted the Spartan constitution to the banks of the Indus. Patala was perhaps really an oligarchy and its people were undoubtedly valorous. But it is not necessary to fancy with the Greeks that the highest valour could only be produced by Spartan political habits. The tribe ruled by Mausikanos (Mucukarṇa) are said to have taken their meals in common and not to have recognised slavery.[5] The latter statement is likely to be true, but the former is again too reminiscent of Sparta. One

[1] Curtius, McCrindle, Invasion of India by Alexander the Great, p. 219.
[2] Strabo, XV, 30.
[3] Diodorus, XVII, 91; McCrindle, Invasion, p. 280.
[4] Diodorus, XVII, 104.
[5] Strabo, XV, 34.

administrative detail about this tribe is more than interesting. Strabo says that their courts took cognisance only of murder and other violent crime.[1] It is possible that criminal justice had been taken over by the state but that civil disputes were still disposed of by heads of families or clans. Reminiscences of Athenian history seem to sway the imagination of the Greek writers when they relate that "at last after many generations had come and gone, the sovereignty, it is said, was dissolved and democratic governments were set up in the cities,"[2] or that "most of the cities adopted the democratic form of government, though some retained the kingly, until the invasion of the country by Alexander."[3] It is noticeable that the Greeks think and write in terms of the city-state about India which was predominantly a land of villages and country states. In all Greek accounts of India this tendency to bring Indian history and politics into line with their own political evolution has to be alllowed for. Arrian has it that beyond the Hyphasis (the Beâs), the country was exceedingly fertile and the inhabitants were good agriculturists, brave in war, and living under an excellent system of internal government; "for the multitude was governed by the aristocracy, who exercised their authority with justice and moderation."[4] Strabo adds that, according to the earlier writers, this aristocracy consisted of "five thousand councillors each of whom furnished the state with an elephant."[5] It has been suggested that this unnamed state was that of the Yaudheyas whose coins have been found in that region in large numbers.[6] In any

[1] Ibid., XV, 34, 54.
[2] Diodorus, III, 38; McCrindle, Megasthenes, etc., p. 38.
[3] Diodorus, III, 39; McCrindle, op. cit., p. 40.
[4] Arrian, Book V, 25; McCrindle, Invasion of India, p. 121.
[5] Strabo, XV, 37; McCrindle, Ancient India as described in Classical Literature, p. 45.
[6] Jayaswal, Hindu Polity, I, 67.

case, the state was a military aristocracy, probably a tribal oligarchy, which comprised some thousands of heads of families. According to Curtius, the Sambastai or Abastanoi (the Ambaṣṭhas) had a democratic form of government; they elected their generals, renowned for their valour and military skill; their army consisted of 60,000 foot, 6,000 cavalry, and 500 chariots. Diodorus adds that having 'adopted the advice of their elders not to fight,' they sent an embassy to Alexander for peace.[1] According to the Greeks the Nysaeans also had an oligarchical form of government. Alexander desired them to send the best hundred men of their governing body to be sent with him. The conversations which followed on this demand betray, on the part of Indians, a familiarity with Greek tradition, Alexander's history and foundation of cities,[2] which is likely to be an effort of the Greek imagination. The only safe conclusion to be drawn from the interesting notice is that the Nysaeans had a ruling class and that Alexander demanded 100 members thereof as hostages for their good faith. The Agsinae or Agalassians (Agraśreṇî ?), in the neighbourhood of the Oxydrakai (Kṣûdrakas) had, according to Diodorus, an army of 40,000 foot and 3,000 horse. Their territory comprised large cities which offered house-to-house resistance to the Macedonians.[3] The Sabarcae are said to have enjoyed a democratic form of government and to have mustered 60,000 foot, and 6,000 cavalry and 500 chariots, commanded by three generals elected for their valour and military skill.[4]

---

[1] Curtius, Book IX, 8; McCrindle, Invasion of India, p. 252.

[2] Arrian, Book V, Ch. I-II; McCrindle, Invasion of India, pp. 79—81. For a discussion of the site of Nysa, see Holdich, Gates of India, p. 122.

[3] Diodorus, Book XVII, Ch. 96; McCrindle, Invasion of India, p. 285.

[4] Curtius, McCrindle, op. cit., p. 282.

The Accae tribes had 40,000 men under arms; their towns had walls of the most formidable strength and were equipped with every means of defence.[1] Much further south, probably in Gujarât, the Automela on the coast had 1,600 elephants, 5,000 cavalry and 1,50,000 foot.[2] Mention is made of the Pandae, the only race in India ruled by women, who had 300 towns.[3] It is, however, doubtful where this tribe lived or if it is to be identified with the Pâṇḍyas of the extreme south. There is an interesting notice that Brâhmaṇas instigated a city to revolt against Alexander who had subdued it. Alexander recaptured the town and put all the Brâhmaṇas concerned to death.[4] Plutarch also says that Alexander hanged many philosophers for encouraging the free states to revolt from his authority.[5] It appears that Brâhmaṇas exercised a good deal of political influence.

Combinations.

Though often at war with one another, the tribes sometimes formed close alliances. The Malloi (Mâlavas) and Oxydrakai (Kṣûdrakas) entered into a confederacy, in the presence of a common foe, cementing it by wholesale inter-marriage, and were able to put into field 90,000 foot-soldiers, 10,000 cavalry, and 900 war-chariots.[6] The two nations, we are told, were proud of their "liberty which for so many ages they had preserved inviolate." But they suffered a defeat at the hands of Alexander. The catastrophe seemed to break up the confederacy. The

[1] The Itinerary of Alexander the Great, by an unknown author, in McCrindle, India as described in Classical Literature, p. 151.

[2] McCrindle, India as described by Megasthenes and Arrian, p. 147.

[3] Ibid., pp. 147, 159, 194-95, 200 202.

[4] Arrian, Book VI, Ch. XVI; McCrindle, Invasion of India, p. 159.

[5] Ibid., p. 306.

[6] Curtius, McCrindle, Invasion of India, p. 234.

Malloi are recorded to have declared that they were willing "to receive whatever satrap Alexander might appoint, pay the tribute he chose to impose and give as many hostages as he required." The Oxydrakai despatched 100 ambassadors, leading men of their cities and their provincial governors. They "all rode in chariots and were men of uncommon stature and of a very dignified bearing. Their robes were of linen embroidered with inwrought gold and purple."[1] The Yaudheyas in the southern portion of the Puñjâb and the Ârjunâyanas in the north-east of modern Râjpûtânâ also represented confederations. They are mentioned by Pâṇini.[2]

Arrian says that the Indian territory, conquered by Alexander, comprised seven nations and 2,000 towns.[3] Pliny puts the number of nations at nine and that of the towns at 5,000, none of which was less than a kos or nearly two miles in extent.[4] Elsewhere Megasthenes remarks of India as a whole that the number of cities was so great that it could not be counted.[5] It may be inferred that the number of towns was strikingly large but of their administrative structure we can gather little beyond what Megasthenes says of Pâṭaliputra.[6] Alexander himself is said to have founded cities and fixed the boundaries of 'satrapies.'[7] The Macedonian conqueror seems to have largely followed the Indian model in his political arrangements. He "not only appointed Poros to govern his own Indians,

Alexander's political arrangements.

---

[1] Arrian, Book VI, Ch. XIV; McCrindle, op. cit., p. 154.

[2] See J. R. A. S., 1897, pp. 887-88.

[3] Arrian, Book VI, Ch. II.

[4] McCrindle, India as described in Classical Literature, p. 108.

[5] Megasthenes, Fragment XXVI; McCrindle, India as described by Megasthenes and Arrian, p. 68.

[6] Infra, Ch. VIII.

[7] Arrian, Book V, Ch. XIV; McCrindle, Invasion of India, p. 156.

but added to his original territory another of still greater extent."[1] He allowed the various districts to be governed by their old rulers under the overlordship of Poros who was to be his own vassal. Besides the satrapy of Poros which extended from the Hydaspes (Jhelum) to the Hyphasis (Beâs) there was the satrapy of Philip at Takṣaśilâ who was also invested with the charge of a province extending as far south as the confluence of the Indus with the Acesinas (Chenâb). But Âmbhi also continued to rule at Takṣaśilâ.[2] According to Curtius, Âmbhi and Eudamos were appointed joint administrators by Alexander.[3] We do not know how their relations were co-ordinated and their spheres demarcated. The third satrapy comprised Sindh and was placed under Pithon, son of Agenor. From the rapidity with which his authority was shaken off, it appears that there were autonomous Indian chiefs under him as well. Alexander left an army of occupation consisting of Macedonians, Thracians and Greek mercenaries but its distribution is uncertain.[4] It is probable that while civil administration was left to Indian chiefs, military authority was concentrated in the hands of Macedonian officers. In any case the Macedonian hold on India was extremely weak. The death of Alexander was the signal for its disappearance. In 321 B.C. at the time of the partition of Triparadisos, Pithon, son of Agenor, had ceased to be the satrap of the lower Indus valley and was ruling only west of that river.[5]

---

[1] Arrian, Book V, Ch. XIX; McCrindle, Invasion of India, p. 109.

[2] Arrian, Book VI, Ch. XV. [3] Curtius, X, 1, 31.

[4] Arrian, Book V, Ch. XV, XXVIII; Curtius, X, 1, 10; Diodorus, Book XIX, Ch. XIV, Book XVIII, Ch. III; Bevan, Cambridge History of India, I, 384-85.

[5] Bevan, House of Seleucus, I, Ch. XIII. If Plutarch can be relied on, the memory of Alexander's exploits lasted for a long while. He records that on his retreat he erected altars to gods which the kings of the Praisai held in veneration even in his (Plutarch's) days. They would cross the river and offer sacrifices there in the Hellenic style (McCrindle, Invasion of India, p. 311).

The Macedonian episode exercised little influence on the development of Hindu political institutions. As Bevan puts it, "India and the Greek world only touched each other on their fringes and there never was a chance for the elements of the Hellenistic tradition to strike deep root in Indian soil."[1]

[1] Cambridge History of India, I. p. 385. See infra, Ch. XVII, Conclusion.

CHAPTER VIII.

The Mauryan Administration.

Magadha.

While in India, Alexander the Great was told of the Gangaridai and Prasii whose reputation for military prowess unnerved the worn-out, home-sick soldiers of Hellas. The term Gangaridai is derived obviously from the Ganges on whose banks the people were settled. Prasii is the Sanskrit Prâcya—eastern. The two terms are used sometimes as if to denote two different peoples and sometimes as if both referred to the same people and country. The various contexts, however, make it clear that the people ruled by the king of Magadha or south Bihâr are meant. Here, as a comparison of the Buddhist and Puranic accounts shows, the Śaiśunâga dynasty had been succeeded by a line of Nandas, probably of lowly extraction, whose last representative, said to be a barber's son, occupied the throne of Pâṭaliputra in 326 B.C.[1] Alexander heard, and Puru confirmed the report, that the king of the Gangaridai possessed an army of 20,000 horse, 2,00,000 infantry, 2,000 chariots and 4,000

[1] Diodorus, XVII, 93; V. A. Smith, Early History of India, 4th edition, pp. 43—51; F. W. Thomas, Cambridge History of India, I, pp. 469—71. S. V. Venkatesvara Aiyar, Ind. Ant., 1915, pp. 41 et seq., regards the Nandas as a continuation of the Śaiśunâga dynasty. Jayaswal (J. B. O R S., IV, 91—95) interprets Navanandâḥ as new Nandas instead of nine Nandas as hitherto accepted. Nanda Râja is mentioned twice in the Hâthîgumphâ inscription of Khâravela, the Jaina king of Orissâ, c. 165 B.C. For the Puranic tradition, Pargiter, Ancient Indian Historical Tradition; Dynasties of the Kali Age.

elephants trained and equipped for war.[1] Plutarch has the version that the kings of the Gandaritai and the Praisoi awaited Alexander with 80,000 horse, 2,00,000 foot, 8,000 war chariots and 6,000 fighting elephants.[2] Pliny records that "the Prasii surpass in power and glory every other people, not only in this quarter, but one may say in all India, . . . Their king has in his pay a standing army of 6,00,000 foot-soldiers, 30,000 cavalry and 9,000 elephants, whence may be formed some conjecture as to the vastness of his resources."[3] Even on the basis of the lowest of these figures for the army, it is manifest that Magadha had become a great military power and that it was almost certainly the strongest state in North India. It seems to have extended its sway over Kaliṅga or Orissâ, Tirhut in North Bihâr, Aṅga, Kośala and Kâśî Its crown passed, after a revolution which left lasting memories, to Candragupta, styled Maurya, in or about 320 B.C.[4] It is certain that Candragupta further extended the bounds of the

[1] Diodorus, XVII, 93.

[2] Plutarch, Alexander, 62.

[3] Pliny, Historia Naturalis, Book VI, Ch. 22.

[4] A tradition recorded in an inscription of the 12th century A.D. states that Kuntala, a large tract including the Western Deccan as well as Northern Mysore, was ruled by the Nandas and that the Kadamba kings claimed descent from Nanda (Rice, Mysore and Coorg from the Inscriptions, p. 3). But this assertion finds no support in earlier tradition. The Matsya, Vâyu and Brahmâṇḍa Purâṇas call Mahâpadma Nanda Sarvakṣatriyântaka, destroyer of 'all Kṣatriyas. The statement supports the tradition that the Nandas were not Kṣatriyas (V. A. Smith, op. cit., pp. 55-56; Thomas, Cambridge History of India, I, pp. 467—73). The course of the revolution is indicated in Viśâkhadatta's Mudrârâkṣasa, which though composed probably in the seventh century A.D. (Rapson, J. R. A. S., 1900, p. 535) or, according to Jacobi, in the 9th century A.D. (Vienna Oriental Journal, II, 1888, p. 212), is, as Hillebrandt emphasises, based on ancient court tradition (Tawney, J. R. A. S., 1908, p. 910). Konow (Ind. Ant., 1914, p. 68) places the play about the 5th century A.D. See also Ind. Ant., 1913, pp. 265—67. For Greek and Roman references to Candragupta, Wilson, Preface to his translation of the Mudrârâkṣasa. The Mahâvaṁśa (tr. Geiger, p. 27) calls Candragupta a scion of the Moriya clan. The Divyâvadâna (ed. Cowell and Neil, 370, 409) calls the Mauryas Kṣatriyas.

kingdom he had won. He probably led the revolt against the Macedonian garrisons and took possession of the territory they guarded. He overran the rest of North India or at any rate got his suzerainty acknowledged throughout the region. He resisted the invasion of Seleucus Nikator and, in exchange for 500 elephants, got the satrapies of the Paropanisadai, Aria, Arachosia and, perhaps, part of Gedrosia, roughly, modern Afghânistân and Baluchistân, about 303 B.C.[1] For the first time North India was united under one sceptre. Kalinga seems to have asserted its independence but a good deal of other territory was added to the empire of Magadha. Candragupta founded a new era.[2]

The seven castes of India.

Magasthenes, who at first represented Seleucus of Bactria at the court of Sibyrtios, satrap of Arachosia (Kandahâr) and who, later, was sent on several missions to Candragupta, wrote what seems to have been the most comprehensive account of India. But it is preserved only in extracts in later writers which sometimes contradict one another. Whether he actually wrote out the monstrosities about gold-digging ants, men with ears large enough to sleep in, men without mouths or noses or with only one eye or spider legs, etc.,[3] which have been put into his mouth may be doubted but it is clear that he knew only Pâṭaliputra and

[1] Plutarch, Alexander, 62. Justin, XV, 4. V. A. Smith, op. cit, pp. 121—26. Thomas, Cambridge History of India, I, pp. 467—73. See also George Macdonald, Hellenic Kingdoms of Syria, Bactria and Parthia, in the Cambridge History of India, I, pp. 427—62.

[2] The Hâthîgumphâ Inscription of Khâravela is dated the year $\frac{165}{164}$ of the Râjâ Muriya (J.B.O.R. S., III, Part IV, pp. 461 et seq.). As Bühler pointed out, the Mauryan era commences from the accession of Candragupta and not from the coronation of Aśoka as Bhagvân Lâl Indrajî supposed. On Candragupta's accession, see also Mahâvaṁśa Ṭîkâ, p. 123.

[3] Strabo, McCrindle, India as described in Classical Literature, pp. 60.—63; also Pliny, Hist. Nat., VII, ii. 14—22.

the districts he passed through. His observations apply only to North India and particularly to Magadha. Megasthenes's account of Indian castes is professedly reproduced by Diodorus,[1] Arrian,[2] Strabo[3] and Pliny,[4] who, however, differ in details. They all agree in summarising that according to Magasthenes, the population of India was divided into seven castes. The Philosophers, though inferior in numbers, prevailed over all "in point of dignity." Exempt from public duties, they were neither the masters nor the servants of others, but engaged themselves in performing sacrifices for others and foretelling the future. The second caste, consisting of the husbandmen, 'far more numerous than the others,' were likewise exempt from 'fighting and other public services.' They devoted the whole of their time to tillage and entirely avoided going into towns. "The third class consists of the neat-herds and shepherds and, in general, of all herdsmen, who neither settle in towns nor in villages, but live in tents." "The fourth class consists of the artisans. Of these some are armourers, while others make the implements which husbandmen and others find useful in their different callings," says Arrian. "This class is not only exempted from paying taxes, but even receives maintenance from the royal exchequer." Strabo, however, enumerates several sub-divisions of the fourth class. It "consists of those who work as traders, of those who send wares, and of those who are employed in bodily labour. Some of them pay tribute and render to the state certain prescribed services. But the armour-makers and ship-builders receive wages and their victuals from the king, for whom alone they work . . . ." The fifth class, second in point of numbers, consisted of fighting men, who, when not engaged in war, gave themselves up to idleness

[1] Diodorus, II, 40-41.
[2] Arrian, Indika, XI, XII.
[3] Strabo, XV, 1, 46—49, also 58—60.
[4] Pliny, VI, 22.

and amusement. "The sixth class consists of the overseers. It is their province to inquire into and superintend all that goes on in India, . . ." (Arrian.) "The seventh caste consists of the councillors and assessors—of those who deliberate on public affairs. It is the smallest class, looking to number, but the most respected, on account of the high character and the wisdom of its members; for from their ranks the advisers of the king are taken, and the treasurers of the state, and the arbiters who settle disputes. The generals of the army also, and the chief magistrates, usually belong to this class. . . . No one is allowed to marry out of his own caste or follow an art except his own: for instance, a soldier cannot become a husbandman or an artisan a philosopher." (Arrian.)

The account of Megasthenes does not harmonise with the traditional Hindu system of caste. But it is difficult to believe that he was ignorant of the latter and failed to portray it with even a distant approach to exactitude. None could have lived even for a short while in India without knowing the salient features of caste. Unless he has been hopelessly distorted, Megasthenes cannot be held to be describing caste. What he seems to do is to observe the dominant occupations and to give his own impressions of the actual division of the population. As a Greek he approaches the question largely, though not exclusively, from the angle of the state. Everywhere he mentions how a particular caste stood in relation to the state. Here lies the chief value of his account. He may have erred in thinking that the classes were endogamic groups, though it is not impossible that the members of a class generally married only among themselves. It must be emphasised that, of the words used by the classical authors, γενος and φυλον alone connote the ideas of race and family. Both are borrowed from the language of Greek social

Value of the Account.

organisation and theory; γενος is used by Plato in the Republic. The terms really mean class or tribe. The two other words μερος and συστημ-α do not imply race at all. They can be used for any groups, organic or mechanical.[1] We cannot be sure of the exact words employed by Megasthenes, for the discrepancies in the four accounts attributed to him prove them to be summaries rather than quotations. In this connection 'class' is a better translation than 'caste.' Megasthenes indicates that there was a ruling class in India, small in numbers but dominating the rest of society through its talents and force of character. It filled the higher ranks of the civil and military services. It was the nobility, the aristocracy of the kingdom. It stood aloof from the large class which furnished the soldiery of the realm. It is again clear that the state employed large numbers of workmen in its factories and put itself in touch with other classes of people who performed certain services.

Life of the king.

The government of the country was despotic. The king not only reigned but ruled from day to day. Curtius, in his History of Alexander the Great, notes that the Indian king's palace "is open to all comers even when the king is having his hair combed and dressed. It is then that he gives audience to ambassadors, and administers justice to his subjects."[2] Strabo says that the king never slept during the day-time and that the hearing of cases occupied him the whole day.[3] All the same he lived in the greatest luxury and pomp. The splendour and magnificence of the palace far surpassed that of Susa and Ekbatana. "In the parks," continues Aelian on the basis of Megasthenes, "tame

[1] I am indebted to Dr. H. N. Randle of the University of Allâhâbâd for an explanation of the Greek terms.

[2] Quintus Curtius, History of Alexander the Great, Bk. VIII, Ch. IX.

[3] Strabo, XV, 1, 55.

peacocks are kept, and pheasants which have been domesticated, and among cultivated plants there are some to which the king's servants attend with special care, for there are shady groves and pasture-grounds planted with trees which the art of the woodsman has deftly interwoven. . . Within the palace grounds there are also artificial ponds of great beauty, in which they keep fish of enormous size but quite tame. No one has permission to fish for these except the king's sons while yet in their boyhood. These youngsters amuse themselves without the least risk of being drowned while fishing in the unruffled sheet of water and learning how to sail their boats."[1] Quintus Curtius has the following general description of Indian potentates:—"The luxury of their kings, or as they call it, their magnificence, is carried to a vicious excess without a parallel in the world. When the king condescends to show himself in public his attendants carry in their hands silver censors and perfume with incense all the road by which it is his pleasure to be conveyed. He lolls in a golden palanquin, garnished with pearls which dangle all round it, and he is robed in fine muslin embroidered with purple and gold. Behind his palanquin follow men-at-arms, and his body-guards, of whom some carry boughs of trees on which birds are perched trained to interrupt business with their cries. The palace is adorned with gilded pillars, clasped all round with a vine embossed in gold, while silver images of those birds which most charm the eye diversify the workmanship . . . (After audience) his slippers being . . . . taken off, his feet are rubbed with scented ointments. His principal exercise is hunting; amid the vows and songs of his courtesans he shoots the game enclosed within the royal park. The arrows, which are two cubits long, are discharged with more effort than effect, for though the force of these missiles depends on their lightness, they are loaded with an obnoxious

---

[1] Aelian, De Arim, XIII, XVIII.

weight. He rides on horseback when making short journey, but when bound on a distant expedition he rides in a chariot mounted on elephants, and, huge as these elephants are, their bodies are covered completely over with trappings of gold. That no form of shameless profligacy may be wanting, he is accompanied by a long train of courtesans carried in golden palanquins, and this troop holds a separate place in the procession from the queen's retinue, and is as sumptuously appointed. His food is prepared by women, who also serve him with wine, which is much used by all the Indians. When the king falls into a drunken sleep his courtesans carry him away to his bed-chamber invoking the gods of the night in their native hymns."[1] Court festivals had already sprung up. It seems a great festival was held when the king washed his hair.[2] Strabo says that "the care of the king's person is entrusted to women, who also are bought from their parents. The body-guards and the rest of the soldiery are posted outside the gates. . . . . . The sons succeed the father. Moreover, the king does not sleep in the day-time and at night he is compelled, as a precaution against attack, to change his couch from hour to hour. . . . ."[3]

The Administration.

Arrian says that the succession was hereditary but if the regular line failed, the most meritorious man was elected to the kingship.[4] It may be assumed that the selection was ordinarily confined to the royal family. The king had a number of counsellors, mostly perhaps the chief officers but occasionally others as well. Royal counsellors commanded the respect of the people. Besides these

[1] Quintus Curtius, Book VIII, Ch. IX.

[2] Strabo, McCrindle, India as described in Classical Literature, p. 75.

[3] Strabo, XV, I, 55.

[4] Arrian, Indika, Ch. VIII.

regular functionaries others were sometimes consulted. According to Strabo, the king employed messengers to obtain the advice of sages who lived in the jungles.[1] Megasthenes makes it clear that the king's government was carried on by a bureaucracy. From Strabo's version of Megasthenes, there appear to have been three classes of officers—the rural, urban and military. The first class was concerned with land revenue, irrigation which had been very remarkably developed, forests, communications and general supervision. To quote Strabo, "some superintend the rivers, measure the land, as is done in Egypt, and inspect the sluices, by which water is let out from the main channels into their branches, so that every one may have an equal supply of it. The same persons have charge also of the huntsmen, and are entrusted with the power of rewarding or punishing them according to their deserts. They collect the taxes and superintend the occupations connected with land, as those of the wood-cutters, the carpenters, the blacksmiths and the miners. They construct roads, and, at every ten stadia, set up a pillar to show the by-roads and distances."

Making allowance for possible exaggerations, it must be admitted that the activity of the state covered a wide range even over the countryside. Unfortunately, Megasthenes gives no idea of the structure of local government. But he makes it clear that the administration of the capital was of a very intense character. Candragupta's capital Pâṭâliputra, called Pâlibothra by the Greeks, was situated

Pâṭaliputra.

on the confluence of the Ganges and the Son[2] and, says Strabo, was "eighty stadia in length and fifteen in breadth. It is of the shape of

[1] Strabo, McCrindle, India as described in Classical Literature, p. 67. Bardesanes, Ibid., p 168.

[2] For the identification of the Erannoboas or Erinnoboas, mentioned by the Greeks with the Son, see Cunningham, Ann. Rep. Arch. Surv., XI, p. 154.

a parallelogram, and is girded with a wooden wall pierced with loopholes for the discharge of arrows. It has a ditch in front for defence, and for receiving the sewage of the city."[1] Pliny also remarks that it was "a very large and wealthy city."[2] The wooden wall was pierced by sixty-four gates and crowned by five hundred and seventy towers.[3] The capital dominated the kingdom which, as well as its ruler, was called by its name.[4]

The administration of the capital.

"Those who have charge of the city," says Strabo, "are divided into six bodies of five each. The members of the first look after everything relating to the industrial arts. Those of the second attend to the entertainment of foreigners. To these they assign lodgings, and they keep watch over their mode of life by means of those persons whom they give to them for assistants. They escort them on the way when they leave the country, or, in the event of their dying, forward their property to their relations. They take care of them when they are sick, and, if they die, bury them.[5] The third body consists of those who inquire, when and how births and deaths occur, with a view, not only of

[1] Strabo, XV, 1, 35-36.

[2] Pliny, Historia Naturalis, Book VI, Ch. 22. For the Greek idea of India's Geography see Ptolemy. Langlois, Géographie de Ptolémée, Paris, 1867, reproduces the map of India from the Ms. of Ptolemy's Geography preserved at the Vatopedi Monastery, Mount Athos.

[3] Fragment XXVI (McCrindle, Ancient India as described by Megasthenes and Arrian, p. 68). Waddell, Discovery of the Exact Site of Aśoka's Classic Capital of Pâṭaliputra, revised edition, 1903. Spooner, Ann. Rep. Arch Surv. of India, Eastern Circle, 1912-13, pp. 55--61. Codrington, Ancient India, etc., pp 20—22; for archæological details, Ann. Rep. Arch. Sur., 1912-13, 53—86: Spooner, Excavations at Pâṭaliputra.

[4] Pliny, Bk. VI, Ch. 22. Strabo, XV, 1, 35-36.

[5] The duties of these officers resembled those of the Greek Proxenoi.

levying a tax, but also in order that births and deaths among both high and low may not escape the cognizance of the government. The fourth class superintend trade and commerce. Its members have charge of weights and measures and see that the products in their seasons are sold by public notice. No one is allowed to deal in more than one kind of commodity, unless he pays a double tax. The fifth class supervises manufactured articles, which they sell by public notice. What is new is sold separately from what is old, and there is a fine for mixing the two together. The sixth and last class consists of those who collect the tenth of the prices of the articles sold. Fraud in the payment of this tax is punishable with death. Such are the functions which these bodies separately discharge. In their collective capacity they have charge both of their special departments, and also of matters affecting the general interest, as the keeping of public buildings in proper repair, the regulation of prices, the care of markets, harbours, and temples."

Thus the affairs of the capital were administered by a board of thirty officers which attended to some of the matters jointly and entrusted the rest to committees of five each. Through these officers the state controlled and regulated the whole economic life of the city, besides performing some other functions. In the Greek account these officers are called Astynomi which was in Greece the designation of some public functionaries who partly corresponded to Roman aediles. It is interesting that in ancient India, Greece and Rome alike public buildings, both religious and secular, were entrusted to a definite class of officers. The record of the census in ancient India is interesting but unfortunately we are not told whether it was confined to the capital or whether it obtained throughout the country. It is probable, though we have no documentary evidence to prove, that the system of administration which prevailed at Pâṭaliputra obtained in other cities also.

Justice.

Megasthenes remarks that Indians decided judicial cases according to unwritten laws. It seems that the Greek writer took Smriti in the literal sense of memory instead of in the sense of "the sacred tradition concerning law" which the term signified.[1] But in any case he makes it clear that there were judicial officers, for the king alone could hardly have disposed of the whole litigation even in the capital. We are told, indeed, that Indians seldom went to law but the elaborate provisions of substantive law and procedure in the Dharma Sûtras, for instance, tell a different tale. Megasthenes has feft on record that theft was a thing of rare occurrence.[2] But the Mauryan criminal code seems to have been a stern one. "A person convicted of bearing false witness," says Strabo, "suffers a mutilation of his extremities. He who maims another not only suffers in return the loss of the like limb, but his hand is cut off. If he causes a workman to lose his hand or his eye, he is put to death." Johannes Stobaios who lived probably about 500 A.D. records a curious ordeal on the authority of Bardesanes. There was a lake of Probation. If the accused denied his guilt but refused the ordeal of the lake, he was assumed to be guilty and punished as such. If he consented to the ordeal, "they conduct him to the lake with his accusers, for these also are subjected to the ordeal by water, lest the charge they prefer should be fictitious or malevolent. On entering the water they pass through to the other side of the lake, which is everywhere knee-deep for every one who goes in. Now, should the accused be innocent he goes in and passes through without any fear and is never wet above the knee, but, if guilty, before he goes

---

[1] Bühler, Indian Palæography, tr. Ind. Ant., 1904, p. 6.

[2] Strabo, XV, 1, 53.

far, the water is above his head. Then the Brâhmaṇas drag him out of the water and deliver him up alive to his accusers, considering him to deserve any punishment short of death. But this is of rare occurrence, since no one cares to deny his guilt through dread of the ordeal by water."[1] Details apart, a water-ordeal might have been known to Mauryan India.

The military administration.

The practice of committee government obtained in the sphere of military administration. There were "six divisions, with five members to each. One division is appointed to co-operate with the admiral of the fleet,[2] another with the superintendent of the bullock trains, which are used for transporting engines of war, food for the soldiers, provender for the cattle, and other military requisites. They supply servants, who beat the drum, and others who carry gongs; grooms also for the horses, and mechanists and their assistants. To the sound of the gongs they send out foragers to bring in grass, and, by a system of rewards and punishments, ensure the work being done with dispatch and safety. The third division has charge of the foot-soldiers, the fourth of the horses, the fifth of the war-chariots, and the sixth of the elephants. There are royal stables for the horses and elephants, and also a royal magazine for the arms, because the soldier has to return his arms to the magazine and his horse and his elephant to the stables. They use the elephants without bridles. The chariots are drawn on the march by oxen, but the horses are led along by a halter, that their legs may not be galled and inflamed, nor their spirits damped by drawing chariots. In addition to the charioteer, there are two fighting men who sit up in the chariot beside him. The war-elephant carries four men—three who shoot arrows and the driver." Megasthenes says that "a private person is not allowed to

[1] Johannes Stobaios, Physica, I, 56.

keep either a horse or an elephant. These animals are said to be the special property of the king, and persons are appointed to take care of them."[1] It is probable that for military reasons the state had the monopoly of these assets of warfare. It was again partly for military reasons that the government attended to the means of communication. Megasthenes speaks of the royal road leading from the western frontier to the capital Pâṭaliputra and measuring 10,000 stadia in length.[2]

Other officers.

The kingdom was divided into several provinces, each ruled by a sort of viceroy. The later Jûnâgaḍh inscription of Rudradâman records that Surâṣṭra or Kâṭhiâwâḍ was governed by the Vaiśya Puṣyagupta in Candragupta's time and by the Yavana Tushâspa under Aśoka. The former governor is designated Râṣṭriya, while the latter is called Adhiṣṭhâya.[3] The details are important for another reason. They show that high officers were sometimes chosen from any class of persons. Throughout the empire there were large numbers of spies who infested towns, camps and the countryside alike. Megasthenes implies that courtesans were employed to assist in the task of espionage. Then there were other numerous employees of state. According to Strabo, armour-makers and shipbuilders could work only for the king. For military reasons the two industries might have been state monopolies. Lastly, the state made allowances of grain to herdsmen and hunters who cleared the land of wild beasts and fowls.[4]

Agriculture seems to have received the serious attention of the state. Rudradâman's Jûnâgaḍh inscription

[1] Megasthenes, Fragment XXXVI; Strabo, XV, 1, 41—43.

[2] Ten stadia=2,022½ yards.

[3] Ep. Ind., VIII, No. 6, pp. 43, 46-47.

[4] Diodorus, II, 40, 41; Strabo, XV, 1, 39—41.

records that Puşyagupta formed the lake Sudarśana by damming a stream between a citadel and a rock. Its supplemental works were executed by Tushâspa.[1] Megasthenes testifies to the work of irrigation officers in rural areas. Besides the scheme of irrigation, there was the unwritten law that agriculturists were exempt from military and other service. "Nor would an enemy coming upon a husbandman at work on his land do him any harm, for men of this class, being regarded as public benefactors, are protected from all injury. The land, thus remaining unravaged, and producing heavy crops, supplies the inhabitants with all that is requisite to make life very enjoyable."[2] We are told that the agriculturists "pay a land-tribute to the king, because all India is the property of the crown, and no private person is permitted to own land. Besides the land-tribute, they pay into the royal treasury a fourth part of the produce of the soil." Most probably, Megasthenes is accurate in his latter statement. Hindu theory fixed the proportion of the state demand at one-sixth of the gross produce but in practice it might well have been raised to one-fourth. But there is nothing in indigenous sources to indicate that this revenue was supplemented by another tax on the supposition that the crown was the owner of the whole land. The distinction between land-revenue and land-tax does not seem to have occurred to the Hindu mind. It is probable that the assertion of Megasthenes applies only to the crown land which was merely cultivated for the king. In Strabo's version Megasthenes is made to say that "the whole of the land is the property of the king, and the husbandmen till

Agriculture.

Revenue.

[1] Ep. Ind., VII, No. 6. For the position of the lake, Arch. Surv. West. Ind., 1898-99, paragraph 49.

[2] Diodorus, II, 40, 41.

it on condition of receiving one-fourth of the produce."[1] But this is clearly wrong. 'Receiving' has, perhaps, been substituted for 'paying.' Arrian in his version of Megasthenes says that the wandering shepherds and neat-herds "are subject to tribute, and this they pay in cattle,"[2] though according to Strabo, they received something from the state. Again, he says that handicraftsmen and retail dealers "have to perform gratuitously certain public services, and to pay tribute from the products of their labour." This rule, of course, would not apply to shipbuilders, sailors and manufacturers of weapons of war who were paid by the state.

In the capital, and probably also in other cities, one-tenth of the prices of the articles sold went into the coffers of the state. "Fraud in the payment of this tax is punishable with death." There seems to have been a license-fee for vendors. "No one is allowed to deal in more than one kind of commodity, unless he pays a double tax." (Strabo.) The sale of certain articles manufactured in government factories brought something. (Ibid.) The presents made to the king must be reckoned among the regular sources of income. We learn from the Greek accounts that at the court festival of the king's hair-washing, they sent great presents to the king and vied with one another in displaying their wealth in that way.[3] Aelian has it that subjects presented animals like cranes, geese, hens, ducks, turtle, doves, partridge, etc., and also tamed tigers, panthers, apes, etc., etc.[4]

Megasthenes notes that philosophers who made any useful suggestions for the improvement of crops or cattle or

[1] Strabo, XV, 1, 39–41.

[2] Arrian, Indika, XI, XII.

[3] Strabo, McCrindle, India as described in Classical Literature, p. 75.

[4] Ibid., 143, 145,

for the promotion of public welfare were exempted from all taxation.[1] It seems that the Mauryas did not follow orthodox Brahmanic theory which would grant such exemption to all Brâhmaṇas. Only those who contributed to the public good received that privilege. There is a statement in Bardesanes that "the Brâhmaṇas pay no taxes like other citizens and are subject to no king." But from the context it seems that this refers only to sages and saints.[2] As already noted, artisans in the service of the state paid no taxes.

Exemptions.

There are a few statements in Megasthenes which seem to indicate that the Mauryan dominions included some protectorates, monarchical or oligarchical. The overseers, as a class, are said to "make report to the king, or where the state is without a king, to the magistrates."[3] According to Arrian, cultivators pay tribute to the king and the independent states.[4] Since the fact of Mauryan overlordship over the whole of North India is well-established, the only probable explanation of these passages is that there were some autonomous principalities within its bounds. It seems that the Western oligarchies, noticed by the Greeks, passed into the orbit of the Mauryan empire without changing their constitution or relinquishing their internal self-government.

Protectorates.

The foundation of the Mauryan empire marked an epoch in Indian history. It is probable that the requirements of the new large state led to some administrative changes. But the paucity of material makes it impossible to trace them in detail.

Bindusâra.

[1] Strabo, XV, 1, 39—41.
[2] McCrindle, India as described in Classical Literature.
[3] Diodorus, II, 40, 41.
[4] Arrian, Indika, XI, XII.

Of Bindusâra, the son and successor of Candragupta,[1] we know little. The range of his diplomacy extended as far as Egypt whose sovereign Ptolemy Philadelphos (285—247 B.C.) sent an envoy to the Mauryan court.[2] The Pâli legends concerning Aśoka's early life show that royal princes were appointed provincial governors. The high-handedness of local officers could sometimes provoke a revolt. Prince Aśoka had to be sent once to Taxila to pacify a popular insurrection. As he neared the town, the people came out to meet him and said, "we are not opposed to the prince nor even to the king (Bindusâra) but the wicked ministers (Duṣṭâmâtyâḥ) insult us."[3] But, according to tradition, history repeated itself in the reign of Aśoka. Once again a royal prince Kuṇâla went to quell a disturbance and met with the same reception from the people. The

Prince.

Pâli legends paint Prince Aśoka himself as a tyrannical governor indulging in calculated cold-blooded atrocities. But here the motive seems to be to create a Kâlâśoka or Caṇḍâśoka for contrast with Dharmâśoka to bring out the divine influence of Buddhism. Nor is it possible to be sure of the truth of the statement in the Ceylonese chronicles that the death of Bindusâra was followed by a fierce civil war, chiefly between the prince-viceroys of Ujjayinî and Takṣaśilâ.[4]

---

[1] For the Jaina tradition of Candragupta's abdication, migration to the south, and death by voluntary starvation in the approved Jaina style, see Rice, Mysore and Coorg from Inscriptions, 1909, pp. 3—9. For a criticism, Fleet, Ind. Ant., XXI, 1892, p. 156, also 287. If the authenticity of the tradition could be established, it would be interesting as showing the influence of religion on politics.

[2] Pliny, McCrindle, Ancient India as described in Classical Literature, p. 108.

[3] Divyâvadâna (ed. Cowell and Neil), p. 371.

[4] Mahâvaṁśa, V, 189. Divyâvadâna, 382. The accompanying tradition that Aśoka slaughtered his brothers—99 in number!—before he ascended the throne is evidently false, as Aśoka speaks of his brothers in his edicts. For Bindusâra, Jayaswal, J. B. O. R. S., II, 79—83.

Aśoka's empire.

After the conquest of Kaliṅga in the ninth year of his reign, the empire of Aśoka comprised the whole of India except the extreme south ruled by the Coḍa, Pâṇḍya, Sâtiyaputra and Keralaputra kings.[1] His edicts, primarily religious and moral, are unpolitical in character but they do indicate that the empire was not governed under a uniform system. Leaving out of account the independent territories mentioned in the edicts, it is possible to distinguish half-independent regions from the king's domains. To the former category, for instance, belong the Ândhras.[2] The regions lying along the frontiers of the empire seem to be autonomous and insecure. The king was particularly anxious to conciliate them. In the second separate Rock Edict Dhauli, he gives the assurance that "this alone is my wish with reference to the borderers . . . that they may not be

[1] For the accession of Aśoka, Dîpavaṁśa, VI, 18, 24: Mahâvaṁśa, V, 34. Buddhaghoṣa, Samantapâsâdikâ, p. 300. The comparison of the dates of the foreign monarchs with the regnal years mentioned in Aśoka's edicts yields slightly divergent dates of Aśoka's accession. Jayaswal (J.A S.B., New Series, 1913, p. 217) holds that Aśoka ascended the throne in 276 B.C. and was consecrated in 272 B.C. See also Senart (Ind. Ant., XX, 242). For the reign of Aśoka, Corpus Inscriptionum Indicarum, Vol. I, New Edition, by Hultzsch. For a criticism, B. M. Barua, Indian Historical Quarterly, II, March, 1926, pp. 88 et seq. Cunningham's old edition (1877) is still useful for topographical details. Senart, Inscriptions de Piyâdâsi, the first reconstruction of Aśoka's history from the inscriptions, is valuable. For its translation, Indian Antiquary. For further discussions, F. W. Thomas, J.R.A.S., 1914, 1915, 1919. Fleet, J.R.A.S., 1903, 1904, 1908, 1909, 1910, 1911. Gauri Shankar Hira Chand Ojha and Shyam Sundar Das, Aśoka kî Pradhâna Dharmalipiyâñ (Hindi) in Devî Prasâda Aitihâsika Pustakamâlâ, No. 4. Among modern narrations may be mentioned V.A. Smith, Aśoka (Rulers of India Series), 3rd edition; D. R. Bhandarkar, Aśoka (Carmichael Lectures, 1923). The Tâmil Saṁgam author Mâmûlnâr makes several references to Mauryan invasions of the south and says that the Mauryas advanced into Tâmil territory as far as Mohur (S. Krishnaswamy Aiyangar, Beginnings of South Indian History, Ch. II; also Contributions of South India to Indian Culture). But these references can only relate to Aśoka's predecessors. On the relations of the Mauryas with the south, see also Târânâtha, Schiefner, p. 89.

[2] Rock Edict XIII. Second Rock Edict, Dhauli, Jaugada.

afraid of me, but may have confidence (in me); that they may obtain only happiness from me, not misery; that they may (learn) this, that Devânâmpriya will forgive them what can be forgiven; that they may (be induced) by me (to) practise morality; (and) that they may attain (happiness in) this world and (in) the other world." The prince-governor and Mahâmâtras of Tosali are repeatedly requested and commanded to set the hearts of the borderers at rest. Special officers, called Antamahâpâlas, had to be appointed to deal with frontiers-men. Even the mild emperor had sometimes to hold out threats to some forest tribes. So faint was the line between autonomy and independence that the frontiers-men within the empire are sometimes confused with those beyond and both are indiscriminately referred to as borderers.[1] In the heart of the empire, too, there seem to be some regions which had not been brought completely under Mauryan rule and which are called Âhâla in the Rûpnâth and Sârnâth edicts. The extreme rapidity with which the empire was built up and the equally striking rapidity with which it broke up point to a confederate rather than a unitary state. Kaliṅga, for instance, owned the sway of the Nanda rulers of Magadha but it soon became independent and had to be reconquered, after a most stubborn fight by Aśoka, only to regain complete independence in the second century B.C.[2] After its incorporation into the empire, a region might retain its identity, in large part its institutions and even its old dynasty in a subordinate capacity and might be able to throw off the imperial yoke at the first favourable opportunity.

The Inscriptions which are the primary authority for the reign of Aśoka, betray a little Persian influence. As

---

1 Rock Edicts V, XIII.

2 Hâthîgumphâ Inscription, J.B.O.R.S., 1917, pp. 425—507.

Senart pointed out, their opening formula resembles the commencement of the proclamations of the Achaemenides from Darius to Artaxerxes Ochus. They come nearest the Naqsh-i-Rustam Inscription in which Darius bequeaths his precepts in policy, morals and religion to his successors.[1] It is possible, but there is no literary or epigraphic evidence to prove, that the whole system of Imperial organisation in India derived suggestions from Persia.[2] From the political point of view, the Inscriptions of Aśoka are valuable, firstly, for a graphic presentation of the practical ideal of the state which the emperor sought to realise and, secondly, for a few glimpses into the structure and working of institutions. In so many words Aśoka enunciates the paternal view of government. "For as one feels confident after having entrusted his child to an intelligent nurse, thinking 'the intelligent nurse will be able to keep my child well,' so the Lâjukas were appointed by me for the welfare and happiness of the country people."[3] He tells the officials of Tosali that confidence should be inspired in the people, "they should be made to learn that Devânâmpriya is to them like a father, that Devânâmpriya loves them like himself, and that they are to Devânâmpriya like his own children."[4] Again, "all men are my children," whose 'complete' welfare and happiness in this world and in the next he must promote.[5] Thanks partly to the vivid realisation of this idea, Aśoka rises above the narrow views of Brâhmaṇas or others and looks to the welfare of all. "I am directing

The Inscriptions.

Paternalism.

[1] Senart, Ind. Ant., XX, 255-56. V. A. Smith, Aśoka, p. 141.

[2] Infra, Conclusion, Ch. XVII.

[3] Fourth Pillar Edict, Delhi-Topra.

[4] Second Separate Rock Edict, Dhauli.

[5] Jaugada Edict I. Separate Rock Edict I, Dhauli. Sixth Pillar Edict, Delhi-Topra.

my attention to all classes"—"to those who are far and near."[1] Even the inhabitants of the forest were pacified and instructed.[2] Beyond the pale of humanity, the lower creatures came within the purview of the Emperor's activities. "On bipeds and quadrupeds, on birds and aquatic animals various benefits have been conferred by me, (even) to the boon of life."[3]

As a corollary of paternalism, the king must ceaselessly exert himself for the public good. "I am never satisfied," he remarks, "with (my) exertion or with (my) dispatch of business. The welfare of the whole world is an esteemed duty with me. And the root of that, again, is this, namely, exertion and dispatch of business."[4] No limits are recognised to the scope of state-activity. The "welfare of the whole world" was to be promoted in every walk of life and by all possible means. Though Aśoka's mission was one of moral amelioration above all, he was alive to the calls of material comfort. " . . . On the roads banyan trees were caused to be planted by me, (in order that) they might afford shade to cattle and men, (and) mango-groves were caused to be planted. And (at intervals) of eight kos wells were caused to be dug by me, and flights of steps (for descending into the water) were caused to be built. Numerous drinking places were caused to be established by me, here and there, for the enjoyment of cattle and men."[5] He encouraged the cultivation of medicinal herbs, roots and fruits. He arranged for the medical treatment of men and cattle not merely in his own dominions, but also in foreign lands.[6] For the relief of distress, charity was organised on

Labour for welfare.

[1] Jaugada Edict I.
[2] Rock Edict XIII.
[3] Pillar Edict II, Delhi-Topra.
[4] Rock Edict VI.
[5] Pillar Edict VII, Delhi-Topra.
[6] Rock Edict II.

a lavish scale on behalf of the emperor and his relations.[1] Members of the royal family followed the example of Aśoka. For instance, the second queen made endowments, registered in her own name, for mango-groves or gardens, almshouses and other charitable purposes.[2] In fact, the emperor was delighted to discover that people in general were imitating his good deeds.[3]

Moral welfare.

The higher concerns of life received more attention. In fact, the Seventh Pillar Edict seems to imply that the provision of material comforts was only subsidiary to the promotion of the Dhamma. In Rock Edicts IX and XI, Aśoka states that there is no such gift as that of Dhamma. His Dhamma, though free from all sectarianism, is not merely the sum of moral duties as Senart supposed.[4] It is also a way of life, an outlook on things in general, a certain measure of the values of social life. Aśoka admits that his predecessors had had the desire to pronote Dhamma, but, he continues, they had adopted no adequate measures and, therefore, men had made no progress. He thought seriously on the promotion of morality, "How could I elevate them by the promotion of Dhamma?" It occurred to him, "I shall issue proclamations on Dhamma, (and) shall order instruction in Dhamma (to be given). Hearing this men will conform to (it), will be elevated and will (be made to) progress considerably by the promotion of Dhamma." So,

[1] Pillar Edict VII, Delhi-Topra. Yuan Chwang (tr. Beal, Si-yu-ki, II, p. 91) says that it was inscribed on a pillar at Pâṭaliputra that Aśoka thrice gave away and purchased back Jambûdvîpa (India). The large bounty of Aśoka may have given rise to this tradition.

[2] Queen's Pillar Edict, Allâhâbâd-Kosam.

[3] Pillar Edict VII.

[4] Ind. Ant., XX, 260.

proclamations were issued all over the realm, including the frontiers. These were inscribed "either in an abridged (form), or of middle size, or at full length," according to local circumstances.[1] The promotion of Dhamma was the true conquest, always to be preferred to conquest by force.[2] There is, however, nothing revolutionary in Aśoka's Dhamma. In one respect, it is remarkably conservative. Aśoka constantly reiterates the injunction to obey one's parents and revere the elders.[3]

Liberalising elements.

The liberalising element in Aśokan ethics is the precept and example of universal toleration. Buddhist Śramaṇas and Brâhmaṇas alike are to be reverenced and supported.[4] Intolerance is declared to be a very short-sighted policy. "For whoever praises his own sect, or blames other sects,—all this out of devotion to his own sect,—if he is acting thus, he rather injures his own sect very severely. Therefore concord alone is very meritorious, (*i.e.*) that they should both hear and obey each other's morals. For this is the desire of Devânâmpriya (*viz.*) that all sects should be full of learning and should be pure in doctrine."[5] Aśoka himself honoured all religions.[6] He declared that "all sects may reside everywhere."[7] He should like the doctrine of all sects to be pure.[8] As part of the regard for others, Aśoka inculcates politeness towards relations, friends and acquaintances.[9]

[1] Rock Edicts XII, XIV, Girnâr. Sahasram Rock Inscription.
[2] Rock Edict XIII.
[3] E.g., Rock Edicts III, IV, VII, IX. Brahmagiri Rock Inscription.
[4] Rock Edicts III, IV, IX, XI, XIII. Pillar Edict V. It will appear that Śramaṇas did not always mean merely Buddhist priest or monk. Cf. Râmâyaṇa, Ayodhyâkaṇḍa, XXXVIII; Araṇyakâṇḍa, LXXIII; Kiṣkindhakâṇḍa, XVIII. See also Beal, Ind. Ant., IX, p. 122.
[5] Rock Edict XII (Girnâr).
[6] Pillar Edict VI.
[7] Rock Edict VII.
[8] Rock Edict XII.
[9] Rock Edicts XIII, IV, XIII. Brahmagiri Rock Inscription.

Aśoka declares that progress in Dhamma was promoted in two ways—by inducing to meditate and by moral restrictions.[1] Both were required for the operation of the humanitarian code on which the emperor had set his heart. He exhorts all to show proper courtesy and kindness to servants and slaves.[2] He imposes restrictions on the slaughter or mutilation of animals. The Fifth Pillar Edict gives the the long list of animals which had been declared inviolable for all times and places. It goes on to lay down that "cocks must not be caponed. Husks containing living animals must not be burnt. Forests must not be burnt either uselessly or in order to destroy (living beings). Living animals must not be fed with other living animals. Fish are inviolable and must not be sold on the three Câturmâsîs (end) on the Tiṣyâ full moon, during three days (*viz.*) the 14th, 15th and 1st (tithi) and invariably on every fast-day. And during these same days also no other classes of animals, which are in the elephant-park (and) in the preserves of the fishermen must be killed." On certain days no animals were to be castrated, no horses or bullocks were to be branded.[3]

Humanitarian elements.

As part of the Dhamma, Aśoka inculcates character-building. Every one must speak the truth,[4] guard one's speech,[5] moderate one's possessions and expenditure[6] and be pure and good.[7] Aśoka prescribes that regular instruction in Dhamma was to be imparted.[8]

Character.

[1] Pillar Edict VII, Delhi-Topra.

[2] Rock Edict IX.

[3] Pillar Edicts II, V.

Cf. Vinaya Texts, Part I, S. B. E., XIII, p. x; Kern, Manual of Indian Buddhism, p. 99. See also Rock Edict I which prohibits the slaughter of animals at sacrifices and promises that the slaughter of a few animals for the royal kitchen which still continued would be stopped.

[4] Pillar Edict VII, Brahmagiri Rock Inscription.

[5] Pillar Edict I.

[6] Rock Edict III. [7] Pillar Edict VII. [8] Ibid.

Besides exhortations, the emperor employed demonstrations to promote righteousness. It had long been customary to summon people by beat of drums to shows and various displays. In a Jâtaka, for instance, a king thus summons a crowd to witness the taming of elephants.[1] The Greeks noted that the sound of shells and drums called crowds to spectacles as also for war.[2] But under Aśoka, as the Fourth Rock Edict records, the sound of drums became the sound of morality, calling the people to sacred representations, generally from the life of the Buddha, or showing glimpses of heavenly bliss.[3] The whole administrative machinery of the state was utilised for the same purpose. The Third Pillar Edict requires all royal officers to help in the ethical mission in their quinquennial tours. Thirteen years after his coronation, the emperor created a special class of officers—a set of censors and missionaries—to further his aims. In the capital, in the country and in the extreme border-lands which were inhabited by Greeks (Yonas), Kambojas, Gandhâras and others, these officers "are occupied with all sects in establishing morality. . . They are occupied with servants and masters . . . for the . . . happiness of those who are devoted to morality, (and) in freeing (them) from desire (for worldly life). They are occupied in supporting prisoners (with money) . . . (if one has) children, or with those who are bewitched (*i.e.*, incurably ill) or with the aged."[4] Elsewhere he observes that his Dhamma Mahâmâtras "are occupied with affairs of many kinds which are beneficial to

Demonstrations.

Censors and Missionaries.

[1] Fick, op. cit., tr. Maitra, p. 189.

[2] McCrindle, Ancient India as described in Classical Literature, p. 68.

[3] D. R. Bhandarkar, Ind. Ant., XLII, 25-26. Khadirangâra Jâtaka.

[4] Rock Edict V, Girnâr.

26

ascetics as well as to householders, and they are occupied with all sects. Some busy themselves with the affairs of the Saṁgha, others with the Brâhmaṇas and Âjîvakas;[1] others with the Nirgranthas; others were ordered by me to busy themselves with various (other) sects; (thus) different Mahâmâtras (are busying themselves) specially with different congregations . . . my Mahâmâtras of morality are occupied with these (congregations) as well as with all other sects."[2] Itthijhaka Mahâmâtras were charged with the performance of censorial and missionary duties towards women.[3]

A few reforms.

In the course of his propagation of Dhamma, Aśoka attempted a few reforms which were necessary in his eyes. He prohibited the slaughter of animals at sacrifices, in defiance of Brahmanic sentiment. He prohibited Samâjas or festive gatherings where they indulged in excesses and where probably animal fights took place.[4] He condemned many "vulgar and useless ceremonies" which women often practised "during illness, at the marriage of a son or daughter or when setting out on a journey." In place of them he recommended the practice of Dhamma.[5]

Aśoka and religion.

These injunctions might have run counter to the received creed of some sections of the population. But their motive was neither intolerance nor persecution. It was purely moral and humanitarian. Whatever might have been the ultimate foundation of his Dhamma in the view of Aśoka,

[1] On Âjîvakas or Âjîvikas, see B. M. Barua, Âjîvikas; also Journal of the Department of Letters, 1920, Vol. II. pp. 1—80; Ind. Ant., XX, p. 362; Annals of the Bhandarkar Institute, 1926-27, Vol. VIII, Pt. II, pp. 183—88; A. P. Banerji Sastri, J. B. O. R. S., March, 1926, p. 53; D. R. Bhandarkar, Ind. Ant., 1912, p. 287. See also J. R. A. S., 1913, pp. 669—74.

[2] Pillar Edict VII, Delhi-Topra.

[3] Rock Edict XII.

[4] Rock Edict I.

[5] Rock Edict IX.

it is non-sectarian and non-theological as it stands. The phenomenon, indeed, is so striking that some scholars are inclined to believe that Aśoka was not a Buddhist at all.[1] Yet the Kausambi Pillar Edict, the Sârnâth Pillar Edict and the Saṁchi Pillar Inscription show that the emperor was not only a Buddhist but, what is more important from our point of view, he also assumed something like the headship of the Buddhist church.[2] Hindu literature and epigraphy prove that priests always exercised some influence on the Hindu state but their lack of organisation and independent means exposed them in their turn to the influence of kings and nobles. The Buddhist Saṁgha certainly had an organisation but it was of an intensely local character and, therefore, ill-adapted to become a real political force or to resist the encroachment of the state. It might be willing to accept the control of a monarch whose piety and holy zeal were above suspicion. Aśoka posed as the guardian of the Buddhist Saṁgha and as the arbiter of its internal controversies. Perhaps there was a real apprehension of schism in the Saṁgha at the time. "My desire," says the emperor in the Saṁchi Pillar Inscription, "is that the Saṁgha may be united and of long duration." He openly threatened disciplinary action against schismatics. "That monk or nun," so runs the inscription on the Sârnâth Pillar, "who shall break up the Saṁgha should be caused to put on white robes and to reside in a non-residence." The edict is communicated to monks and nuns; a copy of it is to be retained by the Mahâmâtras, another deposited with the lay-worshippers, who should study it on the fast-day service. "And as far as your

---

[1] E.g., H. Heras, "Aśoka's Dharma and Religion," Fourth Oriental Conference, 1926. For contrary views, Bühler, Ind. Ant., VII, p. 141; V. A. Smith, Aśoka, 35—39; F. W. Thomas, Cambridge History of India, I, p. 504. See also Fleet, J. R. A. S., 1908, pp. 491-92.

[2] For Aśoka's visit to Buddhist sacred places, Rock Edict VIII.

district (extends), dispatch ye (an officer) according to the letter of this edict. In the same way cause (your subordinates) to dispatch (an officer) according to the letter of this (edict) in all the territories surrounding forts." Elsewhere in the Calcutta-Bairat Rock Inscription he offers friendly advice and guidance to his co-religionists. "The Mâgadha king salutes the Saṁgha and hopes they are well and comfortable . . . Whatever has been spoken by the Buddha has been well-spoken. But, sirs, what would indeed appear to me, 'thus the true Dhamma will be of long duration,' that I feel bound to declare. The following expositions of the Dhamma, sirs, *viz.*, (1) the Vinaya Samukasa, (2) the Aliyavasas, (3) the Anâgata-bhayas, (4) Munigâthâs, (5) the Moneya Sûta, (6) Upatisa-pasina, and (7) the Lâghulovâda which was spoken by the blessed Buddha concerning falsehood,—I desire, sirs, that many groups of monks and (many) nuns may repeatedly listen to these expositions of the Dhamma and may reflect on them." Laymen and laywomen should do the same. In the Brahmagiri Rock Inscription, issued in the course of a tour, the emperor declares that he had not been zealous for a year but that after visiting the Saṁgha, he had become very zealous. It will be too much to infer from this that Aśoka became a monk, though there are Pâli traditions to that effect, but it is apparent that Aśoka was on intimate terms with the Buddhist monastic order. A Burmese Inscription at Bodh-Gayâ of the thirteenth century A.D. credits Aśoka with the erection of 84,000 Caityas.[1] In the paternal attitude, the moral and spiritual leadership of the people at large, in the wide tolerance coupled with zeal for his own persuasion, which Aśoka adopted, there was nothing original in idea. All this had been preached before him or was being preached during his epoch. As incidental passages in his

[1] Ep. Ind., XI, No. 10.

own testament indicate, something had been done by his predecessors to translate the ideal into practice. All the same the Aśokan state is of first-rate importance in the study of Hindu institutions. Amidst the surrounding twilight, it is lighted up by its own glorious bequest and displays its features so clearly. It represents, in a concrete form, the ideal which a Hindu state at its best aspired to attain. It shows more than anything else, that in ancient India the state recognised no limits to its activities; it would regulate everything. It concerned itself as much with the material as with the higher interests of its subjects. It is a culture-state. Under Aśoka it is a missionary state. Aśoka, as is well-known, dispatched missionaries beyond his dominions.[1]

Of the institutions through which the power of the state was exercised, the Aśokan edicts do not say much.

The king.

But they make it clear that the king was the central and most important institution. He thought and planned and advised; he exhorted and guided his officers incessantly. He toured incessantly. Other kings had indulged in vihâra-yâtrâs, pleasure or hunting tours but he had converted them into Dhamma-yâtrâs or spiritual tours.[2] He styled himself Râja. The grandiloquent titles which occur in later inscriptions had not yet come into fashion. Though supreme over the whole of North India and the Deccan, he was primarily the king of Magadha. As such he styles himself in the Calcutta-Bairat Rock Inscription. He has a personal designation of his own, signifying 'king,' beloved of the gods and of affectionate vision[3]— Devânâmpriya Priyadarśi Râja, or briefly Devânâmpriya Priyadarśi, Priyadarśi Râja, Devânâmpriya Râja or Devânâmpriya, as he variously styles himself. It was, perhaps, something like a dynastic appellation. One of the Ceylonese

[1] Rock Edicts II, V, XIII; Dîpavaṁśa, VIII; Mahâvaṁśa, XII.
[2] Rock Edict VIII.

Chronicles calls Candragupta Maurya Piyadassin. Daśaratha, probably a descendant of Aśoka, is called Devânâmpriya, in the Nâgârjunî Hill Cave Inscription.[1] The capital of Aśoka continued to be Pâṭaliputra but he transacted the business of the state wherever he happened to be (Rock Edict VI). The king maintained a huge establishment. The mention of Kâruvâkî as the *second* queen shows that in the harem the grade of queens was fixed. The king's brothers and sons, as the mention of their charities proves, lived in effulgence at Pâṭaliputra and other towns and were often associated in the task of administration.[2] Rock Edict I implies that before his conversion to the Dhamma, hundreds of animals were slaughtered daily in the royal kitchen. This means a huge palace and court establishment though it is probable that part of the meat was distributed free to people. The king seems to have moved about in palanquins.[3] In Pillar Edict V, there is an interesting reference to Nâgavana, the elephant-park of the king.

Aśoka seems to have had a chief minister called Amâtya in the Divyâvadâna. The kingdom was divided into a number of provinces, some of which, perhaps the more important ones, were governed by princes of the blood. The Inscriptions refer to four of the provinces. (1) Ujjayinî in Central India, (2) Takṣaśilâ in the North-west, (3) Kaliṅga or Orissâ with

Provinces.

---

[1] The Dîpavaṁśa (XI, 14, 19, 20, 25) calls the Ceylonese ruler Tissa Devânâmpriya. A Ceylonese inscription applies the designation to other kings. For the Nâgârjunî Hill Cave Inscription, Ind. Ant., XX, 364 et seq. Bhaṭṭojî Dîkṣita in his Siddhânta Kaumudî and Hemacandra in his Abhidhânacintâmaṇi take Devânâmpriya to signify a 'fool' or 'dunce,' but that meaning was obviously unknown in the time of Aśoka. See D. R. Bhandarkar, Aśoka, pp. 5—7; J. R. A. S., 1908, pp. 482-83. The name of Aśoka occurs only in the edict recently discovered at Maski in the Raichur district of Hyderabad-Deccan (Hyderabad Archaeological Series, No. 1, 1915).

[2] Pillar Edict VII.

[3] Rock Edict VI.

its capital at Tosali and (4) Suvarṇagiri probably in the south. From the fact that these were administered by princes and that Aśoka himself had been a provincial governor before his accession to the throne, it may be inferred that royal governors were the rule. The testimony of literature points to the same conclusion. Aśoka's kingdom might have comprised other provinces. For instance, the Jûnâgaḍh Rock Inscirption of Rudradâman seems to show that in Aśoka's time Girnâr was governed by a Yavana potentate Tushâspa. He was probably a Greek by origin who adopted a Persian name and sought service under the Mauryas.[1] It appears that, as a general rule, the province in which the capital was situated, was governed directly by the king. The practice of appointing prince-viceroys could not be free from danger. But, on the whole, it seems to have worked well. At any rate, it warded off the ever-present risk of provincial assertion of independence, so long as the central authority was strong enough.

Advisory Boards.

The king as well as the provincial governors seem to have had advisory boards called Pariṣads, which deliberated on all affairs of state, which acted as a link between the highest officers and the general body of royal servants, and which helped the latter in the discharge of their duties. The Pariṣads seem to have been composed of the higher administrative officers. Their numerical strength is not stated. It will appear that the constitution of these boards represented a further application of the principle which lay at the foundation of the military and urban boards described by Megasthenes. It seems that the Pariṣad freely debated on all questions and that members dared to differ not only among themselves but also from the wishes of the king. In the latter contingency, the matter was at once reported

[1] Ep. Ind., VIII, p. 47.

to the king whose word would, of course, be ultimately decisive. "When," says the king in Rock Edict VI, "in respect of anything that I personally order by word of mouth, for being issued or proclaimed, or again in respect of any emergent work superimposing itself upon the Mahâmâtras, there is any division or rejection in the Pariṣad, I have commanded that it should forthwith be reported to me at all places, and at all hours." The views of the Pariṣad, as soon as formed, were to be reported to the Emperor by the Prativedakas. In Rock Edict III, the Pariṣad is asked to advise and help the Yutas in executing his orders for the promotion of the Dhamma.

Below the viceroys and their advisory boards stood a number of officials divided into various classes. The edicts mention Mahâmâtras, Râjuka or Lâjuka, Virutha or Vyuṭha, Yuta and Puruṣa. It is possible that Puruṣa—"a man"—probably an abbreviation of Râjapuruṣa or king's man, at first only meant a king's servant and applied to all government employees. But in the time of Aśoka the term seems to be confined to a particular class of agents—supervisors, reporters or spies. The high officers of the realm were known as Mahâmâtras—a term which signifies minister or courtier in the Jâtakas. The status of Mahâmâtras may be inferred from the Inscriptions. In the Siddâpur edict, the emperor addresses himself not only to the provincial governor but, through him, also to the Mahâmâtras. In the Jaugada separate edict, he wants his commands to be communicated to Mahâmâtras. It is important to notice that the emperor kept himself in touch with the highest officers throughout the realm. In the Third Rock Edict certain Mahâmâtras are called Prâdeśikas, a term which seems to signify district officers.[1] It appears that a

Mahâmâtras.

[1] The Prâdeśikas are identified with the Pradeṣṭṛi of the Kauṭilīya Arthaśâstra by F. W. Thomas (J. R. A. S., 1914, pp. 383 et seq.; Ibid., 1915, p. 112).

province was divided into a number of districts each under a Prâdeśika. In the Dhauli and Jaugada separate edicts the term Mahâmâtras is applied also to Nagaravyavahârikas, probably judicial officers in towns. This indication supplements the evidence of Megasthenes and corroborates his general observation that towns had an administrative machinery of their own.[1] The application of the term Mahâmâtra to various classes of high functionaries indicates a supreme civil service of the kingdom, which guided the day-to-day administration and from which all important officers were recruited. When Aśoka started censorial and missionary activities, his Dhamma-Mahâmâtras were chosen from the same ranks or assimilated to them.

Râjukas.

Next to the Mahâmâtras in rank stood the Râjukas or Lâjukas. The derivation of the term implies that the Râjukas were fiscal officers but in the Edicts of Aśoka they perform judicial functions. As no other distinct revenue officials are mentioned, it is probable that the Râjukas combined both revenue and judicial functions, an arrangement which was known to Medieval India and still obtains. To the Râjukas or Lâjukas the king could communicate his commands directly or through his agents, possibly Mahâmâtras. As he puts it in the Fourth Pillar Edict, Delhi-Topra, "the Lâjukas also must obey me. They will also obey the agents who know (my) wishes. And these (agents) will also exhort those (people) in order that the Lâjukas may be able to please me." While their subordination is clear, they seem to have enjoyed wide authority. The Dhauli and Jaugada

[1] A terra-cotta seal discovered at Bhiṭâ near Allâhâbâd bears, in characters of the 4th or 3rd century B.C., the legend Sahijitye Nigamasa (Marshall, Ann. Rep. Arch. Surv. Ind., 1911-12, p. 31). As D. R. Bhandarkar has shown, Nigama can only refer to towns, not to guilds as some scholars thought. It is probable that towns early had seals of their own.

Edicts show Mahâmâtras exercising judicial functions in cities but the brunt of the judicial work seems to have fallen on the Lâjukas. "My Lâjukas," says the king, "are occupied with the people, with many hundred thousands of men. I have ordered that either rewards or punishments are left to their discretion, in order that the Lâjukas should perform their duties confidently (and) fearlessly, that they should bestow welfare and happiness on the people of the country and that they should confer benefits on (them)." To their care he entrusted the people as a parent entrusts a child to an intelligent nurse. On them he enjoined that "there should be both impartiality in judicial proceedings and impartiality in punishments."[1] In the First Separate Rock Edict, Dhauli, he expatiates on judicial fairness and impartiality at greater length. He wants the judges to follow not merely a part but the whole of his injunctions on the subject. "It happens in the administration (of justice) that a single person suffers either imprisonment or harsh treatment. In this case you must strive to deal (with all of them) impartially. But one fails to act thus on account of the following dispositions: envy, anger, cruelty, hurry, want of practice, laziness (and) fatigue. You must strive for this that these dispositions may not arise to you. And at the root of all this is the absence of anger and the avoidance of hurry. He who is fatigued in the administration (of justice) will not rise; but one ought to move, to walk and to advance. He who will pay attention to this must tell you: 'see that (you) discharge the debt (which you owe to the king); such is the instruction of Devânâmpriya' . . . If (you) observe this, you will attain heaven, and you will discharge the debt which you owe to me." Thrice a year or more frequently, this edict was to be studied by the officers

Justice.

[1] Pillar Edict IV, Delhi-Topra.

concerned. But to ensure its observance the king arranged the quinquennial or more frequent tours of Mahâmâtras—a sort of inspectors of courts, sent from the central and provincial capitals. "I shall send out every five years (a Mahâmâtra) who will be neither harsh nor fierce (but) of gentle actions (in order to ascertain) whether (the judicial officers), paying attention to this object . . . are acting thus, as my instruction (implies). But from Ujjayinî also the prince (governor) will send out for the same purpose . . . a person of the same description, and he will not allow (more than) three years to pass (without such a deputation). In the same way (an officer will be deputed from Takṣaśilâ also." From the last clause of the edict it will appear that some other duties were also entrusted to these inspectors but all along the emphasis is laid on judicial supervision. Aśoka made a gracious reform in the penal law. "A respite of three days is granted by me to persons lying in prison on whom punishment has been passed (and) who have been condemned to death. (In this way) either (their) relatives will persuade those (Lâjukas) to (grant) their life, or, if there is none who persuades (them), they will bestow gifts, or will undergo fasts in order to (attain happiness) in the other world. For my desire is that when the time (of respite) has expired, they should attain (happiness) in the other world."[1] So, Aśoka aimed at giving the unfortunate condemned men an adequate interval for petitions for mercy and spiritual preparation for the life beyond. None the less justice was to be strict and impartial. Aśoka's reputation for justice lasted through centuries. In the seventh century A.D. Yuan Chwang recorded the tradition that on the representation of the

Inspectors of Courts.

A penal reform.

[1] Pillar Edict IV, Delhi-Topra.

ministers and aged officers, Aśoka sentenced his "extravagant, wasteful and cruel brother" Mahendra to death.[1]

Imprisonment.

Besides death, imprisonment was a regular form of punishment under the Mauryas. In the Fifth Pillar Edict, Aśoka says that within twenty-six years after his Abhiṣeka he had granted amnesty to prisoners twenty-five times. Probably the amnesty was granted regularly on the anniversary of the coronation. As this was the practice of Aśoka even before his conversion to Buddhism, he was, perhaps, only following a time-honoured custom. Rock Edict V, and the First Separate Rock Edict, Dhauli, also testify to the king's concern for prisoners. The aged ones might be released, the infirm might be freed from shackles. In certain cases, the families of prisoners might be provided for. There was, however, a tradition long current in India that, in the early days of Aśoka, prison-life was a veritable hell. Yuan Chwang heard that shortly after his accession Aśoka built a prison enclosed by high walls, with a lofty tower at each corner, full of indescribable terrors and tortures. It was headed by a fierce wicked man. Later, it was demolished.[2]

Yutas, etc.

Below the Mahâmâtras and the Lâjukas stood the Yutas who worked in government offices, codified the royal commands and performed other secretarial duties. Rock Edict III requires the Pariṣad to order the Yutas to register (these rules) both with (the addition of) reasons and according to the letter.[3] It seems that Yutas, too, were appointed for definite territorial areas. The Third Rock Edict requires all the Prâdeśikas, Lâjukas and Yutas to undertake quinquennial

---

[1] Beal, Si-yu-ki, II, p. 91.

[2] Watters, On Yuan Chwang, II, p 88.

[3] As F. W. Thomas pointed out, the Yutas of Aśoka correspond to the Yuktas of the Kauṭilīya Arthaśâstra (J. R. A. S., 1909, pp. 466-7; Ibid., 1914, pp. 387—91).

tours, inspect the whole of their charge and transact administrative business as well as promote Dhamma. Viruthas or Vyuṭhas also toured on business of state but their duties are not clear.[1] Besides Yutas there were a number of clerks, Lipikâras, who are mentioned in Rock Edict XIV. To departments of government were attached a number of Dûtas or messengers whose duties are obvious.[2]

Purușas.

Alongside these officers stood the Puruṣas—'men,' that is, king's men, his agents—acting as spies, reporters and supervisors. They were acquainted with the king's wishes; they are said to control the Lâjukas (Pillar Edict IV), and to be "placed in charge of many people" (Pillar Edict VII). There were three ranks of them—high, middle and low (Pillar Edict I). Aśoka created another similar class of agents, called Prativedakas, who were placed everywhere, as he says, "in order to report to me the affairs of the people at any time, while I am eating, in the harem, in the inner apartment, even at the cowpen, in the palanquin and in the parks."[3]

Revenue.

Into Aśoka's fiscal system, the Rumindei Pillar Inscription affords just a passing glimpse. He made the village of Lummini free of taxes and required it to pay only an eighth share of the produce. It seems that every village besides paying a share of the gross produce had to pay other taxes as well, a surmise which is fully borne out by later evidence. If Aśoka is reducing the land revenue from Lummini to one-eighth of the gross produce, it may be inferred that the usual rate was higher. It might have been in the neighbourhood of the Hindu traditional one-sixth. A later notice in the Samantapâsâdikâ shows that customs yielded a big amount. Aśoka's daily income from the four gates of the

[1] Pillar Edict VII; Rûpanâth Edict.
[2] Rock Edict XIII.
[3] Rock Edict VI, Girnâr.

city of Pâṭaliputra seems to have been 4,00,000 kahâpaṇas. It is also said that he used to get 1,00,000 kahâpaṇas daily in the Sabhâ but this is difficult of interpretation. It may mean revenue from other sources.[1]

The end of Aśoka.

For the rest the institutions of Aśoka may be presumed to be similar to those noticed by Megasthenes. The Divyâvadâna has preserved a tradition that Aśoka's 'waste' of treasure on religion at length forced his ministers to depose him and instal his grandson Samprati on the throne.[2] It is impossible to verify the statement but it is possible that the dedication of the resources of the state to ecclesiastical interests provoked some discontent in political circles.

[1] Samantapâsâdikâ, I, 52.

[2] Divyâvadâna, p. 384. See also Târânâtha, (tr. Schiefner), p. 287.

CHAPTER IX.

After the Mauryan Empire.

A period of darkness.

After Aśoka Indian history enters on a comparatively dark period of five centuries. The Mauryan empire which was never a unitary state soon dissolved into its constituent fragments. The history of the independent kingdoms and confederations which arose is lighted up only by some isolated inscriptions, coins and literary records. A long series of Greek and Scythian invasions from the North-west, which met with varying measures of temporary success, makes the confusion worse confounded and defeats all attempts at the reconstruction of history. Owing to the meagreness of authenticated political facts, no connected account of political institutions in any region at any time during this period is possible. Only a few facts can be gleaned about the activities and institutions of state. The re-appearance of Mauryan institutions in a more developed form under the Guptas and their elaboration in the Smṛitis and the Arthaśâstra suggest that they continued to function with uncertain degrees of efficiency during the interregnum.

The later Mauryas.

The traditional genealogies of the dynastic successors of Aśoka show such divergence that a division of the empire after Samprati has been suggested as a working hypothesis.[1] In the

[1] The Puranic genealogies have been worked out by Pargiter (Dynasties of the Kali Age, pp. 27—30). These, along with other data in the Divyâvadâna, XXIX, Kalhaṇa's Râjataraṅgiṇî, I, 108 et seq., and Târânâtha, tr. Schiefner, pp. 48 et seq., are summarised in the Cambridge History of India, I, pp. 511-12. See also V. A. Smith, Early History of India, 4th edition, pp. 201—205.

absence of further evidence it is impossible to be sure of it. It is, however, clear that the Mauryas continued to rule at Pâṭaliputra until about 184 B.C. According to the Jaina tradition, Samprati was converted to Jainism and did all he could to further the interests of that faith. So, the tradition of the missionary state continued though the objective of the mission partly changed. Samprati also seems to have continued the tradition of large-hearted religious toleration. Similarly, another of the later Mauryas, Daśaratha, probably a grandson of Aśoka, extended his favours to sects other than his own. He allotted some caves to Âjîvakas.[1]

The Śuṅgas.

About 184 B.C. Brihadratha, the last of the Mauryas, was superseded by his over-mighty commander-in-chief, Puṣyamitra, the founder of the Śuṅga line.[2] The fact that the Śuṅgas were Brâhmaṇas proves that ambition or the force of events sometimes violated the rule of Kṣatriya kingship and that Brâhmaṇas, not content with advisory functions or influence, occasionally wielded the sceptre. The accession of Puṣyamitra to power was followed by a reversal of the policy of religious toleration which the Mauryas had uniformly pursued. Puṣyamitra seems to have been a champion of militant Brahmanism and a bitter persecutor of Buddhism. He is said to have burnt Buddhist monasteries throughout the Gangetic valley and to have slaughtered or dispersed the monks.[3] So, the policy of toleration, though generally observed in ancient India, was occasionally violated with a vengeance. In the days of the Śuṅgas North India was divided into a number of principalities, many

[1] Nâgârjunî Hill Cave Inscriptions, Ep. Ind., VIII; Ind. Ant., XX, 1891, p. 361.

[2] Pargiter, op. cit., 31, 70. Bâṇa, Harśacarita, (tr. Cowell and Thomas), p. 193. Jayaswal, J. B. O. R. S., IV, Sep., 1918. Puṣyamitra is also called Puṣpamitra. The former is the more correct of the two (Bühler, Ind. Ant., II, 362).

[3] Divyâvadâna, pp. 433-34. Târânâtha tr. Schiefner, p. 81.

of which acknowledged their suzerainty. The coins and inscriptions which bear the name of a Śuṅga as well as another name clearly bring out the feudal relationship. Bhârhut in Central India, Kauśâmbî, Pañcâla and probably Mathurâ were among the feudatory states.[1] The Hâthîgumphâ Inscription refers to the frightened "kings" of the Uttarâpatha and supports the same conclusion.[2] All through this period there are some non-monarchical feudatories in the Puñjâb and modern Râjpûtânâ, such as the Yaudheyas, Ârjunâyanas and Udumbaras. The coins of the first two date from a period as early as the first century B.C.[3] The tradition preserved in Kâlidâsa that Vasumitra, grandson of Puṣyamitra, was accompanied by a hundred royal princes in his campaigns is another evidence of feudalism.[4] A Śuṅga inscription says that the Senâpati Puṣyamitra performed two sacrifices.[5] It appears that the Śuṅga ruler revived the Râjasûya, imposed his suzerainty on surrounding principalities and only then received formal consecration and titles of royalty. The traditions dramatised by Kâlidâsa in his Mâlavikâgnimitra about the 4th or 5th century A.D. fully accord with epigraphic testimony and prove that until the completion of the sacrifice Puṣyamitra styled himself only Senâpati. He is said to have written to his son, "May it be well with thee! From the sacrificial enclosure the commander-in-chief sends this message to his son Agnimitra, who is in the territory of Vidisâ,[6] affectionately embracing him.

[1] Cunningham, Coins of Ancient India, 73, 79, 85—90; Rapson, Indian Coins, 11—13; Cambridge History of India, I, pp. 523—27. Lüder's Inscriptions, Nos. 687-88.

[2] J. B. O. R. S., III, p. 464.

[3] Fleet, Gupta Inscriptions, No. 1; Cambridge History of India, I, pp. 527—30; J. R. A. S., 1897, pp. 886 et seq.

[4] Kâlidâsa, Mâlavikâgnimitra, Act V.

[5] J. B. O. R. S., Sep., 1924, p. 203.

[6] Vidisâ was governed by Agnimitra, probably as his father's viceroy.

Be it known unto thee that I, having been consecrated for the Râjasûya sacrifice, let loose from all check or curb a horse which was to be brought back after a year, appointing Vasumitra as its defender, girt with a guard of a hundred royal princes. This very horse wandering on the right (or south) bank of the Sindhu was claimed by a cavalry squadron of the Yavanas. Then there was a fierce struggle between the two hosts. Then Vasumitra, the mighty bowman, having overcome his foes, rescued by force my excellent horse which they were endeavouring to carry off. Accordingly, I will now sacrifice, having had my horse brought back to me by my grandson, even as Ansumat brought back the horse to Sagara. Therefore you must dismiss anger from your mind, and without delay come with my daughters-in-law to behold the sacrifice."[1] The nine Śuṅgas who followed Puṣyamitra on the throne of Pâṭaliputra and reigned until about 73 B.C. are more names. Their dominions seem to have diminished considerably in extent.[2]

Kaliṅga.

Even during the lifetime of Puṣyamitra, the supremacy of the Śuṅgas had been challenged and their very existence imperilled from more than one quarter. Kaliṅga had, like Magadha, made a bid for suzerainty. Megasthenes reckoned the Kaliṅga force at 60,000 infantry, 1,000 cavalry and 700 elephants. Aśoka notes that in the Kaliṅga war 1,00,000 men were slain and 1,50,000 persons carried into slavery. The Kaliṅga power was only repressed, not destroyed. Sometime after Aśoka it threw off the yoke of the Mauryas as it had once thrown off that of the Nandas. Kaliṅga reached the zenith of its glory under the Jaina king Khâravela, who twice invaded the north, about 165 B.C. and about 161 B.C.,

[1] Kâlidâsa, Mâlavikâgnimitra, Act V, tr. Tawney, p. 78.

[2] Pargiter, op. cit., 30, 70; V. A. Smith, op. cit., 214-15; Cambridge History of India, I, 518--22,

threatened Pâṭaliputra, defeated Puṣyamitra, reduced him to vassalage at least for a short time and carried his arms up to the foot of the Himâlayas. The Hâthîgumphâ Inscription, which commemorates his exploits and achievements year by year and which now ranks among the most important sources of information regarding ancient India, supplies a few details of administrative importance.[1] Kaliṅga was not yet part of India proper according to the orthodox computation. Khâravela is spoken of as attacking Bhâratavarṣa. Like the Maurya, Khâravela seems to have carried out a census of the population. The inscription puts the population of Kaliṅga at 3½ millions. Considering the figure along with those of armies of various kings mentioned in history and examining the whole data in the light of modern statistics, the whole of India in ancient times seems to have comprised about 100 millions of souls. The education of a prince in Kaliṅga comprised a wide course —state correspondence, currency, state-accounting, law and custom, Dharma injunctions and "all the Vidyâs (arts)." Khâravela seems also to have been taught music. After his 15th year Khâravela was appointed Yuvarâja and consecrated king in his twenty-fourth year according to the rites of the Mahârâjya Abhiṣeka. It is possible that in Kaliṅga, and it may be, in some other parts of the country, the formal consecration was delayed until years of majority. The king assumed several titles—Aira (probably Ârya), Mahârâja, Mahâmeghavâhana, and Kaliṅgâdhipati.[2] This is the first authentic case of a king assuming lofty titles—titles which became loftier still a few centuries later. The

[1] The Hâthîgumphâ Inscription, known since 1825, has only recently been authoritatively edited by K. P. Jayaswal and R. D. Banerji (J.B. O. R. S., Vol. III, 1917, Pt. III, pp 425-507). See also R. C. Majumdar, Ind. Ant., XLVIII, p. 187; V. A Smith, J.R.A.S., 1918, p. 543; Fleet, J. R. A. S., 1910, pp. 824 et seq.; Rama Prasad Chanda, J. R. A. S., 1919, pp. 319 et seq.

[2] Similar titles were assumed by a later Kaliṅga king (Ep. Ind., XIII, p. 160).

capital was a grand city. Khâravela repairs its walls, gates and buildings which had been damaged by a storm, rebuilds the reservoirs and restores the gardens. On the banks of the Prâchi the king built a great 'palace of victory' at a cost of 35 lacs. At the conclusion of a dazzling campaign, he built towers, with richly-carved interiors, to contain trophies and presents. Like the Mauryas, the Kaliṅga kings attended to the needs of irrigation. Khâravela extended a canal which the Nandas had excavated three hundred years before. The king was anxious to please his subjects and win their loyalty. Khâravela entertained the capital by songs, music, dances, theatres, other shows and festivities. One of the interesting celebrations consisted in leading statues of the king's predecessors in procession. His charity was as unstinted as that of the great Mauryan conqueror of his patrimony. The record of the ninth year of his reign mentions his costly gifts. He gave a kalpa tree, a tree of solid gold, with leaves of gold, accompanied by feasts and gifts of elephants, horses, chariots with drivers, to Brâhmaṇas. The qualification of Brâhmaṇas shows the toleration and catholicity of the Jaina king's policy. He made special provision for the dwelling of Kṣatriya ascetics. He does something (which the mutilated inscription does not enable us to specify) for the Śramaṇas. Like Aśoka he prides himself on the respect he paid to all sects. Yet he had some enthusiasm for his own faith. He built numerous Jaina temples. He took pains to recover from Magadha the foot-marks of the first Jina which king Nanda had taken away. Khâravela's army consisted, as usual, of infantry, cavalry, elephants and chariots. In spite of his military activities and glories, Khâravela calls himself King of Peace and Prosperity, the Dharma King, the Bhikṣu (King). Warfare, in fact, was looked upon as an ordinary incident of kingship and did not seem to detract from one's claim to be regarded as peaceful.[1]

The rise of Kaliṅga synchronised with that of another power further south. The Āndhras or Andhras, first mentioned in the Aitareya Brâhmaṇa, VII, 18, 2 and noticed by the Greeks as a powerful people, with thirty walled towns, and an army of 1,00,000 foot, 2,000 cavalry, and 1,000 elephants, had their centre between the Godâvarī and the Kṛiṣṇâ.[2] Aśoka's Rock Edict, XII, mentions them among the southern borderers. On the death of the great Mauryan emperor, they became independent and, under the Śâtavâhana family, rapidly extended their power and measured swords with Kaliṅga. In about 28 B.C. the Āndhra king extinguished the Kâṇva dynasty of Brahmanic origin, which had supplanted the Śuṅgas at Pâṭaliputra about 73 B.C.[3] The Āndhras thus became a northern power and established an empire which, in its extension from north to south and east to west, recalls that of the Mauryas.[4] The coins which form one of the most valuable sources for the study of the Āndhra dynasties, show that different systems of coinage prevailed in different areas and that the imposition of suzerainty on a region rarely implied the extinction of its old coinage. It indicates that the Āndhra empire was not, any more than its predecessors

Āndhras.

[1] For a brief account of Khâravela's campaigns, Cambridge History of India, I, 535—38.

[2] Pliny, Historia Naturalis, Book VI, 21, 22, 23. R. G. Bhandarkar, Early History of the Deccan, p. 6. P. T. Srinivasa Iyengar, Ind. Ant., 1913, pp. 276—78. Nânâghâṭ Cave Inscriptions, Nos. 1112—20.

[3] For the Kâṇva dynasty, Pargiter, op. cit., p. 71. V. A. Smith, op cit., pp. 215—217.

[4] For the Āndhras, Rapson, Catalogue of the Coins of the Āndhra Dynasty, the Western Kṣatraps, Traikûṭaka Dynasty and Bodhi Dynasty; V. A. Smith, op. cit. 217—227; D. R Bhandarkar, Ind. Ant., XLVII, pp. 149 et seq.; Ibid., XLVIII, pp. 77 et seq.; Cambridge History of India, I, 529—35.

or successors, a unitary state; that it left local autonomy more or less undisturbed and that it partook of the nature of a confederation. It is beyond the scope of this work to unravel the tangled skein of Ândhra history which touched the peoples and dynasties of the greater part of India. The fortunes of the Ândhra line vary but it continues in vigour until nearly the end of the second century A.D. and lingers into the latter half of the third century. From the relevant coins and inscriptions, a few facts can be gleaned about the system of administration. The Ândhra Śâtavâhana kings generally assumed the surname Śâtakarṇi which became a dynastic appellation. An inscription of Yajñaśrî Gautamîputra calls him only Râja.[1] The high titles of the Gupta period were not yet in vogue. Queen Nâganikâ's Nânâghâṭ Inscription[2] shows the Ândhra king Śâtakarṇi allied by marriage to the Marâṭhâ king of Râṣṭrikas about the second century B. C. It proves that a woman, though she could not ascend the throne, could act as regent. Another inscription shows that Gautamiputra associated the queen-mother in his administration.[3] The Nânâghâṭ Inscription records the performance of certain great sacrifices in the course of which the priests received large numbers of elephants, thousands of horses, tens of thousands of cows, whole villages and tens of thousands of Kârṣâpaṇas. Twice did Śâtakarṇi perform the Aśvamedha sacrifice.[4] Records of this nature indicate that the revival of Brahmanism was aided by rulers. None the less the Ândhra kings were generally true to the Hindu tradition of toleration for all sects.[5]

[1] Ep. Ind., I, No. 15.
[2] Lüders, No. 1112.
[3] Arch. Surv. West. Ind., IV, p. 105. Ep. Ind., VII, p. 73.
[4] Ind. Ant., XLVIII, p. 77. Arch. Surv. West. Ind., p. 60. R. G. Bhandarkar, J. B. B. R. A. S., XIII, 1877, p. 311
[5] For the grant of a village to monks, Karle Inscription, Ep. Ind., VII, p. 57. See also Ep. Ind., VII, pp. 61, 64; VIII, pp. 60, 65, 71, 82, 94. Arch. Surv. West. Ind., IV, 102, 104, 107, 108, 110, 112, 114.

The cumulative evidence of coins and inscriptions brings out the existence of a ruling class which occupied a two-fold position. Aristocrats, styled Mahârathis, Mahâbhojas and Mahâsenâpatis, are clearly high officers of state at the capital, provincial or district governors. Elsewhere they appear to be feudal lords striking their own coins and making grants of land on their own authority. The line between direct employees of state and vassals is rather faint. Perhaps there never was a clear demarcation. One class faded insensibly into the other. The tendency to the hereditary transmission of office would bring the status of governors nearer that of feudal chiefs. The system of payment in land was another powerful factor in the same direction. An inscription of Siri Pulumâvi of the second century A.D. shows military officers holding large fiefs of land.[1] Marriage alliance between the royal and aristocratic families would tend to produce the same result.[2] Polygamy, always practised by aristocrats in ancient India, would accelerate the conversion of the whole aristocracy into a sort of clan. The government of the state would tend to become government by the clan. It is clear that there were numerous local dynasties under the Ândhra kings. Feudatories assumed titles like those of Cuṭukaḍânanda, Joy of the city of the Cuṭus and Muḍânanda, Joy of the Muṇḍas. In the inscriptions there occur a number of dignitaries, Amâtyas, Mahâmâtras and Bhaṇḍâgârikas, who correspond to officers with similar designations in other inscriptions and in literature. They acted as ministers, treasurers and heads of departments at the central, provincial or feudal capitals. There

The Ruling Class.

[1] Ep. Ind., XIV, No. 9.

[2] E.g., Arch. Surv. West. Ind., IV, p. 99. Ep. Ind., VIII, p. 91.

was a regular secretarial staff, comprising Lekhakas or clerks.[1]

The numismatic and epigraphic materials at our disposal do not permit a fuller picture of institutions, but the literary works dating from the second century A.D. or earlier, show that there existed an elaborate administrative system.[2] There is, however, one important conclusion to which the inscriptions lead, *viz.*, that the state, whether in its suzerain or feudal aspects was not the only form of regulation. Industry had organised itself on the principle of guilds. The Nâsik and Junnar Inscriptions prove the existence of guilds of potters, weavers, braziers, bamboo-workers, artisans, corn-dealers, etc., etc. Guilds acted as banks, receiving deposits at stipulated rates of interest. Their honesty and durability inspired sufficient confidence to induce rulers and others to entrust permanent endowments with them. They were not altogether unconnected with the administrative machinery of the state. Deposits and endowments were sometimes registered in the hall of the town.[3]

Guilds.

The history of North India was influenced during this period not merely by the exploits of the Ândhras but also by events outside India. The movements of the Central Asian Hiungnu and the rise of Parthia were factors of capital importance in the politics of the Middle East and therefore of North India. Parthia cut the Indo-Greeks from the West and, as their coins indicate, forced them to lose their individuality in the midst of Indian conditions. From the close of the

Menander.

[1] Rapson, J. R. A. S., 1903, p. 299; Rapson, Catalogue of the Coins of the Ândhra Dynasty, etc.; D. R. Bhandarkar, Ind. Ant., XLVII, pp. 69 et seq.; R. G. Bhandarkar, Early History of the Deccan.

[2] Infra, Ch. X.

[3] Ep. Ind., VIII, 82—88; X, App., p. 132, Lüders, No, 1133, 1137, 1165, 1180.

third century B.C. to the first century A.D. various Indo-Greek and Indo-Parthian dynasties ruled in the west of India but their history is obscure and little can be ascertained about their institutions. An interesting document is the Taxila Plate of Patika which belongs to about the close of the second century B.C. It applies the title Mahârâya--great king—to Moga whom Cunningham identified with the Moa or Mauos of the coins. So, Mahârâya, corresponding to Mahârâja, was the title of kings at the time in that region. Under the king Patika governed two provinces as satrap. A better-known figure of the second century B.C. is Menander, king of the Bactrian Greeks, who had established themselves in modern Afgḥânistân and the Puñjâb. About 155—53 B.C., Menander annexed the Indus delta, Surâṣṭra or Kâṭhiâwâḍ and other territories, occupied Mathurâ on the Jumnâ and carried his arms up to Pâṭaliputra. He was driven back to the Puñjâb. In spite of the defeat, Bactrian kings continued to hold various districts in the west of India for a long while.[1] Menander is the Milinda of the Milinda Pañha and the Tibetan Tangyur. His capital Śâkala (Siâlkoṭ) is described as "a great centre of trade, . . situated in a delightful country, abounding in parks and gardens and groves and lakes and tanks, a paradise of rivers and mountains and woods."[2] The position of Menander in Buddhist literature and the evidence of coins indicate that the Greeks or Bactrians were rapidly absorbed into the Hindu system. If they had any peculiar political institutions, they perished with their individuality.

---

[1] V. A. Smith, op. cit., 210, 227—29, 233—62. On the successors of Alexander the Great, Cambridge History of India, I, pp. 540—62. For Bactria, Bevan, House of Seleucus. For Parthia, Rawlinson, Sixth Oriental Monarchy. For Indo-Parthian Coins, Catalogue of Coins in the British Museum, pp. 35—62. For some surmises about Indo-Greek kings and viceroys on the basis of numismatic evidence, F.W. Thomas, J.R.A.S., 1906, p. 216. For the Taxila Plate of Patika, Ep. Ind., IV, No. 5.

[2] Milinda-Pañha (tr. Rhys Davids, S. B. E., XXXV), p. 2.

The Satraps of Surâṣṭra.

About the first century A.D. other foreign dynasties ruled in the western regions of India. Bhûmaka Kṣaharâṭa and, some time after him, Nahapâna who assumed the titles Mahâkṣatrapa and Râja exercised sway over southern Râjpûtânâ, Surâṣṭra and some other districts. The line continued until about 119 A.D., when it was extinguished by the Ândhra king Gautamîputra Śri Śâtakarṇi, who annexed its whole territory.[1] It is interesting that the foreigners did not take long to adopt the Hindu title of Râja. Their other title Kṣatrapa is the Sanskritised form of the old Persian Khshathrapâvan, 'protector of the land.' Hindu literature never recognised it but it has been traced on coins and inscriptions from the second century B.C. onwards. The emergence of a new title Mahâkṣatrapa which corresponds to the Hindu Mahârâja indicates an adaptation to Indian conditions. Rudradâman I is said to have won the title Mahâkṣatrapa for himself. The Jûnâgaḍh Rock Inscription of Rudradâman records that he deposed and reinstated many Râjas.[2] It appears that the assumption of the higher title was the symbol of the recognition of suzerainty. For a while the title Mahâkṣatrapa is in abeyance, according to numismatic testimony.[3] Possibly, the suzerainty of the rulers had been destroyed and they had been reduced to vassalage. The rule of Kṣatrapas and Mahâkṣatrapas seems to form part of the federal-feudal conditions which obtained in India. The Jûnâgaḍh Rock

---

[1] V. A. Smith, op. cit., pp. 220-21.

[2] For the inscription, Ep. Ind., VIII, No. 6; Ind. Ant., VII, p. 257; Arch. Surv. West Ind., II, p. 128.

[3] Rapson, Coins, etc., CXLI-CXLII. The distinction between the titles Râja Mahâkṣatrapa and Mahârâja Kṣatrapa is not clear. An Inscription of 180 A.D. (Ind. Ant., X, p. 157) brings to view two hereditary titles, Mahâkṣatrapa and Senâpati. See also Ind. Ant., XIV, p. 325.

Inscription is valuable also for some administrative details.

Administration.

The highest officials of the Mahâkṣatrapa seem to be divided into Matisacivas, counsellors or ministers on the one hand and Karmasacivas or executive officers on the other hand. Amâtya seems to be a general designation of high officers. One of the Amâtyas is a local governor. Amaca, another form of the same term, is the designation in the Nâsik Cave Inscriptions.[1] The Jûnâgaḍh Inscription shows that ministers sometimes dared to differ strongly from their master. When the dam of the lake Sudarśana burst, the ministers did not approve of the monarch's plan to get it repaired. The breach, they held, was too enormous and the expense would be ruinous. The people clamoured in despair. Rudradâman then elected to spend a huge sum of money out of his own private fortune and reconstructed the dam thrice as strong both in length and breadth. The Mahâkṣatrapa prides himself on having accomplished the undertaking without resort to additional taxation and forced labour. Incidentally, it appears that new taxes were often imposed and forced labour exacted for public works. None the less, the care for irrigation is remarkable. An inscription of Rudrasena I also seems to commemorate the construction of a tank.[2] The Nâsik Cave Inscriptions prove that the state levied numerous taxes. Besides, the digging for salt, unless alienated, was a royal monopoly. The visitations of the police were unwelcome to the people, perhaps because they meant some financial exaction. A village, granted for charitable purposes, is to be free from the presence of policemen and the interference of district officers. On the other hand, kings and his relations often displayed unstinted generosity. Uṣavadâta, son-in-law

---

[1] Ep. Ind., VIII, No. 8.

[2] Ind. Ant., XII, 1883, p. 32. Arch. Surv. West. Ind., II, p. 15. J. B. B. R. A. S., VIII, p. 234.

of Nahapâna, gave sixteen villages to gods and Brâhmaṇas, fed 1,00,000 Brâhmaṇas all the year round, built four quadrangular rest-houses, constructed wells, tanks and gardens, established free ferries at many places, founded water-places, halls for meeting, etc. The tradition of religious toleration was maintained. Uṣavadâta dedicated the village of Karajika to the support of all ascetics, "without any distinction of sect or origin" who might keep the Varṣa at the caves at Valûraka. He is said to have given 32,000 stems of cocoanut trees at a village to the congregation of Carakas. It is interesting to note that the money set apart for the cave of ascetics was invested in the guilds at Govardhana—2,000 in a weavers' guild and 1,000 in another weavers' guild.[1]

Another line of Śaka Kṣatrapas ruled in Mâlwâ with its capital at Ujjayinî in the first and second centuries A.D.

Other satraps.

They had to adjust themselves into the network of the relationships of suzerainty and vassalage which extended over the greater part of the country. The satrap Caṣṭana (c. 80—c. 110 A.D.) probably acknowledged the suzerainty of the Kuṣâns in the north. One of his successors, Rudradâman, warred with his father-in-law, the Ândhra king, suffered a defeat at his hands but got back from him most of the old Kṣaharâṭa territory.[2] From coins and inscriptions it appears that Kapiśa, Taxila, and Mathurâ were also centres of satrapal government.[3] The foreign origin of some of these rulers is undoubted but all foreigners were being

[1] Ep. Ind., VII, No. 7; VIII, No. 8.

[2] V. A. Smith, op. cit., 222-23; D. R. Bhandarkar, Kṣatrapa Coins from Sarvania, Ann Rep. Arch. Surv., 1913-14, pp. 227—45. See also Western Kṣatrapas by Bhagvân Lâl Indrâjî, ed. E. J. Rapson.

[3] Cunningham, Coins of Ancient India, p. 85; Numismatic Chronicle, 1889, p. 308; F. W. Thomas, Ep. Ind., IX, p. 139; Bühler, Ep. Ind., V, p. 54. See also, J. R. A. S., 1894, p. 541, ; Ibid, 1905, p. 784.

assimilated, culturally as well as politically, into the Hindu system. The coins of Indo-Scythian kings give Hindu as well as Greek titles. Azes is styled Mahârâja Râjamahata as well as Basileos Basileon Megalon. Gondophares, who seems to have made himself master of the country from Sindh to Arachosia in the second century A.D., has a type of coin on the reverse of which appears Śiva holding a trident. It may be noted in passing that in some of these coins the king and the heir-apparent have the same titles, while in those of the satraps, the king is designated Mahâkṣatrapa and the heir-apparent Kṣatrapa.[1]

The Kuṣân Dynasty.

Perhaps the most remarkable of all foreign dynasties which established themselves in India during this period was that of the Kuṣâns, which belonged to the Yüe-chi. The rise of the Yüe-chi to power in the north of India led to the fall of the Indo-Parthian principalities. The Yüe-chi king Kadphises I (c. 40 A.D.—c. 78 A.D.) ruled a large area from the borders of Persia to the banks of the Indus or the Jhelam. His son who has been called Kadphises II reigned from about 78 A.D. to about 110 A.D., probably conquered the Puñjâb and part of the Gangetic plains up to Benâres and probably annexed the whole of the lower Indus valley. "The conquered Indian provinces were administered by military viceroys, to whom should be attributed the large issues of coins known to numismatics as those of the Nameless king." He maintained diplomatic relations with China and was probably responsible for the Indian embassy which offered its congratulations to Trajan in 99 A.D. He was succeeded by Kaniṣka, one of the great figures of Buddhist history. The date of his accession

[1] Percy Gardner, Catalogue of the Coins of the Greek and Scythic Kings of Bactria and India, VIII, p. 104; R. B. Whitehead, Catalogue of Coins in the Puñjâb Museum, Lâhore, Vol. I, pp. 151-52.

has long been a matter of acute controversy. Most probably it falls in the first half of the second century A.D.[1] The kings of this dynasty adopted the title of Mahârâja which occurs in some inscriptions of Kaniṣka, Huviṣka and Vâsudeva,[2] and sometimes styled themselves Mahârâja Râjâtirâja as in their inscriptions of the years 11, 47, and 87.[3] Some early Brâhmî Inscriptions apply the title Mahârâja Devaputra to Kaniṣka.[4] After the additions made by Kaniṣka, the empire included a large part of North-western regions of India as well as parts of Central Asia. The complex interaction of Hindu, Zoroastrian, Gnostic and Hellenic elements was responsible for some new developments in Mahâyâna Buddhism and Gandhâra sculpture. Under Kaniṣka the foreign state caught up with the Aśokan tradition and stood forth as a culture state. During his latter days Kaniṣka adorned his capital Puruṣapur, modern Peshâwar, with a "great relic tower which seems to have deserved to rank among the wonders of the world. The superstructure of carved wood

[1] On the whole subject, V. A Smith, op. cit., 263—292; Rapson, Scythian and Parthian Invaders, Cambridge History of India, I, 563—92; R. D. Banerji, Scythian Period of Indian History, Ind. Ant, 1908, pp. 25—75; J A. B. S., New Series, 1908, pp. 81 et seq.; K. P. Jayaswal, 'Statue of Wema Kadphises and Kushân Chronology'; J. B. O. R. S, V, p. 511; Ibid., VI, pp. 12—22. Fleet, in various papers, J. R. A. S., 1903, 1905, 1906, 1913, places Kaniṣka in the first century A.D. R. C. Majumdar, (Journal of the Department of Letters, Vol. I, 1920, pp. 65 et seq.) places Kaniṣka after 214 A.D. For fascinating but inconclusive debates on the Kaniṣka question, J. R. A. S., 1913, pp. 627—50, 911—1042.

[2] Ann. Rep. Arch. Surv.. III, Nos. 4, 9, 16, pp. 31, 32, 34. Lüders, J. R. A. S., 1909, p. 645.

[3] Ann. Rep. Arch. Surv., III, Nos. 12, 18, pp. 33, 35. Ind. Ant., X, 326.

[4] Ep. Ind., IX, No. 33.

For a statue of Kaniṣka, J. Ph. Vogel, Journal of the Puñjâb Historical Society. Vol. II, No. 1, pp. 39 et seq.

rose in thirteen storeys to a height of at least 400 feet, surmounted by a mighty iron-pinnacle . . . A monastery of exceptional magnificence which stood by its side was still flourishing as a place of Buddhist education in the ninth century."[1] According to the Buddhist traditions of Tibet, China and Mongolia, Kaniṣka held a great Buddhist council in Kuṇḍalavana near the capital of Kashmir. He is said to have renewed Aśoka's donation of the kingdom of Kashmîr to the Buddhist Church.[2] Though a patron of Buddhism, Kaniṣka was somewhat of an eclectic. In any case, he recognised and favoured other sects as well. On some of his coins appears the figure of Śiva.[3] Similar electicism is apparent from the coins of Wema Kadphises, Huviṣka and Vâsudeva.[4] The Hindu name of the last king is significant. The Mâṇikiâla Inscription which designates Kaniṣka as a Mahârâja brings a few government officials into view. The Daḍanayago may be a general but is more probably a judicial officer. The Navakarmiga is the superintendent of buildings. The Vihâra-karavhaena is the architect of Vihâras.[5]

[1] Song-yun, Beal, Si-yu-ki, I, p. ciii; Yuan Chwang, ibid, 99; Watters, I, 204, 208; Alberûnî, tr. Sachau, II, p. 11; for the monastery, Yuan Chwang, Si-yu-ki, I, 103; Kielhorn, Ghosrâwa Inscription, Ind. Ant., XVII, pp. 307—12. For Kaniṣka's monasteries for Chinese hostages, Beal, Si-yu-ki, I, 56, 173; Watters, On Yuan Chwang, I, 203 et seq.

[2] Yuan Chwang, Beal, I, 117, 151; Watters, I, 270—78; I-tsing, Buddhist Practices, etc., tr. Takakusu, p. xxi; Târânâtha, tr. Schiefner, p. 58; Takakusu, J. R. A. S., 1904, p. 414; Eastern Monachism, p. 188.

[3] British Museum Catalogue of the Coins of the Greek and Scythian Kings of India, p. 132; Catalogue of Coins in the Punjâb Museum, Lâhore, p. 187.

[4] British Museum Catalogue of the Coins of the Greek and Scythian Kings of India, pp. 124 ff; Catalogue of Coins in the Puñjâb Museum, Lâhore, p. 183.

[5] Mâṇikiâla Inscription, Lüders, J. R. A. S., 1909, p. 645.

End of Kaniṣka.

There is a legend that Kaniṣka, advised by a minister named Mâthar, conquered many regions. When he proposed to complete his "universal conquest" by the subjugation of the North, the king's people said, "the king is greedy, cruel and unreasonable; his campaigns and continued conquests have wearied the mass of his servants. He knows not how to be content, but wants to reign over the four quarters. The garrisons are stationed on distant frontiers and our relatives are far from us. Such being the situation, we must agree among ourselves, and get rid of him. After that we may be happy." As he was ill, they covered him with a quilt, a man sat on top of him and the king died on the spot.[1] The death of Kaniṣka occurred probably about 160 A.D. His successors lingered into the third century A.D.

Small principalities.

During this period there were some very small principalities, known after cities or districts, which perhaps acknowledged the suzerainty of some potentates but which were autonomous enough to issue coins of their own. Some Taxila coins have on the reverse the legend Nigamâ[2] which can only refer to cities. There are other coins which bear the legend Janapadasa, which refers to districts.[3] The Bhaṭṭiprolu Inscriptions show nigamas or towns, grâmas or villages and goṣṭhis or groups enjoying a high degree of autonomy.[4]

---

[1] Śrî Dharma Piṭaka, tr. Sylvain Lévi, Notes, etc.; Ind. Ant., 1903, p. 388.

[2] Cunnnigham, Coins of Ancient India, p. 63.

[3] Catalogue of Coins in the Indian Museum, 164-65, 179-80; J. R. A. S., 1907, pp. 92-93; Ibid., 1908, pp. 540-41.

[4] Ep. Ind., II, No. 25

The Mathurâ Jaina Inscription of the year 4 (Lüders, No. 48) refers to a lady who was the wife of a village headman and also daughter-in-law of a village headman. It indicates that the office *might pass from father to son.*

Records of the third and fourth centuries A.D. support the hypothesis of federal-feudalism as the principle of political organisation in ancient India. Sylvain Lévi points out that the Chinese account of an embassy to Siam in the third century A.D. describes Muruṇḍarâja of India as a powerful monarch whose suzerainty was acknowledged by distant kingdoms. His capital might have been somewhere in Eastern India. The Allâhâbâd Inscription of Samudragupta mentions Daivaputra, Ṣâhi, and Ṣâhânuṣâhi as the titles of the chiefs and kings subjugated by the Gupta king. Ṣâhânuṣâhi is the Iranian title of suzerain and corresponds to the Hindu Mahârâjâdhirâja of the Gupta epoch as Ṣâhi corresponds to Râja or Mahârâja.

Aśvaghoṣa.

The best traditions of Kushân rule are perhaps reflected in the writings of Aśvaghoṣa, one of the greatest figures in the Sanskrit Literature of Buddhism. Sprung from a Brâhmaṇa family, he was a master of Sanskrit learning. According to tradition, he was carried off by Kaniṣka from Pâṭaliputra to adorn his court at Puruṣapur. At any rate, the two were contemporaries. As Sylvain Lévi puts it, Aśvaghoṣa's Sutrâlaṅkâra, along with his Buddhacarita, constitutes the first chronological land-mark in the literary history of India. He is probably the forerunner of Kâlidâsa and stands at the head of classical Sanskrit literature.[1] According to Târânâtha, he is identical with the author Mâtṛicetâ. In his Saundara Nandam Kâvyam, Aśvaghoṣa testifies to the supreme need, the indispensability, of the kingship.

[1] For the beginnings of Classical Sanskrit Literature, Macdonell, History of Sanskrit Literature, 318—324. Keith, Classical Sanskrit Literature, 7—21. Sylvain Lévi (tr.) Indian Antiquary, XXXIII et seq. G. K. Nariman, Literary History of Sanskrit Buddhism. The theories of Max Müller and R. G. Bhandarkar on the Sanskrit Renaissance *in the 4th, 5th or 6th century A.D. are exploded by the discovery of the works of Aśvaghoṣa and Bhâsa and the epigraphic researches of Fleet, Bühler and others.*

But the sceptre is always to be wielded for the sake of virtue and not for the sake of selfish gratification. The king should be the guide and teacher of his subjects.[1] Here is a possible reference to Kaniṣka's policy. In the Buddhacarita too, Aśvaghoṣa paints Śuddhodana as the mighty and glorious leader of his people.[2] "He illumined his people on every side, showing them the paths which they were to follow." Here, too, he emphasises the need of a thorough education for the prince.[3] In the Sutrâlaṅkâra, a collection of pious legends of the Jâtaka and Avadâna type, Aśvaghoṣa repeats the same ideas and gives an interesting list of the subjects—literary, military, and conventional—which a prince should study. It includes grammar, writing, rhetoric, eloquence, the Vedas, literature, astronomy, medicine, sacrifices; music and song, playing on the tambourine, playing on the conch, dancing and laughter, computation, chess, dice, the science of precious stones and valuable materials for clothing, silk, sealing, weaving, wax work, strategy, sewing, sculpture, painting, arrangement of garlands, interpretation of dreams, interpretation of the flight of birds, reading horoscopes; the training of elephants, domesticating of horses, carrying the lance, jumping, running and fording a river, archery, rules of battle array, strategy, etc. In another work Vajraśuci, which is attributed, rather doubtfully, to Aśvaghoṣa, caste is attacked on psychological grounds. All human beings are equal "in respect of joy and sorrow, love, insight, manners and ways, death, fear and life."[4] Buddhism could never uproot caste but it is probable that under Buddhist regime it had not the same political importance as Brahmanical literature might lead us to suppose.

[1] Aśvaghoṣa, Saundara Nandam Kâvyam, Canto I, pp. 7-8, Canto II, p. 9.

[2] Buddhacarita, I, 12.

[3] Ibid., II, 24; see also I, 14; II, 42, 44.

[4] G. K. Nariman, op. cit., 36—40, 200-201.

It is during the period reviewed in this chapter that we obtain our first glimpse of the political institutions of the extreme south. The evidence of literature shows that the hereditary monarch was surrounded by five assemblies—of the people, priests, physicians, astrologers or augurs and ministers. Their functions are specified.[1] The subject is not altogether free from doubt but it is clear that southern institutions, even in their first-known stages, differed from those of the north. In spite of manifold points of contact and resemblance, the two pursue different lines of development all through history.

The South.

[1] V. Kanakasabhai Pillai, *Tâmils Eighteen Hundred Years Ago*, pp. 119-20.

CHAPTER X.

The Early Dharma S'âstras, the Arthas'âstras and other Literature.

The period between the fall of the Mauryas and the supremacy of the Guptas was remarkable for the rise of Smṛitis or books of traditional law, etc., Arthaśâstra, or science of welfare and classical Sanskrit literature. From these literary sources it is possible to glean many administrative details which usefully supplement the meagre information yielded by the coins and inscriptions of the period. Theoretical works have, of course, to be used with the utmost caution and never taken as an exact description of the conditions of any period but, as expositions of ideals and even utopias, they inevitably furnish a peep into the institutions they would improve.

The value of theoretical works.

The Smṛitis or Dharma Śâstras occupy a most important place in the Hindu literature on regulation of life,—on religion, ritual, domestic and social life, law, custom and polity. Unfortunately, it is impossible to ascertain their exact dates. Their origin perplexed even ancient writers. For instance, Kumârila Bhaṭṭa remarks in his Tantra Vârtika that owing to the scattering of Śâkhâs, human error or carelessness and the variety of topics, the beginnings of Smṛitis could not be traced. The opinions of modern scholars ranged over an extraordinarily long period. Sir William Jones, for instance, referred Manu to 1200 B.C. Later, some scholars brought him down to the twelfth or thirteenth

The Smṛitis.

century A.D. It is now generally agreed that the Smṛitis assumed their present shape at various epochs in the first millenium of the Christain Era. R. G Bhandarkar placed them in the Kuṣân-Gupta period, that is, between the middle of the second and the end of the fifth century A.D.[1] Hopkins refers Manu to the commencement of or even before the Christian era, while he assigns Viṣṇu to the third, Yâjñavalkya to the fourth and Nârada to the fifth century A.D.[2] Jolly thinks that Manu cannot be later than the second or third century A.D. while Viṣṇu cannot be earlier than the third. He would place Yâjñavalkya in the fourth and Nârada about the commencement of the sixth century while referring Brihaspati and Kâtyâyana to the sixth or seventh century A.D. Bühler, after a searching examination, came to the conclusion that Manusmṛiti existed, pretty much as we know it, in the second century A.D.[3] Manu's references to the Kambojas, Yavanas and Śâkas bar an earlier date for the work as a whole.

The character of Smṛitis.

The Smṛitis, though distinct from Śruti or Revelation, claim to be grounded in Vedic Dharma. In his Jaiminiya Nyâyamâlâvistara, Mâdhavâcârya declares that Smritis are digests collecting and epitomising ordinances which lie scattered in the Vedas. As a matter of fact, they have moved far from the Vedic tradition and only reflect the ideal or positive morality of the various regions in which they arose during the ages following the Dharma Sûtras. Thus Manu belongs to the Gangetic plains, Nârada probably to Nepal, and Yâjñavalkya to Mithilâ in modern Bihâr. The Smṛitis are

---

[1] R. G. Bhandarkar, J. B. B. R. A. S., Vol. XX. No. LVI, p. 356.

[2] Hopkins, Cambridge History of India, Vol. I, p. 279.

[3] Bühler, Introduction to the Laws of Manu, translated with extracts from seven Commentaries. See also the Introduction to A. C. Burnell's translation, entitled 'The Ordinances of Manu.'

attached to different Vedic Schools but the classification of them into Sâtvika, Râjasika and Tâmasika in the Padma Purâṇa is merely fanciful.[1] The discrepancies due to differences of sect, tradition, age and locality perplexed the later writers who were at pains to avoid confusion. The Mîmâṁsâ rules, though relating primarily to ritual, were extended to law, and formed a recognised canon of interpretation. That subject was reduced to what is called a Darśana or system of philosophy. The Pûrva Mîmâṁsâ declares that of two contradictory Smriti texts, the one supported by Śruti shall prevail. But it was argued by some that the other text might accord with a Śruti text which had disappeared. The Purva Mîmâṁsâ replies that a known Śruti text takes precedence of one unknown. It goes further and lays down that a Smriti text, though uncontradicted by Śruti, is liable to be rejected if it can be traced to an unworthy motive.[2] On the other hand, in his Mımâṃsâ Sûtras, Jaimini denies to local usage any authority as a source of law independently of Śruti and Smriti. A similar opinion is expressed by Mâdhavâcârya in his Jaiminiya Nyâyamâlâvistara, though in his Vyavahâra Khaṇḍa he comes round to the different view of Nârada, Kâtyayana and others. The Skanda Purâṇa expressly admits that where the Vedas and Smritis are silent, the Dharmas should be ascertained by observation of the customs of families and countries. Commenting on Manu, Medhâtithi remarks that Âcâra, as understood in Smṛitis, referred to Śiṣṭa practices uncontradicted by Śruti or Smriti. Vijnâneśvara, commenting on Yâjñavalkya, goes further and interdicts action, which, though supported by Smṛitis, is disapproved by usage. Yâjñavalkya himself said that in a conflict between two Smriti texts, reason prevailed according to usage. Nârada expresses himself in a

[1] Padma Purâṇa, Uttarakhaṇḍa, Ch. XLIII.

[2] Pûrva Mîmâṁsâ, I, Part III, 3-4.

similar strain. But later writers insist that the function of reason is limited to the reconciliation of conflicting texts.[1] From this whole scholastic discussion it follows that the provisions of Smṛitis take account both of recognised ideals and current usage, that custom, social or political, was often recognised as authoritative in ancient India and that the state, in spite of its absorbing activity, had to leave a good deal to groups and associations, and to the operation of general conditions.

Manu.

Of all the Smritis that of Manu is admittedly the most important and authoritative. Bṛihaspati remarks that the first rank belongs to Manu, because he has embodied the essence of the Veda in his work, and that the Smriti text which is opposed to Manu is not approved. The Dharma Śâstra of Manu is perhaps based on the Mânava Dharma Sûtra which has disappeared. The Mânavas represent one of the six subdivisions of the Maitrâyaṇî School of the Kriṣṇa Yajurveda. According to a tradition, Manusmriti is addressed to Râjas and other such personages and not to scholars. There are many verses common to the Smṛiti and the Mahâbhârata. Manu treats of the whole of life, and, differing from others, declares that the chief good consists in the combination of Artha, Dharma and Kâma. Needless to say, he is wedded to the recognised Dharma of castes and stages and declares, in a most pronounced and dogmatic fashion, for the supremacy of Brâhmaṇas. Whether ignorant or learned, whether following mean or noble occupations, a Brâhmaṇa is a great divinity. Kṣatriyas derive their origin from Brâhmaṇas and are to be restrained if they become overbearing towards the latter. Learning is the predominant occupation of a Brâhmaṇa, but Manu, obviously compromising with facts, allows him, in 'distress,' that is, in emergencies, to follow

[1] Nârada, I, 40; Yâjñavalkya, XXI; Vijnâneśvara on Yâjñavalkya, I, V, 136.

agriculture, gleaning of corn, etc.[1] From Manu's list of Brâhmaṇas who may not be invited to Śrâddha, it appears that some members of the highest caste worked as players, usurers, actors, singers, makers of bows and arrows, keepers of elephants, camels, horses, cattle, tamers of birds, architects, tradesmen, agriculturists, carriers of corpses, butchers, etc., etc.[2] The Śûdras are barred from all sacred learning. By themselves Śûdras can never form a stable society. A kingdom which is destitute of twice-born people, which contains very many Śûdras and atheists, is soon afflicted with disease and famine and utterly perishes. Brâhmaṇas should not reside in such a state. Manu makes no secret of his contempt for manual labour.[3] He wants the king, that is, the state, to enforce his scheme of caste-superiority and social duties. In particular, Vaiśyas and Śûdras should be compelled to perform their prescribed jobs, for if they swerved from their duties, the whole world would be thrown into confusion.[4] It is not impossible that Manu's advice was partially followed in practice. It was about this period that Gautamiputra Śâtakarṇi prided himself on his restoration of caste rules.

Law.

Besides Śruti and Smṛiti, Manu admits the customs of virtuous men and âtmatuṣṭi or one's own conscience as sources of law. Here is a round-about admission of custom and state-decrees as binding on the people. When he accords equal authority to two conflicting sacred texts, he can only be held to imply that reason or usage was to be the deciding factor. In his chapter on Civil and Criminal Law he is more explicit:

[1] On the whole subject, Manu, I, 21, 89, 91, 96, 98, 100-101; II, 224; IV, 4; VI, 34—37; IX, 313—323; XII, 88—90.

[2] Ibid., III, 151 et seq.

[3] Ibid., IV, 81, 61; VIII, 22; also, III, 154—167; II, 155, 168; IV, 4—6; V, 83-84; VIII, 413-414. But also II, 238, in a slightly different strain.

[4] Ibid., III, 13; VIII, 418. For the ban on Śûdras against propounding the law, VIII, 20.

"What may have been practised by the virtuous, by such twice-born men as are devoted to the law, that he (the king) shall establish as law, if it be not opposed to the (customs of) countries, families and castes." Clearly, local and communal custom must always be respected and for the rest, sound tradition should have its way. Elsewhere, too, Manu lays down that legal disputes of all sorts should be decided "according to principles drawn from local usages and from the institutes of the sacred law." Almost in the same breath he advises the judges to depend on "the eternal law" but, in his view, this involves no inconsistency with the observance of local usage.[1] It seems that even when political autonomy was disturbed by imperialistic ambitions, legal autonomy continued in every region. Manu expatiates at length on the ideal,[2] the majesty[3] of the kingship and the need of a firm policy—Daṇḍa or chastisement, but he holds that the king should "behave like a father towards all men" and please all. He is probably reflecting actual practice when he wants the king to regulate the economic life of the community. The king should watch and control traders—'open cheats.' He must fix the prices of all marketable goods, mark the weights and measures and re-examine them every six months. The followers of various occupations, mechanics, manual workers come in for state supervision. Physicians or veterinary surgeons, who wrong their patients, must be fined.[4] Manu again seems to steer close to facts when he insists on the appointment of a learned Brâhmaṇa as the royal priest and of seven or eight ministers. Every day they should be

The Duties of the State.

[1] Ibid., II, 14; VIII, 3, 8, 46.

[2] Ibid., VII, 37—53, 145-146, 216—226.

[3] Ibid., V; VII, 3—12.

[4] Ibid., VII, 14—21, 22—24, 80, 82—88, 144; III, 134—136, 143; VIII, 309, 386, 401—403; IX, 256—260, 304, 309; XI, 18, 22-23.

consulted on peace, war, finance, endowments and general administration. The king should consult them first individually and then collectively and ultimately decide for himself. Another official of first-rate importance was the Ambassador, a sort of foreign secretary and plenipotentiary, who negotiated alliances and transacted that business by which kings "are disunited or not." Then there are a number of other officials concerned with mines, manufactures, storehouses, revenue, etc.[1]

Local Government.

In local government the ultimate unit was the village. Every village must have a headman. The successively higher areas of local government were formed by groups of ten, twenty, a hundered and a thousand villages. Every town must have "a superintendent of all affairs" with an army of spies to assist him in "exploring" the behaviour of the people. Local government, as a whole, should be placed in charge of a minister at the headquarters. A company of soldiers must be stationed "in the midst of two, three, five or hundreds of villages for the protection of the kingdom." Manu seems to prescribe salaries in land or in kind. The village headman is entitled to certain commodities such as food, drink and fuel which the villagers ought to furnish daily to the king. The head of ten villages is entitled to one kula of land, that is, as much as would suffice for the maintenance of one family; the ruler of twenty villages to five kulas; the lord of a hundred villages is to get a village in Jāgir as the medieval Indian rulers would have called it. The ruler of a thousand villages is entitled to the revenues of a town.[2] All this seems to have a basis in facts. There was no need to idealise here; in fact, the idealistic vein is altogether absent. There is a

[1] Ibid., VII, 54—68, 80-81, 147—51.

[2] Ibid., VII, 113—122

touch of realism in what Manu says of the need of supervising and controlling royal officials. Those, though appointed for the protection of the people, "generally become knaves" and seize the property of others. Evil-minded officials who were guilty of bribery must suffer the confiscation of their whole property and must be banished. Ministers or judges who were at fault in the discharge of their duties should be fined a thousand paṇas.[1]

Revenue.

Manu's maxims on taxation throw some light on contemporary practice. In Manu, as in the Mahâbhârata and elsewhere, the theoretical justification for the large amount and variety of state dues is that they represent the price of the protection which the state extends to all. The land revenue should be one-fourth, one-sixth or one-eighth of the crops, that is, of the gross produce. It is possible that in Manu's age the land-revenue varied from one-fourth to one-eighth in different localities. Besides, a fiftieth of cattle and gold may be taken by the king. He awards the king a sixth part of "trees, meat, honey, clarified butter, perfumes, (medicinal) herbs, substances used for flavouring food, flowers, roots and fruits; of leaves, potherbs, grass, (objects) made of cane, skins; of earthen vessels, all (articles) made of stone." The duties on traders should be fixed on a consideration of the rates of sale and purchase, the means of communication, the charges of securing goods and the necessary expenses of the dealers. Elsewhere Manu gives the state one-twentieth of the value of each saleable commodity as calculated by experts. All who live by traffic should annually pay something, be it a trifle. Any attempt to defraud the customs-house was to be punished with a fine, eight times the amount due. Mechanics, artisans and Śûdras who lived by manual labour should contribute to the state a day's labour in the month.

[1] Ibid., 123—44; IX, 234.

Treasure-trove belonged to the king. Of property inadvertently lost and afterwards found, one-sixth, one-tenth, or at least one-twentieth should go to the king. Lost property, unclaimed for three years, should lapse to the king. Of treasure discovered underground, one-half should go to the king and the other half distributed among Brâhmaṇas. Besides all this, numerous petty dues were levied at ferries: " . . . an (empty) cart shall be made to pay one paṇa, a man's (load) half a paṇa, an unloaded man one-half of a quarter." Carts laden with merchandise should pay according to the value of the goods. In addition to these contributions Manu hints at some state monopolies, as also at some restrictions on exports and perhaps also imports. Those who violated these rules were to suffer the confiscation of their whole property.[1] No theorist could merely invent this extensive list. Whatever the embellishments, Manu is pointing to the extraordinarily large number of sources which the state had begun to tap by the second century A.D. to fill its coffers. He may again be building on facts when he exempts learned Brâhmaṇas, old persons past seventy, the blind, cripples and idiots from taxation.[2]

Civil and Criminal law.

Manu's civil and criminal code is primarily idealistic but a few of its provisions might well have corresponded with reality. In the first place, its eighteen categories are interesting: (1) non-payment of debts, (2) deposit and pledge, (3) sale without ownership, (4) concerns among partners, (5) resumption of gifts, (6) non-payment of wages, (7) non-performance of agreements, (8) rescission of sale and purchase, (9) disputes between the owner and his owners, (10) boundaries, (11) assault, (12) defamation, (13) theft, (14) robbery and violence, (15) adultery, (16) duties of man and wife, (17) partition, (18) gambling and betting. Treason

[1] Ibid., VIII, 30—45, 307-8, 398-99; VII, 127—138; IX, 44.

[2] Ibid., 133—36; VIII, 394.

against the king, murder of Brâhmaṇas, women and children should be punished capitally. A cut-purse should be punished by two of his fingers being cut off for his first offence. If he repeated the crime, he should lose a hand and a foot, while for the third offence, he should be punished capitally. Robbers who cut the walls and committed thefts should be deprived of their hands and fastened on sharp stakes. Those who sheltered or helped the thieves in any way should be punished as thieves.[1] The destruction of the wall or gate of a town or the filling up of the ditch should be punished with instantaneous banishment. Adultery should, as a general rule, be punished with a terrible physical mutilation and banishment, though its detailed provisions are governed by considerations of caste. Various fines and damages of various amounts are prescribed for destroying a bridge or a flag, a pole or images of a temple or a royal palace, stealing a rope or water-pot from a well, damaging a water-hut, breaking the dam of a tank or defiling the sanitation of the highways.[2] Defamation is recognised as a crime though, like adultery, it is governed by notions of caste superiority and inferiority. It may be admitted at once that social status had, at least under rulers of Brahmanical persuasion, something to do with the degree of punishment. But it is doubtful if some of the monstrous penalties prescribed by the Dharma Śâstras were ever carried into effect. If a Śûdra mentioned the names and castes of the twice-born with contumely, "an iron rail, ten fingers long, shall be thrust red-hot into his mouth." If he insulted a twice-born man with gross invective, his tongue should be cut out, "for he is of low origin." If he was so arrogant as to teach

[1] Ibid., VIII, 4—7.

[2] Fines fell into three grades—the first or lowest amercement 250 paṇas, middlemost amercement 500 paṇas, the highest amercement 1,000 paṇas (VIII, 188). Paṇa here is the copper paṇa or kârṣâpaṇa, not silver paṇa (VIII, 136).

Brâhmaṇas their duties, "the king shall cause hot oil to be poured into his mouth and into his ears." Even harsher and sometimes unspeakable are the punishments prescribed by Manu for graver insults which a Śûdra might chance to offer to superior beings. Here the Brâhmaṇas seem to be painting themselves worse than they really were.[1]

Judicial Procedure.

Allowing for obvious ultra-Brahmanical leanings, the judicial procedure of Manu appears to be based on practice. A remarkable feature is the introduction of the popular element into one of the most notable classes of disputes. The question of boundaries between fields and villages has always been a plentiful source of litigation. According to Manu if the inspection of various marks such as tanks, wells, cisterns, fountains and temples, failed to furnish decisive evidence, the case should depend on the testimony of witnesses. These must be examined "in the presence of the crowd of the villagers and also of the two litigants. As they, being questioned, unanimously decide, even so he (the king) shall record the boundary." If no witnesses were available, the case might be left to the decision of people from four neighbouring villages. In certain contingencies Manu allows that the law may be taken in one's hand for recovering one's property.[2]

[1] Ibid., VIII, 15, 319, 267—73, 276-77, 281—84, 352-53, 359, 364-65, 367-68, 374—85; IX, 232, 271, 276—79, 281—83, 285, 289.

[2] Ibid., VIII, 48—50. Manu lays down that the king or his officers should not instigate suits (VIII, 53). Suits are to be taken up in the order of the castes of the plaintiffs (VIII, 24). On the use of logic and reasoning in judicial proceedings, VIII, 44. On the invalidity of contracts, VIII, 163—68. For provision of something like a Court of Wards, VIII, 27—29. For provision of payment in work in case of inability to pay in money, VIII, 177.

The Court should be presided over by the king who should maintain a dignified demeanour but should refrain from ostentation in his dress or ornaments. He must always be assisted by Brâhmaṇas and learned counsellors. Seated or standing, he should raise his right arm and "examine the business of suitors." In the absence of the king, a learned Brâhmaṇa should preside over the Court and should be assisted by three counsellors. The judge should try to find out the truth by inferences as a hunter traces the lair of a wounded deer by the drops of blood. "When engaged in judicial proceedings, he must pay full attention to the truth, to the object, to himself, next to the witnesses, to the place, to the time and to the aspect." Manu bars from the witness-box interested persons, friends, companions, enemies, those convicted of perjury, notorious bad characters, followers of forbidden occupations, men of low caste, those deficient in organs of sense, lunatics, thieves, wrathful people, those who are extremely grieved, intoxicated, tormented by hunger or thirst or desire, or oppressed by fatigue, etc. In grave cases, however, the moral competence of witnesses should not be examined too closely. In Manu witnesses seem to share a little of the character of assessors. "On a conflict of witnesses," we are told, "the king shall accept the majority; if (the parties are) equal in number, those distinguished by good qualities; on a difference between the distinguished, the best among the twice-born." When the parties were assembled, the judge was to exhort them by heaven and hell, with the utmost solemnity, to speak the truth. Besides the evidence of witnesses, the observation of the voice, colour, motions, aspect, eyes and gestures of the parties should aid the judge in discovering the internal dispositions of men. Manu recognises two ordeals, though he does not dilate on them at length. If one could dive under water or carry fire, one should be adjudged

The Court.

innocent.[1] Manu recognises four grades of punishment —admonition, reproof, fines and corporal chastisement. From the last he would exempt Brâhmaṇas. Corporal punishment could fall on any part of the body such as the eyes, ears, the tongue, hands and feet. Imprisonment seems to have been regarded as a variety of corporal punishment.[2]

Spies.

Over all officials, judicial or executive or fiscal, as over the people at large, the king should keep a watch through spies. They are the eyes of the king. They are to 'explore' the behaviour of all.[3]

Viṣṇu.

The ideas of Manu are, for the most part, echoed by Viṣṇu, who, though technically a Sûtrakâra, really represents the Dharmaśâstra line and belongs to about the third century A.D. He stresses caste and wants the traditional social order to be enforced by the state. If the king could not recover stolen property, he must recompense its owners from his own treasury. For administrative purposes Viṣṇu prescribes the same scheme of local government as Manu, except that he omits the subdivision of twenty villages.[4] Viṣṇu's fiscal system is practically the same as that of Manu, though it is far from being definite. The state is entitled to one-sixth of the gross produce of the land, one-tenth of the price of the articles sold within its frontiers and to one-twentieth of those sold outside. The latter is tantamount to an export-duty which might have obtained

[1] Ibid., VIII, 1-2, 9 -11, 20-21, 25-26, 71- 123, 115-117.

[2] Ibid., VIII, 127—130, 43.

If the king fails to recover stolen property, he must make it good out of his own treasury (VIII, 40). The king should inflict a fine of 100 paṇas on ministers or judges who might be guilty of illegalities in the work of adjudication (VIII, 234).

[3] Ibid., VII, 122, 154 ; IX, 256, 298.

[4] Viṣṇu, II, 2-3, 7—16, 65—67, 98 ; XXIV, 1—8 ; XXVI, 4 - 7. See also I, 47 ; II, 17—21.

in practice. The king could charge a sixth on meat, honey, clarified butter, herbs, perfumes, flowers, roots, fruits, liquids and condiments, wood, leaves, skins, earthen pots, stone vessels and anything made of split bamboo. He could take a fiftieth of cattle, gold and clothes. The government is entitled to the whole produce of the mines and to one-half of treasure-trove, the other half going to Brâhmaṇas. As in Manu, labourers are to contribute a day's labour in the month. Attempts at evading the customs mean forfeiture of all the goods. A novel provision is that one-tenth of a debt which might be the subject of a law-suit should go to the king.[1] In Viṣṇu, as in Manu, espionage is an integral part of the machinery of government.

Yâjñavalkya.

Later than Viṣṇu but more systematic, comprehensive and, therefore, more influential is Yâjñavalkya. A compilation rather than an original production, his Smṛiti borrows freely from Dharma Sûtras, Manu, Viṣṇu and the Purâṇas among others. According to him there are fourteen seats or sources of the sciences and Dharma—the Purâṇas, Nyâya, Mimâṁsâ, the Dharma Śâstras, the six Aṅgas and the four Vedas. But he seems to have perceived that these authorities did not always agree among themselves. For the correct interpretation and thorough elucidation of law, Yâjñavalkya would constitute a Pariṣad or legal assembly of members versed in the Vedas, Dharmas and the three sciences. Its decrees should be considered law. Failing such an assembly, the verdict of the foremost of theologians should be law. Like Manu, he recognises âtmatuṣṭi or one's conscience as one of the sources of law. It will appear that the

[1] Ibid., III, 23—32, 55—64; VI, 20. According to Parâśaramâdhava, 152, Viṣṇu permits the king to receive a tenth of the claim from the debtor as fine and a twentieth from the creditor as part of the expenses of the court.

king did sometimes constitute Pariṣads for the solution of legal doubts and that his own conscience, expressed through decrees, was a source of law.[1] In Yâjñavalkya the sphere of government coincides with the whole field of human life.[2] On principles of justice he does not say much that is new. He grants that the customs of families, castes and corporations should be respected but he would allow appeals from their decisions to royal judges. All cases which might have been wrongly decided should be re-tried. His scale of the three amercements differs from that of Manu, being twenty, forty and eighty paṇas respectively.[3] For the safety of the king, the treasury and the people, numerous fortresses should be erected and placed in charge of experts.[4]

The Artha-śâstras.

Contemporaneously with the earliest Smritis arose another class of writings, called Arthaśâstras, treatises on welfare or profit, which treat of politics and economics more or less independently of religion. The Arthaśâstra, in fact, is something like the secular counterpart of the Dharmaśâstra, just as the Kâmaśâstra is the erotic counterpart of it. All the three seem to have arisen at pretty much the same epoch and might have been the result of the same intellectual movement of specialisation. The Mahâbhârata professes to quote from several teachers who are mentioned in Kauṭalya and may be supposed to be his forerunners. But the oldest extant work of its kind is the Kauṭilîya Arthaśâstra, discovered in Southern India less than a generation ago. Its discoverer and first editor, Mr. Shamasastry, accepted and argued for the age-long tradition of its authorship by Câṇakya, or

[1] Yâjñavalkya, I, 3—5, 7, 11.

[2] For the attitude and functions of the king, Ibid., XIII, 309—13, 344, 354-61, 364 et seq., 327—41; XVI, 20; XVIII, 4-5, 12.

[3] Ibid., II, 30, 305; XIII, 366—68.

[4] Ibid., XIII, 353.

Kauṭalya, supposed to be the mighty Chancellor of the first Mauryan emperor in the 4th century B.C. In his Introductory Note Fleet countenanced the conclusion which still finds support with some scholars. But in a few years the conclusions of Mr. Shamasastry were called in question and a battle of articles has ever since raged over the problem. Râmakṛiṣṇa Gopâla Bhâṇḍârkar came to the conclusion that the first or second century A.D. was the earliest date which could be assigned to Kauṭalya. Jolly, a later editor of the work, argues like Winternitz, that the real author was "a theoretician, no statesman but perhaps an official in a state of medium size." The ascription of the work to Kauṭalya or Câṇakya was "entirely due to the myths current regarding the fabulous minister who was looked upon as the master and creator of the art of polity and as the author of all the floating wisdom on the subject of Niti." Both the scholars think that "we might abide by the third century A.D. as the probable date of the work." Berriedale Keith strongly argues for the same view [1]

[1] In support of the fourth century B.C. as the date of the Arthaśâstra, see Shamasastry's Preface to his edition of the Arthaśâstra; Fleet's Introductory Note; T. Gaṇapati Śâstrî's Introduction to his edition of the Arthaśâstra; Jacobi, Ind. Ant., June-July, 1918; K. P. Jayaswal, Hindu Polity I, Appendix C, pp. 203–215; N. N. Law, Calcutta Review, September–December, 1924; D. R. Bhandarkar, Annals of the Bhandarkar Institute, VII, 1925-26, pp. 65 et seq.; Radha Kumud Mookerji's Introductory Essay on the Age and Authenticity of the Arthaśâstra of Kauṭalya in N. N. Law's Studies in Ancient Hindu Polity. See also H. C. Ray, Ind. Ant., 1925, pp. 170, 201. L. D. Barnett in his "Indian Antiquities" does not commit himself but works on the basis of the same hypothesis. V.A. Smith (Early History of India, 3rd and 4th editions) and F. W. Thomas (Cambridge History of India, I) use the Arthaśâstra in connection with the Mauryas.

For R. G. Bhâṇḍârkar's views, Proceedings of the First Oriental Conference, Poona, 1920.

For the third century A.D. as the most probable date of the Arthaśâstra see Introduction to Jolly and Schmidt's edition of the Arthaśâstra, pp. 1—47; Jolly's paper "Kauṭalya and Câṇakya" submitted to the Fourth Oriental Conference, Allâhâbâd, 1926; Winternitz, Calcutta Review, April, 1924; A. B. Keith, J.R.A.S., 1916, pp. 130—38.

To a student of institutions it is apparent in almost every chapter of the Arthaśâstra and particularly in the later ones that the author is writing of very small states. The idea of a big state never enters his horizon. It seems improbable that he flourished during the days of the Maurya, Kaliṅga, or Ândhra empire. For the same reason he cannot be placed during the Gupta period. A lower date being barred by literary evidence, he seems to belong rather to the 3rd century A.D. than to any other epoch. It is impossible to dogmatise on the subject but the 3rd century A.D. is the best working hypothesis.

Hillebrandt ascribes the composition of the Arthaśâstra to a school of Kauṭalya's disciples. Keith ascribes it to some follower of Kauṭalya. But Kauṭalya is really in line with Hindu tradition in introducing his name in his own work. It may be stated, in reply to Keith, that âcâryâḥ is only the customary honorific plural; that on p. 261 (Shamasastry's edition) Kauṭalya distinguishes the views of Ācâryâḥ from those of Kauṭalya and Vâtavyâdhi; that on p. 320 the views of Ācâryâḥ are distinguished from those of Bhâradvâja. On p. 253, the criticism of Kauṭalya by Bhâradvâja and that of the latter again by Kauṭalya only brings together the opinion of two schools of thought. The fact seems to be that the Arthaśâstra, like the Dharmaśâstra, had several traditions and that Kauṭalya represented one, perhaps the most powerful, of them. In his text Kauṭalya quotes, it seems, from four schools and thirteen individual teachers (D. R. Bhandarkar, Carmichael Lectures, 1918, pp. 91—99). Of these Manu, Indra or Bâhudantîputra, Bṛihaspati, Sukra, Viśâlâkṣa, and Bhâradvâja are also mentioned in the Mahâbhârata. Vâtavyâdhi is one of the names of Uddhava, the friend of Kṛiṣṇa in the Purâṇas, specially in the Srîmad Bhâgavata.

For references to Kauṭalya in Hindu Literature, Kâmandaka, I, 4—7, Daṇḍin, Daśakumâracarita, II, 8 and other works cited by Shamasastry, Gaṇapati Sâstri and Jolly in their introductions to the editions of the Arthaśâstra the Jaina Nandisûtra placed the Kauṭilîya among the false sciences though about the 10th century A.D. the Jaina author Samadeva Sûri borrowed the material of his Nîtivâkyâmṛita from Kauṭalya.

The author of the Arthaśâstra is also called Câṇakya or Viṣṇugupta. Hemacandra in his Abhidhânacintâmaṇi (Bombay Edition, p. 34) and Yâdavaprakâśa (Vaijayantî, ed. Oppert p. 96) also call him Drâmila. Hemacandra identifies him with Vâtsyâyana, the author of the Kâmasûtra (Shamasastry, Journal of the Mythic Society, Vol. IV, pp. 210—16). The identification is not corroborated in the rest of Sanskrit literature but the resemblance in the style of the two works is striking.

In Mss. of the Arthaśâstra, both Kauṭalya and Kauṭilya occur as spellings of the author's name. Both may, therefore, be held to

As a scheme of administrative organisation, the Artha-śâstra is unsurpassed in Hindu literature. It is complete in its perspective, detailed in its regulations, thorough in its treatment. It makes provision for all contingencies, for all imaginable possibilities. As a statement of Hindu administrative theory, it leaves hardly anything to be desired. But its supreme merit is its gravest defect as a source of information on administrative practice. Here are no incidental references as in the Brâhmaṇas, Epics and Jâtakas, which, merely on account of their inadvertence, may be held to be true to facts. Nor is politics here subsidiary and, therefore, roughly reflecting current practice as in the Dharma Sûtras and Dharma Śâstras. In the Arthaśâstra everything is elaborately planned, carefully thought out. In its own sphere it is an ideal, an utopia. Kauṭalya's dialectical method points in the same direction. He is fond of inventing problems and riddles. Where possible, he states, discusses and corrects the views of others—and aims at the perfect conclusion. It is thus only in fundamentals and in broad outline of administrative structure which no theoretician could have produced out of his own fancy, that Kauṭalya can be relied on for the practical working of institutions. On the other hand, Kauṭalya's secular tone and freedom from any religious bias tend to show that priestly influence was not always so powerful as the Dharma Śâstras might lead us to suppose.

The value of the Arthaśâstra.

Unfortunately, it is difficult to check Kauṭalya by reference to comtemporary facts. The third century A.D.

be correct. But of the two Kauṭalya is preferable. That is the form which occurs in the Alur Inscription of Vikramâditya V of the tenth century A.D. (Ep. Ind., XVI, No. 7), and also in another inscription of the thirteenth century A.D. (Indian Historical Review, 1925, pp. 569, 786). The name is not, as some scholars have supposed, a nickname signifying 'false' or 'fraudulent.' For the matter of that, as has been pointed out, Sunaśepa means 'dog's tale' and Divodâsa, 'time-server.'

which is his most probable epoch, is, as V. A. Smith puts it, "one of the dark spaces in the spectrum of Indian history, and almost every event of that time is concealed from view by an impenetrable veil of oblivion."[1] It can only be premised that so far as he reflects any actual practice, it is that which prevailed about the 2nd or 3rd century A.D.

General political conditions

The general political conditions in Kauṭalya are the same as in Manu, Viṣṇu and Yājñavalkya and are not out of harmony with what little we know of the country between the fall of the Mauryan empire and the rise of the Gupta Empire. Causes of war among the small states into which the country was divided were always present. The clearing of forests on the frontiers of two or more states seem to have led to complications. The schemes of colonisation which might follow were another fruitful source of misunderstandings. Irrigation from the long rivers which ran through more than one state presented its own difficulties. Frontiers themselves were a problem. Then there were all the petty insults, real or imaginary, to the honour and dignity of sovereigns. Mere aggression, the quest for empire, which public opinion, political philosophy and tradition had sanctified, made confusion worse confounded. It was noticed that a given state—call it A—tended to embroil itself with its neighbours, say, the states of the circle X. These, in their turn, would be at daggers drawn with their adjacent neighbours, say of the circle Y. It seems to follow that these last would be allies of the state A. But as some states of the circles X and Y themselves adjoined one another, and were therefore likely foes, the general rule of political alliance and hostility was disturbed. On a balance of considerations it appeared that some would

[1] Early History of India, p. 212, also p. 276.

be foes, some allies, others neutral, and yet others completely indifferent to A. If you imagine a third circle Z, a more delicate balance will have to be struck. On the whole, a single group of alliances and enmities and neutralities would consist of twelve kings which might be classified as follows:—

I. (1) The Vijigiṣu or would-be-conqueror in the centre.

II. Five kings in front of the Vijigiṣu, thus:

(2) Ari, the enemy.

(3) Mitraprakriti, the friend of the Vijigiṣu.

(4) Arimitra, friend of the friend of Vijigiṣu.

(5) Mitrâmitra, friend of the friend of Vijigiṣu.

(6) Arimitrâmitra—friend of the enemy's friend.

III. Behind the Vijigiṣu:—

(7) Pârṣṇigrâha—a rearward enemy.

(8) Âkranda—a rearward friend.

(9) Pârṣṇigrâhâsâra—friend of the rearward enemy.

(10) Âkrandâsâra—friend of the rearward friend.

IV. (11) Madhyama—intermediary.

(12) Udâsîna—or neutral.

The idea is further subjected to mechanical and mathematical treatment until it gives rise to jig-saw puzzles which stray from reality as they advance in ingenuity. But from all that one thing emerges very clearly. Every state stood in all sorts of relationships with others ranging from complete indifference to deadly hostility or close alliance. In Kauṭalya, interstatal diplomacy knows no morality. Neither unprovoked aggression, nor the violation of the neutrality of other states seems to cause any surprise. Spies and other secret agents revel in falsehood or immorality and freely resort to treachery, poison and the dagger. A strong power is expressly enjoined to embark on a career of conquest, subdue state after state and stand forth as the one all-embracing sovereign. Kauṭalya makes one approach to principle in diplomacy. He unfolds the idea of a balance of power. A king might represent to the neighbouring circle of states that a particular sovereign was growing too powerful, that he might destroy them all and that all should, therefore, march against him. Even this idea of balance, however, is only part of the general calculation which dominates the whole theory of interstatal relationships.

On the other hand, Kauṭalya advises the conclusion of treaties and even defensive and offensive alliances in furtherance of common interests, such as the plantation of colonies, the clearing of forests, reclamation of wild tribes, construction of long trade-routes, fortification of strategic centres and the working of mines.

Protectorates.

Wars and alliances of a certain character resulted in the establishment of the relation of protector and protectorate. Driven to extremities, a weak state might purchase peace by sacrifice of its honour, by consenting to furnish hostages, by paying indemnity, or by binding itself to military service. But under favourable circumstances it might violate its agreements. There were ways and ways of commencing a war of liberation. A hostage might be encouraged to escape in any one of innumerable ways. And so forth. The whole subject is treated with an inexhaustible wealth of detail, supposition and ingenuity. On the other hand, the suzerain should do all he can to keep a permanent hold on his fresh acquisitions. Here force would be of little avail. Conciliation was the right policy. The suzerain should not attempt to bring a new acquisition into uniformity with his original territory. To use a modern term, there should be no annexation. The subdued dynasty should be maintained on the throne. Let the suzerain rescue the dependent princes from misfortunes, redress their grievances, treat them with honour and kindness and even shower on them wealth and dignity. Their family and property rights should be respected. Nor should these principles be departed from on the death of the first vassal. The latter's son should be duly crowned. The people of the feudatory states should be disturbed as little as possible. Manners and customs corresponded to conveniences and should be respected by the suzerain. What was good for one place might not be good for another.

All the same, the strictest watch should be kept on the vassals—the Sâmantas as they are called. All their secrets must be ascertained through spies, through prostitutes, through all other conceivable means, fair and foul. The most shameless falsehoods and immoralities might be employed to keep them disunited. Nor should the secret dagger or poison be spared in case of need. On all this Kauṭalya dilates at great length and in a manner which might have shocked Machiavelli himself. He cannot be taken as an exact mirror of existing conditions. Here, as everywhere else, his imagination, his turn for systematisation, his genius for classification are discernible. But he leaves no doubt that the ordinary state in his time comprised many feudatories whose relations with the suzerain were often clouded by suspicion and occasionally characterised by ferocity and treachery on one side or the other.[1]

[1] Kauṭalya, Arthaśâstra ed. Shamasastry, Book VII, pp. 261—319, 380, 407.

Cf. Kâmandaka (who, according to Winternitz, lived in the 8th century A.D., and according to others in the 6th or 7th century and who based his Nîtisâra almost entirely on Kauṭalya), VIII, 20, 16-17; IX, 45, 2—21, 75; X, 18—22; XVII, 2-3. Also the Agni Purâṇa, Canto CCXL.

Some of the maxims of Kauṭalya are condemned by Bâṇa, in his Kâdambarî, ed. Peterson, Vol. I, p. 109.

For a comparison, not altogether accurate, of Kauṭalya with Machiavelli, see G. B. Botazzi, Precursori di Nicolo Machiavelli in Grecia ad in India, Kauṭalya ad Thucidide, tr. B. K. Sarkar, Indian Historical Quarterly, 1925.

On the whole, Manu stands on a much higher moral pedestal than Kauṭalya. Once he interdicts all treacherous conduct on the part of a king. On the conclusion of a victorious campaign a king should display gentleness and generosity. After ascertaining the desires of the vanquished, he should instal a scion of the fallen dynasty on the throne, if need be, on his own terms. He should honour his new protégé and the latter's principal officials with precious gifts. Promises of safety should be proclaimed and the customs of the people declared authoritative. Even Manu, however, permits the devastation of hostile territory in times of war. When a king has shut up his foe in a town, "let him sit encamped, harass his kingdom, and continually spoil his grass, food, fuel and water. Likewise let him destroy the tanks, ramparts and ditches." Even in Manu, it is almost the duty of a king to sow dissensions in the ranks of his enemies.[1]

Comparison with Manu.

On these matters as on so many others Viṣṇu reads like an echo of Manu. The old dynasty of a conquered country should be maintained, unless it is of ignoble descent. So far as possible, a conqueror should invest a prince of the same line with the 'royal' dignity.[2] In his scheme of foreign policy as in domestic administration spies play an important part.[3]

Viṣṇu.

Yâjñavalkya, too, expounds the usual policies of conciliation, diplomacy, fraud and force. When a country has been conquered, its customs, laws, and family usages must be maintained. On the other hand, a king should attack the enemy when the latter is weak and his realm is filled with corn and provisions. Nothing can be more meritorious than to acquire wealth by war and bestow it on Brâhmaṇas.[4]

Yâjñavalkya.

---

1 Manu, VII, 104, 122, 154, 158—207; IX, 256, 208.
2 Viṣṇu, III, 47—9.
3 Ibid., III, 35.
4 Yâjñavalkya, XIII, 321, 353.

The cumulative evidence of Manu, Kauṭalya, Viṣṇu and Yâjñavalkya, all of whom belong to the great interregnum between the Mauryas and the Guptas tends to show that the country was divided into a large number of states, that they were constantly vacillating between the status of suzerain and that of vassal, that many a state had a number of dependencies and that the internal autonomy of a dependency was generally, though not uniformly, respected, that the status of a protectorate was most difficult to define ranging as it did from almost complete independence to practical annexation, that the acknowledgment of suzerainty might have been merely nominal in some cases, while other states might have been reduced to mere estates. Kauṭalya's reference to some people as Śastropa-jivinaḥ is obscure but it probably means those who lived by their arms and refers to some warlike clans.[1] His characterisation of Dvairâjya as productive of rivalry and mutual conflict leading to destruction indicates some peoples who had not evolved a regular form of monarchical government.[2] In the vocabulary of politics, feudalism is the only word that describes this state of things. The difference between the conditions of medieval Europe and the India of the early Christian era is apparent but the actual position of the state and its head show points of resemblance in either country. It is the institutions of such a small state, ridden by feudalism, that Kauṭalya seeks to portray in what appeared to him an ideal form.

The scope of state-activity.

The scope of the activity of the state in Kauṭalya includes practically everything. It should promote true religion but Kauṭalya wants it to regulate the age and conditions under which one might renounce the world.

[1] Arthaśâstra (ed. Shamasastry), p. 376.

[2] Ibid., p. 323.

Projected Social Legislation.

The state should see that husband and wife, father and son, brother and sister, uncle and nephew, teacher and pupil are faithful to one another and do not play each other false. The state itself should provide support to poor, pregnant women, to their new-born offspring, to orphans, to the aged, the infirm, the afflicted and the helpless.[1] He lays down when men may use witchcraft to gain the affections of their wives or sweethearts and when, for instance, in cases of perversion for incestuous purposes, it was to be punished with mutilation or death.[2] He prescribes the conditions of divorce, separation, second or subsequent marriages, ways of teaching manners to refractory women.[3] Detailed and minute are his provisions for safeguarding the honour of women, the safety of immature girls, relations of lovers, etc.[4] His law of adultery, proceeds on lines of caste.[5] Coming to elopement, he would legislate on every step, on every possibility, in that complicated affair.[6] He classifies prostitutes, places them under a state superintendent, prescribes their fees, checks their tendency to extravagance, limits their expenditure, lays down their conduct in detail towards their paramours, provides for their safety and does not fail to decree that one-fifteenth of their income should go to the state.[7]

[1] Ibid., pp. 47-48; 199. Differing from Manu (VIII, 138) and others, Kauṭalya gives the following scale of fines: the first amercement ranging from 48 to 98 paṇas, the middlemost amercement ranging from 200 to 500 paṇas, and the highest ranging from 500 to 1,000 paṇas.

[2] Ibid., 232—35.

[3] Ibid., 153—59.

[4] Ibid., 124, 183, 228-29.

[5] Ibid., 199, 232—35.

[6] Ibid., 232—35.

[7] Ibid., 124-25, 184.

The state should facilitate, regulate and control public amusements and entertainments. It was to assist the foundation of academies where actors and actresses might learn reading and writing, music and song, dancing and painting and where they might master a complete code of deportment and blandishment. The movements of dancers, rope-dancers, buffoons, jugglers, mimic players and *troubadours* were to be regulated and a fifteenth of their incomes taken as the dues of the state.[1]

Amusements and Entertainments.

Gambling was to be controlled by a Superintendent who should appoint definite places, supply water and other conveniences, of course, for a consideration, and hire out dice at the rate of a Kâkṇí per pair. He was to appropriate five per cent. of all winnings for the state. To play anywhere else should mean a fine of twelve paṇas. The same rules apply to all betting and challenging, except in learning and art. While the play was in progress, the superintendent should exert all his psychological skill in detecting thieves and spies.[2]

Gambling.

The same three fold motive of regulating life, detecting thieves and spies, and securing some revenue for the state underlies Kauṭalya's excise policy. In town and country, camp and forts, the state should itself establish liquor shops at suitable distances from one another or license private individuals to do so according to the laws of supply and demand. Kauṭalya would furnish public houses with beds and seats and enhance their attractions with scents, garlands of flowers, water and other comforts. Stringent regulations on the sale and use of liquor and other fermentations are given

Excise.

[1] Ibid., 48-49, 125, 202.
[2] Ibid., 197-98.

but the code of temperance was to be relaxed for four days on occasions of festivity, fairs and pilgrimages.[1] On the slaughter of animals and the sale of meat, Kauṭalya is equally minute.[2] According to the Arthaśâstra, all professions and occupations are to be controlled by the state. For instance, physicians should report all cases of grave illness to the government. If death occurred in an unreported case, the physician should be punished with the first amercement. If in any case death was due to his carelessness, he should receive the middlemost amercement, while positive neglect or indifference was to be treated as assault or violence.[3] Similarly, rules with an amazing fulness of detail are given for the conduct of goldsmiths, weavers of various descriptions, washermen, and others,[4] while a series of veritable draft statutes of labourers prescribes, *inter alia,* that artisans must fulfil their engagements as to time, place and form of work and obey the instructions duly given, on pain of forfeiting their ways or paying damages or both.[5]

Control of Professions.

In Kauṭalya the state itself appears as the biggest of all business concerns. Details apart, the theory probably reflects a fact. There are some small states even to-day, for instance, in Central India, which stand forth as business corporations to supplement their regular revenue. The proceeds from the crown lands and such of the revenue as was paid in kind are likely to have formed a vast store. The land or 'ocean' mines would yield large quantities of salt, pearls, precious stones and metals. The forests

The state as a business concern.

[1] Ibid., 119—21.

[2] Ibid., 122-23.

[3] Ibid., 202.

[4] Ibid., 201.

[5] Ibid., 201, 204.

would yield valuable timbers, fire-wood, fodder, and various animal products—teeth and tusks, bones, horns, hides and so forth. There seem to have been some state-monopolies. Besides, there were factories of oils, etc., which employed large numbers of men and women. The stores and factories were under the charge of the Koṣṭhâgâra. The sale of raw produce or manufactured articles belonging to the state was managed by a superintendent who fixed the markets, prices and so on, or by Koṣṭhâgâra who also regulated barter, etc.[1] The state is to own ships and boats and ply them on hire at fixed rates.[2]

It need hardly be stated that Kauṭalya would regulate the whole economic life of the community. He would promote the prosperity of the people by all conceivable means. The agricultural population should be more or less evenly distributed. The state should encourage immigration and emigration to remedy the scarcity of population or relieve congestion, and should found new villages. Land which the state cleared of forests should be given to cultivators for life. Crown-lands might be cultivated partly by slaves, prisoners, and hired labourers who, as well as their overseers, should be paid according to the work done. Those who did not cultivate the land themselves should employ labourers or forfeit the property. If the peasants promptly paid government dues, they should be supplied with grains, cattle or money on favourable terms to relieve their distress. Uncultivated land was to be used for pasture. Groups of ten, two hundred, four hundred and eight hundred villages should be guarded by fortresses of varying strength.[3] Kauṭalya wants a meteorological department to study the weather in the interests of agriculture.

Economic life.

Agricultural.

[1] Ibid., 93—5, 98—101. For the rules of work, rewards, bonuses, etc., Ibid., 113—15.

[2] Ibid., 126—28, 140-41.

[3] Ibid., 116—18.

He has an elaborate system of irrigation from tanks, wells, rivers and canals. The charges were to be a third, a fourth, or a fifth of the produce of the irrigated soil, according to the source or method of irrigation. Any wanton interference with irrigation facilities was to be severely punished.[1] For relief of famine, the state granaries should open their doors, the rich should be compelled to yield up their hordes of grain, heavy taxes should be levied on wealthy people, hunting and fishing should be resorted to on a grand scale; emigration to the sea-shore, and to the banks of lakes, rivers, etc., should be encouraged; wherever possible, grains. vegetables, roots and fruits should be intensively cultivated. Relief should be sought from friendly states in the neighbourhood; prayers should go forth to the higher powers; the gods Mahâkaccha, and Indra, the gods of the mountains and the holy Ganges should be worshipped.[2]

Commerce.

Passing from agriculture to commerce, Kauṭalya would license merchants to collect grains and other commodities for wholesale business and would confiscate the goods of unlicensed mercantile houses. On a variety of considerations such as the outlay of capital, the interest thereon, the quantity manufactured, the amount of toll, the expenses of hire, and so forth, the Superintendent of Commerce should strike the balance and fix the prices. In wholesale transactions a five per cent. profit should be allowed on home commodities and ten per cent. on foreign ones. But if the merchants failed to dispose of their stock wholesale, or if obstructions in traffic put them to loss, a higher rate of profit should be allowed.

[1] Ibid., 47, 117, 144, 227. See also p. 228 for protection of harvests For other agricultural measures and for protection against cattle-disease, Ibid., 48-49, 140-41.

[2] Ibid., 206-07.

Frauds in this matter should be punished heavily according to the amounts involved. Combinations among capitalists for fraudulent purposes and any other attempts at deception, or adulteration of goods were to be severely dealt with. Rates of interest on loans and mortgages should be fixed at 15 and 12½ per cent.[1] Kauṭalya would so regulate the customs as to secure the effective control of the market. All sales must be transacted in the market-place. All imports and exports are to be taxed. On flowers, fruits, vegetables, roots, bulbous roots, dried meat and dried fish, 16⅔ per cent. should be charged; on fibrous garments, cotton cloths, silk, mail armour, red arsenic, vermilion, metals, colouring ingredients, sandals, pungents, ferments, dress and so forth, wine, ivory, skins, raw materials for fibrous or cotton garments, carpets or curtains, products from worms, goats, and sheep—10 or 6⅔ per cent.; on some cloths, quadrupeds, bipeds, threads, cotton, scents, medicines, wood, bamboo, fibres, skins, clay-pots, grains, oils, sugar, salt, liquor, cooked rice and so forth, 4 or 5 per cent. The tolls on conch-shells, diamonds, precious stones, pearls, corals, and necklaces should be determined by experts according to the time, cost and finish of the articles. It is emphasised that the sales in the market-place should be made by public proclamation. Smuggling, fraudulent combinations, adulterations were to be severely punished. Besides the principal dues, there are some minor tolls, ferry-charges, road-cesses, from which a number of articles are, according to their destination and purpose, exempted.[2] The state is to provide, manage and regulate the Râja-mârga or the king's highway, Râṣṭra-patha or the state road, and paths for animals, paths for asses and camels, cart-tracks, foot-paths, pasture-paths, shop-paths, defile-paths cremation-paths, etc.

[1] Ibid., 187, 174, 203-04.
[2] Ibid., 113—15.

On the main thoroughfares, pillars at intervals of half a kos, should be set up to serve as sign posts.[1]

Guilds.

Kauṭalya is willing to grant privileges and concessions to guilds, and to protect them from outside competition, but he wants the state to maintain a tight hold on all corporations. The superintendent of accounts should register the professions, customs and professions of various guilds. Three commissioners, enjoying the confidence of the guilds, should be appointed to receive the deposits which should be returned in times of distress. On the other hand, when the state is in need of money, Kauṭalya would permit it to rob guilds by any shameless frauds.[2]

Provisions against calamities, etc.

Besides guiding the day-to-day life of the community, the state should provide for all national calamities. Pestilences are to be fought by organised bands of physicians and by supernatural means; floods by wholesale relief measures and worship of rivers. To guard against fire, villagers should provide themselves with tubs and pots filled with water, ladders, axes, winnowers, hooks and leather bags. Or they must cook their food outside their homes. Many rational and many supernatural expedients are similarly prescribed against rats, snakes, locusts, birds, insects, etc., as also against demons.[3] Social helpfulness in ordinary life as well as in emergencies is prescribed to all on risk of severe penalties.[4] In the course of his treatment of civil law, Kauṭalya regulates inheritance in all its aspects and gives some rather eccentric provisions. He is, however, careful to lay down that unclaimed property except when it happened to belong to

[1] Ibid., 30, 47—49, 54, 298.

[2] Ibid., 185—87.

[3] Ibid., 205—208.

[4] Ibid., 199, 203.

learned men, escheated to the state.[1] For priests and scholars he would provide freeholds.[2]

To discharge these all-embracing functions, Kauṭalya prescribes for the state a corresponding administrative organization. For the king, the centre of the centre, he frames a detailed time-table, which, besides private wants, is to be filled with deliberations on state affairs, administrative plans, review of finance and revenue, inspection of the cavalry, the elephant force, the armoury, etc., supervision of spies, receptions, etc.[3] By the way, the king's harem should stand on a site as secure as possible, should be protected with a parapet and a moat, should consist of many compartments but should be provided with a single gate Inside, a few very old men and eunuchs excepted, all the guards, attendants and servants were to be females, a few of them, prostitutes. The strictest watch should be kept over all "coming and going."[4] Polygamy seems to have produced an atmosphere of suspicion and conspiracy within the palace, which, coupled with treason abroad, led to an extraordinary system of watch and guard. Trusted Amazons should attend the king from room to room. Science should exert its utmost skill and lay down minute rules for the detection of poison, etc.[5] The same harem influences seem to have complicated the problem of the succession. There was backstairs intrigue, conspiracy and treason. Kauṭalya talks of disaffected princes being put under lock and key, of plots hatched to secure their release, of the plans being discovered, of the culprits flying into

The king.

The harem.

The Succession.

[1] Ibid., 160—65.
[2] Ibid., 116—18.
[3] Ibid., 37—39.
[4] Ibid., 40—44.
[5] Ibid., 42—45.

exile. If a prince broke into revolt, kingship knew no kinship, says Kauṭalya. He might be slaughtered like the meanest bondman. Schools of real politics discussed with heartless ingenuity when and how far kings and princes could desert, deceive and slaughter one another or how young princes might be lulled into luxury and vice to keep them from treason.[1]

The Council.

The king should, on all affairs of state, constantly consult his advisory council of which the number had been placed by Manu (probably a representative of Arthaśâstra school occasionally quoted by Kauṭalya) at 12, by Bṛihaspati at 16, by Uśanas at 20. Kauṭalya himself only remarks that the council should consist of as many members as the needs of the state rendered desirable. The utmost secrecy should be observed in regard to the proceedings of the council. One by one the members should express their opinion and debate freely. The final decision should rest with the king alone who, however, is expected by Kauṭalya to accept the view of the majority. The king might also consult only three or four ministers or even single individuals.[2]

Ministers.

In the Arthaśâstra, the ministers are drawn from a sort of governing class, something like a nobility of birth, office and intellect, small in numbers. An excellent intellectual grounding, a blameless private life, a sound judgment, a high sense of duty and

[1] Ibid., 32—37. For the prince's education, comprising theology, philosophy, traditional learning, history, politics, administration, 'science of wealth,' military science dealing with elephant forces, cavalry, chariots, armoury, Ibid., pp. 10-11. Kauṭalya's saying that kingship knew no kinship is identical with the saying of the Mughal Emperor Jahâṅgîr, in the 17th, century A.D. See the Memoirs of Jahâṅgîr (Rogers and Beveridge), pp. 52—54, Motamad Khân, Iqbâlnâmâ, 10-11. David Price's version of the Jahâṅgîrnâma (p. 66, Baṅgabâsî edition, pp. 114-115) has a long discourse on 'kingship knows no kinship' which reminds one of Kauṭalya.

[2] Ibid., 13—29.

a certain amount of popularity are deemed essential qualifications. A discussion recorded by Kauṭalya, though avowedly theoretical, throws a little light on actual conditions. Bhâradvâja advised the king to select ministers from among his old fellow-students, but Viśâlâkṣa demurred to it as ultimately destructive of royal prestige. Parâśara emphasised loyalty as the foremost qualification but Piśuna pointed out that capacity, intellectual and administrative, was the essential desideratum. Kauṇapadanta held that high birth implied a grounding in traditional political wisdom, but Vâtavyâdhi explained that new men versed in the science of politics were safer. Bâhudantiputra, however, decried theoretical knowledge and laid emphasis on birth and capacity. Kauṭalya himself recognised the force of all these arguments but himself pronounced all-round capacity to be the highest qualification. He would, however, bar foreigners from chief offices and confine them to natives of the soil.[1]

The Purohita.

Among the high dignitaries of state, the Purohita occupied an important place. He must be versed not merely in sacred lore but also in the science of government. He must be skilful in reading portents and must be able to ward off providential or human calamities. He must be obedient but in the same breath the king is required to follow him like a student his teacher, a son his father, and a servant his master.[2]

Chief Minister.

Kauṭalya knows of a chief minister, mantrin, the sovereign's representative, the vicegerent of the state, who recalls the Norman-Angevin Chancellor, the Turkish Grand Vizier and, above all, the Vaki of the Indian Mughals.[3] The Senâpati or commander-in-chief who also acted as a sort of secretary for

[1] Ibid., 13—16.
[2] Ibid., 15.
[3] Ibid., 16.

war, was another great officer. A third important minister was the ambassador. Kauṭalya lays down that whosoever has been successful as a counsellor is an envoy. There were to be three grades of envoys.[1] The Samâhartâ or collector-general of taxes, the Nidhâyaka or treasurer, Saunidhâtâ, another treasurer, perhaps of a higher grade, the Vyâvahârika or chief judge, the Karmântika or superintendent of manufactories, the storekeeper, the Nâyaka or chief constable are among the other chief officers.

Departments.

Portfolios should be occasionally exchanged. Every minister should have a number of assistants and, it seems, should control one or more departments officered by Superintendents. Śâsanas, or Royal commands and decisions should be drawn up by Lekhakas or Secretaries in prescribed form and jargon and duly transmitted to departments.[2] The precise grouping of the Departments is not stated by Kauṭalya but his work, as a whole, suffices to give an idea of the working of the Departments of Stores, Forest Produce, Agriculture, Pasture lands, Cows, Slaughter-houses, Weights and Measures, the Goldsmith, Commerce, Tolls, Excise, Passports, Ships, etc. On the military side the chief departments are those of Armoury, Elephants, Horses, Chariots and Infantry.[3] Every department is provided with a regular secretariat. Messengers formed almost a department by themselves. The Department of Accounts was a remarkable one. It should be located in a building called the Accountant's office with a door facing the north or the east. Seats should be duly arranged for the clerks, and shelves provided for the multitudes of account-books. Kauṭalya seems to divide the office into several

Accounts.

---

[1] Ibid., 30—33.

[2] Ibid., 141. For the writs, pp. 70—75.

[3] Ibid., 89—143.

sections, pertaining to the various Departments. A record should be kept of all financial dealings with friendly or hostile sovereigns, together with the treaties and ultimatums which determined them. Corporations or guilds were to be dealt with by a different section. So, too, provinces, villages and families whose customs, professions and transactions were to be duly noted. Gems, precious stones, and other things should be registered with meticulous care—" the rate of their price, the rate of their barter, the counterweights used in weighing them, their number, their weight, and their cubical measure." But the most complicated of all branches of accounts seems to have been that relating to government factories. " The description of the work carried on, and of the results realised, in several manufactories; the amount of profit, loss, expenditure, delayed earnings, the amount of Vyâji (premia in kind or cash) realised—the status of government agency employed, the amount of wages paid, the number of free labourers engaged, pertaining to the investment of capital of any work"—all should be accurately given.[1]

Local Government.

The local officials mentioned by Kauṭalya are interesting. He divides a kingdom into four provinces, each governed by a Viceroy. Antapâlas seem to be officers in charge of frontiers, wardens of the marches. The Âṭavikas took charge of wild tracts. The Durga-pâlas managed the fortifications. There are the same administrative divisions of eight hundred, four hundred and two hundred villages. The Pradeṣṭris were in charge of districts, while at the bottom the Gopa was the village-accountant. Kauṭalya nowhere mentions any self-governing institutions in the village. The Nâgaraka is the superintendent of a city. Mention is made of Daṇḍapâlas and Praśâstris, magistrates or judicial officers.[2]

[1] Ibid., 62.

[2] Ibid., 20, 69-70, 142, 144.

Besides these regular administrative functionaries there were a number of Court and household officers. The High Priest, the sacrificial priest and the royal teacher seem to have ranked among the highest personages of the realm. The Dauvârika or door-keeper and the Antarvâsika or superintendent of the harem come in the second grade. The foreteller, the astrologer, the reader of omens, the reader of Purâṇas, the sacrificial priests, the retinue of the priest, the story-teller, and the bard occupied the same position as the Superintendents of Departments. The sorcerer and, most curious of all, the honourable playmate of the king, came a little lower. The bodyguards and attendants stood much lower. Every Hindu Court patronised poets and scholars whose emoluments in Kauṭalya range from five hundred to a thousand paṇas a year. Many musicians receive two hundred and fifty paṇas a year.[1] In Kauṭalya the salaries and allowances are tremendous in amount.

Court and Household officers.

The highest, 48,000 a year, is given to the preceptor, the High Priest, the teacher, the Chief Minister, the Commander-in-Chief, as also to the Queen, the Queen-mother, and the heir-apparent who, for the purpose, counted as officers of the first rank. The door-keeper, the Superintendent of the harem, the Commander, the Collector-general, and the Chamberlain, receive 24,000 paṇas a year; the prince, his nurse, the Chief Constable, the city officer, the Superintendent of Commerce, the Superintendent of Manufactories, members of the Council, Superintendents of country parts and boundaries, 12,000; chiefs of military corporations, chiefs of elephants, of horses, of chariots, of infantry and commissioners, 8,000; Superintendents of infantry, of cavalry, of chariots, of elephants, guards of timber and elephant forests, 4,000; charioteers, physicians, trainers of horses, chief carpenters,

Salaries.

[1] Ibid., 245—47.

and rearers of animals, 2,000; the foreteller, the reader of omens, the astrologer, the reader of purâṇas, the story-teller, the bard, the retinue of the priest, and all Superintendents of departments, 1,000; musicians, 250; trumpet-blowers, twice as much; artisans and carpenters, 120; servants in charge of quadrupeds and bipeds, workmen doing miscellaneous work, attendants upon the royal person, bodyguards and procurers of free labourers, 60; honourable playmate of the king, the elephant-driver, the sorcerer, miners of mountains, all kinds of attendants, teachers and scholars, 500 to 1,000; a messenger of middle quality, ten paṇas for travelling one yojana, and twice as much for travelling from ten to a hundred yojanas; the king's representative in the Râjasûya and other sacrifices, thrice as much as others; the charioteer of the king, 1,000; principal spies such as those who impersonated the fraudulent, the indifferent, the householder, the merchant, and the ascetic, 100; 'fiery' spies, such as those who served as village servants, poisoners, and those who impersonated mendicant women, 500; servants leading the spies, 250. The remuneration of the subordinate executive and ministerial posts was to be fixed departmentally.[1] So far as possible, all transfers were to be avoided among the guard of royal buildings, forts, and country parts.

Bonuses.

Besides the regular salaries, the government servants expected bonuses from the king when they had to bear the expenses of child-birth, sickness or funerals.

Pensions.

The wives and sons of those who died on duty should receive pensions. So, too, the state should afford relief to the aged or infantine dependents of deceased royal servants.

Promotion.

Promotion depended on good record rather than on seniority. When the treasury was

[1] It is possible, but it cannot be proved, that the higher grades of salaries included part of departmental expenses.

short of money, payment should be made partly in cash and partly in kind.[1] Many government officers, physicians, veterinary surgeons, messengers, are to be provided with land which, however, they could not sell or mortgage.[2]

Payment in kind.

Kauṭalya's judicial system is most elaborate, but there is nothing to indicate how far it corresponded to facts. The details smack too much of theory and must be left out of account. Of course, the king is the highest court of justice. Kauṭalya wants courts to be established in places which formed the headquarters of the circles of eight hundred, four hundred, and two hundred villages and at the meeting-points of districts, and at the headquarters of village circuits. The Courts were of two descriptions, the Dharmasthīya and Kaṇṭaka-śodhana, roughly, civil and criminal, though their spheres overlap and the latter is also invested with some police and executive functions. The judicial bench consists of three judges. The whole administration is presided over by the chief judge.[3] Equity prevails over the letter of the law but the Kauṭalyan penal code is a stern one. Ordinary wounding is to be punished with corresponding mutilation of the offender, perjury with mutilation of the extremities. Injury to a sacred tree, evasion of title on goods sold, and intrusion on the royal procession going to the hunt—all alike might be capitally punished. In a passage of general application, however, Kauṭalya counsels moderation in the infliction of punishments.[4] The procedure prescribed by Kauṭalya with a marvellous fullness of detail, is remarkable for its insistence on recording everything, for its rules on witnesses, their qualifications and disqualifica-

Justice.

[1] Arthaśâstra, 245—47. For the Accounts Department, Ibid., 62.
[2] Ibid., 116—18.
[3] Ibid., 147, 169, 171, 200.
[4] Ibid., 9.

tions in particular cases, their travelling and sumptuary allowances, their cross-examination and punishments in case of perjury.[1] Clerks of the court who neglected their duties or sided with either party to litigation, judges who abused or ill-treated litigants, or accepted bribes were likewise to be chastised.[2] Torture is allowed to elicit confession in certain cases and spies play an ubiquitous role in every stage of judicial proceedings. In Kauṭalya the secret service performs four important duties. Its members noted all happenings, all trends and shades of public feeling and sent regular reports on it to the government—veritable 'newspapers'! They toured in foreign states, tried to fathom the intentions of friends and designs of enemies. As such they closely corresponded to spies in modern Europe. They tried to detect sedition and crime in the land, and thus approximated to the modern Criminal Intelligence Department of India. Lastly, they watched the doings of government servants of all ranks and reported to the highest authorities. Here they bear a partial resemblance to the Wâqiah-navîsas—who, however, were not secret officers—the news-recorders, of the Mughal empire.[3] The spies are to be drawn from both sexes and all grades of society. They should settle on farms, engage in trade, get into prisons, or wander in all conceivable disguises from one end of the kingdom to the other and in regions far beyond. Or they could stoop lower, commit thefts, regale themselves with drink, and lure marked men—natives or foreigners—with their lascivious charms. Throughout his work Kauṭalya displays an abnormal anxiety

Spies.

[1] Ibid., 149, 176.

[2] Ibid., 222—24.

[3] Abul Fazl, Âîn-i-Akbarî, tr. Blochmann. The Hawkins' Voyages, pp. 400-401. Monserrate (tr. Hoyland and ed. Banerji), p. 212. For scattered notices of Wâqiah-navîsas, Abul Fazl, Akbarnâmâ. Extracts from their reports are interspersed throughout Jahâṅgîrnâmâ, Motamad Khân's Iqbâlnâmâ, Maâsir-i-Jahâṅgîrî (Khudâ Bakhsh Ms.), Abdul Hamîd Lâhorî's Pâdshâhnâmâ and other Persian chronicles.

to enlist religion in the service of espionage. He would organise the department in the most thorough-going fashion and devotes many chapters to it. There were to be Saṁsthâs or institutes of espionage to which all classes of spies were to submit their reports. In laying down their methods of work, Kauṭalya sounds the lowest depths of ignominy. All sorts of contemptible fraud, treachery, sacrilege, immorality and cruelty might be resorted to as the occasion demanded.[1] The remuneration of spies varies according to their grade and the nature of their task and sometimes ranges between 250 and 1,000 paṇas.[2]

Defence.

Kauṭalya does not fail to provide a thorough system of military defence. Sthânîya, droṇamukha, khâravâṭika and saṅgrahaṇa fortresses should be set up in the centres of eight hundred, four hundred, two hundred and ten villages respectively. The frontiers should be protected by forts manned by boundary guards.[3] The army comprises regular nationals, mercenaries, recruits from wild tribes, warriors' corporations, immigrants from friendly tracts or deserters from hostile territory. The chief army corps were to be split into divisions and sub-divisions with different flags, trumpets, drums and conch-shells.[4] Kauṭalya provides physicians and surgeons for the battlefield.[5]

Revenue.

The splendours of the court, the salaries of the officers, the expenses of state departments, the army, and the multifarious activities of the state necessitated a vast revenue which seems to have been derived from various sources. In the system of Kauṭalya, the state itself is the biggest landowner and

---

[1] Arthaśâstra, 18—22, 25-26, 208—12, 235—40, 242—44, 376—79, 382—88, 395—401. Kauṭalya (p. 12) calls spies the eyes of the king.

[2] Ibid., 246.

[3] Ibid., p. 46.

[4] Ibid., pp. 139-140.

[5] Ibid., p. 367.

business-concern. It claimed a share in the income of every one else. It exacted a large tribute from the feudatories. It appropriated one-sixth of the land-produce with extra fees for irrigation. A heavy excise on drink, dice and prostitution brought a good deal. Justice, in which heavy fines figure so frequently, might have brought even more. Nothing was manufactured, nothing was distributed, nothing was sold or consumed but something poured into the coffers of the state. The regulation of coinage was in itself a source of income. In the sale of coins which went on, both parties should pay 5 per cent. on their profits to the state. There was a department of the Rûpadarśaka for the purpose.[1]

A large tribute flowed from the feudatories. Kauṭalya frankly recognises the sale of honours for financial purposes. For emergencies he coolly prescribes the fraudulent robbing, through spies, of guilds, religious institutions, wealthy families and individuals. He lays down various devices for collecting money by imposing on popular credulity. In addition to it all, voluntary subscriptions might be called from the people.[2]

In broad outline, such is the administrative system prescribed by Kauṭalya. The details which fill every chapter of his work have to be neglected for our present purpose. But that his general principles are true to facts is borne out by his affinities with Manu, the other Dharma Śâstras and inscriptions. Far in the south, the historical and political data supplied by nearly contemporary Tâmil literature tally with the Arthaśâstra. The pages of V. Kanakasabhai's "Tâmils Eighteen Hundred Years Ago," based on literature, often remind one of

Kauṭalya compared with contemporary southern writers.

[1] The different divisions of the coin standard are the Kârṣâpaṇa, Ardha-Kârṣâpaṇa, Pâda-Kârṣâpaṇa, Caturmâṣaka, Trimâṣaka, Dvimâṣaka, Ekamâṣaka, Ardhamâṣaka, and Kâkaṇika.

[2] Ibid., 240—44.

Kauṭalya. For instance, there are groups of royal attendants —perfumers, garland-makers, betel-bearers, arecanut-servers, armourers, dressing valets, torch or light-bearers and body-guards.[1] Maids and dwarfs are there as in Kauṭalya.[2] Yet more significant are the rules on harlots and courtezans,[3] which, broadly speaking, follow the lines of Kauṭalya. There are tolls and seals on merchandise [4] on which Kauṭalya expatiates at such length.

A similar conclusion emerges from the study of Tiruvalluvar who flourished in the second or third century A.D.

Tiruvalluvar.

His Tâmil ethical classic Muppâl or the Kural, as it is better known, is one of the most popular works south of the Godâvari and has set the standard of literary excellence throughout Tâmilakam.[5] He insists on the same qualities in the king as Kauṭalya—fearlessness, liberality, wisdom, energy, vigilance, learning, bravery, virtue in general,[6] freedom from pride, anger, lust, avarice and from low pleasures,[7] capacity and readiness to hear unpalatable words.[8] "The king who is without the guard of men who can rebuke him will perish even though there be no one to destroy him."[9] As in the Arthaśâstra, so in the Kural, ministers must be of good family and character, should not be ignorant and should not be strangers.[10] The king must be accessible to the people, must personally conduct the administration, examine cases and

[1] Kanakasabhai, Tâmils Eighteen Hundred Years Ago, p. 110.
[2] Ibid., 111.
[3] Ibid., 123.
[4] Ibid., 112
[5] There are numerous Tâmil editions of the Kural. There is an English translation by Pope and another by J. Lazarus who also translates an excellent Tâmil Commentary (Madras, 1885). A selection, with an English translation, by A. Madhaviyah deserves notice. For brief reviews, Gover, Folk-songs of Southern India, pp. 200—245. See also Kanakasabhai, op. cit., p. 138.
[6] Kural, ed. Lazarus, pp. 382—84, 387-88, 390.
[7] Ibid., 431-32, 436.
[8] Ibid., 389.
[9] Ibid., 448.
[10] Ibid., 502, 507—17.

give decisions.[1] The need for consultation is emphasised and the qualifications and duties of the chief officers of state are dwelt upon after the manner of the Arthaśâstras.[2] On ambassadors, the Kural reads like an echo of the Arthaśâstra.[3] On forts,[4] and on the army,[5] the Kural is feeble but in line with the Arthaśâstra. Tiruvalluvar's sayings on espionage might, with slight alterations, pass for those of Kauṭalya. A spy and a book of laws are the eyes of a king.[6] Through spies the king must ascertain daily and quickly what happens among all men.[7] A spy is one who watches all men, to wit, those who are in the king's service, his relatives as well as his enemies.[8] As in Kauṭalya, spies are to assume various disguises, such as those of ascetics.[9] As in Kauṭalya again, the reports of one spy are to be checked by those of another.[10] Honours are not to be conferred publicly on spies lest secrets be divulged.[11] Though avowedly an ethical treatise, the Kural when dealing with diplomatic or foreign affairs, betrays the same temper which made Kauṭalya's name a byeword for fraud and treachery. Its opportunism, its Machiavellian precepts are exactly parallel to the maxims of the Arthaśâstra.[12]

The Bârhaspatya Arthaśâstra.

Another work which must be compared with the Arthaśâstra of Kauṭalya is the Arthaśâstra of Brihaspati in Sûtra form discovered a few years ago by Dr. F. W. Thomas. If its references to Śaiva, Vaiṣṇava and Śâkta sects and to

[1] Ibid., 520, 547—50, 561, 568. See also 551—55, 563—67 on righteous rule.
[2] Ibid., 631—35, 638—40, 643, 646, 655, 660, 675.
[3] Ibid., 681-82, 685-86.
[4] Ibid., 742—50.
[5] Ibid., 761-62, 764, 766—80.
[6] Ibid., 581.
[7] Ibid., 582-83.
[8] Ibid., 584.
[9] Ibid., 585-86.
[10] Ibid., 588-89.
[11] Ibid., 590.
[12] Ibid., 471—74, 488—90

the Yâdavas of Devagiri are genuine, it must be held to be a very late work, not anterior to the 12th century A.D. But these references may be interpolations, for the language and style of the work point to an earlier age. It breathes the Arthaśâstra atmosphere.

The little that this treatise of six short chapters has to say pertains mostly to theory. It is remarkable that it unequivocally declares that the precepts of religion are not to be followed when they are opposed to usage.[1] Right is not to be practised by the king if it is disapproved by the world.[2] The king should keep his wives, relations, friends, counsellors and dependents well in hand. All sorts of means might be employed for the purpose—conciliation, gifts and diplomacy, that is, a policy of divide and rule.[3] An effort should be made to arrive at unanimity in the council-chamber.[4] Youth is declared a disqualification for the delicate office of counsellor.[5]

After emphasising the need of adequate naval and military defence, general protection of the people and enforcement of the social order, Bṛihaspati wants that rest-houses should be provided for the convenience of travellers, temples and schools, tanks and fields should be looked after, festivals should be encouraged and public houses and harlots should be controlled.[6]

That the ideas imbedded in the Arthaśâstras and above all in Kauṭalya remained partly true to facts even in later times is indicated by their persistence in Sanskrit literature. About the 7th or 8th

Kâmandaka.

---

[1] Bârhaspatya Sûtra (ed. F W. Thomas, Puñjâb Sanskrit Series), I, 4, also III, 15. For a rather different view, III, 31—36.

[2] Ibid., I, 4-5.

[3] Ibid., I, 46—48, 52.

[4] Ibid., II, 54; III, 27; IV, 27, 30, 34, 36—44; VI, 4.

[5] On the qualifications of ministers, Ibid., I, 58; II, 51-52.

[6] Ibid., III, 18, 26-27, 38, 49, 53—55, 76—78. For other passages of political significance in Bṛihaspati, see I, 1, 2, 32—35, 51, 93; II, 50; III, 40-41; VI, 8—15.

century A.D. Kâmandaka versified portions of the Kauṭilîya in his celebrated Nitisâra or Essence of Policy.[1] The Agni and Matsya Purâṇas quote whole sections from Kâmandaka. He is likewise profusely drawn upon by later legal writers and commentators, poets and story-tellers. Śaṅkarârya wrote a commentary on Kâmandaka.[2] In the tenth century A.D. Somadeva cried 'back to Kauṭalya.'

About the time of Kauṭalya, the Buddhist author Âryadeva incidentally offered some political reflections in his Catuḥśatikâ. But the only thing noteworthy there is his repudiation of the doctrine of reason of state. Morality or righteousness must everywhere be in supreme, in public as in private life.[3] It is possible that some rulers tried to observe the precept.

Âryadeva.

Another Buddhist writer Ârya Śûra composed his Jâtakamâlâ about the 4th century A.D., but he follows the Jâtakas so closely that he has hardly anything original.[4]

Ârya Śûra.

---

[1] Râjendra Lâla Mitra, M. N. Dutt and B. K. Sarkar hold that Kâmandaka's Nîtisâra was taken to the island of Bâli, in the 4th century A.D., but Jolly (Introduction to the Kauṭilîya Arthaśâstra, pp. 6–8) is inclined to place the author in the 8th century A.D. Winternitz arrives at the same conclusion. See also Dr. Frederick's Report on the Sanskrit Literature of Bâli to the Batavian Society of Arts and Sciences.

In the Nîtisâra, see particularly I, 2–7, 11–14, 21—60; II, 61—71; IV, 33; V, 37; VII, 1-2; XXII, 93; XXXI, 54—68.

[2] The Câṇakya Sûtras (*vide* Appendix to Shamasastry's edition of the Arthaśâstra, 1919) is, in spite of its title, the work of some one else and is, besides, useless for our purpose

[3] Âryadeva, Catuḥśatikâ, pp. 462 - 464.

[4] Târânâtha's identification of Ârya Śûra with Aśvaghoṣa is, on internal grounds, untenable.

In the Jâtakamâlâ see Stories II and III for royal virtues and generosity, Stories VIII and IX for righteous rule and punishment, Stories X for famine relief, XIII for royal righteousness, XXXI for the picture of an ideal prince.

36

CHAPTER XI.

The Gupta Empire and After.

In the fourth century A.D. the centripetal forces re-asserted themselves and an empire of the feudal-federal type embracing the greater part of North India and the Deccan came into existence. The famous Gupta dynasty was founded, as the Allâhâbâd Inscription of Samudragupta records, by a Râja named Gupta. His son was Ghaṭotkaca,[1] whose son and successor Candragupta I. married the Licchavi princess Kumâradevî about 308 A.D. and probably added her patrimony to his dominions. On the obverse of the coins of Candragupta the figure of the Licchavi queen appears along with that of the king himself, while the reverse bears the legend Licchavyaḥ. Probably the Licchavis were a power in eastern India and might have held Pâṭaliputra. The marriage-alliance between the Guptas and Licchavis seems to have resulted somehow in the union of the two principalities. After some additions by conquest, the dominions of Candragupta I. comprised Avadha (Oudh), Tirhut, south Bihâr and the adjoining districts. He assumed the title of Mahârâjâdhirâja and from his reign dates the Gupta era.[2] He was succeeded, in 330 or 335 A.D., by his

The Gupta Dynasty.

[1] Bloch (Ann. Rep. Arch. Surv., 1903-4, p. 102) identifies this ruler with the Ghaṭotkacagupta whose name occurs on one of the Basâḍh seals. V. A. Smith (J.R.A.S., 1905, p. 153) supports the view. But see D. R. Bhandarkar, Ind. Ant., 1912, p. 3

[2] Corpus Inscriptionum Indicarum, Vol. III, Inscriptions of the Early Gupta Kings and their Successors, ed. and tr. Fleet, No. 1. V. A. Smith, Early History of India, 4th edition, pp. 295-96, also Revised Chronology of the Early or Imperial Gupta Dynasty, Ind. Ant., 1902, p. 257. Fleet, op. cit., p. 38, note 5, emphasises that the Gupta era, like other eras, simply grew out of the habit of dating in regnal years. On the calculation of the Gupta era, Ibid., Introduction.

son Samudragupta who, in a series of brilliant campaigns, imposed his suzerainty on many northern Râjas, nine of whom are mentioned in the Allâhâbâd Inscription; on the frontier kingdoms, chiefships or oligarchies; on the chiefs of wild tribes, and on eleven rulers towards the south. He extinguished some of the old dynasties but allowed others to exist under his overlordship. Harişeṇa, the author of the Praśasti on the Allâhâbâd Pillar, boasts that his master conquered the whole earth. He signalised his achievements by celebrating the Aśvamedha sacrifice which seems to have been in abeyance for ages.[1] The range of his alliances extended from the Oxus to Ceylon. Siri Meghavanna or Meghavarṇa of Ceylon (c. A.D. 352 -79) whom Sylvain Lévi, on the basis of evidence from Chinese sources, has proved to be a contemporary of Samudragupta, sent to the latter an embassy, laden with gems, with a view to facilitate the foundation of a monastery The northern emperor was pleased to consider the gifts as tribute.[2] About 375 A.D. Samudragupta was succeeded by his son Candragupta II, surnamed Vikramâditya, who added Mâlwâ, Gujrât and Kâthiâwâḍ to the empire. The Mathurâ Stone Inscription records his boast that he exterminated all kings. He ruled probably until 413 A.D.[3] and was succeeded by Kumâragupta I. who, in spite of a temporary set-back, once again performed the Aśvamedha sacrifice and ruled until 455 A.D.[4] Troubles thickened with the next king

[1] Fleet, Nos. 1, 2. V. A. Smith, op. cit., 297—306. The Aśvamedha was marked by a special issue of gold coins which bear on the reverse the legend Aśvamedha Parâkrama, 'the paramount prince of the horse-sacrifice' and the figure of the queen Dattâdevî, while the obverse has an altar and the figure of the sacrificial horse. See Allan, Catalogue of the Coins of the Gupta Dynasties, etc. See also Rapson, J.R.A.S., 1901, p. 102, for a seal bearing the figure of a horse and the legend Parâkrama.

[2] Sylvain Lévi, Ind. Ant., 1902, p. 192. Fleet, op. cit., No. 1.

[3] Fleet Nos. 3, 4. For an account of the reign of Candragupta II., V. A. Smith, op. cit., pp. 306—16.

[4] V. A. Smith, op. cit., pp. 316-17.

Skandagupta (c. A.D. 455—c. 467), who had to cope with a good deal of internal revolt and with swarms of Huns. The empire fell asunder but the dynasty or its branches continued far into the sixth century A.D.[1]

Records on Gupta Administration.

The administration of the Guptas is to be studied primarily from the inscriptions, supplemented by the coins, of the various kings of the dynasty. A few impressions and opinions are presented by the Chinese pilgrim, Fâ-hien, who travelled in India from 405 to 411 A.D., and who, though engrossed with Buddhist literature and tradition, has incidentally recorded some facts of secular interest. The great poet and dramatist, Kâlidâsa, who belongs most probably to this period, can be noticed in the same connection. So, too, a few other plays like the Mṛicchakaṭikâ and the Mudrârâkṣasa. But since an element of doubt attaches almost invariably to the dates of Hindu writers, this class of evidence is best set forth separately at the end.

Fâ-hien's general observations on Government (405—411).

Fâ-hien's observations are of an entirely general nature and may be noticed first of all. The country was well governed; order was maintained; life and property were secure; the roads were safe for travellers. The government did not interfere much in the life of the people; there were no pass-port regulations, and no registration of households. He remarks that slaughter of animals

[1] Ibid., pp. 326—32. A passage in the Jaina Harivaṁśa Purâṇa (Canto LX, 83—88) has the prophecy that Gupta rule will commence 720 years after the Nirvâṇa of Mahâvîra, that is, about 193-94 A.D., and that it will endure for 231 years. (K. B. Pathak, Ind. Ant., XV, 1886, p. 141.) On the Vâkâṭakas in Gupta history, see Krishnaswamy Aiyangar, Journal of the Mythic Society, Vol. XV, No. 2, pp. 153 et eq.; Annals of the Bhandarkar Institute, Vol. V, Part I, pp. 31 et seq., Y. R. Gupte, Journal of Indian History, December, 1926, pp. 399 et seq.

or drinking was unknown in the country, but he does not mention that either was interdicted by the government. The Guptas were Brahmanists but they observed the rule of toleration and generosity towards all sects. Fâ-hien notes that many Buddhist monasteries enjoyed royal grants of land. The criminal law was mild. Fines were the usual form of punishment. Rebellion or brigandage was punished by amputation of the hand. It may, however, be doubted if Fâ-hien is correct in the statement that capital punishment was altogether unknown. The revenue was derived chiefly from the crown-lands. Fâ-hien mentions free hospitals but only says that they had been founded by benevolent citizens. Those at Pâṭaliputra sheltered the destitute, cripple and diseased from any region. Medicine food, drink, and all comforts were provided free. There is an interesting notice that the kings of Gandhâra were Brâhmaṇas.[1]

Fundamental Political conditions.

The most striking fact which emerges from the study of the Gupta inscriptions is that the empire was dominated by feudalism and that the very idea of a kingdom had become that of a feudal-federal organisation. Râja or even Mahârâja now means only a feudatory. Sâmanta or Mahâsâmanta has the same significance. The higher feudatories have sub-feudatories under them. The idea of a king, as distinct from a feudatory, is conveyed

[1] Travels of Fâ-hien, tr. Giles, Chs. XXVII, XXXVI, XXXVII. The pilgrim's observations on royal generosity and tolerance are borne out by indigenous evidence. Candragupta I. listened to the Buddhist sage Vasubandhu, to whom the prince Samudragupta was made over for education. Naragupta Bâlâditya endowed the Buddhist monastic university of Nâlanda with handsome buildings. The inscriptions which have survived testify abundantly to the generosity of courts. So frequent were the grants that a regular code of agrahâras had grown up. (For instance, see Ep. Ind., XI, Nos. 2, 21.)

only by the grand title of Mahârâjâdhirâja. The suzerain generally assumes two other titles—Parameśvara and Paramabhaṭṭâraka. These are the titles applied to all independent kings in the Gupta as well as later inscriptions. It is significant that the first two rulers of the dynasty—Gupta and Ghaṭotkaca—are not given these high-sounding designations by their descendants and successors. They are only called Mahârâjas.[1] Probably they were only feudatories of more powerful magnates. In Gupta and later inscriptions, feudatories, even when they do not expressly mention their suzerains, are content to call themselves Mahârâjas or adopt a similar title. As soon as the Gupta line started on an independent career of its own and, as was almost inevitable in the political circumstances of the times, stood forth as itself the suzerain of some feudatories, it bedecked itself with titles denoting independence and empire. The inscriptions of the Vardhana dynasty which came into prominence in the first half of the seventh century A.D. tell an identical tale.[2] In this fashion every real kingdom is an empire. An empire or a kingdom is largely a feudal organism. As the internal autonomy of the various regions of an empire is respected, it partakes of the nature of a confederation. The working of this type of polity is well illustrated by the Gupta inscriptions.

The composition of the Gupta Empire.

The Allâhâbâd Inscription states that Samudragupta captured and liberated many kings, while violently uprooting some others of the north. In the latter case is implied annexation, in the former mere imposition of suzerainty. In the same strain the inscription goes on to mention that many royal families which had fallen and had lost their sovereignty were re-established. Autonomy

[1] Fleet, Nos. 1, 4.

[2] For another similar instance, Fleet, No. 47.

carried with it the right to retain or develop different systems of organisation. Thus, the Mâlavas, Ârjunâyanas, Yaudheyas,[1] Mâdrakas, Âbhîras, Prârjunas, Sanakânikas, Kâkas, Kharaparikas and others mentioned in the inscription are clearly tribal oligarchies. The Prahalâdpur Stone Pillar Inscription[2] shows the suzerain appointing a chief as the leader of a tribe. The appointment may be only the recognition of a *de facto* ruler. In any case, the tribal oligarchies retain their individuality and internal self-government. Like other states, they issue coins. Indeed, the large number of punch-marked coins issued from various mints testifies to the large number of autonomous or semi-autonomous regions and groups.[3] There is a notable passage in the Visuddhimagga of Buddhaghoṣa, who flourished about this time, to the effect that a money-changer could recognise from which village, town or capital and from what mint a particular coin was issued. Coinage was thus feudal and local and varied from place to place. So great was this variety that a regular science of coinage grew up as Buddhaghoṣa testifies.[4] There are numerous coins issued by Nigamas or cities and Janapadas or districts, which testify to the existence of very small, partially autonomous areas. The coins, again, prove that some foreign dynasties were allowed to linger. These, however, were being rapidly assimilated to the Hindu tradition. Thus, the coins of the Sytho-Sassanian Varahan V

[1] On the basis of coin-finds, Cunningham placed the Yaudheyas between Delhi and Karnâl (Ann. Rep. Arch. Surv., XIV, p. 140; also Coins of Ancient India, p. 76).

[2] Fleet, No. 57.

[3] On the significance of punch-marks see Spooner, Ann. Rep. Arch. Surv., 1905-6, p. 153; Ibid., 1913-14, p. 220; Walsh, J.B.O.R.S., 1919, pp. 18-19.

[4] D. R. Bhandarkar, Ann. Rep. Arch. Surv., 1913-14, p. 226. On Coinage see also S. B. E., XI, Mahâsudassana Sutta, pp. 252 et seq.

have Śiva and a bull on the reverse.[1] The status of the feudatories shows great variations. In fact, there seem to have been several definite grades among them. In the Allâhâbâd Inscription Pratyantanṛipatis—frontier "kings" or chiefs—are higher than Sâmantas. Mahârâjas are obviously higher than Râjas. Mahârâjas and Mahâsâmantas seem to be of equal status. Both the titles are applied constantly to Samudrasena and his ancestors in an inscription[2] and to others elsewhere.[3] A number of feudatories, in the grants issued by them on their own authority, refer to their feudatories who are therefore sub-feudatories of the emperor. The inscriptions of Mahârâja Hastin, for instance, expressly mention Gupta sovereignty and then proceed to address his own feudatories.[4] It appears that only on acquiring a certain degree of importance could a feudatory be called a Mahârâja. One of the inscriptions makes it clear that after two generations in a family had extended the patrimony and consolidated their power, its third representative assumed the title of Mahârâja. The rise to such a position was duly signalised by a sort of consecration and blessed and acknowledged by the suzerain lord. The Mahârâja Droṇasiṁha was installed "by besprinkling" by his paramount sovereign, 'the sole lord of the circumference of the whole earth,' and the glory of his new position "was purified by his great liberality." Judging from the date of the inscription of his grandson (571-72 A.D.), this event must have taken place during the latter days of the Gupta Empire.[5] It was probably on such occasions that feudatories sometimes ventured to celebrate

[1] Rapson, Indian Coins, No. 15.
[2] Fleet, No. 80.
[3] Ibid., Nos. 3, 10, 12.
[4] Ibid., Nos. 21, 22. See also Ind. Ant., XVII, 1888, p. 183.
[5] Fleet, No. 38.

a sort of Aśvamedha.[1] Vassals specially favoured of the suzerain were given further honorific titles such as Sâmanta-cûḍâmaṇi.[2] Whether these additional titles were hereditary during this period is not clear but the ordinary feudal designations are always transmitted from father to son. Smaller feudatories, those bearing only the title of Râja, also make grants, though, judging from the paucity of their inscriptions, not with the same frequency.[3] It appears that feudatories were sometimes employed in positions of high trust under the suzerain. The Khoh Copper-plate Inscription of the Mahârâja Saṁkṣobha records that the Mahârâja Hastin was placed in charge of eighteen forest chiefships.[4] The grant of Jayabhaṭa II mentions Sâmantas in the same breath with Bhogikas and Viṣayapatis who are undoubtedly government officers.[5] The line between officers of state and feudatories sometimes grows faint and official and feudatory titles are indiscriminately applied to many personages.[6] From another inscription it appears that boundary pillars were sometimes set up to mark off the territories of different feudatories.[7] The king often entered into matrimonial relations with feudatories as with ministers.[8] The feudatories sometimes attended upon the king. The Kahaum Stone Pillar Inscription of the year 460-61 A.D. speaks of the tranquil reign of Skandagupta whose hall of audience (Upasthânabhûmi) was shaken by the wind caused by the falling down (in the act of performing obeisance) of the heads of a hundred Nripatis or feudatory rulers.[9] In the language of etiquette the relations between

1 Ibid., No. 56. Ep. Ind., X, No. 13.
2 Fleet, Nos. 48, 49, 50.
3 Ibid., Nos. 40, 41.
4 Fleet, No. 25, see also Nos. 16, 19.
5 Ind. Ant., V, p. 114.
6 Ind. Ant., V, 105; II, 114.
7 Fleet, No. 22.
8 Ibid., Nos. 12, 55. Ep. Ind., XV, No. 4.
9 Fleet, No 14. Also Bhau Daji, J. B. B. R. A. S., Vol. VIII.

the suzerain and the vassal are summed up in the expression Pâdânudhyâta, "meditating on the feet of—," which emphasises reverence and obedience. The same term is used to typify the attitude of a Mahârâja or Mahârâjâdhirâja towards his parents, preceptors or other superiors.[1] In almost all of the numerous "perpetual," "eternal" grants of villages recorded in the inscriptions, the inhabitants concerned are commanded to obey the grantees. The grants being also expressly free from the entrance of government police and soldiers, it seems that the grantee was expected to arrange for defence and maintenance of order. Since most of the grantees were Brâhmaṇas, some of them might not have discharged these duties by themselves. Perhaps they left them to chief persons of the village. But in any case, this system of grants which are avowedly hereditary, which, in fact, are expected to last "until the sun and moon endure," and the resumption of which is cursed with the heaviest imprecations, would introduce an element of feudalism at the bottom. These small landholders, however, could easily be controlled in the case of any untoward incidents. The great feudatories might have been more difficult to manage. Vassalage faded by insensible degrees into practical independence. It is significant that the Allâhâbâd Inscription counts the king of Ceylon, undoubtedly independent, as a sort of vassal.

The Emperor's Titles.

From the Gupta period onwards, an independent king—generally a real emperor—almost always styles himself Parameśvara, supreme lord, Mahârâjâdhirâja, supreme king of Mahârâjas, and Paramabhaṭṭâraka, the most worshipful one.[2] Sometimes he adds other equally imposing titles—Samrâṭ,[3] Ekâdhirâja,[4] Râjâdhirâja, Cakravartin,

[1] Fleet, Nos. 3, 26. Ep. Ind., X, No. 12. Ind. Ant., XII, p. 249.
[2] For the Gupta period, *i.e.*, Fleet, Nos. 1, 4, 5, 10, 12, 13, 32, 46, etc.
[3] Ibid., No. 33.
[4] Ibid., No. 32.

Paramadaivata.[1] The later Godval Plates of Vikramâditya I, A.D. 674, state that one of his ancestors Pulakeśin I acquired the title of Parameśvara by defeating Harṣavardhana but in the same sentence Pulakeśin's father is also called Parameśvara. So in the Deccan, too, the title must be held to be the ordinary symbol of independence and suzerainty.[2] The Mankuwar Stone Inscription of Kumâragupta, of the Gupta year 129 (=448-49 A.D.), calls him only a Mahârâja.[3] But this solitary instance hardly constitutes an exception to the general rule of titles. If it is not an error, it may mean that the Gupta ruler had been forced at the time to bow to his enemies who, as we know for certain from other inscriptions, assailed him on all sides and reduced him to a sorry plight. He might have been compelled temporarily to acknowledge the overlordship of others. The character of the imperial titles was so well recognised that the Hun ruler Torâmaṇa styled himself a Mahârâjâdhirâja.[4] His son Mihirakula, however, does not style himself so, perhaps because at the time of the inscription in question, he did not retain his independence.[5] Later, sometimes the shorter form Bhaṭṭâraka was coupled with Mahârâjâdhirâja.[6] In point of titles, the practice of the north was the same as that of the Deccan and the south.[7] In later times, the title Bhaṭṭâraka could be used of feudatories,[8] but such instances are not common. One of the Basâḍh seals has Yuvarâja Bhaṭṭâraka, which may mean the chief minister of the heir-apparent but which may also imply that the title

[1] Ibid., No. 39. Kumâragupta's Dâmodarpur Copper-plate Inscriptions, Ep. Ind., XV, 113.

[2] Ep. Ind., X, No. 2.

[3] Fleet, No. 11.

[4] Ibid., No. 36.

[5] Ibid., No. 37.

[6] Ind. Ant., III, p. 26; IX, p. 172.

[7] Ibid., X, p. 103, 189; XI, p. 124.

[8] Ibid., IX, p. 168; XIV, p. 98.

Bhaṭṭâraka was sometimes applied to the heir-apparent. The consort of a suzerain was called Mahâdevî but the title was occasionally applied also to the consort of a Mahârâja.[1]

The Government and people.

As usual, the king personally conducted the administration. He transacted the business of the state even on tours, when he was accompanied by some of his ministers.[2] Towards his subjects he adopts a paternal attitude. Most of the inscriptions discovered record grants to Brâhmaṇas, to groups of scholars or students, or to religious and charitable institutions. So numerous were the gifts that, as the Bihâr Stone Pillar Inscription of Skandagupta indicates, a special officer Agrahârika was deputed to arrange them.[3] The example of the king was followed by his relations, ministers, feudatories and even ordinary subjects. The character of the endowments may be illustrated by a few typical instances. The Bhitârî Stone Pillar Inscription of Skandagupta records the allotment of a village for the maintenance of a temple in which the king had installed an image of Śârṅgin or Viṣṇu.[4] There are gifts dedicated to Satras, charitable alms-houses or halls.[5] Âdityasena's mother built a religious college or monastery.[6] The Sâñchi Stone Inscription of Candragupta's reign records the grant of a village or an area of land and a sum of money to the Ârya Saṁgha at the Buddhist Vihâra of Kâkanâdaboṭa for the purpose of feeding mendicants or maintaining lamps.[7] The

1 Fleet, Nos. 4, 10, 12, 26, 44, 45, 46, 47, 80. For the detailed treatment of the titles and feudal-federal conditions in later times, see infra.

2 Fleet, No. 6.

3 Ibid., No. 12.

4 Ibid., No. 13.

5 Ibid., No. 7. Also Nos. 8, 9, 10.

6 Ibid, No. 42, also No. 43.

7 Ibid., No. 5.

Udayagiri Cave Inscription commemorates the excavation of a cave as a Śaiva temple.[1] A high personage, apparently a minister of Samudragupta, erected a Yûpa or sacrificial pillar.[2] Grants were sometimes made to groups as large as a thousand persons.[3] Some of the endowments were permanently beneficial to the community at large. A queen caused a tank to be excavated.[4] Mayûrâkṣa, a minister, built a temple of Viṣṇu, another of the Divine Mothers, and other temples and halls of the gods, and at the same time supplied the city of his residence with wells for drinking water, pleasure-gardens, irrigation wells, tanks and various kinds of causeways.[5] A private person built a satra or charity-hall and a pillar.[6] Other endowments would be mainly ornamental. Mâtriviṣṇu, a Mahârâja and his brother Dhanyaviṣṇu, erected a column called Dhvaja-stambha, flag-staff, of the God Viṣṇu.[7] All the grants, whether by suzerains or feudatories, are meant to be eternal in duration. The grantor calls upon all his feudatories, officers and people to respect the endowment. He exhorts his descendants and successors to leave it unmolested. A few verses from Vyâsa are almost invariably quoted to consign all disturbers of grants to 60,000 years of hell and to promise their respecters an equal span of bliss in heaven. Every śâsana or charter, as the deed is called,[8] is at pains to limit the boundaries of the areas of land-grants and to specify the accompanying

[1] Ibid., No. 6.

[2] Ibid., No. 12.

[3] Ibid., No. 55.

[4] Ibid., Nos. 44, 45.

[5] Ibid., No. 17.

[6] Ibid., No. 10.

[7] Ibid., No. 19. For other grants of feudatories, Nos. 16, 21, 22, 25, 27–31, 35, etc.

[8] Ibid., *i.e.*, No. 21.

privileges, in the most exact manner. Grants could be made out of any areas.[1] Sometimes only part of the revenue of the area alienated was assigned to the grantee.[2]

The exigencies of endowments serve to give an idea of at least some of the chief officers under the Guptas.

Chief officers.

Numerous inscriptions mention Senâpati, Mahâsenâpati, Balâdhyakṣa or Balâdhikṛita,[3] Mahâbalâdhyakṣa or Mahâbalâdhikṛita, who are all military officers and who perhaps represent four different grades of them. There are two other high military officers—Bhaṭâśvapati, commander of infantry and cavalry, and Kaṭuka, commander of the elephant corps. On the financial side of the military administration was the Raṇabhâṇḍâgârâdhikaraṇa, chief of the treasury of the war office, who is mentioned in the Basâḍh seals. Another minister who had something to do with military policy was the Saṁdhivigrahika or Mahâsaṁdhivigrahika, a sort of foreign secretary.

Military.

It is not clear whether the two terms are used for the same officer or whether the addition of the adjective Mahâ indicates superiority of rank. In the latter case, the Saṁdhivigrahika is the assistant of the Mahâsaṁdhivigrahika. Three other variations in this designation are met with—saṁdhivigrahin, saṁdhvgrahâdhikṛita, saṁdhivigrahâdhikaraṇâdhikṛita. Camûpa is another military officer, perhaps lower than those mentioned above.

In the Gupta age, as in other periods of ancient Indian history, the same officers might perform various functions.

Chief Judges.

There was no real separation of civil and military, executive, judicial and revenue functions. But there were officials who were

[1] Ibid., No. 38.

[2] Ibid., No. 31.

[3] The Basâḍh seals also mention the form Balâdhikaraṇa (Ann. Rep. Arch. Surv., 1903-4, pp. 101 et seq.).

occupied predominantly with only one side of the administration. The chief judicial officers are designated Daṇḍanâyaka, Mahâdaṇḍanâyaka, Sarvadaṇḍanâyaka or Mahâsarvadaṇḍaṇâyaka. Other variations of the designation are Daṇḍâdhipa, Daṇḍanâtha, Daṇḍâbhinâtha, Daṇḍâdhipati, Daṇḍeśa, Daṇḍeśvara. Daṇḍa also means an army in Sanskrit literature. There are inscriptions which equate Daṇḍâbhinâtha with Camûpa and thus make him undoubtedly a military commander. But, on the whole, judicial officers are meant. Possibly, Daṇḍanâyaka, Mahâdaṇḍanâyaka, Sarvadaṇḍanâyaka and Mahâsarvadaṇḍanâyaka represent different grades in the judicial hierarchy.

Other chief officers.

One of the inscriptions (Fleet, No. 55) mentions Sarvâdhyakṣas, Superintendents of all, but it is not clear whether they are central or provincial officers. The Basâḍh seals mention Daṇḍapâśâdhikaraṇa who is probably the chief of police. Numerous inscriptions mention Dûtaka, Dûta or Âjñâdâpaka who communicates royal commands to officers and people concerned. But this office seems often to have been combined with others. In the Gupta Inscriptions the Mahâsaṁdhivigrahika generally acts as the Dûtaka. On some occasions the Dûtaka is dispensed with. The king may declare his commands to officers through his own mouth (svamukhâjñâ).[1]

[1] All these officers are mentioned frequently in the Gupta Inscriptions (Fleet). The other authorities are the Basâḍh seals (Ann. Rep. Arch. Surv., 1903-4, pp. 101—20). The spot of the finds probably represents the home of a maker of seals as D. R. Bhandarkar conjectured from the large number of officials, prominent personages and communities whose seals were made (Ind. Ant., 1912, p. 3). On the official designations see also Ind. Ant., IV, p. 175; VII, p. 70; VIII, p. 20; X, p. 252. The Dûtaka or Âjñâdâpaka is also designated Âjñâmahâmahattara or by similar other titles (Ind. Ant., VI, p. 124; XIII, p. 128; XIV, pp. 160-61).

There are a number of household officers. The Pratîhâra or the Mahâpratîhâra was the chief guard or usher of the palace. The Vinayâsura announced and conducted visitors to the king. The functions of the sthapâlisamrâṭ are not clear but he seems to have been the Superintendent of the host of employees in the women's apartments, that is, in the harem. The Pratinartaka was the bard or herald.[1]

Palace officers.

The king's territory was divided into a number of Bhuktis or provinces, a Bhukti into Viṣayas or districts, a Viṣaya into Grâmas or villages. The governor of a Bhukti bears various designations in the epigrahic records—Bhogika, Bhogapati, Goptâ, Uparika-mahârâja, Râjasthâniya[2]—which convey some idea of his duties. Bhukti or Bhogika has fiscal implications and shows that the provinces were also meant to be fiscal divisions. Uparika-mahârâja has even a more pronounced fiscal significance. Goptâ means protector and, doubtless, the governor was expected to protect the people under his charge. The term Râjasthâniya shows that the governor was considered to be a viceroy, representative of the king. Royal princes were sometimes appointed to this office.[3] The officer called Kumârâmâtya was most probably the minister of a prince-viceroy. Mahâkumârâmâtya may be an honorific synonym thereof, or a higher grade in the same office.

The Provinces

[1] Fleet, Nos. 26, 39. Basâḍh seals, Ann. Rep. Arch. Surv., 1903, pp. 102 et seq.

[2] Fleet, No. 14. Dâmodarpur Copper Plates, Ep. Ind., XV, No. 7. Fleet, No. 14, mentions the qualities desirable in a governor of a province or a ruler of a city. The grants of Dadda II (477-78 A.D.—495 A.D.) from Bharukaccha, modern Baronch, substitute Râṣṭrapati for Bhogika. Râṣṭra had now acquired partially a fiscal significance (Ind. Ant., XVII, 1888, p. 183).

[3] Fleet, No. 14.

The provincial governor had a number of subordinates called Tanniyuktakas. A province had a number of revenue officers. The Basâḍh seals mention the chief of the Uparikas of Tîrabhukti.

The District.

The Dâmodarpur Copper Plates indicate that the king appointed provincial governors and that the latter selected Viṣayapatis or heads of districts. The Sûrat Plates of Vyâghrasena, of the year 490-91 A.D., indicate that âhâra was another name for Viṣâya.[1] In a slightly later record, the Copper Plate Grant of Budhagupta, an Âyukta is mentioned as a Viṣayapati.[2] It seems to imply that an inferior officer had risen by merit or favour to the headship of a district. A district officer had his Adhiṣṭhâna or headquarters in a town. In the Adhiṣṭhâna he had his Adhikaraṇa—office and probably court. He had a large secretariat, consisting of Kâyasthas or scribes, headed by the Prathama Kâyastha. It seems he was expected to maintain close touch with important sections of the people. The Dâmodarpur Copper Plate Inscriptions seem to refer to a sort of advisory council which included a Nagaraśreṣṭhin, a principal citizen; Prathamakulika, representing the craft-guilds, and Sârthavâha, probably representing the trade-guilds

The village.

The lowest administrative division, the village, was under a Grâmika.[3] How he was appointed we are not told. Probably, heredity, informal village opinion and government approval were jointly responsible for his selection. Henceforward, the inscriptions constantly mention Mahattaras, elders of a village, who are addressed in the grants. It is possible, but there is only negative evidence to support the hypothesis, that this

[1] Ep. Ind., XI, No. 21.
[2] Ep. Ind., XV, p. 138.
[3] Fleet, No. 22.

represents a fresh development in village administration. There is no evidence of any village councils in the north. But the Mahattaras seem to be associated in an informal manner with the Grâmika in the administration of village affairs. The Dâmodarpur Plates mention Aṣṭakulâdhikaraṇa, which is difficult to explain but which probably refers to representatives of families, who are likely to have been consulted. There seems to have been a village accountant called Talvâṭaka.[1]

Towns.

Towns seem to have had an administrative machinery of their own. The officer in charge of a town is called Drâṅgika.[2] The term, derived from Udraṅga, has fiscal associations. It is possible that the Drâṅgika was supposed to be as much a fiscal officer as anything else and collected the dues from merchants and others. The town-officer seems to have been appointed by the provincial governor. In one of the inscriptions a viceroy appoints his own son to the charge of a city.[3] Here the young officer becomes very popular with his wards, thanks to his smiling countenance, freedom of conversation, inquiries about welfare and to his habit of conferring honours and presents on the people. On the bursting of a lake, he offered sacrifices to the gods, and built an embankment 100 cubits in length, 68 in breadth and of seven (?) men's height, after "an immeasurable expenditure of wealth." The city-officer is expected to be the leader of the people. Besides these sets of officials whose location is clear, there are numerous others who seem to be associated indiscriminately with the central, provincial and district administrations.

[1] Fleet, *e.g.*, Nos. 46, 38. Ep. Ind., XV, No. 7.

[2] Fleet, No. 38.

[3] Ibid., No. 14.

There are many police officers in evidence—Daṇḍapâśika (policeman), Daṇḍika (chastiser), Cauroddharaṇika (officer apprehending thieves).[1] Câṭas and Bhâṭas also investigated crime.

The Police.

Thus the Sûrat plates of Mahârâja Vyâghrasena, of the year 490-91 A.D., lay down that the small piece of land granted is not to be entered by Câṭas or Bhaṭas unless in order to arrest robbers or persons guilty of high treason.[2] On the other hand, a later writer Lallâ Dîkṣita, commenting on the Mṛicchakaṭika,[3] explains Câṭa as Kṣudraviṣayabhoktâ—the officer of a small district. It will appear that the term had different meanings at different places. Later it came to mean a thief or a bad character.

The inscriptions yield some details about the fiscal administration. The land seems to have been surveyed and measured and the holdings, their boundaries and occupants recorded.

Fiscal Officers.

The surveyors and measurers were called Pramâtṛi, and those who fixed boundaries were designated Sîmâpradâtṛi. The cases arising from these processes seem to come before officers called Nyâyakaraṇikas.[4] The Uparika mentioned in the Bihâr Stone Pillar Inscription of Skandagupta[5] seems to be another revenue officer concerned probably with the tax called Uparikara.[6] The Dhruvâdhikaraṇa seems to be a revenue superintendent.[7] The Utkhetayitâ is a similar dignitary.[8] The exigencies of land-revenue seem to be chiefly responsible for the growth of an elaborate record

---

1 Fleet, Nos. 38, 46.

2 Ep. Ind., XI, No. 21.

3 Ed. Godbole, Bombay, 1896, p. 223.

4 Fleet, No. 38. Ep. Ind., XII, p. 75.

5 Fleet, No. 12.

6 Infra.

7 Fleet, Nos. 38, 12.

8 Ep. Ind., XII, p. 75.

department. The Pustapâla who is mentioned in the Dâmodarpur Plates is the protector, that is, the keeper of books. Akṣapaṭalika or keeper of records and Mahâkṣa paṭalika or great keeper of records seem to be higher officers in the same class.[1] Karaṇika who has charge of Karaṇas or documents seems to be a registrar.[2] The draftsmen are called Kartṛi or Śâsayitṛi.[3] In the Dâmodarpur Copper Plates I—III, they are expected to be familiar with holdings and boundaries and ever ready to report to the government.

Besides those chiefly concerned with land-revenue there were officers who managed other heads of the income of the state. The Śaulkika seems to be in charge of customs and tolls.[4] The Gaulmika seems to be entrusted with forests and the income therefrom and perhaps also forts.[5]

The royal treasure seems to be in charge of a class of officers called Bhâṇḍâgârâdhikṛitas.[6] There are a large

Miscellaneous officers.

number of subordinate employees such as Âyuktapuruṣas[7] and Viniyuktakas, the latter being inferior to the former in status.[8] Diviras and Lekhakas are the terms applied to clerks. Perhaps there were several grades of them.[9]

It appears that from the fiscal point of view the land was divided, broadly speaking, into that fit for cultivation

Bhûmichidra.

and otherwise. Grants are generally made according to the Bhûmichidra Nyâya. Bühler discovered that the term occurs in the Vaiśyâdhyâya of Yâdavaprakâśa's Vaijayantî, verse 18, where it is explained

---

1 Fleet, Nos. 39, 60.
2 Ibid., No. 55.
3 Ibid., No. 88.
4 Ibid., No. 12.
5 Ibid.
6 Ep. Ind., XII, p. 75.
7 Fleet, No. 1.
8 Ibid., No. 38.
9 Ibid., Nos. 27, 80.

as Kṛiṣya yogyâbhûḥ—lands fit for agriculture. It appears that there was a recognised fiscal code applicable to land of one or both the descriptions and that it prescribed the amount of the various dues.[1]

Revenue.

The Gupta Inscriptions bear out the inference suggested by the Dharma Śâstras and Arthaśâstras that the number of taxes was very large in ancient India. Unfortunately, some of the terms used are obscure. The inscriptions seem to assume that they were familiar to all. But they occur rarely in literature. The dictionaries are sometimes silent on them and sometimes contradict one another. Almost every grant is made with the Udraṅga (Sodraṅga). Some scholars have taken it to mean boundary or something like it. But the context supports the view that it was a species of revenue. Bühler drew attention to the fact that in the Śâśvatakoṣa (ed. Zachariaes, pp. xxix, 260) Udraṅga is explained as Uddhâra and Udgrantha (Udgrâha) and thus seems to mean the share of the produce usually collected by the king.[2] It is generally mentioned at the head of all dues in the inscriptions. Probably, it refers to the chief tax. Another term which is mentioned quite as frequently and, in general, immediately after Udraṅga, is Uparikara. A grant of land is usually made Soparikara (with the Uparikara). A few scholars have taken it to refer to a boundary or some variety of land but, most probably, it refers to another species of dues. Fleet held it to be a tax levied on cultivators who had no proprietary rights in the soil. Miscellaneous dues were levied under numerous heads. Thus the Poonâ Plates of the Vâkâṭaka Queen Prabhâvati Guptâ, daughter of Candragupta II and wife of Rudrasena II, speak of the claims of the state on pasturage, hides, charcoal, mines,

[1] For the occurrence of Bhûmichidra Nyâya, Fleet, No. 31.

[2] Ind. Ant., XII, p. 189, note.

purchase of fermenting drugs, hidden treasures, deposits, abundance of milk and flowers, succession of cattle.[1] In several inscriptions reference is made to Dhânya and Hiraṇya as heads of state dues. The former seems to be some special kind of contribution in grain, while the latter, which means gold, undoubtedly pertains to right of the state to gold and probably also other mines. Vâta, another due, defies explanation but Bhûta, which is often mentioned with it, is probably a tax on what is withered. Another source of revenue was the occasional contributions for the royal army, militia or police. Along with the enumeration of exemptions from taxation, it is stated in grant after grant that the plots of land in question are not to be entered by Câṭas and Bhâṭas. Fleet interpreted the last two terms to mean irregular and regular troops. Others have taken Câṭa to mean a thief or robber but it makes no sense to state that particular pieces of land are not to be entered by thieves or robbers. That command would be of universal application. In no case could there be any ground for making such a statement along with exemptions from taxation. Câṭa probably refers to a sort of police force. From the fiscal point of view, the importance of these provisions is that they indicate a distinct source of revenue in the form of levies. It will appear that the petty dues, particularly, those in kind, charged from a village went to pay the village headman and other local officers. Manu (VII, 199) says that the salary of a village headman should ordinarily be those articles which the villagers ought to furnish daily to the king such as food, drink, fuel.[2] Viṣṭika is forced labour which was counted among the regular royal dues. One of the commonest features of ancient Indian grants is that the pieces of land granted are

---

[1] Ep. Ind., XV, No. 4.

[2] For the occurrence of fiscal terms, Fleet, Nos. 3, 8, 21, 22, 31, etc.

declared free from the obligation of supplying forced labour. The grants of feudatories, too, contain that provision.[1] Daśâparâdhâḥ refers to fines levied for ten offences, *viz.*, (*a*) three offences of the body—theft, murder and adultery, (*b*) four offences of speech—harsh, untruthful, libellous, and pointless words, and (*c*) three offences of mind—coveting other's property, thinking of wrong, and devotion to what is not true. This traditional classification throws little light on the actual administration of justice. Thinking could hardly have been punished. Murder would have carried a higher penalty than fines. The term daśâparâdhâḥ is only a generic name for sins and in its administrative sense, only means judicial fines in general. However, it definitely proves that justice was one of the recognised sources of revenue and, as such, could be alienated to favourite grantees.

Tribute.

Tribute and presents from some of the feudatories must be reckoned among the sources of the suzerain's income. Samudragupta's Allâhâbâd Inscription records in a tone of pride that feudatories sought to gratify the emperor by paying various 'taxes' to him.[2]

Government of Feudtaories.

The internal government of the feudatories themselves resembled that of the suzerain. Several inscriptions show that hereditary Mahârâjas like Hastin had their own Amâtyas or ministers, Saṁdhivigrahikas, Dûtakas, Bhogikas, Viṣayapatis, Uparikas, etc.[3]

Combination of offices.

Numerous inscriptions show that in the government of the suzerain, as in that of feudatories, two or more offices were often combined in the same hands. The Kumârâmâtya,

---

[1] Ep. Ind., XI, No. 21. [2] Fleet, No. 1.

[3] Fleet, Nos. 21—23, 27—31. These inscriptions expressly mention Gupta suzerainty.

Saṁdhivigrahika and Dûtaka, for instance, might be the same person.[1] In the inscription of a feudatory Bhogika and Amâtya are the same man.[2] On the other hand, an office could be split up between two persons. Sometimes the same ruler has more than one Dûtaka at the same time.[3]

Official families.

Another fact which epigraphic testimony establishes beyond doubt is that officials were often chosen from the same families and that offices sometimes became hereditary under the suzerain as well as under the feudatories. In the Karmadaṇḍa Inscription of Kumâragupta of the year 436-37 A.D., Pṛithivîṣeṇa, the Kumârâmâtya and subsequently the Mahâbalâdhikṛita of the king is the son of Śikharasvâmin who was the Kumârâmâtya of Candragupta II.[4] In another inscription a son succeeds his father in office.[5] The sons of high officers could be well provided for at court. Hariṣeṇa, the author of the Praśasti on the Allâhâbâd Inscription and a fevourite of the king, was the son of a Mahâdaṇḍanâyaka.[6] In an inscription of Mahârâja Hastin a Saṁdhivigrahika is the son of a Bhogika who himself was the son of a Bhogika.[7]

Guilds.

As in the previous epoch, the economic life of the community was partly regulated by guilds. The Mandasor Stone Inscription of Kumâragupta and Bandhuvarman records that a number of silk weavers migrated from the Lâṭa Viṣaya (central and southern Gujarât) into the centre of Daśapura. Some of them adopted other occupations while those who adhered to their original craft constituted themselves into a guild

[1] Fleet, *en passant*.
[2] Ibid., No. 28.
[3] Ibid., No. 30.
[4] Ep. Ind., X, No. 15.
[5] *Fleet*, No. 6.
[6] Ibid., No. 1.
[7] *Ibid.*, *No. 21*.

which attained great prosperity. During the governorship of Bandhuvarman this guild built a temple of the sun (437-38 A.D.) and a generation later (473-74 A.D.) the same guild repaired it. We are told that the kings treated the guilds like their sons.[1] Another inscription refers to a guild of oilmen and hints at the possibility of their moving away elsewhere.[2] The Basâḍh seals show that many guilds had seals of their own.[3]

After the Gupta Empire.

The system of administration which prevailed under the Imperial Guptas persisted throughout the days of the decline of the empire and also after its fall. Here and there were some variations in titles and administrative details but the framework remained exactly the same. A few of the important inscriptions of the interval between the Guptas and the Vardhanas may be passed in rapid review. The Khoh Copper Plate Inscription shows how offices might rotate in the same families. The father and grandfather of the Mahâsaṁdhivigrahika had been Bhogikas. The grandfather is also given the title of Amâtya or minister. Here are two Dûtakas, one of them being the Mahâbalâdhikṛita.[4] Another inscription of the same feudatory, of the year 533-34 A.D., mentions the usual offices and fiscal arrangements. Like others, it emphasises that the inhabitants should obey the grantees.[5] The Betul Plates of Saṁkṣobha, of the year 518-19 A.D., from the modern Central Provinces show a line of hereditary Parivrâjaka Mahârâjas, who owed allegiance to Guptas, exercising overlordship over a number of forest chiefships. One of the Mahârâjas prides himself on establishing the Varṇâśrama-

[1] Fleet, No. 18.
[2] Ibid., No. 6.
[3] Ann. Rep. Arch. Surv., 1903-4, pp. 102 et seq.
[4] *Fleet, No. 30.*
[5] Ibid., No. 31.

dharma.[1] In the Mandasor Stone Inscription of Yaśodharman, the members of a single family occupy several high offices and one of them constructs a large well for popular use. Here, curiously enough, Yaśodharman is only called Janendra.[2] Another stone-pillar inscription records that a column was erected for the purpose of inscribing a laudation of Yaśodharman's power and glory.[3] The Chamnak Copper Plate Inscription of the Mahârâja Pravarasena II shows how suzerains and feudatories intermarried. Here the charter is written by the Senâpati.[4] The Siwâni Copper Plate Inscription of the same ruler records that he performed four Aśvamedha sacrifices. Evidently, the ceremony was now losing its supreme significance. The privileges conferred with the grant are specific and throw light on contemporary fiscal arrangements. The village granted to some priests "is not to be entered by the regular troops or by the umbrella-bearers; it does not carry with it (the right to) cows and bulls in succession (of production), or to the abundance of flowers and milk, or to the pasturage, hides and charcoal, or to the mines for the purchase of salt in a moist state; it is entirely free from all (obligation of) forced labour; it carries with it the hidden treasures and deposits, and the klripta and upaklripta." The last two terms are obscure. But the inscription suffices to give an idea of the petty dues levied, probably in kind, and the state monopolies. Needless to say, the grant is to be eternal and hereditary. All protection was to be extended to its holders, no hindrance of any kind was to be offered to them.[5] In the Ganeśgaḍ Plates of Dhruvasena I, of the year 526-27 A.D., from

[1] Ep. Ind., VIII, No. 28.
[2] Fleet, No. 35. On Yaśodharman's Exploits against the Huns, J. J. Modi, J. B. B. R. A. S., XXIV. pp. 539—92; also Asiatic Papers, pp. 293–349.
[3] Fleet, No. 33.
[4] Ibid., No. 55.
[5] Ibid., No. 56

Bhâvanagara state, two brothers are big feudatories,—Mahârâja and Mahâsâmanta—and a third one holds the post of Senâpati which he passes on to his son. The feudal dominion has the usual administrative machinery. Drâṅgikas are the town-officers with whom are associated Mahattaras, elders. It appears that, as in the village, the elders were informally consulted on administrative matters in towns. Sthânâdhikaraṇikas are the police-officers in charge of Sthânas (police stations), from which the medieval and modern term thânâ is derived. The nomenclature is interesting. In this inscription the fiscal officers and arrangements are the same as in the foregoing ones.[1] Two other grants of Dhruvasena I from Pâlitânâ introduce big feudatories, Mahâsâmanta Mahârâjas.[2] In the Pâlitânâ Plates of Siṁhâditya, of the year 574 A.D., also appears a line of hereditary Sâmanta Mahârâjas—big feudatories. Among those to whom the Śâsana is addressed are Râjasthânîyas, Drâṅgikas, Mahattaras, riders on elephants and horses who seem to form part of the army.[3] The Pâlitânâ Plates of Dharasena II of the year 571 A.D. mention a few other officers but none which has not been already noticed.[4] These grants prove that Kâṭhiâwâḍ had the same system of administration as the north. Gujarât was quite in line. The Sunao Kala Plates of Saṁgamasiṁha of the year 540-41 A.D., from Bharukaccha, modern Baronch, in Gujarât, furnish an illustration. The Mahâsâmanta Mahârâja, though a feudatory, has a regular administrative system of the usual type. His Śâsana is addressed to Râjasthânîyas, Uparikas, Kumârâmâtyas, Viṣayapatis, Drâṅgikas, Câṭas, Bhaṭas and others. Ârakṣikas and Kulaputrakas are also mentioned. The former are probably

[1] Ep. Ind., III, No. 46.
[2] Ep. Ind., XVII, 7.
[3] Ibid., XI, No. 2.
[4] Ibid., XI, No. 5. See also No. 9.

police-officers. Kulaputrakas are probably not regular officials but merely representatives of families who were consulted by village and town-officers. There is a chamberlain Mahâpratîhâra, while the Saṁdhivigrahika acts as Dûtaka. The fiscal system is the same as that of the Guptas. One of the privileges conferred on the grantee is that his area will not be entered by Câṭas and Bhaṭas whose presence, obviously, was felt as a burden.[1] The foreign rulers who established themselves in India adapted themselves to the Hindu system. In the Eraṇ Stone Boar Inscription Torâmaṇa is called Mahârâjâdhirâja.[2] Elsewhere Torâmaṇa has the titles Śâhi and Jauval as well as Râjâdhirâja.[3] Some of the coins of Mihirakula have the bull-emblem of Siva and the legend Jayatu Vṛiṣaḥ on the reverse.[4]

The shape which the Hindu administrative system assumed under the Guptas never left it afterwards. In the next seven centuries we meet with variations from place to place and time to time but the essentials are the same. From the administrative point of view the Gupta empire stands at the centre of ancient Indian history.

Kâlidâsa.

It is probably the institutions of the Gupta age which are reflected in the works of Kâlidâsa, the greatest of Hindu classical poets and dramatists. His date has long been a matter of acute controversy. There are still a few scholars who argue for the correctness of the tradition that he lived in the first century B.C. Again, a few are still inclined to place him in the sixth century A.D. But the general consensus of opinion, relying on internal literary and

---

[1] Ep. Ind., X, No. 16.

[2] Fleet, No. 36.

[3] Ep. Ind., I, 29. See also Fleet, Coins and History of Torâmaṇa, Ind. Ant., XVIII, 1889, p. 225.

[4] Catalogue of Coins in the Indian Museum, p. 236.

astronomical evidence, favours the 4th century A.D. as the earliest and the 5th as the latest date of the poet. This, at any rate, is at present the soundest working hypothesis. Kâlidâsa is claimed by Kashmir, the Gangetic plains, Bengâl, the Deccan and even Ceylon. But if, as appears probable, his Raghuvaṁśa contains some veiled references to Gupta emperors, he may be presumed to have enjoyed the patronage of the Gupta court or at any rate to have come into contact with it. It may be that he spent some time at Ujjayinî, the capital of Mâlwâ. Bhoja in his Śriṅgâraprakâśikâ says that Kâlidâsa was sent on a political embassy to the Kuntala king. There is no contemporary record to check the statement but internal evidence certainly suggests that the poet lived in intimate touch with men and affairs at a court and was by no means a man of the cloister.[1]

The Raghuvaṁśa.

In his Raghuvaṁśa Kâlidâsa accepts universal dominion as the ideal, the summum bonum of royalty. It is with real poetic fervour that in the fourth canto he describes Raghu's campaigns which bring the whole of India and regions beyond, under his sovereignty. A horse-sacrifice is performed with all the religious solemnities, dazzling

[1] On the date and locale of Kâlidâsa, see Macdonell, History of Sanskrit Literature, pp. 323–25; Keith, Classical Sanskrit Literature, pp. 31-32, Sanskrit Drama, pp. 143 - 47, also J.R.A.S., 1909, pp. 433 et, seq. Vikramâditya, the traditional patron of Kâlidâsa, is identified with Candragupta II by R. G. Bhandarkar (J. B. B. R. A. S., XX, p. 399) and with Skandagupta by D. R. Bhandarkar (Annals of the Bhandarkar Institute, 1926-27, Vol. VIII, Part II, pp. 200–204). Hoernle, J. R. A. S., 1909, pp. 108 et seq., and H. P. Sâstrî, J. B. O. R. S., 1916, p. 391, argue that Kâlidâsa was a contemporary of Yaśodharman. R. D. Banerji, Journal of the Mythic Society, X, pp. 75–96, 364–71; K. G. Shankar (altering his former opinion), Indian Historical Quarterly, I, pp. 309–16; K. Caṭṭopâdhyâya, Allâhâbâd University Studies, II, 1926, pp. 79—170, argue for the first century B.C. On the subject see also K. B. Pathak, J. B. B. R. A. S., XIX, pp. 39 et seq., Ind. Ant., 1912, pp. 266-67; K. G. Shankar, Journal of the Mythic Society, VIII, pp. 278—92, IX, pp. 17—56; Annals of the Bhandarkar Institute, II, pp. 189–91; Ind. Ant., LI, pp. 192–98; J. B. O. R. S., 1920, p. 327; H. P. Sâstrî, J. B. O. R. S., 1915, pp. 197 et seq.

splendour and right royal generosity. Yet annexation in the strict sense of the term is conspicuous by its absence. In the opening lines of the Raghuvaṁśa, the poet expressly refers to the Raghus as anxious to conquer *for the sake of glory.*[1] In the fourth canto he once remarks that Raghu deprived Mahendranâtha of his glory (Śrî) but not of his territory (medinî).[2] All this is in harmony with epigraphic data, but literature with rare exceptions seems to have been too conservative to recognise the grand high-sounding imperial titles which had come into vogue. It is content to apply the ordinary Sanskrit words Râja, Nripa, Narendra, Bhûpati, etc., to all rulers. As a result, the distinction between suzerains and feudatories is never brought out so clearly as in the inscriptions. None the less, the number of small rulers and feudatories within the universal empire postulated by Kâlidâsa is legion. They come in swarms to attend the sacrifices or court ceremonies. There are numbers of them at a svayaṁvara to win the hand of Indumatı. They are ready to war when they are passed over, one by one, in favour of Aja by the princess.[3] In the fifteenth canto Râma divides his kingdom among his sons and nephews. There is nothing in the inscriptions to support such a practice of the distribution of the realm but if it ever took place in any part of the country, it would further promote the feudal tendency.

In the very first canto of the Raghuvaṁśa Kâlidâsa paints the ideal of royalty in terms of glowing eloquence.

The king.

Kings are to combine all physical and intellectual vigour with moral and spiritual

[1] Raghuvaṁśa, I, 7 (Yaśase vijigîṣûṇâm). For Dilîpa's horse-sacrifice, Canto III ; for Râma's horse-sacrifice, Canto XV. On the glorification of dominion, II, 50, in particular.

[2] Ibid., IV, 43.

[3] Ibid., Canto VI.

excellence.[1] A little later he enunciates the doctrine of paternalism in so many words.[2] But the nineteenth and last canto seems to indicate that the ideal was not always translated into practice. Agnivarman entirely neglects the concerns of state and wastes his time, energy and wealth in luxury and vice. As the fifteenth and sixteenth cantos in particular show, kings usually lived in great splendour. They were generally fond of hunting.[3] The Hindu ideal, however, as unfolded by Kâlidâsa, deprecated over-attachment to worldly enjoyment and grandeur. The model kings abdicate in favour of their heirs-apparent and retire to the forest at the approach of old age. Raghu wants to follow the tradition of his predecessors and is persuaded only with the utmost difficulty by his weeping son to remain with him. Then the two share the crown and power.[4] Daśaratha likewise prepares to instal his son Râma on the throne and depart to the forest.[5] The prince who is to receive a thorough education including instruction in Dhanurveda or archery[6] should be installed Yuvarâja or heir-apparent during the lifetime of his father, as in the case of Raghu and his father Dilîpa.[7] As usual, an umbrella is the symbol of sovereignty.[8] It is interesting to notice that in the last canto, on the death of a wicked king, his widow is recognised regent and ceremonies of inauguration are performed for the child in her womb. Everywhere in the Raghuvaṁśa a king has a chief minister and other

[1] Canto I. See also II, 16; III, 25; V. Canto XVII for Kuśa. Cf. Praśasti of Harişeṇa on the Allâhâbâd Pillar.

[2] Ibid., I, 24.

[3] Ibid., IX, 49, 53, etc.

[4] Ibid., VIII.

[5] Ibid., XII. See also XVIII.

[6] Ibid., III, 29–31.

[7] Ibid., III, 35.

[8] Ibid., II, 47.

officers. A king should keep his counsels secret.[1] The land-revenue is fixed at one-sixth of the gross produce.[2] The king must enforce the social order. Râma slays a Śûdra who ventured to perform penances.[3] Every king must also have a Purohita versed in Vedic lore as well as in Daṇḍanîti or science of government and able to ward off all supernal calamities and human misfortunes.[4] In this connection, another work of Kâlidâsa, the Kumârasaṁbhava which moves above the earth, has an interesting passage. Bṛihaspati as chief minister is said to be greater than all the thousand ministers of a deliberative council.[5] It implies the existence of a chief minister and a huge court. The Meghadûta, the finest of Sanskrit lyrics, has little that is political.

The Kumâra-saṁbhava.

Like the Raghuvaṁśa, Mâlavikâgnimitra, perhaps the first dramatic piece of Kâlidâsa, extols the ideal of universal sovereignty in its very first lines. It lays down the precept that enemies should be quickly extirpated but feudatories are in evidence in its pages. There appear a number of border chieftains who often quarrel with one another and sometimes imprison each other's subjects. In the course of its incidents the play indicates that the king had a chief minister and a number of other ministers who held charge of different departments. Once the king is seen holding counsel with his minister in a lonely spot about the doings of the enemy. The Parivrâjikâ in Mâlavikâgnimitra testifies to the existence of female spies and recalls Kauṭalya. The play brings on

Mâlavikâgnimitra.

[1] Ibid., I, 19.
[2] Ibid., II, 66.
[3] Ibid., XV.
[4] Ibid., I, 60.
[5] Kumârasaṁbhava, II, 30.

the stage the turmoils of a polygamous seraglio which, occasionally, must have reacted dangerously on the policy of the state. One or two points of etiquette are interesting. The sovereign must be approached with presents. Officers address him in the most flattering terms.[1]

Vikramorvaśî, another dramatic piece of Kâlidâsa, is feeble and disappointing. But its picture of the royal harem is quite interesting, though it reveals nothing new. In the second Act, the king's time-table partly follows the Kauṭalyan model.

Vikramorvaśî.

The Abhijñâna Śâkuntala, the most charming product of the Hindu genius, has a few interesting political touches. The king is the protector of all—he ought to protect, adjudicate and chastise. He takes one-sixth of the produce of the soil in return for the functions he performs. He also receives one-sixth of the merits and demerits of his subjects. He ought to be the nearest of kin to all. The king, like a tall tree, has to bear the heat and brunt to shelter those under his charge. Royalty, like an umbrella in hand, makes more for inconvenience than for enjoyment.[2] At the same time in actual practice, the king was rather fond of hunting and would spend a long time over it.[3] Hunting, in fact, is eulogised with real poetic fervour. He has a big harem which has its own politics and in which not every one is happy.[4] He was not always easily accessible to the people. "Kings are not to be got at so easily," says a constable when the superintendent is late to return in the sixth Act. In his moods, the king could be arbitrary.

The Abhijñâna Śâkuntala.

[1] Mâlavikâgnimitra, tr. Tawney, pp. 1, 7—9, 29—31 in particular. For the royal sacrifice, supra, Ch. IX.

[2] Abhijñâna Śâkuntala, Act V, Ślokas 4—8.

[3] Ibid., Act I.

[4] Ibid., Act III, see the conversation of Duṣyanta with Śakuntalâ's friends.

In the sorrow of his personal bereavement, Duşyanta forbids the vernal festival in the city.[1]

The king duly published his commands. His orders are proclaimed throughout the city and their reception at the hands of the people is noted.[2] He himself administers justice. In the fifth Act, the king is seen rising from the court of justice for a bath. The royal court was held in the morning. To his hall does the superintendent take a suspect fisherman in the sixth Act. He had a number of officers, some of whom probably received a ring as their signet.[3] In the sixth Act, the king unable to preside himself over the court one morning asks Âryapiśuna to take his place. There seems to be an officer charged with the administration of justice and religion. *Inter alia*, he looked to the interests of hermits, visited their groves and saw that their rites were free from obstruction. It is as such an officer that Duşyanta chooses to reveal himself in the hermitage of Kaṇva. In the sixth Act, the minister is seen devoting considerable time to the preparation of a financial statement and presenting it to the king. The sixth Act also brings into view police officers in charge of the city and police constables. They are seen dragging a poor fisherman whose hands are tied behind his back. A little later they threaten him with death for his suspected theft.

Among court and household employees who appear on the stage in the fifth Act may be mentioned heralds, chamberlains, warders, and a jester, vidûşaka, who is a sort of companion to the king. It may be remarked that priests are always received with respect at the court.

[1] Ibid., Act VI.
[2] Ibid., Act VI.
[3] Ibid., Act I.

An incidental anecdote in the sixth Act shows that the property of those who died without heirs escheated to the state. A conscientious king would satisfy himself thoroughly of the absence of heirs before taking possession. Duṣyanta, on inquiry learns that one of the widows of a childless shipwrecked merchant was pregnant. He gives a decree that the unborn child had a title to its father's property. He continues :

Revenue.

"Rather be it proclaimed that whosoe'er
Of king Duṣyanta's subjects be bereaved
Of any loved relation, and it be not
That his estates are forfeited for crimes
Duṣyanta will himself to them supply
That kinsman's place in tenderest affection."

About the time of Kâlidâsa flourished another dramatist who wrote the Mricchakatikâ, which has a family resemblance with Bhâsa's Cârudatta. The work is ascribed to a king named Śûdraka but the remarks on Śûdraka in the play point to some court poet as its author. Śûdraka himself, in spite of Konow's brilliant hypothesis, must remain a legendary figure.[1] Śûdraka is represented by the Sûtradhâra in the customary prologue as endowed with many of the qualities which the Hindu ideal of kingship demanded. He had knowledge, religious as well as secular. He was versed in the Sâmaveda, in mathematics and in arts. He was warlike and energetic and the delight of those who knew the Vedas.[2] The plot of the play displays a wicked brother-in-law of the king intimidating officers and the

The Mṛiccha-kaṭikâ.

---

[1] See the Introduction to Ryder's translation, styled Little Clay Cart, Harvard Oriental Series, No. 9. Also the introduction (pp. 5—9) of the Bombay edition of Raddi and Paranjpe who refer the play to the first century B.C. For additional criticism, Sylvain Lévi, Théâtre Indien, p. 208; Tawney, J. R. A. S., 1908, p. 910 ; Ibid., 1909, p. 147; Keith, Sanskrit Drama, 128—42.

[2] Mṛicchakaṭikâ, Act I.

court. The picture of the court itself is interesting. Witnesses are summoned and cross-examined; the final judgment is pronounced by the judge who is supposed to represent the king. In Act IX, the magistrate asks the beadle to go to the court-room and make the seats ready (p. 132) When the seats are ready, the judge enters, accompanied by a gild warden, a clerk and others. The judge laments the difficulties of his position:—

> " In court-rooms even the righteous with lies !
> Hide their offences from judicial eyes."

He laments the difficulty of obtaining perfectly true evidence (p. 133). However, the beadle conducts the judge to the court-room. The king's brother-in-law wants to present his case first of all. The judge thinks that the court will be very busy otherwise that day and, accordingly, sends a message through the beadle, "Leave us for to-day. Your suit cannot be considered " (p. 134). Saṁsthânaka says, "I will have this judge removed and another judge appointed." The remark is communicated by the beadle to the judge who is frightened into taking up the case that very day. Saṁsthânaka is seen almost making fun of the court (p. 135). Among witnesses an old woman is called (p. 137). The defendant and the plaintiff are allowed to cross-examine one another, while the court-officers examine both (p. 142). In the course of the proceedings, Saṁsthânaka is once rebuked by the judge (p. 143). No ordeals are employed in this particular case but that they were frequently resorted to is clear from a later speech of the condemned man, Câruddatta. He complains:—

> " If you had proved my conduct by the fire,
> By water, poison, scales and thus had known,
> That I deserved that saws should bite my bone."
>
> . . . . .
>
> (p. 152).

The four ordeals mentioned here are the same as occur in the law-books. To revert to the court scene, when Cârudatta is adjudged guilty of murder, he is at once taken into custody by the guardsmen. But the final order on his fate comes from the king, Pâlaka, who decrees, "Inasmuch as he killed Vasantasenâ for such a trifle, these same jewels shall be hung above his neck, the drum shall be beaten, he shall be conducted to the southern burying ground, and there impaled." The king adds "whoever else shall commit such a crime, shall be punished with a like dreadful doom" (p. 151). The details of the theatrical setting and the terrible punishment have some relation to facts. The execution scene where the temporary tragedy reaches its height (p. 153) may not be equally realistic but is none the less interesting. Act IX speaks of treacherous ministers who involve both princes and peoples in promiscuous ruin. In the tenth and last Act misrule and oppression lead to a revolution resulting in the death of the king.

Bhâsa.

Another outstanding figure in the history of the Sanskrit drama, Bhâsa, can be noticed as conveniently here as anywhere else. T. Gaṇapati Sâstri who recently discovered and edited his plays, ascribed them to the seventh or eighth century B.C. But it has lately been argued that they are not the product of a single mind, that at most they can only be said to belong to one school and that they took shape about the 7th century A.D. Others will bring the date as low as the eleventh century A.D. On weighing the internal evidence and considering the arguments advanced to support the various hypotheses, one is inclined to think that the plays were composed by the same author sometime between the 4th and the 6th century A.D. In the seventh century A.D. Bâṇabhaṭṭa mentioned Bhâsa in the introductory verses of Harṣacarita and placed his name before that of Kâlidâsa.

It is uncertain whether the order of names is merely accidental or whether it implies chronological sequence.[1] But it is impossible not to attach some weight to the arguments of those who hold Bhâsa to be a forerunner of Kâlidâsa. For the present, however, no very definite date can be assigned to him.[2]

Like so many later dramatists, Bhâsa borrows his plots from the Râmâyaṇa, the Mahâbhârata and popular legends. Kings, ministers and ambassadors jostle one another on his stage but his plays are not political. Not even the Abhiṣekanâṭaka fulfils the expectations raised by its title and its plot which begins with the conflict of Râma's ally, the monkey Sugriva, with his brother Bâlin and ends with the fall of the demon Râvaṇa. Another piece, Cârudatta, which might have supplied the plot to Śûdraka's Mricchakaṭikâ, is no better from the political point of view, though it throws interesting side-lights on

[1] Bâṇa, Harṣacarita, verses 15-16.

[2] For the date and authorship of the plays attributed to Bhâsa, T. Gaṇapati Śâstrî. Introduction to Svapnavâsavadattâ and Pratimânâṭakam; Bulletin of Oriental Studies, London Institution, III, p. 627; Bhâsa's Dramas, a criticism. For contrary views, L. D. Barnett, Bulletin of Oriental Studies, London Institution, III, pp. 107, 519. Jayaswal (J.A.S.B., New Series, 1913, pp. 259—70) places Bhâsa about the third century A.D. Keith (Sanskrit Drama, pp. 91—126; Bulletin of Oriental Studies, London Institution, III, p. 295) places him about 300 A.D. On the whole question see also Macdonell, J.R.A.S., 1913, pp. 186—90; F. W. Thomas, J.R.A.S., 1924, pp. 78— 83; Ibid., 1925, pp. 100—104; C. R. Devadhar, Annals of the Bhandarkar Institute, 1925-26, pp. 29—64; A. P. Banerji Sastri, J.B.O.R.S., 1923 (Vol. IX, Part I), pp. 49—113; V. S. Sukthankar, J.B.B.R.A.S., 1917-18, Vol. XXV, No. 1, pp. 230 et seq.; J.A.O.S., 1920, pp. 248 et seq.; Ibid., 1921, pp. 107 et seq.; K. R. Pisharoti, Indian Historical Quarterly, Vol. I, 1925, pp. 103 et seq.; Bhaṭṭanâtha Svâmin, Ind. Ant., 1916, pp. 189—95; J. Ghatak, Journal of the Department of Letters, Vol. XII, 1925, pp. 1—46; Pisharoti, Journal of the Mythic Society, XI, pp. 353 et seq.; XII, pp. 58 et seq.

the manners of those days. In Avimâraka, Kauñjâyana, one of the two ministers of king Kuntibhoja, laments the sad plight of those fools whom vanity prompts to accept the office of ministers. If their projects are successful, the glory falls to the strength of the sovereign. But if they fail, they are denounced for incompetence.[1] Shortly after, the minister wants the king to honour the envoy of the Benâres sovereign. The king exclaims that the ministerial mind looks only to business, not to affection. When called in, he feels how heavy is the burden of the crown. Dharma or the law must be considered at first. The working of the minister's mind must be followed intelligently. The king must conceal his passions—desires and anger. A policy of mercy or sternness must be (determined and) followed as the juncture of events requires. Through spies—eyes of the king—the doings of the people must be perceived; so, too, the maṇḍala of neighbouring kings must be watched. The king must carefully guard his own person and yet expose it on the field of battle.[2] In the second Act, the hero Avimâraka incidentally remarks that according to the injunction of Śâstras one should hold consultation with two (councillors)[3] In a single-act play, Dûtavâkyam, where the plot consists of Krisṇa's futile mission to Duryodhana on the eve of the Great Civil War, sovereignty appears in all its pride. Duryodhana scoffs at the idea of reconciliation. Princes enjoy dominion after defeating their enemies. Dominion is not to be begged in this world. Nor is it to be bestowed on the helpless.[4] The Pratijñâyaugandharâyaṇam enshrines a beautiful picture of ministerial loyalty. It also furnishes an interesting example of aristocratic pride

[1] Avimâraka (ed. Gaṇapati Śâstrî), p. 4.

[2] Ibid., p. 13.

[3] Ibid., p. 31, stanza ii on the same page for another political touch.

[4] Dûtavâkyam (ed. GaṇapatiŚâstrî), p. 38.

(pp. 30-31). Apart from these and similar unimportant political touches, it is clear that Bhâsa upholds the Brahmanic order of things and recognises the supremacy of Brâhmaṇas. In another single-act play, called Madhyamavyâyoga, based on a Mahâbhârata incident, Bhîmasena, proud of his Kṣatriya origin, feels that a Brâhmaṇa deserves the highest worship and is ready to sacrifice himself for his safety.[1] Vâsavadattâ, Act VI, shows that the door-keeper and chamberlain were two distinct officers. There were a number of guards and police officers to maintain order. In Act I, they are seen turning away the people. Vâsavadattâ also shows that the capital of a small kingdom could sometimes be no bigger than a village, but ambitions for wide conquest might still be there. The fourth Act brings a Vidûṣaka—jester—as the companion and confidential friend of the king.

The Uttarâdhhyayana Sûtra.

Here, too, may be noticed another work which is not the product of a single mind or age but which perhaps assumed its present shape sometime after the fall of the Gupta empire The Uttarâdhyayana Sûtra,[2] says Charpentier, "is a collection of materials differing in age and derived from different sources." "It seems at least probable that the main texts already existed in their present shape before the final redaction of the canon at the Council of Valabhî (probably in 526 A.D.)."[3] The text touches government in a rather left-handed manner. But the dialogue between Indra, the king of gods disguised as a Brâhmaṇa, and Nami who had just received enlightenment and renounced his family and dominion of Mithilâ contains a few interesting political references. The federal-feudal idea is there. "Bring into subjection all princes who do not acknowledge you," says

[1] Madhyamavyâyoga (ed. Gaṇapati Śâstrî), p. 17.
[2] Ed. Jarl Charpentier, Archives D'Etudes Orientales, No. 21.
[3] Ibid., Introduction, pp. 40-41, 48.

Indra to Nami. Kings lived in great pomp and glory and constantly multiplied their treasure, jewellery, wardrobe and conveyances. Towns were often enclosed by walls, defended by battlemented gates, moats and those instruments of warfare which were called Śataghnīs. It was felt that the government must severely punish robbers, cut-purses and burglars and thus establish internal tranquillity.[1]

[1] Ibid., Adhyayana, IX, 22—39. For some interesting remarks on Brāhmaṇas, XXV, 24, 33.

CHAPTER XII.

The Later Dharma Śâstras, Purâṇas and other Literature.

The interval between the destruction of the Gupta empire towards the close of the 5th century A.D. and the rise of the Vardhana empire at the dawn of the 7th century A.D. is again an interregnum of confusion and obscurity. The coins and inscriptions supply some names of kings, some outline of certain events such as the invasion, devastation, and the repulse of Huns but they throw little light on institutions. The literature of the period, however, frequently touches on politics. It is not free from difficulties. The dates of the various works are doubtful. The whole literature is bound to the tradition of the past and attempts consciously to move in the old groves. On the other hand, it has suffered from later interpolations. Its data can be held true only in a very general manner and for a rather long period extending beyond the interregnum into subsequent centuries. Once again, its details, precisely worked out and all very fascinating, must be neglected as predominantly theoretical. From the political point of view the extant literature may be viewed under the categories of Dharma Śâstras, Purâṇas and classical literature.

Literature.

Of the later Dharma Śâstras,[1] Nârada and Bṛihaspati are the most important. The former who flourished about the 6th century A.D. draws plentifully on Manu and other Dharma Śâstras and, on the whole, lacks originality. He is concerned

Nârada.

[1] On Dharma Śâstras in general, supra, Ch. X.

primarily with law and touches but incidentally on administrative matters. It is remarkable that the high-sounding imperial or feudatory titles which came into vogue during the Gupta period and lasted for several centuries are not mentioned in Nârada or any other Dharma Śâstra. These adhere to the time-honoured expressions, Râja, Nripati, etc., and show that the pompous style had not originated when the Dharma Śâstra tradition was first chalked out. Nârada places the king and the Brâhmaṇa among the eight sacred objects. He would, like Gautama, exempt them from censure and corporal punishment in this world, "for these two sustain the visible world." The law which Nârada states pertains to the whole of human life. For example, if a man deserts a wife who is obedient and virtuous and who is the mother of male issue, he should be severely punished and brought to his duty by the king. He follows Manu, with his caste discriminations, in his rules on oaths and admission of evidence. He reduces ordeals to a precise system—a subject which is dealt with yet more thoroughly by Bṛihaspati. In the administration of justice, the assessors are given a more important position than in Manu. Nârada is fuller on procedure than his predecessors,[1] but he mostly agrees with Bṛihaspati.

Bṛihaspati.

Bṛihaspati who cannot be placed later than the sixth or seventh century A.D. may be taken as the typical Brahmanical exponent of law and procedure during this period. In the hall of justice in the fort, facing the east, the court should be held all through the morning hours till noon, every day except the holidays. Bṛihaspati divides courts into four classes: (1) stationary, (2) those moving about, (3) those presided over by the chief judge, and (4) those directed by the king.[2]

[1] Nârada, XII, 95; XVI, 20; XVIII, 12, 54, etc.

[2] Bṛihaspati, I, 2-3. See also I, 1, for Bṛihaspati's idea of the need of judicial administration.

As in Manu, the king should be assisted by three assessors.[1] But the popular element enters into the administration of justice in a much more pronounced manner than in Manu. Cultivators, artizans, trade-guilds, artists, money-lenders, dancers, religious mendicants and even robbers are told to administer their disputes according to rules of their own professions. Families, craft-guilds and local assemblies may be authorised by the king to dispose of law-suits among their members except such as concern violent crimes. Bṛihaspati also provides for appeal from meetings of kindred to companies, thence to assemblies and finally to the royal judges on the ground that the lower courts have not duly investigated or deliberated on the cause. The law which the royal courts are told to administer takes account of sacred injunctions, custom and equity. Thus, the king in the court is exhorted to listen to the Purâṇas, codes of law, and rules of polity, to act on the principles of equity, and abide by the opinion of the judges and the doctrine of the sacred law. It was a political necessity to preserve intact the time-honoured institutions of every country, caste and family. "Otherwise the people would rise in rebellion, the subjects would become disaffected towards their rulers; and the army and treasure would be destroyed." Among those who are not to be consulted in adjudication are people ignorant of local customs. A little later, Bṛihaspati expressly lays down that no sentence should be passed merely according to the letter of the law, but the circumstances of a case must be closely examined. Local custom, however, can be overruled by royal edicts, which thus constitute a distinct source of law. As in Manu, the law on defamation and adultery is vitiated by considerations of caste. Bṛihaspati counsels itinerant courts. "For persons roaming the forest, a court should be held in the forest; for warriors,

[1] Ibid., I, 20.

in the camp; and for merchants, in the caravan."[1] It is needless to follow Bṛihaspati into rules of procedure, etc., for they correspond to those enunciated by Manu. But it may be pointed out that, according to him, law-suits fall into two categories, those originating from disputes regarding wealth and those relating to injuries. Roughly, the distinction corresponds to civil and criminal suits.[2] In the absence of the king, some Brâhmaṇa versed in law is to act as judge.[3]

Ordeals.

Like Manu and Nârada, Bṛihaspati stresses the need of evidence, classifies witnesses and hurls anathemas against perjury, but he thinks that various motives, affection, anger or avarice, may render the testimony of witnesses nugatory. When doubts arise with regard to documentary and oral evidence, and when reasoning itself fails, particularly when the offence in question has been committed at night or in solitary places, ordeals should be employed. While Manu had been content with two, Bṛihaspati enumerated nine of them, to be administered according to the character of the accused and the nature of the charge. An ordeal must always be administered according to the established rule by persons versed in the regulations. "If it is administered against the rule, it is ineffective as a means of proving what ought to be proved." In the system of Bṛihaspati there was a general rule that if a certain amount of money or property in question justified an ordeal for a low-class man, double the amount justified it for a middle-class man and four times as much for a high-class man. In the ordeal by balance a person who, when weighed a second time, retained his original weight, was declared innocent while he who weighed heavier was adjudged guilty. It was held that the weight of sin made

[1] Ibid., I, 26—31, 23—25, 33; II, 28, 12, 24, 26-27; XX, 5—15; XXIV, 12. Parâśaramâdhava, pp. 17-18.
[2] Ibid., II, 5.
[3] Ibid., II, 32.

the difference. "Should the scale break, or the balance or beam, or iron hooks split, or the strings burst, or the transverse beam split, he would have to be declared guilty." In the ordeal by water, an individual was immersed in water and three arrows were discharged. In the ordeal by poison, one had to digest poison "given to him according to rule, without the application of spells or antidotes." One should drink three handfuls of water in which the weapon of one's special deity had been bathed. If in a week or fortnight, no calamity happened to him, to his son, wife, or property, he was declared innocent. Or, after a fast and purification, one should chew grains of rice when the sun is not visible. If what he spits out is pure, he is innocent; if it is mixed with blood, he is guilty. If one can take out a hot piece of gold out of heated oil and butter, without one's fingers trembling or being blistered, one is declared innocent. To prove his innocence, one accused of theft should lick with his tongue without injury an iron ploughshare twelve palas in weight. The lighter ordeals are reserved for Brâhmaṇas and women. The Hindu law-givers tend to regard the oath as a kind of ordeal on the ground that it invokes supernatural agency.[1] The law of procedure in Brihaspati bears a family resemblance to the provisions in the Dharmasthîya book of the Kauṭiliya Arthaśâstra.

Other Smṛitis.

A word may be said of the other Smritis which assumed their present shape perhaps a little later but which faithfully continue the old tradition. Their number is legion. Yâjñavalkya had mentioned a number of Dharma Śâstras including those of Atri, Harita, Uśanas, Aṅgiras, Yama, Samavrata, Kâtyâyana,

[1] Ibid., X, 1—33. For actual practice, cf. Yuan Chwang (Watters, I, 172) who, writing in the seventh century, speaks of four ordeals—water, fire, weighing and poison. His description of them is different from that of the Smṛitis. See infra, Ch. XIII.

Parâśara, Vyâsa, Śaṅkha, Likhita, Dakṣa, Śâtâtapa. Vṛiddha Gautama counted 56 or 57 teachers of the law and Nanda Paṇḍita, author of the Vaijayantî, 57. Mitramiśra in his Vîramitrodaya speaks of 18 primary, 18 secondary and 21 other Smritis.[1] Other lists, which are sometimes shorter, do not always agree. Thus Parâśara substitutes Kâśyapa, Gârgya and Pracetâ for Yama, Bṛihaspati and Vyâsa. The Padma Purâṇa omits Atri and adds others to make up its list of thirty-six. Of all these, one of the most important, though rather late, is that of Parâśara.[2] He recognises no finality in law. It changes from time to time. Every age has its own scheme of duties which the government should enforce. In his own scheme of the social order he seeks elaborately to define the occupations which different classes of people may follow under different circumstances. Government should be conducted according to law. In laying down the law, the king must pay heed to Brâhmaṇas. A king should protect the earth, maintain order with a stern hand and conquer the forces of his enemies. Taxes should be mild.[3]

Parâśara.

Atri, describing the duties of various castes, wants a king to punish those who forsake their Dharma.[4] The king should constantly examine the virtue and sin in the various castes.[5] Those (Brâhmaṇas) who do not perform sacrifices are

Atri, etc.

[1] Forty-six of these appear in the list of Stenzler and forty-seven in that of Roer. The Ânanda Âśrama of Poona has published a collection of twenty-seven Smṛitis including the Devala which was composed in Sindh about the time of the Arab invasion in the 8th century A.D.

[2] There is a still later work called Parâśarîya Dharma Śâstra, highly tinged with sectarianism. It is politically valueless. Parâśara deals mainly with Âcâra and Prâyaścitta.

[3] Parâśara Smṛiti (ed. Vinâyak Dharmâdhikârin with the Vidvanmandhara commentary, Benares, 1913), I, 33, 61–67; II, 2, 12–14; VIII, 28-29 ; X, 5–41 ; XI, 50.

[4] Atri, I, 12–15, 17.

[5] Ibid., I, 27.

declared thieves and those who bestow alms on them should be punished by the king.[1] Harita declares as usual that a Kṣatriya should protect his subjects righteously, should duly celebrate sacrifices, and should be devoted to study.[2] Likhita promises high spiritual rewards to those who excavate tanks, plant trees and perform other such works of public beneficence.[3] Vyâsa proclaims the supremacy of Brâhmaṇas in transcendent terms and recommends lavish gifts to them.[4] Śaṅkha is content with the usual remarks on castes and orders.[5] Uśanas, Aṅgiras, Yama, Samavrata, Dakṣa, and Śâtâtapa devote themselves mainly to Śrâddha and other ceremonies. Nor have the rest of the Smritis any political significance. The Dharma Śâstra doctrine exercised a good deal of influence on royal policy. Apart from *a priori* reasons, the inscriptions amply testify to the fact. Not to speak of Vyâsa's imprecatory verses which occur in numberless grants, the inscriptions sometimes expressly refer to Dharma Śâstras.[6]

The Purâṇas.

The composition of the Purâṇas extends even over a longer period than that of the Smritis. From very ancient times there existed accounts of cosmic creation and regal dynasties or heroes in a more or less popular form. The Atharvaveda speaks of Itihâsa-Purâṇa which was, later, loosely called a fifth Veda. The Kauṭilîya Arthaśâstra places the Itihâsa-

---

[1] Ibid., I, 22-23.

[2] Harita, II, 2—5, see also II, 6—10.

[3] Likhita, 1—4.

[4] Vyâsa, IV, 10, 16, 31.

[5] Śaṅkha, I, 2.

[6] For Gupta times, see Fleet, op. cit., pp. 147, 168, 182; for the sixth century A.D. Ep. Ind., III, 80-81, 322; Ind. Ant., IX, p. 48; VIII, p. 97, 303; XVII, p. 198; for the ninth century, Ep. Ind., IV, p. 346; VI, 20; for the south from the ninth to the twelfth centuries, Epigraphia Carnatica, IV, p. 62; V, 22, 151; VII, 50, 59, 85; IX, 85; XI, 13, 41, 45, etc., etc.

Purâṇa on the prince's curricula of study. Purâṇas are frequently mentioned in literature and in the Smritis. It was, however, roughly between the fifth and tenth centuries A.D. that after constant editing, re-editing, additions and subtractions, the Puranic tradition assumed something like its present shape in eighteen books, divided into three schools after Brahman, Śiva and Viṣṇu. Interpolations, however, continued to be made for long afterwards and influences as late as the 16th century A.D. are clearly visible. According to tradition, the Purâṇas comprised altogether 4,00,000 couplets ranging from the 81,000 of the Skanda to 9,000 of the Mârkaṇḍeya but the actual number in each Purâṇa does not always agree with the orthodox computation.[1]

Brahmanical writers will have it that every Purâṇa must deal with primary creation or cosmogony, secondary creation or cosmogony of worlds including chronology, genealogy of gods and patriarchs, reigns of Manus and the history of the solar and lunar dynasties. An ampler analysis splits up these subjects into ten categories but it is applicable really to Upa-Purâṇas, the eighteen sub-Purâṇas, which were composed on the model

[1] For the size, etc., the Matsya Purâṇa, LIII, 13—58.

The Matsya Purâṇa preserves the tradition that the Purâṇas were composed after the Mahâbhârata by Vyâsa. The Kûrma Purâṇa gives a list of nineteen Purâṇas See also Wilson, Introduction to the Viṣṇu Purâṇa. For an 11th century view of Purâṇas, Alberunî, tr. Sachau, Vol. I, 130-31. Recently there has set in a reaction against the nineteenth century underrating of Purâṇas. For instance, Rapson thinks that they have preserved, though in a perverted form, an independent tradition which supplements the priestly tradition of the Vedas and Brâhmaṇas, and which goes back to the same period (Cambridge History of India, Vol. I, p. 302). The Puranic data have been worked out by Pargiter, Dynasties of the Kali Age; Ancient Indian Historical Tradition: various articles in J. R. A. S. The Sthala-Purâṇas or Mahâtmyas are legion but they contain hardly any administrative data.

of Purâṇas. The Kûrma Purâṇa and the Śrimad Bhâgavata give slightly different lists of contents. The political matter introduced into the various sections of the Purâṇas is true only in a general way for a few centuries and unfortunately, directly adds very little to our knowledge of the working of institutions. Some inferences can be drawn from them but it has to be borne in mind that the Purâṇas draw profusely on the epics, including the Harivaṁśa of the Mahâbhârata, on the Smṛitis, Nîti literature and, in some cases, on one another. The Purâṇas give many lists of universal sovereigns, some of whom like Manu, Sagara, Yayâti, Prithu, Dilîpa are mythical, while others may be historical, perhaps only suzerains on a small scale.[1]

The Ag Purâṇa

Politically, the Agni Purâṇa is one of the most remarkable. But in the relevant passages it is largely indebted to the Mahâbhârata, to the Smritis and to Kâmandaka, the author of the Nîtisâra. It thinks of the state as a culture-state, a moral association, with the king, that is, the government, as the supreme instrument for promoting welfare. It describes the qualities and duties of the king in the usual idealistic style. His life is to be one perpetual vow of ameliorating the condition of his subjects. In himself he must be an example of moral discipline, character, energy and fortitude. In particular, he should take care to protect his subjects against the extortions and oppressions of his own officers and favourites and of the usurers.[2]

[1] Kûrma Purâṇa, XX, 31; Padma, IV, 110–18; Brahmâṇḍa. LXIX, 1–8; Mârkaṇḍeya, CXI, 13, etc., etc.

[2] Agni Purâṇa (ed. Manmath Nath Dutt). Uttarakhaṇḍa, CCXVIII, 2-3; CCXX, 22-23; CCXXII, 15–18; CCXXIII, 4–13; 22–26; CCXXV, 1–17; CCXXIX, 6–12. For the king's divinity, CCXVI, 17–20. For the place of politics in the Scheme of Sciences, I, 14–17, also CCXXI.

The Agni, like other Purâṇas, gives elaborate descriptions of the sacrifices and ceremonies which should accompany the consecration of a king. It reproduces numbers of Vedic texts for citation and, on the whole, adheres to the old tradition. Only a few additional details are given. Broadly speaking, the ceremonies are divided into (1) those of Aindra Śânti, performed on the day preceding the consecration, and (2) those performed on the day of consecration. According to this Purâṇa, the consecration should be performed a year after the actual accession to power and the occasion should be signalised by a proclamation of protection to all. The king might celebrate his birthday every year in grand style. He might perform the Abhiṣeka for his successor. The king should every day see his subjects, consider the daily reports of income and expenditure and receive Brâhmaṇas, ministers, officers and others presented by the usher of the court. Every day he should consult his ministers on weighty matters and preside over the court of justice.[1]

The king.

Princes should be instructed in the science of war and the arts of general utility as well as in the moral sciences. They should be taught fine arts in the company of courtiers. If they were not amenable to education, the king should bind them down in a "prison of pleasure" to keep them from mischief. In any case, guards should be set to watch the actions and movements of princes.[2] The Agni Purâṇa jumbles up state and household officials and particularly mentions the Minister, Treasurer, Ambassador, Keeper of the Royal Elephants, Keeper of Stables,

Princes.

Officials.

[1] CCXVIII, 4 - 34; CCXIX; CCXXV. For mantras to be used on the consecration of a king, CCXIX; for the merit of building golden temples, XXXVIII; for the consecration of tanks and ponds, LXIV.

[2] Ibid., CCXXV.

Masters of the Castles and Fortresses, Royal Physicians, Writers. A Brâhmaṇa or a Kṣatriya should be appointed Commander-in-chief, while men of noble descent should occupy the positions of chamberlains and door-keepers. There should be a master of the kitchen who should live in the house where food is cooked for the king. Over and above his efficiency in cuisine and experience of affairs of the world, his supreme qualification is fond attachment to the king. The bearer of the royal betel-vessel may be either a man or a woman who should feel a real attachment to the king. Behind this insistence on affection lies the apprehension of poison being administered to the king. The seraglio employs many women and eunuchs in the offices of ushers and others. Many of the royal officials and servants seem to be hereditary. For the higher officers the Purâṇa prescribes the usual intellectual and moral qualifications. Only it bars atheists from all employment under the king. For local government the old Dharma Śâstra and Arthaśâstra schemes are adopted. The designations are interesting and probably correspond to facts in some locality. The head of the village is called Grâmâdhipati; the superintendent of ten villages is known as Daśagrâmâdhipati; of a hundred villages as Śatagrâmâdhipati and the yet higher officer as Viśveśvara. Their remunerations are to be fixed according to the importance of their charges. A village should be 100 dhanus in extent and a town 200 or 300 dhanus. A town should be enclosed by a wall which a camel could not look over.[1]

The Agni Purâṇa mainly follows its predecessors in laying down the principles and prescribing the items of taxation—the land revenue, the customs, the toll on sales and purchases, the division of treasure-trove, unclaimed property, etc. One-

Revenue.

[1] Ibid., CXIX, 1-8; CCXVII, 20-22; CCXX; CCXXI; CCXXIII, 1-4.

fifth is to be charged on gold; one-sixth on animals, articles of perfumery, cereals, flowers, roots, fruits, leaves, pot-herbs, hays, bamboos, hides, wicker-works, earthen pots, stone-vessels, honey, meat and clarified butter. The sale of female slaves is recognised and a duty according to the time and country of their importation is prescribed. Brâhmaṇas are not to be taxed under any circumstances; they are always to be protected and cherished.[1]

Justice.

On civil and criminal law and on procedure, the Agni Purâṇa dilates at enormous length but there are only a few ideas which are peculiar to it, which are likely to have a practical bearing and which alone need be noted. There are four sources of law—the Scriptures, custom, the practice of the righteous and royal commands. Treason on the part of feudatories or governors should be punished by amputation of the hands and by impalement.[2] Enemies of the public good should be executed publicly, while all other sentences should be carried out privately.[3] In the royal court, assessors and ordeals are admitted. So we have the involved statement that a tribunal should consist of the eight limbs of a law-suit—the king, the judge, the jurors, the scriptures, the astrologer, the clerk, gold, fire, and water.[4] Witnesses should belong to the same caste or social order as the party which cites them.[5]

Feudatories.

The relations of the feudatories to the suzerain power in the Agni Purâṇa are specially noteworthy. In times of war they must be at the beck and call of the sovereign. They should mark out the sovereign's friends from his foes. They should rally

[1] Ibid., CCXXIII, 23–29; CCXXIII, 14–16; CCXII, 15–18, 30—32.
[2] Ibid., CCXXVII, 1—17, 40—48; CCLIII, 3, 50.
[3] CCXLI, 47—53.
[4] Ibid., CCLIII, 3—66.
[5] Ibid., CCLV, 2. On civil and criminal law in general, CCLIV—CCLVIII.

supporters to the king's banner and collect troops for him. They must help him with all their resources. They should appease the public feeling for him.[1]

Foreign Affairs.

On foreign affairs the Purâṇa merely embellishes the precepts of its predecessors. Only its remarks on ambassadors are striking. They are divided into three classes: (1) Śâsanârhaka, those charged simply to deliver a message, (2) Mitrârtha, those charged to conduct negotiations according to instructions from headquarters, and (3) Niḥśriṣṭârtha or plenipotentiaries, those who are authorised to settle affairs according to their own lights. All ambassadors, of whatever grade, must observe the proper etiquette.[2]

The Mârkaṇḍeya Purâṇa.

The Mârkaṇḍeya Purâṇa,[3] one of the earliest, is free from sectarianism, but it wants the rules of the social order to be enforced with the utmost strictness. All must be kept within bounds, within their particular duties and occupations. A royal heir-apparent who married a Vaiśyâ forfeited his right to the throne and had to content himself with Vaiśya occupations.[4] The Purâṇa emphasises the duty and wisdom of conciliating the subjects. But whosoever is an obstacle in the way of promoting popular welfare, be it

[1] Ibid., CCXLI, 16—28.

[2] Ibid., CXXXVI, 17—25; CCXXVI, 4—8; CCXLI, 1—12. For descriptions of military tactics, strategy, manœuvres, auspicious auguries, omens, etc., CCXL, 7—32; CCXXXII—CCXXXIII, CCXXXVI. CCLII for thirty-two varieties of military art. For forts, CCXXII. For the seven factors of government, CCXXXIX.

[3] Wilson assigned the Mârkaṇḍeya Purâṇa to the 9th or 10th century A.D. Pargiter (Introduction to his translation, XIII-XIV) places it in the fourth century. Perhaps the 6th century is the most probable date.

[4] Mârkaṇḍeya Purâṇa, XXVIII, 33—36; CXIII, 19—21.

father or preceptor, kinsman or friend, should be killed by the king.[1]

The Vâyu Purâṇa, one of the oldest like the Mârkaṇḍeya, traces the history of man from the golden age, through its gradual degeneration, to the terrible Kaliyuga. The social order, supposed to be based on hard psychological facts, utility and divine sanction, must be relentlessly enforced by the government.[2]

The Vâyu Purâṇa.

The Viṣṇu Purâṇa throws no additional light on institutions but it gives an interesting picture of a primeval golden age with its bliss and plenty, its gradual degeneration into what is called 'civilisation'—the origin of society, caste, agriculture, industry, commerce, houses, villages and towns, etc., etc. It tends to bring out that the government exists to enforce the social order and to lead and educate the people into righteousness. It repeats the story of Veṇa from the Mahâbhârata as a warning against tyrannical rule.[3]

The Viṣṇu Purâṇa.

The Matsya Purâṇa repeats the same early history of man in yet greater detail and enforces the same conclusion.[4] It looks with horror on Śûdra kingship and counts it as one of the curses of the degenerate Kali age.[5] It will appear that

The Matsya Purâṇa.

[1] Ibid., XXVII, 1; CXXXI, 27-28. For the king's divinity, dignity, qualifications and duties, for ministers, officers, spies, etc., all discussed in the usual refrain, XVII, 21; XXVII, 1—16; 21—31. For punishments in this and the future life, XV, 1—4, 6, 13—16, 19.

[2] Vâyu Purâṇa (ed. Râjendra Lâl Mitra), Canto VIII, 60-61, 64-65, 78—80, 84—90, 92--97. For details of constructions advocated, 98—123; for agriculture, 142-43; for caste, 157—59; for the scheme of duties, 161—64.

[3] Viṣṇu Purâṇa (ed. T. R. Vyâsâchârya, Bombay, 1904), VI, 6, 17—20. Also Canto XIII.

[4] Matsya Purâṇa, Canto XLVII. [5] Ibid., CXLIV, 30—47.

Śûdra kingship was a fact at the time. For the rest it repeats its predecessors and reproduces whole sections from Kâmandaka.[1]

In the Varâha Purâṇa the notices of the creation of the world and the reigns of kings are rather brief and dispersed.

The Varâha Purâṇa.

It mentions several kings who, tired of worldly prosperity, installed their sons on the throne and departed for the forest. It dogmatises on Brahmanic supremacy as usual.[2]

The Kûrma Purâṇa has a long version of the golden age and its gradual degeneration. It exhausts its vocabulary

The Kûrma Purâṇa.

in its denunciation of the Kali age. Speaking in the future tense in the Puranic style, it laments that in that age Brâhmaṇas will associate with Śûdras, and join them in the performance of religious rites. "Princes surrounded by Śûdras, shall persecute the Brâhmaṇas." Śûdras will occupy higher positions than Brâhmaṇas. All alike will insult and disparage the Vedas and gods.[3] These fulminations probably point to Buddhist or Jaina ascendancy in certain quarters. They leave no doubt that in certain ages and regions Brahmanic supremacy was undermined, that Śûdras attained

The Svayambhû Purâṇa.

to the highest positions and guided the policy of the state. The Svayambhû Purâṇa points to the same conclusion.[4] On this matter Puranic evidence unexpectedly corrects the impression which the Dharma Śâstras and even classical literature tend to produce.

[1] Ibid., Cantos CCXXII - CCXVI, for state-craft in general. On finance, law and punishments, CCXXVII-CCXXVIII.

[2] Varâha Purâṇa (ed. H P. Sastri), CCXVIII, 18—20.

[3] Kûrma Purâṇa (ed. Nîlamani Mukhopâdhyâya), Sec. I, Cantos XXIX-XXX.

[4] Svayambhû Purâṇa, Canto VII.

The Padma Purâṇa.

The Padma Purâṇa discusses Nîti or policy, royal duties, diplomacy, manœuvres, etc., in the usual style.[1] It lacks originality. Nor is the Nṛisiṁha Purâṇa more

Nṛisiṁha Purâṇa.

enlightening, though, *inter alia*, it gives a version of the story of Râma.

The Garuḍa Purâṇa, etc.

The Garuḍa Purâṇa has some interesting political passages but they yield no fresh information.[2] Some of the Purâṇas like the Liṅga and Brahma-vaivarta contain hardly anything political. The Brahma Purâṇa, quoted in Vîramitrodaya, Râjanîtiprakâśa adds that the king after the ceremony of consecration went round the capital on an elephant, re-entered the palace, and offered honour to the elders of the city.[3]

The Upa-Purâṇas.

As their title indicates, the Upa-purâṇas depend on the Purâṇas. Only two of them need be noticed in connection with political institutions. The Bṛihaddharma repeats the early history of man, and stresses caste. Relating the episode of Veṇa with abundant details, it sanctions regicide as the last resort against tyranny.[4] On the other hand, it stands for a firm government. If the king has to slaughter in the course of protection, he incurs no sin. The world yields to the control only of those who wield the rod.[5] But Brâhmaṇas, women, old men and children are exempt from capital punishment.[6] No interest on loans

---

[1] Padma Purâṇa (ed. Mahâdeva Chimanji Apte), Vol. III, Cantos CCXVI—CCXXIX.

[2] Garuḍa Purâṇa, CXI—CXIV, CXLIII, CXLIV. It looks on Nîtiśâstra as a science of general morals (CVIII, 1).

[3] Râjanîtiprakâśa, p. 46.

[4] Bṛihaddharma Purâṇa (ed. H. P. Śâstrî), XII, 5—42; I, 4—6, 14, 22-23; II, 8—62; XIII, 13—49, 54—60; XIV, 3—80.

[5] Ibid., III, 10 et seq., III, 6-7, for the divine nature of the king.

[6] Ibid., III, 28—33. For supernatural punishments, 34—37.

should be charged from Brâhmaṇas. Śûdras should be debarred from the study of sacred literature. The brothers of a king should not be given too great a latitude. No minister should continue too long in office. The revenue should be spent on projects of Dharma, on the royal household, and on the succour of Vipras. The government should keep itself in constant readiness for war and should maintain its forces in perfect order.[1]

The Bṛihannâradiya Upa-Purâṇa, one of the latest and most orthodox, prescribes different dresses for different castes. It declares that Dharma varies according to æons and that in the Kali-yuga inter-caste marriage, sea-voyage, Vânaprastha, etc., are forbidden.[2]

The Bṛihannâradîya Purâṇa.

Hindu tradition reckons the Śrîmad Bhâgavata among the Purâṇas, though it is really an independent work.[3] It preaches the doctrine of passive obedience,[4] but qualifies it by approving of the fate which befell Veṇa.[5] It is the king's duty to educate his subjects into virtue, to 'protect' all, to set every one to his duty, and to chastise the undutiful.[6] In an interesting passage it derives the king's right to rule from his setting up idols of gods. The evidence of inscriptions shows that many kings founded or

The Śrîmad Bhâgavata.

[1] Ibid., III, 41—49, 51, 54; IV, 10, 18—24.

[2] Bṛihannâradîya Purâṇa (ed. Hṛiṣikeśa Śâstrî), Canto XXII.

[3] The Śrîmad Bhâgavata inculcates the worship of Kṛiṣṇa and is greatly indebted to the Harivaṁśa and the Viṣṇu Purâṇa. A late passage in the Padma Purâṇa says that Vyâsa, the traditional author of the Mahâbhârata and the Purâṇas, composed the Bhâgavata last of all, and put into it the essence of all. Of the numerous commentaries on this work, that by Śrîdhara Svâmin is the best.

[4] Śrîmad Bhâgavata, IV, 13, 23.

[5] Ibid., IV, 14, 30—35.

[6] Ibid., IV, 20—22, 24.

endowed temples with unstinted profusion.[1] The enumeration of the emblems of sovereignty in the Bhâgavata is interesting. There is the Camara, Vyajana,——fans—— Śaṅkha or conch-shell, chatra or umbrella, the crown, Simhâsana or throne, Śayana or couch.[2]

A few classical writers who belong to this period may be noticed. Bhâravi, who lived probably in the sixth century A.D., has a good deal of political wisdom but is not very enlightening on institutions. From the account of Duryodhana's rule given by Yudhiṣṭhira's agent in the first canto of the Kirâtârjunîya, it will appear that kings would sometimes associate their brothers and other near relations in the task of administration. Spies and secret agents were employed in large numbers, and earnest efforts were made to win popular loyalty and attachment.[3]

Bhâravi.

Daṇḍin who flourished probably in the sixth or in the seventh century A.D. represents a decadent stage in literary style and in political wisdom.[4] His Daśakumâracarita, however, is not without a few points of interest for the student of institutions. We hear of a king of Magadha who had three minis-

Daṇḍin.

[1] For this and some other political touches. Ibid., IV, 2-3, 7-8, 11—19, 21—26, 45; XI, 3, 14-15, 17, 19.

[2] Ibid., X, 26, 61.

[3] On the poem of Bhâravi, F. W. Thomas, J.R.A.S., 1917, pp. 869 et seq. For political references, Kirâtârjunîya, I, 5, 7, 9-10, 13-14, 16, 21, 29—46; II, 1—52. Also Canto III. Bhâravi is mentioned in the Aihole Inscription of 634 A.D. (Ep. Ind., VI, No. 1).

[4] On the date of Daṇḍin, Pâthak, Ind. Ant., XLI, p. 235. Keith, Classical Sanskrit Literature, 70—73. The Avantisundarî Kathâ, lately discovered, develops the same plot as the Daśakumâracarita and appears to be Daṇḍin's work. It has been edited along with its summary by an unknown hand, by Râmakriṣṇa Kavi, in the Dakṣiṇabhâratî Series, No. 3, 1924.

ters. The office of minister was sometimes hereditary and was recognised as such. At its worst, a royal court could be the hot-bed of intrigue, jealousy, favouritism. Poison and the dagger would be freely resorted to and the life, safety, and reputation of all would be endangered.

Bhartṛihari.

Bhartṛihari who, according to the Chinese I-tsing, died about 650 A.D., has just a few political maxims in his Nītiśataka but throws no light on institutions. Yet there may be something in the tradition that he alternated between asceticism and worldly life.[1]

Subandhu.

Another contemporary poet, Subandhu, author of Vâsavadattâ,[2] paints king Cintâmaṇi as an embodiment of moral discipline, beneficent 'protection,' martial glory, and as a patron of poetry and learning.[3] Like so many other heroes of classical Sanskrit literature, Cintâmaṇi is a universal ruler who has humbled all the princes of the earth. It was only he and the elephant of the north that could be called rulers of the world.[4] Behind this imagery there seems to be a feudalistic organisation. Among the king's servants there are bearers of betel which by this time seems to have become a necessary article of luxury for the upper classes.[5]

---

[1] Bhartṛihari, Nītiśataka, 46-47.

[2] Bâṇa, in the Preface to his Harṣacarita, refers to Subandhu's work. Gray (Introduction to his translation) places him in the sixth or seventh century A.D. See also Keith, J. R. A. S., 1914, pp. 1102 et seq., and Classical Sanskrit Literature, p. 77. K. B. Pathak, Ind. Ant., XL, p. 170, holds that Subandhu was a contemporary of the Guptas—Kumâragupta, Skandagupta and Bâlâditya. D. R. Bhandarkar (Ind. Ant., XLI, pp. 1-2) holds Vasubandhu to be the correct reading of the author's name. Vâsavadattâ is an âkhyâyikâ which, as defined in the Sâhityadarpaṇa, should have verse in some places and prose in others. It has come down in two recensions, the Northern and the Southern. Śivarâma Tripâṭhī's Kañcanadarpaṇa commentary on Vâsavadattâ belongs to the eighteenth century (Louis H. Gray, J. A. O. S., XXIII, p. 57).

[3] Vâsavadattâ, tr. Gray, pp. 47 et seq.

[4] Ibid., pp. 48-49.

[5] Ibid., p. 68.

From the 4th century A.D, commences a long line of story-books, presumably under the impulse given by the Buddhist Jâtakas and Avadânas. But the theory that the Indian tales were first composed in some form of Prâkrit and later turned into Sanskrit has now been shown to be entirely untenable. The main purpose of the stories is to impart ethical instruction through the words and actions of human beings, animals and birds. The Tantrâkhyâyika, preserved in Kashmîr and perhaps composed there, is, in any case, earlier than the sixth century A.D. and may be older. It was turned into a yet more popular version in the Pañcatantra, attributed to Viṣṇuśarman. It was probably an earlier version of the present Pañcatantra which was translated into Pahlavi about the middle of the 6th century A.D. and thence into old Syriac in 570 and into Arabic in 750, the last rendering in its turn being translated into Old Spanish in 1251, which, finally was the source of Latin and, later, other European versions. In India the Pañcatantra has influenced all subsequent literature of the didactic tale.[1] We learn from the prologue in which king Amṛitaśakti of Mahilâropya arranges the education of his three sons, that princes were generally made over to Brâhmaṇa Paṇḍitas who taught them grammar, literature, Nîti and other subjects. From the tales one can gather a good deal of the current political wisdom. Some kings nursed their kingdoms, others were too exacting in their demands on the subjects. Experience showed that the prosperity of monarchs was bound up with that of the people. Incidentally, we have an interesting remark that a fort was more useful than a thousand elephants and a

The Pañca-tantra.

[1] On the Pañcatantra, Brown, J. A. O. S., Vol. 39, pp. 1 et seq. See also Max Müller's Essay on the Migration of Fables. Benfrey's work on the Pañcatantra inaugurated what may be called the science of folklore—its motifs and migrations.

hundred thousand horses. No other passages need be quoted. In spite of their intrinsic charm, as political maxims, they are not valuable for the study of practical institutions.[1]

Prabodha Candrodaya.

Perhaps to the seventh century A.D. belongs the Probodha Candrodaya.[2] Though a spiritual drama, it contains an interesting account of the preparations for the king's procession. "Sprinkle the pavement of precious stones," so goes the command, "with water impregnated with sandalwood; open the fountains that their streams may play around; hang up festoons of large brilliant diamonds, and let the flag which bears the bow of Indra wave on the top of the royal residence."

[1] See for instance, Book I, Tale VII, pp. 41, 48.

[2] For the date, J. Taylor, Introduction to the translation, second edition, Bombay, p. 4.

CHAPTER XIII.

The Seventh Century A.D.

Material for study.

The material for reconstructing the administrative outline of the first half of the 7th century A.D. is unexpectedly copious. Besides some coins and inscriptions there is Bâṇa's historical work, Harṣacarita, life of Harṣa, the paramount sovereign of the greater part of North India. Harṣacarita can, for political purposes, be usefully supplemented by Bâṇa's romance Kâdambarî. Additional light is forthcoming from that prince of travellers and scholars, Yuan Chwang,[1] who spent fifteen years in the country and recorded his experiences in an admirable work. Fortunately, the authenticity and chronology of these sources are beyond doubt. They can all be used together.

Harṣavardhana.

These records centre round Harṣavardhana who, in consequence, has been endowed by modern writers with a heroism, power and greatness beyond what a closer study of the originals warrants.[2] The earliest known ancestors of Harṣa were Naravardhana, Râjyavardhana, and Âdityavardhana who are called Mahârâjas and may, therefore, like the

[1] For varieties of the spelling and pronunciation of the Chinese pilgrim's name, Rhys Davids in Watters, I, p. XI.

[2] The chief modern accounts of Harṣa are Ettinghansen's Harṣavardhana, Empereur et Poet (Paris, 1906), K. M. Pannikar's Srî Harṣa of Kanauj (Bombay, 1922), R. K. Mukerji's Harṣa (Milford, 1926), R. C. Majumdar, J. B. O. R. S., 1923, Vol. IX, pp. 311—25, V. A. Smith, Early History of India, 4th edition, pp. 348—72.

ancestors of the imperial Guptas, be presumed to have been feudatories. The dynasty started on an independent career with Prabhâkaravardhana, who was the first to assume the title of Mahârâjâdhirâja.[1] Beginning life as the chief of Sthâṇvîśvara in the land of Śrîkaṇṭha, he brought a number of surrounding chiefs under his control and stood forth as a suzerain.[2] His death seemed at first sight to be the signal for the break-up of his empire but his son and successor Râjyavardhana stemmed the tide of revolt. On the new king's early tragic death, his brother Harṣavardhana more than held his own against the enemies of the dynasty, united his dominions with those of his widowed sister Râjyaśrî, the heir to her childless husband's patrimony of Kanauj, and after six years of campaigning brought many princes under his supremacy. He stood forth as the suzerain of the greater part of North India and one of the most powerful monarchs in the whole country. He died in 648 A.D.[3]

The nature of Harṣa's dominion.

It is, however, a mistake to represent Harṣa as the king of the whole of North India or as the ruler of a unitary state. A close scrutiny of the documents shows him to have been only the suzerain of a very large number of chiefs and his relations with some of the rulers appear to be rather ill-defined. The constitution of Harṣa's empire

1 Sonpat Copper Seal Inscription of Harṣavardhana, Fleet, op-cit., No. 52; Madhuban Plates, Ep. Ind., VII, No. 22.

2 Harṣacarita (tr. Cowell and Thomas), p. 188 Prabhâkaravardhana defeated a confederacy of princes under Devagupta which resisted him. Ep. Ind., VII, 185.

3 According to Yuan Chwang's Life, p. 156, Harṣa died in A.D. 655. Takakusu (I-tsing, pp. LVI and 168) accepts the date but Watters, I, 347, clearly implies that the Emperor was dead in 648 A.D. According to V. A. Smith (Early History of India, 4th edition, pp. 348 et seq.), Harṣa's reign lasted from 606 A.D. to 647 A.D.

follows the lines which the study of the political conditions of the preceding ages would lead one to expect.

Fundamental political conditions.

Yuan Chwang, whose knowledge of the country was close and thorough, says that Yin-tu, as the Chinese called India, was divided into more than seventy kingdoms.[1] Such is likely to have been the number of states which were worth counting. But not all of them were perfectly independent. And besides them there seems to have been a yet larger number of feudatory domains. Putting the evidence of Yuan Chwang, Bâṇabhaṭṭa and the Inscriptions together, it appears that there were several circles of suzerainty, each comprising a suzerain and some feudatories, that within each circle there may be smaller circles of sub-infeudation, that Harṣa and Pulakeśin, who represented the two biggest and most important circles, claimed some sort of hegemony over less powerful suzerains and sometimes imposed their will on them. Thus, Kapis, probably modern Kâfiristân, was an independent state with ten dependencies. Its king celebrated the Mokṣapariṣad, the quinquennial Buddhist assembly, in the style of Harṣa.[2] Kashmîr was also independent and had a number of dependencies such as Râjapur, Taxila and Siṁhapur. Yet Harṣa once compelled the king of Kashmîr to part with a Buddha relic.[3] Another independent state was Cheka with its capital at Sâkala and with its circle of dependencies which included Multân. The praśasti of the temple of Lakkhâ Maṇḍal at Maḍhâ in Jaunsâr (Bâwar) shows the royal race of Siṁhapur reigning in the modern district of Jalandhar. It is probably identical with the Sang-ho-pu-lo of the Chinese.[4] The dynasty

[1] Watters, I, pp. 140-41.

[2] Ibid., I, 123.

[3] Yuan Chwang, Life, p. 181.

[4] Beal, Si-yu-ki, I, 143—47.

is said to have conquered many rulers (Kṣitipâḥ dâpitâḥ) and appears to have been practically independent. Yet in some measure it recognised the suzerainty of Harṣa. Here the line between autonomy and complete independence was faintly drawn.[1] Matipura near Hardwâr was ruled by a Śûdra king and does not seem to have formed part of Harṣa's empire. Thus, practically the whole of the north-west lay outside the limits of the Vardhana regime. Yet Harṣa could arrange that Yuan Chwang should be escorted by a military guard to the frontier, and that the north-western princes should see him safe to the borders of China.[2] Sindh was ruled by a Śûdra king. We know little about its political conditions in the age of Harṣavardhana but the Arab accounts prove that at the dawn of the eighth century A.D., it was dominated by federal-feudalism which is likely to have existed in the seventh century as well. It is remarkable that the tribal oligarchies which the Allâhâbâd Inscription of Samudragupta notices are no longer met with in the seventh century. It seems they had been swept off in the turmoils which followed the decline of the Gupta empire. It may be mentioned that Pâryâtra (Bairât) had a Vaiśya king.[3] Towards the east, epigraphic evidence shows Śaśâṅka as a Mahârâjâdhirâja in Bengal in 619-20 A.D. He had under him some feudatories, one of whom an hereditary Mahârâja Mahâsâmanta issues a grant and acknowledges Śaśaṅka's suzerainty.[4] Yet this Mahârâjadhirâja had been defeated by Harṣavardhana twelve years before. In Yuan Chwang's account of Bengal he appears no longer on the throne. It is probable that

[1] Ep. Ind., I, No. 2.

[2] Yuan Chwang, Life, p. 190. Watters, I, 297.

[3] Harṣa's dominion did not extend over Nepâl which, as Sylvain Lévi has shown, was a Tibetan dependency.

[4] Ep. Ind., VI, 143.

Harṣa, though victorious, failed at first to impose his suzerainty definitely on Śaśâṅka but that, later, he reduced him or his descendants completely to vassalage or exterminated the dynasty. Perhaps it had been assailed both from the west and the east. Bâṇa has it that the king of Kâmarûpa in Âssâm voluntarily offered his allegiance to Harṣa and sent a priceless white umbrella to him. Probably, he wanted to safeguard his position against the common enemy, Śaśâṅka of Bengal. Kumâra retained his practical independence, but he suffered himself to be anointed by his new liege-lord. He attended Harṣa's court and Mokṣapariṣad and took precedence of all feudatories. He was expected to obey Harṣa. When the latter asked him to send the Chinese master, Yuan Chwang, to him, he had the hardihood to reply, "I would rather send my head than let your majesty have the master of the law." But when Harṣa proposed to take him at his word, Kumâra volunteered to bring Yuan himself to Harṣa.[1] Such was one of the forms of the tenure of vassalage which is removed only a step from independence. From the fact that Kumâra's position is definitely regarded as higher than that of other feudatories, it appears that the powers of the latter were more circumscribed. Towards Central India, Mâlwâ appears from Harṣacarita to have acknowledged the overlordship of the Vardhanas. But in the account of Yuan Chwang it is not only independent but counts the rulers of Vadnagar and K'ie-ch'a or K'i-T'a probably Cutch, as its vassals.[2] It is probable that Mâlwâ was really the centre of a political circle and was practically

[1] Yuan Chwang, Life, p. 186, Watters, I, pp. 349-50, Bâṇa, Harṣacarita, p. 139. For Kumâra, also Watters, II, p. 186, Harṣacarita, p. 294. For a Seal of Kumâra found at Nâlanda, J. B. O. R. S., VI, Part I, pp. 151 et seq.

[2] Beal, II, 266, 268, Watters, II, 245, 247.

independent but it acknowledged Vardhana hegemony in a rough and ready manner. The position of Valabhî is difficult to unravel. Its ruler is said to have been the son-in-law of Harṣa though there is nowhere any mention of Harṣa having married. He was certainly defeated by Harṣa ; he attends the latter's Mokṣapariṣad. But in the account of Yuan Chwang he is practically independent. His position seems to resemble that of the rulers of Kâmarûpa and Mâlwâ.[1] The grant of Dhruvasena III from Valabhî of the year 633-34 A.D. speaks of him as having wooed the assembly of kings (Kṣitipasaṁhati), that is, having established his suzerainty over a number of rulers.[2] A proclamation which, as Bâṇa says, Harṣa caused to be engraved soon after his accession, is interesting for the whole subject. It seems to refer both to feudatories and independent princes. "Let all 'kings' prepare their hands to give tribute, or grasp swords; to sieze the realms of space or chowries; let them bend their heads or their bows, grace their ears with my commands or their bowstrings; crown their heads with the dust of my feet or with helmets."[3] Such was the formula of the Digvijaya or conquest of all the quarters, which was a time-honoured institution. Harṣa performed his Digvijaya with 5,000 elephants, 20,000 cavalry and 50,000 infantry. There is no mention of any Aśvamedha sacrifice anywhere. The Digvijaya might well have resulted in some annexations but it left numerous rulers semi-independent within the region which generally acknowledged the suzerainty of Harṣa. Their existence, indeed, is regarded as part of the order of the day. The size of their domains and their prestige varied enormously. Numbers of them appear on many occasions in Harṣacarita. In their very childhood the Princes Râjyavardhana and Harṣavardhana are given

---

[1] Yuan Chwang, Life, p. 185. Also Ind. Ant., XIII, pp. 70 ff.

[2] Ep. Ind., I, No. 13.

[3] Harṣacarita, 218.

the sonsof the 'king' of Mâlwâ as their companions.[1] A little later, we are told that the eyes of "all kings" fell on the Imperial princess Râjyaśrî and that they sent envoys to request her hand.[2] Here independent sovereigns are certainly meant but by implication the great feudatories are also included in the expression 'all kings.' The marriage of the princess was attended by many "kings" and "queens."[3] There is a clearer reference to feudatories when we are told that 'kings' decorated the palace, polished mosaic flowers, erected posts, etc., and that their "queens" enlivened the occasion by their songs.[4] On his death-bed Prabhâkaravardhana charged Harṣa, *inter alia*, to "make prize of feudatory kings."[5] When preparing for his campaigns, Harṣa receives exhortations from princes who already acknowledged the suzerainty of his dynasty and were faithful to it. When actually starting on his campaigns, he was accompanied by a number of Sâmantas.[6] In the encounter between Harṣa and Pulakeśin, in which the former probably suffered a defeat, both the sovereigns were accompanied by a number of feudatories.[7] In Harṣacarita a number of feudatories are seen waiting for an audience of the suzerain.[8] Among others there was a forest chief who had earlier assisted Harṣa in the search for his sister. Bâṇa brings numerous tributary hill-chiefs on the scene.[9] Relating his own experiences, he describes the camps of

---

[1] Ibid., p. 154.

[2] Ibid., p. 155.

[3] Ibid., p. 156.

[4] Ibid., 157—58.

[5] Ibid., 188.

[6] Ibid., 231, 240.

[7] Ep. Ind., V, 202; VIII, 230 ; Ind Ant. VI, 87 ; VIII, 244 ; IX, 125 ; XI, 68 ; XIII, 74. Fleet, Dynasties of the Kanarese District, 350, Yuan Chwang, Watters. II, 239, Life, 147.

[8] Harṣacarita, 170.

[9] Ibid., 259.

'subject kings.' When called for an interview, he has to pass through three courts, crowded with "subject kings," before he meets Harṣa in the fourth.[1] The ranks of feudatories seem to have merged insensibly into those of aristocrats who were only large landowners. Thus, in his bereavement Harṣa is attended closely by many young nobles whose families had long enjoyed the favour of the Vardhana court.[2] The body of the dead king Prabhâkaravardhana was taken by nobles and townsmen headed by the family priest to the Saraswatî.[3]

Relations of the suzerain and feudatories.

Some of the incidents noticed above serve to illustrate the tenure of the relations of the suzerain with the feudatories. The inscriptions and the writings of Yuan Chwang and Bâṇa throw some further light on the question. The vassals adorn the court of the suzerain and send their sons to act as pages at his court and palace. They are sometimes anointed by the suzerain. They assist him with their forces in war. Râjyavardhana, starting on his campaign against the Huns, was attended by feudatories with their forces.[4] Sometimes the suzerain entrusted them with important missions. Thus, the ruler of Jalandhar was placed by Harṣa in charge of matters relating to Buddhism to which he had been converted. "In this capacity (as Protector of the Faith)," continues Yuan Chwang, "the king of Jalandhar rewarded and punished the monks without distinction of persons and without private feeling. He also travelled through all India and erected topes or monasteries at all sacred places."[5] It falls chiefly to him to see Yuan Chwang safe to the frontier.[6] It appears

[1] Ibid., 68, 78.
[2] Ibid., 193.
[3] Ibid., 190-91.
[4] Ibid., 166.
[5] Watters, I, 296.
[6] Life, 189-90.

from the account of Yuan Chwang that Harṣavardhana, without interfering unduly in the internal affairs of feudatory states, tried to encourage good government therein. We are told that "the 'neighbouring' princes, and the statesmen, who were zealous in good works, and unwearied in their search for moral excellence he led to his own seat, and called 'good friends,' and he would not converse with those who were of a different character."[1] It may be presumed that neighbouring princes who consented to be treated in this fashion were not independent sovereigns but feudatories. With their ministers also the suzerain came into some touch. We hear of the presence of 200 such ministers from different kingdoms at the great religious assembly of Kanauj.[2] The occasional meetings of the suzerain and feudatories are likely to have reacted on politics and administration. Of the crowd of feudatories, eighteen or twenty seem to have been the most powerful and important. Yuan Chwang has described how, according to previous arrangement, they marched in Harṣa's train from Kanauj to Prayâga for the sixth quinquennial Mokṣapariṣad.[3] It is clear from the Rohtâsgaḍh Stone Seal-matrix of the Mahâsâmanta Śaśâṅkadeva[4] and the Nirmand Copper Plate Inscription of the Mahâsâmanta Mahârâja Samudrasena[5] that the titles of feudatories were the same as those in the Gupta period. Their consorts could be called Paramadevî and Bhaṭṭârikâ.

Diplomacy.

Beyond the circle of satellites and spheres of influence, the emperor stood in diplomatic relations with many powers. Bâṇa records the presence of ambassadors from Ândhra and Drâviḍa lands at

[1] Watters, I, 344. Beal, I, 214.
[2] Beal, I, 218-19.
[3] Ibid., Life, 177, 186.
[4] Fleet, No. 78.
[5] Ibid., No. 80. Also Ep. Ind., XV, No. 19 (650 A.D.).

Harṣa's court.[1] From Chinese sources we learn that he exchanged diplomatic missions with China [2]

The hypothesis of the relationships of suzerainty and vassalage in the Vardhana Empire is supported by the evidence of Kâdambarî, a prose romance which was composed by Bâṇabhaṭṭa[3] under the patronage of Harṣa and which, details apart, may be held to reflect the dominant political conditions of the times. Feudatories abound in its pages. At the very commencement of the story, Śûdraka is painted as a second Indra, whose commands were honoured by the bent heads of all " kings," . . . who " had an army of neighbouring chiefs bowed down in loyalty to his Majesty." We are assured that he had the signs of a universal emperor.[4] When the Caṇḍâla maiden is ushered in, she beholds the king in the midst of 1,000 chiefs.[5] When the sun reaches its zenith and the hour of bath is at hand, the chiefs are dismissed from the audience-hall but they throng together to pay their respects to the king as he moves.[6] When the time comes for Candrâpîḍa's consecration, he is anointed by the king surrounded by a thousand chiefs.[7]

The Evidence of Kâdambarî.

When he leaves the hall of assembly, he is followed by a thousand chiefs and is soon met by " hosts of kings " who do him homage. Bâṇa's account of the Digvijaya which began on the morrow of Candrâpîḍa's consecration is interesting. " By degrees, as he wandered at will, he bowed the haughty, exalted the humble, encouraged the fearful, protect-

---

[1] Harṣacarita, 170.

[2] Sylvain Lévi, Journal Asiatique, 1900, tr. Ind. Ant., 1911, pp. 111 et seq.

[3] After the death of Bâṇabhaṭṭa the romance was continued by his son.

[4] Kâdambarî, tr. C. M. Ridding, p. 3.

[5] Ibid., 6.

[6] Ibid., 12.

[7] Ibid., 84.

ed the suppliant, rooted out the vicious, and drove out the hostile. He anointed princes in different places, gathered treasures, accepted gifts, took tribute, taught local regulations, established monuments of his visit, made hymns of worship and inscribed edicts . . . " So there were conquests in all quarters.[1] True, Candrâpîḍa is accompanied by an army but there is hardly any fighting. The prince seems to be dealing merely with his own feudatories. Here it must be noted that the suzerain anointed his vassals, took tribute from them and exacted obedience and submission from them. It is a striking proof of Bâṇa's fidelity to his age that the conclusions based on historical evidence are generally supported by his romance.

Change in the status of feudatories.

A few incidental notices in Yuan Chwang show that the status of feudatories sometimes altered and might considerably go down. There were cases of ruling families being replaced altogether by viceroys of the suzerain. By the time of the Chinese pilgrim's visit, the royal family of Gandhâra was extinct and the "kingdom" was governed by deputies from Kapiśa.[2] Nagarahâra (the old capital of Jalâlâbâd territory) had no chief of its own at the time but was governed by a commandant and his subordinates from Kapiśa.[3] In a similar manner Siṁhapur was now a dependency of Kashmir.[4]

Caste of Ruling Families.

Not all the ruling families during this period belonged to the Kṣatriya caste. According to Yuan Chwang, Harṣa belonged to the Vaiśya caste.[5] Yuan Chwang records a tradition that the kings of Kâmarûpa had been Brâhmaṇas for a

[1] Ibid., 89-90.
[2] Beal, I, 98.
[3] Ibid., 91.
[4] Ibid., 143. For a curious tradition about Indian kingship, Ibid., 11.
[5] Beal, I, 209.

thousand generations.[1] As already noted, some other ruling families came from the Brâhmaṇa, Vaiśya or Śûdra caste. Historical testimony thus confirms the impression, which the imprecations and prophecies of the Brâhmaṇas tend to produce, *viz.*, that the orthodox rule of Kṣatriya kingship was not infrequently violated.

The Suzerain's titles.

The titles of the suzerain were the same in the seventh century as in the Gupta age. In the inscriptions, Harṣavardhana is, like his brother and father, called Paramabhaṭṭâraka, Mahârâjâdhirâja.[2] Bâṇa calls the Vardhana suzerain Parameśvara, Cakravartin, lord of the fields bounded by the five oceans, sovereign of all continents.[3] In the inscriptions Harṣavardhana's mother Yaśomatî is called Mahâdevî. According to Yuan Chwang, Harṣavardhana was warned by Avalokiteśvara not to assume the title Mahârâja. Thereupon, he "became king of Kanauj with the title Râjaputra and the style Śîlâditya."[4] The former assertion is contradicted by the inscriptions but it is probable that Harṣa was during his lifetime known by the titles Râjaputra and Śîlâditya. A passage in Harṣacarita indicates that besides the umbrella, there were three other royal emblems—the Siṁhâsana or Lion-throne, a peculiar Śayana or couch and Âsandî or chair.[5]

Harṣa ruled in conjunction with his sister Râjyaśrî because the dominions of the two had been practically united.

Harṣa as administrator.

The capital of the empire was Kanauj, which seems to have been a magnificent city for several centuries. But in Yuan

---

[1] Beal, II, 196. Watters, II, 186. See also Beal, II, 270-71; Watters, II, 250-51.

For instances of Kṣatriya kingship, see Beal, I, 54, 82; II, 209.

[2] Sonpat Copper Seal Inscription of Harṣavardhana, Fleet, No. 52.

[3] Harṣacarita, 85, 100.

[4] Watters, I, 343.

[5] Harṣacarita, 103.

Chwang's account the emperor is seen constantly on the move, except during the rains. Incessant travelling, whether on military expeditions, administrative tours, or from religious motives, was part of the personal conduct of the administration. The emperor never halted long at any place. Temporary buildings were erected at each station for his residence. These pavilions of travel, as they were called, were made of cut grass like huts or built of branches and boughs. They were burnt on the emperor's departure. But while they stood they were furnished with all the paraphernalia of a court. It was at such a temporary court at Kajughira in Bengal that Yuan Chwang first met the emperor. On extraordinary occasions which drew together large numbers of feudatories, such temporary structures could be seen even at Kanauj. The emperor divided the day into three periods, devoting one to affairs of government and two to religious works—a rather disproportionate distribution of time. We are assured that Harṣa found the day too short for him. "He forgot sleep and food in his devotion to good works."[1]

The Emperor's pomp and glory.

In spite of his devotion to duty and religion, Harṣa maintained the traditional pomp and glory of sovereignty. Even while he was on tour, his porters carried his golden foot-stools, water-pots, cups, spittoons and baths. There were bearers of kitchen appurtenances with goats attached to thongs of pig-skin, etc.[2] The royal dress comprised a snow-white lower garment with short silk-threads, a bejewelled girdle, and a thin upper garment spangled with worked stars.[3] There was a certain manner of beating the drums which was a royal monopoly and could be used by no one

[1] Yuan Chwang, Watters, I, 344; II, 183. Beal, I, 215; II, 193. Life, 173, 177.

[2] Harṣacarita, 227, 237.

[3] Ibid., 80.

else.[1] The tradition of keeping women attendants was maintained. There were female chowrie-bearers and shampooers.[2] Eunuchs were also employed at the court and palace.[3] Royal ladies had their own attendants.[4] Court festivities sometimes exceeded all bounds of decorum. Bâṇa's description of celebrations on the birth of Harṣa does not make very pleasant reading.[5]

The Court.

The king's court, consisting of feudatories, ministers, chief personages, poets,[6] and favourites, presented a glittering spectacle. Bâṇa has given an account of Harṣa's camp at Maṇitâra on the Ajirâvatî, surrounded by the camps of renowned "subject kings" with all their separate retinues. There were numbers of elephants, horses and camels. Over the whole scene waved umbrellas with thousands of stirring chowries. It comprised four different sets of apartments, three of which, the outer ones, were filled by feudatory chiefs. In the fourth, under a pavilion, on a throne of pearl-like stone, sat the emperor with his feet resting on a foot-stool of sapphire and ruby. Yuan Chwang has described how the emperor marched to Kanauj followed by several hundreds of thousand people, along the southern bank of the Ganges, while Kumâra Râja, attended by tens of thousands, took his place on the northern bank. The two kings led the way with their gorgeous staff of soldiers, "some also were in boats, some were on elephants, sounding drums and blowing horns, playing on flutes and harps."[7] As in Persia, in the later Roman Empire and, under the medieval Mughals, the

---

[1] Yuan Chwang, Life, p. 173.

[2] Harṣacarita, 83, 177.

[3] Ibid., 78.

[4] Ibid., 142, 181.

[5] Ibid., 144 et seq. For marriage festivities, 157 et seq.

[6] For poets at the court, Ep. Ind., I, 180.

[7] Yuan Chwang, Beal, Si-yu-ki, I, 218.

etiquette of the court smacked of servility. Yuan Chwang relates how on one occasion princes were prostrate at the feet of the suzerain.[1] Yet the fact of being a courtier carried some prestige. When after his reception by Harṣa, the poet Bâṇa returned home, he received an affectionate welcome and congratulations from all and was lionised in the neighbourhood.[2]

The permanent seat of the empire, as usual, presented a glorious spectacle. Bâṇa testifies that Sthâṇvîśvara, when capital of the kingdom, resounded with sounds of triumph, beating of drums, songs of troubadours and minstrels. The palace was magnificent and had a white-washed street wall.[3] Of Kanauj Yuan Chwang writes that "it was very strongly defended and had lofty structures everywhere ; there were beautiful gardens and tanks of clear water, and in it rarities from strange lands were collected . . . ."[4]

The capital.

The household establishment of the king was a large one. There were the bodyguard, chowrie-bearers, chamberlains, door-keepers, ushers, porters, cooks, a chef, etc., etc. There were hereditary royal physicians. Purohitas and Paṇḍitas were there.[5]

The Palace Establishment.

Some passages in Kâdambarî bring out the royal luxury of the 7th century A.D. in extraordinarily vivid colours. When the roar of the drum, followed by the blast of the conch, announced mid-day, the king dismissed

The evidence of Kâdambarî.

[1] Ibid., I, 220.

[2] Harṣacarita, 93. A passage in Harṣacarita, 88-89, shows that the court was dismissed about sunset.

[3] Harṣacarita, 158, 170, 171, 179. Cf. the idealised picture of Ujjayinî in Kâdambarî, tr. Ridding, 47. The towns and villages of the North-west made a poor impression on Yuan Chwang. (Beal, I, 73).

[4] Ibid., 70, 68, 171, 178.

[5] Harṣacarita, 70, 68, 98, 161, 171, 178.

the court, rose from the hall of audience and took exercise in the hall of exercise with princes of his own age. He then entered the bathing place, which was covered with a white canopy, and had numerous inscriptions of bardic verses. "..... It had a gold bath, filled with scented water in its midst, with a crystal bathing seat placed by it, and was adorned with pitchers placed on one side, full of most fragrant waters,........ The handmaidens..... duly besprinkled the king. Straightway there arose a blare of the trumpets sounded for bathing, penetrating all the hollows of the universe, accompanied by the din of song, lute, flute, drum, cymbal, and tabor ..... mingled with the uproar of a multitude of bards ....." After bath and worship, his limbs were "anointed in the perfuming-room with sandal-wood, sweetened with the fragrance of saffron, camphor and musk......" After his meal and chewing of betel, he rose from his dais "with its bright mosaic pavement." A portress, standing close by, hastened to him and "leaning on her arm, he went to the hall of audience, followed by attendants worthy to enter the inner apartments." A long description is given of the hall, which showed as "though walled with crystal by reason of the white silk that draped its ends." Reclining on his couch, "while a maiden seated on the ground, having placed in her bosom the dagger she was wont to bear, gently rubbed his feet...... the king rested for a short time, and held converse on many a theme, with the 'king's' ministers and friends whose presence was meet for the hour."[1]

Royal charity.

While the royal pomp subdued the imagination of the multitude, the unstinted royal generosity won their affection and gratitude. Yuan Chwang has recorded that even while travelling, Harṣa provided food and drink everyday for 1,000 Buddhist

[1] Kādambarī, tr. Ridding, pp. 11—14.

monks and 500 Brâhmaṇas.[1] Every year he gathered Buddhist Śramaṇs from all 'countries' and on the 3rd and 7th days bestowed on them the four kinds of alms—food, drink, medicine and clothing. Yuan Chwang was offered, though he declined, 10,000 pieces of gold, 30,000 pieces of silver, 100 garments of superior cotton, while the eighteen feudatory chiefs wanted to present him rare jewels.

Royal generosity reached its zenith at the quinquennial Mokṣapariṣad. Yuan Chwang has it that Prayâga, as modern Allâhâbâd was called in ancient times, had from of old been the scene of charity on the part of kings and noble families. An extensive area on the bank of the Ganges was called 'the great charity-enclosure.' "At the present time," continues the Chinese pilgrim, "Śîlâditya-râja, after the example of his ancestors, distributes here in one day the accumulated wealth of five years. Immense piles of wealth and jewels were collected in the charity enclosure; the most costly jewels were offered a statue of Buddha. Afterwards, charity to the residentiary priests, then to priests (from a distance) who are present; then to men of distinguished talent; then to resident heretics following the ways of the world; lastly, to the widows and bereaved, orphans and desolate, poor and mendicants. Having exhausted his treasures and given food in charity, he gives away his diadem and his jewelled necklaces . . . ."[2] Such seems to have been the fashion of the age. Yuan Chwang records that the king of Kapiśa held a similar Mokṣapariṣad and gave liberally to the needy, to widows and to widowers.[3] Elsewhere, too, the Chinese pilgrim bears testimony to the generosity of Indian rulers.[4]

[1] Yuan Chwang, Watters, II, 344.

[2] Beal, Si-yu-ki, I, 214, 221, 233. For Prayâga, p. 230.

[3] Yuan Chwang, Watters I, 122-123. Cf. Beal, I, 49.

[4] Ibid., 176.

The succession to the throne was, as usual, hereditary and went by the rule of primogeniture. When on the death of Prabhâkaravardhana, Prince Râjyavardhana offers to resign the throne in favour of his younger brother, the latter violently protests.[1] But the incidents connected with the accession of Harṣa throw light on the manner in which emergencies were got over. When the news of Râjyavardhana's murder was received, the chief minister Bhaṇḍi, who was a near relation of the royal dynasty and whose power and reputation were high and of much weight, addressed the assembled ministers, " The destiny of the nation is to be fixed to-day. The old king's son is dead : the brother of the prince, however, is humane and affectionate, and his disposition, heaven-conferred, is dutiful and obedient. Because he is strongly attached, to his family, the people will trust in him. I propose that he assume the royal authority, let each one give his opinion on this matter, whatever he thinks." All agreed. The chief ministers and officers all exhorted Harṣa to assume the royal authority. ". . . . The opinion of the people, as shown in their songs, proves their real submission to your eminent qualities. Reign, then, with glory over the land; conquer the enemies of your family; wash out the insult laid on your kingdom and the deeds of your illustrious father. Great will your merit be in such a case. We pray you not reject our prayer." According to the account of Bâṇabhaṭṭa it was the Senâpati Siṁhanâda who proposed the installation of Harṣa. In either case the duty is performed by a high officer of state. Yuan Chwang continues that the young prince replied, " The government of a country is a responsible office and ever attended with difficulties. The duties of a prince require previous consideration. As for myself, I

The succession.

[1] Harṣacarita, 200 et seq.

am indeed of small eminence; but as my father and brother are no more, to reject the heritage of the crown, that can bring no benefit to the people. I must attend to the opinion of the world and forget my own insufficiency. . . ." Yuan Chwang adds that in his affliction and crisis, the young man betook himself to a statue of Avalokiteśvara and was warned not to use the lion-throne and "call not yourself Mahârâja." Harṣa duly assumed the royal office and began to issue commands to the ministers.[1] Making all allowance for picturesque effect in the Chinese narrative, the outline may be accepted as true. From the last incident it will appear that several varieties of thrones were known in ancient India, that the lion-throne signified some extravagance or vanity. That the Siṁhâsana or lion-throne was well-known in the 7th century is clear from Yuan Chwang himself. He records of a North-Western state that the large and high lion-throne of the reigning sovereign was much adorned with precious gems, that it was covered with extremely fine drapery, and that its foot-stool was adorned with gems.[2] Perhaps the high-sounding titles too were not universally liked.

Consecration.

The details of a consecration in the 7th century A.D. may be inferred from some passages in Kâdambarî where Prince Candrâpîḍa is anointed king. True, here the ceremony is led by his own father but for the rest, the description may be as applicable to the consecration of a king as of a Yuvarâja. " . . . On an auspicious day," says the romance, "the king, surrounded by a thousand chiefs, raised aloft, with Śukanâsa's help, the vessel of consecration, and himself anointed his son,

[1] Yuan Chwang in Beal, Si-yu-ki, I, 210—213. In the Banskhera Plate of the year 628-29 A.D., Harṣa probably with his own hand subscribes himself as Mahârâjâdhirâja (svahasto mama Mahârâjâśrî Harṣasya). Ep. Ind., IV, No. 29.

[2] Beal, I, 75.

while the rest of the rites were performed by the family priest. The water of consecration was brought from every sacred pool, river and ocean encircled by every plant, fruit, earth and gem . . . and purified by mantras . . . straightway he was anointed from head to foot by Vilâsavatî (his mother) attended by all ladies . . . with sweet sandal white as moonbeams. He was garlanded with fresh white flowers; decked with lines of gorocana; adorned with an earring of dûrvâ grass; clad in two silken robes with long fringes, white as the moon; bound with an amulet round his hand, tied by the family priest; and had his breast encircled by a pearl necklace. . . . " He was completely covered over with wreaths of white flowers. " Then his father him self for that time took the chamberlain's wand to make way for him and he went to the hall of assembly . . . Then, when he had received due homage from the kings (chiefs ?), after a short pause the great drum that heralded his setting out on his triumphal course resounded deeply, under the stroke of golden sticks . . Then, at the roar of the drum, followed by an outcry of 'All hail!' from all sides, Candrâpîḍa came down from the throne, . . . He left the hall of assembly, followed by a thousand chiefs who rose hastily round him . . ."[1] Seated on an elephant, under an umbrella " with a hundred wires enmeshed with pearls . . ." he made his progress and received the homage of hosts of "kings," who bowed low before him "as a trusted general recited their names . . ." Turning slowly towards the eastern quarter, Candrâpîḍa at last reached his palace. It was adorned with many triumphal arches; dotted with a thousand pavilions enclosed in grassy ramparts, and bright with many a tent of shining white cloth. Like a king, he performed all due rites. Next morning he started on his Digvijaya and made "conquests in all quarters." The

[1] Kâdambarî, tr. Ridding, 84—89.

consort was anointed along with the king. "Upon this head," says the widow of Prabhâkaravardhana, "have the subservient wives of countless feudatories poured coronation water from golden ewers."[1] It was in great "conquests" that a Hindu consecration was expected to culminate. It is a striking coincidence that Harṣa's accession to the throne was actually followed by six years of Digvijaya. As usual, the reigns of extraordinarily powerful sovereigns were associated with new eras. The era of Harṣa dates from his accession in October, 606.[2]

The Prince.

On the education of the princes a great deal of care was bestowed by the sovereign. The young princes Râjyavardhana and Harṣavardhana were placed in charge of their maternal uncle Bhaṇḍi who occupied an important position in the state. Sons of a great feudatory ruler were appointed their companions. They were given an excellent military training. Harṣa is reputed to have been a poet and dramatist but even if the plays attributed to him be adjudged the handiwork of a court poet, there is no reason to doubt the tradition of the emperor's literary accomplishments. Bâṇa, in fact, positively asserts that Harṣa was a great poet. Princes were often given high command or provincial governorships. Thus Râjyavardhana was sent by his father Prabhâkaravardhana against the Huns while Harṣa followed with a cavalry force.[3]

A Kâdambarî account.

Bâṇa's Kâdambarî throws some additional light on the practice of the age. Its account of an Ujjain prince's education is obviously romantic but is not without some bearing on actual facts. For his son Candrâpîḍa, six years old, King Târâpîḍa built "a palace of learning outside the

[1] Harṣacarita, 186.

[2] Kielhorn, Ind. Ant., XXVI, 32.

[3] Harṣacarita, 151, 154, 166.

city, stretching half a league along the Siprâ river . . . . with stables for horses and palanquins close by and a gymnasium constructed beneath. He took infinite pains in gathering there teachers of every science, and having placed the boy there, like a young lion in a cage, forbidding all egress surrounding him with a suite composed mainly of the sons of his teachers, removing every allurement to the sports of boyhood, and on an auspicious day he entrusted him, together with Vaiśampâyana (the minister's son), to masters that they might acquire all knowledge." Every day the king visited the prince. In an eloquent, high-flown passage, the novelist relates that the prince mastered the sciences, arts, crafts, music, the Epics, the Purâṇas, foreign languages, all kinds of writing, prosody, etc., etc.[1] On the completion of his education in ten years the prince was asked ceremoniously to return home.[2] Escorted by "three thousand princes, all sons of anointed kings," the prince passed in a procession through the city,[3] and then entered the court to be received affectionately by his parents and all present.[4] Thenceforward, the prince lives a life of comfort, even luxury. He goes out to hunt. He has numerous attendants. Among others, Patralekhâ, daughter of the "king" of Kulûta, captured in war in her childhood, was appointed his betel-bearer by his mother and became his companion and confidential advisor.[5] The king makes over the throne to him and has him regularly anointed with the help of feudatories. Before his consecration, the minister Śukanâsa gives him a lengthy discourse on his position and duties.[6]

---

1. Kâdambarî, tr. Ridding, pp. 59–61.
2. Ibid., pp. 61–63.
3. Ibid., 63–65.
4. Ibid., 70-71.
5. Ibid., 73–75.
6. Ibid., 76–86.

Besides the sons of a king, his other relations might occupy important positions in the state. There is a Chinese notice that in the north-west a king, when starting on a pilgrimage, entrusted the kingdom to his brother.[1]

King's relations.

The administrative system of the seventh century A.D. is practically the same as that of the Gupta age. A few additional details are forthcoming from Bâṇabhaṭṭa, Yuan Chwang and from the inscriptions. A chief minister stands out more clearly than in the data of the Gupta period. Bhaṇḍi, closely related to the royal family, is admittedly superior to all.[2] The incidents connected with the accession of Harṣa make it clear that all the chief ministers met together to discuss important questions. For the north-west outside the dominions of Harṣa there is an interesting Chinese notice that the king and ministers met together for consultation on affairs of state on the 15th and last day of the month, and then took counsel of the chief priest and finally published their decrees.[3] Harṣacarita indicates that ministers were also consulted individually by the king. For instance, Skandagupta, the commandant of the elephant force, is seen urging Harṣa to universal conquest.[4] In Harṣacarita, the chief military officer—'foremost in every fight'—is called Senâpati.[5] The war-elephant on which he rode is covered with coat-of-mail, and his tusks are provided with sharp barbs. There was

Ministers.

---

[1] Beal, I, 22-23.

[2] Harṣacarita, 223; Beal, I, 211; Watters, I, 343. Cf. Kâdambarî (49—51, 76—84) where the Brâhmaṇa Śukanâsa, deeply versed in the arts and sciences and in politics, presides over the administration and gives advice to Prince Candrâpîḍa.

[3] Beal, I, 22.

[4] Harṣacarita, 222, 225, 240.

[5] Ibid., 212.

"a soldier on each side to manage the elephant."[1] The commander of the cavalry was another high military officer.[2] As before, the Mahâsaṁdhivigrahika is the foreign minister.[3] The Pramâtṛi is a counsellor and high officer of state. In the Madhuban Plate Inscription, the office is occupied by the Mahâsâmanta Mahârâja Skandagupta who also acts as the Dûtaka.[4] Incidentally it appears that feudatories were employed in high offices directly under the suzerain. The supposition is strengthened by the mention of Mahâsâmantas and Mahârâjas in the same breath with regular officers in the Madhuban Plates. Among other officers one of the most notable is the Dauḥsâdhanika, one who is entrusted with difficult undertakings, a high police officer.[5] Kumârâmâtyas, Râjasthâniyas (viceroys), Viṣayapatis (district officers), and Uparikas (revenue officers) are common to the Vardhana and Gupta inscriptions. The Mahâkṣapaṭalika was the great keeper of records. Yuan Chwang states that an accurate record of all happenings was kept.[6] The mention of Âyuktakas, subordinate officers,[7] and Câṭas or police, in Harṣacarita supplies another link with the Gupta times. Again, Câṭas are debarred from entering agrahâras, probably because their visitations meant some financial

[1] Watters, I, 171; Beal I, 83.

[2] Harṣacarita, 209, see also 220.

[3] Ibid., 218.

[4] Ep. Ind., I, No. 11. See also the Valabhî grant of Dhruvasena III, Ep. Ind., I, No. 13.

[5] Ind. Ant., XIV, p. 167. The Tipperah Copper Plate grant of Lokanâtha (from East Bengal) of the year 650 A.D., shortly after the death of Harṣa, shows hereditary Mahâsâmantas and Sâmantas occupying the post of Kumârâmâtya (Ep. Ind., XV, No. 19). Two grants of Dhruvasena II, of the year 639-40 A.D., from Central India show the same system of Bhuktis and Viṣayas (Ep. Ind., VIII, No. 20.)

[6] Ep. Ind., IV, 211. Watters, I, 154.

[7] Harṣacarita, 237, 286.

exactions. There are numerous policemen and tax-collectors in Harṣacarita. There is an interesting notice that in the course of the emperor's march through a village, the Akṣapaṭalika or keeper of records, came out with a number of karaṇis or clerks to meet the emperor, to ask for his commands and to receive a golden seal and another emblem from him.[1] Elsewhere, too, there is mention of sakalakaraṇiparikara which shows that many persons were associated in the administration of the village or the next higher unit of rural administration.[2] Drâṅgika, as before, is the town-officer who, from his designation, seems also to have performed some revenue functions. The mention of Mahattaras with him shows that the chief personages of a place were informally associated with the administration or were at least consulted by the officers. There are numerous couriers who carry messages to and fro.[3] The Life of Yuan Chwang supplies an interesting touch that the emperor's letters were written on fine, white cotton stuff and sealed with red wax.[4]

Salaries.

The remuneration of officers seems to have taken the form of grants of land, made according to the importance of the various positions. Yuan Chwang states that the king set apart ¼th of the crown lands for the endowment of great public servants and another ¼ for the expenses of government and state-worship. The two heads partly overlap and it appears that official remuneration consumed more than one-fourth of the revenue. "The governors, magistrates and officials have each a

---

1 Ibid., 227.

2 Ibid., 274.

3 Harṣacarita, 59, 160, 168, 179. Beal, I, 215 ; Life, 169.

4 Life, p. 190. For officials, compare the Tipperah Copper Plate Grant of Lokanâtha (from East Bengal) of the year 650 A.D., which mentions the same official designations and feudatory titles. (Ep. Ind., XV, No. 19.)

portion of land consigned to them for their personal support." Yuan Chwang goes on to state that forced labour was "sparingly used." The assertion may be accepted as true for Harṣa's reign.[1] Bâṇa has recorded that on Harṣa's rush from the north-west to the capital at the news of his father's illness, footmen were sent ahead to secure a relay of villagers to show the way.[2] We are not told that the villagers were paid anything. Perhaps, it was on such occasions that the little forced labour, implied in Yuan's statement, was exacted.

Recruitment of officials.

In the latter half of the seventh century I-tsing made an incidental remark on the recruitment of state-officials which may be equally applicable to the first half of the century. Scholars who defeated their opponents in scholastic controversies were not only gratified with grants of land and the proclamation of their names and achievements in schools but also received high posts in the service of the state.[3] There is nothing improbable in the fact that government recruited men of recognised talents for certain offices which demanded an intellectual background.

Revenue.

The sources of revenue in the 7th century A.D. were the same as in the preceding ages. Yuan Chwang's verdict that the taxes were light may be accepted. Agriculture was, of course, the dominant occupation of the people. "All till the ground for their subsistence." We are told that those who cultivated the royal estates paid $\frac{1}{6}$th of the produce as rent. Yuan Chwang perhaps seems to regard the whole territory directly governed by the king as his estates. Royal estates are opposed to feudatory domains where revenue

[1] Watters, I, p. 176. Beal, I, 87-88.

[2] Harṣacarita, p. 170.

[3] I-tsing, Buddhist Practices, etc., tr. Takakusu, p. 178.

would naturally be paid to feudal chiefs. The Madhuban Plate Inscription mentions the Gupta imposts—Udraṅga, Uparikara, Hiraṇya, etc. Next to the land revenue, customs formed the most important head of receipt. In the Madhuban Plates there is a tax on things sold. It seems that merchants were required to pay some additional tolls at the ferries and fords on the rivers and at many points on the highways. From some passages in Bâṇa it is clear that some of the feudatories, for instance, hill chieftains, paid tribute. Presents came from all who had any occasion to see the king. Bâṇa himself was, for a while, refused admittance to the king's presence, because he had not offered his tribute of respect which, in the context, can only mean a present. In another passage Bâṇa implies that even villagers made presents to the king when he passed through their habitations. It appears that even under excellent kings the collection of regular taxes sometimes led to oppression by petty officials. On one occasion in Harṣacarita, people bitterly complain against revenue and police officials.[1]

Justice.

Bâṇa implies that justice was administered by Mimâṁsakas.[2] It is, however, from Yuan Chwang that one obtains a clear idea of the administration of justice in the 7th century A.D. in the north of India. His account which relates primarily to the North-west, differs markedly in many details from that of the theoreticians Nârada and Bṛihaspati but in principles it confirms them in a most striking manner. Yuan Chwang came to the conclusion that criminals or rebels were few and serious

[1] Harṣacarita, 87—90, 230, 243, 286. Watters, I, 176. Beal, I, 87. Ep. Ind., I, p. 67. The existence of the same fiscal system in Central India is proved by two grants of Dhruvasena II, of the year 639-40 A.D., Ep. Ind., VIII, No. 20. For records and archives, Watters, I, 154.

[2] Harṣacarita, 86.

trouble was only occasional. "When the laws are broken or the power of the ruler violated, then the matter is clearly sifted . . . ." Torture was not used to elicit confession. "In the investigation of criminal cases there is no use of rod or staff to obtain proofs." But there were a few ordeals which were resorted to when the accused persisted in denying the charge. In the water ordeal, "the accused is placed in a sack connected with a stone vessel and thrown into deep water . . . . If the man sinks and the stone floats, he is guilty; but if the man floats and the stone sinks, then he is pronounced innocent." In the ordeal by fire, "they heat a plate of iron and make the accused sit on it, and again place his feet on it, and apply it to the palms of his hands; moreover, he is made to pass his tongue over it; if no scars result, he is innocent; if there are scars, his guilt is proved. In case of weak and timid persons who cannot endure such ordeal, they take a flower bud and cast it towards the fire; if it opens, he is innocent; if the flower is burnt he is guilty." In the ordeal by weight, a man and a stone were placed evenly in a balance. "Then they judge according to lightness or weight." If the accused were innocent, he would weigh down the stone which would rise in the balance. If he were guilty, the man would rise and the stone fall.[1] Lastly, "the poison ordeal requires that the right hind leg of a ram be cut off, and according to the portion assigned to the accused to eat, poisons are put into the leg, and if the man is innocent he survives, and if not the poison takes effect."[2] It will be observed that while the water and particularly, the fire ordeals are serious enough, the others are almost frivolous. Perhaps the theory was that divine opinion and judgment

[1] Yuan Chwang, Beal, I, 84-85; Watters, I, 172.

[2] Watters, I, 172.

had to be invoked. It is again probable that ordeals were resorted to only in cases where no decisive oral or documentary evidence was forthcoming.

The punishments were various and, on the whole, severe. Yuan Chwang's statement that corporal punishment was non-existent is contradicted by himself and opposed to all we know of the ancient Hindu penal code. If a man violated "the rules of propriety, justice, fidelity or filial piety," his nose or his ears were cut off, or his hands or his feet were amputated, or he was expelled from the country or he was driven into the desert wilds. For certain crimes which the Chinese traveller does not specify, the offenders were imprisoned. Yuan Chwang seems to imply, though he is not perfectly clear on the point, that imprisonment was extremely severe. The prisoners were not counted among men and were simply left to live or die.[1] But there is a passage in Bâṇa which shows that prison conditions were not so horrible. On auspicious occasions, like the birth of a prince, the king commanded the release of prisoners.[2] Minor offences were punished with fines. In certain north-western principalities, murder was punished by banishment to the desolate mountains.[3] Treason, though always regarded as a heinous crime, was sometimes punished only by banishment. Five hundred Brâhmaṇas who were implicated in a conspiracy against the king were exiled by Harṣa, though the ministers and feudatories loudly demanded the extermination of the whole tribe. The king's friends urged that the conspirators' agent, who actually assaulted Harṣa, should be instantaneously put to death. The king, however, kept his head and closely interrogated the man. We are not told how he was ultimately punished.[4]

---

[1] Ibid., I, 83, 214.

[2] Beal, I, 188.

[3] Harṣacarita, p. 143.

[4] Beal, 220-21.

Defence.

The army of Harṣa, at the time of his accession, comprised 5,000 elephants, 20,000 cavalry and 50,000 infantry. By the time of Yuan Chwang's visit, the cavalry had gone up to 100,000 and the elephant corps to the staggering figure of 60,000. From a passage in Harṣacarita it appears that there was also a camel corps. As usual, other princes in ancient India also commanded big armies. For instance, Kumâra of Kâmarûpa visited Harṣa with 20,000 elephants. It is clear from Bâṇa that Harṣa acquired a good many elephants as tribute or presents. Horses were imported from Western regions such as Sindh, modern Afghânistân and Persia. Besides the regular military officers there were a number of superintendents of soldiers' barracks. A huge staff or fodderers, grooms and superintendents managed the royal stables.[1] Speaking of a North-western state, Yuan states that troops were levied according to requirements, that recruitment was done by public proclamation and that rewards were promised. A select body of guards were recruited from heroes of choice valour, a sort of hereditary military aristocracy.[2] Some difficulty was experienced in maintaining internal order and security in the seventh century. Soldiers were requisitioned to perform police functions. On his way back, the Chinese pilgrim was provided with a military escort. He has left it on record that the military, besides guarding the frontier, went out to punish the refractory and mounted guard at night round the palace.[3] Towns, even of a small size, appear to have been often enclosed by walls, though these were far from impregnable. Soon after the death of Harṣa, a retributive Tibetan expedition sent by Srong-tsan

[1] Watters, I, 343. Beal, I, 213. Harṣacarita, 66, 70, 72, 228.

[2] Watters, I, 171. Beal, I, 87.

[3] Beal I, 87; Life, p. 191.

Gampo is said to have captured 580 walled towns. Many of these could hardly have been much larger than villages.[1]

The Spirit and Activity of Government.

Speaking of a north-western state, Yuan says that the administration was founded on benign principles and that the rules of government were marked by rectitude. His judgment on Harṣa's regime is even more favourable. It may be accepted that Hindu governance was generally benevolent in the seventh century A.D. But rulers could sometimes be intolerant and oppressive. Śaśâṅka of Bengal persecuted the Buddhists. Even a righteous ruler like Kumâra could sometimes be arbitrary. When Śīlabhadra, the head of the monastery of Nâlanda, twice refused to send Yuan to Kumâra, the latter threatened that he would "let the evil portion of him prevail" and would "equip his army and elephants to raze to the ground the whole monastery of Nâlanda." The poor abbot promptly complied with the peremptory demand.[2] The Chinese pilgrim emphasises that there was no registration of families. But from his own account, as from that of Bâṇa, it is clear that at least the government of Harṣa interested itself most actively in the higher life as well as in the material comforts of the community. Harṣacarita shows that state or private beneficence was responsible for the foundation of numerous alms-houses, rest-houses and water-places.[3] In some respects Harṣa seems to have followed the policy of Aśoka. Throughout his dominions he forbade the slaughter of any living thing and interdicted meat-diet on pain of death without pardon. He erected several thousands of Stûpas on the banks of the Ganges. He erected Saṅghârâmas at all places where there were any holy traces of the Buddha. On all the highways which ran through towns and villages,

[1] Sylvain Lévi, tr. Ind. Ant., 1911, pp. 111 et seq.

[2] Yuan, Life. 170, 171, 187 ; Beal, I, 87.

[3] Harṣacarita, 176.

he established hospitals, appointed physicians therein, arranged for the distribution of medicine, food and drink to travellers and poor people around in an unstinted measure, free of all charge.[1] He arranged scholastic assemblies for discussions and himself judged on the arguments advanced. He honoured character and learning in all individuals, rewarded the good and promoted men of talent.[2] "If there was any irregularity in the manners of the people of the cities, he went amongst them."[3] The higher activities of the state in the 7th century A.D., were according to Yuan Chwang, financed with great generosity. Speaking of the north-west he remarks that the income from the land was divided into four parts, the first was for carrying out the affairs of state and providing sacrificial offerings; the second for providing subsidies to ministers and chief officers of state, the third for rewarding men of distinguished ability and the fourth for charity to religious bodies.[4] Whether Harṣa also actually divided his income regularly in this fashion we cannot be sure. But it is clear that he must have spent a good deal on religion and learning. The accounts of the Buddhist celebrations are interesting. The gorgeous processions were escorted by Harṣa and Kumâra, each with 500 war-elephants clad in armour; in front of the statue of the Buddha as well as behind it marched another 100 big elephants, carrying musicians who sounded their drums and raised their music.[5] When Harṣa made an expedition to Koṅgoda in Orissâ, he held a religious assembly there and summoned to it four Buddhist masters from Nâlanda. He exerted himself energetically in the propagation of Mahâyâna Buddhism and offered to assign the revenue of 80

---

[1] Beal, I, 214.
[2] Ibid., I, 214; Watters, I, 161.
[3] Beal, I, 215.
[4] Ibid. I, 87.
[5] Ibid., 218-219.

towns in Orissâ to the learned Buddhist Jayasena. The practice of the state endowment of religion and piety was common to the whole of north India. For instance the king of Kapiśa commissioned five pure men to make continuous offerings of scents and flowers to Buddhist relics.[1] Other rulers in the north-west favoured various religions.[2] The Chinese pilgrim records numerous instances of Buddhist monarchs and nobles who built Stûpas and Vihâras, organised religious festivals, discussions and assemblies.[3] Harṣavardhana's Brahmanical ancestors had celebrated sacrifices on a grand scale. In his pompous style Bâṇa records that under the rule of Prabhâkaravardhana the golden age seemed to bud forth in close packed lines of sacrificial posts, the evil time to flee in the smoke of sacrifices meandering over the sky and heaven to descend in stuccoed shrines.[4] As to the patronage of learning Bâṇa seems to reflect facts when in his romance he paints king Śûdraka as a founder of literary societies and a refuge for men of taste.[5] In the latter half of the seventh century A.D. I-tsing noted how young scholars went to debate at the courts of kings in the hope of receiving government employment. Often the kings bestowed grants of land on the scholars. At any rate victory in the discussions brought wide fame.[6]

Toleration.

In spite of the career of Śaśâṅka who is said to have uprooted the Bodhi tree and destroyed the "Law" so far as he could,[7] religious toleration must be held to be the rule in the seventh century in India. The "Life" and account of Yuan testify

[1] Ibid., I, 176.
[2] Ibid., II, 107 et seq.
[3] Harṣacarita, 183.
[4] Kâdambarî, tr. Ridding, p. 9.
[5] I-tsing, Buddhist Practices, etc., tr. Takakusu, 177-78.
[6] Watters, I, 343; Life, 171.
[7] Beal, I, 97.

abundantly to the catholicity of the Brahmanic Kumâra. Bâṇa speaks of the presence of Jainas, Ârhatas, Pâśupatas, Brâhmaṇas and mendicants of the school of Parâśara at the court of Harṣa.[1] Planning a big religious assembly, the emperor sent commands from Kajughira in Bengal to the different "kingdoms" that followers of all the various sects and schools should attend. So the Kanauj assembly included 3,000 Mahâyâna and Hînayâna Buddhists, nearly 1,000 Buddhist scholars from Nâlanda, and 3,000 Brâhmaṇas and Nirgranthas.[2] The discussions were conducted in the usual scholastic fashion. For instance, Yuan Chwang propounded a thesis, posted it outside the assembly-hall and challenged its refutation.[3] The practice of holding such assemblies was widespread and of long duration. Yuan was told that king Vikramâditya who had been renowned for his charity all over India had summoned a religious gathering to discuss spiritual doctrines.[4] The Chinese pilgrim speaks of numerous other rulers who had done the same and records some anecdotes. One of the kings is said to have proclaimed that "whoever is defeated shall die, as a proof of his inferiority."[5] On another occasion a great discussion was conducted in a big hall in the presence of a king, his ministers and a vast concourse. When Mâdhava, one of the controversialists, happened to die, his widow occupied his place and took up the cudgels.[6] In such gatherings feeling sometimes ran high. On the occasion of one of Harṣa's assemblies, it was rumoured that the life of Yuan Chwang was in danger. The emperor issued a proclamation to the effect that "if any one should

---

1 Harṣacarita, 170.
2 Beal, I, 218.
3 Ibid., I, 218, 219, 221.
4 Ibid., I, 106.
5 Ibid., II, 99.
6 Ibid., II, 107.

touch or hurt the Master of the Law, he shall be forthwith executed; and whoever speaks against him, his tongue shall be cut out; but all those who desire to profit by his instructions, relying on my good will, need not fear this manifesto."[1]

Harṣa was something of an eclectic. In spite of his strong Buddhist sympathies, he honoured Brâhmaṇas and offered worship to Brahmanic gods. He invited Brâhmaṇa scholars to the Mokṣa-pariṣad and other functions and bestowed valuable gifts on them. But it appears that the lion's share of his charities went to Buddhists. At the sixth Mokṣapariṣad a man attempted the life of the king and, when arrested and closely cross-questioned by the latter, replied, "Great king, you have assembled the people of different countries and exhausted your treasures in offerings to the Śramaṇas, and cast a metal image of the Buddha; but the heretics (Brâhmaṇas) who have come from a distance have scarcely been spoken to. Their minds therefore have been affected with resentment and they procured me . . . to undertkae this unlucky deed."[2]

Jealousies.

During this period royal munificence was responsible for the foundation or maintenance of big monasteries and academies which, without any stretch of language, may be called universities. For instance, the revenues of a hundred villages had been remitted for the support of Nâlanda, the great centre of Buddhist piety and learning. Six successive kings had added to its endowments and buildings until it assumed the status of an all-India institution. Yuan has left a glowing description of its "richly adorned towers, and the fairy-like turrets, like pointed hill-tops," congregated together. "The observatories seem to be lost in the vapours (of the

Nâlanda.

[1] Life, pp. 179-80.

[2] Beal, I, 220-21, 218; II, 198, 261.

morning), and the upper rooms tower above the clouds . . . All the outside courts, in which are the priests' chambers, are of four stages. The stages have dragon-projections, and coloured eaves, the pearl-red pillars, carved and ornamented, the richly adorned balustrades, and the roofs covered with tiles that reflect the light in a thousand shades . . . ." Here were gathered 1,510 teachers who altogether delivered 100 discourses a day on different subjects. The number of students is put at 10,000. Adherents of different persuasions came from all over the country to challenge Nâlanda monks to discussion. The Chinese pilgrim who studied here for several years adds that "the saṁghârâmas of India are counted by myriads but this (Nâlanda) is the most remarkable for grandeur and height."[1] So it appears that there were numerous smaller seats of learning.

Guilds.

In the data of this period guilds occupy a more prominent place than in the preceding epochs. Perhaps this form of economic, and partly social, organisation had developed further. The Vasantagaḍh Inscription of Varmalatâ of the year 625 A.D. (from modern Sirohî state) shows a gosṭhî or guild committee arranging for the construction of a temple.[2] On the occasion of the Princess Râjyaśrî's marriage, guilds of skilled workers—carpenters, painters, modellers, etc.—are summoned to decorate the palace. A reference is also

[1] Yuan Chwang, Life, 110—12. Watters, II, 164-65. For Nâlanda assemblies, Beal, II, 170-71. For a view of Nâlanda in the latter half of the 7th century A.D. I-tsing, tr. Takakusu, p. 177. For the remains of Nâlanda buildings, J. B. O. R. S., 1923 (Vol. IX, Part I), pp. 1—22; also V. A. Smith, J. R. A. S., 1917, pp. 154-55. For a picture of life in Buddhist monasteries and their experiments in communism, I-tsing, op. cit., Ch. XXXVII, pp. 193-94. There were also Brahmanical seats of learning (Harṣacarita, 265,

[2] Ep. Ind., IX, No. 25.

made to Navasevakas or apprentices in guilds.[1] The theory of the status, constitution and working of guilds, as enunciated by Bṛihaspati, indicates that they were a recognised part of the body-politic. From Bṛihaspati as from Nârada it appears that a guild had a general assembly which met from time to time to transact business. There were two, three or five executive officers.[2] Yâjñavalkya and Nârada lay down elaborate rules for the conduct and training of apprentices and their relations with the masters.[3] On the technical side of their affairs, the guilds appear to be self-governing but, according to the theory of the Dharma Śâstras, the state should settle their internal wrangles, regulate and control their relations with the outside world and, in general, should see that they conformed to rules and usages. Yâjñavalkya is perfectly clear on the point. All groups which have strayed from their own laws, whether they be families, guilds, associations, must be subjected to discipline and brought back to the path of duty by the king.[4] In practice, the amount of state control must have varied with distance from the headquarters of government officials, the vigour of the government, the prestige of particular guilds and the character of their work. But it seems clear from the Dharma Śâstras that guilds acted as courts of justice in civil suits, though an appeal might lie from their decisions to the king.

[1] Harṣacarita, 158.

[2] Nârada, X, 3; Bṛihaspati, XVII, 11—19. Bṛihaspati prescribes qualifications of high birth, sterling character, learning and professional excellence for the officers of guilds.

[3] Yâjñavalkya, II, 187; Nârada, V, 16—21.

[4] Yâjñavalkya Saṁhitâ, II, 186—192; I, 361. Nârada, X, 2-3, 5-6. Bṛihaspati, XVII, 5—17, 19—21. Cf. Manu, VIII, 5, 218—20. On other aspects of the life of guilds, also Bṛihaspati, I, 28, 30; XVII, 11-12.

A small amount of supplementary evidence on the politics of the 7th century A.D. can be gathered from a few literary works. To Harṣa himself has been attributed the authorship of three dramatic pieces—Nâgânanda, Ratnâvalî and Priyadarśikâ. There is, however, nothing in them to show that they are the handiwork of an experienced statesman. They are cast in the usual mould and their political touches are far from refreshing. I-tsing, indeed, affirms that Nâgânanda had been dramatised by Harṣa but all that can be asserted with certainty is that the play was composed in the 7th century A.D., probably at the emperor's court. It faithfully reflects contemporary political conditions when, in the very prologue, it refers to the Râjasamûha, the crowd of Râjas, who bowed to the feet of Harṣa. Obeisance of this character is held in the inscriptions also to symbolise the relationship of suzerainty and vassalage. One is reminded of Yuan Chwang's statement when, in the beginning of the fourth Act of Nâgânanda, the chamberlain speaks of the king as one who put everything in order in the cities and who rectified all wrongs by means of punishments according to Nîti. As in the dramatic works of preceding epochs, princes have their boon companions, Vidûṣakas, jesters.[1] In other acts of Nâgânanda there appears a superintendent of the harem, a chamberlain and other household officers.[2] On the basis of tradition as well as internal evidence, Ratnâvalî may be held to belong to the seventh century. In its fourth Act it brings a crowd of feudatories round the suzerain. The description of the royal camp corroborates Bâṇabhaṭṭa and Yuan Chwang.[3]

Literary Evidence.

Nâgânanda.

Ratnâvalî.

[1] Nâgânanda, Act I.
[2] Ibid., Acts II, IV, V.
[3] Ratnâvalî (ed. Cappeller), Act IV.

Bhaṭṭa Nârâyaṇa's Veṇî Saṁhâra which belongs probably to the same century, is an interesting play but the plot which turns on an incident of the Mahâbhârata reflects the temper of the epic. It treats of politics in terms of the family and the clan. It will be unsafe to draw from it any conclusions about the seventh century A.D.

Bhaṭṭa Nârâyaṇa.

The seventh century, so fertile in drama and Kâvya, witnessed the composition of some curious works. The Bhaṭṭikâvya, attributed without adequate reason to Bhartṛihari and belonging probably to this period, seeks to combine grammatical instruction and poetic diction with a narration of the tale of the Râmâyaṇa. It upholds the orthodox Brahmanical order. But its political touches have nothing novel about them.

The Bhaṭṭikâvya.

By the seventh century A.D., the connection of the North with the Deccan had become very close and many political institutions and designations had become common to both regions. The Mauryan, Ândhra, Kaliṅga and Gupta empires, in spite of their respect for autonomy, had served to intensify the centripetal forces. The village institutions of the North always differed from those of the Deccan and yet more markedly from those of the extreme south. There were also other points of difference but the fundamental political conditions, central, provincial and district institutions and fiscal arrangements were remarkably similar in the seventh century. Thus the Sarsavni Plates of Buddharâja of the year 609-10 A.D. (from modern Barodâ territory) present the same type of feudatories—Râjas and Sâmantas—and the same type of administrative officers—Mahâsaṁdhivigrahâdhikaraṇâdhikrita, Mahâbalâdhikṛita, Bhogika, Viṣayapati, etc. Here Âdhikârika appears to denote government employees

The Deccan in the seventh century A.D.

in general. The fiscal system is the same as in the north.[1] Two grants of Dadda IV of the year 641-42 A.D. from Gujarât introduce the title Bhogikapâlaka, literally, protector of Bhogikas. It may refer to the central officer who dealt with the provincial rulers but its exact significance is not clear.[2] The Bagumra Grant of Nikumbhallaśakti of the year 654-55 A.D. from southern Gujarât mentions Râjas or feudatories, Râjasthâniyas or viceroys, and other officers as in the north. It discloses an administrative division Râṣṭra under a Râṣṭrakûṭa. It is perhaps a revenue division. For the rest, the fiscal system is the same as in the north.[3] The Sañjan Plates of the Western Câlukya Buddharasa from the modern district of Thânâ mention the title Râjâdhirâja Parameśvara which appears to be an alternative form of Mahârâjâdhirâja Parameśvara. A cousin of the paramount sovereign is called Râjan which shows that members of the royal family held fiefs. There is mention of a "twelve village," that is, a district which comprised or was supposed to comprise twelve villages, a form of territorial distribution which appears very frequently in the later history of the Deccan.[4] It is curious that some inscriptions of Pulakeśin II do not apply the grand titles to him. In the Chiplun Copper Plate Grant, the king issues his command, *inter alia*, to all Sâmantas, Pṛithivîpâlas and Râjas who are obviously feudatories. But the suzerain styles himself neither Mahârâjâdhirâja nor Parameśvara.[5] The Yekkeri Rock Inscription boasts that Pulakeśin imposed his prowess on the entire number of chieftains and acquired the sovereignty over the whole earth. But he is only designated Mahârâja.[6]

[1] Ep. Ind., VI, No. 29.

[2] Ep. Ind., V, No. 5.

[3] Ind. Ant., XVIII, 1889, pp. 265 et. seq.

[4] Ep. Ind., XIV, No. 8.

[5] Ep. Ind., III, No. 8.

[6] Ep. Ind., V, No. 2.

Yuan Chwang also remarks that Pulakeśin, confident of his martial strength, treated the neighbouring countries with contempt.[1] It appears that the grand titles, while certainly in vogue in the Deccan, were not yet applied there with the uniformity which obtained in the north. Perhaps the titles originated in the North; it is in the northern Gupta Inscriptions that they are first met with in abundance. Thence they were adopted in the Deccan and it was not until some time that they became universal. The Yekkeri and Chiplun Inscriptions as well as the Aihole Inscription[2] present the usual officers, including Viṣayapatis, and the usual fiscal system. The Aihole Inscription also brings to view an hereditary army corps. In the Araṅg Plate of Bhīmasena II of the year 601 A.D. appears a line of hereditary Mahârâjas.[3] A grant of Raṇagraha of the year 640 A.D. shows a Bhogika acting as Dûtaka.[4] In the Nausari Plates of Sryasrava (671 A.D.) âhâra is the subdivision of a Viṣaya.[5] In the Chandalur Plates of Sarvalokasraya (673 A.D.), appears a line of hereditary Mahârâjas. Naiyogika, a term which does not seem to occur in the northern inscriptions, is the title applied to some officers. The Dûtaka is called Âjñapti.[6] The Navalakhi Plates of the year 605-6 A.D. from Jûnâgaḍh in Kâṭhiâwâḍ mention officers of northern designations —Âyuktakas, Viniyuktakas, Kumârâmâtyas, Dûtakas, Câṭas, Bhaṭas, etc. Here Divirapati seems to be a chief clerk, a sort of departmental secretary.[7] It was during this period that a great feudatory title, Pañcamahâśabda, came into vogue in the south. It is rarely met with in the north

[1] Watters, II, 239.
[2] Ep. Ind., VI, No. 1.
[3] Ep. Ind., IX, No. 53.
[4] Ep. Ind., II, No. 4.
[5] Ep. Ind., VIII, No. 22.
[6] Ep. Ind., VIII, No. 24.
[7] Ep. Ind., XI, No. 17.

but in the succeeding centuries it is fairly common in the Deccan. It is almost always applied to feudatories. It signifies that its holder was entitled to the use of five great sounds—musical instruments. Fleet points out that according to the Liṅgâyata Vivekacintâmaṇi these sounds refer to Śriṅga or horn, Tammaṭa or tambour, Śaṅkha or conch-shell, Bherî or kettle-drum and Jayaghaṇṭâ or gong.[1] The privilege of using these instruments in courts or processions seems to have been conferred by the suzerain on big feudatories who won high favour at his hands, though, like all titles in ancient India, it tended to become hereditary.

---

[1] Ind. Ant., XII, p. 95. Also Epigraphia Carnatica, VIII, 168.

CHAPTER XIV.

From the Eighth to the Tenth Century A.D.

After the death of Harṣa c. 648 A.D.

Neither Bâṇabhaṭṭa nor Yuan Chwang nor any of the contemporary inscriptions refers to any wife of Harṣavardhana, or to the fact of his marriage. It is certain that he died childless. When it is remembered that his sister Râjyaśrî is often mentioned, one is inclined to think that the emperor was a celibate all his life. If so, it is interesting to notice that while big seraglios were the rule in aristocratic circles in ancient India, there were occasional exceptions. On the death of Harṣa about 648 A.D. his empire split up into the fragments which had only loosely held together for a few decades. The throne at Kanauj was usurped by a minister of the late king.[1] It is a proof of the great power wielded by ministers that several Hindu empires—the Mauryan, Śuṅga, Kâṇva and Vardhana—ended with ministerial usurpations. From the latter half of the 7th to the 11th century A.D. the history of North India loses unity and clarity. Thanks to Kalhaṇa's Râjataraṅgiṇî, a connected account of the history of Kâshmîr can be constructed. But of the rest of the country only fragmentary glimpses can be obtained through coins, inscriptions, and literature. Towards the ninth century the Gûrjara-Pratihâra ascendancy certainly recalled the glories of Harṣavardhana but it was

[1] For a different view S. Krishnaswamy Aiyangar, Journal of Indian History, December, 1926, pp. 313—15.

short-lived. Besides, the Gûrjara-Pratihâra dominion was held together even more loosely than the Gupta or Vardhana empire. On the whole, then, it may be laid down that the four centuries preceding the Muslim invasions under Mahmûd of Ghaznî were a period of small and, historically, obscure states. The political facts about them, so far as modern research has been able to recover them, are well summarised in the fourth edition of Vincent A. Smith's Early History of India (pp. 366–438), and in a few recent papers notably those of D. R. Bhandarkar and R. C. Majumdar. It is needless to recapitulate them here. All that need be stated is that during the period, the chief states in the north were Kanauj, Kâshmîr, Sindh, Magadha, Kaliṅga or Orissâ, Bengal, Kâmarûpa or Âssâm, Mâlwâ and later, Ajmere, Delhi, Gwalior, Jejâkabhukti and Chedi. Besides them and generally below them lay a huge congeries of petty principalities.

Similarity of Administrative Structure.

As the subsequent analysis of the epigraphic and literary data will demonstrate, the political constitution and administrative structure of these different states were fundamentally similar. Everywhere one meets with the same feudal conditions of suzerainty and vassalage, nearly the same high officers with similar designations, the same fiscal and judicial system and, though not to the same extent, a similar attitude on the part of the state towards the people. Everywhere one meets with the same despotism—often benevolent but sometimes terrible and tyrannical. Everywhere is the same system of village administration—partly informal self-government and partly government and supervision from the district, provincial or central headquarters. This striking similarity is to be attributed to three causes. In the first place the northern plains were governed by the same geographical, economic and social conditions and therefore tended to evolve the same type of polity. In the second place, the human tendency to imitation would conduce to the reproduction of the institutions of one region in others. The multiplicity of states meant a large field for political experimentation. The limits of the experiment, its terms of reference, so to say, were narrow, but within its range it would result in the growth of diverse institutions. Their success and failure would be naturally observed and the more successful ones might be adopted elsewhere. In the third place, the rise of big empires from time to time would assist the process of assimilation. The example of the suzerain would be followed by the vassals and the resulting uniformity of institutions would, in a large measure, survive the break-up of the empire. From the broad administrative point of view North India shows a unity which, from the strict political standpoint, is conspicuous by its absence. Another general conclusion which emerges from the data of this period is that the institutions show little development. The number of officers in a given region may be larger or smaller at one time than in other periods. The number, size and sphere of administrative departments might similarly vary. But there is no change of first-rate importance, no organic evolution, in the institutions of this epoch. When one has arranged all relevant inscriptions and literary documents in the chronological as well as regional order, and compared their data, one fails to detect any marked changes or developments. Monotony and stagnation seem to characterise the politics of these four centuries. This was, perhaps, only part of a general phenomenon. For instance, the literature of this period is wanting in originality, depth and movement. The Purâṇas or Upa-Purâṇas which had been fashioned in earlier epochs were perhaps added to but merely on the old lines. The Smṛitis which were composed during this period slavishly echo the earlier Dharma Śâstras for the most part. Where they attempt something on their own account, they fail miserably. The classical literature is not immune from this deadening tendency. The Kâvya is now bound hand and foot by artificial rules and has perforce to follow a prescribed model. Instead of inspiration and spontaneity, it only shows ingenuity and jugglery of words.[1] The drama which displayed such virility in the days of Bhâsa and which had reached its high-water mark in the Gupta age is now governed by mechanical rules. The Pañcasaṁdhis replace natural movement.[2] A good deal of the literary talent of the period is spent on fashioning these rules of prosody, dramaturgy, etc., in classifying the subject-matter and reducing it to division and sub-division until life is replaced by machine. Other writers exhaust themselves in writing commentaries on old philosophic works, grammarians, the epics, Dharma Sûtras, Dharma Śâstras, Purâṇas and classical pieces. The time came when even commentaries were furnished with a code and composed almost mechanically Such were the general conditions under which government was carried on in North India from the eighth century onwards. For administration it is perhaps best to begin with literature and eke out the little which it has to offer.

Bhavabhûti.

About 700 A.D. Bhavabhûti enriched Sanskrit literature by three remarkable plays—the Mâlatimâdhava, the Mahâvîracarita and, above all, the Uttara Râmacarita.[3] The last two considerably

[1] Daṇḍin's Kâvyâdarśa is probably the first of its kind (Keith, Classical Sanskrit Literature, p. 131). The crop becomes plentiful later on.

[2] See the rules laid down by Bharata, Dhanañjaya, Viśvanâtha and Siṅgabhûpâla. The Bhâratîya Nâṭyaśâstra is probably anterior to Bhâsa and Kâlidâsa (Keith, Classical Sanskrit Literature, p. 129; on the whole subject, Keith, Sanskrit Drama, pp. 290 et seq.) but the domination of rules increases with the lapse of time.

[3] On the date, style, etc., of Bhavabhûti, see Keith, Sanskrit Drama, pp. 186—204. Macdonell, Sanskrit Literature, 362—65 R. G. Bhandarkar's Preface to his edition of the Mâlatimâdhava, Bombay Sanskrit Series, No. XV. Also the introductions by various scholars to the editions and translations of his works, particularly that by S. K. Belvalkar, Harvard Oriental Series, No. 21.

modify the story of the Râmâyaṇa in their plots. The Uttaracarita is a severe indictment of Râma's action in exiling his faithful wife, Sîtâ, to calm irrational rumours, but it admits that a king must pay high regard to popular sentiment and conciliate it at any cost. In the play spies move among the people to detect all shades of feeling and report them to the king who receives them personally. The brothers of a king are associated with him in the task of administration. No great royal sacrifice or ceremony can be complete without the presence of the queen. For the rest, Bhavabhûti, a Brâhmaṇa of the Taittirîya school of the Yajurveda, is an upholder of the orthodox Brahmanical order. In a scene which is hardly necessary to the main plot, King Râma is thrown into consternation when he is told that a Śûdra was, contrary to Śâstric injunctions, practising penances and that this violation of Dharma was bringing ruin and death to some righteous folk. Râma hurriedly takes up the bow, rushes to the scene and slays the Śûdra. The accessibility of the king is one of the remarkable features in Bhavabhûti's plays.

Mâgha.

About the eighth century also comes Mâgha, author of the frightfully artificial Śiśupâlabadha, one of the five Mahâkâvyas of Sanskrit literature. The plot turns on Kṛiṣṇa's killing of his perverse foolhardy relative, Śiśupâla, but the poet, when not enchained to the epic, is subservient to Bhâravi. It is on the Kirâtârjunîya that the political passages of the Śiśupâlabadha are modelled. Mâgha frankly disregards principles in politics. The government should be popular but, above all, efficient, firm and relentless. High ambition and self-interest, adroitly and unflinchingly pursued, swift, decisive action will make the king shine like the sun in the Maṇḍala of twelve kings.[1] The persistence of this school of real

[1] Mâgha, Canto II. particularly Ślokas 26, 29, 30, 65, 81.

politics from the days of the Mahâbhârata onwards indicates that it always had some relation to facts. Machiavelli, said Acton, is "a constant influence" in Europe. His counterparts in ancient India were likewise a permanent phenomenon.

Mudrârâkṣasa.

The fact is well illustrated by Viśâkhadatta's political drama, the Mudrârâkṣasa which belongs to the eighth or ninth century A.D.[1] The play perhaps follows an older tradition and it is not easy to decide how far it is representative of the age in which it was actually composed. None the less, the series of adroit manœuvres in which Câṇakya plays a leading part and which culminate in the replacement of the Nanda by the Mauryan dynasty on the throne of Pâṭaliputra are of fascinating interest. Câṇakya addresses Candragupta as a Vṛiṣala (Śûdra). Râkṣasa, the chief minister of the Nanda king, addresses the goddess of royal power in a soliloquy and asks "was there no chief noble of blood to win thy fickle smiles, that thou must elevate a base-born outcast to imperial sway?" (Act II). In the play the monarch finds his position a source of great uneasiness. It is difficult for him to attend to his own interests as well as to those of others. On the other hand, he runs a fatal risk if he entrusts too much power to his minister. Fortune makes kings her sport. When both the king and the ministers are very powerful, the goddess of royalty deserts one of them. Sovereignty, so to say, is indivisible. If a king relies too much on his ministers, he will, on separation

[1] Charpentier placed Viśâkhadatta in the age of Kâlidâsa, but Jacobi on astronomical evidence brings him down to the latter half of the ninth century A.D. See Keith, J. R. A. S., 1909, p. 145. See also Rapson, J. R. A. S., 1900, p. 535; Tawney, J. R. A. S., 1908, p. 910; Konow, Ind. Ant., 1914, p. 68, also Ind. Ant., 1913, pp. 265—67. Jayaswal places the Mudrârâkṣasa in the time of Candragupta II. Antani (Ind. Ant., LI, p. 49) refutes Jayaswal.

from the latter, feel like a helpless babe. Or the minister may unconsciously usurp too much power. In the play, the king chafes under the control of Câṇakya. In high affairs of state, secret intrigue sometimes played an important, even decisive part. Espionage is there as an integral part of the machinery of government.[1] In the first Act avaricious Nandas are contrasted with Candragupta who "esteems your happiness his wealth." The third Act emphasises that the king must forego his personal comfort for the sake of the general good.

Minor pieces.

Harihara's Bhartṛiharinirveda, in Sanskrit and Prâkrit, brings in the fourth Act, a king listening quietly and attentively to an ascetic's instruction. Râjaśekhara who flourished about 900 A.D. at the court of Mahendrapâla and his successor at Kanauj, wrote four plays: (1) Karpûramañjarî, (2) Bâlarâmâyaṇa, (3) Pracaṇḍapâṇḍava, and (4) Viddhalaśâlabhañjikâ. In the last both the minister Bhâgurâyaṇa and the buffoon Cârâyaṇa are Brâhmaṇas.

The Jaina Âdi Purâṇa.

The Jaina literature of this period, though extensive and magnificent, is from the administrative view-point only of secondary importance. It tells us little that is absolutely new but it confirms, in a most striking manner, the conclusions to which other evidence leads. By far the most important Jaina work of this period is the Âdi Purâṇa, composed by Jinasenâcârya and, after his death, continued by Guṇabhadrâcârya, in the 8th and 9th centuries A.D.[2] It embodies

---

[1] Mudrârâkṣasa (ed. H. R. Kale), particularly Act III, pp. 39, 47, 63.

[2] Mss. of the Âdi Purâṇa are preserved in numerous Jaina temples in India. It has been published in the Syâdvâda Granthamâlâ Series, No. 4. For the author, see the Âdi Puraṇa, Prastâvanâ, 55—58, Uttara Purâṇa, Praśasti, particularly 11-12. The Hindî Jñânaprabodha, 9—17, is unreliable but see Bakhat Râma's Buddhivilâsa. The Vardhamâna Purâṇa and Jinendraguṇastuti, believed to have been written by Jinasena, have not yet been recovered.

a good deal of older tradition. Its conception of government is paternal and patriarchal.[1] When it seeks to demolish the claims of ordinary Brâhmaṇas and in their place to invest Jaina Brâhmaṇas with all the privileges of reverence, stipends, exemption from taxes and severe punishments, it shows that the Brâhmaṇas did really enjoy some privileges. Jaina kings should not accept any blessings from the ordinary Brâhmaṇas.[2]

But the coronation of Ṛiṣabha, the first of the twenty-four Tîrthakaras, in the 16th canto, is conducted in Brahmanic style. The account is also useful for other details which are probably true to facts.

Consecration.

Water was brought from the Ganges, Sindhu (Indus) and other rivers (sacred only in the belief of Brâhmaṇas), for the consecration. The various holy waters, mixed with camphor, sandal, etc., and again with the essence of many kinds of flowers, were poured on Ṛiṣabha by "kings," that is, feudatories, among others. Jewels and many other precious articles were showered on him. His father Nâbhi took the crown off his head and, with his own hands, placed it on that of Riṣabha, saying, 'Riṣabha is the protector of all the crowned heads, not I."[3] On this auspicious occasion, the capital Ayodhyâ was astir with song and music and dance.[4] Later, at the close of his own reign, Riṣabha installed his son Bharata as king and another prince Bâhubali as Yuvarâja.[5] On a yet later occasion in the narration of the Âdi Purâṇa, another

---

[1] Âdi Purâṇa, Parvan XVI, 271—75. For the Jaina conception of the Golden Age, the fall from it, the emergence of 'civilisation,' the creation of society and the state, etc., Ibid., III, XV, 130—190, 241—45, 255—57, 250—52.

For political reflections, LXXV, 105—15, 214—20 in particular.

[2] Ibid., XVI, 241—46; XXXIX, 13-14, 20—22, 108—24, 127—142, 154—57; XL, 40, 63, 67, 139, 192-93; XLI, 45—55; XLII, 181—92.

[3] Ibid., XVI, 211, 225—32.

[4] Ibid., XVI, 197—208.

[5] Ibid., XVII, 76-77.

consecration is performed in a similar style, at first by many great Râjas, then by inmates of the seraglio, by priests and by citizens.[1] Besides Nâbhi and Ṛiṣabha there are other kings or feudatories in the Âdi Purâṇa who renounced the world on the approach of age or even earlier and anointed their sons in their places. Religion could exercise this sort of influence even on those who had no decidedly spiritual turn of mind. For instance, Jayakumâra once entrusted the government to his younger brother, Vijayakumâra, and went to various places for enjoyment.[2] Later, he formally anointed his son and renounced the world.[3] King Atibala suddenly realised that worldly dominion was contemptible and soul-killing and promptly renounced his country, family and all else.[4] Other legends of the Âdi Purâṇa, however, show that kings, so long as they occupied the throne, generally lived a life of luxury and enjoyment. Lalitâṅgadeva, for instance, is said to have had four chief queens and four thousand other wives and to have spent countless years in enjoyment.[5]

Institutions.

The institutions of government in the Âdi Purâṇa are the same as in other literature and in the inscriptions. King Mahâbala, a legendary figure, had four ministers and held counsel with all of them, or three, two or one of them.[6] On finance and local government the Jaina work follows the Brahmanical Dharma Śâstras. It idealises universal conquest in spite of the Jaina emphasis on non-violence as the essence of religion.[7]

[1] Ibid., XXXVII, 2-3, 11, 13-14.

[2] Ibid., XLIII, 256.

[3] Ibid., XLIII, 276—78.

[4] Ibid., IV, 141—56. Cf. Uttara Purâṇa, XLVIII, 9-10, 26-27, 32-33, 90-91; LXVII, 14-17; LIV, 80—82.

[5] Ibid., V, 285—97.

[6] Ibid., IV, 190—96.

[7] Ibid., IV, 106—98; XVI, 254; XXV-XXVI.

The account of Riṣabha, the first of the twenty-four Jaina Tīrthakaras and his son Bharata, the first of the Cakravartins, shows that the small state was the rule but the tendency to expansion brought about an extensive relationship of suzerain and vassal. Feudalism, in fact, is rampant in the Âdi Purâṇa. Not only is the consecration of the suzerain performed primarily by feudatories, but the latter are expected to give him valuable presents on the occasion of his birth-day which, by the way, is celebrated with great festivities.[1] Riṣabha is spoken of as seated on the throne, surrounded by hundreds of Râjas.[2] When he renounces the world, his example is followed by 360 "kings" who, later, fall from the truth.[3] The Digvijaya of Bharata follows the usual course and is said to result in the acknowledgment of his suzerainty all round.[4] A svayaṁvara is attended by numerous 'kings,' who, after it is over, indulge in a free fight.[5] The facts of feudalism are brought out still more clearly in the Uttara Purâṇa as the continuation of Guṇabhadrâcârya, in its relation to the whole as the Mahâpurâṇa, is called. It gives sketches of the twenty-three Tīrthakaras who followed Riṣabha at long intervals of time, of Râma, Kriṣṇa (who are painted as Jaina worthies), Śreṇika, Jīvandhara and numerous other Jaina heroes. Most of the personages were born in royal families and some of them wielded political power. Throughout the pages of the Uttarapurâṇa, feudatories abound. In hundreds they appear as the satellites of the suzerains.

The same conclusion about feudatories emerges from the Jaina Padma Purâṇa and Harivaṁśa Purâṇa. In the latter, for instance, king Śreṇika's example in filling Bihâr with Jaina temples is said to have been followed by his

[1] Ibid., XVII, 1.
[2] Ibid., XVII, 1.
[3] Ibid., XVII, 216.
[4] Ibid., XXVI, 58 et seq.; XXVI.
[5] Ibid., XXXIX, 230 et seq.; XL.

Sâmantas, ministers and subjects in general.[1] Here Sâmanta can have only one meaning, that of feudatory. Here one of the aspects of the relations between suzerain and vassal is that of giving the lead and following the lead.

Sudharmasvâmigaṇabhṛitha's Śripraśnavyâkaraṇâṅgam[2] has some excellent incidental political touches. The term Mâṇḍalika here means a feudatory, a normal feature of the body-politic. Kings are often spoken of as accompanied by them as well as by priests, ministers and commanders. Kings and military commanders sometimes fought among themselves and oppressed the people.[3] Only too often did royal servants misuse their trust. Sudharmasvâmigaṇabhṛitha speaks of them as a species of thieves.[4] Military officers are called rogues[5] and equally severe epithets are applied to police-officers and revenue officers.[6]

Sudharmasvâmigaṇabhṛitha.

Candraprabha Sûri's Prabhâvakacarita[7] also brings out a condition of federal-feudalism. The Anuyogadvârasûtram inculcates loyalty to government as part of the general resignation which is its philosophy, as that of so many other Jaina tracts. In the Gadya Cintâmaṇi written by Vâdibhasiṁhasûri[8] in the style of Bâṇabhaṭṭa about

Other Jaina works.

[1] (Jaina) Harivaṁśa Purâṇa (Gândhî Haribhaî Devakaraṇa Jaina Granthamâlâ No. 2), I, pp. 148-49. See Canto II for royal pomp and splendour. For an instance of stern justice, see Uttara Purâṇa, LXVII. 96 –111, where a king, in spite of the protests of ministers, sentences a defaulting prince to death and remarks that a king should cut off the right hand if it offends.

[2] Published with a commentary by Abhayadevasûri, Nirṇayasâgara Press, Bombay, 1919.

[3] Śrîpraśnavyâkaraṇâṅgam, III, 11.

[4] Ibid., III, 12.

[5] Ibid., III, 11.

[6] Ibid., I, 7.

[7] Ed. H. P. Śâstrî, Bombay, 1909.

[8] Ed. T. S. K. Śâstrî, and S. S. Śâstrî, Tanjore.

the eighth century A.D., King Satyabhadra practically transfers the administration to a scheming minister who usurps the throne. But a posthumous prince recovers his patrimony and shines forth as an ideal ruler. In his Kṣatracûḍâmaṇi[1] the same author speaks of kings as the life of living beings,[2] and condemns disloyalty as a great sin.[3] There is an interesting anecdote that a king, convinced of the futility of worldly grandeur, embraced asceticism to the great grief of Pauras and Jânapadas,[4] city-folk and country-folk. This seems to have been a convenient division of the people from the political point of view.

Haribhadra's Dharmavindu.

There are a few other Jaina works of this period which incidentally touch on politics. Haribhadra's Dharmavindu for instance, which belongs to the ninth century A.D., inculcates loyalty and respect to the sovereign[5] but, on the whole, these works do not reflect the working of institutions and must be passed over. In the tenth century A.D. Somadevasûri composed a remarkable work, Nitivâkyâmṛitam, 'nectar of political sayings' in Sûtra form. It lacks originality of matter. The author cries 'back to Kauṭalya' and frequently draws also on the Mahâbhârata, Vaśiṣṭha, Manu and others. But the dexterity with which he leaves out some of their ideas and weaves the rest into a fine harmonious whole is in itself an index to the political temper of his age. The work was composed under the patronage of a big feudatory but it treats of politics in the usual style. It shows that the governmental machinery of a feudatory state approximated to the usual type. Knowledge is the prime requisite

Somadeva.

[1] Ed. T. S. K. Śâstrî, Tanjore.
[2] Kṣatracûḍâmaṇi, Lamba, I, 46.
[3] Ibid., I, 47.
[4] Ibid., I, 69-70.
[5] Dharamvindu, I, 31.

in public affairs. A perverse ignorant prince should never be installed as heir-apparent.[1] Somadeva wants the king to promote agriculture, to control trade, fix the prices and supervise the markets. In reality there are no greater thieves on earth than tradesmen. Ministers should be well-born Brâhmaṇas, Kṣatriyas or Vaiśyas, but never foreigners. Somadeva puts their number at three, five or seven.[2] Evidently he is thinking of very small states or feudatory domains. The duty of administering impartial justice is extolled in the highest terms and the policy imposing heavy fines from financial motives is condemned. Another possible reference to contemporary politics is implied in the precept that military officers should not be consulted in the determination of policy. They are only too ready to clutch at war. Strife is the law of their being. Besides, if they are placed in control of civil policy, they may grow dangerously proud and powerful.[3] None the less, the commander-in-chief was one of the most important of officers.[4] The ambassador was another notable functionary. A definite code of diplomatic etiquette had been evolved. An envoy might talk as he liked but his life was sacrosanct. On no account was he to be molested.[5] Needless to say, the Purohita was another great personage, who should be instrumental in warding off natural or supernatural calamities.[6]

On espionage Somadeva seems to reflect the facts of his times all over India. Broadly speaking, secret agents fell into two classes, those who busied themselves

---

[1] Somadeva Sûri, Nîtivâkyâmṛitam, 56-57. For the prince's education, 60-61.

[2] Ibid., 62—66, 76—80, 84—90, 93—95, 98—100, 102—104, 106—125, 127—35.

[3] Ibid., 136-37.

[4] Ibid., 149.

[5] Ibid., 170-71.

[6] Ibid., 160—63.

with discovering the misdeeds of officials and the feelings of subjects and those who sought to probe the intentions and plans of neighbouring rulers. In either case they were to disguise themselves as ascetics and scholars, mathematicians and astrologers, physicians and soldiers, tradesmen and artisans, singers and dancers, foresters and snakecharmers, sorcerers and jugglers, and so forth. They must be paid adequately.[1] Another realistic touch is furnished when the author, in spite of his Jaina persuasion, lays down that in law-courts a Brâhmaṇa should take the oath by touching his sacred thread or a piece of gold; a Kṣatriya, by touching a weapon, a jewel or the ground, etc., a Vaiśya by touching his ear or gold, a Śûdra by touching milk or corn. The idea, we are told, is that the form of oath should have some correspondence with the occupation of the person concerned.[2] There are many other political maxims in the Nîtivâkyâmṛtam but they are too theoretical.[3]

Yaśastilaka-campû.

Another of Somadeva's works, the Yaśastilaka-campû, has some political touches, particularly in its third Aśvâsa. But they add nothing to the data available from the Nîtivâkyâmṛitam.

In the eighth century A.D. India felt the impact of the rising power of Islâm for the first time. The Arabs

[1] Ibid., 172—74.

[2] Ibid., 305.

[3] On political deliberation, ibid., 175-76; other qualities in kings and ministers, 177—84, 246—50; on officers, 185—190; on the treasury, 202—206; on the territory, 190—97; on forts, 198—201; on the army, 209—15; on diplomacy and foreign policy, 243—72; on allies, 216—20; on courtiers, 295—305; on taxes, 271. Haribala's commentary on the Nîtivâkyâmṛitam frequently illustrates Somadeva's meaning by parallel quotations from the Arthaśâstra, various Dharma Śâstras and Jaimini, the great master of the rules of interpretation, but it is valueless for administrative practice.

conquered Sindh in 712 A.D. about the same time that their arms were crowned with victory in the far distant Spain. The Arab writers give a full account of the expeditions of the young hero Muhammad-bin-Qâsim and, incidentally, throw some light on the political condition of Sindh and the neighbouring regions. They are not accurate in all their details but in fundamentals they corroborate the conclusions which are reached on the basis of indigenous evidence. The dominant fact which emerges from the Arab accounts is that a feudalised confederation was the type of Hindu polity. The merchant Sulaimân's Salsilatu-t Tawârîkh, written in the middle of the ninth century and added to by Abû Zaidul Hasan of Sirâf in the following century, has it that the Balharâ was the most eminent of the princes of India, that all Indians acknowledged his superiority, that while every prince in India was master in his own state, all paid homage to the supremacy of the Balharâ. The latter's representatives were everywhere received with the profoundest respect. A few pages later, the Arab writer slightly modifies his statement and says that the princes of India did not recognise the supremacy of any one sovereign, each one was his own master, still the Balharâ had the title 'king of kings.'[1] Ibn Khurdabâ's Kitâb-l Masâlik Wa-l Mamâlik, composed towards the close of the ninth or the beginning of the tenth century A.D. also calls the Balharâ king of kings.[2] In the tenth century two other writers, Al Masûdî, author of Murûjul Zahab and Al Idrîsî, author of Nuzhatu-l Mushtak also speak of Balharâ as king of kings and the greatest king in India.[3] Who this Balharâ was is not an easy question to

Sindh.

[1] Elliot and Dowson, History of India as told by its own Historians, Vol. I, pp. 1, 6-7.

[2] Ibid., 13.

[3] Ibid., 21, 75.

answer. Probably he represented the dynasty at Ballabhîpura but the difficulty of the identification does not affect the conclusion that India, so far as known to the Arabs, was split up into a large number of principalities which faintly recognised the suzerainty of an overlord. Another statement of the merchant Sulaimân confirms this view. "When a king subdues a neighbouring state, he places over it a man belonging to the family of the fallen prince, who carries on the government in the name of the conqueror. The inhabitants would not suffer it to be otherwise."[1] This feature of "conquest" which is also well brought out in Hindu literature and epigraphy, would serve to accentuate the federal-feudal character of Hindu political organisation. An idea of the usual size of a Hindu state is given by the Chach Nâmâ or Târikh-i-Hind wa Sind, which, though composed in the 13th century, is based on older, authentic documents which go back to the eighth century A.D. There were no less than seventy chiefs ruling in Sindh.[2] The lines of some of these feudatories survived for long, bearing to the new Muslim power the relation in which they had stood to the Hindu suzerain. About the beginning of the 17th century A.D., the chronicler Mîr Muhammad Mâsûm of Bhakkar, author of the Târîkhu-s Sind, applied the term zemîndâr to all such feudatories.[3] That expression today only means a landholder, but the sense in which the Muslim historians from the 13th to the 17th century A.D. used it to denate the nearly independent or semi-independent Hindu chieftains of the deserts, mountains, Râjpûtânâ, and Central India conveys the idea of the usual relationship of suzerain and vassal in Ancient India.

[1] Ibid., 7.
[2] Ibid., 211.
[3] Ibid., 212.

The sceptre of the suzerain or of the feudatory descended from father to son in the same family. According to Masûdî, the rule was never broken. The Arab writer, however, seems to be wrong when he states that none could ascend the throne until he was forty years of age or that the king never appeared in public except at rare intervals for the inspection of public affairs. But a king who grossly misconducted himself might pay the penalty of his sins. One such ruler, a hopeless drunkard, forfeited the crown. But it seems to have been bestowed on another member of the family.[1] There were, of course, occasional cases of usurpation. For instance, Chach, who occupied the post of chamberlain, usurped the throne on the death of his master.[2] So strong was the sentiment in favour of hereditary succession that the chief offices of state—those of ministers, judges—were practically confined to the same families.[3] The use of the Arabic word Qâzi to denote judges is interesting. It shows that the Hindu judges bore some resemblance to the well-known Muslim officers of the western Muslim countries.

In Sindh the highest office was that of High Chamberlain. According to the Chach-nâmâ, this officer exercised authority over the whole kingdom, and made all appointments and dismissals.[4] The king's territory was divided into four provinces, each under a governor.[5] Alor, the central capital of Sindh, was a large city adorned with all kinds of palaces and villas, gardens and groves, reservoirs and streams, parterres and flowers.[6] The Hindu state had to keep itself constantly in readiness for war. The soldiers were paid regularly.[7]

Ibid., 20.
Ibid., Chach-nâmâ, p. 140.
Ibid., 20.
Ibid., 139, 140.
Ibid., 138.
6 Ibid., 138.
7 Ibid., 138-39.

An instance of influence of the state on social life is recorded. When Chach acquired some tracts in Sindh, he is said to have made the Jâṭas and Lohânas undertake to wear only mockswords, to forswear saddles, to keep their heads and feet uncovered, and to adopt certain occupations like those of carrying fuel and providing guides.[1]

The Arab occupation of Sindh was a mere episode. Muslim rule soon disappeared and for the next four centuries Sindh relapsed into the old political conditions.

The administration of the rest of the northern plains has to be gathered from inscriptions. In the eighth and later centuries the centripetal forces are even weaker than in the former interregnums. Feudalism was now more rampant than ever. The title Râja could be assumed by, or could be bestowed upon, men whose rule was confined to a single village. In the disintegration of the times we can watch the rise of such small feudatories step by step. Udayamâna's lengthy rock inscription at Dudhpani in Magadha, of the eighth century A.D., records that three brothers, Udayamâna, Śrîdhautamâna and Ajitamâna, merchants by profession, on their way back from Tâmalipti in Bengal to Ayodhyâ, after a gloriously successful mercantile adventure, happened to tarry at Bhramaraśâlmali in Magadha. The ruler Âdisiṁha chanced to appear in the forest near by on a hunting trip and demanded an avaloga or avalogan—some sort of supplies or presents—from the villagers. The latter betook themselves to Udayamâna and entreated him to do the king's behest on their behalf. Udayamâna, overflowing with riches, readily complied and found himself a favourite with the king and a recipient of a Śrîpaṭṭa or diadem from royal hands. At his request the ruler sent an assurance to the

Feudalism.

[1] Ibid., 145 et seq.

villagers of Bhramaraśâlmali of his good will towards them. On his return to the village, the benevolent merchant received an affectionate welcome. The grateful people requested him to be their Râja. The ruler approved of the proposal. And so Udayamâna began his rule over the village. He managed to have his brothers Śrîdhautamâna and Ajitamâna appointed Râjas of the neighbouring villages, Nabhûtiṣaṇḍaka and Chiṅgatâ.[1]

In this inscription Âdisiṁha is only called Magadhâdhirâja. The absence of any of the three grand titles—Parameśvara, Mahârâjâdhirâja, Paramabhaṭṭâraka—which were universally employed by independent kings from the Gupta period onwards, shows that Âdisiṁha himself was only a feudatory. Nor does his name appear in any other inscription as that of a suzerain. So there is the interesting spectacle of feudatory Adhirâjas creating sub-feudatory Râjas.

An instance of the emergence of suzerainty.

The emergence of suzerainty like that of vassalage can also be studied in the inscriptions. The Khalimpur Plate of Dharmapâladeva records that Gopâla was induced by the people to assume the sovereignty in order to put an end to lawlessness and disorder. The grant employs the term Mâtsya-Nyâya—the Logic of the Fish—the classical Sanskrit expression for anarchy. So he founded the Pâla dynasty of sovereigns about 730—740 A.D. He married Daddâdevi, daughter of a king of Bhadra, and thus assimilated his line to the bluest blood of the country.[2] Here, then, we can observe how the general popular support would enable a dynasty to rise to supremacy. As in the earlier centuries, the rise to independence was always signalised by the assumption of the grand titles. Thus

[1] Ep. Ind., II, No. 27.

[2] Khalîmpur Grant in Ep. Ind., Vol. IV, No. 34. For Bhadra, Ind. Ant., XXI, p. 258.

the Alina Copper Plate Inscription of Śīlâditya VII of the year 766-67 A.D. designates Dharasena IV, as Paramabhaṭṭâraka, Mahârâjâdhirâja, Parameśvara, and Cakravartin and applies the same titles to his successors but his predecessors are not designated in the same style. The inscription describes powerful princes as bowing before the suzerain.[1]

From vassalage to independence.

The rise from vassalage to independence or suzerainty is also indicated in some other epigraphic records of this period. The Daulatpura Plate of Bhojadeva I of Mahodaya, in the modern state of Jodhpur, dated Harṣa saṁvat 100, that is about 706 A.D., speaks of the grantee and his predecessors as Mahârâjas.[2] On the other hand, the Pehovâ (Pehoa) Inscriptions of Harṣa saṁvat 276, that is, about 882 A.D., speaks of the same monarchs as Mahârajâdhirâjas.[3] It seems that sometime during the interval of 176 years, the dynasty asserted its independence, and contrary to the usual practice, all its previous members were given the grand titles.

The Caste of Rulers.

Most of the rulers of this period are Râjpûts who, according to modern research, had much foreign blood in their veins and who, as an age-long tradition indicates, had been consecrated to Kṣatriyaship. Even non-Kṣatriya kingship was known during this period. Commenting on Manu, VII, 1, 2; VIII, 40, the orthodox Medhâtithi, who lived in the 10th century A.D., admitted the validity of non-Kṣatriya kingship. Later about the 14th century, Vijñâneśvara, who commented on Yâjñavalkya in the Mitâkṣarâ, one of the most influential of all legal commentaries, agreed with Medhâtithi.

[1] Fleet, Gupta Inscriptions, No. 39.

[2] Ep. Ind., V, No. 24.

[3] Kielhorn's List No. 546.

The inscriptions convey a fair idea of administrative structure when they enumerate the personages to whom the royal command is addressed. In the Khalimpur Plate of Dharmapâladeva, Râjans and Râjânakas head the list. The former is undoubtedly a feudal designation. It shows that feudatories were required to respect the suzerain's commands and arrangements. It can also mean that the feudatories were employed in high office in the suzerain's direct administration. The term Râjânaka signified minister in Kashmir and Chambâ. But the context of the Khalimpur Inscription indicates that some feudatories are meant. Perhaps they represent a grade definitely lower than that of Râjas but the point is not free from doubt. The grant in question is made at the request of Nârâyaṇavarman, the Mahâsâmantâdhipati—great chief of Sâmantas, that is, feudatories. It is probable that the greatest and most notable of the feudatories was given this title. The term Râjaputra which follows shows that princes, whether of the suzerain or of the feudal houses, were often employed in high administrative posts. Next, the Râjâmâtyas mean, as usual, the ministers of the king, probably only the highest ministers. The Dûtaka is not mentioned with other officers but he is evidently an officer of the highest importance. In the present inscription, the Yuvarâja himself seems to hold that position. The Senâpatis or commanders of armies stand next in order. Besides them there are a large number of officers. The Dauḥsâdhasâdhanikas and Cauroddharaṇikas are obviously police-officers. The Daṇḍaśaktis and Daṇḍapâśikas may be police-officers but it is more probable that they are judicial officers who are invested with the "power of punishment." The Śaulkikas and Gaulmikas were, as in the preceding epochs, concerned with the supervision of tolls and of forests. The Dûtas,

Administrative machinery. Magadha.

Gamâgamikas[1] and Abhitvarmâṇas are the various classes of messengers. The mention of Kholas between Dûtas and Gamâgamikas indicates that the Kholas were also a class of messengers. The use of four, or at least, three different terms points to a gradation. In any case the frequent mention of messengers with responsible officers is an index of their importance and position. In a far-flung empire their function was necessarily one of great importance. To the central as to the subordinate offices were attached a number of secretaries or clerks, who, again, seem to be divided into grades. Kâyastha was the general term applied to them. Jyeṣṭhakâyasthas or chief writers are specially mentioned in the Khalimpur grant. Among fiscal officers, besides the Śaulkika is mentioned the Śaṣṭâdhikṛita, the superintendent or controller of the Śaṣṭhâṁśa or Śaḍbhâga, the traditional royal sixth of the land produce. The Tarikas were probably overseers of the ferries and collected the ferry tolls. There are a number of military officers, inspectors of the elephants, horse and other troops. Along with them are mentioned inspectors of boats, of cows, buffaloes, goats and sheep. The possibility of these inspectors being civil officers cannot be excluded but from the context and order of their enumeration, it seems that they belonged to the military departments and had charge of the boats which served as a sort of flotilla on the big rivers, and of the animals required for the supply of the army with various articles of diet and comfort. The tadâyuktakas and viniyuktakas are minor employees, perhaps both on the civil and military side. The Bhaṭas, as usual, are soldiers while Câṭas, as usual, are petty miscellaneous, chiefly, police officers.

The Bhâgalapur plates of Nârâyaṇapâla (Ind. Ant., XV, pp. 304 et seq.) also give Mahâsâmantas and Râjarâjânakas

[1] For Gamâgamikas, see also Ep. Ind., III, No. 36; Ind. Ant., XV, p. 306; XVII, p. 11.

as feudatories. Besides other officers there are Kṣetrapa, protector of the fields, Prântapâla, protector of the frontiers, Koṭṭapâla and Khaṇḍarakṣa—police or military officers. It appears that either the king or these officers appointed keepers of elephants, horses, camels, inferior naval and military officers, men in charge of foals, mares, cows, she-buffaloes, goats and sheep. It seems that mercenaries were employed from far and wide. The fiscal system is of the usual type. Besides the three classes of messengers there are Dûtapraiṣaṇikas—those who despatched messengers.

Provincial and local government.

From this inscription some idea of provincial and local government can be formed. Contrary to expectations, Viṣayapatis are mentioned before Bhogapatis. It may be a mistake or it may be that the terms were used rather loosely at some epochs and places. Elsewhere in the same inscription the sequence of local divisions is stated as Bhukti, Viṣaya, and Maṇḍala. Bhogapati was usually in charge of a bhoga or bhukti, that is, a province. Viṣayapati, as before, held charge of a Viṣaya or district. It may be mentioned that in the Alina Copper Plate Inscription of Śîlâditya (VII) (766-67 A.D.) the term Âhâra is used in the sense of Viṣaya. Dâśagrâmika is the officer in charge of a group of ten villages. It appears that this local division was of general prevalence. Karaṇas were another class of government servants charged with registration, etc. The reference to 'other district officers' shows that there were numerous other government employees in local government. The Mahâmahattaras and Mahattaras seem to be village elders who were not government employees. But their frequent mention in the inscriptions shows that they had a voice in village administration and, it may be, also in the administration of the next higher division. The information about the fiscal system in this inscription is rather scanty. The four villages in question are granted with the talapâṭaka and paṭṭika. The former signifies the land revenue paid to the government. Paṭṭika means market dues, usually charged on all markets. This inscription, like others, proves that kings often displayed great generosity. Four villages are here granted for the maintenance of a temple erected by the Mahâsâmantâdhipati Nârâyaṇavarman.[1]

A Nâlanda grant.

The Nâlanda Copper Plate Grant of Devapâladeva of the 10th century A.D. issued by a holder of the three grand titles, mentions practically all the foregoing officers. Râjâmâtya and Mahâkârttâkṛitika alike seem to be high ministers of state. The Râjasthânîya is probably a viceroy, and Uparika, a fiscal officer. The Dâśâparâdhika is a judicial officer. The fiscal system is the same. The large number of officers in all the later grants shows that the administrative structure had attained to the height of its development.[2]

Orissâ.

We meet with essentially the same system in distant Orissâ, though, here, the number of chief officers and departments is smaller. In the ninth century Talcher Grant of Kulastambha the king has the three grand titles. He has big feudatories, Mahâsâmantas, under him. He addresses his command also to Râjaputras. Then there are the Daṇḍapâśikas, Niyuktakas, Câṭas, Bhaṭas and "others." Maṇḍala is used for Viṣaya.[3] The Neulpur Grant of Śubhâkara (8th century A.D.) was issued by an hereditary Mahârâja who was thus a feudatory. He addresses Mahâsâmantas and Mahârâjas which shows that he had big sub-feudatories under him. The mention of Râjaputras shows that princes were employed in high offices. Kumâra is probably a mistake for Kumârâmâtyas,

[1] Ep. Ind., IV, No. 34. Also Ind. Ant., XI, p. 339.
[2] Ep. Ind., XVII, p. 310.
[3] Ep. Ind., XII, No. 20.

counsellors of princes. The Uparikas, Daṇḍapâśikas, Tadâniyuktakas are there as usual. The Antaraṅgas are clearly household officers. The Mahâkṣapaṭalâdhikaraṇâdhikṛita who acts as the Dûtaka is primarily an officer of the Record Department. So, too, the Pustapâlas, keepers of books. Another officer is designated as Mahâkṣapaṭalika-Bhogika which shows that he combined the offices of a provincial governor and a record-keeper. Perhaps, he was in charge of the records of his province. Viṣayapatis, district officers, are there as usual. The reference to two villages as situated in two Viṣayas in North Tosali indicates that the last was the name of a province. The occurrence of the term Bṛihadbhogika shows that the governors of the major provinces might have enjoyed this higher title. There is another officer Sthânântarika but his functions are not clear. From the analogy of other inscriptions he appears to be a police-officer.[1]

The administration was by no means so elaborate everywhere. In Almorâ, a mountainous district in the north of the present United Provinces of Agra and Oudh, the machinery seems to have been much simpler. Two Tâleśvara Grants found there are forgeries but they are none the less valuable for the administration of that district about the eighth century A.D. The monarch, in spite of the undoubtedly small extent of his territory, is called Paramabhaṭṭâraka, Mahârâjâdhirâja which is a clear indication of his independence. In the spurious grant he is made to address chiefs, that is, his feudatories, among others. Besides them, there were many landowners. The prince is one of the counsellors of the king. The chamberlain and the pramâtâra are the chief civil officers mentioned. The masters of

Almorâ.

[1] Ep. Ind., XIV, No. 1.

the elephants and horse are the principal military officers. The mention of Kulacârikas, that is, heads of kulas or families with the landed magnates and officers shows that society in the hills was organised partly on the basis of clans or families and that their heads exercised some regulating authority.[1]

Márwâr.

Another grant discovered in Mârwâr in the modern state of Jodhpur also indicates that the administrative structure in some regions was simpler than in others. The command in question was issued by an independent monarch who bears the three grand titles. But his administrative system is rather elementary.[2] The same remark applies to Bundelkhaṇḍ. From the 9th century A.D. onwards, the Chandel princes of Jejâkabhukti appear as great builders. They beautified the towns of Mahobâ. Kâliñjar and Khajurâho with magnificent temples, palaces, lakes and tanks which still survive somewhere intact, somewhere in ruins But the administrative system of the whole region of Bundelkhaṇḍ never reached the complexity of other regions. In the Pachar Plate of Paramârdideva which is as late as the 12th century A.D. the king of Kâliñjar, like his ancestors, has the three grand titles. His territory is subdivided into Viṣayas but his system of government is not elaborate.[3]

Bundelkhaṇḍ.

Bastar, C.P.

The Sunarpal Stone Inscription of Jayasiṁhadeva of Bastar in the modern Central Provinces, belonging probably to this period, calls the king Râjâdhirâja Mahârâja. He makes the grant in the presence of five officers—the chief minister, the Paḍivâda probably the grand chamberlain, the Cavarikumâra, probably the prince in charge of the whisk, the

[1] Ep. Ind., XIII, No. 7.
[2] Ep. Ind., X, No. 17.
[3] Ep. Ind., X, No. 11.

SarvavÂdi NÂyaka, probably the head of the intelligence department, and the DÂdesan Pâtra CavakÂ, whose position is obscure. In this comparatively backward region, the organisation is different and simpler.[1] Two other inscriptions from near Bastar belonging to the middle of the eleventh century A.D. apply the title MahÂrÂjÂdhirÂja to King Someśvaradeva and call two of his queens MahÂdevîs.[2]

Chhattîsagaḍh, C. P.

In PamparÂjadeva's Kaṅkar Copper Plates, of the beginning of the thirteenth century A.D., belonging to the Chhatt sagaḍh division of the modern Central Provinces, the title Paramabhaṭṭâraka and Mahâmaṇḍaleśvara are used in the ordinary sense.[3]

Mâlwâ.

The Copper Plate Grant of VâkpatirÂja of DhârÂ in MÂlwâ of the year 980 A.D. mentions the usual fiscal arrangements. It is particularly important for local government. It records that a village belonging to the Tiṇisapadra Twelve was alienated to the temple of a goddess.[4] It proves that divisions like the Twelve-village, so common in the Deccan and the south, obtained as far north as Central India. It was on the basis of villages and their combinations that areas of local government were demarcated.

The village.

The majority of the inscriptions of this period refer to the Mahattaras or Mahattamas of a village. The two terms, though apparently representing the comparative and superlative degrees, have the same political significance, that of elders. Their repeated mention shows that generally the elders of a village were associated, it seems informally, with the regular servants of government in the management of

[1] Ep. Ind., X, No. 6.
[2] Ep. Ind., X, No. 5.
[3] Ep. Ind., IX, No. 22.
[4] Ind. Ant., XIV, p. 159.

rural affairs. Sometimes they rose high and obtained recognition at the courts of suzerains and feudatories. In one of the grants a Mahattama appears as the Dûtaka.[1]

The fiscal system.

The tenth century Rajor Inscription of Mathanadeva speaks of numerous dues from a village (the object of a grant), customary and not customary, fixed and not fixed, shares of all sorts of grains—the khalabhikṣâ, prasthaka, skhandhaka, mârgaṇaka. The meaning of these is not clear. The dictionaries give no help.[2] The fines for "ten offences" which are hereby alienated formed a distinct source of revenue. The mention of treasures and deposits shows that the mineral products and treasure-trove were state-perquisites—a fact which is corroborated by the Dharma Śâstras. A little later the inscription mentions a few additional taxes—three viṁśopokas as customary in the market on every sack of agricultural produce brought for sale; two palikâs from every ghaṭakakûpaka of clarified butter and oil; two viṁśopakas per measure for every shop; and fifty leaves for every chollikâ of leaves imported from outside the specified boundaries. The occurrence of the term Maṭṭadâva in this inscription and of Maṇḍapikâ or Śulkamaṇḍapikâ in others shows the existence of a regular customs-house in towns and elsewhere.[3]

Feudatories.

Feudatories appear in numerous inscriptions as making grants on their own authority. In the Rajim Copper Plate Inscription of about 800 A.D. Râja Tîvaradeva refers to his suzerain though the latter's name is not given in the inscription. He grants to some Brâhmaṇas a village in a Bhukti, which seems to

---

[1] Ep. Ind., X, No. 17; III, No. 36.

[2] Khalabhikṣâ apparently means the alms of the threshing floor (Ep. Ind., II, p. 179) but its fiscal significance is obscure. For a discussion of Mârgaṇaka, Ind. Ant., XVIII, p. 83.

[3] Ep. Ind., III, No. 36.

show that his dominions were wide enough to be divided into provinces.[1] In the two Praśastis of Baij Nâth, probably of the ninth century, in the North-western Puñjâb a Râjânaka grants part of the daily receipts at the customs house to Vaidyanâtha.[2]

A tenth century stone inscription of Siyadoni in the modern state of Gwalior in Central India shows that the town was for a while ruled by independent kings who called themselves Mahârâjâdhirâjas. Another personage is distinguished as Samadhigatâ-śeṣamahâśabda and Mahâśamantâdhipati. He enjoys all the Mahâśabdas and is designated as the lord high chief of feudatories and may be regarded as the greatest of all the feudatories under the dynasty.[3] The plates of Pravarasena II, from Dudia in Chhindawârâ in the modern Central Provinces, record a grant by a Mahârâja, a feudatory. It belongs probably to the 8th century A.D.[4] In Balavarman's Plates of the year 893 A.D. the Mahâsâmanta who had attained the five Mahâśabdas declares himself a vassal, as meditating on the feet of the hereditary Paramabhaṭṭâraka, Mahârâjâdhirâja, Parameśvara.[5]

The inscriptions bring out very clearly the activity of guilds or *ad hoc* organisations. An inscription from the temple of Garîbnâth at Paheva in the district of Karnâl in the Puñjâb, of the year 882-83 A.D., applies the three grand titles to the King Bhoja and his father and then proceeds to narrate how a number of horse-dealers, thirty-three or thirty-four in number, from eight different villages in different regions, entered into an agreement to impose upon themselves

Guilds.

[1] Fleet, op. cit., No. 81.
[2] Ep. Ind., I, No. 16.
[3] Ep. Ind., I, No. 21.
[4] Ep. Ind., III, No. 25.
[5] Ep. Ind., IX, No. 1.

certain tithes for distribution among some temples, sanctuaries and priests, in specified proportions.[1] Numerous other inscriptions refer to guilds. Corroborative evidence comes from literature. Commenting on Manu, VIII, 41, in the tenth century A.D. Medhâtithi explained Śreṇî as guilds of merchants, artisans, bankers or priests and thus testified to their existence.

Except in the sphere of village administration, the governmental system of the north resembles that of the regions towards the south in all essentials though there are some differences of details. A few points of comparison and contrast may be noticed. The eighth century plates of Dantivarman of Gujarât show the feudatory Mahâsâmanta as possessed of the five Mahâśabdas and as 'lord of great feudal chiefs.' It appears that sometimes in the North and more often elsewhere in ancient India, suzerains granted lofty titles to their principal feudatories. The administrative system which obtained in the territories of this feudatory followed the usual type. Râṣṭrapati, however, is substituted for Bhogika as the title of the provincial governor. Both the designations have a fiscal significance. It is interesting to note that the grant is made to an academic institution and is to be enjoyed by successive generations of pupils.[2] The ninth century inscriptions from Kâvi near the gulf of Cambay only mention the usual officers.[3]

Gujarât.

The grant of Govind III (806-7A.D.) from Nâsik district mentions the usual officers and items of revenue.[4] In the Cambay Plates, too, Govind III, the Râṣṭrakûṭa king, has the three grand titles. His grants intended for Brâhmaṇas are communi-

The Deccan.

[1] Ep. Ind., I, No. 23.

[2] Ep. Ind., VI, No. 28.

[3] Ind. Ant., V, 1876, pp. 109 et seq.

[4] Ind. Ant., XI, 1882, pp. 156 et seq.

cated to Rāṣṭrapatis, governors of provinces, Viṣayapatis, district officers, Grāmakūṭas, heads of villages, Mahattaras, elders of villages, and to such government servants as Yuktakas, Upayuktakas and Adhikārikas.[1] A Devagiri Inscription of about the 10th century, though spurious and unreliable for the subject of the actual grant, is valuable for a few administrative details. Here a Mahāsāmantādhipati has the hereditary title of the "supreme lord of the town Trikuṇḍapura," which was probably the capital of his territory. He enjoyed the privileges of using the Nandanavana umbrella, the horse-crest and the mirror banner—some of the signs of high feudal rank. By the way, he demands from the villagers a supply of grass for his elephants and horses while on tour.[2]

Titles.

The inscriptions reveal a few peculiarities in titles. Thus, the Hatti-Mattūr Inscription of the Rāṣṭrakūṭa King Kriṣṇa I, of Malkhed of the year 765 A.D , substitutes Bhaṭāra for Bhaṭṭāraka.[3] Further south in Mysore a Doḍḍahuṇḍi Inscription of Nītimārga and Satyakāma, of the 9th century A.D., mentions a line of Dharmamahārājas, presumably a dynasty of feudatories who prided themselves on their attachment to religion.[4] Two Kadamba grants show that a line of Dharma-Mahāmātras assumed the title Mahārājādhirāja.[5] In the Nilgund Inscription of the line of Amoghavarṣa I, of the year 866 A.D., from the Dhārwāḍ district in the Western Presidency, the three grand titles are joined to Pañcamahāśabdas. This juxtaposition of the titles of suzerainty and vassalage is either a mistake or a strictly local peculiarity.[6] In almost all other inscriptions the distinctive

[1] Ep. Ind., VII, No. 6. [2] Ep. Ind., XI, 1.
[3] Ep. Ind., VI, No. 16.
[4] Ep. Ind., VI, No. 6.
[5] Ep. Ind., VI, No. 2; VI, No. 24 (c); V, 18.
[6] Ep. Ind., VI, No. 11.

significance of the titles is observed. In fact in the ninth century in Gujarât it was possible for a sub-feudatory to acquire the five Mahâśabdas. In the Torkhede Grant of the year 812 A.D., of the time of Govindarâja, a feudatory of a feudatory is called Mahâsâmanta and is said to have obtained the Pañcamahâśabda.[1] The phenomenon is extremely rare. It was perhaps confined to cases in which the difference between a feudatory and a sub-vassal was faint.

Local government.

In the sphere of local government one of the most striking facts which emerge from the inscriptions of the Deccan and the south is that administrative divisions were called after (1) the number of villages which they contained or were supposed to contain, and (2) the town which formed the headquarters of the administration. The Banavâsi Twelve-thousand is often mentioned in the inscriptions. In some inscriptions Banavâsi is said to be a great city and its governor is clearly a feudatory. Other epigraphic records speak of the Belgali Three-hundred, the Kundur Five-hundred, the Purigere Three-hundred, the Kundarage, Seventy. A single governor might be in charge of several such areas. The son of one such governor was placed in charge of a smaller area, the Nidugandage Twelve which probably formed part of his father's province. Elsewhere a village called Nilguṇḍ forms part of the Mulaguṇḍa Twelve which itself was part of Belvola Three-hundred.[2]

[1] Ep. Ind., III, No. 9.

[2] Ep. Ind., XI, No. 1; XIII, No. 14; VII, No. 28; VI, 11, 24 (a); XV, No. 21; IV, No. 30; V, No. 25; XVII, No. 10; IV, Nos. 36, 50; XIII, Nos. 2, 14; XVI, Nos. 8, 9, 11. Ind. Ant., XI, 273; XVIII, 309, 362. Rice and others believed that the numbers referred to revenue figures or value of the produce. But they range from twelve to twelve thousand and appear to refer only to the real or supposed number of villages included in such an administrative area

Some southern grants give Bhukti, Viṣaya and Maṇḍala as the successive administrative divisions. Maṇḍala would thus be the lowest subdivision above the village.[1] A few peculiarities in official designations deserve a passing notice. In Anantavarman's Alamanda Plates, Rahasya seems to mean private secretary. The keeper of records is called Akṣaśâlin.[2] In the Mayidavolu Plates of Śivaskandavarman, earlier than the ninth century A.D., the heir-apparent is called Yuvamahârâja. Vyâpṛita is the designation of one of the local officers.[3] Two Anaimalai Inscriptions of the year 770 A.D. from near Madûrâ designate the chief minister as Uttaramantrin.[4] The Konnur Spurious Inscription of Amoghavarṣa I seems to substitute Râṣṭrapati for Viṣayapati.[5]

Official Designations.

The Herbal Inscription of the year 975 A.D. from the Dhârwâr district shows that land could sometimes be alienated as dowry. Here it is recorded that two or three generations earlier some large pieces of territory had been given as the dowry of a princess.[6] Grants were sometimes made for the daily feeding of some people. Thus in the Baloda Plates of Tîvaradeva, called sovereign of Kośala in the south, a village is granted "together with treasures, together with deposits," etc., etc., to feed daily thirty Brâhmaṇas, or others who might alight at the rest-house of Bilvapadraka. It was a condition of the grant that the charity was to be managed by the Adhiṣṭhâna or local authorities.[7] Incidentally, the record

Miscellaneous.

[1] Ep. Ind., XIV, No. 14.
[2] Ep. Ind., III, No. 3. Cf. Ind. Ant., IV, p. 12; XIII, p. 121.
[3] Ep. Ind., VI, Nos. 8, 31.
[4] Ep. Ind., VIII, No. 33.
[5] Ep. Ind., VI, No. 4.
[6] Ep. Ind., IV, 50.
[7] Ep. Ind., VII, 18.

testifies to the royal monopoly of mines. The Mayidavolu Plates of Sivaskandavarman from the Kiṣṭna district bring to view the state-monopoly of salt and other dues. "(Let the area of land granted be) free from diggings for salt, free from (the supply) of bullocks in succession, free from the entrance of soldiers, free from (the supply of) boiled rice, water-pots .... cots and dwellings—with these and all the other immunities prescribed by the rules regarding all Brahmadeyas . . ."[1] The demands for the various articles seem to have been made for soldiers, policemen and petty officials. Like some others this inscription furnishes a vivid explanation of the clause, which occurs so frequently in grants, that the area in question is not to be entered by Câṭas and Bhaṭas.

[1] Ep. Ind., VI, Nos, 8, 31,

CHAPTER XV.

Kashmîr and Chambâ.

The administrative system of the northern plains obtained with some modifications in mountainous regions like Kashmîr and Chambâ. Thanks to Kalhaṇa one can trace the practical working of institutions from age to age in greater detail for Kashmîr than for any other region in the north. The Râjataraṅgiṇî, as the composition of Kalhaṇa is called, is easily the most important of the few historical works in Sanskrit. The author lived in the twelfth century A.D. and writes romance rather than history for the early ages from which his narrative begins. But as he approaches his own times he gains in accuracy, definiteness and fulness. He based his history partly on Nilamatas, blue records, an expression which reminds one of Blue Books. It appears that such records of political and other happenings were regularly kept in Kashmir. Kalhaṇa's long narrative brings to light some novel features of political life.[1]

Kalhaṇa.

As the Râjataraṅgiṇî and later accounts prove, caste in Kashmîr assumed a form different from those which prevailed elsewhere in North India. The fourfold division was certainly known but it lacked rigidity. There was a sharp division between Brâhmaṇas and Śûdras and a still sharper one between Brâhmaṇas and untouchables. The

Caste in Kashmîr.

[1] For Kalhaṇa's life, M. A. Stein, Introduction to the translation of the Râjataraṅgiṇî, Vol. I, Ch. I, pp. 6—12; for the scope and character of his work, Ibid., Ch. II, pp. 22—41.

number of Kṣatriyas and Vaiśyas was small. There are, indeed, some clans of Râjaputras, redoubtable warriors,[1] but there is a passage which shows that these were not native to Kashmir.[2] The number of Brâhmaṇas was so large that the priests practically separated themselves from the ordinary Brâhmaṇas. They organised themselves into corporations in numerous places, became a power in the land and threatened or carried out hunger-strikes.[3] Many Brâhmaṇas took service under the government and, as petty officials and clerks, were included in the generic term Kâyastha.[4] There is a record that all Brâhmaṇas were once exempted from capital punishment[5] but the subsequent narrative does not show that the privilege was universally respected. In marriage the restrictions of caste were disregarded more frequently than in the plains of the north. For instance, in the early years of the eleventh century A.D., King Saṁgrâmarâja married his daughter to a Brâhmaṇa state officer.[6] The mother of King Jayâpîḍa was the daughter of a petty liquor-trader.[7] In the tenth century king Cakravarman made a ḍom, a woman of the very lowest class, his chief queen.[8] High office was within the reach of men of low birth. In the ninth century A.D., one of the chief officers, an engineer of Avantivarman, was a foundling.[9] The son of a Vaiśya who was a watchman in a temple, rose to be the chief minister of another king.[10]

1 Kalhaṇa, Râjataraṅgiṇî, VII, 360, 368, 1617; VIII, 323.
2 Ibid., VIII, 1328.
3 Ibid., VIII, 710, 905, infra.
4 Ibid., VII, 38; VIII, 2383. The term Kâyastha is first mentioned in IV, 621. Later, it occurs frequently, *i.e.*, VIII, 85—87, 131, 560, etc., etc. It does not yet mean a distinct caste or a group of sub-castes as at present.
5 Ibid., IV, 96.
6 Ibid., VII, 11.
7 Ibid., IV, 678.
8 Ibid., V, 389.
9 Ibid., V, 73.
10 Ibid., VII, 207.

Feudal conditions were present in Kashmir as elsewhere. King Meghavâhana in the earlier ages was believed to have conquered many 'kings' in the course of a Digvijaya and made them promise to abstain from slaughter of animals (III, 27, 29). Lalitâditya was believed to have carried his arms far and wide (IV, 144 et seq.) and imposed his suzerainty on many princes. In an apparently incidental passage Kalhaṇa remarks that the terrified Râjas and Râjaputras confined themselves to their homes, "as if in embarrassment" (IV, 447). The number of Râjas, indeed, seems to have been legion. External marks of subjection were sometimes attached to a whole tribe. It was believed that according to the command of Lalitâditya the Puruṣkas carried their arms at their back and shaved half their head. The particular record may be mythical but the fact of such occasional restrictions is probable. In the latter years of the ninth century A.D. Śaṅkaravarman carried out another Digvijaya (V, 139). As he advanced, his army was swelled from place to place by the lines of feudatory chiefs (V, 140). A council summoned by Sugandhâ (904—906 A.D.) to settle the succession included many feudatories (V, 250). Feudal chiefs often played a notable part in the politics of the kingdom as a whole (V, 451-52). They were always expected to help the suzerain in times of war (VII, 48).

Feudal conditions.

The narration of Kalhaṇa reveals the working of the despotism in all its beneficence, its terror and its caprices. There were many pious, noble and generous kings. The court of the half legendary Saṁdhimat is said to have resembled the assembly of Śiva and to have been adorned by ascetics.[1] The shrines built by Lalitâditya, one of the

The despotism; its beneficence.

[1] Ibid, II, 127.

heroes of Kashmir history, were supposed to be numberless.[1] In the tenth century A.D. a single king granted 55 Agrahâras, furnished with various implements, to Brâhmaṇas.[2] Many other kings founded Buddhist vihâras or Brahmanic temples, made grants of land for their maintenance and also showered generous gifts on Brâhmaṇas.[3] Their example was followed by their relations and ministers. For instance, Amṛitaprabhâ, one of the queens of the Buddhist king Meghavâhana, built a lofty vihâra for the benefit of foreign bhikṣus.[4] Other queens followed suit.[5] Kalhaṇa preserves the tradition that Tuñjîna I who ruled in ancient days afforded generous, unstinted relief to his subjects in days of famine.[6] In historic times, too, there were rulers who supplied grain to people at cheap rates.[7] The state does not seem to have founded many hospitals in Kashmir at any epoch but they were not altogether unknown.[8]

Tyranny.

On the other hand, there were many rulers who almost revelled in tyranny or who trampled religion under their feet when they required money. In the eleventh century A.D. King Harṣa plundered most of the temples and took away their accumulated treasures.[9] The requests of his court-favourites succeeded with difficulty in preserving two colossal statues of the Buddha from molestation.[10] An earlier King Śaṅkaravarman

[1] Ibid., IV, 181, 484.
[2] Ibid., VI, 89.
[3] Ibid., I, 99, 121, 145—48; II, 132; III, 8; IV, 673; V, 124, 158; VII, 1096, 1098; VIII, 243—46, 2391, 3316-17, 3343-44.
[4] Ibid., III, 9.
[5] Ibid., III, 11—14; for a similar later instance, VIII, 2433. For the pious foundations of ministers, VIII, 2419.
[6] Ibid., II, 27—33.
[7] Ibid., VIII, 61.
[8] Ibid., III, 461.
[9] Ibid., VII, 1090.
[10] Ibid., VII, 1081, 1098.

(883—902 A.D.) straightway plundered sixty-four temples and resumed the endowments of many others.[1] Starting on a campaign, Lalitâditya appropriated ten millions from the shrine of Bhûteśa, though on returning victorious, he more than made up for it and presented eleven times as much to the shrine.[2] All through the Râjataraṅgiṇî there are many kings who confiscate previous grants, or divert them from their original object or who plunder the temples.[3] Kings sometimes adopted other lines of conduct which bore even more heavily on the poor. They would sometimes take possession of a whole harvest in a given area leaving hardly anything to the cultivators.[4] In 1090-1100 A.D. when a terrible famine and inundation devastated the land, King Harṣa, far from thinking of any relief to the miserable, imposed heavy fines on the people, tormented them through his petty officers, and commanded the governors to kill or disperse certain over-powerful tribes.[5] There were some kings who wasted the resources of the state on their own festivities and drinking.[6] Others indulged in forms of debauchery too horrible to recapitulate.[7] Yet others practised diabolical cruelties which make the flesh creep.[8]

Protest by hunger-strikes.

In the Râjataraṅgiṇî the people of Kashmîr show extraordinary capacity to bear oppression but even their patience was occasionally exhausted. They protested by means of hunger-strikes which often achieved their immediate object. Thus,

[1] Ibid., V, 16—69.

[2] Ibid., IV, 189.

[3] Ibid., II, 132; IV, 395; V, 52, 170; VI, 175; VII, 48, 106, 570, 696, 1344; VIII, 2756.

[4] Ibid., IV, 347, 628, 639; VII, 1107.

[5] Ibid., VII, 1219—27.

[6] Ibid., V, 206; VI, 10, 150; VII, 285; VIII, 868, 1866.

[7] Ibid., IV, 659; V, 440-41; VI, 151—71; VII, 1109—14.

[8] Ibid., VIII, 676—80.

when the system of forced carriage of loads introduced by Śaṅkaravarman (V, 174) led to great oppression, the Brâhmaṇas started a fast to be exempted from it (VII, 1088, also VIII, 2513). Hunger-strike, in fact, became a common resort of people who felt themselves aggrieved. We find the door-keeper of King Yaśaskara in the tenth century, reporting once at the close of business to his master, 'A Brâhmaṇa stands outside to commit suicide unless he can see (you), though I have told him that your Majesty has done with business for to-day, and that there is time to-morrow for his communication' (VI, 43). The king felt obliged to postpone his dinner and redress the Brâhmaṇa's wrong (VI, 44—60). Once in the 11th century, the Brâhmaṇa counsellors of a king led the Purohitas and other Brâhmaṇas to go on a hunger-strike at Parihâsapura to bring about the fall of an obnoxious royal favourite (VII, 13). For the time being, the king yielded (VII, 15). When a bitter civil war between a king and his son in the 11th century threatened to plunge the country into ruin, Brâhmaṇas organised a solemn fast which forced the combatants to make peace for a while (VII, 400-401). It will appear that such a hunger-strike roused popular sympathy and had a tendency to inflame the public feeling.

Sometimes there arose popular leaders who acquired the reputation of experts in the art of arranging fasts. They were generally the leaders of the priestly corporations. They are reckoned among those who delight in the king's misfortunes (VIII, 710).

In the early years of the 12th century when royal servants plundered the Agrahâra of Akṣosura, the local Brâhmaṇas went on a solemn fast (VIII, 898). Soon other fasts broke out in the city (VIII, 899-900) and yet others followed on an alarming, unprecedented scale (VIII, 901-2). The king tried to pacify them in vain (VIII, 903). Large numbers of citizens came every day to watch the hunger-strikers and discussed numberless plans with them but to no purpose (VIII, 905). The atmosphere was soon charged with electricity and the outbreak of a storm was not long delayed (VIII, 907). In the face of the crisis the first care of the king was to go to the hunger-strikers and try once again to conciliate them. But his endeavours failed once more (VIII, 903). The war went on. It was only when the Brâhmaṇas were frightened at certain exigencies in the struggle that they gave up the fast (VIII, 939-40). So familiar was the weapon of hunger-strike that even rulers sometimes resorted or threatened to resort to it to achieve their ends. At the commencement of the twelfth century King Uccala vowed that if any accused person or any litigant starved himself to death by way of protest against miscarriage of justice, he would himself commit suicide. So, we are told, the judges became very careful.[1] There were other forms of similar protest. Once a thief having died from an over-severe beating, the kind-hearted minister resigned and went off on a pilgrimage.[2]

Assassination, Insurrection, etc.

In the political life of Kashmir matters sometimes took a more serious turn. There were attempts at the assassination of tyrannical rulers or their agents. Insurrections broke out. There were many who would fish in troubled waters and make the situation worse confounded. The pages of the Râjataraṅgiṇî are full of such incidents. For instance, Yudhiṣṭhira I was expelled from the kingdom and he and his wives had to undergo terrible hardships.[3] A new dynasty from abroad now filled the throne. On a subsequent vacancy of the throne, Sandhimati who had resisted

[1] Ibid., VIII, 51.
[2] Ibid., VII, 602.
[3] Ibid., I, 178.

the tyranny of the late king, was persuaded by the people to assume the sceptre.[1] On the extinction of the Gonanda dynasty a Kârkoṭa prince was consecrated "with sacred water poured out from golden jars."[2]

Political Reflections.

Often in the course of his narrative Kalhaṇa pauses to moralise on the events in the usual style.[3] There is one set of precepts which came down to posterity as the political testament of Lalitâditya and which deserves notice. Its tone is so realistic that it must be held to reflect certain practical tendencies in the administration. "Those who wish to be powerful in this land, must always guard against internal dissension . . . ."(IV, 345). "Those who dwell there in the (mountains) difficult of access, should be punished, even if they give no offence, because sheltered by their fastness, they are difficult to break up if they have (once) accumulated wealth" (346). "Every care should be taken that there should not be left with the villagers more food supply than required for one year's consumption, nor more oxen than wanted for (the tillage of) their fields" (347). If they kept more wealth, they would neglect the commands of the king (348, also, 349—52).

The Scope of State-activity.

The scope of the activity of the state in Kashmir is the same as elsewhere in India. Irrigation, for instance, was cared for by the state. In the 8th century A.D., Lalitâditya distributed the water of the Vitastâ by constructing a series of water-wheels (IV, 212). Besides the cases of the foundation temples and vihâras, etc., already referred to, it may be mentioned that, according to the traditional history, the ancient king Meghavâhana began his reign by commanding

---

[1] Ibid., II, 116.

[2] Ibid., II, 528.

[3] Ibid., I, 118—20; IV, 342, 344—48, 352, 701; V, 183—91, 210 et seq.; VIII, 1—61, 195, 993.

his officials to proclaim everywhere by beat of drum that no living beings were to be slaughtered anywhere on any account (III, 5). With the same object in view he undertook a Digvijaya (III, 27) and made the conquered 'kings' take a vow of abstinence from slaughter (III, 29). Butchers and others who had hitherto lived on the sale of meat were encouraged by grants from the royal treasury to adopt a sinless livelihood (III, 6). In strictly historical times, in the latter half of the ninth century A.D., Avantivarman issued a command—which was to be observed till the end of the world—prohibiting the killing of fishes and birds on a vast take (V, 119). It appears that the king exercised some supervision over the temples (V, 169). King Harṣa (1189—1201 A.D.) introduced new fashions in dress. Jayâpiḍa revived Sanskrit learning by attracting famous scholars and poets to his court towards the close of the 8th century A.D.

The general tenor of the king's personal share in the administration is clear from the foregoing narrative. A few further details may be added. A king was sometimes on terms of friendship and familiarity with powerful or wealthy subjects (IV, 13-14). Righteous kings were accessible to all, even to the poorest, and ever ready to redress their wrongs (VI, 44—60). There were kings who discharged the functions of ministers (VI, 117). At times of festivity, music or dance, the court presented a brilliant appearance. Singers and artists from abroad were readily welcomed (V, 355-6). The magnificence of the Kashmir court reached its zenith under King Harṣa (1089—1101 A.D.). The chronicler goes into lyrics over it. "Nobody in his court was seen without brilliant dress, without gold ornaments, with a small following, or without a resolute bearing." People from various countries presented themselves. The riches of all countries seemed to be piled up at the Kashmir court. The palace witnessed the movement of numberless counsellors, chamberlains

Kings.

and attendants adorned with golden chains and bracelets. On journeys, a minister would always be mistaken for the king. At night the assembly-hall, illuminated by a thousand lamps, was the scene of scholastic discussions, musical performances and dances (VII, 881—83, 895, 944). And so on (VII, 946—949). Over and above it all, the king practised magnificent charity (VII, 955). But all this expenditure ultimately led to oppressive exactions from tax-payers (VII, 1100-1101).

The king's harem.

A king had usually a big harem which was sometimes increased by questionable means. For instance, a king falls in love with a girl, much younger than himself, daughter of a merchant who was on friendly terms with him.[1] On the other hand, ministers sometimes intrigued with the ladies of the royal seraglio.[2] The king's household expenditure was generally heavy. In the ninth century A.D. the household was placed in charge of a superintendent designated Gṛihakṛitya.[3]

Harem influences.

Harem influences sometimes seriously affected the administration. A singer's daughters, Haṁsí and Nâgalatâ were taken by the infatuated King Cakravarman into his harem in the thirties of the tenth century A.D. Haṁsí was at once designated chief queen. Her relations tended to monopolise all power and office with the result that the kingdom fell into troubles.[4] Female intrigue, again, was one of the forces which complicated the problem of the succession on failure of direct heirs. Women were, as a rule, barred from the throne. There is indeed the case of

The Succession.

[1] Ibid., IV, 23—30.
[2] Ibid., III, 497—500; V, 282, 281—8
[3] Ibid., V, 167, 176.
[4] Ibid., V, 354, 361—90, 404—12.

queen Diddâ who actually reigned for a long while in the latter half of the tenth century A.D.[1] She is one of the extremely few queens who regularly occupied a throne in ancient India. But even in Kashmîr ambitious women had generally to content themselves with power behind the scenes. Once a royal lady, Sugandhâ, wielded actual power for two years (904—906 A.D.). Anxious to perpetuate her influence, she planned the elevation of one of her own creatures to the throne. To achieve her purpose she summoned an assembly of feudal chiefs, ministers, Tantrins and Ekâṅgas. But dissensions arose and two civil wars followed in the course of which Sugandhâ herself was put to death.[2]

Sometimes a mere false move on the part of a king might lead to trouble of the most serious description. In 1063 A.D. King Ananta, urged by his wife, but against the advice of his ministers, abdicated in favour of his son Kalaśa. But when the latter proved his incapacity by his disgraceful rule, the old "king" and "queen" thought of replacing him by their grandson Harṣa. The altercations which followed led to two bitter civil wars at the end of which Ananta committed suicide.[3]

In the troubles over the succession, Brâhmaṇas sometimes played a leading part. On the deposition of the child-king Śûravarman in 939 A.D. the Brâhmaṇas gathered from all sacred places, debated the succession for five or six days but the man whom they set up at last kept them at arm's length lest they should become too powerful.[4] In his political testament Lalitâditya Muktâpiḍa laid down that "the elder should be placed on the throne . . . .

[1] Ibid., VI.
[2] Ibid., V, 249—62, 288—340.
[3] Ibid., VII, 230—456.
[4] Ibid., V, 461—66; VI, 2—4.

Do not make the younger king. If, however, through a fault of judgment, this should happen, then his commands should be obeyed and he (himself) protected, though he may be of bad character."[1]

Ministers.

According to Kalhaṇa, there were only seven high officials of state until the time of Jalauka, *viz.*, the judge, the revenue superintendent, the treasurer, the commander of the army, the envoy, the Purohita and the astrologer. Jalauka established 18 offices or Karmasthânas,[2] but the king is represented as the son of Aśoka and is not quite an historical figure. All that we can say is that the number of state departments in Kashmîr was at first much smaller than eighteen. Much later Lalitâditya instituted another five offices—Mahâpratipîḍa or high chamberlain, Mahâsaṁdhivigraha, minister for peace and war, Mahâśvaśâla, chief master of the horse, Mahâbhâṇḍâgâra, high keeper of the treasury, Mahâsâdhanabhâga, chief executive officer, rather vague.[3] It will appear that the administration developed gradually and the number of ministers rose accordingly.

Pañcamahâśabda.

The context of the Râjataraṅgiṇî indicates that it was the titles of these five offices which were denoted by the term Pañcamahâśabda. In the inscriptions of the plains of India, however, the expression will not bear that meaning. There it seems in practically every case to refer to feudatories who had the privilege of using certain fine musical instruments, or beating some instruments five times a day. The most likely solution of the difficulty which has exercised several scholars, seems to be that the term had different significations in different localities.[4] In Kashmîr ministers were

[1] Ibid., IV, 356—58.

[2] Ibid., I, 118—20.

[3] Ibid., IV, 137, 140, 142-43.

[4] Ind. Ant., IV, 106, 180, 204; XII, 95; XIII, 134; XIV, 202.

called Râjânakas.[1] Above the rest was a chief minister called Sarvâdhikâra.[2] Two or even more of the higher offices were sometimes combined in the hands of a single person (IV, 140). Sometimes princes of the blood were appointed to the highest posts.[3] Other relatives of the king also sometimes occupied high offices and exercised influence. Sometimes they made merry if a king died heirless.[4] The actual power and prestige of a minister would depend on the personal equation but the general importance of their position is clear from a few well-attested incidents. On the death of Avantivarman in 883 A.D., a number of members of the royal family aspired to the throne and quarrelled among themselves. The Chamberlain placed Śaṅkaravarman, a son of the late king, on the throne. Another minister installed a different member of the royal family as Yuvarâja. A civil war was the result.[5] Ministers could sometimes conspire and imperil the safety of the king.[6] The commanders of the standing army or bodyguard of infantry were particularly dangerous.[7] One of the most important military commands seems to have been that of the Dvârapati or warden of the marches.

Other officials.

One of the important offices was that of the Koṣâdhyakṣa who superintended the treasury.[8] The department of the Grihakṛitya not only looked after palace finance but was also responsible for the management of gifts and endowments to gods, Brâhmaṇas, royal servants, paupers, strangers, cows, etc.[9] A new fiscal office or Karmasthâna was established by King

[1] Kalhaṇa, VI, 117.
[2] Ibid., VII, 364.
[3] Ibid., IV, 142-43.
[4] Ibid., IV, 680; V, 127—30.
[5] Ibid., V, 127—30.
[6] Ibid., VIII, 294 et seq.
[7] Ibid., V, 248.
[8] Ibid., V, 232.
[9] Ibid., VII, 42-43.

Kalaśa in the 11th century.[1] A little later King Harṣa created some fresh revenue offices to manage his new imposts.[2] It appears that every head of revenue was managed by a separate official and his department. The organisation of new offices indicates that the administrative system developed according to needs. Justice seems to be the charge of the Râjasthâna.[3] In the plains the term Râjasthânīya meant viceroy but in Kashmīr the cognate Râjasthâna stood for the chief justice or the chief court of justice. The chief administrative and household offices were often filled by aristocrats.[4] But according to the evidence of the Râjataraṅgiṇī as a whole the tendency to the hereditary transmission of offices was less strong in Kashmīr than elsewhere in north India.

Minor functionaries.

Among the minor functionaries of state may be mentioned Adhikaraṇalekhakas or official recorders. Their duties were important enough to tempt others to offer bribes to them.[5] There was a large secretariat of which the members called Diviras discharged specified functions in separate departments. The number of Diviras was increased or decreased by individual kings.[6] Below the Diviras seem to have stood the Lekhakas, or clerks. The minor functionaries of state, as a whole, were called Kâyasthas.[7] They do not yet form a caste; they are only a class by themselves. But later the class developed into a series of subcastes which filled the minor ranks of government service under the Muslim rulers of medieval India.

[1] Ibid., VII, 570.
[2] Ibid., VII, 1105-6.
[3] Ibid., VIII, 573.
[4] Ibid., VIII, 713.
[5] Ibid., VI, 30, 38.
[6] Ibid., V, 177.
[7] Ibid., V, 181.

Local government in Kashmir followed the type of the northern plains, not that of the Deccan or the South. The representatives of the state in the village were known as Grâmakâyasthas.[1]

Local Government.

A city was under a prefect who, *inter alia*, was responsible for the maintenance of order.[2] Prefects were sometimes very corrupt and, what was worse, kings sometimes, though of course rarely, condescended to share their ill-gotten wealth.[3] On the other hand, there are cases of prefects carefully looking after their charges and reforming the administration and improving the condition of the people.

There were only too many officials of all ranks who were corrupt and oppressive. King Uccala (1101—1111 A.D.) always thought that "officials in truth are eager to kill, desirous of evil, robbers of others' property, rogues and demons; he (the king) should protect the people against them."[4] The historian pauses to comment on the king's opinion in yet stronger terms, comparing the petty officials to cholera, colic, exhaustion, crabs, poison, trees, etc.[5] King Uccala punished them relentlessly.[6] He degraded them, dismissed them from office, imprisoned them, inflicted fancy punishments on them and reduced many of them to utter poverty, ridicule and humiliation.[7] The king felt it necessary to endeavour all day long to know what the people thought and how they fared.[8] He went about incognito among the people.[9] Such strict supervision on the part of a king must have gone a long way to secure good government.

[1] Ibid., V, 175.
[2] Ibid., VIII, 814.
[3] Ibid., VI, 70.
[4] Ibid., VIII, 85—87.
[5] Ibid., VIII, 88—91, 131; also, V, 18.
[6] Ibid., VIII, 53.
[7] Ibid., VIII, 92—106.
[8] Ibid., VIII, 46.
[9] Ibid., VIII, 55; also 74.

Revenue.

The income of the state was derived from crown-lands,[1] the usual land-revenue which seems to have been paid often in kind,[2] and customs. Towards the close of the ninth century A.D., the collection of tolls on merchandise was entrusted to a distinct office, Aṭṭapatibhâga (the share of the lord of the market).[3] Tolls were levied on the bridges and on frontier posts, particularly at fortified stations.[4] Goods which had paid customs were stamped with a seal bearing the king's name in red lead.[5] As already observed, the number of state-dues was sometimes increased by kings. Forced labour amounted to a tax. In the ninth century Śaṅkaravarman compelled the villagers who were not called upon to render the forced labour, to pay an equivalent in money.[6] Unscrupulous kings could reduce the weights and thus defraud all whom they had to pay.[7] They would make deductions from the salary of village clerks and other government employees. Similar other devices might be resorted to.[8] Śaṅkaravarman, in fact, reduced fiscal oppression to an art[9] (883—902 A.D.).

Justice.

Justice still retained a primitive element in Kashmir. Once a fine is levied on the head of a family for misconduct on the part of a married woman.[10] A king once sent for the books of a merchant and detected a forgery in his accounts. He promptly banished the merchant, deprived him of his property and made it over to the party wronged.[11]

[1] Ibid., V, 170.
[2] Ibid., IV, 347, 628, 639; VII, 1107.
[3] Ibid., V, 167.
[4] Ibid., VIII, 136.
[5] Ibid., VIII, 2010.
[6] Ibid., V, 172—76.
[7] Ibid., V, 171—76.
[8] Ibid., V, 175-76.
[9] Ibid., V, 128—227.
[10] Ibid., VIII, 3336.
[11] Ibid., VI, 41.

Kashmir was the only region in ancient India which developed the art of historiography at all. Besides Kalhaṇa there were a few other chroniclers. On one of them, Ratnâkara Purâṇa, Hasan based his Persian History of Kashmir which is abstracted in the Kashmiri writer Ânand Kaul's History of Kashmir. But it adds little to the foregoing information on administration.

Other historical works.

Two other writers who flourished in Kashmir about the same time as Kalhaṇa may be briefly noticed. In the latter half of the eleventh century Vidyâpati Bilhaṇa, author of the play Karṇasundarî, wrote the Vikramâṅkadevacarita in which love, politics and warfare march side by side. The ideal of conquest and universal dominion in the narrow feudal sense of the term is there. The picture of Anantadeva of Kashmir as a model of virtue, generosity, veracity and heroism is interesting.[1] His brother Kṣitipati is not only a scholar himself but a patron of learning and withal a warrior.[2] The poet is employed as a tutor to the king's daughter who falls in love with him. The incensed monarch sentences the poet to death but reprieves him afterwards. Bilhaṇa winds up the story of his own life by a solemn exhortation to princes, in view of the fleeting nature of all prosperity, to worship those true poets "who work the salvation of your bodies of glory through the nectar of their verse, and renouncing pride make them your spiritual guides."[3]

Vidyâpati Bilhaṇa.

Kṣemendra, who lived in Kashmir in the eleventh century and probably came of a line of ministers, stands in a class by himself among later Sanskrit writers. In his Râmâyaṇamañjarî and his Bhâratamañjarî he summarises the epics, reproduces their

Kṣemendra.

[1] Vikramâṅkadevacarita, XVIII, 33—39.

[2] Ibid., XVIII, 47—50.

[3] Ibid., XVIII, 106-07.

political teachings and seeks to re-capture their spirit and atmosphere. None the less, the influence of Dharma Śâstras and Nîti Śâstras is there.[1] The same writer in his Bodhisattvâvadânakalpalatâ epitomised numerous Buddhist Jâtaka and Avadâna tales with equal success. Here, however, the political ideas are given in a Brahmanical setting. In the Bṛihatkathâmañjarî, based on Guṇâḍhya's Bṛihatkathâ, the politics of the age find a reflection. There is nothing new here. But it is worth while observing that federal-feudalism is reflected in these works as elsewhere.

Chambâ.

Kalhaṇa's evidence on administration is corroborated and supplemented by the inscriptions from the neighbouring state of Chambâ[2] which recognised the suzerainty of Kashmîr for long. The fundamental political conditions are the same here as prevailed in Kashmîr and the rest of North India. It was about 700 A.D. that Meruvarman assumed the title Râjâdhirâja which here corresponded to the Mahârâjâdhirâja of the plains. Evidently the light yoke of Kashmîr was shaken off and the dynasty of Meruvarman started on an independent career. These rulers stood forth as the ultimate suzerains of the petty chiefs who had so far been their sub-feudatories. Meruvarman further extended the area of his suzerainty and imposed his yoke on other chiefs. By the tenth

[1] Ibid., Bhâratamañjarî (ed. Śivadatta and Kâshînâtha Pâṇḍuraṅga Parab), Śânti Parvan, Râjadharmâḥ, 298—307, 320, 328, 330—33, Âpaddharma, 581—96.

[2] The Chambâ inscriptions are published in J. Ph. Vogel's Antiquities of Chambâ State, Archæological Survey of India, New Imperial Series, Vol. XXXVI, Calcutta, 1911. Pp. 1-136 discuss the geography, ancient history and chronology of Chambâ and the general character of the inscriptions. Some of the inscriptions are also given in Ann. Rep. Arch. Surv., 1902-3, pp. 239—71. See also Ind. Ant., XVII, 1888, pp. 7 et seq., Chambâ Copper Plate Inscription of Somavarmadeva and Asatadeva (middle of the 11th century A.D.).

century A.D. the line was firmly established with its capital at Chambâ.[1] Henceforward, Kalhaṇa never calls them sâmantas or vassals but addresses them as bhûpâla, nripati, etc.[2] The feudatories are called Râjas while the terms Râṇâs and Râjânakas seem to be applied to small feudatories or sub-feudatories who exercised various governmental prerogatives.[3] A few centuries later their position was well understood by the Musalmân historians who call them zamîndârs, a designation which they applied to the feudatories of the central Muslim power in North India. In some respects the position of these petty feudatories and sub-feudatories resembled that of the feudal nobility in medieval France.

After a while the suzerains adopted the three grand titles, Parameśvara, Mahârâjâdhirâja, Paramabhaṭṭâraka, which were now in vogue all over India. The administrative system of Chambâ also resembles that of the plains in many particulars. Feudatories were often given high office under the suzerain, a practice which, together with the custom of making grants of land and the tendency to hereditary transmission of office, sometimes made the line between feudatories and regular officers rather faint. In the inscriptions feudatories are generally mentioned before the officers. The occurrence of the term Râjaputra in the same connection suggests that the sons of rulers—suzerains or feudatories—were given high administrative posts. The term Kumârâmâtya, minister of the prince, points to the same practice and suggests that a prince-governor or officer had a special minister to assist him. The latter in some

Administrative Machinery.

[1] J. Ph. Vogel, Antiquities of Chambâ State, Inscriptions, Nos. 6, 8, 9, 14-15.

[2] Ibid., p. 103.

[3] Ibid., Nos. 13, 32.

cases might have been the real administrator. There seems to be a chief minister called Râjâmâtya or Mahâmâtya as in No. 24. Amâtya was the general term for ministers. In Chambâ as in Kashmîr, Râjasthâna relates to justice. The Râjasthânîya who figures in the inscriptions seems to be in charge of justice and is, so to say, a minister of justice. The Pramâtâr was charged with the administration of justice perhaps only in civil cases. Daṇḍika and Daṇḍavâsika also seem to be judicial officers. Kṣetrapa, wrongly written as Kṣatrapa, means a police-officer specially charged with the protection of fields, that is, of agriculture. Cauroddharaṇika, 'one who is entrusted with the extermination of thieves,' was another high police-officer. The Uparika is a fiscal officer as in the plains, probably charged with the collection of the main head of land revenue. The Śaulkika was in charge of customs; Gaulmika in charge of forests and forest produce. The Akṣapaṭalikas or Mahâkṣapaṭalikas kept the records. Kâyasthas wrote out the legal documents. Among household officers may be mentioned the Khaṇḍarakṣa, probably a vernacularised form of the Sanskrit Khaḍgarakṣa, 'sword guard,' obviously belonging to the body-guard; the Chatrachâyika, parasol-bearer, who held the royal umbrella; the Vetakali, a betel-bearer.

On the military side the Hastyaśvoṣṭrabalavyâpṛitakas are the officers in charge of elephants, horse, camels, and infantry. Chariots are replaced by camels. The former had gone out of vogue all over India by this time and would be perfectly useless in a region like Chambâ. Vîrayâtrika is another military officer but his status and functions are obscure. The mention of tribes with officers—Khaśa, Kulika—shows that tribesmen headed by their own chiefs, occupied a notable place in the army.

The scheme of administrative sub-divisions in Chambâ seems to have been a little different from that of the plains,

Bhogika or Bhogapati and Viṣayapati are there, as usual, in charge of provinces and districts. But two other local officers—Nihelapatis and Tarapatis—are peculiar to the mountainous regions. They seem to be in charge of sub-divisions known as Nihelas and Taras, probably sub-divisions of the Viṣaya. Tara appears to be smaller than Nihela. The sub-division, immediately above the village, was supervised by an officer called Câṭa, a term which bears a different meaning in the plains. Câṭa is still the designation of the head of a paraganâ in Chambâ. In the earlier inscriptions the Câṭa, *inter alia*, collects road-carriers and supplies for the king, his. relations or officers when on tour. Here Bhaṭas seem to be subordinate to Câṭas. As in the plains, Viniyuktakas seem to be the assistants, something like secretaries, of divisional officers, Bhogikas and Viṣayapatis. Here, as elsewhere, are a large number of messengers, classified into Dûtas, Gamâgamikas and Abhitvaramâṇas.[1]

Local Government.

No. 15, the Suṅgal Copper Plate Inscription of Vidagdha, shows the fiscal system of Chambâ and the neighbouring states to be the same as that of Kashmir. Here, as in the rest of India, justice was a source of revenue. The daśâparâdhâḥ—ten offences, that is to say, the fines from ten offences, are enumerated among the privileges granted to favourites, with well-defined pieces of land. From the inscriptions of Chambâ as from the others in the rest of India, it appears that the land was carefully measured and

The fiscal system.

[1] For the various officials, Ibid., Inscriptions, pp. 137—255, particularly the Suṅgal Copper Plate Inscription of Vidagha No. 15; the Chambâ Copper Plate Inscription of Somavarman and Âsaṭa, No. 25; the Ṭhuṇḍhu Copper Plate Inscription of Âsaṭa, No. 26. For the use of the term Câṭa in modern Chambâ, pp. 131-32.

boundaries of fields and villages recorded with the most meticulous precision. The Suṅgal Copper Plate Inscription speaks of the "regular share and use, tax in kind and cash, and every other tribute due to the king," showing that the royal dues were many. It appears that on extraordinary occasions the king's officers demanded or perhaps forcibly appropriated many other perquisites. "Of our district officers and their subordinates and others," so runs a passage in the royal Suṅgal grant, "no one will be allowed to alight at his (grantee's) house, to cut or crush his corn, sugar-cane or pasture (?), whether green or ripe, nor to take rocika or ciṭolâ or to take cow's milk, nor to carry off stools, benches or couches, nor to seize his wood, fuel, grass, chaff, and so on. Not even the slightest oppression or vexation should be inflicted on him, nor on his ploughmen, cowherds, maids, servants and all other people that are dependent on him." It may be mentioned in passing that here as elsewhere grants were made sometimes to groups.[1]

[1] Ibid., No. 25.

CHAPTER XVI.

The Eleventh and Twelfth Centuries A.D.

The Arab occupation of Sindh in the eighth century A.D. was an episode in itself which left no permanent impress on the country. The long series of invasions by Mahmûd of Ghazni in the first quarter of the eleventh century A.D. was more important as showing the way to India and leading to the final loss of the gateways and the Western Puñjâb to the Islamic power. Until the close of the tenth century A.D. the Gûrjara-Pratihâras carefully guarded the North-western frontier but the decline of their power now facilitated the enterprise of the Sultân of Ghazni.[1] The Râjpûts, torn by hereditary feuds and lagging behind in military sciences, had to give way at almost every turn.

Musalmân Invaders.

Nevertheless the exploits of Mahmûd, though they reached as far as Gujarât towards the south and the banks of the Ganges towards the east, were essentially raids. Except in the north-west, there was no permanent annexation. As soon as the avalanche had receded, the old surface re-appeared and life resumed its normal course. It was not until the close of the twelfth century that Mohammad Ghorî and his redoubtable lieutenants, Bakhtiyâr Khiljî and Qutb-ud-dîn Aiyabek, finally reduced the north of India

[1] On the Gûrjara-Pratihâras, A. M. T. Jackson, Bombay Gazetteer, Vol. I, Part I, App. III; R. C. Majumdar, Journal of the Department of Letters, Calcutta, Vol. X, 1923, pp. 1—76; Hoernle, J. R. A. S., 1904, pp. 639—62; Ibid., 1905, pp. 1—32; V. A. Smith, J. R. A. S., 1909, pp. 53—76, 247—81; D. R. Bhandarkar, J. B. B. R. A. S., XXI. pp. 405 et seq.

and stamped out Hindu sovereignty. Another century was to roll by before Muslim arms penetrated into the south. For the whole of India, the eleventh and twelfth centuries A.D. are to be reckoned as part of the Ancient Age, and for the North, as its last period.

The materials for the study of the administrative practices of these two centuries fall into three classes. In the first place, there are Muslim accounts, chiefly that of Alberûnî, the first and foremost of all Muslim students of Sanskrit, who lived for a while in India and wrote about 1030 A.D. In the second place, the contemporary Sanskrit literature, both Brahmanic and Jaina, can be made to yield something. In the third place, the inscriptions supply numerous administrative details.

Alberûnî is entitled to special weight from his scientific habits of observation and mastery of Sanskrit. He is concerned with the culture rather than with the politics of India. None the less, here and there he notices the laws or institutions of the country. Caste inevitably attracted his notice. He makes the arresting remark that between the last two classes, the Vaiśyas and Śûdras, there was no very great distance.[1] As these constituted the mass of the people, it follows that Brâhmaṇas and Kṣatriyas formed the social aristocracy of the land. It appears that in the districts which came under Alberûnî's observation, political administration was not run by Brâhmaṇas at all. He reports the tradition current in his time that "originally the affairs of government were in the hands of the Brâhmaṇas but the country became disorganised since they ruled according to the philosophic principles of their religious codes, which proved impossible when opposed to the mischievous and perverse elements of the

Alberûnî.

Caste.

[1] Alberûnî, India, tr. Sachau, Vol. I., pp. 100-101, on caste in general, pp. 99—103.

populace. They were even near losing also the administration of their religious affairs. Therefore they humiliated themselves before the lord of their religion. Whereupon Brahman entrusted them exclusively with the functions which they now have, whilst he entrusted the Kṣatriyas with the duties of ruling and fighting. Ever since the Brâhmaṇas live by asking and begging, and the penal code is exercised under the control of the kings, not under that of scholars."[1]

Law and Justice.

It is on law and justice that Alberûnî is most illuminating. Here he supplies details which are not to be found in the Hindu literature or the inscriptions. He rightly observes that the Hindus believed their religious law and its simple precepts to be derived from Ṛiṣis .... "Further no law can be exchanged or replaced by another, for they use the laws simply as they find them." But he adds presently "laws can be abrogated, for some practices allowed before the coming of Vâsudeva are now forbidden."[2] In the Court a suitor had ordinarily to submit some documentary evidence, in prescribed form, to substantiate his claims before the judge. In the absence of such documentary evidence, the case was settled by means of witnesses. Witnesses should not be less than four but they might be more in number. Only where the facts were perfectly clear, adds Alberûnî, would the testimony of a single witness suffice. Even then the judge would employ all sorts of tricks and secret means to elicit the truth. If the plaintiff could not prove his claim, the defendant had still to swear to his innocence. On the other hand, the defendant himself might, evidently at an earlier stage, tender the oath to the plaintiff saying, "Swear thou that thy claim is true and I will give thee what thou claimest." Oaths were of many kinds in accordance with the value of the object of the claim. If

[1] Ibid., II, 161-62.
[2] Ibid., I, pp. 106-7.

the object were not very important and the plaintiff agreed, the defendant merely swore, in the presence of five learned Brâhmaṇas, that "if I lie, he shall have as recompense as much of my goods as is equal to the eightfold of the amount of his claim."[1]

The oath itself was regarded as a kind of ordeal. There were five other ordeals successively more serious. In the first, the ordeal by water, the accused, brought to a deep rapid river or a deep well, spoke as follows: "Since thou belongest to the pure angels (gods?), and knowest both what is secret and public, kill me if I lie and preserve me if I speak the truth." He was then thrown by five persons into the water. It was believed that if he had spoken the truth, he would not drown and die. In the second ordeal, the judge would send both parties to the most venerated temple of the place, where the defendant would fast for a day and then, dressed in new garments, post himself with the plaintiff in the temple. "The priests pour water over the idol and give it him to drink. If he, then, has not spoken the truth, he at once vomits blood." In the ordeal by balance, the accused was first weighed on the scale. He then called on the gods to testify to his innocence and wrote down his invocations and declarations on a piece of paper. The paper was fastened to his head. "He is a second time placed in the scale of the balance. In case he has spoken the truth, he now weighs more than the second time." In the fourth ordeal, "they take butter and sesame-oil in equal quantities, and boil them in a kettle. Then they throw a leaf into it, which by getting flaccid and burned is to them a sign of the boiling of the mixture. When the boiling is at its height, they throw a piece of gold into the kettle

Ordeals.

[1] Ibid., II, 158-59.

and order the defendant to fetch it out with his own hand. If he has spoken the truth, he fetches it out." In the highest ordeal, a piece of iron, red-hot and almost molten, was, with a pair of tongs, put on the hand of the accused; "there being nothing between the hand and the iron save a broad leaf of some plant, and under it some few and scattered corns of rice in the husks. They order him to carry it seven paces, and then he may throw it to the ground."[1] It will be observed that while some of the ordeals were extremely mild and even trivial, others were very harsh and severe. Their choice probably depended on the nature of the charge and the sex, rank and character of the accused.

Punishments.

According to the Hindus of the 11th century A.D. the most serious crimes were the murder of a Brâhmaṇa, slaughter of a cow, drinking wine, and adultery, particularly with the wife of one's own father or teacher. Alberûni's description of judicial punishments shows that the Smṛiti regulation of justice on lines of caste had some basis in facts. He notes the theory that if a Brâhmaṇa murdered a man of another caste, the former was only bound "to do expiation consisting of fasting, prayers and alms-giving." But if a Brâhmaṇa murdered another Brâhmaṇa, he was not to be allowed to do any expiation but must be compelled to suffer the full rigour of punishment in the next world. In practice it appears, a Brâhmaṇa or a Kṣatriya, guilty of any of the deadly crimes mentioned above, was deprived of his property and banished. Alberûinî seems to imply that for a similar offence a Vaiśya or a Śûdra forfeited his life.

If a man other than a Brâhmaṇa or a Kṣatriya killed a man of his own caste, he had to perform expiation and undergo an exemplary punishment. For theft the punishment

[1] Ibid., II, 159-60.

varied according to the value of the objects stolen. "If the object is very great, the kings blind a Brâhmaṇa and mutilate him, cutting off his left hand and right foot, or the right hand and left foot, whilst they mutilate a Kṣatriya without blinding him, and kill thieves of the other castes." A woman, guilty of adultery, was driven from home and exiled.[1]

It will appear that the priestly injunction to deprive the Śûdras of sacred knowledge was respected by the state.

Disabilities of Śûdras.

Alberûnî, in fact, records that a Vaiśya or a Śûdra who dared to hear, pronounce, or recite Vedic texts was hauled up by Brâhmaṇas before magistrates who ordered his tongue to be cut out.[2] From the mention of Vaiśyas, the whole passage smacks of exaggeration but it certainly has a substratum of fact in it. Alberûnî is more correct in a later passage where he singles out the Śûdra for punishment for daring to arrogate the Dvija privileges of saying prayers, reciting the Veda and offering sacrifices to the fire.[3]

The Muslim historians who wrote accounts of the relations of Sabuktigîn and Mahmûd of Ghaznî in the latter

Muslim Historians.

half of the tenth century and the first half of the 11th century A.D. do not display any deep knowledge of Indian political conditions and view all events from Ghaznî. But the incidental touches in their writings fully confirm the previous conclusions. Al'Utbi, author of Târîkh Yamînî or Kitâbu-l Yamînî speaks of the vassals collected by Jaipâl for his march on Afghânistân which, after the Arab occupation of Sindh, represented the first armed conflict between Hindus and Musalmâns.[4] Again, there is a reference

[1] Ibid., II, 162.
[2] Ibid., I, 125.
[3] Ibid., II, 136.
[4] Elliot and Dowson, History of India as told by its own Historians, II, p. 19.

to chieftains.[1] Mention is made of vassals in the course of Mahmûd's campaigns in India.[2] Numerous Râis, as Hindu rulers are called in Muslim narratives, flourished in the north-western plains.[3] Hasan Nizâmi's Taju-l Maâsir which describes the campaigns of Mohammad Ghori and his lieutenants—the real conquest of North India—is also silent on the Hindu system of government and, in broad outline, merely confirms the foregoing accounts.[4] There was a custom that a king, when taken prisoner, should not reign after his release. Jaipâl on return from Mahmûd's captivity, committed suicide by fire.[5] Kings and chiefs adorned their bodies. The necklace worn by Jaipâl was composed of large pearls and shining gems and rubies set in gold, estimated at two hundred thousand dînârs. Twice that value was obtained from the ornaments on the necks of the king's relations.[6]

The Inscriptions.

It is only from inscriptions that any connected account of the administrative structure can be given. From the epigraphic data it appears that there were differences of detail in the institutions of various regions during this period but the framework was the same all over North India.

Kanauj.

The Candrâvatî plates of Candradeva of Kânyakubja, that is, Kanauj, belonging to the last decade of the eleventh century A.D., give the designations of many court officials as well as strictly political officers. As usual, the grants are made by the king after a bath, in the present instance, in the sacred river Sarayû at Ayodhyâ. The king styles himself Mahârâjâdhirâja Parameśvara. In the usual manner, he

[1] Ibid., II, 27.
[2] Ibid., II, 38.
[3] Ibid., II, 42.
[4] Ibid., II, 204—43.
[5] Ibid., II, 27.
[6] Ibid., II, 26.

respects, informs and commands a number of personages, beginning with Râjas and Râjñis, feudatory chiefs and their consorts. Yuvarâjas, heirs-apparent to the various domains, come next. In the list of officers which follows, the central and local functionaries of state and the household officers are all mixed up together. Mantrins or ministers proper head the list. Then come Senâpatis or commanders of troops, Purohitas, chaplains, Pratihâras, chamberlains, Akṣapaṭalikas, keepers of records, Bhâṇḍâgârikas, treasurers or superintendents of stores, Bhiṣags or physicians, Naimittakas or astrologers, Antaḥpurikas, superintendents of seraglio departments or of gymnasiums, Dûtas or envoys, then officers in charge of elephants, horses, towns (paṭṭana), mines (âkara), stations or police stations (sthânas), officers in charge of districts (Viṣaya), cattle-stations (gokulas) and others (apara). The inhabitants of the villages granted to some Brâhmaṇas are called upon to render to the latter the bhâgabhogakara, the turuṣkadaṇḍa, viṣayadâna, etc. Bhâgabhogakara is the usual term for taxes of all kinds, including the royal share of the gross produce, the customs, tolls on sales, ferry dues, etc., etc. Turuṣkadaṇḍa is obscure. It may refer to ransom-money which had to be paid to Turuṣkas or western invaders and which had to be raised from the whole population. As such it would correspond to the Danish tax levied in England for a while. Or it may mean a sort of poll-tax imposed on Turuṣkas or settlers from the north-west. There is no reason to suppose that Turuṣkas were settled in every place of which the grants mention the Turuṣkadaṇḍa. But when once the tax had found a place in the fiscal system, it would be mentioned as an ordinary impost along with others. Viṣayadâna may mean some peculiar district tax. In any case, the number of imposts is strikingly large.[1]

[1] Ep. Ind., XIV, No. 15.

Twenty-one Copper-plates of the kings of Kanauj ranging from the second to the seventh decade of the 12th century A.D. throughout mention the three grand titles and indicate the same feudal system. They show that Pattalâ was one of the divisions of local government and comprised a number of villages. The clerks were all called Kâyasthas. All the foregoing taxes are here with a few additions. Besides the Turuṣkadaṇḍa there is the Kumâragadiaṇaka and Pravaṇikara, rather obscure (which occur in many other grants), Gokara, probably a tax on the increase of cattle and Jâtakara. Any or all of the taxes might be alienated to the grantees.[1] Five Copper-plate Inscriptions of Govindacandra[2] and two later Copper-plate Grants of Jayacandra of Kanauj,[3] all belonging to the 12th century A.D., mention all the above officers and state dues. Some other inscriptions of Kanauj kings repeat the same.[4] Six Copper-plates of Jayacandra record grants to a Kṣatriya, an hereditary Râut and Mahâmahattaka. They prove that local dignities were often hereditary and that grants could be made to non-Brâhmaṇas as to Brâhmaṇas.[5] The Saheth-Maheth Plate of Govindacandra is particularly interesting for its feudal indications.[6] The Benâres Copper-plate Inscription of Karṇadeva of the year 1042 A.D. gives the usual information and is important for its clear indication of the claim of the state to the mineral products of the country.[7]

[1] Ep. Ind., IV, No. 11. For another inscription of the same import, Ep. Ind., VII, No. 11.

[2] Ep. Ind., VIII, No. 14.

[3] Ind. Ant., XV, pp. 6 et seq.

[4] Ind. Ant., XVIII, 1889, pp. 9 et seq.

[5] Ibid., XVIII, 136—42.

[6] Ep. Ind., XI, No. 3, J. R. A. S., 1909, pp. 1066 et seq.

[7] Ep. Ind., II, No. 23.

The Lucknow Museum Plate of Kîrtipâla of the year 1111-12 A.D. is interesting as indicating the existence of some religious dignitaries at some courts. Here the Paramabhaṭṭâraka Mahârâjâdhirâja Parameśvara mentions Mahâpurohita, Dharmâdhikaraṇika, Daivâgârika, Śaṅkhadhâri, two Paṇḍitas, three Upâdhyâyas, Daivajña, Vaṭhakkura. Then come a few administrative officers—Mahâkṣapaṭalika, Âṣṭavargika, Karaṇakâyastha (registrar), Mahâtthâśâsanika, and Mahâsâdhanika. The term Mahâtthâśâsanika is obscure.[1]

In the Sevâḍi Stone Inscription of Aśvarâja of the year 1110-11 A.D. from Mârwâr in Râjputânâ, the titles are confused. There appears a new administrative term. Mahâsâhaṇīya is the great master of stables.[2] In another inscription of the year 1179-80 A.D. (Mârwâr) mention is made of the bhukti of the queen.[3] Perhaps the proceeds of the province had been made over to her.

In the Goharwa Plates of Karṇadeva, 1047 A.D., appear the chief officers of other inscriptions but Mahârâjaputra is used for Râjaputra, Mahâmantrin for Mantrin. Mahaśvasâdhanika is the great officer in charge of horses.[4]

Bengal.

The Tarpaṇḍighi Grant of Lakṣmaṇasena, of the year 1122 A.D., shows that the same feudal-federal administrative and fiscal systems prevailed in Bengal as elsewhere.[5] The conclusion is strengthened by the Bârrackpur Grant of Vijayasena of the 12th century A.D. Here also occur Mahâdharmâdhyakṣa, a great judicial officer, Mahâmudrâdhikrita, a great mint officer or keeper of the royal seal, and the same administrative

[1] Ep. Ind., VII, No. 10.
[2] Ep. Ind., XI, No. 4 (III).
[3] Ep. Ind., XI, No. 4 (XVII).
[4] Ep, Ind., XI, No. 13.
[5] Ep. Ind., XII, No. 3.

divisions of Bhukti, Viṣaya and Grâma.[1] The Bengal grants of this period give unusually full lists of officers and state demands.

The Belava Copper-plate Inscription of Bhojavarmadeva of East Bengal, in the 11th century A.D., shows the fundamental political conditions to be the same but mentions a few additional offices which seem to have existed there. The king has all the three grand titles and addresses his command first to Râjans, Râjanyakas, Râjñīs (consorts of Râjans) and Râṇakas. Here are the various bodies of feudatories. After Râjaputras or princes who may, in many cases, have occupied high offices, comes the Râjâmâtya or chief minister. After the Purohita comes the Piṭhikâvitta whose functions are not clear. Then there are the Mahâdharmâdhyakṣa or chief judge, Mahâsaṁdhivigrahika, minister of peace and war, Mahâsenâpati, commander-in-chief, Mahâmudrâdhikṛita, as before, Antaraṅgabṛihaduparika, chief private secretary or superintendent of the seraglio or chief physician, Mahâkṣapaṭalika, chief keeper of records, Mahâpratihâra, grand chamberlain, Mahâbhogika, chief revenue officer, or provincial governor, Mahâvyûhapati, chief master of military arrays, Mahâpilupati, chief keeper of elephants, Mahâgaṇastha, chief commander of a gaṇa squadron, Dauḥsâdhika, a special police-officer, or porter, or superintendent of villages, Cauroddharaṇika, a police-officer who had to deal with thieves, then inspectors of the flotilla, elephants, horses, cows, buffaloes, goats, sheep, etc., Gaulmikas, superintendents of forests or commanders of gulma squadrons, Daṇḍapâśikas, police-officers or executioners, Daṇḍanâyakas (magistrates), Viṣayapatis or district officers, other Adhyakṣas, superintendents or chief officers, Câṭas, petty police-officers, Bhaṭas, soldiers.[2]

East Bengal.

[1] Ep. Ind., XV, No. 15.

[2] Ep. Ind., XII, No. 8.

Another East Bengal document, the Râmpâl Copper-plate Grant of Śrîcandradeva, gives the same list of officers.[1] So, too, the Khairah Plate of Yaśaḥkarṇadeva.[2] In another inscription the word Râṣṭra is used in the sense of a district.[3]

Orissâ.

The records of the Somavaṁśî kings of Kaṭak (Cuttack) in Orissâ disclose the same practices of suzerainty and vassalage as prevailed elsewhere in India. The suzerain, as usual, employed the three grand titles. Not only feudatories but also high government officials here make grants of land on their own account. Perhaps the system of remunerating high officials with assignments of land prevailed. Petty officials and clerks are called Kâyasthas.[4] The Kudopali Plates of the time of Mahâbhavagupta II, about the 12th century A.D., show that a feudatory could enjoy lofty titles and yet possess a very small territory. Puñja was a Mâṇḍalika, a Râṇaka and had obtained the five Mahâśabdas but he ruled only over fifteen villages.[5] The plates of Vidyâdharabhañjadeva bring to view feudatories and sub-feudatories.[6] In the Orissâ grants the number of officials is smaller than in the Gangetic plains. It appears that administrative development there had not reached the stage which the Kanauj and Bengal grants, for instance, reveal.

Kâmarûpa.

The Copper-plate Grant of Vaidyadeva of the middle of the 12th century A.D. is of absorbing interest as giving a picture of contemporary Assamese administration. Probably a Brâhmaṇa by birth, Vaidyadeva was a capable general of King Kumâ-

[1] Ep. Ind., XII, No. 18.
[2] Ep. Ind., XII, No. 24.
[3] Ep. Ind., XII, No. 17.
[4] Ep. Ind., III, No. 47.
[5] Ep. Ind., IV, No. 35.
[6] Ep. Ind., IX, No. 37.

rapâla and, politically, a man of first-rate importance. His grant shows that suzerains sometimes displaced disloyal feudatories and put loyal ones in their places. The highest offices might be hereditary. In the present case the office of Mantrin descended from father to son for no less than four generations. There is negative evidence that the number of imposts was not so large as elsewhere. The suzerain, by the way, has all the three grand titles.[1]

Mâlwâ.

The Mândhâtâ Plates of Jayasiṁha of Dhârâ in Mâlwâ of the year 1055-56 A.D. disclose the usual feudal and fiscal system. Here the village officer is called Paṭṭakila. The grant is made to a Paṭṭaśâlâ, probably the same as Pâṭhśâlâ, a seat of learning.[2]

Central India.

The Ratnapur Stone Inscription of Jâjalladeva of the year 1114 A.D. shows the central Indian rulers founding new towns and beautifying new and old alike. Here the word maṇḍala was used to denote spheres of diplomacy dominated by one or other of the numerous princes.[3] Two Candella Inscriptions show hereditary ministers.[4] Another two Candella Inscriptions from Ajayagaḍh of the thirteenth century A.D., show a queen constructing a well and a hall.[5]

Local Government.

The Nâdol Stone Inscription of Râyapâla (Mârwâr, Râjpûtânâ) of 1141 or 1142 A.D. is extremely important for local administration. Here sixteen Brâhmaṇas, inhabitants of eight different wards of the town of Dhâlopa, and another man named Devaica, a mediator, head all the men of the

[1] Ep. Ind., II, No. 28.

[2] Ep. Ind., III, No. 7.

[3] Ep. Ind., I, No. 5.

[4] Ep. Ind., I, No. 25.

[5] Ep. Ind., I, No. 38. See also three Candella Copper Plate Grants of the eleventh century A.D., Ind. Ant., XVI, p. 301.

town in presenting a document, drafted by them, to the ruler. They promise to find out, in accordance with the custom of the country, through the Caukaḍikâ or pañcâyata, whatever is lost by or snatched away from the Bhaṭa, the Baṭṭaputra, Dauvârika, Kârpaṭika, Vaṇijjâraka and others on their way. The individuals responsible for a particular ward were to busy themselves in person in tracing out any articles lost therein. The Mahârâja Śrîrâjyapâla supplied the people with money, weapons and watchmen, etc., for tracing lost articles. The document ended with an imprecation that if a Brâhmaṇa refused to share in this task of investigation, he might die like a cur, a donkey or a caṇḍâla, and no blame would rest on the chiefs or Râṇakas. Apart from its feudalism, the document shows that a town was divided into a number of wards, at least eight in this particular case, that the inhabitants with recognised leaders at their head undertook some important police duties, that all, even Brâhmaṇas, were expected to give their personal services in the task and that the whole thing was managed with the knowledge and assistance of the ruler. The document was signed by many witnesses, including the Bhaṭṭârakas of temples.[1]

A thirteenth century document from the same area—the Sâñcor Stone Inscription of Sâmantasiṁha styled Mahârârâjakula—brings the administration of a village to view. The local authority in the village was exercised by the pañca, literally a committee of five, consisting of the Mahanta Hîrâ and others appointed by the king.[2]

It is in the case of Mârwâr alone in North India that there is any epigraphic evidence of organs of even partial local self-government. Neither in the inscriptions nor in literature is there anything to enable us to trace their origin and development. But their existence in

[1] Ep. Ind., XI, No. 4 (IX).

[2] Ep. Ind., XI, No. 4 (XXI).

Mârwâr in the last period of the ancient age is undoubted. Elsewhere in the North we only find the village elders—Mahattaras or Mahattamas—informally associated with village officers from the Gupta period onwards. In this respect the North offers a strong contrast to the South which had by this time evolved a regular system of village self-government through assemblies, committees and elective officers working under the general supervision of the government.

The Fiscal System.

Besides the regular taxes of the foregoing epochs, the inscriptions of this period bring into view some peculiar imposts. The Nadlai Stone Inscription of Râyapâla of the year 1132-33 A.D. from Mârwâr, Râjpûtâna, mentions the grant of two palikâs out of those due to the state from each oil machine (ghaṇaka) to some Jaina saints. To this benefaction there were a number of witnesses.[1]

Feudatories.

A Paṭnâ inscription of the beginning of thirteenth century A.D. is interesting from more than one point of view. Under the suzerain Yâdavasiṁhana were two feudatories, the brothers Soideva and Hemâdideva who ruled over "the country of 1,600 villages." They liberally endowed with land and 'other sources of income' a college founded by the Yâdava king's chief astrologer, grandson of the famous astronomer Bhâskarâcârya for the study of Siddhântaśiromaṇi and other works of his grandfather and relations.[2]

Endowments.

Most of the extant inscriptions are grants to persons, temples or institutious. They testify abundantly to the generosity of Hindu courts. Recipients also sometimes commemorated their gratitude. For instance, the Govindpur Stone Inscription of the poet Gaṅgâdhara, of the year 1137-38 A.D., records

[1] Ep. Ind., XI, No. 4 (VII, also XV).

[2] Ep. Ind., I, No. 39.

that the poet and his ancestors enjoyed the patronage of Magadha rulers for generations.[1] Of the seats of learning endowed by royal munificence during this period, Vikramaśilâvihâra is probably the finest example. It was founded by Dharmapâla, second of the Pâla dynasty, in the 9th century A.D. The institution was housed in a magnificent building which made room for 107 temples within its precincts. It included six different scholastic institutions where teaching was imparted by 108 masters. Altogether, it could accommodate 8,000 men. The head called Adhinâyaka was appointed by the king. This seat of learning had an all-India fame and attracted scholars and students from far and near. There was a tradition that even its gate-keepers were Paṇḍitas and had to be defeated in scholastic discussion before one could enter the precincts. The institution flourished until the 12th century A.D. when it was engulfed in the rushing tide of the Muslim conquest.[2]

The evidence of literature.

Nîtiśâstras.

The evidence of the inscriptions and of the Muslim writers of this period is supplemented by literature in several particulars. The close of the ancient age produced several Nîtiśâstras—compositions which, in their method and treatment stand midway between the Arthaśâstras and Dharma Śâstras and represent a partial fusion of the two. According to the theory of the Garuḍa Purâṇa,[3] the Nîtiśâstras are concerned with ethics in general of which the Arthaśâstra forms

[1] Ep. Ind., II, No. 26.

[2] Nundo Lal Dey, J.A.S.B., New Series, 1909, pp. 1 et seq., quoting Indian Paṇḍitas in the Land of Snow, 39, 58. Journal of the Indian Buddhist Text Society, 1893. Kern, Manual of Indian Buddhism, 133. Satîśchandra Vidyâbhûsaṇa, Bhâratî, Baiśâkh, 1315, identifies Vikramaśila with Sultânganj in the district of Bhâgalpur.

[3] Garuḍa Purâṇa, CVIII, 1.

a part. So far as contents are concerned, the line between Arthaśâstra and Nitiśâstra is very faint, almost non-existent. It need hardly be stated that the Nitiśâstras, in spite of their profuse classifications, divisions, sub-divisions, and multitudes of details, are essentially theoretical and can be used for the study of practical administration only with the utmost caution.

The Yuktikalpataru.

King Bhoja of Dhârâ in Mâlwâ, of the 11th century A.D., is known to Hindu tradition as a second Vikramâditya.[1] To him is attributed the authorship of many works on Yoga, philosophy, astronomy, medicine, prosody, and Alaṅkâra. He is said to have written the Yuktikalpataru which treats of a huge number of topics, covering law, government, military tactics and accoutrements, ship-building, architecture, precious stones, draught animals, etc., etc.[2] Here the royal preceptor, priest, minister, counseller, commander and ambassador are the chief officers of state (pp. 3—6). There are various superintendents, including those of forests. Towns had an administrative machinery of their own. Espionage plays an important part in the working of the administration.[3]

Vaiśampâyana.

A Nîtiprakâśikâ, attributed to Vaiśampâyana,[4] enjoyed some vogue in the Middle Ages but it contains hardly anything new. It pays special attention to archery.[5]

The Câṇakya Sûtras, as one of the versions of the composition wrongly ascribed to the author of the Arthaśâstra

[1] For the date of Bhoja, Ind. Ant., 1907, pp. 170—72. Ibid. 1912, p. 20.

[2] The Yuktikalpataru has recently been published in the Calcutta Oriental Series.

[3] For the purport of Yuktikalpataru (p. 1); foreign policy and war (pp. 7—14, 17—20); for daṇḍa, p. 15.

[4] Ed. Gustav Oppert, Madras, 1882.

[5] For its history of Nîti, I, 20—28.

is called, is almost valueless. It stresses the importance of discipline on the part of the king but preaches passive obedience and servility to the 'chief god' as the king is called.[1] The work called Vriddha Câṇakya Râjaniti[2] is even more disappointing. It is concerned merely with ethics and worldly wisdom. It is a symptom of decline that Niti and Râjaniti had altered their meaning.

The Câṇakya Sûtras.

About the eleventh century A.D. Padmagupta in his Navasâhasâṅikacarita[3] celebrated the glories of Sindhurâja in the usual manner and reflected a state of feudalism.

Padmagupta.

The Jaina writer Merutuṅgâcârya composed his Prabandha Cintâmaṇi[4] only in the 14th century but he based his work on older tradition and may be noticed here. He is half-mythical in his earlier narration and, though he gains in sobriety as he descends to later times, he retains his passion for tales which rebound to the glory of Jainism. The old stories of fabulous kings reflect the traditional patronage of learning at Hindu courts.[5] Ministers are seen offering wholesome advice to kings and giving them instruction from Niti works.[6] On the other hand, the pages of Merutuṅgâcârya show some royal officers oppressing the people. The king, however, comes to the rescue, redresses their grievances and grants them certain exemp-

Merutuṅgâcârya.

[1] Câṇakya Sûtras, 14, 87, 372, 445, 532-33.

[2] Published Ahmedâbad, 1903.

[3] Ed. Bombay Sanskrit Series, No. 53. For a criticism, J. R. A. S., 1907, p. 1072.

[4] Translated from Sanskrit Mss. by C. H. Tawney. On the reliability of the dates, R. Sewell, J.R.A.S., 1920, pp. 331—41.

[5] Ibid., 75—77, 38.

[6] Ibid., 88.

tions from taxes.[1] Palmists and astrologers are there at the court.[2] The ideal of a prince's education is set forth when Bhoja is said to have studied all the treatises on 'king-craft,' learnt the use of thirty-six weapons and "attained the further shore of the ocean of 72 accomplishments."[3] The king holds religious assemblies of representatives of all sects.[4] There is a tragic touch in the fourth chapter where king Bhîmasena, unwilling to give the throne to Kumârapâla, his son by a low-caste woman, seeks to encompass his destruction. But the prince flies away.[5]

The Kathâsaritsâgara.

In the latter half of the eleventh century A.D. Somadeva composed the Kathâsaritsâgara—'the Ocean of the Rivers of Stories'—largely on the basis of the Bṛihatkathâ, which, as already noted, had been written by an earlier creative author Guṇâḍhya in the Paiśâci dialect.[6] In spite of some indubitable Buddhist influence, the tone and spirit of the Kathâsaritsâgara are mainly Brahmanic. It is, therefore, all the more interesting to find at the very outset a Brâhmaṇa sentenced to death by the king. The fictitious story serves to indicate that the Brahmanic claim to exemption from capital punishment was not always respected in practice. In the stories the ideal of kingship is high,[7] but there were kings who fell into ease and luxury and left the cares of state to ministers.[8]

[1] Ibid., 77-78.

[2] Ibid., 9, 32.

[3] Ibid., 32.

[4] Ibid., 62.

[5] Ibid., 116.

[6] On the Bṛihatkathâ, Keith, J.R.A.S., 1909, pp. 145 et seq. J. S. Speyer, Studies on the Kathâsaritsâgara.

[7] Kathâsaritsâgara, tr. Tawney, Vol. I, Part I, p. 163, for the king's duties of the day.

[8] Ibid., p. 67.

The grant of a large area of land to a Brâhmaṇa by royal charter is interesting in the light of contemporary inscriptions.[1] Later, the rule of Mlecchas is painted as one of persecution of Brâhmaṇas, interruption of sacrifices and abduction of hermits' daughters.[2]

The Puruṣaparîkṣâ.

Vidyâpati Ṭhâkura's Puruṣaparîkṣâ, though actually composed in the 14th or 15th century A.D., belongs to the older tradition and can be noticed here. Kings were only too often arbitrary. For instance, king Nanda of Kusumpur deprives his minister Śakaṭâra of all his property and throws him into prison. Another tyrannical king whom even the sages failed to bring to duty is expelled by the people and his brother is placed on the throne.[3] There were ministers who drew the minds of their masters away from duty and themselves practically usurped all authority. Ministers, we are told, are naturally of crooked minds.[4] Every king had a sort of council which, it is urged, should consist of men versed in the Śâstras.[5]

Amitagati Sûri.

The eleventh century saw another story-book of some literary merit, the Dharmaparîkṣâ by the Jain writer Amitagati Sûri, author of Subhâṣitaratnasaṁdoha, Pañcasaṁgraha, Śrâvakâcârya, and other works. In spite of its strong sectarian animosities, the Dharmaparîkṣâ adopts the current political maxims of Brâhmaṇas. In its pages, small Râjas flit to and fro. Another Jaina "treasury of

[1] Ibid., p. 43.

[2] Ibid., Vol. II, Book XVIII, Canto CXX.

[3] Puruṣaparîkṣâ, No. XXXII, Tale of a Repentant Sinner.

[4] Ibid., XIII, Tale of a Base Informer.

[5] Ibid., XVII, Tale of a Man learned in the Śâstras. See also the Story of One well-versed in Wisdom. For royal patronage see XXII, Tale of a Man knowing the Art of Singing.

stories," the Kathâkoṣa[1] gives many tales of princes and princesses and shows the small feudalised state to be the norm in Indian politics. At the same time it discloses intrigues, conspiracies and assassination at courts. Kings were sometimes whimsical. A king forcibly seized the wife of another man.[2] There is another interesting political touch in an earlier story in which a king appoints a favourite merchant keeper of the Great Seal.[3]

The Kathâkoṣa.

Only a few other works need be noticed. In the Nalodaya wrongly ascribed to Kâlidâsa, a kingdom is treated like private property which can be pawned, lost and regained at dice. The theme recurs in Trivikramabhaṭṭa's Nalacampû. The same story was worked out towards the close of the 12th century A.D. by Śrī Harṣa into the Naiṣadhīya, one of the five Mahâkâvyas of Sanskrit Literature.[4] The dramatic piece Satya Hariścandra Nâṭaka[5] also regards the realm as private property which can be given away to a saint as if it were a piece of furniture. Ballâlasena's Bhoja Prabandha,[6] reproducing the old political maxims holds forth the king as the guide, teacher and exemplar of his subjects.[7] Kavirâja's Râghavapâṇḍavīya simultaneously relates the tales of the Râmâyaṇa and the Mahâbhârata and thus represents the height of artificiality.[8] It

Miscellaneous.

---

[1] Translated from Sanskrit Mss. by C. H. Tawney (Oriental Translation Fund, New Series II).

[2] Kathâkoṣa, p. 33.

[3] Ibid., p. 5.

[4] Ed. with Nârâyaṇa's commentary by Śivadatta, Bombay, 1907.

[5] Ed. B. R. Apte and S. V. Puranik, 3rd edition, Bombay, 1923.

[6] Ed. Vâsudeva Sharma, Bombay, 1921.

[7] Ibid., pp. 8, 10.

[8] Ed. with the commentary of Śaśadhara by Kâśinâth Pâṇḍuraṅg Parab, in the Kâvyamâlâ, No. 62, Bombay, 1897. The work was supposed to belong to the ninth century A.D. but see Keith, Classical Sanskrit Literature, 56, who dates it about 1190 A.D.

echoes the old politics and is hardly representative of its age.

An Apabramśa work.

To the last age of ancient India belongs an interesting Apabhraṁśa Jaina work, Bhavisattakahâ by Dhanapâla.[1] The incidental political references in the story, particularly in the thirteenth and fourteenth saṁdhis or chapters, show that the western half of North India was divided into a number of principalities, some of which were independent, while the rest acknowledged the suzerainty of others. Sâmanta is the term used to denote vassals of this character. A circle of suzerainty comprising an overlord and his vassals was known as a Maṇḍala.

Western India.

During this period, as in the preceding one, the institutions of the North generally resemble those of the Deccan and, to a slightly lesser extent, those of the extreme south. There were, of course, many differences of detail and nomenclature. It is worth while bringing out a few points of comparison and contrast by analysing some typical inscriptions. In the Bhandup Plates of the year 1026 A.D., found in the Thânâ district of the modern Bombay Presidency, Chittarâjadeva is called Mahâmaṇḍaleśvara, and Mahâsâmantâdhipati who has attained the Pañcamahâśabdas. Like all big feudatories he has sub-feudatories under him and runs an administration which resembles the prevailing system of the country. But his chief officers seem to fall into three categories, Mantrin, Amâtya, and Pradhâna. They may be translated as counsellor, minister and chief but the exact degree of the difference between

[1] Ed. C. D. Dalal and P. D. Gune, Gaekwad Oriental Series, XX. The work is also called Bhavisattakahâ or Suyapañcamîkahâ. From internal references it is clear that the work was composed after the 9th century A.D. while linguistic evidence fixes the lower limit at the 12th century A.D. (Introduction, pp. 1—4).

them cannot be ascertained. Mention is made of the Sarvâdhikârin, chief executive head, and two Saṁdhivigrahikas. Probably, they would fall under one or other of the above categories. Between the Mantrin and the Amâtya is mentioned the Purohita. There are two general terms for minor officers: Apradhâna ('not chief') and Naiyogika, functionaries. Four classes of local officers are mentioned—Râṣṭrapati, probably the governor of a province, Viṣayapati, district-officer, Nagarapati, city-officer, Grâmapati, village-officer. Niyuktas seem to be lower government servants, Râjapuruṣa is probably the general name for servants of state.[1] A distinction is drawn between Janapada, people of the country and Pauratrivarga, three classes of citizens.[2] It will be observed that the administrative nomenclature of Western India was different from that of the North.

The titles of suzerainty and vassalage are generally applied in the Deccan and south exactly as in the north.

Titles.

The few peculiarities may be noticed. In an inscription of 1072 A.D, for instance, Jayasiṁha III is called Mahârâjâdhirâja, Parameśvara and Śrîprithvivallabha.[3] In the Pithampur Plates of Vira Colâ, Râjaparameśvara is substituted for Parameśvara and the fact of suzerainty over Râjas is brought out more prominently.[4] In another inscription one of the three grand titles is omitted.[5] In the Soraikkavur Plates of Virûpâkṣa of the 13th century A.D., a Mahâmaṇḍaleśvara styles himself Râjâdhirâja Râjaparameśvara.[6] This is one of the rare instances of big feudatories assuming partly the titles of

[1] Compare the grant of the Raṣṭrakûṭa King Govind IV, dated Śaka 853 (A.D. 930) which mentions inter alia Râṣṭrapati, Grâmakûṭa, Yuktakas, and Upayuktakas (Ep. Ind., VII, 39-40).

[2] Ep. Ind., XII, No. 31.

[3] Ep. Ind., IV, No. 30.

[4] Ep. Ind., V, No. 10.

[5] Ep. Ind., V, No. 15.

[6] Ep. Ind., VIII, No. 31.

suzerainty. Perhaps the ruler had many big sub-feudatories under him and was developing into a suzerain. For great suzerains some new grandiloquent titles like Sakalabhuvanacakravartin and Tribhuvanacakravartin had emerged.[1] The Chebrolu Inscription of Vikrama Cola (c. 1126 A.D.) calls the king Mahârâjâdhirâja, Râjaparameśvara, Paramabhaṭṭâraka, Râjarâjendra, Vîramahendra.[2]

The Kalbhan Jaina Inscription from the Sampgaum Tâlukâ of the Belgaum district of the modern Bombay Presidency belonging to the 11th century A.D. throws some additional light on feudatories. A Mahâmaṇḍaleśvara who paid homage as usual to a Paramabhaṭṭâraka Mahârâjâdhirâja Parameśvara, had been duly invested with the five Mahâśabdas. His capital is called the best of cities. He had been decorated with the binding on of the Koṅguṇi fillet of rulership (Paṭṭabandha); he was entitled to be heralded in public by the sounds of the victorious drum of a Śâsanadevi; he had for an ornament the banner of a bunch of feathers; he was governing the Gaṅgavâḍi Ninety-six thousand.[3] In the Gadag Inscription of Vira-Ballâla II, of the year 1192 A.D., Jagaddeva, probably a feudatory of the Western Câlukya king Vikramâditya VI, is called a Saptâṅga. Elsewhere he is designated a Mahâmaṇḍaleśvara. It appears that Saptâṅga was now one of the new feudal titles.[4]

The Pithampuram Inscription of Pṛithvîśvara of the 12th century A.D. from the Kiṣṭnâ district shows a line of hereditary Mahâmaṇḍaleśvaras ruling a territory divided into Viṣayas and conducting an administration of the regular type.[5] The Salotji Pillar Inscription of the 11th

---

[1] Ep. Ind., VII, No. 23.

[2] Ep. Ind., VI, No. 21 (A). Here a Mahâmaṇḍaleśvara has got the five Mahâśabdas.

[3] Ind. Ant., XVIII, 1889, pp. 309 et seq.

[4] Ep. Ind., VI, No. 10. [5] Ep. Ind., IV, No. 4.

or 12th century A.D. from the Bijâpur district shows that feudatories had banners with peculiar emblems of their own. A golden Garuḍa marked the banner of a Mahâmaṇḍaleśvara who had attained to the five Mahâśabdas.[1] The Nadagam Plate of Vajrahasta, of the year 1058 A.D. has a two-fold interest. It discloses a line of hereditary Mahârâjas becoming Mahârâjâdhirâjas. Next it shows that Viṣayas could be created *ad hoc* and that some of the Viṣayas were very small. Vajrahasta calls together his ministers and other people, clubs twelve villages together, designates the aggregate as the Viṣaya of Velpura and makes a grant of it.[2]

The Gañjam Plates of Pṛithivivarmadeva of the 12th or 13th century give the three grand titles as well as that of Mahârâja to the king. The latter is spoken of as having brought the whole Sâmanta-cakra (circle of feudatories) under him.[3]

The same system is reflected in the Managoli Inscriptions of the 12th century.[4] The Ablur Inscriptions of the same century show several grades of feudatories.[5] In the six Inscriptions at Tirunamanallur, too, feudatories abound.[6] An inscription of the time of Pratâparudra of the Tâmil country speaks of the ruler of a province as Mahâmaṇḍala-cakravartin. Obviously, he was a feudatory.[7]

The Belaturn Inscription of the year 1057 A.D. of the time of Râjendradeva from Mysore vividly pictures the process of elevation in feudal rank. The Chola king presents the chief of Kudiyas, who, by the way was a Śûdra, with a pearl umbrella, a conch, cymbals, and a royal elephant. So he

[1] Ep. Ind., IV, No. 6 (c).
[2] Ep. Ind., IV, No. 24.
[3] Ep. Ind., IV, No. 26.
[4] Ep. Ind., V, No. 3.
[5] Ep. Ind., V, No. 25.
[6] Ep. Ind., VII, No. 19.
[7] Ep. Ind., VII, No. 18.

was created a Mâṇḍalika.[1] An Inscription of Buddharâja brings into view a line of hereditary Mahâmaṇḍaleśvaras.[2] In the Saṁgamner Copper Plate Inscription of the Yâdava Bhillama II a Mahâsâmanta who had obtained the five Mahâśabdas is described as the supreme lord of the city of Dvârâvatî. That city was probably his headquarters.[3]

The Kolhâpur Inscription of the Śilahara Vijayâditya of the year 1143 A.D., from Kolhâpur State, shows a Mahâmaṇḍaleśvara, who has attained the five Mahâśabdas, making a grant to a Jaina shrine in the usual style.[4]

The Bhâdâna Grant of Aparâjita, belonging to the close of the 10th century A.D., shows a Mahâsâmantâdhipati Mahâmaṇḍaleśvarapañcamahâśabda commanding sub-feudatories, regular officers, heads of towns, people of Sthânas—police-stations—chief men and common people of the three principal castes. A Koṅkan Viṣaya comprised 1,400 villages. Here part of the revenue is not alienated to the grantee.[5] It also proves that warfare often resulted in the enslavement of large numbers of men and women. The Gaṇapeśvara Inscription of the time of Gaṇapati, of the year 1231 A.D., from the Kiṣṭnâ district, refers to families which supplied hereditary servants of state. One of them, a special favourite with the king, received the dignity of a general and of a commander of the elephant troop along with a palanquin, a parasol and other emblems.[6]

The Dirghasi Inscription of Vanapati or Banapati of the year 1075-76 A.D. shows a feudatory—a Mâṇḍalika—occupying the position of a Pratihârin or chamberlain at the court of his suzerain, Râjarâja.[7]

[1] Ep. Ind., VI, No. 10.
[2] Ep. Ind., VI, No. 26.
[3] Ep. Ind., III, No. 10.
[4] Ep. Ind., III, No. 27, also 29, 33.
[5] Ep. Ind., III, No. 37, also 40. For sub-feudatories, also 42, 43.
[6] Ep. Ind., III, No. 15.
[7] Ep. Ind., IV, No. 45.

The Anmakonda Inscription of Prola (1117 A.D.) shows that a Mahâmaṇḍaleśvara had his headquarters at a chief town, employed a sub-feudatory as his Daṇḍâdhinâtha, judicial officer, and was served by an hereditary chief minister.[1] An old-Kanarese Inscription at Terdâl in the southern Marâṭhâ country, of the year 1123-24 A.D., shows that a Mahâmaṇḍaleśvara, with his headquarters at a fine city, having attained the five Mahâśabdas, "had a trivale played before him." He also had the device of an elephant and the figure of a golden eagle on his banner.[2]

A Kadambâ Inscription at Siddâpur near Dhârwâḍ, of the 12th century, throws some light on fiscal arrangements. Various dues were to be collected from various persons for worship and repair of temples. From a body of 60 tenants was to be collected a set of earthern pots for oil; from the gardening tenants, one pâga for caitra and one pâga for pavitra; from another body of 504 tenants, one pâga for caitra and one pâga for pavitra, and one pâga for gâtra; from another body of 300 tenants, one pâga for caitra and one pâga for pavitra.[3]

A few of the officials in Deccan and southern inscriptions may be mentioned by way of contrast with the North. An

Officials.

inscription of the time of Pratâparudra from the Tâmil region calls a general Nâyaka.[4] Several inscriptions use the terms Kaṭakâdhîśa, Kaṭakeśa and Kaṭakarâja to denote either a governor or a superintendent of the royal camp.[5] In the Kaluchumbarru Grant of the eastern Câlukya king Vijayâditya-Amma II, of the year 945 A.D., the Yuvarâja, heir-apparent, is called

[1] Ep. Ind., IX, No. 35.

[2] Ind. Ant., XIV, pp. 14 et seq.

[3] Ind. Ant., XI, 1882, pp. 273 et seq.

[4] Ep. Ind., VII, No. 18.

[5] Ep. Ind., VII, No. 25; Ind. Ant., VII, 17, 183, 189; XII, 93; XIII, 138; XX, 17, 106, 417.

Bhûpati. Here the office of Grâmakûṭa or village headman is given to a man in perpetuity.[1] In the 14th century Raṅganâtha Inscription of Goppana the chief minister is called Mahâpradhâna.[2] The Nilagunḍa Plates of Vikramâditya VI (1087—1123 A.D.) mention Âyuktakas and Niyuktakas as subordinate officers.[3]

Female sovereigns.

Two grants of Daṇḍimahâdevî from the Gañjam district of the modern Northern Circars (in the Southern Presidency), of the thirteenth century A.D., are unusually interesting as bringing to view female sovereigns who appear so rarely in the annals of ancient India. The queen Daṇḍimahâdevî is styled Paramabhaṭṭârikâ, Mahârâjâdhirâja Parameśvarî. Her mother had also been a sovereign. Daṇḍimahâdevî issues the grant in the usual manner and addresses her command first to Mahâsâmantas and Mahârâjas—the big feudatories. Later, special mention is made of the Sâmantas and Sâmavâjins who dwelt in the eastern sub-division of Vardûkhaṇḍa-viṣaya and who constituted a class of feudatories by themselves. Towards the end mention is made of a Râṇaka, probably a small feudatory, who acts as the Dûtaka. The central local officers mentioned here are the same as in the Northern grants of the last age of ancient India. The village is granted with the weavers, Gokuṭas, distillers of spirituous liquors, other artisans, hamlets, thickets, and landing-places in accordance with the Bhûmichidra maxim. The meaning is that some dues were usually levied from those who followed the occupations or used the places enumerated and that all such dues were now alienated to a Brâhmaṇa.[4]

[1] Ep. Ind., VII, No. 25.

[2] Ep. Ind., VI, No. 33.

[3] Ep. Ind., XII, No. 19.

[4] Ep. Ind., VI, No. 13.

CHAPTER XVII.

Conclusion.

Medieval India.

The close of the twelfth and the beginning of the thirteenth century A.D. saw the destruction of Hindu independence and the establishment of Musalmân rule over the greater part of North India. After another century the daring Khiljî leader Alâ-ud-dîn planted the Muslim standard on the southern edge of the peninsula. The four or five centuries which follow may be designated 'the Medieval Period' of Indian history, in preference to 'Mohammadan Period' which term implies a serious underrating of the presence and strength of the Hindu elements all through. It may be admitted at once that the military strength of the Islamic dynasties was the dominating factor in Indian politics for five centuries but Hindu culture, literature, art and social life were never swept away. They received some influences from Islam but in their turn they exercised yet deeper influence on the higher life of the Muslims.[1] Nor did the influence of Hindu political ideas and institutions die out with the thirteenth or fourteenth century. There were regions where the Hindu administration survived, though in a modified form, while it was vital enough to affect the political arrangements of the Musalmâns all over the country.

---

[1] For illustrations of this phenomenon, see Macauliffe, Sikh Religion, particularly Vol. VI. Beni Prasad, Introduction to Saṁkṣipta Sûra Sâgara (Hindî); Kabîr—a study, Tomorrow (Ahmedâbâd), 1922, pp. 521—40; Kabîr, his Song and his Mission, Ibid., 1923, pp. 41—47.

The Vijayanagara Empire.

South of the Kṛiṣṇâ, the old Hindu life re-asserted itself soon after the first Muslim shock and resumed its cultural and political career under the ægis of the Vijayanagara Empire which lasted in vigour until the battle of Tâlikoṭa in 1565. There the old stream of Hindu political thought and institutions continued and developed into a new phase. The Vijayanagara empire was essentially a feudal-federal structure of the ancient Hindu type; the suzerains and feudatories used high-sounding titles as of old; the state regulated the economic life of the people; the courts patronised learning, poetry and art; the traditions of religious toleration were, as a rule, maintained.[1] Even after the fall of Vijayanagara, the Hindu system did not come to an end. Neither the Deccan Sultâns who had humbled Vijayanagara nor the great Mughal Emperor Auraṅgzeb, before whom they went down in their turn in the last quarter of the seventeenth century, succeeded in establishing any stable Muslim administration in the south. Hindu principalities lingered on until they were engulfed in the currents and cross-currents of the Anglo-French struggle for supremacy in the south which terminated in the latter half of the eighteenth century. Certain features of their polity were adopted by the English East India Company whose dominion was established over nearly the whole of the present Madras Presidency by the close of the eighteenth century. Thus, as Krishnaswamy Aiyangar puts it, the administration of the great Cholâs is, through the Vijayanagara Empire, the ancestor of the present Madras revenue and fiscal administration.

[1] S. Krishnaswamy Aiyangar, Sources of Vijayanagar History; Contributions of South India to Indian Culture; South India and her Musalmân Invaders; R. Sewell, A Forgotten Empire; Major, India in the Fifteenth Century. The inscriptions of the period are given in Epigraphia Indica, Epigraphia Carnatica, Madras Government Epigraphist's Reports, South Indian Inscriptions.

Further north, the Koṅkan, the narrow strip of land between the Western Ghats and the sea retained its autonomy throughout the medieval period. The Marâṭhâs whose homeland it formed were indeed deeply influenced by their contact with the Deccan Sultâns, particularly, by the Nizâmśâhî court of Ahmadnagar, where they played the game of high politics with skill and dexterity. Through the Sultanates the Marâṭhâs also received ideas and suggestions from the Mughals whose impact roused their energies in the seventeenth century A.D.[1] Nevertheless, the new Marâṭhâ State which reared its head in the latter half of the seventeenth century and which, within two generations, developed into an empire, reproduced certain features of ancient Hindu polity. The coronation of Śivâjî, the founder of the Marâṭhâ power, which symbolised the emergence of a new factor of first-rate importance in Indian politics, was performed at Râigaḍh in 1674 A.D. in studiously orthodox Brahmanic style. The administrative system of the Marâṭhâs represented a fusion of Hindu and Musalmân elements. The number of the Aṣṭapradhâna or Council of Eight which Śivâjî instituted reminds one of the Mahâbhârata and Manusmṛiti. The Council of Bârbhâis or Twelve Brothers which emerged later and which was destined to be set aside by Nânâ Fadnavîs, also carries the mind to ancient India. The designations of some of the officers —Amâtya, Mantrî, Sacіva, Senâpati—were borrowed from old Hindu practice. The numerous Lekhakas formed the counterpart of Kâyasthas.[2] The eighteen Kârkhânâs,

The Marâṭhâ Administrative System.

[1] On Marâṭhâ History, Grant Duff, History of the Mahrattas; Kincaid and Parasnis, History of the Marâṭhâ People; Ranade, Rise of the Marâṭhâ Power; J. N. Sarkar, Śivâjî and his Times; G. S. Sardesai, Marâṭhî Riyâsat (Marâṭhî) and Main Currents of Marâṭhâ History.

[2] Chiṭṇîs, p. 168.

and twelve Mahâls, altogether thirty departments which Śivâji organised, were designed, of course, primarily to meet the exigencies of the situation. But naturally they were based partly on old Marâṭhâ practice and on contemporary institutions in other parts of India. Their description in the Marâṭhâ chronicles reminds one as much of Abul Fazl's Âin-i-Akbarî, the astounding Imperial Gazetteer of the Mughal Empire as of the Kauṭiliya Arthaśâstra and the inscriptions which lie between the Gupta period and the last age of ancient India. They included Treasury, Cash, Jewellery, Harem, Agriculture, Liquor, Chariots, Mints, etc.[1] In the domain of local government the designation of the Marâṭhâ village officer, the Pâṭil, corresponded to the Paṭṭakila of the inscriptions which, in its turn, was akin to the Akṣapaṭalika or Mahâkṣapaṭalika which occurs so frequently in ancient epigraphic records. The Pâṭil answered also to the ancient Grâmâdhipati and, like him, performed some police, judicial and fiscal duties. The other Marâṭhâ village officer, Kulakarṇi, is reminiscent of the ancient Karaṇika. The dues levied from the people again recall the ancient inscriptions and are, in fact, more numerous than those mentioned in any single inscription of old. A list of twenty-two of them has been compiled from a Marâṭhi deed of sale. Besides the usual land revenue, they include a bundle of fuel, a quantity of grain, and twenty-five bundles of jawâr sticks from each cultivator, nine ṭâkas of oil from each oil-mill, thirteen leaves per day from each seller of betel leaves, one goat from each herd on the Daśerâ (Vijayadaśami) day, one piece of cloth per loom per year from all classes of weavers, half a cocoanut from every marriage-negotiation, every ordinary marriage as well as every widow-remarriage, some

[1] Sabhâsad, pp. 94-95.

vegetables from vegetable-growers, usual tolls from each seller in the market and every petty trader's stall, ¼th seer per bag of grocery from a grocer's shop, etc., etc. These payments in kind went to support the local officials as in ancient times. In spite of all their weaknesses, the Marâṭhâ rulers were, like the kings and statesmen of old, often conscious of high ideals. "Propagate the Dharma of Mahârâṣṭra," said Râmadâsa, the preceptor of Śivâji to the latter's son Sambhâji.[1] The Marâṭhâ regime was the Augustan age of Marâṭhi literature and was equally remarkable for the intense cultivation of Sanskrit learning. The Marâṭhâ rulers covered the country with temples and images, forts and palaces, tanks and anicuts, many of which still survive intact or in ruins. Their charity halls were almost innumerable. Religious toleration was the rule in Mahârâṣṭra. In all this the Marâṭhâs were in line with the ancient Hindu tradition. They were in line with it also at some weak points. The administrative organisation was not rigid enough. The Marâṭhâ empire of the eighteenth century was a mere confederacy. The Gâekwâḍ of Barodâ, Sindhiâ of Gwâlior, Holkar of Indore and the Bhonslâ of Nâgpur recognised the hegemony of the *de facto* king, Peśwâ of Poonâ, or the *de jure* monarch, the Râja of Satârâ, in a very rough and ready fashion. They would sometimes rally to his standard and sometimes war with him. Sometimes they would fight among themselves and sometimes band together against the common foe. With obvious differences of setting and detail, they acted the political drama of ancient India on the stage of the eighteenth century.

Even in the North where, thanks to the continuous influx from the North-west, Muslim influence was much deeper

[1] For the political reflections of Râmadâsa (1608—82 A.D.), see his Marâṭhî Classic, Dâsabodha, Daśaka X, Samâsa 6; XII, 10; XIV, 6; XV, 3; XVI, 10; XIX, 6, etc.

and more extensive, there were a few small tracts and one large area which retained their autonomy for long. There Hindu institutions survived, of course, in a modified form. The subject is too vast to be treated here in detail but a few instances from a late period may be given to illustrate the persistence of the Hindu system. As late as the seventeenth century A.D , Khurdâ, a small, rather primitive district on the borders of Orissâ and Golkuṇḍâ, modelled its army on the Hindu system which had become antiquated by that time.[1] In the seventeenth century, again, the small state of Kiṣṭwâḍ to the south of Kashmir, close to the Puñjâb border, had a fiscal system which bore some affinity to that of the Hindus. Every customer had to pay four rupees per two seers of saffron purchased. Fines, always heavy and particularly severe in the case of rich folk, formed the greatest source of the public income.[2] The annals of Kâṅgrâ in the north-eastern Puñjâb, which, in spite of 52 sieges did not surrender to Musalmânas until 1620 A.D., disclose the old Hindu feudal-federalism in full force. The 'zemindârs,' as the Hindu chiefs are called by Muslim historians, stood in relations of suzerainty and vassalage to one another.[3] The Bâra Bhuñyas or Twelve Landholders who exercised sway in some Bengal tracts in a semi-independent capacity after the Muslim conquest and who created trouble

In the North.

[1] Bahâristân-i-Ghaibî, Paris Ms., summarised by J. N. Sarkar, J. B. O. R. S., II, Part I, pp. 53—56. Jahâṅgîrnâmâ (ed. Rogers, tr. Beveridge), I, 438.

[2] Motamad Khân, Iqbâlnâmâ, pp. 143—46; Jahâṅgîrnâmâ (Rogers and Beveridge), II, 137—39 ; Shâh Nawâz Khân, Maâsir-ul-umarâ (tr. Beveridge), I, 490.

[3] Jahâṅgîrnâmâ (R. and B.), II, 184 : Fath Kâṅgrâ in Elliot and Dowson, History of India as told by its own Historians, VI, 526 See also Elliot and Dowson, II, 34, 444-45; III, 405—7, 515, 570 ; IV, 67, 415, 455.

for Muslim rulers until the seventeenth century, also organised themselves, rather loosely, after the traditional Hindu system.[1]

Râjputânâ

It is, however, Râjpûtânâ which furnishes the most striking example of the survival of Hindu institutions in the North. Here the Râjpûts established themselves after they had been driven out of the Gangetic plains. Though forced to acknowledge Muslim suzerainty from time to time, the Râjpût States, with the exception of Ajmer, the *point d'appui*, were never annexed to Muslim empire. In the eighteenth century and early years of the nineteenth, the Marâṭhâs harassed the Râjpûts but did not extinguish their autonomy. In modern times the British Government has left them pretty much to themselves. The old institutions were certainly modified by three factors—the presence of a large aboriginal population, constant pressure from outside and the example of Muslim organisation. Nevertheless, before modern influences and, particularly, the modern means of communication, warfare and industrial organisation affected Râjpûtânâ, its institutions resembled those of ancient India in many points. In Tod's Annals and Antiquities of Râjasthân, supplemented by more recent additions to our knowledge, Râjpûtânâ appears in some respects as a miniature edition of ancient India.[2] The small size of the state, internecine warfare, relationships of suzerainty and vassalage, constant attempts to throw off the yoke—all

[1] James Wise, J. A. S. B., 1874, pp. 194—214; Ibid., 1875, pp. 181—83; Beveridge, J. A. S.B., 1904, pp. 57—63; Hosten, J. A. S. B., 1913, pp. 437—49. The Bengalî works, Pratâpâditya by Nikhil Nath Roy and 'The Life of Pratâpâditya, the last Hindu King of Bengal' by Satya Charan Śâstri give the traditions which cluster round the figure of the leader of the Bâra Bhuñyas. See also two other Bengalî works, 'History of Murshidâbâd' by Nikhil Nath Roy and 'History of Bengal' by R. D. Banerji.

[2] Tod, Annals and Antiquities of Râjasthân (Routledge and Sons); Kavirâja Shyamal Das, Vira Vinoda (Hindî); Gauri Shankar Hirachand Ojha, Râjasthâna (Hindî); Naiṇasîkhyât, a valuable original work, pub. 1925; Tessitori, Historical and Bardic Survey of Râjpûtânâ.

this carries the mind to the ancient age. In Râjpûtânâ there were gradations of feudal chieftains, in some places, four in successive order.[1] Here, too, vassals were sometimes associated in the administration of the suzerain's territory.[2] Suzerains and feudatories alike had big harems which, as in ancient India, sometimes reacted dangerously on the politics of the state. A state was parcelled out into a number of districts. In certain tracts a district comprised generally from fifty to one hundred townships and villages, though the proportion was sometimes exceeded. Many of these divisions were called Caurâsis—'eighty fours'—collections of 'eighty-four' villages, an expression which reminds one of Central Indian and Southern administrative jargon. Caurâsi, however, is like eighteen, a sort of sacred number among the Hindus. It only indicates that the average number of villages in such a district would range from somewhere about seventy-five to somewhere about a hundred. The chief officer of the district performed both civil and judicial functions. There was also another officer charged with military, fiscal and some judicial duties. The judicial procedure reminds one of ancient India. A town or a village had a Cabûtrarâ or court where the headman or the judicial officer, assisted by some inhabitants of the locality, marked out by public opinion for indefinite periods, administered justice.[3] Taxes and tolls were numerous as in ancient India. Besides the land revenue and customs, we read of Ganim-burrâr, war-tax, corresponding perhaps to the Turuṣkadaṇḍa of the eleventh and twelfth centuries A.D., Ghar-burrâr, house-tax, Hal-burrâr, plough-tax, Neotâ-burrâr, marriage-tax.[4] There were various other imposts in different

[1] Tod, Annals and Antiquities of Râjasthân (ed. Routledge), I, p. 117.

[2] Ibid., I, 116.

[3] Ibid., I, 119-20.

[4] Ibid., I, 118, 119.

regions, such as those on sales.[1] As in ancient days there were special frontier-officers always appointed from the head-quarters and corresponding to the Antapâlas of literature and the inscriptions.[2] At the top of the administration stood a few ministers, often four in number, generally headed by a Pradhâna or chief minister who, needless to say, was responsible to the Râja.[3] As in ancient days again, government servants, high and low alike, were not infrequently hereditary. Payments were often made in grants of land which, along with the hereditary transmission of office, must have accentuated feudalism. There were numerous court and household officers who held large grants of land. As in antiquity there were titles and other insignia of dignity such as standards, kettledrums, heralds.[4] Râjpût magnates followed the ancient tradition of making grants to poets, scholars, priests, or favourites and remitting the whole or part of the revenues. The state sometimes concerned itself with minute affairs of life. Thus, it was once enacted that none shall attempt to carry anything away from the public feast. A Jaina obtained a charter to the effect that none shall eat after sunset.[5] It may be added that custom and usage regulated the rights and tenures of land and public affairs in general in Râjpûtânâ as in ancient India.[6]

Evidence of Literature.

The fundamental political conditions of Râjpûtânâ are well reflected in the great Hindi epic Pṛithvirâjarâso which, though ascribed by tradition to Candabardâi, the bard of Pṛithvirâja Cauhâna, the renowned, though ultimately unsuccessful, champion of Hindu India against Muhammad

[1] Ibid., I, 111.
[2] Ibid., I, 116.
[3] Ibid., I, 119.
[4] Ibid., I, 115, 116.
[5] Ibid., I, 111.
[6] Ibid., I, 110; on feudal incidents, Ibid., I, Ch. III, pp. 128—41.

Ghorí in the 12th century A.D., is really a collection of bardic lays composed in Ḍiṅgal Hindi, the peculiar mixed idiom of heroic poetry, by various minstrels through several centuries in medieval Râjpûtânâ. Some passages are as late as the seventeenth century A.D.[1] Râjas, Sâmantas, aristocrats abound throughout the Râso. Its feudalism is sometimes several layers deep. The government which is mirrored in its pages has fallen from the ancient cultural standards but its structure, while certainly less elaborate, follows the old pattern. The conclusions to which the study of the Râso leads are amply supported by other Râjpût compositions of a similar type which are preserved in Mss. in palace libraries and private collections, particularly in Jaipur, Jodhpur, Udaipur, and Bûndi. The prefaces or conclusions of many ordinary Hindi and Sanskrit books which were written or copied in the latter half of the sixteenth or in the seventeenth century and which may be read in Mss. in various collections in the modern state of Jaipur bring out one very interesting fact. At the commencement or at the end they glorify Râjâ Mân Singh who, as a vassal of the Mughal emperors Akbar and Jahâṅgir, ruled his hereditary patrimony of Âmer (Amber or modern Jaipur) and also occupied one of the very highest positions in the service of his suzerain. He governed an important imperial province like Bengal. He commanded imperial armies on momentous expeditions, even against the Râjpût state of Chittor or modern Udaipur. In the notices of Jaipur Mss. his campaigns are represented as a Digvijaya and celebrated as the conquest of the

[1] The work has been edited and published by the Kâśî Nâgarî Pracâriṇî Sabhâ, Benâres and the Nâgarî Pracâriṇî Sabhâ, Ārrâh. For criticism, Miśra Brothers, Miśra Bandhu Vinoda, I, pp. 227—36; Hindî Navaratna, Ch. I; Kavirâja Shyamal Das, J.A.S.B., 1886, Pt. I, pp. 5—65. In reply to the last, Mohan Lal Vishnu Lal Pandya, A Defence of Pṛithvîrâja Râso, Benâres, 1887.

whole world or the whole of India. Yet he was only a feudatory and an imperial officer. Once again the Hindu mind failed to grasp firmly the distinction between autonomy and independence. It may be added that the career of Mân Singh was by no means unique in the annals of medieval India. Other Râjpût princes like Bhagvân Dâs, Sarbuland Râi, Jaswant Singh, Jai Singh, while governing their own territories, managed to play a high role in imperial politics and to rank in the highest grade of imperial officers—Mansabdârs as they were called. The conclusions on feudalism in Râjpûtânâ hold good of Central India as the genealogies, bardic lays and notices in general books, preserved in Ms. collections in central India, particularly in the palace library of Chhatarpur, prove. Of all this we can be perfectly sure, thanks to the contemporary Persian chronicles. Similar seems to have been the position of vassals in ancient India as indicated by the inscriptions. Like the Râjpût princes of medieval India, they received titles, commands and governorships from the suzerain and at the same time generally ruled their own territories as autonomous princes. If the ancient Hindus had cared to write their history, the statements and indications to this effect in the inscriptions and in Yuan Chwang might have been borne out in ample detail.[1]

Influence of the Hindu on Muslim administration.

It is not merely the Hindu principalities of Medieval India which testify to the persistence of the Hindu administrative tradition. Hindu influence is perceptible on the systems of Muslim administration which prevailed over the greater part of the country from the thirteenth to the seventeenth century and lasted far into

[1] For the careers of Râjpût princes in Mughal service, see Abul Fazl, Akbarnâmâ, Jahângîrnâmâ, Motamad Khân, Iqbâlnâmâ, Kâmgar Husainî, Maâsir-i-Jahângîrî (Khudâ-Bakhsh Ms.), Abdul Hamîd Lâhorî, Pâdshâhnâmâ, Shâh Nawaz Khân, Maâsir-ul-umarâ.

the eighteenth. It may be admitted at once that both the so-called Paṭhân administration (13th—15th century A.D.) and the Mughal administration (16th—18th century A.D.) hit upon devices of their own to meet the circumstances of the times. Then there was the law of the Qurân and Hadis, binding on the whole body of the Faithful, to exercise a deep influence on Muslim politics in India as elsewhere. There is again enough evidence to show that the institutions of Musalmâns in India were affected by the political ideas and practices of the western Muslim countries particularly by the example of the courts of Baghdâd and Cairo and, from the sixteenth century onwards, by Persia, the glory and mistress of the Muslim world. Nevertheless in several important branches the Muslim administration in India largely retained the old practices. Throughout the medieval period the ancient revenue and fiscal arrangements lasted in India. The Muslims simply took over the old fiscal divisions, the old fiscal system and the old classes of officers. For long they did not directly collect the taxes but employed for the purpose agencies which adhered to the old methods. Many of the old divisions and sub-divisions of ordinary local administration were retained. They all appear in the Âin-i-Akbarî, the great imperial gazetteer compiled by the Allâmî Abul Fazl in the reign of Akbar towards the close of the sixteenth century. The Âin, supplemented by Persian chronicles, shows that under the pressure of tradition and environment the Muslim administration was reproducing some of the old conditions. Certain Âin descriptions of even unimportant matters like the imperial harem,[1] ensigns of royalty, *inter alia*, musical instruments,[2] division and sub-division of precious stones,[3] specific gravity,[4] remind one of the

[1] Âin-i-Akbarî, Âin, 15.

[2] Ibid., Âin, 19.

[3] Ibid., Âin, 3.

[4] Ibid., Âin, 14.

Kauṭilīya Arthaśāstra. In the sixteenth century A.D. when the Muslim state in India, after three centuries of unsettlement, had caught up with antiquity, some of the prominent features of Hindu administration re-appeared. Survey and record of land, administrative sub-divisions, ubiquitous espionage, regular secretariats, pomp and glory of the court—all resembled the Hindu system. What was even more important, the regime of Sher Shâh and, following it, the Mughal empire revived the tradition of religious toleration, religious discussion and patronage of learning.[1] The Persian chroniclers have preserved long lists of the literate whom the generosity of the Mughal court raised above want, even to affluence.[2] As one studies the biographies of contemporary Hindī poets, one is struck by the large number of those who received the patronage of Muslim courts. In the lives of some of them, the only certain fact is that they visited the Mughal court at some time.[3] Such was the force of the ancient tradition that the Mughal state

[1] Ābul Fazl, Āīn-i-Akbarī, Akbarnâmâ, Father Anthony Monserrate, Mongolicae Legations Commentarius, ed. Hosten, Asiatic Society of Bengal Memoir, III, No. 9, pp. 508—704, with translation of important passages. Another translation and notes by J. S. Hoyland and S. N Banerji. Father Pierre Du Jarric of Toulouse, Histoire des Choses plus memorables, etc, or Thesaurus Rerum Indicarum, etc. E. D. Maclagan, Jesuit Missions to the Court of Akbar, J. A. S. B., Part I, Vol. LXV, 1896, pp. 38-113. Sir Thomas Roe, Embassy to India, ed. Foster, p. 314; Edward Terry in Purchas His Pilgrims, IX, p. 52; Della Valle, Travels, I, 30, 120—29.

[2] For the reign of Akbar (1556—1605), Āīn-i-Akbarī; for that of Jahâṅgīr, Jahâṅgīrnâmâ, (R. and B.), I, 46; II, 257, 345; Motamad Khân, Iqbalnâmâ, 308; Mohammad Hâdī, p. 20; for the reign of Shâh Jahân (1627—1658), Abdul Hamīd Lâhorī, Pâdshâhnâmâ.

[3] Reports on the Search for Hindī Mss. Kâśī Nâgarī Pracāriṇī Sabhâ; Saiṅgar, Śiva Singh Saroja, Miśra Brothers, Miśra Bandhu Vinoda, Vols. I and II; Beni Prasad, A Few Aspects of Education and Literature under the Great Mughals, Proceedings of the Fifth Meeting of the Indian Historical Records Commission, pp. 44—56.

could not lose sight of Sanskrit in its effort to encourage and guide education. One of the regulations recorded by Abul Fazl lays down that "in studying Sanskrit students ought to learn the Bayakaran (Vyâkaraṇa), Niyai (Nyâya), Bedânta (Vedânta) and Patañjal (Patañjali).[1] Once again, the state, in spite of its predominantly non-Hindu character, made an effort to regulate social life, though in a different manner. Akbar sought to abolish Satî or widow-burning and compulsory widowhood and to discourage child-marriage and polygamy.[2] Jahâṅgîr forbade a new peculiar form of Satî prevalent among Hindu converts to Islâm who buried their widows with their husbands.[3] He interdicted the practice of intermarriage between Hindus and Musalmâns prevalent in some hill-tracts.[4] Another point at which the Muslim state now linked itself with antiquity was philanthropic activity. For instance, following the example of Akbar, Jahâṅgîr commanded the erection of rest-houses and mosques, schools and hospitals and the appointment of physicians in big towns at the expense of the state.[5] The Muslim sovereigns made numerous grants of land to poets, priests, scholars, and favourites The farmâns as they were called, have exactly the same significance as the Sanskrit Śâsana which used to denote grants in ancient India. In form some of the Muslim farmâns bear an astounding resemblance to Hindu

[1] Âîn-i-Akbarî, tr. Blochmann, pp. 278-79.

[2] Al Badâûnî, Muntakhâb-ut-tawârîkh, II, tr. Lowe, p. 367.

[3] Jahâṅgîrnâmâ (R. and B.), II, 181.

[4] Ibid.

[5] Âîn-i-Akbarî. Jahâṅgîrnâmâ (R. and B.), I, Regulations Nos. 2, 10, pp. 8-9. Alî Muhammad Khân, Mirat-i-Ahmadî, I, 209; Khafî Khân, Muntakhâb-ul-lubâb, I. 249. For some minor reforms, Jahâṅgîrnâmâ (R. and B), I, 8, 370-71; II, 150, 151, 168. For the management of a typical rest-house at Ahmedâbâd, P. Della Valle, Travels, I, 95-96, 67. For a typical instance of imperial charity, Jahâṅgîrnâmâ (R. and B.), I, 440.

Tâmrapatras. Thus a Persian farmân of the emperor Jahângîr largely follows the Hindu Sanskrit style of composition.[1] It will be too much to claim that the Musalmâns borrowed all such practices and ideas from Hindus. But apart from *a priori* considerations, a comparison of the Hindu and Muslim administrative systems of the country shows that the latter, in spite of undoubtedly foreign influences in its make-up, steadily approached the old model and derived suggestions from its ever-living tradition in some tracts. In the day-to-day administrative routine, the employment of the same class of Hindu servants under Muslim rule would tend to the perpetuation of old practices. Throughout the Persian chronicles it is the Hindu Kâyasthas on whom the brunt of inferior official work falls. It will be remembered that in the post-Vardhan inscriptions. Smṛitis, Kalhaṇa's Râjataraṅgiṇî and elsewhere the same term is used to designate secretaries, clerks and petty officials in general. By the close of the ancient age the Kâyasthas had formed a class or rather a set of local classes throughout the north of India and in some parts of Gujarât and the Deccan. It is these officers who passed, almost *en bloc*, to service under Muhammadans. They retained their old designation but they exchanged the study of Sanskrit for that of Persian. They retained their Brahmanic faith but, thanks to their environment, they were influenced by Muhammadans in matters of dress, diet, manners and culture. The Kâyastha classes now developed into a caste or rather a number of sub-castes. But whatever the social or cultural transformations which they underwent, the Kâyasthas faithfully handed down and preserved the administrative tradition which their

[1] Jahângîr's farmân is reproduced in J. B. B. R. A. S., 1920-21, pp. 419 et seq.

forefathers had fashioned.[1] At the lowest rung of the ladder the village officers were always drawn from the old classes. This personal element formed an important factor in the transmission of Hindu administrative practices.

Justice.

One of the most obscure topics of Indo-Muslim administration is that of rural justice. It is clear that there were Muslim judicial officers, Qâzis and Mir Adls in towns but neither the Persian chronicles nor the Persian Dastûr-ul-amals, manuals of official regulations and procedure, nor the contemporary European accounts nor general literary works reveal the practices of civil adjudication in villages. The silence of our authorities, which are generally so full and detailed, indicates that the vast mass of Hindu population on the countryside was left to settle civil suits by itself according to time-honoured law and custom. This was probably one of the spheres in which old Hindu practice survived for long even outside the territories of Hindu feudatories. It would be particularly strong in tracts which, in spite of direct Muslim rule, managed largely to escape, Muslim influence. The hypothesis is borne out by the recent discovery of a Sanskrit judgment in Mithilâ.

A Sanskrit judgment from Mithilâ.

Mithilâ in north Bihâr still forms a centre of Sanskrit learning and Brahmanic orthodoxy. Throughout the middle ages it retained its cultural autonomy and, partly, its freedom of administrative and juridical practice. Its Hindu landowners were recognised by Muslim sovereigns

[1] Besides the inscriptions and works referred to in the foregoing chapters, some facts and traditions about Kâyasthas are given in Brâhmaṇotpattimârtaṇḍa which forms part of Bṛihajjyotiṣârṇava and in Jwala Prasad Miśra's Jâti Bhâskara (Veṅkaṭeśvara Press, Bombay). The Kâyasthas who continued to serve the surviving Hindu principalities retained their orthodox manners on which their descendants still pride themselves.

and suffered to stick to old ways. This state of things survived the break-up of the Muslim power and lasted until the close of the eighteenth century when the East India Company had established its sway all over the lower Gangetic valley. The date on the Sanskrit Jayapatra, as a judgment was called, is equivalent to the 10th of June, 1794 A.D. As the only available document of its kind the Jayapatra deserves notice in some detail. It comes from the village of Dharmapur which had long been held by Hindus under a Muslim imperial grant. The judgment is given and signed by Sacala Miśra who is evidently the Prâḍvivâkâ or chief justice referred to in the course of the document. It begins by mentioning the names of the parties and then gives the case of the plaintiff as stated in his plaint. Next the nature and substance of the defendant's answer are recapitulated. There follows a discussion as to the party on whom the burden of proof lay. The issues are determined and summarised. Next adjournments are dealt with. The plaintiff having made default, the fact that proceedings thereafter are in retrial is noted. Once the defendant objected that on principles of the Hindu law of evidence a single witness to prove a case was inadmissible The plaintiff prays for leave to resort to the mode of proof extraordinary, or non-secular, that is, by ordeal. To this the defendant objects and cites authority in support of his contention. The judge quotes and discusses legal digests and arrives at the conclusion that the ordeal was inapplicable to the case in question. The judge and Pâṣat members refuse the request preferred by the plaintiff. Ultimately, the plaintiff is adjudged to have failed in establishing the claim preferred.[1] It is possible

[1] Jayaswal, J. B. O. R. S., March, 1920, Vol. VI, Part I, pp. 246-58. See also Gaṅgâ Nâtha Jhâ, Ibid., 1921, pp. 121-2. Cf. Jolly, Ibid., 117-20, a Javanese Jayapatra. For the Hindu view of the nature of a judgment, Bṛihaspati in Parâśaramâdhava, p. 150.

that old Hindu judgments were written in something like this form and that something like the procedure indicated here was followed in ancient Mithilâ.

The survival of Hindu administrative practices in Medieval India had its counterpart in theory. Now, as ever, Hindu theory kept at a distance from facts but it could never lose sight of them completely. Sanskrit literature, which did not die out with the loss of Hindu independence, now concerned itself less and less with politics until it ceased to care for it at all. Though concerned primarily with literary form, commenting and explaining of old matter, custom and usage, it produced a few works which belong to the old tradition of Hindu social and political thought. The most important of them was Śukranitisâra the bulk of which was composed probably about the thirteenth century, and which, in its present shape, includes some matter as late as the 16th or even the 17th century A.D.[1] Conscious, perhaps, that he had appeared on the scene rather late, the author of Śukraniti is at pains to connect his handiwork with hoary antiquity.[2] He touches on all topics of government, embellishing and improving on all the details.

Medieval Hindu Political Theory.

There is one passage in Śukra which is peculiarly valuable for the organisation of the last age of ancient India and its medieval survivals. On the basis of annual

[1] Śukranîti was edited by Gustav Oppert, Madras, 1882. The editor (Introduction, p. VIII) ascribed it to the 4th century A.D., but besides other difficulties, this hypothesis supposes the existence of guns and gunpowder in ancient India. In support of Oppert's view, see B. K. Sarkar, Positive Background of Hindu Sociology, Book II, Part I, pp. 63—71. K. P. Jayaswal places the work in the 8th century A.D. Râjendra Lâla Mitra perceived long ago that the Śukranîti could not be older than the 16th century A.D.

[2] Śukranîti, tr. B. K. Sarkar, pp. 1, 2, 4.

income the author divides rulers into various grades as follows :—

Designation.		Annual Revenue in Karṣas.
Sâmanta	...	... 1 lac to 3 lacs
Mâṇḍalika	...	... 3 lacs to 10 lacs.
Râja ..	..	... 10 lacs to 20 lacs.
Mahârâja	..	... 20 lacs to 50 lacs.
Svarâṭ ..	...	... 50 lacs to 100 lacs.
Samrâṭ	...	.. 1 crore to 10 crores.
Virâṭ ..	...	... 10 crores to 50 crores.
Sârvabhauma	..	... Universal Monarchy.[1]

On the very face of it the scheme is theoretical. Elsewhere Śukra applies some of these designations to government officers who were placed in charge of districts of various sizes.[2] Taken together, the passages imply that federal-feudalism was the order of the day and that vassals were often employed in high positions under the sovereign. Śukra advocates tighter control on feudatories than his predecessors in political theory had contemplated. They must be closely watched and, if they misbehaved, might be deposed or pensioned off.[3]

---

[1] Ibid., pp. 36-37.

[2] Ibid., 25, 27, 269.

[3] Ibid., 47-48, also 52.

For the succession, the royal council, the chief officers, and other government employees, Ibid , 25, 27, 54—89, 97-8, 100-101, 269.

On the court, its seating arrangements and etiquette, Ibid., 48—51. On royal supervision over the administration, 40, 46, 51-2, 269. On the capital and council-chamber, 27—35. On communications, 34-5, 43, 184-5, 189—91, 192, 194—206, 209, 211, 213-14, 217--19, 255-56. rest-houses, 35-36. On law, justice and procedure, 134-35, 183—209. On revenue, 138, 140, 89. On expenditure, 43-4. On foreign policy, 130, 261.

The seventeenth century works like Mitra Miśra's Vîramitrodaya and Nîlakaṇṭha's Nîtimayûkha discuss politics on old lines and here and there give a new turn to political ideas. But they throw no fresh light on institutions. The same remark applies to the bulky legal work, the Nṛisiṁhaprasâda of Dalapati, minister of

A Profound Change.

In one essential matter, the Indo-Muslim state of the Middle Ages marks a great departure from ancient practice. It struck at the root of feudal-federalism and inaugurated the era of the unitary state. It is true that many Hindu principalities were allowed to subsist for long as autonomous vassals. Again, a close study of medieval India shows, what scholars have generally failed to notice, that certain epochs and regions witnessed a sort of feudalism among Musalmâns themselves. In the last years of the fifteenth century and the first quarter of the sixteenth, the Lodîs whose dominion comprised the major part of North India, never understood the meaning of a unitary state and persisted in a sort of clan-feudalism which their ancestors on the north-western frontier had evolved. Much later in the eighteenth century, the Rohillâs who dominated the north of the present United Provinces reproduced a similar type of feudalism. Nevertheless, when all allowance has been made for such exceptions, the fact remains that the Muslim state was predominantly a unitary one. The Muslim conquerors destroyed one Hindu dynasty after another, annexed its

---

the Nizâmshâhî ruler of Ahmednagar in the sixteenth century. Legal digests like those of Jîmûtavâhana (15th or 16th century A.D.) rarely touch administration proper. Medieval vernacular literature in the North rarely touches politics. The Bundeloṅ kî Vaṁśâvalî (Chhatarpur Ms.) is one of the few exceptions. For a detailed notice, Beni Prasad, Journal of the U. P. Historical Society, 1922. For slight political touches in Sûra Dâsa, the greatest of Medieval lyricists, Sûra Sâgara, IX, 170; X, 160, 221, 1008, 2377, 2503, 2505, 2507, 2569. Similarly for Tulasî Dâsa, the greatest of Hindî poets, Râmacaritamânasa (Indian Press, Allâhâbâd edition, pp. 233, 270-71, 338, 373, 392, 399). Krittivâsa's Bengalî version of the Râmâyaṇa is no better. Southern literature is much more useful for politics. For instance, the Telugu classic attributed to King Krishṇâdeva Râya (1509—30 A.D.) has a number of political maxims with a bearing on practice For a summary, Raṅgaswâmî Saraswatî, Journal of Indian History, January, 1926, pp. 64—77.

dominions and, for the most part, ruled them as their own. The conclusions of wars among Muslim rulers themselves meant, so far as possible, direct, downright annexation and the extermination of the defeated royal houses. Here Muslim policy was an antithesis of the Hindu tradition. As a result, the Musalmâns gave a tremendous impetus to the process of the political unification of India. The tendency, at its strongest, is represented by the Mughal empire which was founded by Bâbur in 1526 and which, with a short interregnum under Humâyûn, flourished in vigour until the death of Aurangzeb in 1707. It effectively united the north under one sceptre and for a time brought nearly the whole of the Deccan and the south under the same dominion, free from the presence of any feudatories in recently conquered territories. It is in matters other than the fundamentals of organisation that the Muslim state displays Hindu influence.

The indigenous origin of institutions.

The Hindu administrative system which flourished until the 12th or 13th century A.D., and which left its influence behind to last for many generations was almost entirely free from foreign influence in historical times. The recent discoveries made by the Archæological Department at Mohenjo-Daro and Harappa reveal a pre-Âryan culture which bears a striking resemblance to that of Anon, Sura, Babylon and Crete, but the fact of borrowing on one side or the other has yet to be established. No administrative interaction of any kind is perceptible. It is impossible to form an idea of the pre-Âryan institutions of North India. It is probable that such as existed before the Âryan immigration were not obliterated but assimilated into the Âryan system. Indeed, on *a priori* grounds it may be argued that the older institutions, being the natural growth of climatic conditions and economic environment, would gradually grip the Âryans. As we have seen, there is an indication in Vedic literature[1] that the development of the Âryan kingship owed something to the example of the aborigines. But after this possible fusion of Âryan and aboriginal institutions had been completed, there was, in historical times, little outside influence forthcoming to give a different turn to Hindu political development. There was, for instance, no such metamorphosis of the organs of governance in ancient India as came over Anglo-Saxon institutions with the Norman Conquest. Scholars now agree that general Greek influence on India was neither so deep nor so far-reaching as was once, almost naturally, supposed. Even in the case of the Hindu theatre the fact of the Greek influence, so strongly argued for by Weber,[2] has been denied by later writers.[3] The latest surveyor of the Sanskrit Drama thus sums up the situation: "We cannot assuredly deny the possibility of Greek influence, in the sense that Weber admitted the probability; the drama or the mime, may, as played at Greek courts, have aided in the development of a true drama, but the evidence leaves only a negative answer to the search for positive signs of influence."[4] Greek influence on the art of Gandhâra is generally admitted but its extent is still a matter of controversy. Nor is the ground any surer in regard to philosophy. The new spirit which appeared in Buddhism about the first century B.C. has been traced by Sylvain Lévi to Hellenic influences, but here, as elsewhere, the evidence is very scanty. The fact remains that the growth of ideas and cultural styles in India can be adequately explained on the basis of Indian causes. On Hindu political theory Greek influence is conspicuous by its absence. Nowhere in

Greek influence on India.

[1] Supra, Ch. I.
[2] History of Indian Literature, p. 17.
[3] Sylvain Lévi, Theâtre Indien, pp. 343 -6
[4] Keith, Sanskrit Drama, p. 68.

the entire range of that speculation is there any such break or new turn as the impact of the virile, profound political philosophy of Greece would tend to produce. The little development which Hindu political thought displays is fully explicable on variations in the degree of secularity in different groups of compositions, on the rise of new creeds which necessitated a re-statement of the political theory attached to old religious schools and on the mutual approach of the various lines of thought thus started. In Manu and a few other writers the term Yavana is used loosely to indicate one of the hordes which lay beyond the Hindu pale. There are indeed a few isolated passages which, *prima facie*, suggest Greek influence. For instance, Aśvaghoṣa in his Saundara Nandam Kâvyam remarks that some princes founded a city but discovered that if its affairs were to prosper they must have a king. So they raised to rulership one of themselves who was senior to the rest in age, discipline and accomplishments.[1] Here a city is a state, its government is elective and secular in origin. But even here is nothing essentially new to Hindu thought, nothing that could not have arisen from the impact of Buddhist philosophy on the line of thought represented by the Mahâbhârata. The deeper problems with which the Greek mind grappled with lasting, amazing results—the sociality of man, the ethos of society or state, the classification of states, etc.—do not appear in Hindu political speculation. If the Greek intellectual genius, always so potent in moulding the thought of peoples, found no opportunity for making itself felt in India, it was hardly likely that the Greeks should influence Hindu government. In the domain of administrative practice the only tangible evidence of Greek influence is the Greek titles or legends on some coins and a few inscriptions. The Indo-Greek coins, however, show a rapid

Saundara Nandam Kâvyam, I, 7-8.

assimilation to the Hindu type. There is no evidence to support the view that the formation of big empires in India was inspired by the example of Alexander's vast dominion. As the foregoing chapters will have proved, the nature and character of Hindu empires were essentially different from those of the Macedonian regime. The latter approached the Roman model. The Hindu empire, on the other hand, was the exact antithesis of Rome which stood for rigidity and uniformity. The process of empire-building had commenced in India, after the characteristic genius of her people, long before Alexander appeared on the scene. The Mauryan empire only represented a further stage in the development. The fact is that Alexander's stay in India was far too short to cast any influence on Indian institutions. The effort of Seleucus to revive the glories of the great Macedonian empire ended in failure. The Greeks who appeared on the Indian scene after Seleucus were themselves fast losing touch with the mainsprings of Greek life. At last the rise of Parthia, one of the central events in the history of the Middle East, cut them off almost completely from the centres of Hellenism. Then the Hindu capacity for assimilating foreign elements told with decisive effect. The Indo-Greeks ceased to be Greek and became Indian. Whatever their original political ideals, they were cast aside in favour of Hindu tradition. When all the evidence on administrative practices from coins, inscriptions, literature and foreign accounts is put together, it shows nothing which was Greek in origin or which assumed its historical form under Greek influence. In a like manner the Scythians and others who entered India after the Greeks and who were rapidly Hinduised exercised little influence on the development of institutions in ancient India.

There is, however, one possible source of foreign influence which needs some examination in detail. For centuries India maintained constant intercourse with Persia. The early literature, religion and culture of the Irânians were akin to those of the Hindus. It is more than probable that the two branches of the Âryan race had a good deal of social and political organisation in common. After their separation their environment, climatic or economic, was, of course, different but not so radically different as to give rise to fundamentally and entirely different systems of polity. Accordingly, the Persian system of administration, as reconstructed in the light of the latest researches, presents many points of affinity with the institutions examined in the foregoing chapters. It is now recognised that "the discussion as to the respective merits of democracy, oligarchy and monarchy attributed by Herodotus to Darius and his six companions after the death of Gaumata, interesting as it may be as an illustration of Greek political philosophy, is valueless for the Persian theory or practice of government."[1] Like the Hindu, the Persian monarchy was hereditary; pretenders to the Persian throne sought to pass for scions of the royal house. But the principle of primogeniture was not recognised so well in Persia as in India.[2] In Persia, the king's word was law, a principle which Hindu theory, wedded to Theology, would not recognise. In practice, however, the Persian and Hindu systems came near each other. The king's word in Persia was "generally determined in consultation with the Persian nobles and officials (which custom required of the king), and by regard for the usages of the country concerned. The 'royal judges,' as Herodotus calls them, or 'law-bearers' as they were probably called in Persian (dâtabara), advised the king what was law

India and Persia.

[1] G. B. Gray and H. Cary, Cambridge Ancient History, Vol. IV, Ch. VII, p. 184.

[2] Ibid., p. 184.

or custom."[1] The difference with the Hindu practices lay in the large part played by the priest in the latter. In Persia "the king acted in consultation with his ministers, the heads of great departments of state, which must have existed in the capital, though of them little is directly known. . . . . Certain lines of policy characteristic of the Persian government seem clear. While supreme authority resided in the king, great regard was paid, so far as the supremacy of the central authority allowed, to the traditional life and custom of the many diverse peoples gathered into the vast empire. The Persian was a tolerant government.

"Not only were the Persians prepared to be tolerant to the various religions within their empire; they went further and actively supported the temple-worship of the gods of their subjects, or contributed to the building of their temples, and conferred on priesthoods and religious institutions special privileges . . . . "[2] *Mutatis mutandis*, this is true of the great empires which arose from time to time in ancient India.

The education of the princes in Persia is another point of resemblance with Hindu practice. "At the court of the king himself, or at the minor courts of the satraps, 'all the boys of the foremost Persians,' as Xenophon phrases it, were educated. The stress laid on old Persian habits of life and accomplishments—riding, shooting with the bow, plainness of diet, the chase—formed a counteractive to the luxury which tended to increase with the increase and increasing wealth of the empire . . . "Instruction in history and religion, attendance at judicial proceedings, familiarity with the king's methods of awarding or withholding favours, are

[1] Ibid., pp. 185-86.

[2] Ibid., pp. 185—87.

other elements in this education on which the Greek writers who describe it lay stress."[1] In Persia as in India there was a ruling class which supplied, "not indeed exclusively, but very largely, the generals and officers of the army, the ministers of the central administration, and the satraps and governors of provinces and districts throughout the empire."[2] The king's audience chamber, and the system of his correspondence and communications again are reminiscent of ancient India.[3]

A similar likeness is observable in the systems of provincial and local administration. The Persian empire, at least from the time of Darius, "was divided into twenty satrapies, or provinces, under satraps or governors appointed by the king; and within these large provinces there were again smaller districts under subordinate governors to whom however, at least often, the same term satrap was applied." This system indeed goes back to Cyrus and Cambyses and recalls the similar system which prevailed in the Assyrian, Median and Babylonian empires. It is indeed so natural that it developed everywhere. It is, however, interesting that the term satrap or Kṣatrapa had a long history in India. It is again instructive to read that in Persia, as in India, the local administrators were "appointed for indefinite terms, often retaining their position over a long period of years and through more than one reign."[4] Again, like the Hindu governors, the Persian "satraps were men of high birth, . . . in some cases members of the royal family by birth or marriage."[5] Nor is the final touch of resemblance lacking. In Persia, "these powerful administrators, as early as the reign of Darius,

[1] Ibid., p. 191.

[2] Ibid., p. 191.

[3] Ibid., pp. 192-3.

[4] Ibid., p. 194.

[5] Ibid., p. 196.

showed a tendency to independence, and later the satrapic system facilitated the break-up of the empire."[1] In Persia, as in India, numerous dues were levied in cash or kind.[2] It may be noted that the term 'king's eye' which denoted secret agents and reporters in ancient India was applied to inspectors of local administration in Persia.[3] In fundamentals there is, indeed, one great difference. Annexation was far more frequent and far more thorough in ancient Persia than in ancient India. Across the Hindu-Kush conquered princes, as a rule, were not treated so gently. Persian organisation had much less of federal-feudalism than ancient India. None the less the resemblances in the two systems of administration are striking enough. It must be borne in mind that similarity of beginnings and similarity of environment account for a good deal. But owing to the facilities of communication between the two countries and the direct, intimate touch supplied by the extension of the Persian dominion into India under Darius, the possibility of some influence cannot be ruled out. In point of time the Persian system, as all the evidence at our disposal for the two countries indicates, developed earlier than the Hindu. It is possible that the latter owed some suggestions to the former. The almost identical form of the commencement of Darius's Naqsh-i-Rustam Inscription and the Aśokan inscriptions supports the hypothesis. The prevalence of the title Kṣatrapa of Persian origin in India points the same way. Beyond this there is no direct evidence of influence but its probability is well-established.

It is only the Persian empire which lends itself to ready comparison with the ancient Hindu system. The Roman

---

[1] Ibid., p. 197.

[2] Ibid., pp. 199-200.

[3] Ibid., p. 198.

Empire was built on different principles and in several respects was the antithesis of the Hindu system. Rome stood for centralisation, uniformity, rigidity, efficiency at all costs. The Hindu system made for localism, variety, flexibility. Only a few court and palace officers are common to the two. After the fall of 'the city on the Tiber,' the Byzantine Empire or the later Roman Empire as Bury prefers to call it, partly received Oriental influences and thus came slightly nearer the contemporary Hindu state. Even here, the difference is striking enough. The Byzantine Empire was "mainly an aggregate of cities which were originally independent states, and which still were allowed to retain enough of independence and of their municipal government to stand in their old relation of exclusiveness to one another."[1] The Hindu system had never known the city-state and treated the city almost as an accident. Again, while the aristocracy of the Roman Empire was an aristocracy of officials,[2] the Hindu aristocracy was based on birth as well as partly on office. None the less a few of the officers remind one of India. In the Roman Empire, "the grand chamberlain was a functionary rendered necessary by the oriental tincture, given to the imperial surroundings by the policy of Diocletian. He issued commands to all the officers connected with the palace and the emperor's person, including the count of the wardrobe, the count of the residence, the officer of the bed-room, and also to the officers of the palace bodyguard, called Silentiarii. His constant attendance on the person of the emperor gave this minister an opportunity of exercising a vast influence for good or evil, especially if the emperor happened, like Arcadius, to be of a weak and pliable

Comparison with the later Roman Empire.

[1] Bury, Later Roman Empire, I, pp. 37-38.

[2] Ibid., pp. 38—42.

disposition." Again, "the count of the sacred bounties was the lord-treasurer or chancellor of the exchequer, for the public treasury and the imperial fisc had come to be identical; while the count of the private estates managed the imperial demesnes and the Privy purse." The magister officiorum, the master of the offices, performed some miscellaneous duties. "He had control over the bureaux of imperial correspondence, over messengers despatched on imperial orders, over the soldiers on guard at the palace, over manufactories of arms . . . ."[1] These arrangements recall ancient India. For the rest, the Roman and Hindu systems were so utterly divergent that chance analogies hardly count for anything.

Different views on Hindu Government.

The Hindu system of administration has not yet received adequate scientific treatment. For long it was regarded as hardly worthy of serious study. More than one modern writer on Indian history has quoted with approval Gibbon's epigram that all oriental history is "one unceasing round of valour, greatness, degeneracy and decay." Relying apparently on the generalisations of some noted historians, T. H. Green laid down that "the great empires of the east are, in the main, tax-collecting institutions. They exercise coercive force on their subjects of the most violent kind, for certain purposes and at certain times, but they do not impose laws as distinct from particular and occasional commands. Nor do they judicially administer and enforce customary law."[2] The reaction against this attitude touched the other extreme. In a series of brilliant articles (in the Modern Review, Calcutta, 1913), later expanded into "Hindu Polity," K. P. Jayaswal endeavoured

[1] Ibid., pp. 44-45.

[2] T. H. Green, Lectures on the Principles of Political Obligation, ed. Bosanquet, 1901, p. 99.

to prove that the ancient Hindu political system was one of republics, partly of the Athenian type, and of constitutional limited monarchies, not unlike that of Great Britain, with institutions like the assemblies of the Pauras or citizens and Janapadas or country-folk.[1] These organisations, as painted by Jayaswal, were more advanced than anything which modern Switzerland or the United States of America can show. The lead thus given was followed by several scholars who sought to reinforce Jayaswal's conclusions or to fill in the details of his outline. To all these attempts, however, there are a few objections. In the first place, the basis of these hypotheses is rather narrow. They rest on a very small number of passages in Hindu literature and Greek accounts and a yet smaller number of inscriptions which are more than counterbalanced by numerous other passages and inscriptions. It is these latter pieces of evidence which escaped the zealous pioneers. In the second place, the authenticity of some of the passages utilized is far from established. For instance, the Greek extracts, as given in the versions of much later writers, cannot always be taken at their face value. In the third place, the interpretation of some passages, for instance, in the Sûtras of Pâṇini or the work of Kâtyâyana, is more than doubtful. In the fourth place, many of the conclusions in question have been reached by combining data from widely distant epochs. To discuss the evidence of the Vedas and Brâhmaṇas in the same breath with that of Śukranîti is a violation of the canon of historical criticism. In like manner, to combine northern with southern and Ceylonese evidence and to draw therefrom conclusions for the whole of India is rather unscientific. In the fifth place, the connecting link in some of the arguments is lacking or extremely weak. To equate the theory

[1] Jayaswal, Hindu Polity, II, pp. 60–108.

of the procedure of the Buddhist monastic order with the practice of contemporary political assemblies, is, in the absence of definite evidence, hardly convincing. In the sixth place, the theory of the Epics, the Arthaśâstra or the Dharma Śâstras has often been taken to be an exact statement of contemporary practice. The scientific order of treatment seems to be that Hindu political theory should be extracted primarily from literature and secondarily from inscriptions but political practice should be gleaned primarily from coins and inscriptions, next from foreign accounts and, lastly, from literature. It may be added that some of the conclusions of recent writers do not harmonize with what we know with certainty about the intellectual influences, social institutions and economic conditions of ancient India. Real democracy, for instance, could not be reared on the social chasms of caste. Nor could a 'national' assembly 'of country-folk' function regularly in a large area which was split up into thousands of villages and which lacked the modern means of communications.

Development of Northern administration.

It may be desirable to indicate the broad generalisations which emerge from a study of the administrative data of ancient India. It is clear that in spite of some fundamental similarities and identical details, the administrations of the North and the South develop on independent and different lines. Northern imperialism like that of the Mauryas and Guptas or southern imperialism like that of the Ândhras and Râṣṭrakûṭas occasionally linked the political fortunes of the north and the south together but the peculiarities of the administrative system in either region were not obliterated. The most striking difference lies in the sphere of local government. The south developed regular organs of local self-government, while the north was generally content with the informal association of elders with officers. Guilds also developed more in the south than in the north. Other divergences need not be dwelt upon here but it must be emphasised that, from the administrative point of view, the north and the south must be treated apart. Confining our view to the North, it must be admitted that here the extent of organic development is rather limited. Not only were the ancient Hindus a conservative race but they experienced little economic change which has always been so fruitful of political change in European history. After the Vedic period at any rate, the main features of economic life remain the same. We can watch the institutions of the Ṛigveda—the heritage with which the Indo-Âryans started on their historical career—change under the impact of geographical factors, economic environment and social organisation. We can notice that caste gains in strength age after age and begins to dominate the structure and working of governmental institutions. We can watch the Vedic tribal assembly recede in the background and ultimately give way to the pageant of a court. We can see the average size of the state become larger and a correspondingly elaborate system of administration spring up. A large number of new offices arise, areas of local government are demarcated. At the same time a network of relationships of varying degrees of suzerainty and vassalage extends over the country. In all these spheres of development the Mauryan empire, founded about 320 B.C., marks a decisive stage. It knows nothing of popular assemblies; it has a machinery of central, provincial and district government, of fiscal and judicial administration, more elaborate than anything known to previous ages. It displays the workings of federal-feudalism on a grand scale. In another matter the Mauryan regime marks the culminating point of statecraft. The Hindu state which never recognised any limits to its scope of activity and which, off and on, concerned itself with every aspect of the material and moral life of the people, now stood forth as a great instrument of material comfort. Above all it shone forth as a missionary state which must promote morality and righteousness all around. The ideals proclaimed by the Emperor Aśoka were not always followed by the kings who came after him but the idea of the state as the great agency of moral and spiritual welfare never disappeared from India. After the Mauryan empire Indian History enters on a period of obscurity. But the facts and inferences which can be gathered from coins, inscriptions and literature prove that the Mauryan institutions of government did not die out. When the curtain rises again. the Gupta empire displays the Mauryan institutions in a more advanced stage of development. The central officers are more numerous and more definitely posted. The administrative subdivisions are better marked out; offices like those of Bhogapatis and Viṣayapatis are familiar to all. The number of taxes has also increased. The facts of federal-feudalism are recognised by all and symbolised in the gradations of titles and insignia. The Gupta empire stands at the centre of ancient Indian history. All previous history flows into it; all later history issues from it. In the development of the Sanskrit drama, classical literature, Dharma Śâstra thought and Puranic compositions, it marks the decisive epoch. Under its auspices the Hindu system of administration reaches almost the limit of organic development which it was destined to undergo in the north. After the fall of the Gupta empire, the Vardhana empire alone displays any novel features of importance. Thenceforward, organic development ceases altogether; the number of state departments or officers may increase or decrease but there is no essential change, no departure in principle or policy. In the old rut the northern administration ran for five centuries until its free independent life was extinguished by the Musalmâns. It will be observed that, compared to Greek, Roman or English political development, the range of Hindu administrative evolution was very narrow. But it must be emphasised that besides the small amount of organic development, Hindu administrative practices show considerable variation from age to age and place to place. The foregoing chapters will have demonstrated that the structure and working of institutions, as revealed by the original authorities, was not, except in essentials, uniform over the whole of North India or throughout the ancient age. During the last few centuries for which authentic epigraphic evidence is most abundant, the administration was much less elaborate in some regions than in Kanauj, Magadha or Bengal. As part of the variety which Hindu administration shows, must be reckoned the existence of clan or tribal oligarchies. Their existence is well-attested by Jaina and Buddhist literature, by Greek accounts and by Samudragupta's Allâhâbâd Inscription. They did not all follow a uniform type. Negatively the absence of monarchy as commonly understood and positively, the presence of the oligarchic principle was the only common feature. An interesting passage of rather uncertain date, in the Jaina Âcârânga Sûtra speaks of six different kinds of polity as prevalent in north India—" arâyâṇi vâ, gaṇarâyâṇi vâ, juvarâyâṇi vâ, dorajjâṇi vâ, verajjâṇi vâ, viruddharajjâṇi vâ."[1] The import of the statement is not perfectly clear; the last two terms are particularly obscure; perhaps the classification proceeds as much on the basis of difference of administrative structure as of quality of administration. But one can distinguish kingless, gaṇa-ruled and two-ruled states. In any case it appears that the oligarchies differed in constitution among themselves as monarchies did. They were confined to a part of the north and disappeared altogether after the fall of the Gupta empire. It must be remembered

[1] Âcârânga Sûtra, II, 3, 1, 10.

that in spite of the important difference in constitution the oligarchies formed part of the general political system, which was predominantly monarchical, of North India. For instance, the Śâkyas of Kapilavastu acknowledge the suzerainty of the king of Kośala. The Ârjunâyanas, Yaudheyas and others were included in the Gupta empire.

Principles of Hindu governance.

The principles which underlay the Hindu system of governance as a whole were different from those of ancient Rome or modern Europe. They bear a partial resemblance to the principles of medieval European polity. The state in ancient India was not unitary in the strict sense of the term. It was saturated through and through with the principles of what for convenience may be called federalism and feudalism. It must, of course, be emphasised that the modern notions of federalism—written constitutions, clear demarcation of spheres of power, the idea of the co-ordination of federal and state authorities—were unknown to ancient India. Nor was the economic side of medieval European feudalism present in the Hindu system of organisation. These words have to be used for the sake of convenience. But when applied to ancient India they must be shorn of some of their European associations. They are only meant to imply that, as a general rule, a Hindu kingdom comprised a number of feudatories who enjoyed varying degrees of autonomy, that they themselves might have sub-feudatories of a similar status under them and so on to the third, fourth or fifth degree. A big empire was partly a series of alliances, partly a series of relationships of suzerainty and vassalage and partly an area of directly administered territory. The high-sounding Digvijaya could lead only to such a consummation on a large or small scale. The bond which held an empire together was so slight that it could be snapped at any favourable moment. Under every regime, suzerain or feudal, the village was the ultimate unit of society. Even in the north it enjoyed a sort of social or legal autonomy, and was administered, at least from the Gupta period onwards, in consultation with village elders. Here was another type of localism. Finally, there were a number of associations and corporations, religious, economic and social, which enjoyed a fair degree of autonomy. Sovereignty *de facto* was diffused among all these organisations and the influences which supported them.

The Scope of State Activity.

Within the limits prescribed by the force of circumstances and principles of social and political organisation, the Hindu state recognised no restrictions on its activities. While there was much which had been fashioned by other associations and on which the state could only set its imprimatur, the seal of its force, there was much else which it essayed to perform by means of its own resources. From time to time it elected to propagate Dharma, to inculcate and enforce morality, to maintain or improve the social order, to encourage learning, education and art, to subsidise various academies, to regulate industry and commerce, to foster agriculture, to relieve the distress from famine and calamities, to establish hospitals, rest-houses, charity-halls, etc. All this it essayed to do in addition to its primary functions of defence, order and justice. As Hindu theory emphasises times without number, the king was to be the father of the people. As the Aśokan inscriptions testify, the state was to be paternal in the widest sense of the term. Laissez-faire never commanded the allegiance of India. At its highest, the Hindu state was not merely a culture state but an all-pervasive moral and spiritual association. The glory of the situation was that in spite of the missionary zeal which moved its spirit at several epochs, it was generally tolerant of all forms of religious belief. A few bitter religious persecutors like Puṣyamitra and Śaśāṅka certainly flit across the stage of ancient India but, as a rule, Hindu monarchs, even burning enthusiasts like Aśoka, tolerated all creeds, preached toleration and even went to the extent of patronising sects other than their own. It seems that metaphysical inquiries pursued for long had resulted in the rise and persistence of so many divergent schools of thought that every one was forced to adjust himself to differences and to recognise the imperative necessity of toleration.

Checks on Despotism.

The ideals of the Hindu state were certainly high. Its weak point was the despotic character of the hereditary monarchy. Sooner or later the sceptre was bound to fall into incapable, wicked or oppressive hands. The tyranny revealed in Kalhaṇa's Râjataraṅgiṇî makes the flesh creep. The high-handedness of officials, particularly of those in the lowest rung, was not easy to restrain. Nevertheless there were certain checks which operated to mitigate the evils inseparable from the system. Custom could not be lightly disregarded. Following the earlier writers Śukra defines Deśadharma as "custom which may or may not owe its origin to Śruti but is always followed by the people in different climes."[1] The local practices could be violated only at the risk of trouble. Religion which always had a mighty hold on ancient India was another tempering, stabilising and conservative influence in politics. The idea of Dharma was deeply imbedded in the Hindu mind. Dharma, said the Mahâbhârata, upheld all creatures.[2] Even earlier, the Bṛihadâraṇyaka Upaniṣad had laid down that Dharma had been created by Brahman, that Dharma was the king of kings and that there was nothing higher than Dharma.[3] The idea, in fact, had appeared with the Vedas. In the Vedic hymns, as Max Müller puts it, ṛita from meaning

---

[1] Śukranîti, IV, III, 64.

[2] Mahâbhârata, Śânti Parvan, CIX, 8—13.

[3] Bṛihadâraṇyaka Upaniṣad, I, 4, 11—14.

the order of the heavenly bodies became in time the name for moral order and righteousness.[1] It sustained the world.[2] From the Brâhmaṇas the idea of Dharma passed to Buddhists. "Dharma is not simply law," says Rhys Davids speaking of Buddhism, "but that which underlies and includes the law—a word often most difficult to translate and best rendered by truth or righteousness."[3] Mrs. Rhys Davids explained it as the normal, necessary, eternal order and law of all moral and spiritual things.[4] The Jainas always define Dharma so as to include the law of inanimate matter. The Hindu view of Dharma as the foundation of order and, therefore, transcending all merely human authority could not fail to exercise some influence on rulers and to serve as a check on the passive loyalty of the people. Besides these moral checks there were what may be called the checks of expediency or enlightened self-interest. Princes who were often anxious to extend their dominions and who were always liable to aggression from neighbouring states must, for purposes of effective defence and offence alike, keep their subjects contented and well-disposed. In his discussion of foreign policy Kauṭalya emphasises that a king desirous of conquests should keep his subjects well-pleased lest they should be won over by the enemy. The presence of feudatories, ever ready to strike a blow for independence, was another check of expediency on a king. With his own subjects disaffected, a suzerain would hardly be able to control his feudatories. Lastly, the Hindu monarchy, like every other despotism, was tempered by assassination and insurrection. This explains the extraordinary severity of the law of treason in ancient India.

---

[1] Max Müller, Hibbert Lectures, 1878, p. 235.

[2] Cf. Mahâbhârata, Karṇa Parvan, CXIX, 59; Manu, IV, 176; Matsya Purâṇa, CXLV, 27; CCXLI, 3, 4.

[3] Rhys Davids, Buddhism, p. 45.

[4] Mrs. Rhys Davids, Buddhism, p. 35.

The Hindu State and Caste.

The Hindu state was never a theocracy. The occasional appearance of Brahmanic ruling dynasties was a mere accident like the existence of Vaiśya and Śûdra dynasties. As a rule, the sceptre was wielded by Kṣatriyas or those who were fictitiously recognised as Kṣatriyas.[1] The inscriptions and the foreign accounts indicate that the extreme Brahmanic claims, set forth in the Dharma Sûtras, Dharma Śâstras and Purâṇas, were not fully conceded in practice. The privileges which Brâhmaṇas did actually enjoy in practice were seriously curtailed under Buddhist and Jaina regimes. Nevertheless the Hindu state, though not a theocracy, was often influenced by the Brâhmaṇas, who posed as the depositories of learning, law and religion. The Purohita was always beside the king. Brâhmaṇas supplied many counsellors, judges and other officials. Doubtful points of law were often referred to Brâhmaṇa pariṣads. The state recognised the facts of caste and sat rather hard on the lower classes. Apart from the evidence of the theoretical Dharma Sûtras, Dharma Śâstras, Arthaśâstras and Purâṇas, Alberûnî testifies to the disabilities imposed on Śûdras in the matter of justice and all that pertains to the higher life of man. The inscriptions show that most of the grants of land or presents of money and articles were made to Brâhmaṇas. Suzerains or feudatories, in the north or south, when addressing their subjects through inscriptions, begin by mentioning the Brâhmaṇas and thus recognise their social primacy. Forced labour, which is alluded to in so many inscriptions, must have fallen on the lower classes. It is from the dominance of caste that Hindu administration

[1] For alleged early contests between Brâhmaṇas and Kṣatriyas for supremacy (Muir, Original Sanskrit Texts, Part I, Ch. III) there is no tangible evidence. No safe inference can be drawn from the myths of Paraśu Râma's extermination of Kṣatriyas in the Purâṇas and the Mahâbhârata (Âdi Parvan, LXIV).

draws its darkest stain. In spite of its anxiety to promote morality and righteousness, it was alien to all ideas of democracy, of equality or equal opportunity. The influence of caste on administration is clear from authentic records. It is worth while inquiring how far the state in its turn influenced the development of caste. Buddhist and Jaina kings would naturally reduce its political significance, though nothing could obliterate it. Foreign or mixed tribes and clans which possessed themselves of political authority got installed as Kṣatriyas and thus affected the old order. Some rulers claim in their inscriptions that they actually enforced the rules of caste.[1] If so, such action would promote the tendency of the community to split into innumerable sub-castes. The size of a principality, whether that of a suzerain or a feudatory, was usually small. A ruling of the state on a matter of caste would operate over a restricted area and thus differentiate one group of a wide-spread caste from all others. In course of time they would be permanently disunited. Government servants of various grades would come to form classes of their own; classes which, after the Hindu fashion, would develop into castes. Kâyasthas, already referred to, furnish an example. More direct means might sometimes be employed. Sir William Hunter has recorded the tradition that certain rulers of Orissâ, finding themselves in need of more Brâhmaṇas than existed in their dominions, promoted whole groups to Brâhmaṇahood. As the old Brâhmaṇas refused to admit the new ones to commensality and intermarriage, the latter formed themselves into new castes. The Jaina tradition recorded in the Âdi Purâṇa that King Bharata, son of the first Tîrthakara Ṛiṣabha, created Jaina Brâhmaṇas out of Kṣatriyas, Vaiśyas and Śûdras is suggestive. The Râjas of Chambâ are said to have bestowed on some

[1] See, for instance, Ep. Ind., I, No. 45.

people the right to wear the sacred thread in return for gifts and services. Alberûni has preserved a tradition that "the kings of antiquity who were industriously devoted to the duties of their office, spent most of their care on the divisions of their subjects into different classes and orders, which they tried to preserve from inter-mixture and disorder. They did not allow anybody to transgress the limits of his class, and even punished those who would not be content with their class."[1] The statement cannot be taken at its face value but it does seem to indicate that governmental action had something to do with the development and maintenance of the system of castes and sub-castes. For later times Tod reports the tradition of a Râjpût prince who regulated the dress of all even to the tie of a turban and who would thus accentuate the outward distinctions of caste.

Aspects of the Administration.

A few salient features of the Hindu administrative structure may be briefly touched upon. Ancient India had no perception of the necessity or desirability of separation of functions. The same men wielded civil and military authority at the same time. There were, indeed, judges who were nothing else but in addition to them high executive officers performed judicial duties. Any capable officials might be appointed ambassadors. Aśoka entrusted missionary and censorial work partly to ordinary officers of state.

The organisation of departments under superintendents with a regular secretarial and other staff and all grouped under different ministers is one of the striking features of the Hindu system. It is under this head that the administration displays the greatest amount of development. Kalhaṇa speaks of successive increases in the number of portfolios, superintendents and ministers in Kashmîr.

[1] Alberûnî, India, tr. Sachau, I, pp. 99-100.

A comparative study of the inscriptions reveals the fact that the number of officers steadily increased in the north with the lapse of time until the last age presented the greatest number of them. Of the status of ministers, who next to the king, formed the highest rung of the official ladder, enough has been said before with reference to various epochs and regions. But it may be emphasised here that, though creatures of the king, they occupied a position of the highest dignity and responsibility. As the Jûnâgaḍh Inscription of Rudradâman shows, they sometimes dared to oppose the king. Somadeva Sûri lays down that one of the essential features of ministership was that the king should be afraid of ministers.

The division of a territory into provinces, districts and even lower administrative areas is another noticeable feature of the Hindu system at least from the Mauryan period onwards. Some of the provinces were governed by princes of the blood and others by men drawn from a sort of ruling class. The tenures of offices were generally long. The employment of feudatories in high office, the practice of payment through grants of land, the occasional hereditary transmission of offices and the practical restriction of all high offices to a small class gave a deep feudal tinge to the whole administration. But that was only part of the order of the day. So long as the central power was not assailed by enemies and was wielded by capable hands, it could make itself felt.

The position of the village as the lowest unit of administration need not be discussed again. But it may be emphasised that a village would naturally tend to develop a consciousness of its own. The ancient Hindu village bore some resemblance to that of China, Indo-China and Siam. The functional organisation, typified by the guild, could not have the same fixity and permanence or the same keen sense of autonomy. Nevertheless, as the inscriptions, coins, seals and literature alike prove, the guild became a real factor in the economic life of the community and appropriated some social and judicial functions. Add to all this the numerous castes and sub-castes with customs and usages of their own and it is clear that Hindu government, in the widest sense of regulation, was essentially a pluralistic one. The whole Hindu system of social and political organisation seems to have developed concurrently on the bases of race, occupation and region. There could be no question of unified loyalty and allegiance. Social development had been multilinear. Loyalty, like sovereignty, was split up. In the multitude of associations and organisations, the task of the state was (1) to secure and maintain those conditions of life in which each group could express itself in the best and fullest manner and without detriment to the rest and (2) to adopt all direct means for the furtherance of popular good and happiness.

The failure and success of the Hindu State.

How far the Hindu state succeeded in this task is a question difficult to answer in the lamentable absence of adequate data. Nor is a single judgment possible. Owing to the vicissitudes of Indian history, each region and epoch should be discussed by itself. But for that there is not sufficient material. Taking a broad, comprehensive view, it is not possible to make any unqualified statement on the achievements of the Hindu state. It must be admitted that the despotism could occasionally lead to oppression, sometimes severe, even diabolical. Not to speak of the Râjataraṅgiṇî, Nâgasena remarks in Milinda-Pañha that "some people have left the world at the tyranny of kings."[1] The personal expenditure of princes, the heavy bill of the palace, the pomp and pageantry of the court, and frequent wars are likely to have told grievously

[1] Milinda Pañha, II, 1, 6. See also IV, 22.

on the tax-payer—on the poor peasant, artisan or labourer. The Hindu state sanctioned too many tolls and petty dues and too much forced labour. It failed signally to reclaim the tribes on the frontiers or in the centre of India. It fell a victim to caste and deliberately refused to bring the lower classes into line with the rest of Hindu society or to encourage their higher life. It allied itself with priestcraft and conservatism and helped perpetuate the distinctions between man and man. Lastly, the Hindu state, parochial, short-sighted and isolated from the rest of the world, failed to keep abreast of the times and to organise the resources of the country against successive foreign invasions. At last in the thirteenth century it shipwrecked in the storms it was incapable of weathering.

On the other hand, the Hindu state was generally alive to some vital interests of the people. It encouraged agriculture and looked after irrigation. It stepped in to save the consumer from exorbitant profiteering and allowed all classes of craftsmen to band together. It cared for the means of communication and had no small share in promoting the homogeneity of culture throughout the country. The rulers often provided for the comforts of travellers and sick people and showed unstinted generosity to the poor people. The Hindu courts favoured poets and scholars and endowed academies and veritable universities which won the enthusiastic admiration of great Chinese scholars. The Hindu state succeeded in maintaining conditions favourable to the rise of systems of philosophy which still command respect, religions which, in certain aspects, touch the sublimest heights, and a literature which ranks among the great literatures of the world. Sometimes the state directly took the lead in moral and religious reform. Under Aśoka and Kaniṣka it helped transform the higher life of India and transmitted to the Far East a gospel which still warms and illumines its spiritual life.

BIBLIOGRAPHY[1]

I. Vedic Literature.

Ṛigveda, Saṁhitâ and Pada text with Sâyaṇa's commentary. Edited by F. Max Müller. 2nd Edition, 1890—2.

———Saṁhitâ text only. Edited by Th. Aufrecht 2nd Edition. Bonn, 1877.

———Translation by R. T. H. Griffith, Benares, 1896-7. In part only, by Max Müller in the Sacred Books of the East Series, Vol. XXXII, Oxford, 1891, and in part by H Oldenberg, Ibid., Vol. XLVI, 1897.

Kaegi, A. The Ṛigveda Translated by R. Arrow Smith. Boston, 1886.

Muir, J. Original Sanskrit Texts, Vol V, 3rd Edition, 1884.

Sâmaveda, Edition with translation by Th. Benfey, Leipzig, 1848; by Satyavrata Sâmaśrami, Calcutta, 1873.

———Translation by Griffith. Benares, 1893.

Yajurveda:—Taittirîya Saṁhitâ. Edited by A. Weber. Berlin, 1871-2; with the commentary of Mâdhava Calcutta, 1854—9. Kâṭhak Saṁhitâ. Edited by L. Von Schroeder Leipzig, 1900—11.

Maitrâyaṇî Saṁhitâ. Edited by Schroeder. Leipzig, 1881—6.

Vâjasaneyi Saṁhitâ, with Mahîdhara's Commentary. Edited by Weber. London, 1852.

Translation by Griffith, Benares, 1899, and by A. B. Keith, Cambridge (Mass.), 1914.

Atharva Veda, Saṁhitâ text. Edited by R. Roth and W. D. Whitney. Berlin, 1856.

———Saṁhitâ and Pada text, with Sâyaṇa's Commentary. Edited by Śaṅkara P. Pandit. Bombay, 1895—8.

———Translation by R. T. H. Griffith, Benares, 1897; W. D. Whitney (with additions by Lanman), Cambridge (Massachusetts), 1905; in part, by M. Bloomfield in the Sacred Books of the East, Vol. XLII. Oxford, 1897.

Aitareya Brâhmaṇa. Edited by Th. Aufrecht. Bonn, 1879 (best edition). Also edited and translated by Haug, 2 volumes, Bombay, 1863.

[1] The minor works, referred to in the text, are not included in this Bibliography.

Aitareya Âraṇyaka. Edited with translation by A. B. Keith. Oxford, 1909.

Kauṣitaki Brâhmaṇa. Edited by B. Lindner. Jena, 1887.

Śâṅkhâyana Âraṇyaka. Edited by Keith. Oxford, 1909 (Bks. VII--XV); by Friedländer, Berlin, 1900 (Bks. I-II); by E. B. Cowell, Calcutta, 1861 (Bks. III--VI=Kauṣîtaki Brâhmaṇa Upaniṣad).

——Translation by Keith. London, 1908

Pañcaviṁśa Brâhmaṇa. Edited by A. Vedântavâgîśa, Calcutta, 1869—74

Jaiminiya or Talavakâra Brâhmaṇa; the Upaniṣad Brâhmaṇa. Edited by H. Oertel with translation and notes. Journal of the American Oriental Society, XVI, pp. 79 -260.

Taittirîya Brâhmaṇa. Edited by Râjendra Lâla Mitra, Calcutta, 1855 70; N. Godbole, Poona, 1898.

Taittirîya Âraṇyaka. Edited by H. N. Apte. Poona, 1898.

Śatapatha Brâhmaṇa. Edited by A. Weber, London, 1855

—— Translation by J Eggeling S. B E., Bks. XII, XXVI, XLI, XLIII, XLIV, Oxford, 1882—1900.

Gopatha Brâhmaṇa. Edited by Râjendra Lâla Mitra and H. Vidyâbhûṣana, Calcutta, 1872.

Brihadâraṇyaka Upaniṣad. Edited with translation by O. Böhtlingk, Leipzig, 1889.

Chandogya Upaniṣad. Ibid.

Kâṭhaka Upaniṣad. Edited by Apte. Poona, 1889.

All the principal Upaniṣads have been translated by F. Max Müller in the S. B. E., Vols. I and XV.

Bloomfield, M. The Atharva Veda. Strassburg, 1899 (in Bühler's Encyclopedia).

Hopkins, E. W. Transactions of the Connecticut Academy of Arts and Sciences, XV. 21 sq. (on the Pañcaviṁsa Brâhmaṇa).

Macdonell, A. A. and ***Keith, A. B.*** Vedic Index, 1912.

Macdonell, A. A. Vedic Mythology, Strassburg, 1897.

Bloomfield, M. The Religion of the Veda. New York, 1908.

II. The Sûtras.

A. ŚRAUTA SÛTRAS.

Śâṅkhâyana Śrauta Sûtra. Edited, together with the commentary of Varadattasuta Ânatîya, by Alfred Hillebrandt (Bibliotheca Indica). Calcutta, 1888.

Baudhâyana Śrauta Sûtra, belonging to the Taittirîya Saṁhitâ. Ed. W. Caland. Calcutta, 1904.

Srauta Sûtra of Âpastamba, belonging to the Taittirîya Saṁhitâ. Edited with the commentary of Rudradatta by Richard Garbe. Calcutta, 1882

Śrauta Sûtra of Lâṭyâyana. Edited. with the commentary of Agnisvâmî, by Ânandachandra Vedântavâgîśa (Bibliotheca Indica). Calcutta, 1872.

B. GṚIHYA SÛTRAS.

Mânava Gṛihya Sûtra. Ed. F. Knauer. St. Petersburg, 1897.

Pâraskara Grihya Sûtra. Ed. A. F Stenzler. Leipzig, 1876.

Âśvalâyana Gṛihya Sûtra. Ed. A. F. Stenzler. Leipzig, 1864.

Khâdira Gṛihya Sûtra. Ed. and tr. Oldenberg, S. B. E., XXIX.

Gobhila Gṛihya Sûtra. Ed. F. Knauer. Dorpat, 1884.

Śâṅkhâyana Gṛihya Sûtra. Ed. Oldenberg, in Ind. Stud XV.

C. DHARMA SÛTRAS.

Gautama Dharma Śâstra (Sûtra). Ed. Stenzler. London, 1876.

Baudhâyana Dharma Śâstra. Ed. E. Hultzsch. Leipzig, 1884.

Âpastambîya Dharma Sûtra. Ed. Bühler, Bombay, 1868 and 1872 (in two parts).

Vâśiṣṭha Dharma Sûtra. Ed A. Führer. Bombay, 1883.

Translations in S. B. E., Vols. II and XIV.

III. The Epics.

The Bṛihaddevatâ, edited and translated by A. A. Macdonell. Cambridge, Massachusetts, 1904.

The texts of the epics, the Mahâbhârata and the Râmâyaṇa, have come down in various recensions, but no one edition can be said to be wholly accurate.

The Calcutta edition of the *Mahâbhârata* (1834—9) includes the Harivaṁśa. The Bombay edition (1888) does not contain it and also differs in some places from the Calcutta edition. The text handed down by South Indian tradition and published at Kombakonam differs substantially from the northern recensions. It has been published in Bombay, 1906—10. The northern texts are in general use. The earliest surviving, though fragmentary, commentary on the Mahâbhârata is that by Sarvajña Nârâyaṇa, going back at least to the 14th century A.D. The best known is that of Nîlakaṇṭha, 16th century A.D.

The Râmâyaṇa text has a similar history. The Bengal text, without the last book, was published by G. Gorresio in Paris, 1843–50. The Bombay edition, with the complete text, appeared in 1895. The South Indian readings given in another edition (published in Bombay, 1905) do not materially differ from the above edition.

Translations. The Mahâbhârata in the northern recension was translated into English by P. C. Ray in Calcutta, 1883–96; also by M. N. Dutta (Calcutta, 1896). R. C. Dutta published an abridged translation (London, 1899). P C. Ray's translation has been generally followed in the text.

G. Gorresio edited the epic with an Italian translation in 1843 67. A beautiful commentary was published by Jacobi (Bonn, 1893).

R. T. H. Griffith published an abridged translation (Benares, 1895).

J. Muir's Original Sanskrit Texts (London, 1868–84) gives copious extracts from the religious chapters of the epics.

Hopkins, E. W. The Great Epic of India, and India Old and New (New York, 1901).

——— J.A.O.S., Vol. XIII, 1888, for the social and military position of the ruling caste.

IV. Arthaśâstras.

Arthaśâstra of Kauṭalya. Edited by R. Shamasastry, Mysore, 1909. The Ms. came from a village near Conjeevaram in Tâmîlakam ——Translation by the same, Bks. I–IV, Mysore, 1908. Bks. V–XV, Ind. Antiquary, 1909-10. Complete in one work. Bangalore, 1915; second edition, 1919.

Jolly and Schmidt's Edition of the Arthaśâstra, with the Nayacandrikâ Commentary on a section of the work, has been published in the Puñjâb Sanskrit Series (Lahore, 1925); *Gaṇapati Śâstrî's edition* with a commentary of his own in the Trivandrum Sanskrit Series.

Kâmandaka's work is styled *Nîtisâra* but it is for the most part a summary of Kauṭalya. The Nîtisâra, with the Jayamaṅgala Commentary by Śaṅkarârya has been edited by Gaṇapati Śâstrî and published in the Trivandrum Sanskrit Series 1912.

The Bârhaspatya Sûtra has been edited and translated by F. W. Thomas in the Puñjâb Sanskrit Series, 1921. It appeared at first in Le Museon, 1916, pp. 131–166.

V. Dharma Sâstras.

The Mânava Dharma Śâstra. Edited by N N. Mandalik with commentaries, Bombay, 1886; by J. Jolly, London, 1887. Earlier editions appeared at Calcutta, 1813; London, 1825; and at Paris in 1830.

Translations First by Sir W. Jones; by Bühler in S. B. E., Vol XV, with an excellent introduction; and by A. C. Burnell and E. W. Hopkins (London, 1884). By Gaṅgâ Nâtha Jhâ, with the commentary of Medhâtithi, Calcutta, 1921—23.

Vaiṣṇava Dharma Śâstra. Edited by Jolly. Calcutta, 1881.

Yâjñavalkya Dharma Śâstra. Edited by Stenzler. Berlin, 1849

Mitâkṣarâ. Bombay, 1909. Translation by S. C. Vidyâratna. Allâhâbâd, 1918.

Nârada Smṛiti. Edited by Jolly Calcutta, 1885.

Bṛihaspati Smṛiti. Edited in the Ânandâśrama Sanskrit Series. Poona. Translated by Jolly in S. B. E., Vol. XXXIII.

The Dharma Śâstra Saṁgraha. Edited by Pandit Jîvânanda Vidyâsâgara. Calcutta, 1876.

(Contains the texts attributed to Atri, Viṣṇu, Harita, Yâjñavalkya, Uśânas, Aṅgiras, Yama, Âpastamba, Samavarta, Kâtyâyana, Bṛihaspati, Parâśara, Vyâsa, Śaṅkha, Likhita, Dakṣa, Śâtâtapa, Vaśiṣṭha, Gautama and Vṛiddha Gautama.) Vol. VII of the S. B. E. Series contains translation of the Viṣṇu by Jolly. The Nârada Smṛiti and some parts of Bṛihaspati are in Vol. XXXIII.

Bâlambhaṭṭî—a gloss on the Mitâkṣarâ by Bâlambhaṭṭa, ed. Govind Das, Bibliotheca Indica Series.

Aparârka's Commentary on Yâjñavalkya Smṛiti, 2 vols, Ânandâśrama, Poona, 1903-4.

Viśvarûpa's Commentary, ed. S. S. Setlur, 1912, Madras. It forms the basis of Vijñâneśvara's Mitâkṣarâ. Nîlakaṇṭha's Vyavahâra-Mayûkha was translated by Borradaile in 1827. His Nîtimayûkha was lithographed at Benares in 1880.

VI. Purânas.

Padma Purâṇa, Ed. V. N. Mandalika. Poona, 1894.

Varâha Purâṇa. Ed. Pandit Hṛiṣîkeśa. Calcutta. 1893.

Vâyu Purâṇa. Ed. Râjendra Lâla Mitra. Calcutta, 1880.

Kûrma Purâṇa. Ed. Nîlamaṇi Mukhopâdhyâya. Calcutta, 1890.

Bhâgavata Purâṇa. Edited by Nityasvarûpa Brahmacârin, Bṛindâvana, 1916-7.

Brahma Vaivarta Purâṇa. Published by Kṣemarâja Śrî Kṛiṣṇadâsa. Bombay, 1809.

Garuḍa Purâṇa. Ibid., 1906-7.

Brahma Purâṇa. Ibid., 1906.

Nârada Purâṇa. Ibid., 1905.

Śiva Purâṇa. Ibid., 1906.

Mârkaṇḍeya Purâṇa. Ed. Pandit Kanhaiyâ Lâla. Ibid , 1910.

Viṣṇu Purâṇa. Published by Kṣemarâja Śrî Kṛiṣṇadâsa, Bombay, 1910.

Liṅga Purâṇa. Ibid., 1907.

Skanda Purâṇa. Ibid., 1909.

Agni Purâṇa. Published in Bibl. Indica, 1873–9.

Bhaviṣya Purâṇa. Ibid., 1910.

Vâmana Purâṇa. Jagaddhitecchu Press, Bombay, 1886.

Matsya Purâṇa. Ānandâśrama Sanskrit Series, No. 54. Poona, 1907.

TRANSLATIONS.

Mârkaṇḍeya Purâṇa. Translated by F. E. Pargiter. Calcutta, 1904.

Viṣṇu Purâṇa. Translated by H. H. Wilson Vols. I–V. Edited by F. Hall. Vols. VI—X. London, 1864—70. (A storehouse of information about the legendary history of the Epics and Purâṇas.)

Brahma Vaivarta Purâṇa. Part 1. Translated by Râjendra Nâth Sen. Sacred Books of the Hindus Allahabad, 1920.

Matsya Purâṇa. (Chaps. 1—291.) 2 Vols. Translated by "A Taluqdar of Oudh." Ibid., 1917.

Garuḍa Purâṇa. Translated by Ernest Wood and S. V. Subrahmanyam. Ibid., 1911.

Pargiter, F. E. The Purâṇa Text of the Dynasties of the Kali Age. Oxford, 1913. An excellent collection of different useful texts with translations.

Pargiter, F. E. Earliest Indian Traditional History. J. R. A. S., 1914.

Fleet, J. F. The Kaliyuga Era. J.R.A.S., 1911.

UPAPURÂṆAS.

Brahmâṇḍa Purâṇa. Śrîveṅkateśvara Press. Bombay, 1906.

Gaṇeśa Purâṇa. Gopâla Nârâyaṇa and Co. Bombay, 1892.

Bṛihaddharma Purâṇa. (Bibl. Indica.)
Saura Purâṇa. Ānandâśrama Sanskrit Series, 1889, Poona.
Kalikâ Purâṇa. Veṅkateśvara Press, Bombay, 1891.
Bṛihannâradîya Purâṇa. (Bibl. Ind.)
Narasiṁha Purâṇa. Grantha Ratnamâlâ. Edition by Uddhavâcârya. Bombay, 1889.

VII. Buddhist Literature.

Aṅguttara Nikâya. Ed. by R. Morris and E. Hardy. Pali Text Society. London, 1885—1900.
Apadâna. Not yet edited.
Atthaśâlini. Ed. by Eduard Müller. P. T. S. London, 1897.
Dhammapada. Edited by Sûriyagoḍa Sumaṅgal Thera. P. T. S. London, 1914.
——Translation by Max Müller. S. B. E., Vol. X.
——Commentary. Edited by H. C. Norman. P. T. S. London, 1906—14.
Dîgha Nikâya. Edited by J. W. Rhys Davids and J. E. Carpenter. P. T. S. London, 1890—1911.
——Commentary Sumaṅgala Vilâsinî. Edited by R. Davids. P. T. S. London, 1886.
Dîpa Vaṁśa. Edited and translated by Oldenberg. London, 1879.
Divyâvadâna. Edited by E. B. Cowell and R. A Neil. Cambridge, 1886.
Jâtakas. Edited by V. Fausböll. London, 1877—97.
——Translation by various scholars under the editorship of E. B. Cowell. Cambridge, 1895—1913.
Jâtakamâlâ by Arya Śûra, tr. from the Sanskrit by J. S. Speyer, London, 1895.
Buddhist Legends. Tr. from the original Pâli text of the Dhammapada Commentary, by E. W. Burlingame. Cambridge, Mass., 1921.
Lalita Vistara. Edited by Râjendra Lâla Mittra. Calcutta, 1877; by S. Lefmann. Halle, 1902—1908.
Mahâvaṁśa. Edited by W. Geiger. P. T. S. London, 1908; and translated by the same in 1912.
Mahâvastu. Edited by E. Senart. Paris, 1882—97.
Majjhima Nikâya. Edited by V. Trenckner and R. Chalmers. P. T. S. London, 1888—99.

66

Milindapañha. Edited by V. Trenckner. London, 1880.
———Translation by R. Davids. S. B. E. Vols. XXXV, XXXVI, Oxford, 1890—4.

Samantapâsâdikâ. A Commentary on the Vinaya. An edition of it has just been published by the Pâli Text Society.

Saṁyutta Nikâya. Edited by Léon Feer and Mrs. Rhys Davids. P. T. S. London, 1884—1904.

Thera Gâthâ and Therî Gâthâ are Psalms of the Buddhist Brethren and Sisters. Edited by Oldenberg and Pischel respectively, and translated by Mrs. Rhys Davids. P. T. S. London.

Udâna. Edited by P. Steinthall. P.T.S. London, 1885; and translated by D. M. Strong. London, 1902.

Vimânavatthu. Edited by E. R. Goonaratne. P.T.S. London, 1886.

Vinaya. Edited by H. Oldenberg. London, 1879—83.

Vinaya Texts. Translated by Rhys Davids and Oldenberg. S. B. E. XIII, XVII, XX. Oxford, 1881—5.

The Sanskrit Buddhist Literature of Nepâl, by Râjendra Lâla Mitra. Calcutta, 1882.

VIII. Jaina Literature.

Caritra Saṅgraha Ahmedabad, 1884.

Jaina Kathâratna Koṣa. 8 vols. Bombay, 1890.

The Kumâra Pâla Carita, by Hema Candra. Edited by S. P. Pandit (Bom. Sans. Series). 1900.

Sthavirâvali Carita, by Hema Candra. Edited by Jacobi (Bibliotheca Indica). Calcutta, 1891.

The Hammîra Mahâ Kâvya of Nayacandra Sûri (Indian Antiquary, Vol. VIII, pp. 55—73). Bombay, 1879.

The Sukṛita Saṁkîrtana, of Arisiṁha Translated by E. H. Burgess. (Indian Antiquary, Vol. XXXI, 1902.)

Indian Studies. G. Bühler. The Jagaḍû Carita of Sarvânanda, a historical romance from Gujarât. Wien, 1892.

Dhanañjaya's Dvisandhâna. Edited by Pandit Śivadatta and K. P. Parab. Kâvyamâlâ No. 49. Bombay, 1895.

Yaśastilaka Campû by Somadeva Sûri. Ibid., No. 70. Bombay, 1901.

Bâla Bhârata by Amaracandra Sûri. Ibid., No. 45. Bombay, 1894.

Hema Candra's Jaina Râmâyaṇa. Calcutta, 1876. Poona, 1890.
——— *Laghu Arhannîti.* Ahmedâbâd.

The Kathâ Koṣa, or Treasury of Stories. Translated from Sanskrit Manuscripts by C. H. Tawney. London, 1895.

Prabandhacintâmaṇi, of Merutuṅgâcârya. Edited by Râmacandra Dînanâtha Bombay, 1888. Translated by C. H. Tawney (Bibl. Ind.). Calcutta, 1899.

Śripâlacarita or Śri Pâla Râjano Râs. Second Edition, Bombay, 1876.

Somadeva Sûri. Nîtivâkyâmṛitam with a commentary by an unknown paṇḍit, in the Mâṇika Candra Granthamâlâ, 22. Bombay, Vikrama Era 1979.

The Mahâ Purâṇa, comprising the Âdi Purâṇa by Jinasenâcârya and its continuation, the Uttara Purâṇa by Guṇabhadrâcârya has been published with a Hindî translation by Lâlâ Râma Jaina, in the Syâdvâda Granthamâlâ, Bombay.

Kirti Kaumudî by Someśvaradeva. Edited by A. V. Kâthavaṭe (Bom. Sans. Series), No. 25. Bombay, 1883.

The Gauḍavaho. An historical poem in Prâkrit, by Vâkpatirâja. Edited by S. P. Pandit (Bom. Sanskrit Series, No. XXXIV). Bombay, 1887.

H. Jacobi. On Mahâvîra and his predecessors. (Ind. Antiq., Vol IX.) Bombay, 1880.

J. Klatt. Extracts from the historical records of the Jainas (Ind. Antiq., Vol. XI, pp. 245—256). 1882.

Bhadrabâhu, Kalpa Sûtra. Ed. H. Jacobi, Leipzig, 1879.

IX. Nîti Śâstras.

Kâmandaka, Nîtisâra. Edited by Gaṇapati Śâstri in Trivendram Sanskrit Series.

Śukra Nîtisâra. Edited by Gustav Oppert. Madras, 1882. Translated with notes by B. K. Sarkar in the S. B. H., Allâhâbâd.

Vîramitrodaya, Râjanîti Prakâśa. By Mitra Miśra. Edited in the Chowkhambhâ Sanskrit Series, Benâres.

Nîlakaṇṭha's Nîti Mayûkha. Lithographic edition. Benâres, 1880.

Râjanîti of Chaṇḍîśvara, ed. K. P. Jayaswal.

Vaiśampâyana, Nîtiprakâśikâ, ed. Gustav Oppert. Madras, 1882.

Yuktikalpataru (attributed to Bhoja), ed. Iśwara Chandra Śâstri, Calcutta, 1917.

X. General Literature.

Aśvaghoṣa Buddha Carita. The Śariputra Prakaraṇa and other fragments of plays. Published by Lüders.

Bhâsa. All his dramas have been edited by T. Gaṇapati Śâstrin in the Trivendram Sanskrit Series, 1912—15. The chief of them are the Dûta Ghaṭotkaca, Urubhaṅga, Dûtavâkya, Bâla Carita, Avimâraka, Pratijñâyaugandharâyaṇa, and Svapnavâsavadattâ.

Śûdraka. The Mṛicchakaṭikâ. Edited by Stenzler, Bonn, 1847; and by Pandit Jîvânanda Vidyâsâgara. Calcutta, 1891. A good translation by Ryder styled " The Little Clay Cart."

Kâlidâsa. The Raghuvaṁśa and Kumâra Sambhava. Edited by Stenzler in 1832 and 1838, London, and later by several scholars. The Abhijñâna Śâkuntala (edited by M. R. Kale, Bombay, 1894, and by Monier-Williams, Oxford, 1876. Translation by the same,16th Edition, London, 1894). Vikramorvaśî, edited by Vaidya, Bombay, 1895. Mâlavikâgnimitra, edited by Bollensen, 1879, Leipzig; S. P. Pandit, Bombay, 1869. Several other editions.

Bhâravi. Kirâtârjunîya. Edited by J. Vidyâsâgara. Calcutta, 1875. Translated by Schütz Bielefield, 1843. Many later editions.

Subandhu. Vâsavadattâ. Edited with Introduction by F. Hall in Bibliotheca Indica, 1859.

Bâṇabhaṭṭa. Harṣacarita. Edited by Vidyâsâgara, Calcutta, 1883. Translation by Thomas and Cowell, Royal Asiatic Society. London, 1897. Kâdambarî, edited by Peterson, Bombay Sanskrit Series, 1889. Edited with Commentary and published by the Nirṇaya Sâgara Press, Bombay, 1896. Translated with occasional omissions by C. M. Ridding, Royal Asiatic Society, London, 1896.

Daṇḍin. Daśakumâracarita, Part I, edited by Bühler. Bombay Sanskrit Series, 2nd Edition, 1888. Part II by Peterson, ibid., 1891. Edited also by P. Banerji, Calcutta, 1888.

Pañcatantra. Edited by J. Hertel, 1910, and translated in 1909.

Bhartṛihari. Nîtiśataka. Several editions.

(*Attributed to*) *Harṣa.* Ratnâvali with Commentary. Nirṇaya Sâgara Press, Bombay, 1895.

Nâgânanda. Edited by J. Vidyâsâgara. Calcutta, 1873. Ed. R. D. Karmakar, 2nd edition, Bombay, 1923. Priyadarśikâ. Edited by R. V. Kriṣṇamachariar, Srirangam, 1906. Translated by G. Strehly, Paris, 1888.

Bhaṭṭikâvya. Attributed without solid reasons to Bhartṛihari. Edited by M. R. Kalé. Bombay, 1897 (with translation).

Bhavabhûti. Mâlatimâdhava. Edited by R. G. Bhandarkar. Bombay, 1905.

Mahâvîra Carita. Edited by F. H. Trithen. London, 1848. Tr. by J. Pickford. London, 1892. Uttararâmacarita. Edited and translated by S. K. Belvalkar, P. V. Kane and others.

Mâgha. Śiśupâlabadha Edited with Commentary by Vidyâsâgara, 1884. Ed. with Mallinâtha's Sarvaṁkaṣâ commentary by Durgâ Prasâda and Śivadatta. 4th edition, Bombay, 1905.

Viśâkhadatta. Mudrâ Râkṣasa. Edited by Hillebrandt. Breslau, 1912. Translated by Wilson. Also edited with translation by M. R. Kale.

Bhaṭṭa Nârâyaṇa. The Veṇî Saṁhâra. Edited by J. Grill. Leipzig, 1871. Translated by S. M. Tagore. Calcutta, 1880.

Nârâyaṇa. Hitopadeśa. Edited by Peterson. Bombay, 1887.

Bilhaṇa. Vikramâṅkadeva Carita Bombay Sanskrit Series, No. 14.

Râjaśekhara. Bâla Râmâyaṇa and Bâla Bhârata.

Karpûramañjarî. Edited by Stein Konow. Tr by Lanman. 1901.

Śrîharṣa. Naiṣadhîya Carita. Edited with the Commentary of Nârâyaṇa by Śivadatta Śâstrî. Bombay, 1894.

Kavirâja. Râghavapâṇḍavîya. Edited with Commentary in the Kâvyamâlâ Series, Bombay.

Padmagupta. Navasâhasâṅkacarita. Edited in the Bombay Sanskrit Series, 1895 (No. 53).

Kalhaṇa. Râjataraṅgiṇî. Edited by M. A. Stein. Bombay, 1892. Translated, London, 1900.

Kṣemendra. Bṛihatkathâmañjarî, Bhârata Mañjarî and Râmâyaṇa Mañjarî in the Kâvyamâlâ.

Somadeva. Kathâsaritsâgara.

Câṇakya Sûtras (appendix to R. Shamasastry's edition of the Arthaśâstra, 1919).

XI. Epigraphy.

Epigraphia Indica. Bombay.

Corpus Inscriptionum Indicarum, Vol. I (Revised edition by F. Hultzsch). Vol. III, by Fleet.

Inscriptions of Aśoka, ed. D. R. Bhandarkar and S. N. Majumdar. Calcutta, 1920.

Annual Reports of the Archæological Survey of India.

Inscriptions of the Madras Presidency. Edited by V. Rangâchârya Madras, 1919.

Epigraphia Carnatica. Lewis Rice, Vols. I to IV. Bangalore, 1886–98. Vol. V. Mangalore, 1902. Further volumes. Bangalore, 1902–5.

Madras Government Epigraphist's Reports.

Annual Reports of the Archaeological Survey of Western India.

Hyderabad Archæological Survey.

J. Ph. Vogel. Antiquities of Chambâ State. Calcutta, 1911.

Bhagvâna Lâla Indrâji (ed. Bühler). Twenty-three Inscriptions from Nepâl. Bombay, 1885.

Numerous Inscriptions are edited, often with translations, in *Indian Antiquary; Journal of the Royal Asiatic Society; Journal of the Bengal Asiatic Society; Journal of the Bombay Branch of the Royal Asiatic Society; Journal of the Bihâr and Orissâ Research Society.*

Prâcînalekhamâlâ ed. Bhavadatta Śâstrî, Śivadatta and Kâśînâth Pâṇḍurang Parab. Bombay, 1897, 1903.

Jainalekhasaṁgraha (in Jaina Vividha Sâhitya Śâstramâlâ Series). Ed. Pûraṇacandra Nâhara. Calcutta, 1918.

Behistân Inscriptions. Ed. and tr. L. W. King and R. C. Thompson. The Sculptures and Inscription of Darius the Great on the Rock of Behistûn in Persia. London, 1907.

XII. Numismatics.

Cunningham, A. The Coins of Alexander's Successors in the East. London, 1873 (Numismatic Chronicle, 1868–73).

Gardner, P. Coins of the Greek and Scythic Kings of Bactria and India. British Museum Catalogue, 1886.

Whitehead, R. B. Indo-Greek Coins. Lahore Museum Catalogue, I. Oxford, 1906.

Smith, V. A. Catalogue of Coins in the Indian Museum, Calcutta, Vol. I. Oxford, 1906.

Rapson, E. J. Catalogue of the Coins of the Āndhra Dynasty, the Western Kṣatrapas, Traikûṭaka Dynasty and the Bodhi Dynasty. London, 1908.

Allan, John. Catalogue of the Coins of the Gupta Dynasties and of Śaśâṅka, King of Gauḍa. London, 1914.

A large number of coins are noticed in the *Journals mentioned above in Section XI.*

XIII. Foreign Accounts.

A. GREEK.

Herodotus. History, tr. G. Rawlinson. London, 1858–60.

Xenophon. Cyropædia. Ed. and tr. W. Miller, London and New York, 1914.

Megasthenes. Fragments of the Indica. Ed. E. A. Schwanbeck. Bonn, 1846, tr. J. W. McCrindle, Ancient India as described by Megasthenes and Arrian. Calcutta, Bombay, and London, 1877.

Other translations by McCrindle are :—

The Commerce and Navigation of the Erythraian Sea. Calcutta, 1879. This volume contains a translation (with commentary) of Periplus Erythraei Maris by an unknown writer of the first Christian century, and of the second part of the Indika of Arrian, in which is described the memorable voyage of Nearchos from the mouth of the Indus to the head of the Persian Gulf.

Ancient India as described by Ktêsias the Knidian. Calcutta, 1882. Ktêsias was the first writer who gave the Greeks a special treatise on India. The work is lost but we have an epitome of its contents by Phôtios, and fragments of it in other writers.

Ancient India as described by Ptolemy. Calcutta, 1885. This volume contains not only Ptolemy's Geography of India, but also his Geography of Central and Eastern Asia, and a copy of his map of India.

The Invasion of India by Alexander the Great. First Edition, Westminster, 1893. New Edition, 1896. Contains translations of the accounts of Alexander's campaigns in India and Afghânistân found in Arrian, Q. Curtius, Diodorus Siculus, Plutarch and Justinus.

Ancient India as described in Classical Literature. Being a collection of Greek and Latin texts relating to India, extracted from Herodotus, Strabo, Diodorus Siculus, Pliny, Aelian, Philostratus, Dion Chrysostum, Porphyry, Stobaeus, the Itinerary of Alexander the Great, the Periêgêsis of Dionysius, the Dionysiaka of Nonnus, the Romance History of Alexander and other works. Westminster, 1901.

B. CHINESE.

Fâ-hien, tr. Giles, London and Shanghai, 1877.

——tr. Legge, Oxford, 1886.

Watters. "Fa-hsien and his English Translators." China Review, VIII.

Si-yu-ki. Buddhist Records of the Western World. Translated from the Chinese of Hiuen-Tsiang by Samuel Beal. 2 volumes. Latest reprint, London, 1906.

The Life of Hiuen-Tsiang by the Shaman Hwui Li, with an Introduction containing an account of the works of I-tsing. Tr. Samuel Beal. New Edition, London, 1911.

On Yuan Chwang's Travels in India by Thomas Watters, ed. T. W. Rhys Davids and S. W. Bushell. Oriental Translation Fund. New Series. Vol. XIV, London, 1904.

I-tsing. A Record of the Buddhist Religion as practised in India and the Malay Archipelago, tr. J. Takakusu, Oxford, 1896.

C. ARAB.

Alberûnî's India, tr. with notes and indices by Edward C. Sachau, in two volumes. London, 1910.

Elliot and Dowson's History of India as told by its own Historians. Vol. I. containing translations from various Arab writers.

XIV. General Modern Works.

The Cambridge History of India. Vol. I (Ancient India), edited by E. J. Rapson. Cambridge, 1922.

Dutta, R. C. History of Civilisation in Ancient India. London, 1893.

Smith, V. A. The Early History of India. 4th Edition. Oxford, 1924. Edited by Edwardes.

——The Oxford History of India. Oxford, 1919.

Rapson, E. J. Ancient India. Cambridge, 1914.

Barnett, L. D. Antiquities of India. London, 1913.

Krishnaswami Aiyangar, S. Ancient India. Madras, 1911. The work is devoted chiefly to the history of South India.

Duff, C. M. The Chronology of India. Westminster, 1899.

Bhandarkar, R. G. Early History of the Deccan. Second Edition. Bombay, 1895.

——A Peep into the Early History of India (322 B.C. to 500 A.D.). J.B.B.R.A.S. (Vol. XX, pp 356 408). Bombay, 1902.

Law, *N. N.* Aspects of Ancient Indian Polity. Oxford, 1921.

Ghoshal, *U.* A History of Hindu Political Theories. Oxford University Press, 1923.

Aiyangar, *K. V. R.* Some Aspects of Ancient Indian Polity. Madras, 1916.

Banerji, *P. N.* Public Administration in Ancient India. London, 1917.

Jayaswal, *K. P.* Hindu Polity. Calcutta, 1924.

Majumdar, *R. C.* Corporate Life in Ancient India. Calcutta, 1919.

Sarkar, *B. K.* Positive Background of Hindu Sociology. Bk. II. Allâhâbâd, 1921.

———Political Institutions and Theories of the Hindus. Leipzig, 1922.

Mookerji, *R. K.* Local Government in Ancient India. Clarendon Press, Oxford, 1919.

Fick, *Richard.* Social Organisation in North-East India in Buddha's Time. Translated from the German by S. Maitra. Calcutta, 1920.

Max Müller, *F. W.* History of Ancient Sanskrit Literature. 2nd Edition. London, 1860.

Weber, *A.* History of Indian Literature. 2nd Edition. London, 1882. English Translation by J. Mann and Th. Zachariae.

Macdonell, *A. A.* A History of Sanskrit Literature. London.

Keith, *A. B.* Classical Sanskrit Literature.

———-Sanskrit Drama.

Nariman, *G. K.* Literary History of Sanskrit Buddhism from Winternitz, Sylvain Lévi, Hüber. Bombay, 1920.

Hopkins, *E. W.* The Religions of India. Boston, 1895.

———India, Old and New. New York, 1901.

Beni Prasad. Theory of Government in Ancient India (post-Vedic). Indian Press, Allâhâbâd, 1927.

Subrahmanya Aiyar, *K. V.* Historical Sketches of Ancient Dekhan. Madras, 1917.

INDEX.

67